REGG
FAMILY

Ethnic Diseases SOURCEBOOK

Health Reference Series

First Edition

Ethnic Diseases SOURCEBOOK

Basic Consumer Health Information for Ethnic and Racial Minority Groups in the United States, Including General Health Indicators and Behaviors, Ethnic Diseases, Genetic Testing, the Impact of Chronic Diseases, Women's Health, Mental Health Issues, and Preventive Health Care Services

Along with a Glossary and a Listing of Additional Resources

Edited by
Joyce Brennfleck Shannon

615 Griswold Street • Detroit, MI 48226

Bibliographic Note

Each new volume of the *Health Reference Series* is individually titled and called a "First Edition." Subsequent updates will carry sequential edition numbers. To help avoid confusion and to provide maximum flexibility in our ability to respond to informational needs, the practice of consecutively numbering each volume will be discontinued.

Edited by Joyce Brennfleck Shannon

Health Reference Series

Karen Bellenir, *Series Editor*
Peter D. Dresser, *Managing Editor*
Maria Franklin, *Permissions Assistant*
Joan Margeson, *Research Associate*
Dawn Matthews, *Verification Assistant*
Jenifer Swanson, *Research Associate*

EdIndex, Services for Publishers, *Indexers*

Omnigraphics, Inc.

Matthew P. Barbour, *Vice President, Operations*
Laurie Lanzen Harris, *Vice President, Editorial Director*
Kevin Hayes, *Production Coordinator*
Thomas J. Murphy, *Vice President, Finance and Comptroller*
Peter E. Ruffner, *Senior Vice President*
Jane J. Steele, *Marketing Coordinator*

Frederick G. Ruffner, Jr., Publisher

Library of Congress Cataloging-in-Publication Data

Ethnic diseases sourcebook : basic consumer health information for ethnic and racial minority groups in the United States, including general health indicators and behaviors, ethnic diseases, genetic testing, the impact of chronic diseases, women's health, mental health issues, and preventive health care services; along with a glossary and a listing of additional resources / edited by Joyce Brennfleck Shannon.-- 1st Ed.
p. cm. -- (Health reference series)
Includes bibliographical references and index.
ISBN 0-7808-0336-1 (lib. bdg. : alk. paper)
1. Minorities--Health and hygiene--United States. 2. Minorities--Diseases--United States. 3. Genetic disorders--United States. 4. Ethnic groups--Diseases--United States. I. Shannon, Joyce Brennfleck. II. Health reference series (Unnumbered)

RA563.M56 E838 2001
362.1'089'00973--dc21

00-052853

∞

This book is printed on acid-free paper meeting the ANSI Z39.48 Standard. The infinity symbol that appears indicates that the paper in this book meets that standard.

Printed in the United States

Table of Contents

Part III: Genetic Testing

Part IV: The Impact of Chronic Diseases

Part V: Mental Health Services

Part VI: Ethnic Women's Health

Part VII: Improving the Health of Ethnic and Racial Groups

Part VIII: Additional Help and Information

Preface

About This Book

In 1970, persons in racial and ethnic minority groups accounted for 16% of the population; by 1998, this proportion had increased to 27%. The proportion is expected to continue increasing, to nearly 50% by 2050. Recognition of the disparities in risk for chronic disease and injury that exist between non-Hispanic whites and persons belonging to other racial or ethnic groups has become the foundation for current efforts to improve health care research, delivery, and education to racial and ethnic groups in the United States. Health disparities include:

- Infant death rates among blacks, American Indians and Alaska Natives, and Hispanics were all above the national average of 7.2 deaths per 1,000 live births. The greatest disparity exists for blacks, whose infant death rate (14.2 per 1,000 in 1996) is nearly 2½ times that of white infants (6.0 per 1,000 in 1996).

- In 1996 blacks had the highest death rates for seven causes of deaths, and American Indians or Alaska natives had the highest death rates for two of the causes. Conversely, Asians or Pacific Islanders had the lowest death rates for six of the causes of death, and Hispanics had the lowest death rates for four causes.

- Sickle cell anemia occurs in approximately 1 of every 500 African American births and 1 in ever 1,000 Hispanic American births. Approximately 1 in 12 African Americans, carries the sickle cell trait.

- The carrier rate for Tay-Sachs disease among non-Jewish people is one in 250. Among Jewish people, one in 27 carries the Tay-Sachs gene. Some other diseases are especially prevalent in Jewish populations. For example, one in 37 is a carrier of Canavan disease; and approximately one in every 10 Jewish individuals of central and eastern European ancestry carries the gene for Type I Gaucher Disease.

This *Sourcebook* provides health information about genetic and chronic diseases that affect ethnic and racial minorities in the United States. Readers will learn about diseases that are prevalent within ethnic and racial groups, the availability of genetic tests and counseling, and the impact of chronic diseases. Information about mental health services, women's health, and tips for improving health are also included along with a glossary and a listing of additional resources.

How to Use This Book

This book is divided into parts and chapters. Parts focus on broad areas of interest. Chapters are devoted to single topics within a part.

Part I: General Health of Ethnic and Racial Groups in the United States provides an overview of health indicators and behaviors by race and ethnicity; immunization rates; infant mortality rates; alcohol, tobacco, and drug use; and the challenges of aging.

Part II: Diseases of Ethnicity reviews inherited diseases prevalent within ethnic groups and offers specific information on Thalassemia, Gaucher disease, Lupus, Niemann-Pick disease, sickle cell anemia, and Tay-Sachs disease.

Part III: Genetic Testing gives practical information on genetic counseling, testing, and the potential affects of genetic information on employment and insurance.

Part IV: The Impact of Chronic Diseases looks at the burden of disease within racial and ethnic groups caused by asthma, cardiovascular disease, cancer, diabetes, hepatitis, and acquired immune deficiency syndrome (AIDS).

Part V: Mental Health Services addresses cultural diversity which affects the mental health perspectives and needs of racial and ethnic groups.

Part VI: Ethnic Women's Health presents statistics and behaviors pertinent to Asian American, African American, Hispanic American, Native American, and older minority women. It reviews risk factors, cultural differences, predisposition to disease, drug use during pregnancy, and leading causes of death among women by racial and ethnic group.

Part VII: Improving the Health of Ethnic and Racial Groups examines access to health care, development of cultural competency in health care situations, and offers healthy ethnic food recipes.

Part VIII: Additional Help and Information includes a glossary, listings of minority health resources, sources of health education materials arranged by racial and ethnic groups, and a listing of genetic testing laboratories in the United States.

Bibliographic Note

This volume contains documents and excerpts from publications issued by the following U.S. government agencies: Agency for Healthcare Research and Quality; Centers for Disease Control and Prevention (CDC); Department of Health and Human Services (DHHS); Health Resources and Services Administration (HRSA); *Mortality and Morbidity Weekly Report* (MMWR); National Cancer Institute (NCI); National Center for Human Genome Research (NHGRI); National Heart, Lung, and Blood Institute (NHLBI); National Institute on Alcohol Abuse and Alcoholism (NIAAA); National Institute of Allergy and Infectious Diseases (NIAID); National Institute of Arthritis and Musculoskeletal and Skin Diseases (NIAMS); National Institute of Diabetes and Digestive and Kidney Diseases (NIDDK); National Institute on Drug Abuse (NIDA); National Institutes of Health (NIH); National Institute of Mental Health (NIMH); National Women's Health Information Center (NWHIC); Office of Minority Health (OMH); and the U.S. Public Health Service.

In addition, this volume contains copyrighted documents from the following organizations and individuals: Dystonia Medical Research Foundation (DMRF); Kenneth Bridges, M.D.; Cooley's Anemia Foundation; National Niemann-Pick Disease Foundation (NNPDF); and the National Tay-Sachs and Allied Diseases Association, Inc. (NTSAD).

Full citation information is provided on the first page of each chapter. Every effort has been made to secure all necessary rights to reprint the copyrighted material. If any omissions have been made, please contact Omnigraphics to make corrections for future editions.

Acknowledgements

Special thanks to the many organizations, agencies, and individuals who have contributed materials for this *Sourcebook* and to the series editor Karen Bellenir, permissions specialist Maria Franklin, researchers Joan Margeson and Jenifer Swanson, verification assistant Dawn Matthews, indexer Edward J. Prucha, and document engineer Bruce Bellenir.

Note from the Editor

This book is part of Omnigraphics' *Health Reference Series*. The series provides basic information about a broad range of medical concerns. It is not intended to serve as a tool for diagnosing illness, in prescribing treatments, or as a substitute for the physician/patient relationship. All persons concerned about medical symptoms or the possibility of disease are encouraged to seek professional care from an appropriate health care provider.

Our Advisory Board

The *Health Reference Series* is reviewed by an Advisory Board comprised of librarians from public, academic, and medical libraries. We would like to thank the following board members for providing guidance to the development of this series:

Health Reference Series *Update Policy*

The inaugural book in the *Health Reference Series* was the first edition of *Cancer Sourcebook* published in 1992. Since then, the Series has been enthusiastically received by librarians and in the medical community. In order to maintain the standard of providing high-quality health information for the lay person the editorial staff at Omnigraphics felt it was necessary to implement a policy of updating volumes when warranted.

Medical researchers have been making tremendous strides, and it is the purpose of the *Health Reference Series* to stay current with the most recent advances. Each decision to update a volume will be made on an individual basis. Some of the considerations will include how much new information is available and the feedback we receive from people who use the books. If there is a topic you would like to see added to the update list, or an area of medical concern you feel has not been adequately addressed, please write to:

Editor
Health Reference Series
Omnigraphics, Inc.
615 Griswold Street
Detroit, MI 48226

The commitment to providing on-going coverage of important medical developments has also led to some format changes in the *Health Reference Series*. Each new volume on a topic is individually titled and called a "First Edition." Subsequent updates will carry sequential edition numbers. To help avoid confusion and to provide maximum flexibility in our ability to respond to informational needs, the practice of consecutively numbering each volume has been discontinued.

Part One

General Health of Ethnic and Racial Groups in the United States

Chapter 1

Health Indicators and Behaviors by Race and Ethnicity

In the United States, disparities in risks for chronic disease (e.g., diabetes, cardiovascular disease, and cancer) and injury exist among racial and ethnic groups. This report summarizes findings from the 1997 Behavioral Risk Factor Surveillance System (BRFSS) of the distribution of access to health care, health-status indicators, health-risk behaviors, and use of clinical preventive services across five racial and ethnic groups (i.e., whites, blacks, Hispanics, American Indians or Alaska Natives, and Asians or Pacific Islanders) and by state.

Description of System

The BRFSS is a state-based telephone survey of the civilian, non-institutionalized, adult (i.e., persons aged greater than or equal to 18 years) population. In 1997, all 50 states, the District of Columbia, and Puerto Rico participated in the BRFSS.

Results

Variations in risk for chronic disease and injury among racial and ethnic groups exist both within states and across states. For example, in Arizona, 11.0% of whites, 26.2% of Hispanics, and 50.5% of American Indians or Alaska Natives reported having no health insurance.

"State-Specific Prevalence of Selected Health Behaviors, by Race and Ethnicity—Behavioral Risk Factor Surveillance System, 1997," *Mortality and Morbidity Weekly Report* (MMWR), March 24, 2000/49 (SS02);1-60, National Center for Chronic Disease Prevention and Health Promotion.

Across states, the median percentage of adults who reported not having this insurance ranged from 10.8% for whites to 24.5% for American Indians or Alaska Natives. Other findings are as follows. Blacks, Hispanics, American Indians or Alaska Natives, and Asians or Pacific Islanders were more likely than whites to report poor access to health care (i.e., no health care coverage and cost as a barrier to obtaining health care). Blacks, Hispanics, and American Indians or Alaska Natives were more likely than whites and Asians or Pacific Islanders to report fair or poor health status, obesity, diabetes, and no leisure-time physical activity. Blacks were substantially more likely than other racial or ethnic groups to report high blood pressures. Among all groups, American Indians or Alaska Natives were the most likely to report cigarette smoking. Except for Asians or Pacific Islanders, the median percentage of adults who reported not always wearing a safety belt while driving or riding in a car was greater than or equal to 30%. The Papanicolaou test was the most commonly reported screening measure: greater than or equal to 81% of white, black, and Hispanic women with an intact uterine cervix reported having had one in the past 3 years. Among white, black, and Hispanic women aged greater than or equal to 50 years, greater than or equal to 63% reported having had a mammogram in the past 2 years. Approximately two-thirds of white, black, and Hispanic women aged greater than or equal to 50 years reported having had both a mammogram and a clinical breast examination in the past 2 years; this behavior was least common among Hispanics and most common among blacks. Screening for colorectal cancer was low among whites, blacks, and Hispanics aged greater than or equal to 50 years: in each racial or ethnic group, less than or equal to 20% reported having used a home-kit blood stool test in the past year, and less than or equal to 30% reported having had a sigmoidoscopy within the last 5 years.

Interpretation

Differences in median percentages between racial and ethnic groups, as well as between states within each racial and ethnic group, are likely mediated by various factors. According to published literature, socioeconomic factors (e.g., age distribution, educational attainment, employment status, and poverty), lifestyle behaviors (e.g., lack of physical activity, alcohol intake, and cigarette smoking), aspects of the social environment (e.g., educational and economic opportunities, neighborhood and work conditions, and state and local laws enacted to discourage high-risk behaviors), and factors affecting the health care system (e.g., access to health care, and cost and availability of screening for diseases and health-risk factors) may be associated with these differences.

Action Taken

States will continue to use the BRFSS to collect information about health-risk behaviors among various racial and ethnic groups. Analysis of these data will enable states to monitor factors that may affect the rate of chronic disease- and injury-related morbidity and mortality and to develop public health programs and policies to address these problems.

Introduction

Behaviors (e.g., physical inactivity, excessive alcohol consumption, and cigarette smoking) can contribute to chronic disease- and injury-related morbidity and mortality in the United States.[1] Preventive health practices (e.g., cholesterol screening, mammography, the blood stool test, and sigmoidoscopy) can help identify early stages of chronic disease (e.g., heart disease, breast cancer, and colorectal cancer), thereby reducing the morbidity and mortality rates from these leading causes of death among the U.S. adult (i.e., persons aged greater than or equal to 18 years) population.[2] Increasing the use of screening for chronic disease and reducing high-risk behaviors were among the year 2000 national health objectives.[3]

In the United States, disparities in risk for chronic disease and injury exist between non-Hispanic whites and persons belonging to other racial or ethnic groups.[4] For example, in 1996 blacks had the highest death rates for seven causes of deaths, and American Indians or Alaska Natives had the highest death rates for two of the causes (Table 1.1). Conversely, Asians or Pacific Islanders had the lowest death rates for six of the causes of death, and Hispanics had the lowest death rates for four causes. In 1970, persons in racial and ethnic minority groups accounted for 16% of the population; by 1998, this proportion had increased to 27%. The proportion is expected to continue increasing, to nearly 50% by 2050.[5]

Although persons in racial and ethnic minority groups are accounting for increasingly larger proportions of the U.S. population, information about the health behaviors of persons in minority groups is insufficient, especially at the state and local levels.[6] Ongoing state-specific information is important in identifying or monitoring the prevalence of access to health care, health-status indicators, health-risk behaviors, and use of clinical preventive services among various racial and ethnic groups. These data can be used to identify disparities among racial and ethnic groups and to plan, implement, and evaluate culturally appropriate prevention programs at the state and local levels.

State-specific data about modifiable risk factors for chronic diseases and other leading causes of death among adults are collected each year through the Behavioral Risk Factor Surveillance System (BRFSS), an ongoing surveillance system. The BRFSS is administered by state health departments each month in all 50 states, the District of Columbia, and Puerto Rico (for simplicity in this report, the term state hereafter includes the District of Columbia and Puerto Rico). This system can be used to measure achievement toward national health objectives[3] and specific state objectives. The history, rationale and use of the BRFSS have been previously described.[7-10] In this report, 1997 state-specific BRFSS estimates of access to health care, health-status indicators, health-risk behaviors, and use of clinical preventive services are presented for five racial and ethnic groups.

Methods

Sampling

Each state health department used random digit dialing to select samples of adults in households with a telephone. The samples represent each state's civilian, non-institutionalized, adult population.[7] States used the three-stage cluster sampling based on the Waksberg method[11] or simple random sampling, stratified random sampling, or other sampling designs.

Questionnaire

The BRFSS includes a core set of questions asked in all participating states each year and a rotating set of core questions asked every other year. Rotating core questions asked in 1997 were about awareness of high blood pressure and high blood cholesterol, alcohol use, safety belt use, testing for cholesterol, and colorectal cancer screening. Because the rotating core question regarding leisure-time physical activity was not asked in 1997, the 1996 data for this health behavior are used in this report.

Language Barriers

If a substantial portion of a state's population does not speak English proficiently, the state can use a Spanish version of the core questionnaire provided by Centers for Disease Control and Prevention (CDC). If the interviewer determines that the respondent is not proficient in the available languages, the interviewer does not administer the survey and notes language barrier as the reason for ending the telephone call.

Data Collection and Processing

In each state, during the interview period in each month, BRFSS data are collected from randomly selected adults. The data are sent to CDC after the monthly interviewing cycle ends. CDC edits and checks the reliability of the data collected.

A computer-assisted telephone interviewing (CATI) system, which permits direct entry of data into a computer file during an interview, was used in 49 states in 1997. CATI helps reduce errors in data collection by facilitating data coding and entry and by enabling monitoring of the interviewers.

Data Weighting and Analysis

CDC aggregates the edited monthly data files to create a yearly sample for each state. Each state's yearly data file is weighted to the respondent's probability of selection and to the age- and sex-specific or race-, age-, sex-specific population from the most current census data (or intercensal estimates) for each state.[9,12] CDC uses these weighted data to estimate the prevalence of risk factors for each state's population. SUDAAN, a software package for analyzing complex survey data, is used to calculate the standard errors and the 95% confidence intervals (CI) around the prevalence estimates.[13]

In 1997, the number of interviews completed in each state ranged from 1,505 to 4,923 (median: 2,340). Response rates were calculated according to the methodology of the Council of American Survey Research Organization (CASRO)[14] and ranged from 36.7% to 88.9% (median: 62.1%).

Each BRFSS respondent reports his or her race and ethnicity. These self-reports were the basis of the five categories used in this report: white, black, Hispanic, American Indian or Alaska Native, and Asian or Pacific Islander. Any respondent reporting Hispanic ethnicity was categorized as Hispanic, regardless of race. Survey respondents who reported they were of another race and not Hispanic (0.6% of respondents) and those who replied "don't know" or refused to answer the questions on both race and ethnicity (less than 0.5% of respondents) were excluded from this analysis. In this report, state-level estimates for any race- and ethnicity-specific group that had less than 50 respondents are considered unstable and are not shown. No statistical testing was performed for comparisons presented in this report; therefore, these findings should be considered descriptive.

Results

In the 1997 BRFSS, whites comprised 75.4% of the respondent group (Table 1.2). Blacks represented 9.7% of the cohort, Hispanics represented 11.1%, American Indians or Alaska Natives accounted for 1.0%, and Asians or Pacific Islanders accounted for 2.8%. The number of respondents was sufficient (i.e., greater than or equal to 50) in 51 states for whites, 35 states for blacks, 36 states for Hispanics, 11 states for American Indians or Alaska Natives, and 10 states for Asians or Pacific Islanders. Survey questions that were restricted to adults of a certain age (e.g., colorectal cancer screening among persons aged greater than or equal to 50 years) or sex (e.g., breast cancer screening among women) further reduced the number of states that had a sufficient number of respondents for analysis.

The factors related to access to health care, health-status indicators, and health-risk behaviors {less than a high school education, no health care insurance, etc.} are those that place adults at high risk for chronic disease and injury. In contrast, use of clinical preventive services reduces the risk of chronic disease, because screening allows early detection and treatment.

Access to Health Care

Low Educational Attainment

The median percentage of adults who reported having less than a high school education was 9.8% for whites (range: 0.7%-22.2%), 17.2% for blacks (range: 2.8%-31.0%), 20.9% for Hispanics (range: 11.3%-47.4%), 17.0% for American Indians or Alaska Natives (range: 3.4%-32.0%), and 9.5% for Asians or Pacific Islanders (range: 3.5%-23.9%).

Lack of Health Care Coverage

The median percentage of adults who reported that they did not have any kind of health care coverage, including prepaid plans (e.g., health maintenance organizations) and government plans (e.g., Medicare), varied considerably between states and between racial and ethnic groups. Hispanics and American Indians or Alaska Natives were more than twice as likely as whites to lack health care coverage. The median percentage of respondents who were uninsured was 10.8% for whites (range: 6.4%-18.4%), 16.4% for blacks (range: 5.8%-34.9%), 22.6% for Hispanics (range: 1.3%-44.9%), 24.5% for American Indians or Alaska Natives (range: 12.5%-50.5%), and 14.3% for Asians or Pacific Islanders (range: 4.8%-31.1%).

Cost as a Barrier to Obtaining Health Care

The median percentage of adults who reported they needed to see a doctor in the last 12 months but could not because of the cost, irrespective of insurance status, ranged from 9.4% to 16.2%. Whites were the least likely racial or ethnic group to report that cost was a barrier to obtaining health care. The median percentage was 9.4% for whites (range: 5.4%-24.3%), 13.2% for blacks (range: 6.6%-27.7%), 16.2% for Hispanics (range: 7.9%-30.1%), 12.6% for American Indians or Alaska Natives (range: 9.2%-26.7%), and 11.6% for Asians or Pacific Islanders (range: 4.7%-16.3%).

No Routine Physical Examination

Blacks were the least likely racial or ethnic group to report having had no routine physical examination within the past 2 years. The median percentage of BRFSS participants who reported not having had a recent, routine physical examination was 18.0% for whites (range: 11.6%-28.4%), 8.7% for blacks (range: 4.7%-19.3%), 18.2% for Hispanics (range: 7.7%-33.9%), 14.5% for American Indians or Alaska Natives (range: 8.8%-30.0%), and 17.1% for Asians or Pacific Islanders (range: 5.9%-25.2%).

Health Status Indicators

Fair or Poor Health Status

The race- and ethnicity-specific median percentage of adults who reported fair or poor health status ranged from 8.8% to 19.4%. The median percentage was 11.6% for whites (range: 3.4%-21.7%), 19.4% for blacks (range: 10.3%-30.5%), 16.1% for Hispanics (range: 2.1%-35.2%), 17.5% for American Indians or Alaska Natives (range: 10.1%-35.4%), and 8.8% for Asians or Pacific Islanders (range: 5.6%-17.2%).

Obesity

A United States man or woman having a body mass index of greater than or equal to 30 kg/m2 is considered obese.[15] This criterion conforms to World Health Organization guidelines.[16] In the 1997 BRFSS, respondents were asked their weight and height, and body mass index was calculated. More than one-fourth of blacks and American Indians or Alaska Natives were determined to be obese. The median percentage of respondents who were obese was 15.6% for whites (range: 5.8%-21.2%), 26.4% for blacks (range: 7.6%-33.2%), 18.2% for Hispanics (range: 8.1%-34.7%), 30.1% for American Indians or Alaska Natives (range: 13.0%-32.3%), and 4.8% for Asians or Pacific Islanders (range: 1.7%-16.9%).

Awareness of Certain Medical Conditions

High Blood Pressure

The median percentage of adults who reported having ever been told by a health professional that their blood pressure was high was 23.0% for whites (range: 11.0%-29.6%), 30.9% for blacks (range: 21.9%-45.4%), 18.6% for Hispanics (range: 11.4%-28.4%), 20.7% for American Indians or Alaska Natives (range: 16.6%-30.7%), and 16.3% for Asians or Pacific Islanders (range: 4.5%-27.9%).

Diabetes

The median percentage of adults who reported having ever been told by a health professional that they had diabetes was less than 8% in each racial and ethnic group. The median percentage was 4.4% for whites (range: 0.7%-6.2%), 7.6% for blacks (range: 2.6%-17.9%), 5.5% for Hispanics (range: 0.4%-14.4%), 7.6% for American Indians or Alaska Natives (range: 3.3%-14.0%), and 4.6% for Asians or Pacific Islanders (range: 0.0%-8.2%).

High Blood Cholesterol

The racial- and ethnic-specific median percentages of adults who had had their blood cholesterol checked and reported having ever been told by a health professional that they had high blood cholesterol were very similar, from 25.6% for Hispanics to 29.7% for whites. The median percentage was 29.7% for whites (range: 14.3%-35.2%), 26.0% for blacks (range: 7.6%-36.7%), 25.6% for Hispanics (range: 12.5%-41.0%), and 27.3% for Asians or Pacific Islanders (range: 16.3%-35.8%). In the states that had a sufficient number of American Indian or Alaska Native respondents for this question, the percentage was 26.0% (95% CI: 17.7%-34.2%) for Alaska, 28.6% (95% CI: 14.2%-42.9%) for Oklahoma, and 26.5% (95% CI: 9.3%-43.8%) for Washington.

Health Risk Behaviors

No Leisure-Time Physical Activity

The BRFSS rotating core question on leisure-time physical activity was asked in 1996 but not in 1997. Leisure-time physical activity is exercise, recreation, or physical activities (e.g., running, calisthenics, golfing, gardening, or walking) that are not performed as part of regular job duties. The median percentage of persons who reported no leisure-time physical activity was greater than or equal to 25% in each racial and ethnic group. For each group, the percentage varied by greater than or equal to 17 percentage points across states. The percentage ranged from 13.0% to 50.6% for whites (median: 25.1%), from 17.8% to 54.6% for blacks (median: 38.2%), from 15.0% to 51.9% for Hispanics (median: 34.2%), from 26.7% to 43.2% for American Indians or Alaska Natives (median: 37.2%), and from 21.5% to 40.3% for Asians or Pacific Islanders (median: 28.9%).

Alcohol Consumption

Current Drinking

For each racial and ethnic group, the median percentage of adults who reported current drinking (i.e., consumption of greater than or equal to 1 drink of beer, wine, wine cooler, or liquor in the past month) varied across states by greater than or equal to 33 percentage points. The range was 27.0%-71.3% for whites (median: 55.4%), 25.1%-73.2% for blacks (median: 40.4%), 26.5%-70.0% for Hispanics (median: 50.8%), 30.8%-64.2% for American Indians or Alaska Natives (median: 50.5%), and 10.2%-58.5% for Asians or Pacific Islanders (median: 38.2%).

Binge Drinking

Asians or Pacific Islanders were the group least likely to report binge drinking (i.e., consumption of greater than or equal to 5 drinks on at least one occasion in the past month); American Indians or Alaska Natives were the most likely to report this behavior. The median percentage of adults who reported binge drinking was 14.3% for whites (range: 7.2%-23.6%), 8.7% for blacks (range: 3.0%-23.6%), 16.2% for Hispanics (range: 4.3%-28.0%), 18.9% for American Indians or Alaska Natives (range: 11.4%-30.2%), and 6.7% for Asians or Pacific Islanders (range: 0.0%-31.9%).

Cigarette Smoking

The median percentage of adults who reported having ever smoked greater than or equal to 100 cigarettes and currently smoked varied almost fourfold across the racial and ethnic groups. The median percentage was 23.6% for whites (range: 13.3%-30.8%), 22.8% for blacks (range: 14.8%-37.0%), 23.1% for Hispanics (range: 10.5%-43.6%), 41.3% for American Indians or Alaska Natives (range: 3.1%-48.6%), and 10.7% for Asians or Pacific Islanders (range: 4.7%-36.1%).

Lack of Safety Belt Use

The median percentage of adults who reported not always wearing a safety belt while driving or riding in a car was greater than or equal to 30% for each racial and ethnic group except Asians or Pacific Islanders. The median percentage of adults who reported this behavior was 30.0% for whites (range: 13.0%-60.6%), 37.6% for blacks (range: 11.7%-63.0%), 30.3% for Hispanics (range: 10.9%-57.5%), 40.9% for American Indians or Alaska Natives (range: 20.6%-75.1%), and 18.6% for Asians or Pacific Islanders (range: 9.4%-27.4%).

Clinical Preventive Services

Blood Cholesterol Checked

The median percentage of adults who reported having had their blood cholesterol checked within the last 5 years was greater than or equal to 55% in each racial and ethnic group. The median percentage was 71.2% for whites (range: 56.1%-82.8%), 67.4% for blacks (range: 45.3%-81.7%), 59.3% for Hispanics (range: 45.7%-81.7%), 54.7% for American Indians or Alaska Natives (range: 49.9%-75.4%), and 67.8% for Asians or Pacific Islanders (range: 36.7%-74.1%).

Papanicolaou (Pap) Test

The median percentage of white, black, or Hispanic women with an intact uterine cervix who reported having had a Pap test in the past 3 years was greater than or equal to 81%. The median percentage was 84.7% for whites (range: 77.7%-93.4%), 91.1% for blacks (range: 83.5%-97.0%), and 80.9% for Hispanics (range: 69.2%-92.9%). In Alaska, the only state that had greater than or equal to 50 Native American or Alaska Native respondents for this question, the percentage of women with an intact uterine cervix who reported having had a recent Pap test was 95.5% (95% CI: 91.1%-100.0%). In the states that had a sufficient number of Asian or Pacific Islander respondents for this question, the percentage was 84.2% for Hawaii (95% CI: 80.5%-88.0%), 75.9% for New York (95% CI: 63.5%-88.3%), and 84.1% for Washington (95% CI: 73.6%-94.5%).

Breast Cancer Screening

Mammogram

The percentage of women aged greater than or equal to 50 years who reported having had a mammogram in the past 2 years was 73.7% for whites (range: 58.7%-89.7%), 76.1% for blacks (range: 44.3%-85.5%), and 63.5% for Hispanics (range: 59.7%-79.6%). Alaska was the only state that had greater than or equal to 50 Native American or Alaska Native respondents to this question; the percentage who reported having had a recent mammogram was 93.5% (95% CI: 87.7%-99.2%). Hawaii was the only state that had greater than or equal to 50 Asian or Pacific Islander respondents; the percentage was 80.7% (95% CI: 75.2%-86.2%).

Clinical Breast Examination

The median percentage of white, black, or Hispanic women aged greater than or equal to 50 years who reported having had a clinical breast exam in the past 2 years was greater than 75%. The median percentage was 77.5% for whites (range: 64.7%-88.4%), 78.2% for blacks (range: 57.6%-90.0%), and 75.5% for Hispanics (range: 58.3%-78.7%). In Alaska, the only state that had greater than or equal to 50 American Indians or Alaska Native respondents for this question, the percentage of women who reported having had a recent clinical breast exam was 93.4% (95% CI: 87.1%-99.7%). In Hawaii, the only state with a sufficient number of Asian or Pacific Islander respondents, the percentage was 77.8% (95% CI: 71.3%-84.3%).

Mammogram Plus Clinical Breast Exam

The median percentage of women aged greater than or equal to 50 years who reported having had both a mammogram and a clinical breast exam in the past 2 years was 67.6% for whites (range: 51.3%-81.3%), 67.8% for blacks (range: 35.7%-79.5%), and 57.8% for Hispanics (range: 53.7-72.3). Alaska was the only state that had greater than or equal to 50 American Indian or Alaska Native respondents for this question; 88.5% reported having had both a mammogram and a clinical

Table 1.1. Death Rates* for Selected Causes of Death, by Race or Ethnicity, United States—National Center for Health Statistics, 1996.

Cause of Death	White	Black	Hispanic+	American Indian or Alaska Native	Asian or Pacific Islander
Heart disease	129.8	191.5	88.6	00.8	71.7
Stroke	24.5	44.2	19.5	21.1	23.9
Chronic obstructive pulmonary disease	21.5	17.8	8.9	12.6	8.6
Diabetes	12.0	28.8	18.8	27.8	8.8
Chronic liver disease and cirrhosis	7.3	9.2	12.6	20.7	2.6
Lung cancer	38.9	48.9	15.4	24.4	17.4
Colorectal cancer	11.8	16.8	7.3	8.5	7.7
Breast cancer	19.8	26.5	12.8	12.7	8.9
Motor vehicle-related injuries	16.3	16.7	16.1	34.0	9.5
Pneumonia and influenza	12.2	17.8	9.7	14.0	9.9

*Age-adjusted rates per 100,000. Rates are adjusted to the 1940 population

+In this table only, Hispanics may be of any race, therefore this category is not mutually exclusive with the four categories for race.

breast exam in the past 2 years (95% CI: 80.1%-96.8%). Hawaii was the only state that had greater than or equal to 50 Asian or Pacific Islander respondents; 71.2% reported having had both screening procedures recently (95% CI: 64.3%-78.2%).

Colorectal Cancer Screening

Home-Kit Blood Stool Test

A blood stool test (also called fecal occult blood test) is a test to determine whether the stool contains blood. The test may be done at home with a special kit. The median percentage of adults aged greater than or equal to 50 years who reported having used a home-kit blood stool test in the past year was 18.2% for whites (range: 9.1%-31.2%), 20.3% for blacks (range: 3.0%-43.3%), and 14.2% for Hispanics (range: 5.8%-28.6%). In Alaska, the only state that had greater than or equal to 50 Native American or Alaska Native respondents, the percentage who reported having recently used a home-kit blood stool test was 12.3% (95% CI: 4.3%-20.4%). Two states had greater than or equal to 50 Asian or Pacific Islander respondents for this question; the percentage was 2.6% in California (95% CI: 0.0%-6.2%) and 23.8% in Hawaii (95% CI: 18.9%-28.7%).

Sigmoidoscopy

Sigmoidoscopy (also called proctoscopy) is a procedure involving a thin tube being inserted into the rectum to view the bowel for signs of cancer and other health problems. The median percentage of adults aged greater than or equal to 50 years who reported having had a sigmoidoscopy within the last 5 years was 30.4% for whites (range: 15.6%-49.1%), 28.2% for blacks (range: 10.9%-38.3%), and 22.4% for

Table 1.2. Racial and Ethnic Distribution of Survey Respondents Totals for U.S.—Behavior Risk Factor Surveillance System, 1997.

White		Black		Hispanic		American Indian or Alaska Native		Asian or Pacific Islander	
No.	%*	No.	%	No.	%	No.	%	No.	%
109,222	75.4%	11,308	9.7%	9,296	11.1%	1,640	1.0%	2,692	2,8%

*Weighted percentages

Table 1.3. Medians and Ranges of Values for Access to Health Care, Health Status Indicators, Health Risk Behaviors, and Clinical Preventive Services, by Race or Ethnicity—Behavioral Risk Factor Surveillance System, 1997.

	Total		White		Black		Hispanic		American Indian or Alaska Native		Asian or Pacific Islander	
Health behavior	**%**	**(Range*)**	**%**	**(Range)**	**%**	**(Range)**	**%**	**(Range)**	**%**	**(Range)**	**%**	**(Range)**
Access to health care												
Low educational attainment	11.2	(7.0–29.6)	9.8	(0.7–22.2)	17.2	(2.8–31.0)	20.9	(11.3–47.4)	17.0	(3.4–32.0)	9.5	(3.5–23.9)
Lack of health care coverage	12.0	(6.1–24.2)	10.8	(6.4–18.4	16.4	(5.8–34.9)	22.6	(1.3–44.9)	24.5	(12.5–50.5)	14.3	(4.8–31.1)
Cost as a barrier to obtaining health care	9.9	(6.3–25.3)	9.4	(5.4–24.3)	13.2	(6.6–27.7)	16.2	(7.9–30.1)	12.6	(9.2–26.7)	11.6	(4.7–16.3)
No routine physical examination	16.8	(7.8–29.1)	18.0	(11.6–28.4)	8.7	(4.7–19.3)	18.2	(7.7–33.9)	14.5	(8.8–30.0)	17.1	(5.9–25.2)
Health-status indicators												
Fair or poor health status	13.0	(9.4–35.1)	11.6	(3.4–21.7)	19.4	(10.3–30.5)	16.1	(2.1–35.2)	17.5	(10.1–35.4)	8.8	(5.6–17.2)
Obesity	16.6	(11.9–22.0)	15.6	(5.8–21.2)	26.4	(7.6–33.2)	18.2	(8.1–34.7)	30.1	(13.0–32.3)	4.8	(1.7–16.9)
Awareness of certain medical conditions												
High blood pressure	23.0	(16.2–34.5)	23.0	(11.0–29.6)	30.9	(21.9–45.4)	18.6	(11.4–28.4)	20.7	(16.6–30.7)	16.3	(4.5–27.9)
Diabetes	4.8	(3.0–10.5)	4.4	(0.7–6.2)	7.6	(2.6–17.9)	5.5	(0.4–14.4	7.6	(3.3–14.0)	4.6	(0.0–8.2)
High blood cholesterol	28.6	(18.2–34.2)	29.7	(14.3–35.2)	26.0	(7.6–36.7)	25.6	(12.5–41.0)	++		27.3	(16.3–35.8)
Health-risks behaviors												
No leisure-time physical activity	28.0	(17.2–51.4)	25.1	(13.0–50.6)	38.2	(17.8–54.6)	34.2	(15.0–51.9)	37.2	(26.7–43.2)	28.9	(21.5–40.3)

Alcohol consumption						
Current drinking	53.5 (26.6–70.4)	55.4 (27.0–71.3)	40.4 (25.1–73.2)	50.8 (26.5–70.0)	50.5 (30.8–64.2)	38.2 (10.2–58.5)
Binge drinking	14.4 (6.3–23.2)	14.3 (7.2–23.6)	8.7 (3.0–23.6)	16.2 (4.3–28.0)	18.9 (11.4–30.2)	6.7 (0.0–31.9)
Cigarette smoking	23.2 (13.7–30.8)	23.6 (13.3–30.8)	22.8 (10.5–43.6)	23.1 (10.5–43.6)	41.3 (3.1–48.6)	10.7 (4.7–36.1)
Lack of safety belt use	30.7 (12.8–59.8)	30.0 (13.0–60.6)	37.6 (11.7–63.0)	30.3 (10.9–57.5)	40.9 (20.6–75.1)	18.6 (9.4–27.4)
Clinical preventive services						
Blood cholesterol checked	69.2 (55.0–79.3)	71.2 (56.1–82.8)	67.4 (45.3–81.7)	59.3 (45.3–81.7)	54.7 (49.9–75.4)	67.8 (36.7–74.1)
Papanicolaou test	84.8 (71.8–92.3)	84.7 (77.7–93.4)	91.1 (83.5–97.0)	80.9 (69.2–92.9)	++	++
Breast cancer screening						
Mammogram	73.7 (56.5–83.6)	73.7 (58.7–89.7)	76.1 (44.3–85.5)	63.5 (59.7–79.6)	++	++
Clinical breast examination	77.0 (63.5–86.4)	77.5 (64.7–88.4)	78.2 (57.6–90.0)	75.5 (58.3–78.7)	++	++
Mammogram plus clinical breast examination	66.4 (49.2–76.1)	67.6 (51.3–81.3)	67.8 (35.7–79.5)	57.8 (53.7–72.3)	++	++
Colorectal cancer screening						
Home-kit blood stool test	18.1 (9.3–28.5)	18.2 (9.1–31.2)	20.3 (3.0–43.3)	14.2 (5.8–28.6)	++	++
Sigmoidscopy	30.1 (15.6–41.5)	30.4 (15.6–49.1)	28.2 (10.9–38.3)	22.4 (18.1–40.7)		

*Lowest and highest state estimates.

++Median is not considered meaningful for the three or fewer states that had<=50 respondents in this racial or ethnic category and is not shown

Hispanics (range: 18.1%-40.7%). In Alaska, the only state that had greater than or equal to 50 American Indian or Alaska Native respondents for this question, the percentage who reported having had a recent sigmoidoscopy was 27.6% (95% CI: 16.7%-38.5%). Two states had greater than or equal to 50 Asian or Pacific Islander respondents to this question; the percentage was 24.3% in California (95% CI: 11.4%-37.2%) and 40.7% in Hawaii (95% CI: 34.9%-46.5%).

Discussion

Adults in the United States continue to engage in behaviors that increase their risk of chronic disease and injury.[1] Since 1984, BRFSS data have documented substantial state-to-state variation in the prevalence of these behaviors.[8,17-24] This report presents 1997 BRFSS data by state and documents disparities in the prevalence of health-status indicators, health-risk behaviors, and receipt of clinical preventive services across five racial and ethnic groups.

The differences in median percentages between racial and ethnic groups, as well as between states within each racial and ethnic group, are likely mediated by various factors. Socioeconomic factors (e.g., age distribution, educational attainment, employment status, and poverty), lifestyle behaviors (e.g., lack of physical activity, alcohol intake, and cigarette smoking), aspects of the social environment (e.g., educational and economic opportunities, neighborhood and work conditions, and state and local laws enacted to discourage high-risk behaviors), and factors affecting the health care system (e.g., access to health care, and cost and availability of screening for diseases and health-risk factors) are thought to be major reasons for such differences.[25-28] Level of education is highly correlated with the prevalence of many health risks (e.g., obesity, lack of physical activity, and cigarette smoking).[27, 29-31] In this report, the percentage of adults who did not have at least a high school education in 1997 varied more than twofold across the five racial and ethnic groups. Persons in the United States who have more education usually have higher incomes, are more likely to have health care coverage, and perhaps are better able to access and use the health care system.[4,31] In addition, having health insurance is closely associated with employment status. If a person is unemployed or is employed in a part-time or low-wage job, employee health benefits may not be available or the portion of the cost the employee must bear may be prohibitive.[32] Persons in the United States who do not have health insurance are less likely to receive clinical preventive services.[33,34] Thus, education, employment, and health insurance all affect the health and health behavior of U.S. adults.

The literature indicates that recent immigration and lack of fluency in English may affect the prevalence of risks for chronic disease and injury among certain racial and ethnic groups. In 1997, 61% of the Asian or Pacific Islander portion and 38% of the Hispanic portion of the U.S. population were foreign born; in contrast, only 8% of the white portion, 6% of the black portion, and 6% of the American Indian or Alaska Native portion were foreign born.[5] Although some immigrants are highly educated and have high incomes,[5] lack of familiarity with the U.S. public and private health systems, different cultural attitudes about the use of traditional and U.S. conventional medicine,[6] and lack of fluency in English may pose barriers to obtaining appropriate health care.[35]

Conditions associated with very poor urban areas (e.g., high rates of circulatory diseases, accidents, homicide, crime, infection with the human immunodeficiency virus, and exposure to environmental hazards) can negatively affect health.[36] On the other hand, living outside metropolitan areas can also be a risk factor for poor health, because fewer opportunities may exist for health care and clinical preventive services.[37] Racial and ethnic groups tend to distribute differently in urban and rural settings. For example, American Indians or Alaska Natives are the most likely group to live outside metropolitan areas.[5] More than one half of Hispanics and blacks and nearly one half of Asians or Pacific Islanders, but only one fourth of whites, live in central cities.[5]

Of the five racial and ethnic groups in this report, Hispanics reported the highest median prevalence of three of the four factors associated with limited access to health care (i.e., less than a high school education, cost as a barrier to obtaining health care, and no routine physical examination). Hispanics also reported the second-highest prevalence of no health care coverage. The latter finding is consistent with observations from the 1997 Current Population Survey,[38] the 1998 National Health Interview Survey,[4] and the 1996 Medical Expenditure Panel Survey[39] that Hispanics and blacks were the groups most likely to report having no health insurance. These three surveys did not present data for American Indians or Alaska Natives or for Asians or Pacific Islanders. All four national surveys found that whites were the least likely racial and ethnic group to report that they had no health care coverage. The BRFSS and Medical Expenditure Panel Survey also found that whites were the least likely to report that cost was a barrier to obtaining health care. In the BRFSS, blacks were the least likely to report not having a recent physical examination, and Asians or Pacific Islanders were the least likely to report having less than a high school education.

The National Cholesterol Education Program recommends that all adults in the United States have their total blood cholesterol checked every 5 years,[40] but in this report, the median percentage of adults who reported having had this screening procedure within the last 5 years ranged from only 54.7% among American Indians or Alaska Natives to 71.2% among whites. Only seven states had achieved the year 2000 national health objective that greater than or equal to 75% of adults have had their blood cholesterol checked within the last 5 years.[3] In this report, a timely Pap test was the most frequently reported clinical preventive service: the median percentage of white, black, or Hispanic women with an intact uterine cervix who reported having had a Pap test in the past 3 years was greater than or equal to 81%. For any racial or ethnic group, only three states had reached the national health objective that greater than or equal to 95% of women have had a timely Pap test, but most states had reached the objective that greater than or equal to 60% of women aged greater than or equal to 50 years have had both a mammogram and a clinical breast exam within the past 2 years.[3] The median percentage of white, black, or Hispanic adults who reported having been screened for colorectal cancer was low. The data from this report and a previous report indicate that less than or equal to 20% had used the home-kit blood stool test in the past year and less than or equal to 30% had had a sigmoidoscopy within the last 5 years.[41] The American Cancer Society recommends that all persons aged greater than or equal to 50 years have a blood stool test each year and a sigmoidoscopy every 5 years.[42]

Interpretation Cautions

Caution must be used in interpreting these BRFSS data. In 1997, only 11 states had a sufficient number of (i.e., greater than or equal to 50) American Indian or Alaska Native respondents to produce stable state-level estimates, and only 10 states had a sufficient number of Asian or Pacific Islander respondents. When responses to BRFSS questions were stratified by age and sex, as few as one state had greater than or equal to 50 respondents in a racial or ethnic group. Thus, the prevalence reported may not be representative of the nation for these groups.

In addition, combining several populations into a broad category may mask important differences between the populations. BRFSS surveys conducted among Chinese, Korean, and Vietnamese persons in California have demonstrated that each sub-population has some distinct characteristics in educational attainment, income, prevalence of health-risk behaviors, and use of clinical preventive services.[6,35,43] Thus, a median prevalence for the broader category of Asian or Pacific Islander may not accurately reflect the prevalence among the subpopulations in this group.

The racial and ethnic categories used in this report may be not only too broad, but also imprecise. The proportion of persons in the United States who identify their race as American Indian or Alaska Native has increased since the 1960s.[44] The increase is larger than can be accounted for by deaths, births, immigrations, and improvements in census coverage. This disproportionate increase suggests that persons are now more likely to identify themselves on censuses and surveys as American Indian or Alaska Native.

The BRFSS-estimated prevalences of access to health care, health-status indicators, health-risk behaviors, and clinical preventive services pertain only to the U.S. adult population living in households with telephones. Overall, 95% of U.S. households have telephones; coverage ranges from 87% to 98% across states and varies for subpopulations as well.[45] In 1996 an estimated 5.0% of white; 14.6% of black; 14.6% of Hispanic; 16.8% of American Indian, Aleut, or Eskimo; and 4.7% of Asian or Pacific Islander households had no telephone.[46] Approximately 8% of households in the South, 5.5% in both the Northeast and West, and 5.3% in the West had no telephone. Persons in lower socioeconomic groups also typically had lower telephone coverage. The BRFSS uses no direct method to compensate for no telephone in the home, but post-stratification weights are used and may partially correct for any bias caused by non-telephone coverage. BRFSS weights adjust for differences in probability of selection, non-response, and non-telephone coverage, and they must be used to derive representative population-based prevalence estimates.

Conclusion

Most of the risks behaviors associated with chronic disease and injury and described in this report are modifiable. Lack of health insurance, cost as a barrier to obtaining health care, obesity, high blood pressure, high blood cholesterol, lack of leisure-time physical activity, binge drinking, cigarette smoking, not always wearing a safety belt, and screening for cancer could be improved through more effective state and local public health programs. Health care practitioners could do more to encourage their patients to reduce harmful behaviors and adopt healthier behaviors.[47] In addition, health care delivery systems could offer patients more counseling on preventive measures (e.g., losing weight, stopping smoking, wearing safety belts, or getting a timely mammogram) and facilitate patients' access to clinical preventive services (e.g., by coordinating mammography vans that visit work sites or neighborhoods, or hosting health fairs at shopping centers that offer blood pressure and cholesterol screening).[48] Rapid improvements in modifiable risks and particularly in preventive services are possible, as evidenced by the doubling of timely screening for breast cancer in the United States from 1987 through 1992.[49] In the early 1980s, use of mammography had been underused by women, especially among black women, but the gap between whites and blacks disappeared by 1992.

State-specific data and racial- and ethnic-specific data from the BRFSS can provide a sound basis for developing and evaluating public health programs to reduce racial and ethnic disparities in health risks. In Georgia, analysis of BRFSS data has prompted implementation of a parallel, local survey in a large urban county to further investigate such disparities. In Alaska, according to BRFSS data, the median percentage of adults who smoke is higher than that for the nation, and in this state American Indians or Alaska Natives have the highest percentage of smokers of all racial or ethnic groups. Alaska is using BRFSS data to support state tobacco control efforts to reduce the prevalence of smoking and its harmful health effects.[50]

This report is a first step toward understanding some of the reasons for racial and ethnic disparities in health and health behaviors. More analytic work is needed to shed light on the reasons for these differences. A better understanding of these differences should help states develop effective, culturally sensitive public health prevention programs to decrease the prevalence of high-risk behaviors and increase the use of preventive services. The BRFSS is also a valuable tool in monitoring progress toward national year 2000 and state health objectives for racial and ethnic populations.

References

1. McGinnis JM, Foege WT. Actual causes of death in the United States. *JAMA* 1993;270:2207-12.

2. Hahn RA, Teutsch SM, Rothenberg RB, Marks JS. Excess deaths from nine chronic diseases in the United States, 1986. *JAMA* 1990;264:2654-9.

3. Public Health Service. Healthy people 2000: national health promotion and disease prevention objective-full report, with

commentary. Washington, DC: US Department of Health and Human Services, Public Health Service, 1991; DHHS publication no. (PHS)91-50212.

4. National Center for Health Statistics. Health, United States, 1998 with socioeconomic status and health chartbook. Hyattsville, MD: US Department of Health and Human Services, CDC, National Center for Health Statistics, 1998; DHHS publication no. (PHS)98-1232.

5. Council of Economic Advisors for the President's Initiative on Race. Changing America: indicators of social and economic well-being by race and Hispanic origin. Washington, DC: Council of Economic Advisors for the President's Initiative on Race, 1998.

6. CDC. Behavioral risk factor survey of Vietnamese–California, 1991. *MMWR* 1992;41:69-72.

7. Nelson DE, Condon K. Objectives and design of the Behavioral Risk Factor Surveillance System. In: American Statistical Association 1998 proceedings of the Section on Survey Research Methods. Alexandria, VA: American Statistical Association, 1999:214-8.

8. Powell-Griner E, Anderson JE, Murphy W. State- and sex-specific prevalence of selected characteristics—Behavioral Risk Factor Surveillance System, 1994 and 1995. In: CDC surveillance summaries (August 1). *MMWR* 1997;46(No. SS-3).

9. Frazier EL, Franks AL, Sanderson LM. Behavioral risk factor data. In: Using chronic disease data: a handbook for public health practitioners. Atlanta: US Department of Health and Human Services, Public Health Service, CDC, 1992:4-1-4-17.

10. Remington PL, Smith MY, Williamson DF, Anda RF, Gentry EM, Hogelin GC. Design, characteristics, and usefulness of state-based behavioral risk factor surveillance: 1981-87. *Public Health Rep* 1988;103:366-75.

11. Waksberg J. Sampling methods for random digit dialing. *J Am Stat Assoc* 1978;73:40-6.

12. Gentry EM, Kalsbeek WD, Hogelin GC, et al. The behavioral risk factor surveys: II. Design, methods, and estimates from combined state data. *Am J Prev Med* 1985;1:9-14.

13. Shah BV, Barnwell BG, Bieler GS. SUDAAN: software for the statistical analysis of correlated data. User's manual, release 7.0 [Software documentation]. Research Triangle Park, NC: Research Triangle Institute, 1996.

14. White AA. Response rate calculation in RDD telephone health surveys: current practices. In: American Statistical Association 1983 proceedings of the Section on Survey Research Methods. Washington, DC: American Statistical Association, 1984:277-82.

15. National Heart, Lung, and Blood Institute. Clinical guidelines on the identification, evaluation, and treatment of overweight and obesity in adults. The evidence report. Bethesda, MD: US Department of Health and Human Services, Public Health Service, National Institutes of Health, 1998; NIH publication no. 98-4083.

16. World Health Organization. Obesity: preventing and managing the global epidemic. Report of a WHO consultation of obesity, Geneva, 3-5 June 1997. Geneva: World Health Organization, 1998.

17. Frazier EL, Okoro CA, Smith C, McQueen DV. State- and sex-specific prevalence of selected characteristics—Behavioral Risk Factor Surveillance System, 1992 and 1993. In: CDC surveillance summaries (December 27). *MMWR* 1996;45(SS-6).

18. Siegel PZ, Frazer EL, Mariolis P, Brackbill RM, Smith C. Behavioral risk factor surveillance, 1991: monitoring progress toward the nation's year 2000 health objectives. In: CDC surveillance summaries (August 27). *MMWR* 1993;42(SS-4).

19. Siegel PZ, Brackbill RM, Frazer EL, Mariolis P, Sanderson LM, Waller MN. Behavioral risk factor surveillance, 1986-1990. In: CDC surveillance summaries (December). *MMWR* 1991;40(SS-4):1-23.

20. Anda RF, Waller MN, Wooten KG, Mast EE, Escobedo LG, Sanderson LM. Behavioral risk factor surveillance, 1988. In: CDC surveillance summaries (June 1). *MMWR* 1990;39(SS-2).

21. CDC. Behavioral risk factor surveillance—selected states, 1986. *MMWR* 1987;36:252-4.

22. CDC. Behavioral risk factor surveillance in selected states—1985. *MMWR* 1986;35:441-4.

23. CDC. Behavioral risk factor surveillance—selected states, 1984. *MMWR* 1986;35:253-4.

24. CDC. Behavioral risk factor surveillance system: reprints from the *MMWR*, 1990-1998. Atlanta: CDC, 1999.

25. Lillie-Blanton M, Laveist T. Race/ethnicity, the social environment, and health. *Soc Sci Med* 1996;43:83-91.

26. Lillie-Blanton M, Parsons PE, Gayle H, Dievler A. Racial differences in health: not just black and white, but shades of gray. *Annu Rev Public Health* 1996;17:411-48.

27. CDC. Prevalence of selected risk factors for chronic disease by education level in racial/ethnic populations—United States, 1991-1992. *MMWR* 1994;43:894-9.

28. Otten MW Jr, Teutsch SM, Williamson DF, Marks JS. The effect of known risk factors on the excess mortality of black adults in the United States. *JAMA* 1990;263:845-50.

29. Guralnik JM, Leveille SG. Annotation: race, ethnicity, and health outcomes—unraveling the mediating role of socioeconomic status. *Am J Public Health* 1997;87:728-30.

30. Shea S, Stein AD, Basch CE, et al. Independent associations of educational attainment and ethnicity with behavioral risk factors for cardiovascular disease. *Am J Epidemiol* 1991;134:567-82.

31. Winkleby MA, Fortmann SP, Barrett DC. Social class disparities in risk factors for disease: eight-year prevalence patterns by level of education. *Prev Med* 1990;19:1-12.

32. Kuttner R. The American health care system: employer-sponsored health coverage. *N Engl J Med* 1999;340:248-52.

33. CDC. Health insurance coverage and receipt of preventive health services—United States, 1993. *MMWR* 1995;44:219-25.

34. Makuc DM, Freid VM, Parsons PE. Health insurance and cancer screening among women. Advance data from vital and health statistics; no. 254. Hyattsville, MD: US Department of

Health and Human Services, Public Health Service, CDC, National Center for Health Statistics, 1994.

35. CDC. Behavioral risk factor survey of Korean Americans–Alameda County, California, 1994. *MMWR* 1997;46:774-7.

36. Geronimus A, Bound J, Waidmann TA, Hillemeier MM, Burns PB. Excess mortality among blacks and whites in the United States. *N Engl J Med* 1996;335:1552-8.

37. Mueller KJ, Patil K, Boilesen E. The role of uninsurance and race in healthcare utilization by rural minorities. *Health Serv Res* 1998;33(pt 1):597-610.

38. Bennefield RL. Health insurance coverage: 1997. *The haves and have-nots*. Washington, DC: US Department of Commerce, Economics and Statistics Administration, Bureau of the Census, 1998. (Current population report P60-202).

39. Kass BL, Weinick RM, Monheit AC. *Racial and ethnic differences in health,* 1996. Rockville, MD: Agency for Health Care Policy and Research, 1999; AHCPR publication no. 99-0001. (MEPS chartbook no. 2).

40. Expert Panel on Detection, Evaluation, and Treatment of High Blood Cholesterol in Adults. Summary of the second report of the National Cholesterol Education Program (NCEP) Expert Panel on Detection, Evaluation, and Treatment of High Blood Cholesterol in Adults (Adult Treatment Panel II). *JAMA* 1993;269:3015-23.

41. CDC. Screening for colorectal cancer—United States, 1997. *MMWR* 1999;48:116-21.

42. Byers T, Levin B, Rothenberger D, Dodd GD, Smith RA. American Cancer Society guidelines for screening and surveillance for early detection of colorectal polyps and cancer: update 1997. *CA Cancer J Clin* 1997;47:154-60.

43. CDC. Behavioral risk factor survey of Chinese—California, 1989. *MMWR* 1992;41:266-70.

44. Passel JS. The growing American Indian population, 1960-1990: beyond demography. In: Sandefur GD, Rindfuss RR, Cohen B, eds. *Changing numbers, changing needs: American Indian demography and public health*. Washington, DC: National Academy Press, 1996:79-102.

45. US Bureau of the Census. *Phoneless in America*. Washington, DC: US Department of Commerce, Economics and Statistics Administration, Bureau of the Census, 1994. (Statistical brief 94-16).

46. Giesbrecht LH, Kulp DW, Starer AW. Estimating coverage bias in RDD samples with Current Population Survey (CPS) data. In: American Statistical Association 1996 proceedings of the Section on Survey Research Methods. Alexandria, VA: American Statistical Association, 1997:503-8.

47. US Preventive Services Task Force. *Guide to clinical preventive services. 2nd ed.* Baltimore: Williams & Wilkins, 1996.

48. Walsh JM, McPhee SJ. A systems model of clinical preventive care: an analysis of factors influencing patient and physician. *Health Educ Q* 1992;19:157-75.

49. Anderson LM, May DS. Has the use of cervical, breast, and colorectal cancer screening increased in the United States? *Am J Public Health* 1995;85:840-2.

50. Owen P, Ingle DE, Schumacher C. The prevalence of tobacco use among Alaska adults. *Alaska Med* 1996;38:21-51.

—Julie C. Bolen, Ph.D., Luann Rhodes, M.P.A., M.P.H., Eve E. Powell-Griner, Ph.D., Shayne D. Bland, M.Sc., Deborah Holtzman, Ph.D.

Chapter 2

Immunization Rates of Youth and Persons Over 65

Goal: Eliminate Disparities in Child and Adult Immunization Rates

The reduction in incidence of vaccine-preventable diseases is one of the most significant public health achievements of the past 100 years. This success is best illustrated by the global eradication of smallpox, achieved in 1977. The major factor in this success is the development and widespread use of vaccines, which are among the safest and most effective preventive measures. Billions of dollars are saved each year through the use of vaccines.

Childhood immunization rates are at an all-time high, with the most critical vaccine doses reflecting coverage rates of over 90 percent. The 1996 immunization coverage targets for all five vaccines (measles, mumps, and rubella [MMR]; polio; diphtheria, tetanus, and pertussis [DTP]; Haemophilus influenza type B [Hib]; and hepatitis b [Hep B]) were exceeded. Although immunization rates have been lower in minority populations compared with the white population, minority rates have been increasing at a more rapid rate, thus significantly narrowing the gap. For example, four of the five 1996 coverage targets were met for blacks. Current efforts must be sustained in order to achieve and maintain at least 90 percent coverage for all recommended vaccines in all populations.

"Race and Health: Immunizations: How to Reach the Goals," Department of Health and Human Services (DHHS), September 13, 1999.

Although coverage for preschool immunization is high in almost all states in the U.S., pockets of need, or areas within each state and major city where substantial numbers of under-immunized children reside, continue to exist. These areas are of great concern because, particularly in large urban areas with traditionally under-served populations, there is a potential for outbreaks of vaccine-preventable diseases.

In addition to the very young, older adults are at increased risk for many vaccine-preventable diseases. Approximately 90 percent of all influenza-associated deaths in the United States occur in people aged 65 and older, the fastest growing age group of the population. Reduction of deaths in this age group has been hindered in part by relatively low vaccine utilization. Immunization is one of the most cost-effective strategies to prevent needless morbidity and mortality. Each year, however, an estimated 45,000 adults die of infections related to influenza, pneumococcal infections, and hepatitis B despite the availability of safe and effective vaccines to prevent these conditions and their complications. In addition, the overall cost to society for vaccine-preventable diseases exceeds $10 billion each year.

There is a disproportionate burden of these diseases in minority and under-served populations. Although vaccination levels against pneumococcal infections and influenza among people 65 years and over have increased slightly for blacks and Hispanics, the coverage in these groups remains substantially below the general population and the year 2000 targets.

Table 2.1. Childhood Immunization Rates*

Race	**1994**	**1997**
White	78%	80%
Black	69%	74%
Asian/Pacific Islander	86%	75%
American Indian/Alaska Native	74%	78%
Hispanic	68%	74%

*Immunization rates reflect those children ages 16-33 months who have received 4 doses of DTO (diptheria, tetanus, pertussis), 3 polio, and 1 MMR (measles, mumps, rubella).

Sources: CDC, NIP, NCHS, National Immunization Survey

Childhood Immunization

The goal is to enhance current immunization efforts in order to achieve and maintain at least 90 percent coverage for all recommended vaccines in all populations and to eliminate remaining disparities among groups. The near-term goal is to achieve and maintain at least 90 percent coverage for all recommended childhood vaccines in all populations.

Adult Immunization

The goal is to increase pneumococcal and influenza immunizations among all adults aged 65 years and older to 60 percent and eventually

Table 2.2. Influenza Immunization Rates among Persons Ages 65 Years and Over

Race	1991	1995
White	43.2%	60.0%
Black	27.2%	39.7%
Asian/Pacific Islander	29.2%	50.8%
American Indian/Alaska Native	47.0%	49.0%
Hispanic	34.0%	49.9%

Source: CDC, NCHG, National Health Interview Survey

Table 2.3. Pneumococcal Immunization Rates among Persons Ages 65 Years and Over

Race	1991	1995
White	21.9%	35.3%
Black	14.1%	21.9%
Asian/Pacific Islander	15.4%	23.4%
American Indian/Alaska Native	30.7%	33.4%
Hispanic	12.1%	23.2%

Source: CDC, NCHG, National Health Interview Survey

to eliminate disparities among groups. The 1994 influenza rates need to nearly double among blacks, Hispanics, and Asians and Pacific Islanders. The 1994 pneumococcal immunization rates among these groups need to nearly quadruple. The near-term goal is to increase pneumococcal and influenza immunizations among all adults aged 65 years and older to 60 percent.

Chapter 3

Infant Mortality Rates

Goal 1: Eliminate Disparities in Infant Mortality Rates

Infant mortality is an important measure of a nation's health and a worldwide indicator of health status. Although infant mortality in the United States has declined steadily over the past several decades and is at a record low of 7.2 per 1,000 live births (1996 data), the United States still ranks 24th in infant mortality compared with other industrialized nations.

Infant mortality rates (IMR's) vary substantially among and within racial and ethnic groups. Infant death rates among blacks, American Indians and Alaska Natives, and Hispanics in 1995 or 1996 were all above the national average of 7.2 deaths per 1,000 live births. The greatest disparity exists for blacks, whose infant death rate (14.2 per 1,000 in 1996) is nearly two and a half times that of white infants (6.0 per 1,000 in 1996). The overall American Indian rate (9.0 per 1,000 live births in 1995) does not reflect the diversity among Indian communities, some of which have infant mortality rates approaching twice the national rate. Similarly, the overall Hispanic rate (7.6 per 1,000 live births in 1995) does not reflect the diversity among this group which had a rate of 8.9 per 1,000 live births among Puerto Ricans in 1995.

To achieve further reductions in infant mortality and morbidity, the public health community, health care providers, and individuals

---

"Race and Health: Infant Mortality: How to Reach the Goals," Department of Health and Human Services (DHHS), September 13, 1999.

must focus on modifying the behaviors, lifestyles, and conditions that affect birth outcomes, such as smoking, substance abuse, poor nutrition, other psychosocial problems (e.g., stress, domestic violence), lack of prenatal care, medical problems, and chronic illness.

Women who receive prenatal care in the first trimester have better pregnancy outcomes than women who receive little or no prenatal care. For example, the likelihood of delivering a very low birth weight (VLBW) infant (less than 1,500 grams or 3 lb. 4 oz.) is 40 percent higher among women who receive late or no prenatal care compared with women entering prenatal care in the first trimester. Approximately 95 percent of VLBW infants are born pre-term (less than 37 weeks gestation). The risk of early death for VLBW infants is about 65 times that of infants who weigh at least 1,500 grams. In 1996, the proportion of pregnant women across the nation receiving prenatal care in the first trimester reached 81.8 percent—a consistent improvement for the seventh consecutive year and up from 75.5 percent in 1989. Yet, one in five pregnant women, or three-quarters of a million women, still did not receive timely prenatal care; almost 47,000 women received no prenatal care at all. In addition, there are substantial racial disparities in the timely receipt of prenatal care.

In 1996, 84 percent of white pregnant women, compared with approximately 71 percent of black and Hispanic pregnant women, received early prenatal care. Eliminating these disparities requires the removal of financial, educational, social, and logistical barriers to care.

Among the leading causes of death in infants, the racial and ethnic disparity (expressed as the ratio of the infant mortality rate for black infants to that for white infants, representing the greatest disparity) is greatest in the following: disorders relating to short gestation (preterm birth [PTB]) and unspecified low birth weight, respiratory distress syndrome, infections specific to the perinatal period and newborns affected by maternal complications of pregnancy, and sudden infant death syndrome (SIDS). Overall, 13 percent of infants die from disorders relating to short gestation. A much higher incidence of PTBs occurs among black mothers than among white mothers (17.7 compared with 9.7 percent). Underlying factors, such as chronic hypertension and bacterial vaginosis, which have higher incidences among blacks, play a role in PTBs.

SIDS accounts for approximately 10 percent of all infant deaths in the first year of life. Minority populations are at greater risk for SIDS. In addition to the greater risk among blacks, the rates are three to four times as high for some American Indian and Alaska Native populations.

We will have a significant impact on infant mortality by increasing our efforts to address the racial disparities that exist in both PTB and SIDS rates. Racial and ethnic differences in PTBs and SIDS most likely reflect variations in the prevalence of risk factors, including socioeconomic and demographic factors, certain medical conditions, quality of and access to health care, and practices such as placing

Table 3.1. Infant Mortality Rates by Race and Ethnicity of Mother Per 1,000 Live Births

Race/Ethnicity	1990	1997
White	7.3	6.0
Black	16.9	13.7
Asian/Pacific Islander	6.6	5.0
American Indian/Alaska Native	13.1	8.7
Hispanic	7.5	6.0
Puerto Rican	9.9	7.9

Source: CDC NCHG, National Vital Statistics System, Linked Birth and Infant Death dataset.

Table 3.2. Sudden Infant Death Syndrome Rates by Race and Ethnicity of Mother Per 100,000 Live Born Infants

Race/Ethnicity	1990	1997
White	110.7	64.4
Black	230.6	143.2
Asian/Pacific Islander	93.2	51.2
American Indian/Alaska Native	307.3	155.6
Hispanic	84.2	46.5

Source: CDC NCHG, National Vital Statistics System, Linked Birth and Infant Death Dataset.

babies on their backs to sleep to prevent SIDS. We can work toward addressing all of these issues and measure their impact on reducing the rates of infant deaths due to PTB and SIDS.

Near-Term Goal

The goal is to continue progress in reducing overall infant mortality rates and to eventually eliminate disparities among groups. As a major step toward that end, we have set a near-term goal to reduce infant mortality among blacks (the group with the greatest disparity in terms of infant death rates) by at least 22 percent from the 1996 rate—or from 14.2 per 1,000 to 11.0 per 1,000 live births. We also will work to reduce infant mortality rates among American Indian and Alaska Natives, and Puerto Ricans, whose rates also are above the national average. In addition, we will continue to monitor progress in reducing the SIDS rates for all racial and ethnic groups as an indicator of our progress toward reducing the national infant mortality rate.

Chapter 4

Alcohol and Minorities

Do blacks, Hispanics, American Indians, and Asians and Pacific Islanders in the United States drink more or less than whites drink? Do they have more alcohol-related medical problems? Do they receive treatment in proportion to their problems? In 1990, 68.3 percent of whites, 64.5 percent of Hispanics, and 55.6 percent of blacks used alcohol.[1] Although these percentages appear similar, different patterns of use and abuse and varying prevalence of alcohol-related problems underlie the numbers.[2-9] This chapter considers why some minorities have more medical problems than others and whether minorities receive adequate treatment and prevention services. It examines genetic and environmental factors that may put minorities at risk for or protect them from alcohol problems. It also reviews research on screening to identify those at risk for alcoholism or alcohol abuse.

Medical Consequences and Alcohol-Related Trauma

Given major underreporting of alcohol-related diagnoses, minimum estimates from one survey of non-Federal, short-stay hospitals in 1991 found 54.5 patient discharges for alcohol-related diagnoses for every 10,000 people in the United States over age 15.[10] The rate for whites was 48.2 per 10,000; however, the rate for blacks was 102.9 per 10,000 population.[10] Because it is not known whether the rates

---

"Alcohol and Minorities—Alcohol Alert No. 23-1994," National Institute on Alcohol Abuse and Alcoholism (NIAAA), January 1994.

of underreporting are equal among ethnic groups, it is difficult to interpret the meaning of such reported differences.

A study of alcohol-related mortality in California showed that blacks and Hispanics had higher rates of mortality from alcoholic cirrhosis than did whites or Asian-Americans. Nationwide, death rates attributed to alcohol dependence syndrome also were highest for blacks, although a higher percentage of blacks than whites abstain from using alcohol.[5,11] The high rates of medical problems seen in blacks thus occur among a smaller percentage of the black population when compared with whites.

The California study suggests that for many alcohol-related causes of death such as alcohol dependence syndrome and alcoholic hepatitis, Hispanics had either similar or lower mortality rates compared with whites. However, the mortality rate among Hispanics from alcohol-related motor vehicle crashes was 9.16 per 100,000, significantly higher than the rates for whites (8.15) or blacks (8.02).[11]

The group identified as "Asian/Other" in the California study had lower rates of alcohol-related mortality than any other group for most causes of death. Their mortality rate from motor vehicle crashes, for example, was 5.39 per 100,000.[11] Asians tend to have lower rates of drinking and alcohol abuse than whites.[2]

Although highly variable among tribes, alcohol abuse is a factor in five leading causes of death for American Indians, including motor vehicle crashes, alcoholism, cirrhosis, suicide, and homicide. Mortality rates for crashes and alcoholism are 5.5 and 3.8 times higher, respectively, among American Indians than among the general population. Among tribes with high rates of alcoholism, reports estimate that 75 percent of all accidents, the leading cause of death among American Indians, are alcohol related.[7]

Fetal Alcohol Syndrome (FAS)

The prevalence of FAS among select groups of Navajo, Pueblo, and Southwestern Plains Indians has been studied. Among two populations of Southwestern Plains Indians ages newborn to 14 years, 10.7 of every 1,000 children were born with FAS. This was compared with 2.2 per 1,000 for Pueblo Indians and 1.6 for Navajo.[12] Overall rates for FAS in the United States range from 1 to 3 per 1,000.[15] Cultural influences, patterns of alcohol consumption, nutrition, and differing rates of alcohol metabolism or other innate physiological differences may account for the varying FAS rates among Indian communities.[13]

The incidence of FAS among blacks appears to be about seven times higher than among whites, although more blacks than whites abstain from drinking.[5,14,15] The reasons for this difference in FAS rates are not yet known.[14,15] Paradoxically, one study has found that black women believe drinking is acceptable in fewer social situations than do white women.[6] Ten percent of black compared with 23 percent of white women surveyed said that drinking more than one or two drinks at a bar with friends is acceptable.[6] This attitudinal difference could help to explain why fewer black women are frequent, high-quantity drinkers than are white women.[6] Nevertheless, FAS seems to be more prevalent among blacks than among whites.

Genetic Influences

Certain minority groups may possess genetic traits that either predispose them to or protect them from becoming alcoholic. Few such traits have so far been discovered. However, the flushing reaction, found in the highest concentrations among people of Asian ancestry, is one example.

Flushing has been linked to variants of genes for enzymes involved in alcohol metabolism. It involves a reddening of the face and neck due to increased blood flow to those areas and can be accompanied by headaches, nausea, and other symptoms. Flushing can occur when even small amounts of alcohol are consumed.[16]

Japanese-Americans living in Los Angeles have been studied. Among those with quick flushing responses (flushing occurs after one drink or less), fewer consumed alcohol than did those with no or with slow flushing responses (flushing occurs after two or more drinks).[17] In another group of Japanese-American students in Los Angeles, flushing was far less correlated with abstention from alcohol than it was in the first group.[17] Thus, although flushing appears to deter alcohol use, people with the trait may nevertheless consume alcohol.

Another genetic difference between ethnic groups occurs among other enzymes involved in metabolizing alcohol in the liver. Variations have been observed between the structures and activity levels of the enzymes prevalent among Asians, blacks, and whites.[18] One enzyme found in Japanese, for example, has been associated with faster elimination of alcohol from the body when compared with whites.[19] Interesting leads relating these varying rates of alcohol metabolism among minorities to medical complications of alcoholism, such as liver disease, are now being followed.

Influence of Acculturation

Acculturation has a dramatic effect on drinking patterns among immigrants to the United States and successive generations. Comparisons of drinking among immigrant and second and third generation Mexican-American women reveal that drinking rates of successive generations approach those of the general population of American women. Seventy-five percent of Mexican immigrant women in one study abstained from alcohol; only 38 percent of third generation Mexican-American women abstained. This rate is close to the 36-percent abstention rate for women in the general U.S. population.[20] Rates of alcohol-related problems also may be affected by acculturation. A study has found that Hispanic women who are at least second generation Americans have higher rates of social and personal problems than either foreign born or first generation Hispanic women.[3] Studies of Asian-Americans have suggested that their drinking rates conform to those of the U.S. population as acculturation occurs.[17,21]

Identification and Treatment

Do screening instruments for alcohol-related problems, validated in primarily white populations, accurately detect alcohol problems among minorities? One study evaluated the Self-Administered Alcoholism Screening Test (SAAST), translated into Spanish, in Mexico City and the original English version in Rochester, MN. The Spanish translation identified alcoholics and non-alcoholics at rates comparable to those of the English version. The study found that the questions that best predicted alcoholism were the same in both versions.[22] This study suggests that translations or other revisions of screening tools may be just as accurate as the original instruments, but more studies are needed before firm conclusions can be drawn.

It is not known whether all treatment programs are effective for members of minority groups. Among minority patients who enter treatment programs for the general population, success rates are equal to those of whites in the same programs.[23,24] Also, despite the existence of programs designed to treat specific minority groups, no evidence exists that either supports or denies their ability to produce improved outcomes.[25,26]

Do minorities have the same access to alcoholism treatment as do whites? Access to treatment for minorities has not been assessed widely, but several factors have been studied. There is evidence that not everyone in these groups who needs treatment receives it. For example, Hispanics and blacks are less likely to have health insurance and more likely to be below the poverty level than whites, factors that may decrease their access to treatment.[24,27,28]

No studies focus on access to alcoholism treatment for the U.S. Hispanic population as a whole.[28] Some culturally sensitive programs exist for Hispanics and are often aimed at specific cultures within this group, such as Puerto Ricans. These programs have not been evaluated.[24,28]

Prevention

Prevention efforts that work among the general population have been shown to be effective among some minorities.[29] However, it is unclear whether interventions designed for specific minorities also would be beneficial. For example, programs incorporating peer counseling, enhancing adolescents' coping skills, and alcohol education appear to be effective among American Indians. One study has demonstrated that specific populations of American Indian adolescents who completed such a program used less alcohol when compared with their peers 6 months after completion of the program.[29] A second study showed that American Indian participants in another program decreased their own use of alcohol when evaluated 12 months after the program's completion.[30]

The effectiveness of warning labels on alcoholic beverage containers has been evaluated in a group of black women.[31] A study showed that 6 months after the label was mandated by law, pregnant black women who were light drinkers slightly reduced their drinking during pregnancy, whereas black women who were heavier drinkers did not change their drinking habits.[31]

Alcohol and Minorities—A Commentary by NIAAA Director Enoch Gordis, M.D.

The increasing number of studies of alcohol problems among minorities has produced both important findings and new questions to answer. Higher abstention rates among African-Americans coexist with higher cirrhosis mortality. Native American groups vary greatly in their drinking practices, but the specific contributions of social, cultural, and genetic influences to these variations are not yet known. We need to understand why acculturation seems to increase drinking among successive generations of Hispanics and diminishes the "protective" effect of the flushing reaction among succeeding generations of Asian-Americans. Finally, we need to know more about disparities in access to treatment and prevention among minority groups and whether culturally relevant treatment approaches improve treatment outcome.

References

1. National Institute on Drug Abuse. *National Household Survey on Drug Abuse: Main Findings 1990*. DHHS Pub. No. (ADM) 91-1788. Washington, DC: Supt. of Docs., U.S. Govt. Print. Off., 1991.

2. Ahern, F.M. Alcohol use and abuse among four ethnic groups in Hawaii: Native Hawaiians, Japanese, Filipinos, and Caucasians. In: *Alcohol Use Among U.S. Ethnic Minorities*. National Institute on Alcohol Abuse and Alcoholism Research Monograph No. 18. DHHS Pub. No. (ADM) 89-1435. Washington, DC: Supt. of Docs., U.S. Govt. Print. Off., 1989. pp. 315-328.

3. Caetano, R. Drinking patterns and alcohol problems in a national sample of U.S. Hispanics. In: *Alcohol Use Among U.S. Ethnic Minorities*. National Institute on Alcohol Abuse and Alcoholism Research Monograph No. 18. DHHS Pub. No. (ADM) 89-1435. Washington, DC: Supt. of Docs., U.S. Govt. Print. Off., 1989. pp. 147-162.

4. Herd, D. Subgroup differences in drinking patterns among black and white men: Results from a national survey. *Journal of Studies on Alcohol* 51(3):221-232, 1990.

5. Herd, D. The epidemiology of drinking patterns and alcohol-related problems among U.S. blacks. In: *Alcohol Use Among U.S. Ethnic Minorities*. National Institute on Alcohol Abuse and Alcoholism Research Monograph No. 18. DHHS Pub. No. (ADM) 89-1435. Washington, DC: Supt. of Docs., U.S. Govt. Print. Off., 1989. pp. 3-50.

6. Herd, D. An analysis of alcohol-related problems in black and white women drinkers. *Addiction Research* 1(3):181-198, 1993.

7. Manson, S.M.; Shore, J.H.; Baron, A.E.; Ackerson, L.; and Neligh, G. Alcohol abuse and dependence among American Indians. In: Helzer, J.E., and Canino, G.J., eds. *Alcoholism in North America, Europe, and Asia*. New York: Oxford University Press, 1992. pp. 113-130.

8. Manson, S.M.; Shore, J.H.; Bloom, J.D.; Keepers, G.; and Neligh, G. Alcohol abuse and major affective disorders: Advances in epidemiologic research among American Indians. In: *Alcohol Use Among U.S. Ethnic Minorities*. National Institute on Alcohol Abuse and Alcoholism Research Monograph No. 18. DHHS Pub. No. (ADM) 89-1435. Washington, DC: Supt. of Docs., U.S. Govt. Print. Off., 1989. pp. 291-300.

9. Windle, M. Alcohol use and abuse: Some findings from the National Adolescent Student Health Survey. *Alcohol Health & Research World* 15(1): 5-10, 1991.

10. Caces, M.F., and Dufour, M.C. *Surveillance Report #28: Trends in Alcohol-Related Morbidity Among Short-Stay Community Hospital Discharges*, United States: 1979-91. National Institute on Alcohol Abuse and Alcoholism. Division of Biometry and Epidemiology. Dec. 1993.

11. Sutocky, J.W.; Shultz, J.M.; and Kizer, K.W. Alcohol-related mortality in California, 1980 to 1989. *American Journal of Public Health* 83(6): 817-823, 1993.

12. May, P.A. Fetal alcohol effects among North American Indians: Evidence and implications for society. *Alcohol Health & Research World* 15(3): 239-248, 1991.

13. Aase, J.M. The fetal alcohol syndrome in American Indians: A high risk group. *Neurobehavioral Toxicology and Teratology* 3(2): 153-156, 1981.

14. Chávez, G.F.; Cordero, J.F.; and Becerra, J.E. Leading major congenital malformations among minority groups in the United States, 1981-1986. *Journal of the American Medical Association* 2 61(2): 205-209, 1989.

15. Sokol, R.J.; Ager, J.; and Martier, S. Significant determinants of susceptibility to alcohol teratogenicity. *Annals of the New York Academy of Sciences* 477: 87-102, 1986.

16. Thomasson, H.R., and Li, T.K. How alcohol and aldehyde dehydrogenase genes modify alcohol drinking, alcohol flushing, and the risk for alcoholism. *Alcohol Health & Research World* 17(2): 167-172, 1993.

17. Nakawatase, T.V.; Yamamoto, J.; and Toshiaki, S. The association between fast-flushing response and alcohol use among

Japanese Americans. *Journal of Studies on Alcohol* 54(1): 48-53, 1993.

18. Burnell, J.C., and Bosron, W.F. Genetic polymorphism of human liver alcohol dehydrogenase and kinetic properties of the isoenzymes. In: Crow, K.E., and Batt, R.D., eds. *Human Metabolism of Alcohol: Volume 2. Regulation, Enzymology, and Metabolites of Ethanol.* Boca Raton, FL: CRC Press, 1989. pp. 65-75.

19. Meier-Tackmann, D.; Leonhardt, R.A.; Agarwal, D.P.; and Goedde, H.W. Effect of acute ethanol drinking on alcohol metabolism in subjects with different ADH and ALDH genotypes. *Alcohol* 7(5): 413-418, 1990.

20. Gilbert, M.J. Acculturation and changes in drinking patterns among Mexican-American women. *Alcohol Health & Research World* 15(3): 234-238, 1991.

21. Johnson, R.C., and Nagoshi, C.T. Asians, Asian-Americans and alcohol. *Journal of Psychoactive Drugs* 22(1): 45-52, 1990.

22. Davis, L.J., Jr.; de la Fuente, J.-R.; Morse, R.M.; Landa, E.; and O'Brien, P.C. Self-Administered Alcoholism Screening Test (SAAST): Comparison of classificatory accuracy in two cultures. *Alcoholism: Clinical and Experimental Research* 13(2): 224-228, 1989.

23. Gilbert, M.J., and Cervantes, R.C. Alcohol services for Mexican Americans: A review of utilization patterns, treatment considerations and prevention activities. *Hispanic Journal of Behavioral Sciences* 8(3): 191-223, 1986.

24. Institute of Medicine. Populations defined by structural characteristics. In: *Broadening the Base of Treatment for Alcohol Problems.* Washington, DC: National Academy Press, 1990. pp. 356-380.

25. Institute of Medicine. Patient-treatment matching and outcome improvement in alcohol rehabilitation. In: *Prevention and Treatment of Alcohol Problems: Research Opportunities.* Washington, DC: National Academy Press, 1989. pp. 231-246.

26. Westermeyer, J. Alcoholism and services for ethnic populations. In: Pattison, E., and Kaufman, E., eds. *Encyclopedic*

Handbook of Alcoholism. New York: Gardner Press, 1982. pp. 709-717.

27. Anderson, R.M.; Giachello, A.L.; and Aday, L.A. Access of Hispanics to health care and cuts in services: A state-of-the-art overview. *Public Health Reports* 101(3): 238-252, 1986.

28. Caetano, R. Priorities for alcohol treatment research among U.S. Hispanics. *Journal of Psychoactive Drugs* 25(1): 53-60, 1993.

29. Gilchrist, L.D.; Schinke, S.P.; Trimble, J.E.; and Cvetkovich, G.T. Skills enhancement to prevent substance abuse among American Indian adolescents. *International Journal of the Addictions* 22(9): 869-879, 1987.

30. Carpenter, R.A.; Lyons, C.A.; and Miller, W.R. Peer-managed self-control program for prevention of alcohol abuse in American Indian high school students: A pilot evaluation study. *International Journal of the Addictions* 20(2): 299-310, 1985.

31. Hankin, J.R.; Firestone, I.J.; Sloan, J.J.; Ager, J.W.; Goodman, A.C.; Sokol, R.J.; and Martier, S.S. The impact of the alcohol warning label on drinking during pregnancy. *Journal of Public Policy & Marketing* 12(1): 10-18, 1993.

Chapter 5

Tobacco Use in U.S. Ethnic and Racial Minority Groups

"Cigarette smoking is the leading preventable cause of disease and death in the United States. We have an enormous opportunity to reduce heart disease, cancer, stroke, and respiratory disease among members of racial and ethnic minority groups, who make up a rapidly growing segment of the U.S. population."—David Satcher, MD, Ph.D., Surgeon General.

Major Conclusions of the Surgeon General's Report

- Cigarette smoking is a major cause of disease and death in each of the four population groups studied in this report. African Americans currently bear the greatest health burden. Differences in the magnitude of disease risk are directly related to differences in patterns of smoking.
- Tobacco use varies within and among racial and ethnic minority groups; among adults, American Indians and Alaska Natives have the highest prevalence of tobacco use, and African American and Southeast Asian men also have a high prevalence of smoking. Asian American and Hispanic women have the lowest prevalence.

"Surgeon General's Report on Tobacco," National Center for Chronic Disease Prevention and Health Promotion, April 1998; and "Ethnicity, Gender, and Risk Factors for Smoking Initiation," by Robin Mermelstein, Ph.D. from *Addicted to Nicotine, A National Research Forum, Section II: Nicotine—Individual Risk Factors for Initiation* Richard R. Clayton, Ph.D., Chair, 1998.

- Among adolescents, cigarette smoking prevalence increased in the 1990s among African Americans and Hispanics after several years of substantial decline among adolescents of all four racial and ethnic minority groups. This increase is particularly striking among African American youths, who had the greatest decline of the four groups during the 1970s and 1980s.
- No single factor determines patterns of tobacco use among racial and ethnic minority groups; these patterns are the result of complex interactions of multiple factors, such as socioeconomic status, cultural characteristics, acculturation, stress, biological elements, targeted advertising, price of tobacco products, and varying capacities of communities to mount effective tobacco control initiatives.
- Rigorous surveillance and prevention research are needed on the changing cultural, psychosocial, and environmental factors that influence tobacco use to improve our understanding of racial and ethnic smoking patterns and identify strategic tobacco control opportunities. The capacity of tobacco control efforts to keep pace with patterns of tobacco use and cessation depends on timely recognition of emerging prevalence and cessation patterns and the resulting development of appropriate community-based programs to address the factors involved.

African Americans

- In the 1970s and 1980s, death rates from respiratory cancers (mainly lung cancer) increased among African American men and women. In 1990-1995, these rates declined substantially among African American men and leveled off in African American women.
- Middle-aged and older African Americans are far more likely than their counterparts in the other major racial and ethnic minority groups to die from coronary heart disease, stroke, or lung cancer.
- Smoking declined dramatically among African American youths during the 1970s and 1980s, but has increased substantially during the 1990s.
- Declines in smoking have been greater among African American men with at least a high school education than among those with less education.

American Indians and Alaska Natives

- Nearly 40 percent of American Indian and Alaska Native adults smoke cigarettes, compared with 25 percent of adults in the overall U.S. population. They are more likely than any other racial and ethnic minority group to smoke tobacco or use smokeless tobacco.
- Since 1983, very little progress has been made in reducing tobacco use among American Indian and Alaska Native adults. The prevalence of smoking among American Indian and Alaska Native women of reproductive age has remained strikingly high since 1978.
- American Indians and Alaska Natives were the only one of the four major U.S. racial and ethnic groups to experience an increase in respiratory cancer death rates in 1990-1995.

Asian Americans and Pacific Islanders

- Estimates of the smoking prevalence among Southeast Asian American men range from 34 percent to 43 percent—much higher than among other Asian American and Pacific Islander groups. Smoking rates are much higher among Asian American and Pacific Islander men than among women, regardless of country of origin.
- Asian American and Pacific Islander women have the lowest rates of death from coronary heart disease among men or women in the four major U.S. racial and ethnic minority groups.
- Factors associated with smoking among Asian Americans and Pacific Islanders include having recently moved to the United States, living in poverty, having limited English proficiency, and knowing little about the health effects of tobacco use.

Hispanics

- After increasing in the 1970s and 1980s, death rates from respiratory cancers decreased slightly among Hispanic men and women from 1990-1995.
- In general, smoking rates among Mexican American adults increase as they learn and adopt the values, beliefs, and norms of American culture.

- Declines in the prevalence of smoking have been greater among Hispanic men with at least a high school education than among those with less education.
- Factors that are associated with smoking among Hispanics include drinking alcohol, working and living with other smokers, having poor health, and being depressed.

Choosing Health

- More than 10 million African Americans, American Indians and Alaska Natives, Asian Americans and Pacific Islanders, and Hispanics smoke cigarettes. Without intervention, this number may swell in the coming decade.
- Both direct and passive exposure to tobacco smoke poses special hazards to pregnant women, babies, and young children. Babies and children who are exposed to tobacco smoke have more ear infections and asthma and die from SIDS more often. Mothers who smoke during pregnancy are more likely to have low birth weight babies and put their babies at increased risk of SIDS.
- Smoking trends today will determine how heavy the health burden will be among communities tomorrow. Programs that reflect cultural diversity will be the foundation in the battle against tobacco use.

Table 5.1. Cigarette Smokers among U.S. Racial and Ethnic Minority Populations. These four groups now make almost a fourth of the U.S. adult population of 194 million

Racial/ethnic group	1995 adult population	1994-1995 smoking prevalence	Number of adult smokers
African Americans	21.4 million	26.5%	5.7 million
American Indians and Alaska Natives	1.3 million	39.2%	0.5 million
Asian Americans and Pacific Islanders	6.2 million	15.3%	0.9 million
Hispanics	17.3 million	18.9%	3.3 million

Source: National Center for Health Statistics, CDC, and U.S. Bureau of the Census.

Powerful Influences Undermine Public Health Efforts

- Smoking is associated with depression, psychological stress, and environmental factors such as peers who smoke and tobacco marketing practices.
- Tobacco advertisements promote the perception of cigarette smoking as safe and far more widespread and socially acceptable than is actually the case.
- Tobacco companies garner community loyalty by hiring community members, providing communities with tobacco sales and advertising revenues, funding community organizations, and supporting educational, political, cultural, and sports activities.

Helping People Enjoy Smoke-Free Lives

- Group approaches for quitting smoking generally have not been successful with members of racial and ethnic minority groups, possibly because the processes used have not been culturally relevant or because of a lack of transportation, money, or access to health care.
- To be effective in discouraging tobacco use among young people, strategies should include restricted access to tobacco products, school-based prevention programs, and mass media campaigns

Table 5.2. Percentage of U.S. Adult Smokers Who Would Like to Stop Smoking

	African Americans	**American Indians/ Alaska Natives**	**Asian Americans/ Pacific Islanders**	**Hispanics**	**Whites**
Characteristic	**%**	**%**	**%**	**%**	**%**
Total	71.4	65.0	60.2	68.7	70.4
Men	68.6	57.3	58.3	63.8	67.8
Women	74.9	79.3	65.3	70.3	72.4

Source: National Health Interview Survey, National Center for Health Statistics, CDC, 1993.

geared to young people's interests, attitudes, and cultural values.

- Most successful programs for quitting smoking do more than deliver culturally appropriate messages. They provide practical information about the health consequences of tobacco use, resources to help people quit, and specific techniques for quitting.

Facts at a Glance

- In the 1970s and 1980s, smoking rates declined substantially among African American youths, regardless of gender, self-reported school performance, parental education, and personal income, but have increased markedly since 1992.
- If current patterns continue, an estimated 1.6 million African Americans who are now under the age of 18 will become regular smokers. About 500,000 of those smokers will die of a smoking-related disease.
- Studies show that adverse infant health outcomes (e.g., the likelihood of pregnant women delivering low birth weight babies, SIDS, and high infant mortality) are especially high for African Americans and American Indians and Alaska Natives. Cigarette smoking also increases these risks, especially for SIDS, among Asian Americans and Pacific Islanders and among Hispanics.
- In all four racial and ethnic minority groups, the percentage of persons who have ever smoked and have quit increases with increasing age.
- In all racial and ethnic minority groups except African Americans, men are more likely than women to use smokeless tobacco.
- Asian Americans and Pacific Islanders are the least likely of the four U.S. racial and ethnic minority groups to smoke, but several local surveys report very high smoking rates among recent male immigrants from Southeast Asia.
- Most African American, Asian American and Pacific Islander, and Hispanic smokers smoke fewer than 15 cigarettes a day. Heavy smoking—25 or more cigarettes a day—is most common among American Indians and Alaska Natives, but still lower than among whites who smoke.

Ethnicity, Gender, and Risk Factors for Smoking Initiation

The prevalence of cigarette smoking has increased significantly among youth over the past several years. In 1991, 27.5 percent of high school students smoked cigarettes, compared with 36.4 percent in 1997. These overall rates mask important racial, ethnic, and gender differences, however. Smoking is more common among white students (39.7 percent) than among Hispanic (34.0 percent) and black students (22.7 percent). The racial and ethnic differences are particularly striking among females; more than two times as many white females currently smoke (39.9 percent) as black females (17.4 percent), and almost five times as many white females are frequent smokers (20.1 percent) compared with black females (4.3 percent). Earlier data have shown high prevalence rates among American Indians and low prevalence rates among Asian American and Pacific Islander youth, especially females. Smoking among black youth has shown the greatest increase since 1991, almost doubling from 12.6 percent in 1991 to 22.7 percent in 1997.

What might explain these ethnic and gender differences? What accounts for the relative resiliency of black and Asian American females, and how do they differ from white females? This section presents highlights of racial, ethnic, and gender differences in risk factors for smoking and identifies questions for researchers to address.

What We Know

Although there is a plethora of studies on risk factors for initiation, the majority focus almost exclusively on white youth, and as a result, we know much less about how risk factors for smoking may differ among the racial, ethnic, and gender subgroups. Generalizing findings from the studies of white youth may be inappropriate, and few studies have specifically compared racial, ethnic, and gender subgroups. There are, however, some hints at important differences across the subgroups.

The Relative Role of Family Versus Peer Influences

Peer smoking and peer-group identification are consistently strong predictors of smoking among white adolescents, but are far less consistent predictors of smoking among other adolescents, especially among African Americans. Among whites, parent and family factors play a much less important role in predicting onset. Cultural differences in the importance of family and value on family messages may moderate the power of peer influence. Data from qualitative studies of several ethnic groups found that nonwhite youth reported stronger antismoking messages and perceived consequences for smoking from parents than did white youth. Youth who were not white reported the strong belief that youth smoking was disrespectful to parents, and there was a strong value placed on not "shaming" the family (especially among females).

Perceived Negative Consequences of Smoking

Although the majority of youth acknowledge the health consequences of smoking, survey data show that American Indian students are less likely to agree with such statements. Asian American female students are more likely than other groups to agree that there is strong social disapproval of smoking. Racial, ethnic, and gender subgroups may also differ dramatically in the perceived negative consequences of smoking that are not health related. Qualitative data indicate that African American girls are unique in their view of smoking as "risky." For African American girls, smoking may be seen as the first step "down a slippery slope" and incompatible with a promising, successful, and healthy future.

Societal and Cultural Expectations

Such expectations may place white female adolescents at increased risk and may be protective of females in other ethnic groups. White females may be at increased risk for smoking because of smoking-related expectations that are reinforced through broader sociocultural attitudes of the mainstream society. These include beliefs that smoking helps to (1) control weight, and thinness is desirable; (2) control mood, notably anger, stress, and depression, for which white females may be at increased risk; and (3) enhance one's image of being independent and sophisticated, characteristics that are idealized in cigarette advertisements targeted to females and that might uniquely apply to white female adolescents.

Identification with mainstream, white society may influence how much youth from other ethnic groups endorse these beliefs as well. In contrast, strong cultural antismoking norms for females may protect some ethnic minority females notably Asian Americans and Pacific Islanders and, to some extent, less acculturated Hispanic females.

There is a strong sentiment among these groups that smoking is not appropriate for girls, is "unladylike," and ruins a girl's reputation.

Popular Media/Entertainment

Celebrities and other public figures may influence the appeal of smoking and be differentially relevant to racial, ethnic, and gender subgroups. Messages about smoking appear everywhere to youth, notably in entertainment outlets (music, television, and movies) that may appeal to youth. Qualitative data suggest that youth are very aware of the smoking status of public personalities (e.g., music and entertainment figures) and often cite that appealing personalities have positive smoking messages (through image, behavior, in music). The prevalence of smoking in the entertainment media may have increased during recent years.

What We Need to Know

Specific Examination of Ethnic and Gender Effects

The relationship between smoking and certain risk factors may vary by racial, ethnic, and gender subgroups, and the prevalence and relative importance of risk factors may vary as well. We need to identify and compare more specifically predictors of smoking and protective factors among the racial, ethnic, and gender subgroups.

Parental/Familial Influence

Qualitative data suggest that parental messages about smoking matter, although quantitative data may suggest that parental influences wear off over time, primarily for white youth. We do not know, though, how parental smoking and verbal messages about smoking interact and are interpreted by youth from different subgroups. We need to know more about the consistency and strength of parental messages, how they vary developmentally with the youth, how they interact with other risk factors, and how these can be enhanced to inhibit youth smoking.

How Youth Cope with Negative Moods

Mood management is a primary reason for smoking across all youth subgroups. We need to know more about why some youth choose to cope with negative moods by smoking, whereas others might choose other substances, behaviors, or coping strategies and whether these vary by gender and ethnicity.

Investigate if Factors That Protect Youth in Some Subgroups Can Be Diffused to Others.

We need to explore whether some of the strong "counter-mandates" against smoking that exist for African American and Asian American females can be diffused to other subgroups or whether these protective factors are truly culture specific.

Recommended Reading

Bachman, J.G.; Wallace, J.M., Jr.; O'Malley, P.M.; Johnston, L.D.; Kurth, C.L.; and Neighbors, H.W. Racial/ethnic differences in smoking, drinking, and illicit drug use among American high school seniors. *Am J Public Health* 81(3):372-377, 1991.

Centers for Disease Control and Prevention. Tobacco use among high school students–United States, 1997. *MMWR Morb Mortal Wkly Rep* 47:229-233, 1998.

Conrad, K.; Flay, B.R.; and Hill, D. Why children start smoking cigarettes: Predictors of onset. *Br J Addict* 87:1711-1724, 1992.

Flay, B.R.; Hu, F.; Siddiqui, O.; Day, L.E.; Hedeker, D.; Petraitis, J.; Richardson, J.; and Sussman, S. Differential influence of parental smoking and friends' smoking on adolescent initiation and escalation of smoking. *J Health Soc Behav* 35:248-265, 1994.

Landrine, H.; Richardson, J.L.; Klonoff, E.; and Flay, B. Cultural diversity in the predictors of adolescent cigarette smoking: The relative influence of peers. *J Behav Med* 17:331-435, 1994.

For More Information

Office on Smoking and Health

National Center for Chronic Disease Prevention and Health Promotion
Centers for Disease Control and Prevention
4770 Buford Highway, NE (Mail Stop K-50)
Atlanta, GA 30341-3717
Tel: 770-488-5707
Toll Free: 800-CDC-1311
Fax: 770-332-2552
E-mail: tobaccoinfo@cdc.gov
Website: http://www.cdc.gov/tobacco

Chapter 6

Drug Use in Racial and Ethnic Minorities

Among Puerto Ricans, African Americans, and Asians, cultural influences and ethnic identification may significantly influence drug use. Studies conducted by National Institute on Drug Abuse (NIDA) researchers in New York City suggest that Puerto Rican and African American adolescents who strongly identify with their communities and cultures are less vulnerable to risk factors for drug use and benefit more from protective factors than do adolescents without this identification. In San Francisco, NIDA-supported research demonstrated different patterns of drug use among different subgroups of the Asian community. These findings suggest that incorporating ethnic and cultural components into drug abuse prevention programs can make these programs more effective.

Adolescents who strongly identify with their communities and cultures are less vulnerable to risk factors for drug use. In one study, Dr. Judith Brook at the Mount Sinai School of Medicine in New York City examined the extent to which ethnic and cultural factors influenced drug-related behavior in Puerto Rican adolescents. She and her colleagues interviewed 275 males and 280 females aged 16 to 24. The researchers asked the participants to describe the importance in their lives of cultural and ethnic factors such as observation of Hispanic

---

"Ethnic Identification and Cultural Ties May Help Prevent Drug Use," by Patrick Zickler, *NIDA Notes* Research Findings, Volume 14, Number 3, 1998; and "Race and Drugs: Perception and Reality, New Rules for Crack Versus Powder Cocaine," by Barry R. McCaffrey, Director Office of National Drug Control Policy, 1997.

holidays and customs, preference for speaking Spanish or English, feelings of attachment to their ethnic group, ethnic affiliation of their friends, and the value placed on the family. The participants also answered questions designed to assess their personal risk for drug use; these risk factors included the use of drugs by parents or siblings, peer use or tolerance of drug use, perception of the risks of drug use, and the availability of illegal drugs in their environment. The participants were categorized into stages of drug use: no reported drug use, used alcohol or tobacco only, used marijuana but no other illicit drug, or used illicit drugs other than or in addition to marijuana.

"Other studies have looked at ethnic identification in isolation, not as an interactive part of a young person's cultural and social context," Dr. Brook says. "We wanted to determine the extent to which ethnic and cultural factors might mitigate risk factors or enhance protective factors and lead to lower stages of drug use. We found that strong ethnic identification acts to offset some risks, resulting in less drug use.

"For example, strong identification with Puerto Rican cultural factors offsets drug risks such as a father's drug use, peer tolerance of drugs, and the availability of drugs. Identification with Puerto Rican friends offsets risks associated with family tolerance for drug use and drug availability," Dr. Brook notes. Ethnic identification also serves to amplify the effect of protective factors, Dr. Brook says. For example, among participants whose siblings were not drug users, those with a strong Puerto Rican affiliation were significantly more likely to be in a lower stage of drug use than those whose affiliation was weaker.

In a related study that focused on late-adolescent African Americans in New York City, Dr. Brook and her colleagues found a similar interaction between ethnic and cultural identification and drug use. The study involved 627 participants—259 male and 368 female—aged 16 to 25 years. The researchers found that components of ethnic identity—such as awareness of African American history and tradition, identification with African American friends, or participation in African American cultural activities such as Kwanzaa—interacted with other factors to reduce risk or to enhance protection. "In isolation, few specific components of ethnic identity play a role as main effects on drug use. Instead, they act in combination with family, personality, or peer influences to blunt the negative impact of risk factors and magnify the positive value of protective factors," Dr. Brook says.

"Together, the research with Puerto Rican and African American populations points out the importance of incorporating ethnic identity into drug programs," Dr. Brook concludes. "It can be a valuable part of drug prevention programs in communities and can also be applied to individual treatment programs."

Cultural Differences Lead to Different Patterns of Drug Use

In another NIDA-supported study, Dr. Tooru Nemoto and his colleagues at the University of California, San Francisco, have identified patterns of drug use among Asian drug users that are unique to ethnicity, gender, age group, and immigrant status. "Large multiracial studies have not distinguished between Asian ethnic groups," Dr. Nemoto says. "The purpose of our study was to describe the patterns of drug use in Chinese, Filipino, and Vietnamese groups and to assess the relationship between cultural factors and drug use among the groups."

The San Francisco study was based on qualitative interviews with 35 Chinese, 31 Filipino, and 26 Vietnamese drug users who were not enrolled in treatment programs. All participants were 18 years or older, with an average age of 32.5, and had used illicit drugs more than three times per week during the preceding 6 months. Overall, immigrants and women represented 66 percent and 36 percent, respectively. However, all Vietnamese were immigrants. Overall, participants born in the U.S. began using drugs at an earlier age, 15 years, than did immigrant Asians, 19 years, and were more likely than immigrants to use more than one drug. In general, women started drug use at about the same age as men, about 17.5 years, but ethnic groups showed a varied pattern. Chinese women began earlier at 15.2 years than Chinese men at 18.5 years. Filipino women began using drugs later at 15.5 years than Filipino men at 13.1 years. Vietnamese women in the study started drug use much later at 27.8 years than did Vietnamese men at 19.9 years.

Dr. Nemoto and his colleagues identified differences in drug use among the ethnic groups. Filipino drug users were most likely to have begun drug use with marijuana, while Vietnamese drug users in the study most often started with crack or powder cocaine. Chinese and Vietnamese were twice as likely as Filipinos to be using crack as their current primary drug. Filipinos were four times more likely to be using heroin than were Chinese or Vietnamese. Filipino study participants were more likely than Chinese or Vietnamese to be injecting and less likely to be smoking drugs. There were also significant differences in the characteristics of drug user networks among the ethnic groups. For example, Filipinos were more than twice as likely as

Chinese or Vietnamese participants to use drugs in groups that included members of other races or ethnic groups.

"These differences among ethnic groups have important implications for the way we design programs aimed at Asian drug users," Dr. Nemoto says. "Prevention programs should address the common factors among Asian drug users, such as stigma associated with injection drug use, but we should also be careful to incorporate factors that are unique to each target group."

Sources

Brook, J.S., et al. Drug use among African Americans: Ethnic identity as a protective factor. *Psychological Reports* 83:1427-1446, 1998.

Brook, J.S.; Whiteman, M.; Balka, E.B.; Win, P.T.; and Gursen, M.D. Drug use among Puerto Ricans: Ethnic identity as a protective factor. *Hispanic Journal of Behavioral Sciences* 20(2):241-254, 1998.

Nemoto, T., et al. Drug use behaviors among Asian drug users in San Francisco. *Addictive Behavior* (in press).

Perception and Reality, New Rules for Crack Versus Powder Cocaine

"Would you close your eyes for a second, envision a drug user, and describe that person to me?" This question appeared on a survey, the results of which were published in 1995 in the *Journal of Alcohol and Drug Education* (Burston, Jones, and Robertson-Saunders, "Drug Use and African Americans: Myth Versus Reality"). Ninety-five percent of respondents pictured a black drug user while only 5 percent imagined other racial groups. The truth is most drug users in the United States are white. African Americans constitute only 15 percent of current U.S. drug users. Before falsely stigmatizing any minorities, we should bear in mind that more whites than blacks use both forms of cocaine (according to the 1995 National Household Survey on Drug Abuse). Cocaine is a problem that afflicts the entire country.

The controversy over federal sentencing disparities for "crack" versus powder cocaine reflects and contributes to racial tension. At present, federal laws pertaining to crack cocaine are a hundred times more severe than for powder cocaine. As a result of the 1986 Anti-Drug Abuse Act, a five-year minimum prison sentence is required for anyone possessing five grams of crack or five hundred grams of powder cocaine. By comparison, simple possession (no distribution intended) of small quantities of powder cocaine—on the part of first-time offenders—is only a misdemeanor punishable by no more than a year in prison. Because crack cocaine is less expensive and more common in inner cities, harsher punishment for crack has been interpreted as discrimination against blacks.

The current federal sentencing policy has produced disproportionally severe punishment for African Americans. According to the most recent figures, African Americans constitute 15 percent of cocaine users. However, 38 percent of those charged with powder cocaine violations, and 88 percent of those convicted of crack cocaine charges, are black. (Crack accounts for about half of total U.S. cocaine consumption.) For crimes involving 50 to 150 grams of cocaine, crack defendants received median sentences of 120 months in prison compared to 18 months for powder. Since nearly all cocaine is smuggled into our country and transported over state lines in powdered form (one gram of powder cocaine converts into .89 grams of crack), the federal sentencing disparity has produced long incarceration for low-level crack dealers rather than for international, interstate, and wholesale traffickers.

Chapter 7

The Challenges of Aging

Health and Older Minorities

Many of the people who participate in the Asian Seniors Health Project have been denied health care in the past. A history of discrimination tends to obscure any desire they have to get help, says Carlina Yeung, director of the project. The result is that "older Asians in our area seek health care on a crisis basis when a health problem becomes a real emergency."

The seniors find they are unable to communicate health needs because of language barriers. They are discouraged by the lack of cultural understanding that plagues the mainstream health care system. Recent immigrants view the system as intimidating and too hard to understand. Some harbor a general distrust of western medicine. Recognizing how these factors influence the help-seeking behavior of a population is critical to delivering high-quality health services, Ms. Yeung said.

The Asian Seniors Health Project, a grantee of the Office of Minority Health, is part of Asian Americans for Community Involvement (AACI), a community health center in San Jose, California. The project targets Chinese, Vietnamese, Cambodian, and Laotian individuals who are aged 55 years and older. Services include mental health and nutrition counseling, health education seminars, and screenings to test for diabetes and hypertension.

Excerpts from "Aging," *Closing the Gap*, May/June 1996, Office of Minority Health.

The project takes a health promotion and case management approach. "We make doctor's appointments, provide transportation and translation services, and ensure that appropriate steps are taken for follow-up care," Ms. Yeung said. It's a holistic method that requires the project's health educators to understand a client's family relationships, advocate on a patient's behalf, and refer a client for additional services when necessary.

Across all four Asian populations that the project reaches, hypertension and stroke persist as the biggest health problems. While the groups share some similarities, their differences are just as notable. For example, Chinese and Vietnamese seniors are more independent, Ms. Yeung said. "They're much more willing to take the bus to get to appointments, whereas Cambodians and Laotians are inclined to confine themselves to home."

To meet the needs of those seniors who are more homebound, the Asian Seniors Health Project is developing teams of nurses and health promoters to conduct home visits more frequently. Additionally, the center is recruiting bilingual/bicultural volunteers who can provide cultural competency training to health providers.

This training is essential because of the limited choice of providers offered through managed care. Managed care is overwhelming to AACI clients, said Ms. Yeung. "They sign up for health plans and then don't understand how they're supposed to use the system," she said. Most health plans don't have literature in English that is easily understandable, she added. And finding material in Asian languages is much harder. A major point of conflict is that a managed care system, by its nature, seeks to cut costs. So spending the money it takes to make a plan more accessible to minority groups may be regarded as more costly.

Surviving Managed Care

The pressing question is whether clinics that serve elderly Asians can survive in a managed care climate, says Don Watanabe, executive director of the National Asian Pacific Center on Aging (NAPCA) in Seattle, Washington. Small clinics are in a precarious position, he said. "They are trying to access and maintain the funding and resources they need to keep operating." But with the build-up of health maintenance organizations, their livelihood is threatened.

Clinic directors are wondering whether to compete with HMOs or join them. "There are no easy answers," said Mr. Watanabe. "But without community clinics, health care for the Asian elderly is likely to fall by the wayside." Asian and Pacific Islander (API) advocacy and direct service provider organizations are urging legislators and other mainstream decision makers in the health care industry to address this issue of inclusion for API elderly.

One role of NAPCA is to develop coalitions and get as many agencies as possible talking about shared concerns such as managed care, said Jeffry Young, Phi, director of advocacy and demonstration projects. "The goal is to increase dialogue about alternatives for those individuals whose needs aren't being met by the one-size-fits-all health care system," he added.

To address the lack of Asian language materials, NAPCA has launched a new program called Facsimile Information in Translation (FAX-IT). Callers can dial into FAX-IT and choose from more than 300 documents in 15 languages on health, nutrition, culture, and social services. Callers make selections using the touch-tone keys on the telephone handset of their fax machine. When a caller hangs up, FAX-IT immediately faxes back the requested information. Callers may reach FAX-1T at 206-624-0185.

AARP Works to Improve Minority Health

Office of Minority Affairs

AARP's Office of Minority Affairs works to change the thinking and actions of older minorities, their families, and the general public, in order to advance the health and well-being of this population. The office provides health education in a range of areas including nutrition and disease prevention. "We work to help reduce the incidence of diseases endemic to minorities," Ms. Bacon said.

Minority Health Facts

- Leading causes of death for African Americans aged 65 and older. Men: heart disease, lung cancer, stroke, chronic obstructive pulmonary disease. Women: heart disease, stroke, diabetes, lung cancer, and colorectal cancer.
- Leading causes of death for Hispanics/Latinos aged 65 and older. Men: heart disease, lung cancer, stroke, chronic obstructive pulmonary disease, and prostate cancer. Women: heart disease, stroke, diabetes, lung cancer, and colorectal cancer.
- Leading causes of death for Asians and Pacific islanders aged 65 and older. Men: heart disease, stroke, lung cancer, chronic

abstractive pulmonary disease, and colorectal cancer. Women: heart disease, stroke, lung cancer, diabetes, and colorectal cancer.

- Leading causes of death for American Indians/Alaska Natives aged 65 and older. Men: heart disease, lung cancer, stroke, diabetes, and chronic pulmonary disease. Women: heart disease, stroke, diabetes, chronic obstructive pulmonary disease, and lung cancer.

The Growth of the Older Population

In 1994 the older population, aged 65 and up, numbered 33.2 million, almost 12.7 percent of the U.S. population. By 2030, the number will be about 70 million or 20 percent of the future population. In 1994 minorities made up 14 percent of all older Americans. Eight percent were African American, four percent were Hispanic/Latino, two percent were Asian or Pacific islander, and 1 percent was American Indian/Alaska Native. By 2030, the total minority representation will climb to 25 percent of the elderly population. (Source: A Profile of Older Americans, AARP)

Educating Hispanic/Latino Elderly

For many Hispanic/Latino elderly persons, God is the only doctor. On one hand, this culturally grounded belief can provide a sense of peaceful feeling that everything in life will turn-out as God wants it. No need to worry about the uncontrollable. But on the other hand, the belief can interfere with the practice of prevention.

According to one study of the American Association of Retired Persons (AARP), religious beliefs were a major reason that Hispanic elders postponed medical appointments and failed to seek health education. The study, which assessed health attitudes of Mexicans, Salvadorans, Guatemalans, Puerto Ricans, and Dominicans in New York City and Los Angeles, sought to identify cultural barriers to delivering health education.

In addition to holding strong spiritual convictions, many of the elders practiced folk medicine, especially for colds and stomach problems. The study also found that the respondents considered Hispanic physicians, friends, and family members the most credible sources of health information. And the most effective way to deliver health messages to large audiences turned out to be through Spanish-language radio and television stations, churches, and social clubs. Also popular are toll-free 800 lines with Spanish-speaking operators.

"Mainstream health personnel should be aware of these factors," said Amelia Castillo, a clinical consultant for El Paso Senior Opportunities and Services in Texas. "Knowing that older Hispanics, more so than younger ones, really adhere to religion and traditional medicines," she said, "would help health providers and educators tailor their services."

Other elements that can affect health education for older Hispanics, she added, include a lack of resources, lack of transportation, and lack of mobility. At the top of the list of prevalent diseases among Hispanic elderly persons are diabetes, hypertension, cancer, cardiovascular disease, and glaucoma, she said.

Also of significance are arthritis, substance abuse, and smoking, said Marta Sotomayor, executive director o the National Hispanic Council on Aging (NHCoA), Located in Washington, DC. NHCoA works to improve life for Hispanic/Latino elderly persons. This includes improving health status and education. As an advocacy network with chapters and affiliates across the country, the council shapes policy, conducts research, and administers programs.

NHCoA conducts a multi-site, national program funded by the Centers for Disease Control and Prevention. The program aims to increase the number of older Latinas who seek screening services for breast and cervical cancer. Hispanic women are twice as likely as non-Hispanic whites to suffer from cervical cancer, and are much less likely to know the warning signs.

The Impact of Falls

A large number of elderly African Americans treated for falls suffer pain and limited activities long after the fail, according to a study conducted by the Philadelphia Department of Public Health and the University of Pennsylvania, and supported by a grant from the Centers for Disease Control and Prevention (CDC). The study, which was published in the *Journal of the American Geriatrics Society* a few years ago, was the first to assess falls in elderly African Americans and to identify predictors of recovery. And it is the most recent CDC study to examine falls in this population.

After examining medical records and conducting a series of interviews with 197 African Americans age 65 and up in Philadelphia who were treated in the emergency room after a fall, researchers found that 61 percent were hospitalized for injuries related to the fall. "The circumstances of the fall were such that if they had occurred in younger persons, in all likelihood few persons would have been injured and even fewer would have been subsequently disabled," the authors state.

Factors related to poor recovery included leg injuries. Those who recovered slowest were less likely to be married and more likely to be female. Twenty-six percent of those who had reported continued pain or restricted activity at the time of the first interview had not seen a doctor since the emergency room visit. Because of the apparent lack of follow-up care in some cases, researchers recommend that follow-up programs be implemented for elderly persons who seek emergency room treatment.

Results revealed that the most common time of day for falls was in the morning. The most common place was on stairs. Though researchers couldn't assess whether the pattern of falls among African Americans is different than those among whites, there was a need to conduct a specialized study because race had not previously been considered.

"The impact of falls in this elderly community is substantial," the authors write. "Not only did a number of persons sustain fractures and require hospitalization, but even more importantly, the ability to carry out basic activities of daily living was restricted in a large proportion of cases." Physical frailty, which affects millions of older Americans, is a major contributor to disability from injuries caused by falls.

Asians among Those at High Risk for Osteoporosis

It may be hard to believe, but we experience a cycle of bone loss and replacement throughout our lives. Our bones undergo tremendous growth when we're young, and when we reach our 30s, bone loss begins. The older we get, the faster bones break down sometimes faster than new bone can be formed. The National Osteoporosis Foundation (NOF) says that osteoporosis occurs when too little bone is formed, when too much bone is lost, or a combination of both.

Osteoporosis is preventable and treatable, and it affects both women and men. Women are at high risk for the disease largely because women have less bone mass and lose bone faster than men, particularly with the onset of menopause. At highest risk for osteoporosis are women who are post menopausal and small-boned, as well as those whose diets are low in calcium and Vitamin D. Being white or Asian is also a high risk factor. Whites and Asians have the disease more often than African Americans and Hispanics because of differences in bone mass and density between these groups. Still, African Americans and Hispanics are at significant risk for the disease.

Persons with osteoporosis are susceptible to hip, spine, and wrist fractures. Each year, more than 300,000 hip fractures occur in older people. NOF reports that one out of every five persons who has a hip fracture will not survive more than one year.

American Indian/Alaska Native Elders Face Challenge of Long-Term Care

From 1980 to 1990, the number of American Indian/Alaska Native elders doubled. This population growth, coupled with the shift from acute and infectious diseases to chronic and degenerative diseases in this population, is making long-term care the biggest problem American Indian/Alaska Native elders face, said Dave Baldridge, executive director of the National Indian Council on Aging (NICOA) in Albuquerque, New Mexico.

"One of the key issues," Baldridge said, "is that American Indians/ Alaska Natives are served on an entirely different health care system than the mainstream elderly population." Since 1955, the Indian Health Service (IHS), part of the U. S. Department of Health and Human Services, has been the federal entity responsible for delivering public health service functions to American Indians/Alaska Natives in IHS service areas, generally defined as those areas on or near reservations. This includes 1.3 million people.

Baldridge acknowledged that IHS has made significant strides, such as improving Indian life expectancy, which has gone up to age 72 from age 61 since 1972. "But the fact remains that IHS does not operate nursing homes or other long-term health care facilities," he said.

Some members of the public believe the myth that all Indian tribes participate in gaming the practice of gambling, Baldridge said. "And they take it a step further to say that gaming tribes are making so much money that they have enough to invest in long-term care. But as of 1993, there were only 12 tribally operated nursing homes in the United States."

IHS is beginning to address the issue of long-term care through its Elder Care Initiative, which IHS director Michael Trujillo, M.D., M.P.H., introduced in October of 1995. According to Louise Kiger, M.N., R.N., coordinator of the initiative, "the effort will explore ways to improve Indian health care and increase community/tribal capacity to develop community-based elder care services."

It's important to know that long-term care does not only encompass nursing homes, said Patrick Stenger, D.O., a member of the Elder Care Initiative. IHS uses a definition that was published in 1995 White Papers called *A National Agenda for Geriatric Education*: "Within medicine, long-term care refers to a comprehensive range of medical, psychological, and social services developed and coordinated to meet the physical, emotional, and social needs of chronically ill persons over a period of time, and may be delivered in a person's own home, in the community, or in an institutional facility."

"Many needs assessments and elders health surveys done in Indian country have shown that Indian elders and tribal leaders want IHS to emphasize home and community-based services." Dr. Stenger said. Examples of these services include primary health care; alcohol, drug, and mental health care; social services; nutrition services; and home visits by public health nurses and community health representatives all services which IHS provides. So while IHS does not have future plans to start operating nursing homes, the agency's Elder Care Initiative will work to develop home and community care programs and supportive services for Indian elders.

Undoubtedly, the question of who has the primary responsibility for delivering long-term care services to American Indian/Alaska Native elders is complicated by budget constraints. Currently, the HIS Elder Initiative has no funding, and overall, the agency is funded at only 50 to 60 percent of the level it needs to be, said Cliff Wiggins, operations research analyst in the Office of the Director at HIS.

Aging Resources

The American Society on Aging
833 Market St., Suite 511
San Francisco, California 94103
Tel: 415-974-9600
Fax: 415-974-0300
E-mail: info@asaging.org
Website: http://www.asaging.org

National Association for the Hispanic Elderly
1452 West Temple Street
Los Angeles, California 90026-1724
Tel: 213-487-1922
Fax: 213-208-5905

Administration on Aging
330 Independence Ave., SW, Room 4755
Washington, DC 20201
Tel: 202-619-7501
Toll Free: 800-677-1116 (Eldercare Locator)

Fax: 202-260-1012
E-mail; aoainfo@aoa.gov
Website: http://www.aoa.dhhs.gov

National Asian Pacific Center on Aging
Melbourne Tower
1511 3rd Ave., Suite 914
Seattle, Washington 98101
Toll Free: 800-336-2722
Tel: 206-624-1221

National Caucus and Center on Black Aged
1424 K St., NW, Suite 500
Washington, DC 20005
Tel: 202-63 7-8400
Fax: 202-347-0895
Website: http://www.ncba-blackaged.org

National Hispanic Council on Aging
2713 Ontario Rd., NW
Washington, DC 20009
Tel: 202-265-1288
Fax: 202-745-2522
E-mail: nhcoa@wowrldnep.att.net
Website: http://www.incacorp.com/nhcoa

National Indian Council on Aging
10501 Montgomery Blvd., NE
Albuquerque, New Mexico 87111
Tel: 505-292-1922
Website: http://www.nicoa.org

National Institute on Aging
National Institutes of Health, Public Information Office
Building 31, Room 5C27
Gaithersburg, Maryland 20898-2292
Toll Free: 800-222-2225
Toll Free TTY: 800-222-4225
Tel: 301-496-1752
Fax: 301-496-1072
E-mail: niainfo@access.digex.net
Website: http://www.nih.gov/nia

American Association of Retired Persons

Office of Minority Affairs
601 E St., NW
Washington, DC 20049
Toll Free: 800-424-3410
Tel: 202-434-2277
Website: http://www.aarp.org

National Resource Center on Minority Aging Populations

University Center on Aging, San Diego State University
College of Health and Human Services
San Diego, California 92182
Tel: 619-594-6765
Fax: 619-594-2811

Part Two

Diseases of Ethnicity

Chapter 8

Allied Diseases Profiled

Tay-Sachs and the allied diseases are genetic conditions classified as storage diseases. They are caused by the abnormal accumulation, or storage, of certain waste products in the cells or tissues of affected individuals. As these products build up, cells become damaged and gradually lose their ability to function properly, causing disease symptoms. While the specific clinical courses of these related disorders differ, they have certain points in common, and children and adults affected with Tay-Sachs or any of the allied diseases share many issues associated with chronic, progressive illness. Table 8.1 provides a quick reference for the major characteristics of the allied diseases. The Omim # refers to the catalogue citation on the Online Mendelian Inheritance In Man, the hypertext version of Victor McCusick's landmark catalogue of human genetic disease.

Additionally, the following Allied Diseases are profiled in more depth in their own chapters: Tay-Sachs Disease, Sandhoff Disease, Gaucher Disease, Niemann-Pick Disease, and Canavan Disease. This information is provided in response to a growing demand for knowledge and in the hopes of increasing awareness and understanding of these rare, but often devastating, diseases.

Table 8.1. Tay-Sachs & the Allied Diseases

Disease	Enzyme Defect	Omim #	Prenatal Diagnosis?	Carrier Testing?	Chromosome Location	Inherits Pattern
Lysosomal Storage Disorders						
Disorders of Lipid and Sphingloid Degradation						
GM1 Gangliodsidosisb	b-Galactosidase	230500	Yes	Yes	3	AR
Tay-Sachs Disease	b-Hexosaminidase	A272800	Yes	Yes	15	AR
Sandhoff Disease	b-Hexosamindase A&B	268800	Yes	Yes	5	AR
GM2 Gangliosidosis: AB Variant	GM2 Activator Protein	272750	Yes	No	5	AR
Fabry Disease	a-Galactosidase A	301500, 230800	Yes	Yes	X	X-Linked
Gaucher Disease	Glucocerebrosidase	230900, 231000	Yes	Yes	1	AR
Metachromatic Leukodystrophy	Arylsulfatase A	250100	Yes	Yes	22	AR
Krabbe Disease	Galactosylceramidase	245200	Yes	Yes	14	AR
Niemann-Pick, Types A and B	Acid Sphingomyelinase	257200	Yes	Yes	18	AR
Niemann-Pick, Type C	Cholesterol Esterification Defect	257200	Yes	Yes	18	AR
Farber Disease	Acid Ceramidase	228000	Yes	Yes	?	(AR)
Wolman Disease	Acid Lipase	278000	Yes	Yes	10	AR
Cholesterol Storage Disease	Acid Lipase	278000	Yes	Yes	10	AR
Disorders of Mucopolysaccharide Degradation						
Hurler Syndrome (MPS III)	a-L-Iduronidase	252800	Yes	Yes	4	AR
Scheie Syndrome (MPS IS)	a-L-Iduronidase	252800	Yes	Yes	4	AR
Hurler-Scheie (MPS IH/S)	a-L-Iduronidase	252800	Yes	Yes	4	AR

Hunter Syndrome (MPS II)	Iduronate Sulfatase	309900	Yes	Yes	X	X-Linked
Sanfilippo A (MPS IIIA)	Heparan N-Sulfatase	252900	Yes	?	17	AR
Sanfilippo B (MPS IIIB)	a-N-Acetylglucosaminidase	252920	Yes	Yes	17	AR
Sanfilippo C (MPS IIIC)	Acetyl-CoA-Glucosaminide Acetyltransferase	252930	Yes	?	14	AR
Sanfilippo D (MPS IIID)	N-Acetylglucosamine -6-Sulfatase	252940	Yes	?	12	AR
Morquio A (MPS IVA)	Galactosamine-6-Sulfatase	253000	Yes	Yes	16	AR
Morquio B (MPS IVB)	b-Galactosidase	253010	Yes	Yes	3	AR
Maroteaux-Lamy (MPS VI)	Arylsulfatase B	253200	Yes	Yes	5	AR
Sly Syndrome (MPS VII)	b-Glucuronidase	253220	Yes	Yes	7	AR
Disorders of Glycoprotein Degradation						
Mannosidosis	a-Mannosidase	248500	Yes	?	19	AR
Fucosidosis	a-L-Fucosidase	230000	Yes	?	1	AR
Asparylglucosaminuria	N-Aspartyl- b-Glucosaminidase	208400	Yes	Yes	4	AR
Sialidosis (Mucolipidosis I)	a-Neuraminidase	256550	Yes	?	20	AR
Galactosialidosis	Lysosomal Protective Protein	256540	Yes	?	20	AR
Schindler Disease	a-N-Acetyl-Galactosaminidase	104170	Yes	Yes	22	AR
Other Lysosomal Storage Disorders						
Batten Disease						
(Juvenile Neuronal Ceroid Lipofuscinosis)	Unknown	204200	Yes	?	16	AR
(Infantile Neuronal Ceroid Lipofuscinosis)	Palmitoyl-Protein Thioesterase	256730	Yes	Yes	4	AR

Table 8.1. **(continued on next page)**

Table 8.1. Tay-Sachs & the Allied Diseases **(Continued)**

Other Lysosomal Storage Disorders (continued)						
Pompe Disease	Acid-a1, 4-Glucosidase	232300	Yes	Yes	17	AR
Mucolipidosis II (I-Cell Disease)	N-Acetylglucosamine-1-Phosphotransferase	252500	Yes	Yes	4	AR
Mucolipidosis III (Pseudo-Hurler Polydystrophy)	Same as ML II	252600	Yes	Yes	4	AR
Mucolipidosis IV	Unknown		?	No	?	(AR)
Cystinosis	Cystine Transport Protein	219750	Yes	Yes	17	AR
Salla Disease	Sialic Acid Transport Protein	269920	Yes	?	6	AR
Infantile Sialic Acid Storage Disease	Sialic Acid Transport Protein	269920	Yes	?	6	AR
Saposin Deficiencies	Saposins A, B, C or D	176801	Yes	No	10	AR
B. Non-Lysosomal Diseases						
Abetalipoproteinemia	Microsomal Triglyceride Transfer Protein	200100	Yes	?	4	AR
X-Linked Adrenoleuk-odystrophy	Peroxisomal Membrane Transfer Protein	300100	Yes	Yes	X	X-Linked
Refsum Disease	Phytanic Acid a-Hydroxylase	266500	Yes	?	?	(AR)
Canavan Disease	Aspartoacylase	271900	Yes	Yes	17	AR
Cerebrotendinous Xanthromatosis	Sterol-27-Hydroxlase		No	Yes	2	AR
Pelizaeus Merzbacher Disease	Lipophlin	312080	Yes	Yes	X	X-Linked
Tangier Disease	Apo-Gln-1	205400	No	No	?	(AR)

More Information

National Tay-Sachs & Allied Diseases Association
2001 Beacon Street, Suite 204
Brighton, MA 02135
Toll Free: 800-906-8723
Fax: 617-277-0134
Website: http://www.ntsad.org/ntsad/contact.htm

Chapter 9

Canavan Disease

Canavan Disease (CD) is named for Myrtelle Canavan, who first described the disorder in 1931. Since that time, much has been learned about the genetic and biochemical bases of the disease. Recent developments in the understanding of the genetic defect involved in Canavan Disease have increased not only the ability to diagnose CD accurately, but also the accuracy of carrier screening and prenatal detection for at-risk families.

Clinical signs in an individual with CD usually begin during infancy. Parents may begin to notice subtle changes, such as visual inattentiveness or an inability to perform motor tasks, at around three to nine months. One of the earliest signs of CD recognized by many parents is overall low muscle tone and lack of head control. As the child grows, motor skills and mental functioning deteriorate. The child eventually becomes blind, but hearing remains sharp. Affected children continue to recognize and respond to the voices of their primary caregivers. Difficulties which arise as the child grows include stiffness, weakness of the muscles, seizures, and feeding problems.

It is not possible to describe all children with CD in the same way, since the presentation and progression of illness varies from child to child. Although many children with CD die in infancy, some survive into adolescence and even occasionally into adulthood.

- Fact: One of the earliest signs of Canavan Disease recognized by many parents is overall low muscle tone and lack of head control.

Canavan Disease belongs to a group of conditions known as leukodystrophies, which result from defects in myelin. Myelin, a substance made up of proteins and lipids, is an integral component of the nervous system. It is commonly known as the "white matter" in the brain; its function is to protect nerves and allow messages to be sent to and from the brain. In CD the white matter deteriorates because affected children have a deficiency of the enzyme aspartoacylase, which leads to the accumulation of a chemical, called N-acetyl-aspartic acid (NAA), in the brain. It is not known exactly how this chemical imbalance causes the destruction of myelin but all of the symptoms of CD can be explained by this progressive loss of myelin.

Canavan Disease, like Tay-Sachs, is inherited as an autosomal recessive trait. Both of the parents of an affected child are carriers of an altered gene on chromosome 17, which is responsible for synthesizing aspartoacylase. A parent who is a carrier is healthy because he or she has one functional copy of the gene which produces a sufficient amount of the enzyme. A child who receives two altered copies of the gene, one from each parent, is unable to produce any aspartoacylase and will develop the symptoms of CD.

Canavan Disease is most commonly found in people of Ashkenazi Jewish descent, although it is seen also in other ethnic groups. Biochemical tests for aspartoacylase activity are not sensitive enough to detect carriers, but DNA testing of Ashkenazi Jewish couples can tell with over 95% certainty whether either or both parents is a carrier. If neither or only one parent carries a mutation in the aspartoacylase gene, the couple is not at risk for having a child with Canavan Disease. If both parents are carriers, there is a 25% chance with each pregnancy that their child will have Canavan Disease. Genetic counseling is important to assist at-risk couples in exploring their options in planning their families. Accurate and reliable DNA-based prenatal testing, using samples obtained through CVS or amniocentesis, is available to couples who are both carriers of identified mutations.

- Fact: In situations where at least one parent is not of Ashkenazi Jewish ancestry, DNA testing for Canavan Disease may be less informative.

Many of the DNA mutations which cause Canavan Disease in children of other ethnic backgrounds are unique to individual families.

In situations where a non-Ashkenazi individual has a family history of Canavan Disease, it may be possible to identify the mutation in that family and use the information for prenatal diagnosis. However, identifying individual mutations is costly and time-consuming and requires initiative on the part of the individuals seeking the information, since it is not routinely done. Another method of prenatal diagnosis which may provide information to families with unidentified mutations is linkage analysis, a form of DNA testing which compares the DNA of the fetus to that of affected and unaffected relatives to determine whether the fetus is likely to be affected. A third method relies on the measurement of NAA levels in amniotic fluid; accurate determination of NAA levels in amniotic fluid is difficult but it is performed at one or two laboratories in the U.S.

Because of the severity of Canavan Disease, the lack of treatment for it, and its high incidence in the Ashkenazi Jewish population, population screening within the Jewish community is beginning to be offered using the model developed for population screening for Tay-Sachs Disease. The goal of population-based screening is to identify carriers with no family history of Canavan Disease who may not realize they are at risk for having an affected child. As was done earlier for Tay-Sachs Disease, it is important that population-based screening for CD be coupled with thorough education and genetic counseling services so that test results are interpreted correctly.

Breakthroughs in Canavan Disease Detection

Recent medical breakthroughs have made it possible to prevent a second allied disease, one that is very similar to Tay-Sachs. It is Canavan Disease which strikes babies and is fatal in childhood. As with Tay-Sachs, through a simple blood test, we can now identify carriers of the Canavan-causing gene.

The following questions and answers have been prepared to help you understand what Canavan Disease is and how it affects your family.

Why Would I Want to Be Tested for Canavan?

The same logic that motivated you to be tested for the Tay-Sachs gene applies to Canavan. As with Tay-Sachs children, Canavan babies appear healthy at birth. Then, at around six months, certain Canavan symptoms begin to appear, such as lack of head control and a diminished ability to turn over or grasp objects. Over time, muscle weakness causes most body functions to deteriorate, so that Canavan children cannot crawl or walk, sit or swallow easily, play or perform simple tasks. Some Canavan victims live to age ten or eleven; most die much younger.

How Likely Is It That I Am a Carrier of the Canavan Gene?

Canavan is most prevalent among Jewish families of Eastern European descent. One in 37 Jews is a carrier (compared to one in 27 carriers of the Tay-Sachs gene). Canavan does occur among all ethnic groups, so interfaith couples will want to consider getting tested. Since testing is so new, we do not yet know the carrier rate for Canavan among non-Jews. (Carrier rate for Tay-Sachs among non-Jews is one in 250)

If I've Been Tested for Tay-Sachs, Why Do I Need to Be Tested for Canavan?

The diseases are similar, but are caused by different gene defects. The fact that you are or are not a Tay-Sachs carrier has no bearing on whether you have the Canavan gene.

If I Have the Gene, Wouldn't I Know It?

Carriers are perfectly healthy individuals. The Canavan gene can be passed unknowingly in a family for years, from one generation to the next, until one day a baby is born with Canavan Disease. Therefore, even if there are no known cases of Canavan in your family, you may still be at risk. Moreover, there is a very real possibility that a child with Canavan would have been misdiagnosed since little has been written about the disease in medical literature. Even today, most physicians are unaware of Canavan Disease and prevention.

What Is the Test for the Canavan Gene?

It's a simple blood test. However, while Tay-Sachs is a blood serum test, Canavan screening requires DNA analysis. This makes it more complex, and a little more costly. You will want to discuss the cost when you call for information or an appointment.

What Happens if I Learn I Have the Canavan Gene?

The strategy of prevention, successfully applied to Tay-Sachs disease for the past 25 years, can now be applied to Canavan. That is, couples get tested to learn if they have the Canavan gene. When both partners are carriers, there is a one-in-four chance with each pregnancy the child will be born with the disease. Genetic counseling is recommended for carrier couples so they learn their many options for having a healthy family. It is important to note that prenatal testing for Canavan is also available and can be done early in pregnancy.

If I Already Have a Child, Should I Be Tested?

If you are planning to have more children, you may still be at risk for having a Canavan child. If you have completed your family, one parent may have passed the gene to a child, making him or her a carrier. You can either be tested now, or be prepared to have the children tested when they become young adults. The important thing is that Canavan and Tay-Sachs information become a permanent part of your family's health history.

Today, you may feel overwhelmed with health care issues, which often include conflicting recommendations about preventive tests. The Tay-Sachs Association encourages you to consider Canavan testing with the same reasoning you applied to Tay-Sachs testing. The National Tay-Sachs & Allied Diseases Association's mission is to prevent the birth of even one more child with the deadly Tay-Sachs or Canavan Disease. To achieve this goal, they recommend Canavan screening for everyone of Jewish ancestry.

For More Information

National Tay-Sachs & Allied Diseases Association
2001 Beacon Street, Suite 204
Brighton, MA 02135
Toll Free: 800-906-8723
Tel: 215-887-0877
Fax: 617-277-0134
Website: http://www.ntsad.org/ntsad/contact.htm

Tay-Sachs Prevention Program
Thomas Jefferson University
Tel: 215-955-8320, to make an appointment for testing.

Chapter 10

Dystonia

What Is Dystonia?

Clinically, dystonia is a neurological disorder that is characterized by involuntary muscle contraction which forces parts of the body into abnormal, sometimes painful, movements or positions.

Dystonia is the third most common movement disorder after Parkinson's disease and Tremor, affecting an estimated 300,000 persons in North America. The disorder is often misunderstood by the public and misdiagnosed by medical doctors. It is not a psychological disorder nor does it affect intellect. Dystonia is not fatal, but, depending on the form, it can be debilitating.

Dystonia is not a single disease, but a syndrome—a set of symptoms that cannot be attributed to a single cause. Thus, both genetic and non-genetic events must be accounted for before we finally have a full understanding of the common elements—namely, the twisting, repetitive movements around an axis, such as an arm or the neck. Dystonia may result from hereditary condition or as a result of brain injury.

What Are Genes?

Genes are made of DNA (deoxyribonucleic acid), a long threadlike molecule coiled inside our cells. Each cell in the body has a large central

Reprinted with permission, "The Genetics of Dystonia," © 1999 Dystonia Medical Research Foundation.

body called the nucleus. Within this cell nucleus, the DNA is packaged into 23 pairs of chromosomes, which contain a complete set of genetic instructions known as the human genome.

Each chromosome, in turn, carries thousands of genes arrayed like beads on a string. There are over 100,000 or so genes which determine, at least in part, many of our traits such as eye color, height, blood types, and bodily functions. Genes, which are simply short segments of DNA, are packets of instructions that tell cells how to behave. They do so by specifying the instructions for making particular proteins.

Every gene oversees the body's production of a certain protein. Proteins are how your body communicates and they help cells make other chemicals that your body needs like hemoglobin, antibodies, and enzymes.

The hereditary instructions are written in a four-letter code, with each letter corresponding to one of the chemical constituents of DNA: A (Adenine), T (Thymine), C (Cytosine), G (Guanine). Genes are, in essence, the "recipe" which is written in DNA language, with a certain sequence of As, Ts, Cs, and Gs constituting a recipe for a specific protein. Your DNA plan contains recipes for making about fifty thousand different types of proteins, and every second your cells are using gene recipes to make the proteins they need.

How Do Genetic Disorders Occur?

If the DNA language becomes garbled, the cell may make the wrong protein, or too much or too little, of the right one—mistakes that sometimes result in disease. Errors in our genes are responsible for an estimated 3,000 to 4,000 clearly hereditary diseases, including certain forms of dystonia. But finding disease genes can be very difficult.

In the case of dystonia, the proteins involved are crucial to the brain's communication with the muscles. The muscle spasms of dystonia are what happens when your body isn't making the correct proteins and your muscles aren't getting the right message.

Known Inherited Forms of Dystonia

Researchers have identified several genes associated with dystonia. They include:

- **Early-Onset Childhood Dystonia** (Generalized Dystonia or Idiopathic Torsion Dystonia, ITD) usually starts in childhood or adolescence. Symptoms typically start in one part of the body, usually in an arm or leg and can eventually spread to the rest of the body, causing it to twist into unnatural positions. It is the most common hereditary form of dystonia, resulting, in most cases, from the DYT1 gene.

- **Dupa-Responsive Dystonia** (DRD) usually starts in childhood or adolescence with progressive difficulty in walking. It may be misdiagnosed since it mimics many of the symptoms of cerebral palsy or even parkinsonism. The affected gene, located on chromosome 14, is the gene for GTP cyclohydrolase, an enzyme that helps in the synthesis of dopamine. DRD symptoms are relieved with very low doses of levodopa.
- **Paroxysmal Dystonia** refers to relatively brief attacks of dystonia movements and postures with a return to normal posture between episodes. Paroxysmal dystonias take two main forms. Paroxysmal kinesigenic dystonia (PDK) refers to brief attacks triggered by sudden movement, occurring frequently many times a day. Paroxysonal dystonic choreoatherosis (PDC) refers to attacks that may last for several hours and may occur three to four times a day. One gene maps to chromosome 2q.
- **X-linked Dystonia-Parkinsonism** (Lubag) is a form of dystonia found almost entirely among men from the Philippine Island of Panay. Females are believed to the carriers of the gene, mapped to chromosome Xq13. It usually begins focally, progresses to generalized, and can be replaced by parkinsonian features.
- **Myoclonic Dystonia** is characterized by rapid lightening-like movements (jerks) alone or in combination with sustained postures of dystonia. Inherited as a dominant disease no genes or linkages have been identified at this time.
- **Rapid-Onset Dystonia-Parkinsonism** (RDF) is a newly described autosomal dominant movement disorder with abrupt onset of slowness of movement (parkinsonism) and dystonic spasm. The classic features include involuntary dystonic spasms in the arms more than legs, prominent involvement of the speech and swallowing muscles, slowness of movement and poor balance. RDF usually occurs in adolescence or young adulthood with little progression after the sudden appearance. There is no treatment for RDF, although levodopa/carbidups (Sinemet) and dopamine agonists may provide some mild improvement in some affected individuals.

- **Late-Onset Dystonia** has an average age of onset of 48 years but can range from the third to the eighth decades. The dystonic symptoms tend to remain focal. Several common forms of focal dystonia include cervical dystonia (spasmodic torticollis), blepharospasm, spasmodic dystonia, and writer's cramp. Probably at least 25% of focal dystonias are inherited and these seem to be dominant. A gene has been linked to chromosome 18p in a family with torticollis but many other focal dystonia families do not show linkage to this region, suggesting there are more genes, as yet unidentified, for focal dystonias.

DYT1 Gene Discovery

One of the most important breakthroughs in understanding the genetics of dystonia was announced in September 1997. Researchers identified the DYT1 gene on chromosome 9 for early-onset childhood dystonia. Also discovered was that 80% of affected individuals carry the same mutation—the deletion of three "letters" (GAG) in the genetic code that spells out the sequence of amino acids in proteins. This is the culmination of more than 15 years of effort by Drs. Xandra O. Breakefield and Laurie Ozellus and their genetic research team. The discovery of this gene gives us our first clues toward understanding the mechanisms behind this disorder and allows us to devise testable hypotheses based on these clues.

The DYT1 gene codes for a previously unknown protein, named "torsinA," and it has significant similarities to the heat-shock proteins and chaperone proteins.

Found in virtually all living organisms, the heat-shock proteins help cells recover from stresses including heat, traumatic injury, and chemical poisoning. Until now, no human disease has been associated with these proteins.

In patients with early-onset dystonia, the DYT1 gene has a mutation that results in the loss of an amino acid, glutarmic acid, in the torsinA protein. Somehow this defective protein disrupts communication among the neurons responsible for movement and muscle control, leading to the symptoms of the dystonia disorder.

The vulnerability to early-onset dystonia seems to disappear after age 28 years. If the mutated gene product acts, there seems to be no stopping its consequences, but if the process does not start by age 28, people with the mutation are virtually free from the risk of developing symptoms. We now have important clues to help us find that trigger, and, we hope, to stop it.

Researchers believe that the same mutation in the DYT1 gene appeared independently in several ethnic populations throughout history and is possibly one of only a few mutations that result in early-onset dystonia. Exactly how the abnormal gene causes the dystonia is presently unknown.

How Is the Gene Inherited?

Early-onset dystonia appears when a person has one copy of the mutated gene and one copy of the normal gene. This means that the disease is dominant, because only one copy of the mutated gene is needed to cause it, but less than half (30%) of the people who have the mutated gene will develop symptoms. Therefore, 70% of the people who carry the gene will not develop symptoms. Geneticists call this phenomenon "variable penetrance."

Another aspect to the inheritability is that the severity of the illness may differ markedly within a family. For example, the affected mother may have mild dystonia; one of her children may have severe generalized dystonia; while another may have mild focal dystonia. And in the same family there may be still another child who is actually carrying the gene, has no symptoms at all, but who can pass it on to his/her children.

What Does This Discovery Mean for Those Who Don't Carry the Gene?

For individuals who have early-onset dystonia but do not have the DYT1 gene or for the individuals with late onset and/or focal dystonias, the impact of this gene discovery is less defined. Research is ongoing to determine whether there are other mutations in the DYT1 gene that can account for the other 20% of early onset patients who do not have the GAG deletion.

Detection of other mutations would allow these individuals to undergo genetic testing and may also reveal something about the mechanism of action of this protein.

From the screening of focal dystonia patients for the GAG deletion, it seems fairly clear that this mutation is not directly involved in most of these forms of dystonia, with the possible exception of writer's cramp. However, this does not mean that the DYT1 gene does not have a role in these diseases.

Further understanding how the DYT1 Gene functions and ultimately results in dystonia will have implications for focal patients.

The DYT1 gene is part of a gene family; that is, there are other genes located on other chromosomes that are similar in structure (about 50% homology) and therefore, probably share similar functions with the DYT1 gene. These genes may be involved in other forms of dystonia.

It is also reasonable to surmise that the brain pathways involved in the generation of movements that are disrupted in dystonia are similar for focal and generalized dystonia. Therefore, understanding the role of DYT1 in this pathway may lead to clues about other aspects of the pathway.

Testing for the DYT1 Gene

Direct molecular diagnostic testing for the DYT1 gene for the early-onset (9q34) form is available for anyone affected with early-onset, or limb-onset dystonia, regardless of ethnic background or family history. It also allows for better diagnostic testing, testing for confirmation of the diagnosis, and prenatal testing.

This test analyzes for the presence of the known GAG deletion using DNA obtained from a small blood sample. Prenatal testing is also available for the DYT1 gene. This test is unlikely to be positive for individuals with late-onset, primarily cervical or cranial dystonia, or blephaospasm, unless there is a family history of early-onset dystonia.

Currently, the test is performed through the DNA Diagnostics Laboratory at Massachusetts General Hospital in Boston. All genetic testing is done through a neurologist or genetics counselor knowledgeable in dystonia and costs approximately $135.

Some insurance carriers reimburse for genetic counseling and testing, other do not, so individuals should check with their insurance companies before ordering this test. With any genetic test, there may be potential for insurance or employment discrimination. These issues should be explored as part of genetic counseling before choosing to undergo testing. Legislation protecting privacy and preventing this potential discrimination has been developed and is pending.

A listing of genetic counselors in your area is available from the National Society of Genetic Counselors, Inc. They can be reached online at www.nsgc.org or you can contact the Dystonia Medical Research Foundation

What Are the Next Steps?

Determining the function of torsinA is the next problem researchers face. One of their present, testable hypotheses is that this protein may be involved in protecting dopamine-producing cells from environmental insult. Dopamine is known to be involved in the appearance of dystonia symptoms.

Genetic research has potential to help all. Dystonia is a complex disease. Its causes, treatment, progression, and variability of symptoms are difficult to explain, but all dystonias have similar symptoms which involve the same area of the brain and similar neurotransmitters. The discovery of the DYT1 gene is a major step to finding new treatments and leading us to answers that will be applicable to all dystonia patients. Until now, we have directed treatments to the symptoms of dystonia. Now we can expect to have direct treatment efforts to the causes of dystonia.

For More Information

Dystonia Medical Research Foundation
One East Wacker Drive, Suite 2430
Chicago, IL 60601-1905
Tel: 312-755-0198
Fax: 312-803-0138
E-mail: dystonia@dystonia-foundation.org
Website: http://www.dystonia-foundation.org

Chapter 11

Familial Mediterranean Fever

Gene Identified for Familial Mediterranean Fever

An international consortium of researchers, led by investigators at the National Institute of Arthritis and Musculoskeletal and Skin Diseases (NIAMS) and the National Human Genome Research Institute (NHGRI) at the National Insitutes of Health (NIH) has—for the first time—identified a gene for familial Mediterranean fever (FMF) and found three different gene mutations that cause this inherited rheumatic disease.

The gene holds the code for making a protein the researchers call pyrin. They hypothesize that pyrin normally plays a role in keeping inflammation under control, and that mutations in the gene lead to a malfunctioning protein and uncontrolled inflammation.

Discovery of the gene mutations, published in the August 22, 1997 issue of *Cell*, "will allow immediately a simple diagnostic blood test for FMF," says lead researcher Daniel L. Kastner, M.D., Ph.D. from the NIAMS. "One reason that's important is that in the U.S. physicians are often unfamiliar with FMF. Now it will be possible to develop a simple diagnostic test for FMF that could be used in patients with unexplained, recurring fevers," says Kastner.

Researchers hope that studying how pyrin works will ultimately lead to new, improved treatments for FMF and perhaps for other diseases

---

"NIH Researchers Lead International Group in Identifying Gene for Familial Mediterranean Fever," National Human Genome Research Institute (NHGRI), Media Release, 1997.

involving excess inflammation. The FMF gene is one of an increasing list of human disease genes that have been found using the resources of the Human Genome Project (HGP), the multi-year, international effort to map all of the genes in the human body.

"Successful identification of the FMF gene, which was a particularly challenging target because of the subtlety of its mutations, is another example of the way that the tools and technologies of the Human Genome Project have made possible gene discoveries considered impossible only a decade ago," said Francis Collins, M.D., Ph.D., director of the NHGRI. "In this instance, finding the FMF gene may well shed light on the whole mechanism by which the human body mounts an inflammatory response, and may well have spin-offs that extend far beyond those individuals with this genetic disorder," Collins said.

People with FMF suffer from recurring bouts of fever, most commonly with severe abdominal pain due to inflammation of the abdominal cavity (peritonitis). Attacks can also include arthritis (painful, swollen joints), chest pain from inflammation of the lung cavity (pleurisy), and skin rashes. Some patients develop amyloidosis, a potentially deadly buildup of protein in vital organs such as the kidneys. The only treatment for FMF is a drug called colchicine, which patients have to take every day for life and which causes side effects such as diarrhea and abdominal cramps.

FMF occurs most commonly in people of non-Ashkenzi Jewish, Armenian, Arab, and Turkish background living in the U.S. and abroad. As many as 1 in 200 people in these populations have the disease, and as many as 1 in 5 to 1 in 7 carry a mutated FMF gene. A person must inherit two mutated copies of the gene—one from each parent—in order to get FMF.

The research groups identified the gene for FMF after years of collaboration with several U.S. groups, as well as investigators from Israel and Australia. The researchers analyzed genetic material from people in 62 families with FMF, most of them recruited through clinics in Tel Aviv and Los Angeles. Out of the three FMF gene mutations identified so far in these families, the same two mutations are found in ethnic populations that have been geographically separated for over 2,000 years, suggesting that most individuals with the disease are descended from a small, ancient group of individuals.

Researchers at NHGRI, including Dr. Francis Collins, Dr. Pu Paul Liu and Trevor Blake of the Laboratory of GeneTransfer, made key contributions to the cloning of the FMF gene by generating a physical map in the study and in the isolation of candidate genes in the region. The NHGRI team made several critical discoveries during screening for gene mutations which ultimately led to the identification of the FMF gene.

The three gene mutations found to date lead to changes in the same region near one end of the protein, suggesting that this region is critical to pyrin's function. Computer analyses done by the researchers show that the gene mutations in FMF lead to an alteration in the shape of the pyrin protein. This shape change presumably interferes with pyrin's normal functioning.

The pyrin protein, named from the Greek word for fire, bears a strong resemblance to several proteins found in the nucleus of cells. Some of these proteins are known to regulate inflammation. The researchers found that the FMF gene is decoded to make the protein only in white blood cells called peripheral blood leukocytes, which are the first line of the body's defense system in an infection or after certain other challenges to the body. In attacks of FMF, these leukocytes rush into the affected part of the body in massive numbers, triggering inflammation—a typical response of tissues to injury or disease that is characterized by redness, swelling, heat, and pain.

The researchers think that pyrin may normally act as a switch to shut down or dampen the inflammatory reaction. In FMF, Kastner hypothesizes, "this switch is not working quite right, so that even if you get a small provocation you can end up getting a strong inflammatory response, whereas in normal people the protein would [eventually] shut down this response." This over-reaction leads to disease symptoms such as fever and excessive inflammation.

The fact that mutations in the FMF gene are so common in several Middle Eastern populations suggests that people with only one mutated FMF gene—who are carriers for the disease but do not have FMF—may have some type of survival advantage such as an increased resistance to one or more disease-causing organisms, perhaps ones that are very common in the Mediterranean region.

Identifying the genetic cause of FMF is in some ways just the beginning of the story. The researchers now must pursue work such as looking at the minority of patients in whom they have not yet found mutations, and studying the pyrin protein to better understand the role it plays under normal circumstances and in people with FMF. "The longer-term payoff [of this work] is in terms of therapeutics," Kastner says. "Eventually understanding this protein [pyrin] or proteins in this same pathway might give rise to a new class of anti-inflammatory drugs."

Chapter 12

Gaucher Disease

Introduction

How do scientists investigate diseases? We take for granted that medical researchers will use test tubes and computers in their search, but what exactly are they searching for? They are looking for the answers to three basic questions:

- Is there a disease?
- What causes it?
- Can we prevent, treat, or cure it?

The answers to the questions above do not always come in that order, and answering all three questions usually takes years of work, done by many investigators. That is why Dr. Roscoe Brady's team at the National Institute of Neurological Disorders and Stroke (NINDS) is rare. Dr. Brady's research into Gaucher disease answered all three questions, and continues to strive for better treatments and a cure for Gaucher disease.

Is There a Disease?

In 1882, the French medical student Phillipe Charles Ernest Gaucher described a 32-year old woman whose spleen was very enlarged. A

"Researching Disease: Dr. Roscoe Brady and Gaucher Disease," National Institute of Health (NIH), and "Gaucher Disease," © The National Tay-Sachs & Allied Diseases Association, Inc., reprinted with permission.

postmortem exam revealed that cells in the spleen were themselves enlarged. Gaucher described these clinical and pathological findings in his doctoral thesis. The enlarged cells (now called "Gaucher cells") and spleen became signs of the disease, and Gaucher's description of them enabled other physicians to diagnose people with Gaucher disease, and introduce the term into medical literature. Did people with Gaucher disease exist before 1882? Yes, they did. But because a set of symptoms wasn't identified with the condition, "Gaucher disease" as a disease diagnosis did not exist.

As more was learned about Gaucher disease, the list of identifiable symptoms or signs grew. In addition to an enlarged spleen and liver, people with Gaucher disease may have lung, kidney, and digestive problems; bone problems, including growth retardation in children, joint pain, spontaneous fractures, and acute bone crises; nosebleeds, bruising, anemia, and other blood-related problems; and general fatigue. Sometimes, in more severe cases, the central nervous system is also affected.

Beyond the emotionally-draining effects that chronic diseases can have, Gaucher disease also has other psychological consequences. Children must deal with looking different from their friends and having physical limitations of their activities. Adults may question whether to get married or to have children, and they face uncertainty about how severe their disease may become. Many people with Gaucher disease must change their life plans and dreams.

What Causes It?

In 1934, the French chemist, A. Aghion, discovered the chemical cause of the enlarged spleens and liver: a buildup of a lipid (fatty substance) called "glucocerebroside." This discovery led researchers to speculate why there was too much lipid—did people with Gaucher disease make too much of the lipid for their bodies to handle? Or did their bodies not break it down and dispose of it? The answer to this question came during the early 1960s, when Dr. Roscoe Brady's group showed that people with Gaucher disease made the lipid normally but did not make enough of the enzyme "glucocerebrosidase" to break it down and clear it out of the body.

In 1967, Brady's group developed a convenient diagnostic test for Gaucher disease which works by measuring the activity of the enzyme glucocerebrosidase in white blood cells. The amount of enzyme one's body makes directly relates to how severe a case of Gaucher disease one has. The enzyme activity is also one way that may help to distinguish the three types of Gaucher disease described in Table 12.1.

Table 12.1. Three Types of Gaucher Disease

	Type 1	Type 2	Type 3
Whom it strikes	young adults/ adults	infants	children/ young adults
Distinguishing symptom	no nervous system problems	early nervous system problems	later onset of nervous system problems
Effects of disease	varies from mild to severe	dies in infancy	becomes severe
Glucocerebrosidase activity	some activity but much less than normal	very little activity	little activity

All three types of Gaucher disease are inherited storage diseases, and all result from the deficiency of an enzyme called glucocerebrosidase, which is necessary for the breakdown of a particular fatty substance, glucocerebroside. This fatty substance is normally present in very small amounts in all body cells, but in patients with Gaucher disease, glucocerebroside is not broken down as it should be and becomes abnormally stored, primarily in unique cells called Gaucher cells.

The major disease manifestations are due to the progressive storage of glucocerebroside in Gaucher cells in the bone marrow, spleen and liver. Gaucher cells in the bone marrow can cause bone and joint pain, fractures, and other orthopedic problems. Accumulation of Gaucher cells in the spleen and liver causes enlargement of these organs as well as blood abnormalities such as anemia, easy bruising and impaired blood clotting. In a small number of persons with Gaucher disease, glucocerebroside also accumulates in the central nervous system, leading to neurological damage.

The three types of Gaucher disease are distinguished by their clinical severity and course, and by the presence or absence of neurological complications. Type I is the most common form and does not have mental or neurological involvement. This disease primarily affects Jewish individuals of central and eastern European ancestry (Ashkenazi Jews), although it is also seen in people of other ethnic groups. Type II has its onset in infancy and is a fatal neuro-degenerative disorder with death occurring in the first or second year of life. It is an extremely rare type and does not occur with a higher frequency in any particular ethnic or demographic group. Type III begins in early childhood, has mild to severe neurological involvement, and is very rare, except in Sweden, where most patients have been found. Each of these three types of Gaucher disease is genetically distinct and "breeds true" in affected families—that is, no two types of Gaucher disease occur in the same family. Type I Gaucher disease is the most common form of the disease.

- Fact: Unlike many more severe recessive disorders, most people with Type I Gaucher disease can have children.

The clinical manifestations of Type I Gaucher disease usually become apparent in childhood or early adulthood, but some persons remain asymptomatic into their 50's and 60's. Common early symptoms include an enlarged spleen and hematologic or orthopedic problems. Since there is marked variability in the severity of Type I Gaucher disease even within a family, it is difficult to predict the future severity and extent of complications in individual patients. Although there is no classic, predictable disease course, prognosis generally depends on the severity at the time of diagnosis and the intervals between the onset of new disease complications in each affected individual.

Gaucher disease, like Tay-Sachs, is an autosomal recessive disorder. Affected individuals have one copy of the altered gene. As in other recessive disorders, a couple where both people are carriers of the Gaucher disease gene faces a 25% chance in each pregnancy that their child will inherit two copies of the altered gene and, in all probability, have the disease.

Unlike many more severe recessive disorders, most people with Type I Gaucher disease (with two altered copies of the gene) will, of course, pass one of those nonfunctional genes on to each of his or her children. Therefore, all children of a person with Gaucher disease will carry at least one altered copy of the Gaucher disease gene. Thus, the children will be carriers, they will not have the disease unless the other parent is also a Gaucher carrier and passes his or her inactive gene on to the child.

The gene responsible for Gaucher disease, called the glucocerebrosidase gene, is located on chromosome 1. Mutations in this gene cause Gaucher disease symptoms in most individuals; however, some individuals with mutations in both copies of this gene show no symptoms whatsoever. Nine mutations are seen with some frequency in patients with Type I Gaucher disease, and attempts have been made to correlate the mutations with the clinical presentation of the disease. Some correlations have been made between specific mutations and expression of clinical symptoms, but it is not possible to predict with certainty how severely an individual with a given pair of mutations will be affected.

Type I Gaucher disease occurs primarily, but not exclusively, in individuals of Ashkenazi Jewish ancestry. It is estimated that about one in every 10 Jewish individuals of central and eastern European ancestry is a carrier of a Type I Gaucher disease gene and that one in every 450 Ashkenazi Jews has two altered copies of the gene. Although some of these people show no symptoms of Gaucher disease, most do. Gaucher disease is, therefore, one of the most common genetic diseases in the Ashkenazi Jewish population.

Concerned couples and individuals have options for carrier testing for Type I Gaucher disease. DNA-based testing, which looks for mutations in the glucocerebrosidase gene, is the most reliable method, as measurements of the level of the enzyme glucocerebrosidase do not distinguish all carriers from non-carriers. DNA mutation analysis detects about 84% of all carriers, but the detection rate is higher (about 90%) for persons of Ashkenazi Jewish descent. Some affected but asymptomatic individuals learn that they have two copies of the Gaucher disease gene when they undergo carrier testing.

- Fact: Enzyme replacement therapy has become commercially available and has been successful in slowing and reversing the progression of many symptoms of Gaucher disease.

Can We Prevent, Treat, or Cure It?

The third question that medical researchers try to answer is the most important, and often depends on the answer to the question, "What causes it?" For Gaucher disease, physicians initially attempted to address the symptoms that accompany the disease. They removed enlarged spleens, and performed liver transplants, blood transfusions, and orthopedic procedures. Only bone marrow transplantation for people with Type I Gaucher disease was sometimes successful. To be truly successful, a treatment would have to address the cause of the disease, not just the symptoms.

In 1966, Dr. Roscoe Brady suggested a therapy for Gaucher disease based on replacing the enzyme. Using human placentas, Dr. Peter Pentchev of Dr. Brady's team isolated a tiny sample of purified glucocerebrosidase. In 1973, two patients received this enzyme; because of the good biochemical results, Brady decided to develop a procedure to obtain larger quantities of the enzyme for further clinical trials.

A large-scale purification method was completed in 1977. The enzyme had to be treated with an alcohol to make it stick to the purifying columns. But this preparation of the enzyme produced inconsistent results during clinical trials. The alcohol had removed a lipid (fat) that activates the enzyme and targets it to the affected cells, called macrophages. Dr. Brady's challenge was now to get the purified enzyme into the targeted cells.

About this time, two facts became known. First, the enzyme has sugar side-chains attached to amino acid backbone of its structure. Second, macrophages react with enzymes whose sugar chains end with the sugar called "mannose." The problem was that the mannose on the sugar side-chains of glucocerebrosidase was inside of the chains, not on the end of the chains. The mannose therefore could not interact with macrophages. Dr. Brady's team needed to develop a method to strip off some of the sugars on the ends of the side chains to expose the mannose, which would allow the enzyme to bind to the macrophages.

In the first clinical trial with macrophage-targeted glucocerebrosidase, eight people with Gaucher disease received a fixed dose of the modified enzyme. Only the smallest one—a child—experienced beneficial effects. His hemoglobin and platelet counts increased; the size of his spleen and liver decreased; and the damage to his bones lessened. The other seven people were adults and had not received enough of the enzyme to improve their condition.

Brady's team then selected a different dose amount of replacement enzyme for a trial of twelve people with Gaucher disease. All of these people had strikingly good clinical responses within a few months. For example, their height and weight increased; their anemia improved; their liver and spleen sizes decreased; and their bone damage lessened. Because of these findings, macrophage-targeted glucocerebrosidase was approved as a specific treatment for Gaucher disease by the Federal Drug Administration on April 5, 1991. Enzyme replacement therapy worked.

In a few short years, people with Gaucher disease were able to receive the enzyme replacement therapy at home. Enzyme replacement therapy is an effective treatment for most people with Type I Gaucher disease.

Dr. Brady is conducting genetic research to provide a cure for all people with Gaucher disease. At the National Institutes of Health in

May 1995, a young man with Gaucher disease received the first gene therapy for that disease. He received back his own cells into which the correct genes for making the enzyme glucocerebrosidase had been inserted. He had no adverse reaction, proving the safety of the procedure. Current trials are attempting to determine the efficacy of gene therapy for Gaucher disease.

Treatment

Treatment for Type I Gaucher disease has traditionally included periodic blood transfusions, partial or total spleen removal, and the use of pain relievers. More recently, enzyme replacement therapy has become commercially available and has been successful in slowing and reversing the progression of many symptoms of the disease. The treatment involves infusions of Ceredase^{tm}, a chemically modified enzyme derived from glucocerebrosidase that has been specifically targeted to Gaucher cells. The disadvantages of this therapy are its high cost and the need for repeated infusions of the enzyme. In patients with severe clinical symptoms, bone marrow transplantation is sometimes performed; if successful, it provides a lifelong cure. It is possible that in the future, gene therapy using a patient's own bone marrow stem cells may be available to provide a permanent cure without the immunological complications of bone marrow transplantation from a donor.

The availability of treatment and the uncertainty of prognosis for individuals with two copies of the Gaucher disease gene make it especially difficult for at-risk couples to make decisions about whether they wish to undergo prenatal testing and to decide what to do with the information they may learn from test results. Carrier and prenatal testing for people with a family history of Gaucher disease should be offered in conjunction with genetic counseling so that people can be aware of their options and make informed decisions.

Prenatal testing methods for Gaucher disease include direct DNA testing to identify mutations in the glucocerebrosidase gene, linkage analysis (another form of DNA testing which compares the DNA of the fetus to that of affected and unaffected relatives) and biochemical testing to measure the amount of glucocerebrosidase in the fetus. All types of testing can be done from samples obtained through amniocentesis or chorionic villus sampling (CVS); however, none of these types of testing can predict the degree to which the child will be affected clinically if it is determined that he or she has two copies of the altered glucocerebrosidase gene.

Additional Readings

Living with Gaucher Disease: A Guide for Patients, Parents, Relatives, and Friends.

Genzyme Corporation
One Kendall Square
Cambridge, MA 02139
Toll Free: 800-745-4447
Website: http://www.genzyme.com/cerezyme/patient/broch.htm

Gaucher Disease: Current Issues in Diagnosis and Treatment

A National Institutes of Health Technology Assessment Conference Statement, February 27-March 1, 1995.

NIH Office of Medical Applications of Research
Federal Building
Room 618
7550 Wisconsin Avenue, MSC 9120
Bethesda, MD 20892-9120
Tel: 301-496-1143

"Development of Effective Enzyme Therapy for Metabolic Storage Disorders," by Roscoe O. Brady and Norman W. Barton. *International Pediatrics*, Vol. 9, No. 3, 1994. Pages 175-180.

"Enzyme Replacement Therapy for Gaucher Disease: Critical Investigations Beyond Demonstration of Clinical Efficacy," by Roscoe O. Brady and Norman W. Barton. *Biochemical Medicine and Metabolic Biology*, Vol. 52, 1994. Pages 1-9.

"Development of Effective Enzyme Replacement Therapy for Hereditary Metabolic Disorders," by Roscoe O. Brady. *Resident and Staff Physician*, Vol. 41, No. 8, August 1995. Pages 38-40.

For More Information

The National Gaucher Foundation
11140 Rockville Pike
Suite 350
Rockville, Maryland 20852
Tel: 301-816-1515
Toll Free: 800-925-8885

National Tay-Sachs & Allied Diseases Association, Inc.
2001 Beacon St.
Suite 204
Boston, MA 02135
Tel: 617-277-4463
Fax: 617-277-0134
E-mail: nstad-boston@worldnet.att.net

Chapter 13

Lupus

Seeking Answers to the High Prevalence of Lupus among Minorities

Does a person's ethnicity influence his or her experience with lupus? New research supported by the National Institute of Arthritis and Musculoskeletal and Skin Diseases (NIAMS) says it can, at least to a certain extent. Ethnicity includes race (and a given genetic background) as well as cultural values and beliefs and practices, which in the United States are associated with a certain socioeconomic status. Ethnicity, in fact, may have greater influence on lupus than genetics.

This information comes from the study LUpus in MInorities: NAture versus Nurture (LUMINA), conducted by researchers from the University of Alabama at Birmingham, the University of Texas–Houston Health Sciences Center, and the University of Texas Medical Branch at Galveston. The study, which includes over 300 African American, Hispanic, and Caucasian lupus patients aged 20 to 50 years, is designed to identify the relative contribution of genetic and socioeconomic factors on the course and outcome of lupus among these

---

"Seeking Answers to the High Prevalence of Lupus among Minorities," National Institute of Arthritis and Musculoskeletal and Skin Diseases (NIAMS), January 2000; and "Genetic Risk Factor Identified for Lupus Kidney Disease in African Americans," National Institute of Arthritis and Musculoskeletal and Skin Diseases (NIAMS) Research News, March 6, 1996.

three ethnic groups. LUMINA researchers are looking at features such as:

- socioeconomic and demographic characteristics (e.g., age, gender, marital status, income, health insurance);
- clinical attributes (e.g., disease onset and duration, clinical manifestations, treatments);
- behavioral and psychosocial factors (e.g., social support, abnormal illness-related behaviors, feelings of helplessness, acculturation [Hispanics only]);
- immunologic factors (e.g., autoantibodies); and
- genetic factors (e.g., genotypes, allotypes).

An essential part of this study is patient recruitment, and a difficult issue for researchers is recruiting minority research participants. Seemingly, various barriers exist among the different minority groups, including trust, language, and cultural mores. African American patients in general, and particularly in Alabama, have been leery of participating in medical research as a result of the Tuskegee Syphilis Study—a 40-year research study of 399 African American males who were not informed of changes made in the protocol, and who were not notified when effective treatment became available. As a result, many of the patients died from complications caused by syphilis. For Hispanic patients, language differences between the patient and the researcher form a barrier for communication and understanding. Cultural values, beliefs, and practices exist as barriers for both minority groups.

Fortunately for the LUMINA researchers, these barriers have been overcome through targeted recruitment efforts, including the use of a community hospital treating African American patients, and through local radio advertisements targeted at the Hispanic community. As a result, 86 Hispanic and 135 African American patients have been recruited. The same recruitment barriers have not existed for the 92 Caucasian patients.

To date, the LUMINA study reveals that ethnicity, above several factors, makes a significant impact on some aspects of the disease. Both African American and Hispanic lupus patients tend to develop lupus earlier in life, experience greater disease activity at the time of diagnosis (including kidney problems), and have more severe disease overall than Caucasian patients. Further, African American patients have a higher frequency of neurologic problems such as seizures, hemorrhage, and stroke, while Hispanic patients experience cardiac disease more frequently.

Ethnicity does not act alone in influencing disease course and outcome, however. LUMINA researchers found that after ethnicity, socioeconomic and demographic factors such as age, income, employment, education, and health insurance seem to play a major role in the course of lupus. Many of these factors are associated more with the African American and Hispanic patients than Caucasian patients, which may begin to explain the worse disease outcomes experienced by these two groups.

Feelings of helplessness (e.g., despair over the disease and its symptoms), insufficient social support, and overall abnormal illness-related behaviors such as denial have been found to influence both mental and physical functioning of patients, independent of ethnicity. Having identified these behavioral and psychosocial factors as applicable across all ethnic groups studied, LUMINA researchers believe this to be a good starting point for intervention directed by the healthcare provider. Interaction between the healthcare provider and patient may be one way to address these contributing factors.

Although LUMINA results to date do not implicate genetic influences as commonly responsible for differences in the early course of disease among these ethnic groups, researchers believe there are relevant genetic factors to be identified. LUMINA researchers hope to further this study of nature versus nurture by including more patients. What roles genetic and socioeconomic-demographic factors play in the course and outcome of lupus in these ethnic groups remains under investigation.

References

1. Reveille JD, et al. Systemic lupus erythematosus in three ethnic groups: I. The effects of HLA Class II, C4, and CR1 alleles, socioeconomic factors, and ethnicity at disease onset. *Arthritis and Rheumatism* 1998; (41): 1161-1172.

2. Alarcón GS, et al. Systemic lupus erythematosus in three ethnic groups: II. Features predictive of disease activity early in its course. *Arthritis and Rheumatism* 1998; (41): 1173-1180.

3. Alarcón GS, et al. Systemic lupus erythematosus in three ethnic groups: III. A comparison of characteristics early in the natural history of the LUMINA cohort. Lupus in minority populations: Nature vs. Nurture. *Lupus* 1999; (3): 197-209.

4. Friedman AW, et al. Systemic lupus erythematosus in three ethnic groups: IV. Factors associated with self-reported functional outcome in a large cohort study. *Arthritis Care and Research* 1999; (12): 256-266.

5. Alarcón GS, et al. Systemic lupus erythematosus in three ethnic groups: V. Acculturation, health-related attitudes and behaviors, and disease activity in Hispanic patients from the LUMINA cohort. *Arthritis Care and Research* 1999; (12): 267-276.

Genetic Risk Factor Identified for Lupus Kidney Disease in African Americans

Researchers supported by the National Institutes of Health (NIH) have identified a gene associated with increased risk of lupus kidney disease in African Americans. Variations in this gene affect the ability of immune cells to remove potentially harmful molecules from the body. This finding is a significant step towards enabling doctors to predict who is at risk for lupus and its complications and to take steps to minimize that risk. Systemic lupus erythematosus (SLE, or lupus) is an autoimmune disease that is three times more common in African Americans than in white Americans, and also tends to be more severe in African Americans.

"We found an inherited susceptibility factor that is important in determining the severity of disease in a population [African Americans] that gets more severe disease," said Jane E. Salmon, M.D., of The Hospital for Special Surgery/New York Hospital, Cornell University Medical College, in New York City, who led the collaborative, multicenter research study.

Research indicates that lupus is caused by a complex interplay of genetic and environmental factors. "These results are very important in helping us understand the genetic factors that play a role in determining who is at risk for the potentially lethal complications of lupus," said Stephen I. Katz, M.D., Ph.D., director of the NIH's National Institute of Arthritis and Musculoskeletal and Skin Diseases (NIAMS), which funded the study. The results also provide clues to the cause of lupus, particularly lupus nephritis, the kidney disease that can be a serious complication of SLE and can lead to kidney failure.

This study, reported in the March 1, 1996 issue of the *Journal of Clinical Investigation*,* also involved NIAMS researchers at the NIH campus in Bethesda, Md., as well as researchers at University of Texas Health Science Center in Houston, Texas; State University of New York Health Science Center, Brooklyn, N.Y.; and Northwestern University School of Medicine, Chicago, Ill.

Investigators at these medical research centers studied 257 African Americans with lupus and 139 African Americans without the disease. The researchers looked at a gene that controls production of proteins called Fc receptors, which help certain white blood cells capture and destroy potentially harmful molecules called immune complexes. The researchers found that, among African Americans with lupus, those with lupus nephritis had an increased likelihood of having the gene for a form of the Fc receptor that has a low efficiency for capturing immune complexes. Excessive buildup of immune complexes in the kidneys is known to be associated with lupus nephritis.

"Our results suggest that inheriting a low capacity for removing immune complexes plays a role in determining predisposition to lupus kidney disease," Salmon said. "By unraveling the causes of the disease we can begin to design better treatments, and predict those who are likely to get lupus nephritis and take steps to prevent it."

Immune complexes are formed when normal antibodies react with foreign substances that invade the body, such as viruses or bacteria. In lupus, the immune system goes awry and produces abnormal antibodies—called autoantibodies—that combine with substances from the body's own tissues to form immune complexes. These immune complexes circulate in the bloodstream and are deposited in various tissues.

Excessive buildup of immune complexes in tissues or organs can trigger the inflammation that causes tissue injury in lupus. The joints, skin, kidneys, lungs, heart, nervous system, and blood vessels can be affected. Defects in removal of immune complexes from the body are particularly profound in people with kidney complications of lupus. The signs and symptoms of lupus differ from one person to another, and the disease can range from mild to severe. Ninety percent of people with lupus are women, and the disease most often strikes during the childbearing years.

The particular Fc receptor gene that the investigators studied comes in two forms: one form (H131) codes for Fc receptors that are highly efficient at removing immune complexes; the other form (R131) codes for Fc receptors with low efficiency. The researchers examined the distribution of these two forms of the Fc receptor gene among African Americans with and without lupus, and among those African American lupus patients with or without kidney disease. They found that people with lupus more often had the gene for the less efficient form of this particular Fc receptor. People with lupus nephritis had an even more pronounced tendency to have the low-efficiency Fc receptor gene.

"We are exploring genes for additional Fc receptor molecules and other genes that may predispose people to lupus and its complications," said Robert P. Kimberly, M.D., director of the multipurpose arthritis center at the Hospital for Special Surgery, and a study collaborator. "This will allow us to define biological risk factors in different ethnic groups, and the degree to which these factors contribute to the prevalence and severity of lupus in various populations."

Researchers supported by the NIAMS are working to identify other genes involved in determining susceptibility to lupus. They have evidence that multiple genes contribute to disease susceptibility, and that no single gene can by itself cause the disease.

"In the future," said Salmon, "we will be able to put together a risk factor profile that predicts outcome for lupus patients, and we'll be able to decide whether we should use more or less aggressive treatments, depending on the person's likelihood of getting severe disease." She added: "Being able to do these studies in a collaboration between multiple research centers was one of the crucial components to success."

*Reference: FcgRIIA alleles are heritable risk factors for lupus nephritis in African Americans. Jane E. Salmon, Sean Millard, Leah A. Schachter, Frank C. Arnett, Ellen M. Ginzler, Mark F. Gourley, Rosalind Ramsey-Goldman, Margaret G.E. Peterson, and Robert P. Kimberly. *Journal of Clinical Investigation*, March 1, 1996.

Chapter 14

Niemann-Pick Disease

In 1914 Albert Niemann, a German pediatrician, described a young child with an enlarged liver and spleen, enlarged lymph glands, swelling and a darkening of the skin of the face. The child had brain and nervous system impairment and died in less than six months, before the age of two. Later, in the 1920's, Luddwick Pick studied tissues after the death of such children and provided evidence of a new disorder, distinct from other storage disorders.

Today, there are three separate diseases that carry the name Niemann-Pick: Type A, Type B, and Type C. The majority of the infants affected with the acute infantile form of Niemann-Pick already described (now called Type A) are of Ashkenazi Jewish ancestry. The less common Niemann-Pick disease, Type B, a chronic non-neurological form, shows the same ethnic predilection as Type A. It has been estimated that about 1 in 1000 Ashkenazi Jews is a carrier for one of these forms of Niemann-Pick disease. Niemann-Pick Type C, a biochemically and genetically distinct form of the disease, does not show this ethnic predilection and occurs with similar frequency in all populations.

Infantile, or Type A, Niemann-Pick disease occurs most frequently and it accounts for about 85% of all cases of the disease. Its effects

---

This chapter includes the following documents reprinted with the permission of the National Niemann-Pick Disease Foundation © 1999: "What Is Niemann-Pick Disease?" "How Is NPD Transmitted?" "What Are the Signs and Symptoms of NPD?" "How is NPD Diagnosed?" and "What Treatment Is Available for NPD?" Also included is "Niemann-Pick Disease," © National Tay-Sachs & Allied Diseases Association, Inc., reprinted with permission.

begin in the first few months of life; by six months of age feeding difficulties, progressive loss of early motor skills, and enlargement of the abdominal organs are usually present. Continued poor feeding causes children to take on an emaciated look accompanied by abdominal distension. Their skin may develop a brownish-yellow discoloration, and about one-third of affected children have a cherry-red spot in the eye similar to that found in children with Tay-Sachs disease. There is progressive loss of motor and mental function and death usually occurs between two and three years of age.

Type B Niemann-Pick has a more variable course with the first symptoms of disease usually being enlargement of the liver and/or spleen in early childhood. The child experiences progressive organ enlargement, poor growth, and susceptibility to chest infections but no nervous system involvement. Many persons with Type B Niemann-Pick survive into adulthood.

Persons with Type C Niemann-Pick, on the other hand, exhibit normal development for two or more years followed by a slow loss of speech and other nervous system skills. The disease progresses with symptoms of increased clumsiness, lack of coordination, eventual seizures, and a gradual failure of physical and mental function. Most children with Type C die between the ages of 5 and 15 years.

- Fact: All forms of Niemann-Pick are autosomal recessive diseases, so they affect both males and females equally.

Niemann-Pick disease ("Niemann-Pick") is actually a term for a group of diseases which affect metabolism and which are caused by specific genetic mutations. The three most commonly recognized forms of the disease are Types A, B, and C.

Types A and B Niemann-Pick are both caused by the deficiency of a specific enzyme activity, acid sphingomyelinase (ASM). This enzyme is ordinarily found in special compartments within cells called lysosomes and is required to metabolize a special lipid, called sphingomyelin. If ASM is absent or not functioning properly, this lipid cannot be metabolized properly and is accumulated within the cell, eventually causing cell death and the malfunction of major organ systems.

Although Types A and B are both caused by the same enzymatic deficiency, the clinical prognosis for these two groups of patients is very different. Type A Niemann-Pick is a severe neurologic disease that generally leads to death by 2 to 3 years of age. It is believed that the majority of Niemann-Pick cases are Type A.

In contrast, patients with Type B generally have little or no neurologic involvement and may survive into late childhood or adulthood. The underlying reason for this dramatic difference in the two forms of the disease is not really understood, and, at present, it is not possible to accurately predict the severity of the disease by enzyme testing.

Type C Niemann-Pick, although similar in name, is very different at the biochemical and genetic level. Patients with Type C are not able to metabolize cholesterol and other lipids properly. Consequently, excessive amounts of cholesterol accumulate within the liver and spleen and excessive amounts of other lipids accumulate in the brain.

The defect in metabolism occasionally leads to a secondary reduction in ASM activity in some cells, which is why these diseases were all called Niemann-Pick disease in the early days, before the biochemical differences were understood.

Type D Niemann-Pick has only been found in the French Canadian population of Yarmouth County, Nova Scotia and is now thought to be a variant of Type C. Geneological research indicates that Joseph Muise (c. 1679-1729) and Marie Amirault (1684-c. 1735) are common ancestors to all Type D cases. This couple are the most likely origin for the Type D variant.

A **Type E Niemann-Pick** has also been suggested based on a number of adults who have been found with some of the same tissue and chemical changes as Type C, but with very late adult onset of symptoms.

Niemann-Pick affects all segments of the population with cases reported from North America, South America, Europe, Africa, Asia, and Australia. However a higher incidence of has been found in certain populations:

- Ashkenazi Jewish population (types A and B)
- French Canadian population of Nova Scotia (type D)
- Maghreb region (Tunisia, Morocco, and Algeria) of North Africa (type B)
- Spanish-American population of southern New Mexico and Colorado (type C)

Pick's disease is sometimes confused with Niemann-Pick but it is a different disease.

How Is NPD Transmitted?

All types of Niemann-Pick are autosomal recessive. This means that both parents carry one copy of the abnormal gene, without having any signs of the disease themselves. (They are carriers or heterozygotes.) Children with Niemann-Pick disease have two copies of the abnormal gene. When both parents are carriers, there is a 1 in 4 chance that a child will be affected with the disease and 1 in 2 chance that a child will be a carrier.

Carrier detection testing for all families is not yet reliable. The mutations for Types A and B have been extensively studied, particularly among the Ashkenazi Jewish population, and DNA tests for these forms of Niemann-Pick are available. Antenatal diagnosis (diagnosis in the fetus) of NPD is available in a limited number of centers. Carrier detection is possible for other families only after their specific mutation is identified.

In mid-1999, the Ara Parseghian Medical Research Center announced plans for a Genetic Testing and Counseling Center for Type C which opened in 2000. The NNPDF funded continuing research in 1999 to identify and describe all known mutations in the Type C gene. Dr. Wenda Greer of Dalhousie University is closing in on the gene for Type D. Discovery of the gene and description of its mutations will allow for genetic testing of families with this form of Niemann-Pick in the future.

What Are the Signs and Symptoms of NPD?

Type A Niemann-Pick begins in the first few months of life. Symptoms may include:

- feeding difficulties
- a large abdomen within 3 to 6 months
- progressive loss of early motor skills
- cherry red spot in the eye
- (generally) a very rapid decline leading to death by two to three years of age.

Type B is biochemically similar to Type A but the symptoms are more variable. Abdominal enlargement may be detected in early childhood but there is almost no neurological involvement, such as loss of motor skills. Some patients may develop repeated respiratory infections.

Type C Niemann-Pick usually affects children of school age, but the disease may strike at any time from early infancy to adulthood. Symptoms may include:

- jaundice at (or shortly after) birth
- an enlarged spleen and/or liver
- difficulty with upward and downward eye movements (Vertical Supranuclear Gaze Palsy). VSPG is highly suggestive of Type C.
- unsteadiness of gait, clumsiness, problems in walking ("ataxia")
- difficulty in posturing of limbs ("dystonia")
- slurred, irregular speech ("dysarthria")
- learning difficulties and progressive intellectual decline ("dementia")
- sudden loss of muscle tone which may lead to falls ("cataplexy")
- tremors accompanying movement and, in some cases, seizures.

A child showing signs before one year of age may not live to school age. Children showing symptoms after entering school may live into their mid to late teens, with few surviving into their twenties.

Symptoms of all forms of Niemann-Pick are variable—no single symptom should be used to include or exclude Niemann-Pick as a diagnosis. A person in the early stages of the disease may exhibit only a few of the symptoms. Even in the later stages of the disease, not all symptoms may be present.

In addition, symptoms are progressive but the rate of progression is different from person to person. Finally, the symptoms of Niemann-Pick are also found in other, more common, diseases. These factors make it difficult to diagnose Niemann-Pick without appropriate testing.

How Is NPD Diagnosed?

Type A and B Niemann-Pick are diagnosed by measuring the ASM (acid sphingomylinase) activity in white blood cells. The test can be performed after taking a small blood sample from suspected individuals. While this test will identify persons with Type A and B (two mutated genes), it is not very reliable for detecting persons who are carriers (only one mutated gene).

However, it is possible to diagnose Types A and B carriers by DNA testing because the gene containing the blueprint for ASM has been cloned and many of its mutations identified. This is particularly useful in the Ashkenazi Jewish community where known mutations account for more than 92% of the mutations surveyed and the Maghreb North African population where a single mutation accounts for virtually all cases. In other families, the mutations must first be identified for each family before DNA testing can be performed. Both the Mount Sinai School of Medicine and the University of Pittsburgh can perform DNA testing for Types A and B.

Type C Niemann-Pick is initially diagnosed by taking a small piece of skin ("skin biopsy"), growing the cells ("fibroblasts") in the laboratory, and then studying their ability to transport and store cholesterol. The transport of cholesterol in the cells is studied by measuring conversion of the cholesterol from one form to another ("esterification"). The storage of cholesterol is assessed by staining the cells with a compound ("filipin") which glows under ultraviolet light. It is important that both of these tests be performed, since reliance on one or the other may lead to the diagnosis being missed in some cases.

Because Niemann-Pick Type C is rare and its symptoms are quite variable, it is not widely known even in the medical community. While education efforts by NNPDF have increased awareness of the disease, there are still instances of misdiagnosis and/or delayed diagnosis. If your child is exhibiting symptoms of Niemann-Pick, you may need to ask your doctor to consider the possibility of NP.

Since 1997, research funded by the NNPDF has cataloged over 100 of the genetic mutations related to Type C, representing over 90% of the known cases of Type C. This research led to the establishment of a Genetic Counseling and Carrier Testing Center in December 1999. Located at the Mayo Clinic, and funded in part by the Ara Parseghian Medical Research Foundation, the Center will provide DNA testing and counseling for patients and families with NP Type C.

For Additional Information

Mayo Clinic
200 1st Street SW
Rochester, MN 55905
Tel: 507-284-8198

What Treatment Is Available for NPD?

The news concerning treatments for all forms of Niemann-Pick is improving but there is still much to do before effective therapies are available. Just a few years ago, the cause of Niemann-Pick was unknown. Now the genetic sources of several types of Niemann-Pick have been identified and research is focusing on how the biochemical mechanisms work and how they can be corrected.

Potential treatments are described for informational purposes only. You should consult with your physician for medical advice about individual cases.

For Types A and B Niemann-Pick the ASM gene has been isolated and extensively studied—it resides on chromosome 11 in man. Many of the molecular abnormalities in this gene which cause Types A and B NPD have been identified and DNA testing and prenatal diagnosis has begun.

Research into therapies for Types A and B NPD has progressed rapidly since the early 1990's. Mount Sinai School of Medicine is conducting research on bone marrow transplantation, enzyme replacement therapy, and gene therapy. All of these therapies have had some success against Type B Niemann-Pick in a laboratory environment. Unfortunately, none of the potential therapies has been effective against Type A.

Bone marrow transplantation has proven effective in mouse models for many aspects of Type B when the transplant occurs early in life. It is unclear if transplantation later in life is also effective.

Enzyme replacement could not be evaluated until the discovery of the ASM gene allowed researchers to produce large quantities of the enzyme for evaluation. Test results on mice indicate that enzyme replacement has the potential to be an effective treatment for Type B NPD. Genzyme Corp. and Mount Sinai Medical Center announced plans for clinical trials of enzyme replacement therapy that began in 2000.

Gene therapy would allow the defective gene to be replaced by normal genes. Positive results have been obtained with individual cells but testing on Niemann-Pick mice is just beginning. Despite these encouraging beginnings, research has a long way to go before all patients with Types A and B NPD can be effectively treated or accurate predictions made about which form of the disease patients will develop.

For Type C Niemann-Pick, no specific treatment is available. A healthy low-cholesterol diet is recommended. However research into low-cholesterol diets and cholesterol-lowering drugs do not indicate that these halt the progress of the disease or change cholesterol metabolism at the cellular level.

In July, 1997, the primary gene causing Type C ("NPC1" on Chromosome 18) was isolated. The identification of this gene opens the door for progress toward more accurate diagnosis and a treatment for this disorder. Research also indicates that a second gene, currently unidentified, may be involved in some forms of the disease. Studies to identify this second gene and to understand how it interacts with NPC1 may also suggest treatment options.

The first steps toward a treatment of Type C Niemann-Pick are being taken as a result of the gene discovery. Bristol Myers Squibb conducted an assay of 50,000 compounds to identify those that have potential as therapies for Type C. A small number of compounds were identified which might be effective as treatments. These compounds are being analyzed to determine if they truly affect Type C.

In addition, a drug (OGT 918) which appears to slow the onset of neurological problems in other diseases may prove to be of benefit for people with Type C. As of December 1999, clinical trials were underway for one other neurological disease. Research on the effectiveness of OGT 918 on Type C for animal models is underway. While there is currently no treatment for Niemann-Pick Type C, many of its symptoms, such as seizures and cataplexy, can be controlled or tempered by drugs.

Chapter 15

Sandhoff Disease

Sandhoff disease is much less common than Tay-Sachs disease but is so similar to Tay-Sachs in the way it affects children that most cases cannot be distinguished without biochemical laboratory tests. As in Tay-Sachs disease, motor weakness begins in the first 6 months of life and is progressive. The same exaggerated startle reaction to sound, early blindness, progressive mental and motor deterioration, doll-like face, cherry-red spot, and enlargement of the heart are all present in Sandhoff Disease. The same loss of swallowing function occurs progressively together with increased risk for aspiration and subsequent chest and lung infections. Death usually occurs due to the latter problems at about 3 years of age. Some involvement of the bones and abdominal organs may occur which is distinct from the child with Tay-Sachs.

Sandhoff disease is also inherited as an autosomal recessive disorder but, unlike Tay-Sachs, occurs more commonly in the non-Jewish population. In fact, given the higher incidence of Sandhoff in non-Jews and the clinical similarity of the two diseases, it is probable that some of the non-Jewish children diagnosed before the availability of the laboratory tests actually had Sandhoff disease.

- Fact: Sandhoff disease is also inherited as an autosomal recessive disorder. But, unlike Tay-Sachs occurs more commonly in the non-Jewish population.

The fatty material (GM2 ganglioside) which accumulates in the child's brain cells is the same in Sandhoff and Tay-Sachs diseases. However, the enzyme deficiency in Sandhoff disease arises from mutations in a different gene on a different chromosome (i.e. the b-subunit gene on chromosome 5 instead of the a-subunit gene on chromosome 13 for Tay-Sachs). Mutations in this beta subunit gene affect both Hex-A and Hex-B activity. As a result, children with Sandhoff disease have almost no hexosaminidase unlike children with Tay-Sachs who still have Hex-B activity but not Hex-A. Because of the nearly total absence of hexosaminidase activity in affected individuals, laboratory diagnosis of an affected child as well as prenatal diagnosis is accurate and reliable. However, biochemical testing for the adult carrier requires special care and careful standardization of the laboratory test. DNA-based tests are also available for families in which the specific beta-subunit mutations have been identified; when these are known, the DNA-based tests provide the highest level of specificity and accuracy for both carrier testing in relatives and for prenatal diagnosis. NTSAD has current information available on where to obtain the tests that are critical to the diagnosis and management of Sandhoff Disease within families.

Chapter 16

Sickle Cell Anemia

What Is Sickle Cell Anemia?

Sickle cell anemia is an inherited blood disorder, characterized primarily by chronic anemia and periodic episodes of pain. The underlying problem involves hemoglobin, a component of the red cells in the blood. The hemoglobin molecules in each red blood cell carry oxygen from the lungs to the body organs and tissues and bring back carbon dioxide to the lungs.

In sickle cell anemia, the hemoglobin is defective. After the hemoglobin molecules give up their oxygen, some of them may cluster together and form long, rod-like structures. These structures cause the red blood cells to become stiff and to assume a sickle shape. Unlike normal red cells, which are usually smooth and donut-shaped, the sickled red cells cannot squeeze through small blood vessels. Instead, they stack up and cause blockages that deprive the organs and tissue of oxygen-carrying blood. This process produces the periodic episodes of pain and ultimately can damage the tissues and vital organs and lead to other serious medical problems.

Unlike normal red blood cells, which last about 120 days in the bloodstream, sickled red cells die after only about 10 to 20 days. Because they cannot be replaced fast enough, the blood is chronically short of red blood cells, a condition called anemia.

"Facts about Sickle Cell Anemia," National Heart, Lung, and Blood Institute (NHLBI), NIH Publication No. 96-4057, November 1996.

What Causes Sickle Cell Anemia?

Sickle cell anemia is caused by an error in the gene that tells the body how to make hemoglobin. The defective gene tells the body to make the abnormal hemoglobin that results in deformed red blood cells.

Children who inherit copies of the defective gene from both parents will have sickle cell anemia. Children who inherit the defective sickle hemoglobin gene from only one parent will not have the disease, but will carry the sickle cell trait. Individuals with sickle cell trait generally have no symptoms, but they can pass the sickle hemoglobin gene on to their children.

The error in the hemoglobin gene results from a genetic mutation that occurred many thousands of years ago in people in parts of Africa, the Mediterranean basin, the Middle East, and India. A deadly form of malaria was very common at that time, and malaria epidemics caused the death of great numbers of people. Studies show that in areas where malaria was a problem, children who inherited one sickle hemoglobin gene—and who, therefore, carried the sickle cell trait—had a survival advantage: unlike the children who had normal hemoglobin genes, they survived the malaria epidemics; they grew up, had their own children, and passed on the gene for sickle hemoglobin. As populations migrated, the sickle cell mutation spread to other Mediterranean areas, further into the Middle East, and eventually into the Western Hemisphere.

In the United States and other countries where malaria is not a problem, the sickle hemoglobin gene no longer provides a survival advantage. Instead, it may be a serious threat to the carrier's children, who may inherit two abnormal sickle hemoglobin genes and have sickle cell anemia.

How Common Is Sickle Cell Anemia?

Sickle cell anemia affects millions of people throughout the world. It is particularly common among people whose ancestors come from sub-Saharan Africa; Spanish-speaking regions (South America, Cuba, Central America); Saudi Arabia; India; and Mediterranean countries, such as Turkey, Greece, and Italy.

In the United States, it affects approximately 72,000 people, most of whose ancestors come from Africa. The disease occurs in approximately 1 of every 500 African American births and 1 of every 1,000-1,400 Hispanic American births. Approximately 2 million Americans, or 1 in 12 African Americans, carry the sickle cell trait.

What Are the Signs and Symptoms of Sickle Cell Anemia?

The clinical course of sickle cell anemia does not follow a single pattern; some patients have mild symptoms, and some have very severe symptoms. However, the basic problem is the same—the sickle-shaped red blood cells tend to get stuck in narrow blood vessels, blocking the flow of blood.

The presence of two defective genes (SS) is needed for sickle cell anemia. If each parent carries one sickle hemoglobin gene (S) and one normal gene (A), with each pregnancy, there is a 25 percent chance of the child inheriting two defective genes and having sickle cell anemia; a 25 percent chance of inheriting two normal genes and not having the disease; and a 50 percent chance of being an unaffected carrier like the parents.

This results in the following conditions:

- **Hand-foot syndrome.** When the small blood vessels in the hands or feet are blocked, pain and swelling can result, along with fever. This may be the first symptom of sickle cell anemia in infants.
- **Fatigue, paleness, and shortness of breath**—all symptoms of anemia, or a shortage of red blood cells.
- **Pain** that occurs unpredictably in any body organ or joint, wherever the sickled blood cells block oxygen flow to the tissues. The frequency and amount of pain varies. Some patients have painful episodes (also called crises) less than once a year, and some have as many as 15 or even more episodes in a year. Sometimes the pain lasts only a few hours; sometimes it lasts several weeks. For especially severe, ongoing pain, the patient may have to be hospitalized and treated with painkillers and intravenous fluids. Pain is the principal symptom of sickle cell anemia in both children and adults.
- **Eye problems**. When the retina, the "film" at the back of the eye that receives and processes visual images, does not get enough nourishment from circulating red blood cells, it can deteriorate. Damage to the retina can be serious enough to cause blindness.
- **Yellowing of the skin and eyes**. These are signs of jaundice, resulting from the rapid breakdown of red blood cells.

- **Delayed growth and puberty** in children and often a slight build in adults. The slow rate of growth is caused by a shortage of red blood cells.
- **Infections**. In general, both children and adults with sickle cell anemia are more vulnerable to infections and have a harder time fighting them off once they start. This is the result of damage to the spleen from the sickled red cells which prevents the spleen from destroying bacteria in the blood. Infants and young children, especially, are susceptible to bacterial infections that can kill them in as little as 9 hours from onset of fever. Pneumococcal infections used to be the principal cause of death in young children with sickle cell anemia until physicians began routinely giving penicillin on a preventive basis to infants that are identified at birth or in early infancy as having sickle cell anemia.
- **Stroke.** The defective hemoglobin damages the walls of the red blood cells, causing them to stick to blood vessel walls. This can result in the development of narrowed, or blocked, small blood vessels in the brain, causing a serious, life-threatening stroke. This type of stroke occurs primarily in children.
- **Acute chest syndrome**—a life-threatening complication of sickle cell anemia, similar to pneumonia, that is caused by infection or trapped sickled cells in the lung. This is characterized by chest pain, fever, and an abnormal chest x-ray.

How Is Sickle Cell Anemia Detected?

Early diagnosis of sickle cell anemia is critical so that children who have the disease can receive proper treatment. More than 40 states now perform a simple, inexpensive blood test for sickle cell disease on all newborn infants. This test is performed at the same time and from the same blood samples as other routine newborn screening tests. Hemoglobin electrophoresis is the most widely used diagnostic test.

If the test shows the presence of sickle hemoglobin, a second blood test is performed to confirm the diagnosis. These tests also tell whether the child carries the sickle cell trait.

How Is Sickle Cell Anemia Treated?

Although there is no cure for sickle cell anemia, doctors can do a great deal to help sickle cell patients, and treatment is constantly being improved. Basic treatment of painful crises relies heavily on pain-killing drugs and oral and intravenous fluids to reduce pain and prevent complications.

Blood transfusions are used to treat and to prevent some of the complications of sickle cell anemia. Transfusions correct anemia by increasing the number of normal red blood cells in circulation. Transfusions are used to treat spleen enlargement in children before the condition becomes life-threatening. Regular transfusion therapy also can help prevent recurring strokes in children at high risk of crippling nervous system complications.

Giving young children with sickle cell anemia oral penicillin twice a day, beginning when the child is about 2 months old and continuing until the child is at least 5 years old, can prevent pneumococcal infection and early death in these children. Recently, however, several new strains of pneumonia bacteria that are resistant to penicillin have been reported. Since the vaccines for these bacteria are ineffective in young children, studies are being planned to test new vaccines.

The first effective drug treatment for adults with severe sickle cell anemia was reported in early 1995, when a study conducted by the National Heart, Lung, and Blood Institute showed that daily doses of the anticancer drug hydroxyurea reduced the frequency of painful crises and of acute chest syndrome in these patients. Patients taking the drug also needed fewer blood transfusions. The long-term side effects of hydroxyurea and its effects in children with sickle cell anemia are still being studied.

Sickle cell anemia patients with severe chest or back pain that prevents them from breathing deeply may be able to avoid potentially serious lung complications associated with acute chest syndrome by using an incentive spirometer. This is a small plastic device, shaped like a tube, with a ball inside. The patient must breathe into it hard enough to force the ball up the tube, so using it helps the patient breathe more deeply.

Most complications of sickle cell anemia are treated as they occur. For example, laser coagulation and other types of eye surgery may be used to prevent further vision loss inpatients with eye problems. Surgery may be recommended for certain kinds of organ damage—for example, to remove gallstones or replace a hip joint. Leg ulcers may be treated with cleansing solutions and zinc oxide, or with skin grafts if the condition persists.

Regular health maintenance is critical for people with sickle cell anemia. Proper nutrition, good hygiene, bed rest, protection against infections, and avoidance of other stresses all are important in maintaining good health and preventing complications. Regular visits to a physician or clinic that provides comprehensive care are necessary to identify early changes in the patient's health and ensure that the person receives immediate treatment.

Today, with good health care, many people with sickle cell anemia are in reasonably good health much of the time and living productive lives. In fact, in the past 30 years, the life expectancy of people with sickle cell anemia has increased. Many patients with sickle cell anemia now live into their mid-forties and beyond.

The Future of Sickle Cell Anemia Treatment

Scientists have learned a great deal about sickle cell anemia during the past 30 years—what causes it, how it affects the patient, and how to treat some of the complications. They also have begun to have success in developing drugs that will prevent the symptoms of sickle cell anemia and procedures that should ultimately provide a cure.

Some researchers are focusing on identifying drugs that will increase the level of fetal hemoglobin in the blood. Fetal hemoglobin is a form of hemoglobin that all humans produce before birth, but most people stop making shortly after birth. Most humans have little fetal hemoglobin left in their bloodstream by the time they reach the age of 6 months. However, some people with sickle cell anemia continue to produce large amounts of fetal hemoglobin after birth, and studies have shown that these people have less severe cases of the disease. Fetal hemoglobin seems to prevent sickling of red cells, and cells containing fetal hemoglobin tend to survive longer in the bloodstream. Hydroxyurea appears to work primarily by stimulating production of fetal hemoglobin. There is some evidence that administering hydroxyurea with erythropoietin, a genetically engineered hormone that stimulates red cell production, may make hydroxyurea work better. This combination approach offers the possibility that lower doses of hydroxyurea can be used to achieve the needed level of fetal hemoglobin. However, both of these drugs may produce serious side effects, so researchers continue to search for safer agents that are just as effective.

Butyrate, a simple fatty acid that is widely used as a food additive, is also being investigated as an agent that may increase fetal hemoglobin production.

Clotrimazole, an over-the-counter medication commonly used to treat fungal infections, is under investigation as a treatment to prevent the loss of water from the red blood cells that contributes to sickling.

It is hoped that this medication, used alone or in conjunction with other antisickling agents, may eventually offer an effective long-term therapy for sickle cell anemia patients.

Bone marrow transplantation has been shown to provide a cure for severely affected children with sickle cell disease. Although many of the risks of this procedure have been reduced, it still is not entirely without risk. In addition, the marrow must come from a healthy matched sibling donor, and only about 18 percent of children with sickle cell anemia are likely to have a matched sibling. Researchers are working on techniques to further reduce some of the risks of bone marrow transplantation for patients with sickle cell disease.

The ultimate cure for sickle cell anemia may be gene therapy. In sickle cell anemia, the gene that switches on production of adult hemoglobin shortly before birth, is defective. Two approaches to gene therapy are being explored. Some scientists are looking into whether correcting this gene and inserting it into the bone marrow of people with sickle cell anemia will result in the production of normal adult hemoglobin. Others are looking at the possibility of turning off the defective gene and simultaneously reactivating another gene that turns on production of fetal hemoglobin. In both cases, the research is at a very early stage. Progress is being made, however, and there is a real possibility of an eventual clinical cure for sickle cell anemia.

Although the genetic defect that causes sickling was identified more than 40 years ago, until very recently, research into the development of treatments for the disease was hampered by the lack of an animal model that could be used to test experimental drugs and gene therapy. Recently, however, scientists were able to genetically engineer a line of mice that exhibit some of the characteristics of sickle cell disease in much the same way humans do. This is an important advance in the search for an effective treatment and eventual cure for sickle cell disease.

Frequently Asked Questions

How Can Patients and Their Families and Friends Be Helped to Cope with Sickle Cell Anemia?

Sickle cell patients and their families may need help in handling the economic and psychological stresses of coping with this serious chronic disease. Sickle cell centers and clinics can provide information and counseling on handling these problems. Parents should try to learn as much about the disease as possible so that they can recognize early signs of complications and seek early treatment.

Is It Possible to Detect Sickle Cell Anemia in an Unborn Baby?

Yes. By sampling the amniotic fluid or tissue taken from the placenta, doctors can tell whether a fetus has sickle cell anemia or sickle cell trait. This test can be done as early as the first trimester of pregnancy.

What Should Future Parents Know?

People who are planning to become parents should know whether they are carriers of the sickle cell gene, and, if they are, they may want to seek genetic counseling. The counselor can tell prospective parents what the chances are that their child will have sickle cell trait or sickle cell anemia. Accurate diagnostic tests and information are available from health departments, neighborhood health centers, medical centers and clinics that care for individuals with sickle cell anemia.

For More Information

National Heart, Lung, and Blood Institute (NHLBI)
Information Center
P.O. Box 30105
Bethesda, MD 20824-0105
Tel: 301-592-8573

The Sickle Cell Disease Program Division of Blood Diseases and Resources
National Heart, Lung, and Blood Institute
II Rockledge Centre
6701 Rockledge Drive MSC 7950
Bethesda, MD 20892-7950
Tel: 301-435-0050

Sickle Cell Disease Association of America
200 Corporate Pointe, Suite 495
Culver City, CA 90230-8727

Toll Free: 800-421-8453
Tel: 310-216-6363
Fax: 310-245-3722
E-mail: scdaa@siclecelldisease.org
Website: http://www.sicklecelldisease.org

National Maternal and Child Health Clearinghouse
2070 Chain Bridge Rd., Suite 4450
Vienna, VA 22182
Tel: 703-821-8955

Agency for Healthcare Research and Quality
2101 E. Jefferson Street
Rockville, MD 20852
Tel: 301-594-1364

Chapter 17

Tay-Sachs Disease

What Is Tay-Sachs Disease?

The classical form of Tay-Sachs disease (TSD) is a fatal genetic disorder in children that causes progressive destruction of the central nervous system.

The disease is named for Warren Tay (1843-1927), a British ophthalmologist who in 1881 described a patient with a cherry-red spot on the retina of the eye. It is also named for Bernard Sachs (1858-1944), a New York neurologist whose work several years later provided the first description of the cellular changes in Tay-Sachs disease. Sachs also recognized the familial nature of the disorder, and, by observing numerous cases, he noted that most babies with Tay-Sachs disease were of eastern European Jewish origin.

Tay-Sachs disease is caused by the absence of a vital enzyme called hexosaminidase A (Hex-A). Without Hex-A, a fatty substance or lipid called GM2 ganglioside accumulates abnormally in cells, especially in the nerve cells of the brain. This ongoing accumulation causes progressive damage to the cells. The destructive process begins in the fetus early in pregnancy, although the disease is not clinically apparent until the child is several months old. By the time a child with TSD is three or four years old, the nervous system is so badly

---

affected that life itself cannot be supported. Even with the best of care, all children with classical TSD die early in childhood, usually by the age of five.

A baby with Tay-Sachs disease appears normal at birth and seems to develop normally until about six months of age. The first signs of TSD can vary and are evident at different ages in affected children. Initially, development slows, there is a loss of peripheral vision, and the child exhibits an abnormal startle response. By about two years of age, most children experience recurrent seizures and diminishing mental function. The infant gradually regresses, losing skills one by one, and is eventually unable to crawl, turn over, sit, or reach out. Other symptoms include increasing loss of coordination, progressive inability to swallow, and breathing difficulties. Eventually, the child becomes blind, mentally retarded, paralyzed, and non-responsive to his or her environment.

To date, there is no cure or effective treatment for TSD. However, there is active research being done in many investigative laboratories in the U.S. and around the world. The uses of enzyme replacement therapy to provide the Hex-A which is missing in babies with TSD has been explored. Although this approach is promising, scientists still face serious obstacles. Because the disease affects brain cells which are protected by the blood-brain barrier, enzymes like Hex-A are blocked from entering the brain from the blood. Bone marrow transplantation has also been attempted but to date has not been successful in reversing or slowing damage to the central nervous system in babies with TSD.

Although a cure for Tay-Sachs disease does not exist at the present time, support for families of affected children is available through organizations such as the National Tay-Sachs and Allied Diseases Association.

How Is Tay-Sachs Disease Transmitted?

All of us carry genes, in pairs, located along 23 pairs of chromosomes. TSD is controlled by a pair of genes on chromosome 15; these are the genes that code for the enzyme Hex-A. If either or both Hex-A genes are active, the body produces enough of the enzyme to prevent the abnormal build-up of the GM2 ganglioside lipid. Carriers of TSD—people who have one copy of the inactive gene along with one copy of the active gene—are healthy. They do not have Tay-Sachs disease. The only significance of being a carrier is the possibility of passing the inactive gene to one's children.

A carrier has a 50% chance of passing the inactive gene on to his or her children; any child who inherits one inactive gene is a Tay-Sachs carrier like the parent. If both parents are carriers and their child inherits the inactive TSD gene from each of them, the child will have Tay-Sachs disease since he or she has inherited two inactive recessive genes and, therefore, cannot produce any functional Hex-A.

When both parents are carriers of the inactive Tay-Sachs gene, they have a 1 in 4 chance (25%) with each pregnancy that their child will have Tay-Sachs Disease, and a 3 in 4 chance (75%) that their child will be healthy. Of their unaffected children, there is a 2 in 3 chance that each child will be a carrier, like the parents. This pattern of inheritance is called autosomal recessive.

Are Certain Populations at Higher Risk?

Recessive diseases such as Tay-Sachs often occur more frequently, though not exclusively, in a defined population. A person's chances of being a TSD carrier are significantly higher if he or she is of eastern European (Ashkenazi) Jewish descent. Approximately one in every 27 Jews in the United States is a carrier of the TSD gene. There is also a noticeable incidence of TSD in non-Jewish French Canadians living near the St. Lawrence River and in the Cajun community of Louisiana. By contrast, the carrier rate in the general population as well as in Jews of Sephardic origin is about one in 250.

While there are certain populations known to be at higher risk for carrying an altered Hex-A gene, anyone in any population can be a carrier of TSD. If two such individuals have children, they will have the same one in four chance, with each pregnancy, of having a child with TSD. In fact, over the past 25 years, carrier screening and genetic counseling within high-risk populations have greatly reduced the number of children born with TSD in these groups. At the same time the number of children born with TSD to couples not known to be at high risk of being carriers of TSD has remained more or less constant. Therefore, a great percentage of the babies born with Tay-Sachs disease today are born to couples who were not previously thought to be at significant risk.

Is There a Test to Identify Carriers?

Tay-Sachs most often appears in families with no prior history of the disease. The TSD gene can be carried without being expressed through many generations. Before 1970, the only way to learn if one was a Tay-Sachs carrier was to be the parent of a baby with TSD. Now, safe and reliable carrier testing is available to identify Tay-Sachs carriers. Most important, testing can identify carrier couples who are at risk for bearing a child with TSD—before a tragedy occurs. With this vital information, couples can explore the various options that will enable them to protect their families from this devastating disease.

A simple blood test can distinguish Tay-Sachs carriers from non-carriers. Blood samples can be analyzed by either enzyme assay or DNA studies. The enzyme assay is a biochemical test that measures the level of Hex-A in a person's blood. Carriers have less Hex-A in their body fluid and cells than non-carriers. (Babies with Tay-Sachs disease have a total absence of Hex-A in their cells.) The biochemical test is able to detect all Tay-Sachs carriers of all ethnic backgrounds.

Accurate biochemical testing requires laboratories to be proficient in specialized laboratory procedures and experienced in the interpretation of test results. To ensure accuracy, persons seeking such carrier testing for TSD should verify that the analysis is being performed at a laboratory that participates in the Tay-Sachs Quality Control Program supported by NTSAD. A complete list of laboratories affiliated with the Quality Control Program is available from NTSAD.

- Fact: Tay-Sachs carrier testing is vital for individuals in High-Risk populations who are planning to have children and for the close relatives of families with an affected child.

DNA-based carrier testing looks for specific mutations, or changes, in the gene that codes for Hex-A. Since 1985, when the Hex-A gene was isolated, over 50 different mutations in this gene have been identified. Some are more prevalent than others, and a few are associated with a later-onset form of the disease, rather than with the infantile form described here.

The limitation of DNA-based carrier testing is that not all known mutations in the Hex-A gene are detected by the test, and others have yet to be identified. The tests currently available detect about 95% of carriers of Ashkenazi Jewish background and about 60% of non-Jewish individuals. Therefore, some people who are carriers will not be identified by DNA analysis alone.

DNA testing can provide very important information when used in conjunction with biochemical testing, especially in cases where both members of a couple are determined to be carriers. Knowing information about the mutations carried by each parent, and whether they are classical or Late-Onset Tay-Sachs mutations, is important if a couple chooses to undergo prenatal diagnosis.

Tay-Sachs carrier testing is vital for individuals in high-risk populations who are planning to have children. Even if your childbearing years are over, your carrier status can provide extremely important information. If you are a carrier, your close relatives (children, brothers, sisters, cousins, aunts, and uncles) should be alerted to be tested as well. Tay-Sachs carrier testing is also vital for the close relatives of families with an affected child, regardless of ethnic background, since all parents of children with Tay-Sachs are, by definition, carriers.

Note: Some special considerations are involved in carrier testing of pregnant women. The best advice for women is to be tested before pregnancy. The standard biochemical test used to test males and non-pregnant women cannot be used in pregnant women because of changes in serum enzyme levels during pregnancy. Pregnant women must instead be tested using leukocytes (white blood cells). The leukocyte test is as reliable as the blood serum test, but is considerably more complex and costly. Another advantage to testing before pregnancy is that a couple is given time to consider the information they receive. If a couple is found to be at risk, they can review their options and make the necessary decisions about planning and protecting their families.

If There Is No Cure, Is There a Way to Prevent the Tragedy of Tay-Sachs Disease?

Tay-Sachs today is a preventable tragedy. Recent medical advances offer high-risk couples the means of having full, healthy families. In 1969, researchers discovered that Tay-Sachs babies lack Hex-A and that carriers of TSD have reduced amounts of Hex-A in their blood. Two years later, Hex-A levels were measured in amniotic fluid, introducing the first prenatal diagnosis for Tay-Sachs Disease.

Today, at-risk couples can choose from two available prenatal diagnostic procedures: amniocentesis and chorionic villus sampling (CVS). Amniocentesis involves removing and testing a small quantity of the fluid that bathes the fetus in the uterus. This procedure is done at approximately the 16th week of pregnancy. If Hex-A is found to be present, the fetus is not affected by TSD. On the other hand, if Hex-A is missing in fetal cells, the infant will have TSD. If the fetus is affected, the family may elect to have a therapeutic abortion. In this way, even at-risk couples can be helped to have children, as many as they wish, who are free of Tay-Sachs disease.

- Fact: Recent medical advances offer high-risk couples the means of having full, healthy families.

Chorionic villus sampling (CVS) is a newer technique. It is performed earlier in pregnancy, by the 10th week, and usually provides a test answer much sooner than amniocentesis. The cell sample is obtained by withdrawing a small bit of the developing placenta (afterbirth). Because the procedure is performed earlier than amniocentesis—often before the pregnancy shows—CVS offers couples greater privacy in their decision making as well as a safer pregnancy termination, should therapeutic abortion be necessary.

Recently, assisted reproductive technologies have become available to at-risk couples who wish to have children but for whom abortion is not an option. One option is artificial insemination by a non-carrier sperm donor. Another option, available only for couples with identified DNA mutations in the Hex-A gene, involves in-vitro fertilization using the couple's own eggs and sperm. Here, in-vitro fertilization is followed by an analysis of the DNA of the newly formed embryos to determine which carry two copies of the TSD gene and which do not; only those embryos determined not to be affected with TSD are implanted in the woman. This latter method is complex and quite expensive but is sometimes covered by insurance.

Genetic counseling is an important service available to all carrier couples to assist them in assessing their reproductive options. In addition to reviewing the various options for family planning which are currently available to high-risk couples (prenatal diagnosis by amniocentesis or CVS and selective termination of affected fetuses; adopting children; assisted reproductive technologies such as in-vitro fertilization followed by pre-implantation diagnosis or artificial insemination by a non-carrier donor; or taking a 25% risk of bearing a child with TSD), the genetic counselor can help carriers fulfill their responsibility of informing family members that they, too, may be carriers and should be tested.

Late Onset Tay-Sachs Disease

Late-onset Tay-Sachs disease (LOTS) is a variant of Tay-Sachs which is much less common than the infantile form of the disease. As the name suggests, LOTS affects adults rather than infants, and manifests itself as a progressive loss of functioning of the nervous system. The enzyme defect, a deficiency of Hex-A, is the same as that of classical Tay-Sachs, but people with the late-onset condition have significantly reduced amounts of Hex-A rather than a complete absence of the enzyme.

The onset of symptoms in people with LOTS is usually between adolescence and the mid-30's, with much variation among individuals. The symptoms worsen over time, beginning with subtle signs such as clumsiness and mood alterations which may be noticed only in retrospect after a diagnosis has been made. Neurological manifestations of the disease can include: muscle weakness, cramping, wasting, and twitching; lack of coordination; slurred speech; and dystonia (distortion of posture caused by muscle contractions). Affected individuals often have some, but not all, of these symptoms.

Some individuals with LOTS have impaired intellectual functioning, which may involve memory impairment, difficulty with comprehension, and deterioration in school performance. Behavioral alterations can include short attention spans and changes in personality. About 40% of persons with LOTS have psychiatric symptoms such as psychotic episodes or depression.

- Fact: LOTS affects adults, not infants as in classical Tay-Sachs, who display a significantly reduced level of Hex-A, rather than a complete absence of the enzyme.

Since LOTS is a recently recognized condition, there is much that remains to be learned about the disease. The long-term prognosis for persons with LOTS is uncertain, especially because there is considerable variability from individual to individual. It appears that life-expectancy for people with LOTS is similar to that of the unaffected population. While there is no known cure, current medical treatment for LOTS is directed towards managing the symptoms of the disease. Additionally, support services for individuals and families can be helpful in dealing with the personal and social aspects of living with a progressive chronic disease.

LOTS, like classical Tay-Sachs disease, is inherited in an autosomal recessive manner. A person with LOTS has two altered copies of the same Hex-A gene that causes infantile Tay-Sachs disease. The gene is altered in a slightly different way from that of a classical Tay-Sachs mutation, so that an individual with LOTS is able to produce small amounts of Hex-A. A person with LOTS may have two late-onset mutations or one late-onset mutation and one infantile mutation. In either case, there is a deficiency of Hex-A, but the small amount of Hex-A that is produced in persons with LOTS accounts for the difference in the clinical course of LOTS as compared to infantile Tay-Sachs disease.

As is true for all autosomal recessive conditions, the parents of a person with LOTS are both Tay-Sachs carriers, and therefore have a 25% chance with each pregnancy of having an offspring with LOTS. Often, however, the diagnosis of the individual affected with LOTS is not made until the parents have completed childbearing. Since individuals with LOTS are often able to have children, genetic counseling may be helpful in explaining the possibility that the children of an affected person may be healthy, affected with LOTS, or affected with infantile Tay-Sachs disease, depending on whether the affected person's spouse is also a Tay-Sachs carrier.

Additional Information

Late Onset Tay-Sachs Foundation
1303 Paper Mill Road
Erdenheim, PA 19038
Tel: 215-836-9426
Toll Free: 800-672-2022

March of Dimes Birth Defects Foundation
1275 Mamroneck Ave.
White Plains, NY 10605
Tel: 914-428-7100
Toll Free: 888-663-4637

National Foundation for Jewish Genetic Diseases, Inc.
250 Park Ave.
Suite 1000
New York, NY 10177
Tel: 212-371-1030

National Organization for Rare Disorders (NORD)
P O Box 8923
New Fairfield, CT 06812-8923
Tel: 203-746-6518
Toll Free: 800-999-6673

National Tay-Sachs & Allied Diseases Association, Inc
2001 Beacon Street
Suite 204
Brookline, MA 02146
Tel: 617-277-4463
Toll Free: 800-906-8723

Genetic Alliance
4301 Connecticut Ave NW
Suite 404
Washington D.C. 20008-2304
Tel: 202-966-5557
Toll Free Helpline: 800-336-4363
E-mail: info@geneticalliance.org
Website: http:www.geneticalliance.org

Chapter 18

Thalassemia

What Is Thalassemia?

Thalassemia is the name of a group of genetic blood disorders. To understand how thalassemia affects the human body, you must first understand a little about how blood is made.

Hemoglobin is the oxygen-carrying component of the red blood cells. It is made of two different kinds of proteins, called alpha and beta globins. If the body doesn't produce enough of either of these two proteins, the red blood cells do not form properly and cannot carry sufficient oxygen. The result is anemia that begins in early childhood and lasts throughout life.

Since Thalassemia is not a single disorder but a group of related disorders that affect the human body in similar ways, it is important to understand the differences between the various types of thalassemia.

Alpha Thalassemia

People who do not produce enough alpha protein have alpha-thalassemia. It is commonly found in Africa, the Middle East, India, Southeast Asia, southern China, and occasionally the Mediterranean region.

This chapter includes "What Is Thalassemia?" "Alpha Thalassemia," "Beta Thalassemia," "Other Forms of Thalassemia," "Treatment," and "Thalassemia Trait," all reprinted with permission © 1999, 2000 Cooley's Anemia Foundation.

There are seven types of alpha thalassemia that range from mild to severe in their effect on the body.

Silent Carrier State. This condition generally causes no health problems because the lack of alpha protein is so small that the hemoglobin functions normally. It is called "Silent Carrier" because of how difficult it is to detect. Silent Carrier state is "diagnosed" by deduction when an apparently normal individual has a child with Hemoglobin H Disease or alpha thalassemia trait. It can also be diagnosed by special DNA testing.

Hemoglobin Constant Spring. This is an unusual form of Silent Carrier state that is caused by a mutation of the alpha globin. It is called Constant Spring after the region of Jamaica in which it was discovered. As in Silent Carrier state, an individual with this condition usually experiences no related health problems.

Alpha Thalassemia Trait or Alpha Thalassemia Minor. In this condition, the lack of alpha protein is somewhat greater. Patients with this condition have smaller red blood cells and a mild anemia, although many patients do not experience symptoms. However, physicians often mistake alpha thalassemia minor for iron deficiency anemia and prescribe iron supplements that have no effect on the anemia.

Hemoglobin H Disease. In this condition the lack of alpha protein is great enough to cause moderate to severe anemia and serious health problems such as an enlarged spleen, bone deformities, and fatigue. It is named for the abnormal hemoglobin H (created by the remaining beta globin) that destroys red blood cells.

Hemoglobin H-Constant Spring. This condition is more severe than Hemoglobin H Disease. Individuals with this condition tend to have a more severe anemia, and suffer more frequently from enlargement of the spleen and viral infections.

Homozygous Constant Spring. This condition is a variation of Hemoglobin H-Constant Spring that occurs when two Constant Spring carriers pass this gene on to their child (as opposed to Hemoglobin H Constant Spring, in which one parent is a Constant Spring Carrier and the other a carrier of Alpha Thalassemia Trait). This condition is generally less severe than Hemoglobin H Constant Spring and more similar to Hemoglobin H Disease.

Hydrops fetalis or Alpha Thalassemia Major. In this condition, there are no alpha genes in the individual's DNA, which causes the gamma globins produced by the fetus to form an abnormal hemoglobin called hemoglobin Barts. Most individuals with this condition die before or shortly after birth. In some extremely rare cases where the condition is discovered before birth, in utero blood transfusions have allowed the birth of children with hydrops fetalis who then require lifelong blood transfusions and medical care.

Beta Thalassemia

People who do not produce enough beta protein have beta thalassemia. It is found in people of Mediterranean descent; such as Italians and Greeks, and is also found in the Arabian Peninsula, Iran, Africa, Southeast Asia, and southern China.

There are three types of beta thalassemia that also range from mild to severe in their effects on the body.

Thalassemia minor or thalassemia trait. In this condition, the lack of beta protein is not great enough to cause problems in the normal functioning of the hemoglobin. A person with this condition simply carries the genetic trait for thalassemia and will usually experience no health problems other than a possible mild anemia. As in alpha thalassemia minor, physicians often mistake the small red blood cells of the person with beta thalassemia minor as a sign of iron-deficiency anemia and incorrectly prescribe iron supplements.

Thalassemia Intermedia. In this condition the lack of beta protein in the hemoglobin is great enough to cause a moderately severe anemia and significant health problems including bone deformities and enlargement of the spleen. However, there is a wide range in the clinical severity of this condition, and the borderline between Thalassemia Intermedia and the most severe form, Thalassemia major, can be confusing. The determining factor seems to be the number of blood transfusions required by the patient. The more dependent the patient is on blood transfusions, the more likely they are to be classified as thalassemia major.

Thalassemia major or Cooley's anemia. This is the most severe form of beta thalassemia in which the complete lack of beta protein in the hemoglobin causes a life-threatening anemia that requires regular blood transfusions and extensive ongoing medical care. These extensive, lifelong blood transfusions lead to iron-overload which must be treated with chelation therapy to prevent early death from organ failure.

Other Forms of Thalassemia

In addition to the alpha and beta thalassemias, there are other related disorders that occur when the abnormal gene for alpha or beta thalassemia combines with another abnormal or mutant globin gene.

E Beta Thalassemia. Hemoglobin E is one of the most common abnormal hemoglobins. It is usually found in people of Southeast Asian ancestry, such as Cambodians, Vietnamese, and Thai. When combined with beta thalassemia trait, Hemoglobin E produces E Beta Thalassemia, a moderately severe anemia which has similar symptoms to Beta Thalassemia Intermedia.

Sickle Beta Thalassemia. This condition is caused by a combination of beta thalassemia trait and Hemoglobin S trait, the abnormal hemoglobin found in people with Sickle Cell Disease. It is commonly found in people of Mediterranean ancestry, such as Italians, Greeks, Turks, and in people from the Caribbean. The severity of the condition varies according to the amount of normal beta globin produced by the beta gene. When no beta globin is produced by the beta gene, the condition is almost identical with sickle cell disease. The more beta globin produced by the beta gene, the less severe the condition.

Treatment

Blood Transfusions

The most common treatment for all severe forms of thalassemia is red blood cell transfusions. These transfusions are necessary to provide the patient with a temporary supply of healthy red blood cells with normal hemoglobin capable of carrying the oxygen that the patient's body needs.

While thalassemia patients were given infrequent transfusions in the past, clinical research led to a more frequent program of regular blood cell transfusions that has greatly improved the patients' quality of life. Today, there is great variation in the transfusion practices between different countries, and between medical centers in the same country. In the USA, while some centers practice transfusions every two weeks, more often the interval is every three to four weeks.

Iron Overload

Because there is no natural way for the body to eliminate iron, the iron in the transfused blood cells builds up in a condition known as "iron overload" and becomes toxic to tissues and organs, particularly the liver and heart. Iron overload typically results in the patient's early death from organ failure.

Chelation Therapy

To help remove excess iron, patients undergo the difficult and painful infusion of a drug, Desferal. A needle is attached to a small battery operated infusion pump and worn under the skin of the stomach or legs for up to twelve hours five to seven times a week. Desferal binds iron in a process called "chelation." Chelated iron is later eliminated, reducing the amount of stored iron.

The Compliance Problem

Compliance with Desferal is vital to the thalassemia patient's long term survival. However, many patients find the treatment so difficult that they do not keep up with it or abandon treatment altogether. Lack of compliance with chelation therapy leads to accelerated health problems and early death. To combat the compliance problem, researchers are at work on better tolerated new chelators that can improve patient compliance.

Who Carries the Thalassemia Trait?

Thalassemia was originally believed to be common only to people of the Mediterranean region, such as Italians, Greeks, and Turks. (An early name for thalassemia major or Cooley's anemia was Mediterranean anemia.) Since then, scientists have discovered that the thalassemia trait is found in people of many other regions, including the Arabian Peninsula, Africa, the Indian subcontinent, China, Southeast Asia, and the Caribbean. Today, due to the migration and intermarriage of different ethnic populations, the trait for thalassemia is found throughout the world, sometimes in people with no obvious ethnic connection to the disorder.

It is estimated that over 2 million people in the United States carry the genetic trait for thalassemia. For this reason, the National Institutes of Health recommends that all US citizens should be tested for the thalassemia trait.

Inheritance of Thalassemia

- If two people who carry the trait for the same genetic type of thalassemia (alpha or beta) have a child, there is a 25% chance with each pregnancy that the child will inherit a serious blood disease.
- If both parents carry the genetic trait for beta thalassemia, there is a 25% chance with each pregnancy that their child will be born with Thalassemia Major or Cooley's anemia, a serious blood disease that is fatal without treatment.
- If one parent carries the trait for beta thalassemia and the other carries the trait for Hemoglobin E, there is a 25% chance with each pregnancy that the child will be born with E Beta Thalassemia.
- If one parent carries the trait for Beta Thalassemia and the other carries the trait for Hemoglobin S, there is a 25% chance with each pregnancy that their child will be born with Sickle Beta Thalassemia.
- If both parents carry the trait for Alpha Thalassemia and if only one parent has the "cis" type of alpha trait (two alpha globin mutations on the same chromosome), there is a 25% chance with each pregnancy that their child will be born with Hemoglobin H Disease.
- If both parents carry the trait for Alpha Thalassemia and if both parents have the "cis" type of alpha trait (two alpha globin mutations on the same chromosome), there is a 25% chance with each pregnancy that their child will inherit hydrops fetalis which is almost universally fatal in utero.
- If one parent carries a thalassemia trait and the other parent has normal hemoglobin, there is no chance that the child will inherit a serious blood disease—however, there is a 50% chance that the child will inherit the thalassemia trait.

As you can see, the possibilities for inheriting the various forms of thalassemia are very complicated. Therefore, if you belong to any of the ethnic groups at risk, it is recommended that you be tested for the thalassemia trait and, if you are found to be a trait carrier, seek the advice of a genetic counselor.

Thalassemia Trait Testing

Finding out if you have the genetic trait for thalassemia begins by determining the size of your red blood cells.

If you have a routine blood test known as a Complete Blood Count, or CBC, already on file at your doctor's office, ask your doctor to look at the Mean Corpuscular Volume, or MCV. The MCV reading determines the size of your red blood cells. For adults, if the MCV reading is less than 75 you may be a trait carrier. For children, the MCV reading may be lower and varies according to their age.

If your MCV reading indicates that you may have the thalassemia trait, your doctor should then perform additional tests to make sure. Although the MCV reading is a good indicator of whether a person may have either the alpha or the beta thalassemia trait, finding out for certain if you have either trait involves two different kinds of tests.

A special test called hemoglobin electrophoresis is a reliable way of determining whether or not a person has the trait for beta thalassemia (beta thalassemia minor). This test is available at most large hospitals and clinics.

Testing for alpha thalassemia trait (alpha thalassemia minor) is usually done by a process of exclusion; people who have microcytosis but a normal hemoglobin electrophoresis and are of the appropriate ethnic origin are presumed to have alpha thalassemia minor.

Note: This information is for educational purposes only and is not intended to substitute for informed medical advice. You should not use this information to diagnose or treat a health problem or disease without consulting a qualified health care provider. The Cooley's Anemia Foundation strongly encourages you to consult your health care provider with any questions or concerns you may have regarding your condition.

Part Three

Genetic Testing

Chapter 19

What Is Genetic Counseling?

Stop the presses! "BRCA1 Gene Found." "Gene Unlocks Mystery of Huntington's Disease." Genetic testing has been in the headlines lately, with the discovery of genes that can play a role in predicting an individual's risk of illnesses such as breast cancer, Huntington's disease, and more. Reading about these breakthroughs might have made you wonder whether this cutting-edge scientific technology has something to offer your family. Could genetic tests provide valuable information that could benefit your child's health? It's possible—in some cases, genetic testing can literally be a lifesaver.

But it's even more likely that you might seek and benefit from genetic counseling. This is a broader category that encompasses not only testing but also some old-fashioned medical detective work and professional counseling.

What Is Genetic Counseling?

Genetic counseling is a health service that helps people identify and understand what particular traits they might pass on to their children. It is performed by doctors and nurses, as well as by specially educated health professionals who are certified as genetic counselors and come from a variety of disciplines, including biology, genetics, psychology, public health, and social work.

"Genetic Counseling," The Office on Women's Health, U.S. Department of Health and Human Services, July 1999.

"Genetic counselors blend the knowledge of the science of genetics and the interpersonal skills needed to interpret information for individuals and couples," explains Bea Leopold, executive director of the National Society of Genetic Counselors, an organization in Wallingford, Pennsylvania. Genetic counselors are trained to be sensitive to the background and values of the people they advise. A responsible counselor will never push you toward or dissuade you from a particular course of action but will only supply the information you need to make your own decisions.

Genetics Refresher Course

Understanding what determines your child's risk of an inherited disorder means taking a quick trip back to biology class. Here are the simple basics of genetics:

DNA (deoxyribonucleic acid) is a large molecule that holds the instructions for making all the proteins a cell needs.

A **gene** is a piece of DNA that contains the instructions for making a specific protein. The human body has approximately 80,000 genes. Each plays a different part in determining a person's heath tendencies and physical makeup—everything from his eye color to his risk of heart disease. A child gets half of his genes from each of his parents.

Genes are contained in **chromosomes**, structures in the nucleus of the body's cells. Human cells have 46 chromosomes, arranged in pairs.

Genetic inheritance patterns are classified as **dominant** or **recessive**. If a parent passes on the gene for a dominant disorder (such as Marfan's syndrome, a connective tissue disease), her child has a 50 percent chance of inheriting it. If both parents carry a gene for a recessive disorder (such as cystic fibrosis), their child has a 25 percent chance of inheriting it. If only one parent has the gene for a recessive trait, it will be overridden by the other parent's normal gene and will not cause the child to be affected.

Why Might I Want to Consult a Genetic Counselor?

Genetic counseling can help you make important decisions, such as whether to have more children and whether to seek preventive or early treatment for a disease or disorder for which you or your child is at high risk. Situations in which people commonly seek genetic counseling include planning a pregnancy after age 34; having suffered two or more miscarriages; being aware of a family history of an inherited disorder; or already having a child with an inherited disorder or birth defect.

"People usually go for genetic counseling because a child or another family member has an inherited disorder, which usually falls into one of two categories," says Christopher Cunniff, MD, FAAP, chair of the Section of Medical and Molecular Genetics and an associate professor of pediatrics at the University of Arizona, in Tucson. "It may be a structural problem, such as cleft lip or palate, or it may be a functional problem, such as mental retardation or a developmental disability." Some people also seek genetic counseling to address concerns about serious disorders that affect their particular race or ethnic group. Such disorders include sickle cell anemia, a blood disorder that affects mainly Blacks; thalassemia, another blood disorder, which afflicts mostly people of Mediterranean (usually Greek or Italian) ancestry; and Tay-Sachs disease, a degeneration of the brain that strikes primarily Jews of Central or Eastern European descent.

When Is the Best Time to Get Genetic Counseling?

If you are concerned about passing on an inherited disorder, it's best to seek genetic counseling before becoming pregnant. If you become aware of an inherited disorder in your family while you are pregnant, however, genetic counseling is still a good idea. It can help you understand the likelihood that your child will be affected and help you prepare emotionally and medically.

If you are interested in genetic counseling because you suspect your child has an inherited disorder, bring the matter to your pediatrician's attention so that she can refer you to a testing and counseling facility when appropriate. "Children can be evaluated at any age," says Dr. Cunniff, "but the earlier it's done, the better it is for supervising their health care. Potential problems can be treated or at least anticipated as soon as possible."

What Is Genetic Testing?

Genetic testing is one tool used in the genetic counseling process. There are several types of genetic tests. The more sophisticated blood tests analyze DNA to determine a person's risk of developing, or passing on to his children, specific inherited disorders.

What Disorders Can Genetic Tests Predict?

In addition to the ethnic specific conditions already mentioned, serious disorders that can be detected (or risk predicted) include cystic fibrosis, a disorder that causes overactivity of the exocrine glands, which produce mucus; and Huntington's disease, a degenerative disorder that affects the brain and nervous system.

Scientists have already identified the gene that causes idiopathic ventricular fibrillation, a condition that can cause a younger person's heart to stop beating for no apparent reason and that leads to an estimated 15,000 to 36,000 deaths each year. They are also close to isolating the gene responsible for autism, a brain disorder that originates in infancy and is characterized by repetitive behavior, language dysfunction, and the inability to interact socially.

Through sophisticated research, genes responsible for specific conditions are being located all the time, and genetic tests are being developed to identify them. The Human Genome Project is an ongoing effort by scientists throughout the world to map the estimated 80,000 genes in human DNA.

Does Genetic Counseling Always Involve Genetic Tests?

No. Genetic tests are an important tool in genetic counseling, but they are not always needed to predict the risk of developing or passing on a disorder. A genetic counselor can often glean a great deal of information based on your family health history, your personal health history, and any signs and symptoms of the disorder that you or your child might exhibit. In some cases, standard, non-genetic medical tests can also reveal the presence of inherited disorders.

Creating a Family Health History

To help a genetic counselor accurately assess the risk of a particular disorder, it's important to furnish your child's complete family health history. In fact, even if you never seek genetic counseling, it's wise to have this record. It can be just as valuable to your child's pediatrician as to your own physicians in helping them make decisions about your care. Gather information on your parents (your child's grandparents), siblings, aunts, uncles, and cousins. Make sure you canvass both sides of your child's family—yours and your spouse's; the risk of some diseases vary according to which side of the family the disease has appeared in.

Here are three starting points for assembling a family health history:

1. **Interview family members**. Providing a form for them to fill out may help jog their memory and will make your record keeping easier. You can obtain standard forms by calling the March of Dimes Birth Defects Foundation, or you can visit the American Health Information Management Association Web site at http://www.ahima.org/consumer/healthinfo.forms.html.

2. **Gather hospital and other medical records**. These should include copies of any exam results, hospital discharge summaries, and genetic tests performed on family members living and dead.

3. **Request copies of death certificates**. These records, available from state health departments, note the person's age and cause of death.

If Our First Child Has an Inherited Disorder, Can a Genetic Counselor Tell Us Whether Our Next Child Will Have the Same Condition?

As a genetic counselor will explain, the risk of inheriting a condition is the same for each child of the same two parents. For instance, if both parents are carriers of a recessive disorder (neither parent has the condition, but they are able to pass on the gene for it), each of their children will have a 25 percent chance of inheriting the disorder, a 50 percent chance of being a carrier but not having the condition, and a 25 percent chance of having neither the disorder nor the gene for it. These risks will be the same for each of the couple's children, no matter how many offspring they have.

Some birth defects, however, are thought to result from a combination of genetic and other factors, such as the mother's diet, health, and exposure to environmental influences. These defects include spina bifida, and cleft lip and palate. According to the March of Dimes Birth Defects Foundation, these defects are much less likely to happen more than once in a family. The risk of a second child's suffering from one of these problems is estimated at about five percent.

Are Genetic Tests Ever Performed on Children, or Only on Parents?

Some genetic tests can be performed on children as well as on parents. In fact, screening tests for certain genetic disorders, such as sickle cell anemia, are routinely performed on newborns. Some inherited disorders, such as Wilson's disease (a liver and mental disorder) and glaucoma (a sight-threatening buildup of pressure inside the eye), are not always apparent at birth. If you have a family history of such a disorder, ask your pediatrician about having your child examined or tested for it as early as possible.

What Is the Benefit of Knowing That my Child Has an Inherited Disorder or Is at Increased Risk of Having One?

Once they have been identified, some conditions can be successfully treated and their symptoms prevented or minimized. Metabolic disorders, for example, can cause serious problems if they aren't addressed, but they can be treated effectively by avoiding certain foods or nutrients or by taking certain supplements.

Knowing your child's prognosis can also enable her pediatrician and other healthcare providers to anticipate possible complications and be ready to treat them early on. Dr. Cunniff cites neurofibromatosis, a genetic disorder that causes multiple growths on the skin or tumors inside the body, as an example. "If your child has such a disorder, your pediatrician can schedule screenings for tumors at regular intervals so they can be caught in the early stages," he says.

Discovering an inherited disorder in the prenatal period can help you make choices that may dramatically affect your child's well-being. "It can affect the management of your delivery, as well as the care and testing the newborn receives," says Dr. Cunniff. As an example, he says, "When we know a baby has spina bifida, a failure of the bones in the spine to fully fuse, we generally recommend Cesarean delivery, which can improve the neurological outcome because it lessens the risk of trauma to the spine."

Prenatal diagnosis also provides other benefits, says Leopold. "Knowing about an inherited disorder in advance gives parents time to adjust to the reality of the situation and to get in touch with other families and support systems that can help ease their way."

As a child grows, being aware of his disorder can help parents set realistic expectations for his development and prepare emotionally for the challenges of dealing with his condition.

How Can I Find a Qualified Genetic Counselor?

Your obstetrician or pediatrician can help you decide whether genetic counseling might be helpful in your situation and refer you to a genetic counselor if necessary. Other referral sources include the March of Dimes Birth Defects Foundation at (888) 663-4637 and the National Society of Genetic Counselors at (610) 872-7608.

—Nancy Arnott

Nancy Arnott is a writer in New York City who specializes in health topics.

Chapter 20

Safe and Effective Genetic Testing

The remarkable advances in genetics in recent decades are the fruition of almost a century of basic research. Our ability to identify the underlying defects in single-gene (Mendelian) diseases, most of which are rare, has improved diagnosis in symptomatic individuals, and the prediction of risks of future disease in asymptomatic individuals. We have learned how to prevent a few of these diseases by early intervention and how to treat a few others after symptoms appear. Gene therapy, in which a normal gene is introduced into cells of patients with defective genes, is being investigated in over 1,000 individuals, including some with Mendelian disorders such as cystic fibrosis and adenosine deaminase deficiency.[2]

We now know that a small percentage of people with common disorders have inherited rare, single mutations that make them much more susceptible to developing the disease. Occasionally, single mutations that markedly increase susceptibility to disease reach frequencies as high as 1% in some population groups;[3] usually the combined frequency of all such mutations is under 5% of all those who will develop the disease. More common genetic variants (polymorphisms) less markedly increase susceptibility.

Excerpts from "Promoting Safe and Effective Genetic Testing in the United States," Final Report of the Task Force on Genetic Testing, edited by Neil A. Holtzman, M.D., MPH, and Michael S. Watson, Ph. D., Department of Energy Working Group on Ethical, Legal, and Social Implications of Human Genome Research, National Institutes of Health (NIH), September 1997.

Over the past half century, scientists have discovered the existence of DNA polymorphisms in which the most common form (allele) occurs in no more than 99% of the population. We are beginning to learn that some of these polymorphisms are associated with increased risks of common diseases, but usually not to the same degree as the rare variants. Conversely, some forms of polymorphisms convey resistance to disease. Before disease develops in people with either predisposing rare variants or polymorphisms, other genetic and environmental factors must be present.

Genetic discovery can benefit people in other ways than by discovering the inherited components. In the case of cancer, scientists have learned that acquired (somatic) mutations play a significant role.[16] By comparing the molecular genetic profiles of cells from diseased organs and tissues to the comparable normal cells, scientists are beginning to learn which gene functions have been altered and how they might affect the development of chronic conditions like osteoporosis and arthritis.OFP.[17] With this knowledge, interventions can be devised to avert or treat the triggering events or treat the disease effectively in its early stages.

Despite this remarkable progress much remains unknown. The unknowns have a strong impact on genetic testing, particularly when it is used as a predictive factor in healthy or apparently healthy people.

- No effective interventions are yet available to improve the outcome of most inherited diseases. It has proven far more difficult to devise a means of preventing or treating most Mendelian genetic diseases than to diagnose or predict increased risk of them. A "therapeutic gap" exists.
- Negative (normal) test results might not rule out future occurrence of disease. In the case of single-gene disorders, some tests do not detect all of the mutations capable of causing disease. In the case of common disorders, the disease often occurs even when tests for inherited susceptibility mutations or predisposing polymorphisms are negative.
- Positive test results might not mean the disease will inevitably develop. This is particularly a problem for the common disorders. For those who get the disease, the age at which it occurs and its severity and response to treatment cannot always be predicted. These problems arise in some Mendelian disorders, as well as in the common disorders. For instance, the severity of

> the lung disease, the most life-threatening aspect of cystic fibrosis, cannot be predicted by the mutations a person with CF possesses.[22]

It is primarily in the context of their unknown potential risks and benefits that the Task Force considered genetic testing.

Research and discovery in the first century of the new millennium will reduce the uncertainties, but the nature of human variation is such that it will never be possible to have genetic tests that are perfect predictors of disease. Even today, however, tests for the disorders for which these problems have not been solved can be of benefit.

- A negative test result in someone from a family in which affected relatives are known to have a disease-related mutation indicates a low risk of the disease. This can decrease anxiety and, for some diseases, reduce the frequency of periodic monitoring for early signs of the disease (e.g., mammography for breast cancer). A negative result can, depending on the disease, also enable a person to purchase health or life insurance at the standard rate.
- A positive test result enables a person to prepare for disease. Parents who learn from carrier screening that they are at risk of having an affected child can take steps to avoid the conception or birth of an affected child. People at risk of disease later in life can take steps to avoid passing the disease-causing allele on to their future children or can plan for the disease.
- Knowing that one is a carrier or has inherited a susceptibility to disease enables the person to inform relatives that they also might be at risk.

Nevertheless, problems will remain, especially as long as the means of preventing or treating genetic disease in those born with it are not fully at hand. The Task Force was created to make recommendations to ensure that genetic tests are safe and effective in view of the persistence of problems in the foreseeable future.

Definition of Genetic Tests

Genetic test—The analysis of human DNA, RNA, chromosomes, proteins, and certain metabolites in order to detect heritable disease-related genotypes, mutations, phenotypes, or karyotypes for clinical purposes. Such purposes include predicting risk of disease, identifying carriers, establishing prenatal and clinical diagnosis or prognosis. Prenatal, newborn, and carrier screening, as well as testing in high-risk families, are included. Tests for metabolites are covered only when they are undertaken with high probability that an excess or deficiency of the metabolite indicates the presence of heritable mutations in single genes. Tests conducted purely for research are excluded from the definition, as are tests for somatic (as opposed to heritable) mutations, and testing for forensic purposes.

The Task Force is primarily concerned about predictive uses of genetic tests performed in healthy or apparently healthy people. Predictive test results do not necessarily mean that the disease will inevitably occur or remain absent; they replace the individual's prior risks based on population data or family history with risks based on genotype. The Task Force divides predictive tests into presymptomatic tests, which are performed to detect highly "penetrant" conditions, and predispositional tests, which are performed for incompletely penetrant conditions. The Task Force cannot limit its definition to predictive tests because some tests intended for diagnostic use can also be used predictively. The Task Force also decided that it cannot limit genetic tests only to those for which the analyte is DNA. Clinical laboratories will continue to use protein and enzyme and metabolite analyses for the purposes listed in the definition, including prediction.

Some, but not all, predictive genetic testing falls under the rubric "genetic screening." The Task Force follows the definition used in a National Research Council report. "Genetic screening may be defined as a search in a population for persons possessing certain genotypes that

1. are already associated with disease or predispose to disease,
2. may lead to disease in their descendants, or
3. produce other variations not known to be associated with disease."[26]

Under this definition, testing an asymptomatic person in a family with several relatives affected with disease does not constitute screening but predictive genetic testing.

Review of Genetic Testing

Over 500 commercial, university, and health department laboratories provide tests for inherited and chromosomal disorders, and genetic predispositions in the United States. Virtually every newborn is screened for phenylketonuria and congenital hypothyroidism and many are screened for sickle cell disorders.[27] Screening for carriers of Tay-Sachs and sickle cell is performed among populations at risk. Based on the recommendations of a recent consensus panel,[28] cystic fibrosis carrier screening might increase. Approximately 2.5 million pregnant women are screened each year to see if their fetuses are at high risk of neural tube defects or Down syndrome.[29] Of 467 organizations that responded fully to the survey conducted for the Task Force, 56.7% indicated that they were testing for at least one of 44 inherited conditions that were listed in the questionnaire. A few commercial and university laboratories were offering tests for inherited susceptibility mutations to breast and colon cancer. Of 197 health maintenance organizations who responded to a recent survey, 45% said they were covering predictive tests for breast cancer and 42% were covering for colon cancer for some of their subscribers.[30]

For the most part, genetic testing in the United States has developed successfully, providing options for avoiding, preventing, and treating inherited disorders. There are some problems with genetic testing. Sometimes, genetic tests are introduced before they have been demonstrated to be safe, effective, and useful.

- There is no assurance that every laboratory performing genetic tests for clinical purposes meets high standards.
- Often, the informational materials distributed by academic and commercial genetic testing laboratories do not provide sufficient information to fill in the gaps in providers' and patients' understanding of genetic tests.

The Need for Recommendations

In the past few years, scientific and professional societies, as well as consumer groups, have felt impelled to publicly express concern when predictive tests were introduced with insufficient evidence of safety and effectiveness. These included prenatal screening with alpha-fetoprotein and other markers,[31,32] carrier screening for cystic fibrosis,[33,34] testing for susceptibility to cancer[35,36] and breast cancer in particular,[37,38] and Alzheimer disease.[39,40] These statements often expressed a reaction to the imminence or appearance of a test and undoubtedly reduced inappropriate use of tests. The publication of each statement depended on mobilizing individuals with interest and expertise and then getting ratification by the sponsoring organization, tasks not easily accomplished in a short period without extraordinary effort. This becomes an impossible task as the number of tests expands but the problems persist.

Although professional societies must play a major role in solving problems of genetic testing, they are only one of several stakeholders, some of whose interests conflict with others' interests. The Task Force believes that all stakeholders must be involved. As this report demonstrates, they often will succeed in resolving disagreements and reaching consensus.

Except for neonatal and prenatal screening and diagnosis, the volume of testing has not been great and much of the testing has been performed in genetic centers or in consultation with highly-trained geneticists and genetic counselors. In the next few years, the use of genetic testing is likely to expand rapidly while the number of genetic specialists remains essentially unchanged. A greater burden for making genetic testing decisions will fall on providers who have little formal training or experience in genetics and are less equipped to deal with the complex and special problems raised by some predictive genetic tests. Consulted primarily by people who are sick, and who expect doctors to tell them what to do to get better, many physicians adopt a directive stance when asked how they would deal with genetic tests and results that have reproductive implications.

Until the 1980s most genetic and cytogenetic testing was performed in the laboratories of non-profit organizations, most of them in academic medical centers. These labs were often directed by the same professionals who cared for patients. In the last decade, genetic testing has been commercialized. As a result, providers who were close to patients and families at risk of illness might not have as much influence on testing policy as they once did.

Although formal comparisons have not been made, there is little evidence that the problems encountered in the development and delivery of genetic testing technologies have been more frequent or severe than for other medical technologies. Some problems encountered in other specialties have not been trivial. Amendments to the Food, Drug and Cosmetic Act, and to the Clinical Laboratory Improvement Act were passed by Congress because of problems in the clinical use of some new medical technologies.[41-45] In 1996, recognizing the challenge posed by genetic tests, two Congressional committees held hearings related to the validity and quality of genetic tests.[46,47]

The Ethical, Legal and Social Implications (ELSI) component of the Human Genome Project was founded on the concept that the new technologies of gene identification will engender problems that can be minimized if anticipated and dealt with promptly. The recommendations of the Task Force are very much in this vein. In this document, the Task Force does not recommend policies for specific tests but suggests a framework for ensuring that new tests meet criteria for safety and effectiveness before they are unconditionally released, thereby reducing the likelihood of premature clinical use.

The focus of the Task Force on potential problems is not intended to detract from the benefits of genetic testing. Its overriding goal is to recommend policies that will reduce the likelihood of damaging effects so testing benefits can be fully realized undiluted by harm.

Overarching Principles

In making recommendations on safety and effectiveness, the Task Force concentrated on test validity and utility, laboratory quality, and provider competence. It recognizes, however, that other issues impinge on testing, and problems can arise from testing. Regarding these issues, the Task Force endorses the following principles.

Informed Consent

The Task Force strongly advocates written informed consent, especially for certain uses of genetic tests, including clinical validation studies and predictive testing. The failure of the Task Force to comment on informed consent for other uses does not imply that it should not be obtained.

Test Development

Informed consent for any validation study must be obtained whenever the specimen can be linked to the subject from which it came. As long as identifiers are retained in either coded or uncoded form, the possibility exists to contact subjects even if the intent of the original protocol was not to do so. As part of the disclosure for consent, individuals must be informed of possible future uses of the specimen, whether identifiers will be retained and, if so, whether the individual will be contacted again.

Testing in Clinical Practice

1. It is unacceptable to coerce or intimidate individuals or families regarding their decision about predictive genetic testing. Respect for personal autonomy is paramount. People being offered

testing must understand that testing is voluntary. Their informed consent should be obtained. Whatever decision they make, their care should not be jeopardized. Information on risks and benefits must be presented fully and objectively. A non-directive approach is of the utmost importance when reproductive decisions are a consequence of testing or when the safety and effectiveness of interventions following a positive test result have not been established. Obtaining written informed consent helps to ensure that the person voluntarily agrees to the test.

2. Prior to the initiation of predictive testing in clinical practice, health care providers must describe the features of the genetic test, including potential consequences, to potential test recipients. Individuals considering genetic testing must be told the purposes of the test, the chance it will give a correct prediction, the implications of test results, the options, and the benefits and risks of the process. The responsibility for providing information to the individual lies with the referring provider, not with the laboratory performing the test.

Newborn Screening

1. If informed consent is waived for a newborn screening test, the analytical and clinical validity and clinical utility of the test must be established, and parents must be provided with sufficient information to understand the reasons for screening. By clinical utility, the Task Force means that interventions to improve the outcome of the infant identified by screening have been proven to be safe and effective. Using newborn screening to identify couples who are at risk of having a future child with sickle cell anemia or other disorder because their screened infant is found to be a carrier (heterozygote) is not of primary benefit to the infant screened. Using newborn screening to identify parents at risk should only be done after this intention is communicated to parents (prior to screening) and their written consent is obtained. The Task Force recognizes that newborn screening programs have succeeded in significantly reducing the burden of a number of inherited disorders by timely diagnosis and institution of preventive therapies. Sometimes, however, newborn screening is undertaken before tests are validated and interventions are established to prevent or reduce clinical problems. A recent consensus development conference on cystic

fibrosis concluded that the evidence to warrant routine screening of newborns for cystic fibrosis was insufficient. [28]

2. For those disorders for which newborn screening is available but the tests have not been validated or shown to have clinical utility, written parental consent is required prior to testing. The Task Force also recognizes that specimens collected for newborn screening become an important resource for developing new tests. When the infant's name or other identifying information is retained on these specimens, the Task Force believes that parental informed consent is needed.

Prenatal and Carrier Testing

Respect for an individual's or couples' beliefs and values concerning tests undertaken for assisting reproductive decisions is of paramount importance and can best be maintained by a non-directive stance. One way of ensuring that a non-directive stance is taken and that parents' decisions are autonomous, is through requiring informed consent.

Testing of Children

Genetic testing of children for adult onset diseases should not be undertaken unless direct medical benefit will accrue to the child and this benefit would be lost by waiting until the child has reached adulthood. The Task Force agrees with the American Society of Human Genetics and the American College of Medical Genetics that, "timely medical benefit to the child should be the primary justification for genetic testing in children and adolescents."[48] Although sympathetic to the considerable difficulties inherent in living with uncertainty about the health status of the child, the Task Force does not feel that these warrant foreclosing the child's right to make an independent decision in regard to testing in adulthood. We are aware, however, that there are situations (e.g., testing for inherited mutations in the ademomatous polyposis coli gene) in which the benefit of avoiding medical surveillance (if the test result is negative) is sufficient to warrant testing even though no treatment will usually be undertaken until a later age (if the test result is positive). In addition, the Task Force realizes that legal adulthood is a somewhat arbitrary concept. For example, in families with a considerable burden of disease and in which several adults are undergoing genetic testing, older teenagers might request testing for themselves in order to reduce uncertainty and anxiety. It is unfortunate that almost no research evidence currently exists on the risks and benefits of genetic testing to teenagers and younger children. The Task Force believes that such psychosocial research must be pursued as vigorously as research on issues of analytic validity or utility of tests. However, unless and until such time as contradictory research findings emerge, testing of minors for presumed psychological benefits should be avoided.

Confidentiality

Protecting the confidentiality of information is essential for all uses of genetic tests.

1. Results should be released only to those individuals for whom the test recipient has given consent for information release. Means of transmitting information should be chosen to minimize the likelihood that results will become available to unauthorized persons or organizations. Under no circumstances should results with identifiers be provided to any outside parties, including employers, insurers, or government agencies, without the test recipient's written consent. Consent given for minors should expire when the minor reaches adulthood.

Unless potential test recipients can be assured that the results will not be given to individuals or organizations they have not specifically named, some will refuse testing for fear of losing insurance, employment, or for other reasons. Aggregate results, stripped of identifiers, can be reported to government agencies for statistical and planning purposes.

2. Health care providers have an obligation to the person being tested not to inform other family members without the permission of the person tested, except in extreme circumstances.

The Task Force agrees with recommendations of The President's Commission for the Study of Ethical Problems in Medicine and Biomedical and Behavioral Research[49] and the Institute of Medicine[23] that disclosure by providers to other family members is appropriate only when the person tested refuses to communicate information despite reasonable attempts to persuade him or her to do so, and when failure to give that information has a high probability of resulting in imminent, serious, and irreversible harm to the relative, and when communication of the information will enable the relative to avert the harm. When test results have serious implications for relatives, it is incumbent upon providers to explain to people who are tested the reasons why they should communicate the information to their relatives and to counsel them on how they should convey the information so the communication itself does not result in undue harm. Great care must be taken to avoid inadvertent release of information.

Recently, a subcommittee of the American Society of Human Genetics[50] endorsed these same principles for disclosure to relatives, but suggested that "the health care professional should be obliged to inform the patient of the implications of his/her genetic test results and potential risks to family members. Prior to genetic testing and again upon refusal to communicate results, this duty to inform the patient of familial implications is paramount." The Task Force is of the opinion that, as part of this duty, providers must make clear that they will not communicate results to relatives, except in extreme circumstances, which the provider should define. If left with the impression that the provider will inform relatives when the person considering testing does not want them informed, some people will decline testing. This would have the effect not only of denying information to the relative but to the person offered testing as well. Providers should be explicit in describing the extreme situations in which they would inform other relatives.

Harm can also result when relatives communicate genetic information. Strategies to assist individuals in communicating information to relatives should be developed.

Discrimination

No individual should be subjected to unfair discrimination by a third party on the basis of having had a genetic test or receiving an abnormal genetic test result. Third parties include insurers, employers, and educational and other institutions that routinely inquire about the health of applicants for services or positions. Discrimination can take the form of denial or of additional charges for various types of insurance, employment jeopardy in hiring and firing, or requirements to undergo unwanted genetic testing. Protection from unfair discrimination has been the subject of legislation at both the State and Federal levels.[51] The problem has not been completely solved.[52,53]

Consumer Involvement in Policy Making

Although other stakeholders are concerned about protecting consumers, they cannot always provide the perspective brought by consumers themselves, the end users of genetic testing. Clearly, there are technical issues that cannot be decided primarily by consumers, but consumers must be involved in decision making on matters of policy in test development and in clinical use that directly affects their well-being. Consumers should be involved in policy (but not necessarily in technical) decisions regarding the adoption, introduction, and use of new, predictive genetic tests.

Issues Not Covered

There are aspects of genetic testing with which we have not dealt. Several respondents asked the Task Force to comment on genetic testing for non-medical conditions, such as homosexuality or other behavioral traits, or for gene enhancement. Although the Task Force has drawn upon examples of past and current testing, it has not made pronouncements about specific types of testing. As already stated, its intent is to develop generic policies that cover predictive testing for a wide range of medical conditions.

The Task Force recognizes that patenting and licensing can have a profound effect on the costs of medical tests. The payment of license fees is likely to be passed on to third-party payers or to consumers if they do not have or wish to use their health insurance. This issue has been highlighted recently by lawsuits by a patent holder to force laboratories performing prenatal screening for Down syndrome to pay royalties.[54] The issue of patenting and licensing needs further exploration but is beyond the scope of the Task Force.

The Task Force has not dwelled in depth on the use of stored tissues for genetic research, including the development of genetic tests. Recommendations on this issue have been made by others[55-58] and are still being actively discussed and modified.

References

1. Scriver CR, Beaudet AL, Sly WS, Valle D, editors: *The Metabolic and Molecular Bases of Inherited Disease*. Seventh Edition. New York, McGraw-Hill, Inc. 1995.

2. Friedmann T: Overcoming the obstacles to gene therapy. *Scientific American* 1997;276:96-101.

3. Struewing JP, Hartge P, Wacholder S, et al: The risk of cancer associated with specific mutations of BRCA1 and BRCA2 among Askhenazi Jews. *New England Journal of Medicine* 1997;336:1401-1408.

4. Szabo CI, King M: Invited editorial: Population genetics of BRCA1 and BRCA2. *American Journal of Human Genetics 1997*;60:1013-1020.

5. Kinzler KW, Vogelstein B: Lessons from hereditary colorectal cancer. *Cell* 1996;87:159-170.

6. Morrison-Bogorad M, Phelps C, Buckholtz N: Alzheimer disease research comes of age. The pace accelerates. *JAMA* 1997;277:837-840.

7. Seshadri S, Drachman DA, Lippa CF: Apolipoprotein E e4 allele and the lifetime risk of Alzheimer's disease. What physicians know, and what they should know. *Archives of Neurology* 1995;52:1074-1079.

8. Tisch R, McDevitt H: Insulin-dependent diabetes mellitus. *Cell* 1996;85:291-297.

9. Vyse TJ, Todd JA: Genetic analysis of autoimmune diseases. *Cell* 1996;85:311-318.

10. Ridker PM, Miletich JP, Hennekens CH, Buring JE: Ethnic distribution of Factor V Leiden in 4047 men and women. Implications for venous thromboembolism screening. *JAMA* 1997;277:1305-1307.

11. Frosst P, Blom HJ, Milos R, et al: A candidate genetic risk factor for vascular disease: A common mutation in methylenetetrahydrofolate reductase. *Nature Genetics* 1995;10:111-113.

12. Reynolds MV, Bristow MR, Bush EW, et al: Angiotensin-converting enzyme DD genotype in patients with ischaemic or idiopathic dilated cardiomyopathy. *Lancet* 1993;342:1073-1075.

13. Nebert DW: Polymorphisms in drug-metabolizing enzymes: What is their clinical relevance and why do they exist? *American Journal of Human Genetics* 1997;60:265-271.

14. Smith MW, Dean M, Carrington M, et al: Contrasting genetic influence of CCR2 and CCR5 variants on HIV-1 infection and disease progression. *Science* 1997;277:959-968.

15. Bell J: The new genetics of clinical practice. *BMJ* 1997.

16. Vogelstein B, Kinzler KW: The multistep nature of cancer. *Trends in Genetics* 1993;9:138-141.

17. Haseltine WA: Discovering genes for new medicine. *Scientific American* 1997;276:92-97.

18. Treacy E, Childs B, Scriver CR: Response to treatment in hereditary metabolic disease: 1993 survey and 10-year comparison. *American Journal of Human Genetics* 1995;56:359-367.

19. Burke W, Petersen G, Lynch P, et al: Recommendations for follow-up care of individuals with an inherited predisposition to cancer. I. Hereditary nonpolyposis colon cancer. *JAMA* 1997;277:915-919.

20. Schrag D, Kuntz KM, Garber JE, Weeks JC: Decision analysis — effects of prophylactic mastectomy and oophorectomy on life expectancy among women with BRCA1 or BRCA2 mutations. *New England Journal of Medicine* 1997;336:1465-1471.

21. Burke W, Daly M, Garber J, et al: Recommendations for follow-up care of individuals with an inherited predisposition to cancer. II. BRCA1 and BRCA2. *JAMA* 1997;277:997-1003.

22. Cystic Fibrosis Genotype-Phenotype Consortium: Correlation between genotype and phenotype in patients with cystic fibrosis. *New England Journal of Medicine* 1993;329:1308-1313.

23. Andrews L, Fullarton JE, Holtzman NA, Motulsky AG, eds. *Assessing genetic risks: Implications for health and social policy.* Washington DC, National Academy Press; 1994.

24. Task Force on Genetic Testing: Interim principles. *Available at www.med.jhu.edu/tfgtelsi 1996.*

25. National Institutes of Health: Proposed recommendations of the Task Force on Genetic Testing; Notice of meeting and request for comment. *Federal Register* 1997;62:4539-4547.

26. Committee for the Study of Inborn Errors of Metabolism: *Genetic screening: Programs, principles, and research.* Washington DC, National Academy of Sciences; 1975.

27. Hiller EH, Landenburger G, Natowicz MR: Public participation in medical policy making and the status of consumer autonomy: The example of newborn screening programs in the United States. *American Journal of Public Health* 1997; 87(8):1280-1288.

28. Howell RR, Borecki I, Davidson ME, et al: National Institutes of Health Consensus Development Conference Statement: Genetic testing for cystic fibrosis. 1997;in press.

29. Palomaki GE, Knight GJ, McCarthy JE, Haddow JE, Donhowe JM: Maternal serum screening for Down syndrome in the United States: A 1995 survey. *American Journal of Obstetrics and Gynecology* 1997;176:1046-1051.

30. Myers MF, Doksum T, Holtzman NA: Coverage and provision of genetic services: Surveys of health maintenance organizations (HMOs) and academic genetic units (AGUs). *American Journal of Human Genetics* 1997;in press. (Abstract)

31. Council on Scientific Affairs: Maternal serum a-fetoprotein monitoring. *JAMA* 1982;247:1478-1481.

32. American Society of Human Genetics: Maternal serum alpha-fetoprotein screening programs and quality control for laboratories performing maternal serum and amniotic fluid alpha-fetoprotein assays. *American Journal of Human Genetics* 1987;40:75-82.

33. American Society of Human Genetics: The American Society of Human Genetics Statement on cystic fibrosis screening. *American Journal of Human Genetics* 1990;46:393.

34. National Institutes of Health: Statement from the National Institutes of Health Workshop on population screening for the cystic fibrosis gene. *New England Journal of Medicine* 1990;323:70-71.

35. National Advisory Council for Human Genome Research: Statement on use of DNA testing for presymptomatic identification of cancer risk. *JAMA* 1994;271:785.

36. American Society of Clinical Oncology: Statement of the American Society of Clinical Oncology: Genetic testing for cancer susceptibility, Adopted on February 20, 1996. *Journal of Clinical Oncology* 1996;14:1730-1736.

37. American Society of Human Genetics Ad Hoc Committee: Statement of The American Society of Human Genetics on genetic testing for breast and ovarian cancer predisposition. *American Journal of Human Genetics* 1994;55(5):i-iv.

38. National Breast Cancer Coalition. *Presymptomatic genetic testing for heritable breast cancer risk.* Washington DC, 1995.

39. American College of Medical Genetics: Statement on use of apolipoprotein E testing for Alzheimer disease. *JAMA* 1995;274:1627-1629.

40. National Institute on Aging: Apolipoprotein E genotyping in Alzheimer's disease. *Lancet* 1996;347:1091-1095.

41. Higgs R: *Hazardous to our health? FDA regulation of health care products*. Oakland, Independent Institute; 1995.

42. Merrill RA: Regulation of drugs and devices: An evolution. *Health Affairs* 1994;Summer:46-69.

43. Bogdanich W: False negative. Medical labs, trusted as largely error-free, are far from infallible. *Wall Street Journal* Feb. 2, 1987:1.

44. Bogdanich W: Risk factor. Inaccuracy in testing cholesterol hampers war on heart disease. *Wall Street Journal* Feb. 3, 1987:1.

45. Nash P: Discussion Session I. *Clinical Chemistry* 1992; 38:1220-1222.

46. Subcommittee on Technology, Committee on Science, U.S. House of Representatives Hearing on Technological advances in genetics testing: Implications for the future. 1996.

47. U.S.Senate Committee on Labor and Human Resources. Hearing on Advances in Genetics Research and Technologies: Challenges for Public Policy. 1996.

48. American Society of Human Genetics, American College of Medical Genetics: Points to consider: Ethical, legal, and psychosocial implications of genetic testing in children and adolescents. *American Journal of Human Genetics* 1995;57:1233-1241.

49. President's Commission for the Study of Ethical Problems in Medicine and Biomedical and Behavioral Research: *Screening and Counseling for Genetic Conditions*. Washington DC, U.S. Government Printing Office; 1983.

50. American Society of Human Genetics Social Issues Sub-Committee on Familial Disclosure: Professional disclosure of

familial genetic information. *American Journal of Human Genetics* 1997.

51. Rothenberg KH: Genetic information and health insurance: State legislative approaches. *Journal of Law, Medicine & Ethics* 1995;23:3112-319.

52. Hudson KL, Rothenburg KH, Andrews LB, Kahn MJE, Collins FS: Genetic discrimination and health insurance: An urgent need for reform. *Science* 1995;270:391-393.

53. Rothenberg KH, Fuller B, Rothstein M, et al: Genetic information and the workplace: Legislative approaches and policy challenges. *Science* 1997;275:1755-1757.

54. Eichenwald K: Push for royalties threatens use of Down Syndrome test. *New York Times* May 23, 1997;A1.

55. Clayton EW, Steinberg KK, Khoury MJ, et al: Informed consent for genetic research on stored tissue samples. *JAMA* 1995;274:1786-1792.

56. American College of Medical Genetics: ACMG Statement. Statement on storage and use of genetic materials. *American Journal of Human Genetics* 1995;57:1499-1500.

57. American Society of Human Genetics: ASHG report. Statement on informed consent for genetic research. *American Journal of Human Genetics* 1996;59:471-474.

58. Academy for Clinical Laboratory Physicians and Scientists, et al. Uses of human tissue. August 28, 1996. 1996;draft.

Ensuring the Safety and Effectiveness of New Genetic Tests

Some predictive genetic tests become available without adequate assessment of their benefits and risks. When this happens, providers and consumers cannot make a fully informed decision about whether or not to use them. Although extensive use has eventually proven most tests to be of benefit, a few have not proven helpful and were discarded or modified. In the meantime, people were wrongly classified as at-risk and subjected to treatments that, in their case, proved unnecessary or sometimes harmful. Others, who could have benefited from treatment were classified as "normal" and not treated.

Harmful effects can be avoided or at least reduced if systematic, well-designed studies to assess a test's safety and effectiveness are undertaken before tests become routinely available and after they are significantly modified. In this section, criteria for assessing genetic tests prior to routine use, policies for ensuring that the necessary data are collected and, finally, recommendations for review of the data before tests are routinely used is presented.

Ensuring the Quality of Laboratories Performing Genetic Tests

Over 500 clinical laboratories in the United States perform chromosomal, biochemical, and/or DNA-based tests for genetic diseases. These laboratories must comply with regulations under the Clinical Laboratory Improvement Amendments of 1988 (CLIA), which include biennial inspection, some proficiency testing, and requirements of the specialty in which the laboratory is certified. Although clinical cytogenetics is a specialty under CLIA, there is no broader genetics specialty and, consequently, no special requirements for laboratories performing DNA-based and other types of genetic tests. No proficiency testing programs in genetics or cytogenetics are required under CLIA. New York State requires any laboratory performing tests on New York residents (even if those laboratories are outside of New York) to participate in its quality assurance programs in DNA-based and biochemical genetics. These programs involve onsite inspection but not formal proficiency testing. A number of organizations have voluntary programs for quality control of genetic tests. In a survey conducted for the Task Force in early 1995, 11% of biotechnology companies that provide genetic tests and 16% of nonprofit (primarily university-based) molecular (DNA) labs reported that they neither participated in a formal proficiency testing program nor shared samples informally for quality control. According to the survey, about 15% of laboratories performing clinical DNA-based tests were not registered under CLIA.

Principles for Laboratories Adopting New Genetic Tests

No clinical laboratory should offer a genetic test whose clinical validity has not been established, unless it is collecting data on clinical validity under either an IRB-approved protocol or conditional premarket approval agreement with FDA. The service laboratory should justify and document the basis of decisions to put new tests into service. A clinical laboratory that develops a genetic test would have to submit its data on analytical and clinical validity to external review before offering the test for clinical practice. If the test has been developed elsewhere, clinical laboratories should carefully review evidence for test validity. If external review by professional societies has led to the publication of indications and guidelines for use, laboratories should adhere to them. Regardless of where the test to be adopted was developed, clinical laboratory directors are responsible for ensuring the analytic validity of each genetic test their laboratory intends to offer before they make the test available for use in clinical practice (outside of an investigative protocol).

Before routinely offering genetic tests that have been clinically validated, a laboratory must conduct a pilot phase in which it verifies that all steps in the testing process are operating appropriately. In establishing the pilot phase, the laboratory should define endpoints, such as number of tests to be performed, and the procedures to be used to review the findings, including the organizational body that will review them. If the outcome of this review reveals that the laboratory is not as competent as other laboratories in performing the test, or the test does not detect as many people with the genetic alteration as anticipated, the laboratory should not proceed to report patient-specific results without attempting to rectify the problems. If demand is not sufficiently high to be able to maintain a high level of quality, the laboratory should institute special procedures to ensure quality.

Clinical Laboratory Improvement Amendments (CLIA) of 1988

A statutory framework for ensuring laboratory quality was laid down by Congress in the Clinical Laboratory Improvement Act of 1967 and greatly expanded in the Clinical Laboratory Improvement Amendments of 1988 (CLIA). Any laboratory performing "examination of materials derived from the human body for the purpose of providing information for the diagnosis, prevention, or treatment of any disease or impairment of, or the assessment of the health of, human beings" must comply with CLIA.[2] Implementation of CLIA is the responsibility of the Health Care Financing Administration (HCFA) and the Centers for Disease Control and Prevention (CDC). Under CLIA, these Federal agencies have developed requirements for laboratory quality assurance and control, personnel, patient test-management and, if a proficiency program is not available, interlaboratory comparison of assays. The stringency of these requirements depends on the complexity level and specialty to which tests are assigned. Despite these basic provisions, the Task Force has serious concerns as to whether CLIA adequately assures the quality of genetic tests in clinical use.

Complexity Ratings

CDC assigns a complexity level to a test according to predetermined criteria. Simple tests are categorized "waived." The remainder are assigned ratings of either "moderate" or "high" complexity. Laboratories performing high complexity tests have more stringent personnel and quality control requirements.

Over 17,000 clinical laboratory tests have been assigned a complexity level. Any test for which CDC has not determined test complexity is considered to be high complexity by default. Any home-brew method, or change in procedure that can affect laboratory performance (sensitivity, specificity, accuracy, precision) falls under the high complexity category until it is rated differently by CDC. Under the rating scheme, a genetic test that can be used predictively might receive a rating of moderate complexity despite the importance of ensuring that the provider and the patient understand the uncertainty of the prediction and the implications for decision-making. Both the creatine phosphokinase test, which can be used as a screening test for Duchenne muscular dystrophy, and alpha-fetoprotein (AFP), which is used as a predictive prenatal test for neural tube defects and Down syndrome, are rated as moderate complexity. Despite multiple uses, a test method gets only one rating based on the seven criteria that reflect the complexity of performing the test. All cytogenetic tests are rated high complexity, which seems appropriate. The Task Force recommends that tests that can be used for purposes of predicting future disease be given a rating of high complexity.

CLIA Specialties

Laboratories performing tests of moderate or high complexity must also conform to the requirements of the specialties to which tests are assigned. Laboratories can perform tests only in specialties for which they are certified. Although there is a cytogenetics specialty, there is no genetics specialty. The specialty categories under CLIA are based on traditional laboratory practice; each specialty tends to involve somewhat similar technologies, although this is not the case in all instances. Each analyte is assigned to only one specialty.

Establishing a specialty for genetics presents a number of problems. For example, specialty designations are administratively linked to Medicare payment specialty designations, and any changes in specialty designations must take this into account. In addition, genetic tests use a wide variety of technologies, some of which are used in other (non-genetic) types of tests. For instance, DNA is the analyte in some tests for predicting genetic susceptibility and also in some tests for infectious agents. Sometimes the same test is used for purposes of genetic prediction (in healthy individuals), genetic diagnosis (in individuals with symptoms), and non-genetic diagnosis or prognosis. For instance, the creatine phosphokinase assay can be used to screen for carriers of muscular dystrophy and affected infants, but it is also used in the diagnosis of myocardial infarction. Despite these problems a genetics specialty is needed.

Monitoring Laboratory Performance

Proficiency Testing

Proficiency testing (PT) is mandated by CLIA to externally evaluate the quality of a laboratory's performance. For PT, a laboratory is provided with specimens whose composition of an analyte is known to the supplier but not to the recipient laboratories. They are expected to analyze the specimen the same way they would a patient's specimen. Each laboratory performing moderate or high complexity tests is required to enroll in an approved PT program for all specialties/subspecialties, analytes, or tests for which the laboratory is certified and for which a PT program has been recognized by HCFA. Any laboratory that fails a proficiency test must take corrective action. HCFA takes an educational approach to PT and works with the laboratories that have problems to help improve performance. Sanctions can be applied to those laboratories repeatedly unable to perform satisfactorily. These include suspension of the CLIA certificate to perform that test or specialty. If its certificate is suspended, the laboratory is not eligible for Medicare/Medicaid reimbursement, since such reimbursement requires a CLIA license with no restrictions.

Although genetic tests do not appear on the list of regulated analytes for PT purposes under CLIA, laboratories must establish the accuracy and reliability of a test by methods of their own choosing. This can include participation in one of the voluntary PT programs. As the PT programs mentioned above are not approved by CLIA, no laboratory is obliged to use them and can establish accuracy and reliability by another method, although it must make the data available for onsite inspection under CLIA. If they do participate and do not perform adequately, laboratories will usually improve performance. If, however, they continue to fail to meet PT criteria, they are not obliged to stop testing as participation is voluntary. A few laboratories participating in the PT programs recently surveyed do not always correctly analyze all PT specimens. According to the Tay-Sachs program, one or two per year do not improve and usually stop testing.

Information collected in conjunction with PT sometimes reveals outliers among laboratories. For instance, a survey conducted by the FBR/CAP prenatal screening PT program found a few laboratories that did not follow established criteria in accepting specimens.

Onsite Inspection

All CLIA-certified laboratories are routinely inspected on a two-year survey cycle by one of three types of organizations: (1) HCFA regional offices and State agencies; (2) private non-profit organizations that have applied for and received deemed status because they provide reasonable assurance that the laboratories they accredit, which enables the laboratory to obtain a CLIA certificate, meet the conditions required by Federal law and regulation; (3) State-exempt licensure programs. States that have programs that license laboratories and provide HCFA with reasonable assurance that their criteria are equivalent to or more stringent than those specified under CLIA can apply for exempt status. So far New York, Oregon, and Washington (state) have exempt status. California, Florida, and Georgia were under review as of July 1997. Regardless of the organization under whose auspices inspections are conducted, the surveyors are laboratory professionals who are trained to determine compliance with CLIA regulations (or a program that is determined to be equal to or more stringent than CLIA). Even though genetics is not a specialty, surveyors are expected to examine the quality of genetic tests. This should include inspection of the records of how the laboratory performed on genetic PT programs in which it participated voluntarily. It is not clear, however, that all CLIA surveyors currently are sufficiently knowledgeable to assess the performance of molecular genetics laboratories.

CAP [College of American Pathologists] has deemed status to conduct inspections in several specialties, but since genetics is not a specialty under CLIA, the CAP program does not have deemed status in genetics. In the CAP genetics program, laboratories that voluntarily (and for a fee) participate in the program are inspected. The surveyors use a checklist covering all aspects of quality assurance and quality control, from specimen accessioning to final sign-out. Compliance with some items on the checklist is optional; for others, compliance is mandatory. Following inspection, the laboratory receives a written report and is expected to respond to CAP in writing regarding correction of any deficiencies in the mandatory categories. In areas in which it does not have deemed status, such as genetics, CAP has no authority to grant accreditation for CLIA purposes.

Making Laboratory Performance Assessments Public

HCFA annually publishes a list ("Laboratory Registry") that identifies all poor performance laboratories, the reason enforcement actions were taken and type of enforcement, and the name of the laboratory director. The Registry is available to the public upon request, and is accessible on the Internet at http://www.hcfa.gov. Survey findings are also available through the Freedom of Information Act, once the laboratory has the opportunity to respond with its Plan of Action. CAP reports PT results for regulated analytes (i.e., those for which CLIA requires PT) to HCFA. It does not report PT results directly to the public because it maintains that PT alone is insufficient to demonstrate laboratory quality. CAP does make accreditation status available through its toll-free hotline (1-800-LAB-5678), and a CAP-published list of accredited laboratories. As CAP is not deemed to accredit in areas of genetics, it does not make the results of its assessments of genetic test performance public.

The Importance of the Pre- and Post-Analytic Phases of Testing

In the pre-analytic phase, laboratories sometimes give information about the test to providers and consumers. Informed consent can be obtained, and data are requested from those to be tested. In the post-analytic phase, test results are given to the provider and patient, often with an interpretation. Genetic counseling services can be provided or arranged by laboratories, but are the responsibility of the referring provider.

Pre-Analytic Phase

The Task Force is concerned about the quality of information made available to providers and consumers who are considering testing. Some materials have serious omissions that impair the ability of providers and consumers to make informed decisions about testing. In a comparison of four different brochures made available by organizations offering testing for genetic susceptibility to breast cancer, the Task Force found striking discrepancies. Physicians or consumers reading one brochure might, as a result, make a different decision than if they read another organization's brochure. It is the responsibility of health care providers, not the clinical laboratory, to provide information to the individual offered or considering testing, but material made available by laboratories is often used. The completeness and accuracy of this material is, therefore, extremely important.

Obtaining informed consent helps ensure that the person voluntarily agrees to testing and has some understanding of the reasons for testing. Informed consent is appropriate for predictive genetic tests, particularly those for which stringent scrutiny is needed. The Task Force is of the opinion that laboratories should obtain documentation of informed consent when appropriate and should not perform an analysis if documentation is lacking. The most rigorous documentation is for the laboratory to be sent a signed copy of the patient's consent. It is less rigorous to ask the ordering physician to check a box on the laboratory requisition indicating that consent has been obtained.

Because of the complexities of assessment and interpretation, requisitions for many genetic tests require more intake information than those for virtually any other clinical laboratory procedure. In addition to routine information, genetic test requests often must include the reason for requesting the test, any relevant clinical or laboratory information, the person's age and ethnicity, and notation of family history of the disorder in question (along with a full pedigree for tests involving linkage analysis). If information that is critical to the performance or the interpretation of the test cannot be obtained, or if the information that is provided suggests that the patient is not an appropriate candidate for testing, the physician must be contacted. There is consensus, for instance, that minor children should not be tested for adult-onset disease for which no diagnostic or therapeutic interventions are needed before adulthood, yet some laboratories report testing children Most authorities agree that healthy women without a family history of breast cancer should not be tested for inherited susceptibility mutations for breast cancer except under investigative protocols to gather data on the penetrance of these mutations, and that women with a family history of the disease should only be tested if an inherited susceptibility mutation is found in an affected relative.[5-7] Consequently, laboratories must ascertain the presence of a family history before accepting a specimen. At least one laboratory is offering testing to Ashkenazi Jewish women without a family history.[8] In general, laboratory personnel must be competent to recognize what information is needed and what the criteria are for accepting specimens. When in doubt, they must communicate with the ordering provider.

Post-Analytic Phase

Increasingly, genetic tests will be requested by providers without much or any training in genetics. Accurate and comprehensible interpretation of genetic test results by the clinical laboratories is critical to ensure that the provider understands the implications and can explain them to the persons who were tested. Genetic test results must be written by the laboratory in a form that is understandable to the non-geneticist health care provider. The quality of laboratories' written interpretations of genetic test results should be included in the overall assessment of laboratories providing genetic tests.

Some laboratories also make genetic counselors available to discuss results with physicians. If testing of other relatives is an option, a potential conflict of interest arises as the counselor might want to promote additional business.

Direct Marketing of Genetic Tests to the Public

Many clinical laboratories advertise the availability of tests directly to the public. Great care must be taken that information on genetic tests presented directly to the public is accurate and includes risks and limitations, as well as benefits. The informational material should be sensitive to the knowledge level of the general public. In addition to describing the benefits and risks of the genetic test(s), including discrimination issues and the potential emotional impact on individuals and family members, the material should describe those for whom testing is appropriate (e.g., couples planning to have children for carrier tests, and individuals with a family history of a late-onset disorder for which genetic predispositions can be detected), and should emphasize that all genetic testing is voluntary, often requiring informed consent. Consumers should discuss testing options with a health care provider competent in genetics prior to having specimens collected for analysis.

In accord with laws in most States, clinical laboratories in the U.S. require that specimens for the vast majority of tests come from a physician or are reported to a physician. A few laboratories accept specimens for predictive genetic testing directly from consumers without the intervention of their own physician. In such cases, a physician affiliated with the testing laboratory, who is a specialist but may be previously unknown to the patient, can order the test. As DNA can be isolated and amplified from cells in saliva or scraped from the buccal mucosa, it is possible for lay people to collect their own specimens. FDA has the authority to regulate this practice if the laboratory supplies or requires use of a specially designated collection device or container to send specimens from the person's home to the laboratory. The Task Force discourages advertising or marketing of predictive genetic tests to the public.

References

1. Kaback M, Lim-Steele J, Dabholkar D, Brown D, Levy N, Zeiger K: Tay-Sachs disease—carrier screening, prenatal diagnosis, and the molecular era. An international perspective, 1970 to 1993. The International TSD Data Collection Network. *JAMA* 1993;207:2307-2315.
2. Bogdanich W: False negative. Medical labs, trusted as largely error-free, are far from infallible. *Wall Street Journal* Feb. 2, 1987:1.
3. Public Law 100-578: Clinical Laboratory Improvement Amendments of 1988. 1988;42 USC 263a.
4. Palomaki GE, Knight GJ, McCarthy JE, Haddow JE, Donhowe JM: Maternal serum screening for Down syndrome in the United States: A 1995 survey. *American Journal of Obstetrics and Gynecology* 1997;176:1046-1051.
5. Burke W, Kahn MJE, Garber JE, Collins FS: "First Do No Harm" applies to cancer susceptibility testing too. *Cancer Journal from Scientific American* 1996;2:250-252.
6. Weber B: Breast cancer susceptibility genes: Current challenges and future promises. *Annals of Internal Medicine* 1996;124:1088-1090.
7. Blue Cross and Blue Shield Association Technology Evaluation Center (TEC): Executive Summary of TEC Assessment on Genetic Testing for inherited BRCA1 or BRCA2 mutations. 1997.
8. Schulman JD, Stern HJ: Genetic predisposition testing for breast cancer. *Cancer Journal from Scientific American* 1997;2:244-249.

Genetic Testing for Rare Inherited Disorders

The vast majority of single-gene (Mendelian) disorders are rare, occurring less often than 1 in 10,000 live births. Exceptions are sickle cell anemia, cystic fibrosis, thalassemia, and Tay-Sachs disease in some populations, and heterozygous familial hypercholesterolemia, Duchenne muscular dystrophy, and the hemophilias more generally. Phenylketonuria, for which newborns are routinely screened, occurs in slightly less than 1 in 10,000 births. Most of the several thousand other known inherited diseases occur much less frequently, but their combined incidence is by no means rare. Between 10 and 20 million Americans may suffer from one of the several thousand known rare diseases over their lifetimes.[1] With the discovery of the role of inherited mutations in common diseases, such as breast and colon cancer and Alzheimer disease (albeit in a small proportion of affected people), the Task Force is concerned that research might shift away from the multitude of rare diseases. Commercial genetic test developers, for instance, expend a greater effort on the common, complex disorders than on rare ones. The development and maintenance of tests for rare genetic diseases must continue to be encouraged.

There is no uniform definition of a rare disease. The Orphan Drug Act (ODA) defines orphan disease as one affecting less than 200,000 persons in the U.S., or approximately 1 in 1,250 Americans. For devices (which include genetic tests), the 1988 ODA Amendments define rare disease as "any disease or condition that occurs so infrequently in the United States that there is no reasonable expectation that a medical device...will be developed without [financial] assistance." As already noted, the Humanitarian Device Exemption of the Safe Medical Devices Act of 1990 applies to diseases or conditions that affect fewer than 4,000 persons in the United States (1 in 62,500 Americans). It is silent on what constitutes a disease or condition (e.g., whether rare variants of a common genetic disease constitute a separate disease, or whether carriers are excluded). The carrier (heterozygote) frequency for autosomal recessive disorders with an incidence of 1 in 10,000 is 1 in 50.

Dissemination of Information about Rare Diseases

Research Activity

The NIH Office of Rare Diseases (ORD), founded in 1994, maintains a database of clinical studies involving rare diseases that are funded by NIH. At the end of 1996, approximately 300 studies were contained in the database. ORD plans to expand the database to include clinical research supported by private organizations, including the biotechnology and pharmaceutical industries. When fully operational, the database will contain abstracts of studies, enrollment criteria, and the names of principal investigators and how to contact them. The database is available to patients, providers, and other researchers on the World Wide Web at http://rarediseases.info.nih.gov/pages. In the future, people may be able to contact principal investigators of clinical studies through the databases. ORD would also like to coordinate rare disease research by the establishment of an information center, which would also respond to inquiries about rare genetic disorders.

The Metabolic Information Network (MIN) (Dallas, Texas) is a registry containing medical information on approximately 10,000 living and deceased patients with any one of 86 metabolic disorders. Funded originally by the National Institute of Child Health and Human Development, MIN currently receives most of its support from pharmaceutical companies. Through MIN, an investigator doing research on a particular disease can locate other investigators doing related research. Names of patients are not included in the registry and requests for investigator-to-investigator contact are reviewed by a scientific advisory board.

Finding Information on the Interpretation of Clinical Findings

Some rare genetic diseases present with unusual symptoms or signs, making diagnosis relatively easy for knowledgeable physicians. Many rare inherited metabolic disorders present with commonly encountered problems for which the usual explanation is not a rare disease.[5] When the clinical problem persists or recurs despite treatment, health care providers must be aware that a rare disease could be the explanation. Prompt recognition can often save the patient's life by leading to initiation of effective therapy before irreversible damage occurs. Many of these metabolic disorders appear in infants and children; early diagnosis can alert the parents to their risk of having another affected child. Several tests can be used predictively for prenatal diagnosis. Carrier testing in collateral relatives is often possible.

Finding Clinical Diagnostic Laboratories

Because of the rarity of many diseases, only one or a few laboratories in the United States, or the world, accurately perform tests for them. This raises the problem of how physicians caring for patients will be able to identify these laboratories in time to benefit patients who present with acute illness.

The Helix Directory of Medical Genetics Laboratories, supported by the National Library of Medicine, lists approximately 300 laboratories that perform tests on over 480 genetic diseases. Helix began by listing laboratories performing DNA-based tests including fluorescent in situ hybridization (FISH), but will extend to biochemical tests in the future. As of July 1997, Helix had 4,500 registered users and received 150 requests per day. (Personal communication, Maxine L. Covington, Helix Directory Manager, July 23, 1997) Helix provides information by phone and fax, but it is encouraging inquiries via the World Wide Web at http://www.hslib.washington.edu/helix. As many of the laboratories entered in the database do not want to be contacted directly by patients, passwords for entry to the database are available only to health care providers. Consequently, Helix is not listed in ORD's databases.

Through ORD's database on clinical research studies, physicians can get help in the diagnosis of patients in whom they suspect particular rare diseases. To maintain and expand its database, ORD should identify laboratories worldwide that perform tests for rare genetic diseases, the methodology employed, and whether the tests they provide are in the investigational stage, or are being used for clinical diagnosis and decision making.

Ensuring the Quality of Genetic Tests for Rare Diseases

Neither the clinical nor the laboratory diagnosis of rare inherited diseases is easy. If clinicians do not mention the possibility of a rare disorder when they order clinical laboratory tests, the laboratory might not test for them. Clinical laboratories, too, might misinterpret abnormal findings, often neglecting rare disorders in favor of more common situations, such as poisoning. Some clinical laboratories do not have the equipment or expertise to diagnose a rare disorder, but clinicians might not realize it. Many rare disorders will be diagnosed only by special laboratories accustomed to looking for rare diseases and having the equipment and expertise to do so.

References

1. National Commission on Orphan Diseases: Report of the National Commission on Orphan Diseases. 1989;(Abstract).

2. Public Law 97-414: 1995;U.S.C. Sec 360aa et:(Abstract).

3. Public Law 100-290: Orphan Drug Amendments of 1988. 1995;U.S.C. Sec 360cc(a):(Abstract).

4. Public Law: Safe Medical Devices Act of 1990. 1995;U.S.C. Sec 360j(m):(Abstract).

5. Holtzman NA: Rare diseases, common problems: Recognition and management. *Pediatrics* 1978;62:1056-1060.

6. Shoemaker JD, Lynch RE, Hoffmann JW, Sly WS: Misidentification of propionic acid as ethylene glycol in a patient with methylmalonic acidemia. *Journal of Pediatrics* 1992;120:417-421.

7. Woolf AD, Wynshaw-Boris A, Rinaldo P, Levy HL: Intentional infantile ethylene glycol poisoning presenting as an inherited metabolic disorder. *Journal of Pediatrics* 1992;120:421-424.

Chapter 21

Genetic Information and the Workplace

Recent advances in genetic research have made it possible to identify the genetic basis for human diseases, opening the door to individualized prevention strategies and early detection and treatment. These advances hold much promise for improving health. However, genetic information can also be used unfairly to discriminate against or stigmatize individuals on the job. For example, people may be denied jobs or benefits because they possess particular genetic traits—even if that trait has no bearing on their ability to do the job. In addition, since some genetic traits are found more frequently in specific racial or ethnic groups, such discrimination could disproportionately affect these groups. This chapter discusses why American workers deserve federal legislation to protect them from genetic discrimination in the workplace.

The Promise of Genetic Information

Unprecedented progress in identifying and understanding the 50,000 to 100,000 or so genes that make up the human genome provides an opportunity for scientists to develop strategies to prevent or reduce the effects of genetic disease. Scientists have shown that straightforward inherited errors in our genes are responsible for an estimated 3,000 to 4,000 diseases, including Huntington's disease, cystic fibrosis, neurofibromatosis, and Duchenne muscular dystrophy.

The National Human Genome Research Institute (NHGRI), January 20, 1998.

More complex inheritance of multiple genetic errors also can increase an individual's risk of developing common disorders such as cancer, heart disease, and diabetes. Genetic technologies, such as simple DNA tests, increasingly are becoming available to identify people who might have an increased likelihood of developing a disorder. The majority of diseases Americans encounter, however, do not result solely from genetic predisposition but from the interaction of genes with environmental factors, including occupation, diet, and lifestyle. Consequently, genetic tests alone cannot predict with certainty whether a person with a particular genetic error will in fact develop a disease.

With tools from the Human Genome Project, a new gene discovery is reported nearly every week. For example, scientists recently reported the discovery of a genetic alteration that, in early studies, appears to double a person's risk of colon cancer. The genetic alteration, which can be identified with a $200 blood test, is most prevalent among Jews of Eastern European descent. Once identified, people who carry this mutation can use regular colon examinations to detect cancer growth early when it is most easily treated.

Where effective means of early detection and treatment have been established, knowledge of genetic alterations can help a person prevent or reduce the likelihood of illness, and in some instances actually reduce health care costs. For example, genetic testing for hemochromatosis, glaucoma, and some cancers can alert the individual to begin preventive measures before the disease causes harm.

Genetic Information and Discrimination

There are several ways to gather genetic information. It can be deduced from a family's medical history or during a physical examination. Routine laboratory tests that measure the body's output of specific substances might also suggest the genetic make-up of the individual. But the most direct approach to obtaining genetic information is through analysis of DNA, the material that makes up genes. Such genetic tests identify specific DNA features in people who have already developed a disease, in healthy people who may be at risk of developing a genetic disorder later in life, or in people who are at risk of having a child with an inherited disorder. Thus, genetic information includes information about genes, gene products, and inherited characteristics that may derive from individuals or their family members.

While genetic technology increases the ability to detect and prevent health disorders, it can also be misused to discriminate against or stigmatize individuals. A 1996 survey of individuals at risk of developing a genetic condition and parents of children with specific genetic conditions identified more than 200 cases of genetic discrimination among the 917 people who responded. The cases involved discrimination by insurance companies, employers, and other organizations that use genetic information. Another recent survey of genetic counselors, primary care physicians, and patients, identified 550 people who had been denied employment or insurance based on their genetic predisposition to an illness. In addition, because an individual's genetic information has implications for his or her family members and future generations, misuse of genetic information could have intergenerational effects that are far broader than any individual incident of misuse.

Many Americans are reluctant to take advantage of new breakthroughs in genetic testing for fear that the results will not be used to improve their health but rather to deny them jobs or health insurance.

- A 1995 Harris poll of the general public found that over 85 percent of those surveyed indicated they were very concerned or somewhat concerned that insurers or employers might have access to and use genetic information.
- Sixty-three percent of the participants in a 1997 national telephone survey of more than 1000 people reported that they would not take genetic tests for diseases if health insurers or employers could get access to the results.
- Eighty-five percent felt that employers should be prohibited from obtaining information about an individual's genetic conditions, risks, and predispositions.
- Researchers conducting a multi-year Pennsylvania study designed to understand how to keep women with breast cancer gene mutations healthy reported that nearly one-third of the high-risk women invited to participate in the study refused because they feared discrimination or a loss of privacy.
- Another study of 332 people who belonged to support groups for families with genetic disorders found that fear of genetic discrimination resulted in 17 percent of the participants not revealing genetic information to employers.

In addition, people have hidden genetic information about themselves due to fear of the effects of disclosure. For example, an 18-year-old man, at risk for inheriting Huntington's disease from one of his parents, who wished to enlist in the Marines to serve in the Persian Gulf War, believed that knowledge of his risk status would disqualify him from service, even though it was unlikely that he would become symptomatic during his tour of duty. He therefore answered "no" to questions regarding hereditary disorders on his application and did not include Huntington's disease in his family medical history. Another individual whose parent died of Huntington's disease also chose to hide the truth from his employer. Fearing adverse consequences at work if this cause of death was known, the individual arranged for the diagnosis of asphyxiation to be reported as the cause of death to avoid mention of the disease in an obituary. Fear of genetic discrimination and the consequences of this fear have been reported in both the scientific literature and the popular press.

Genetic Information in the Workplace

Two types of genetic testing can occur in the workplace: genetic screening and genetic monitoring. Genetic screening examines the genetic makeup of employees or job applicants for specific inherited characteristics. It may be used to detect general heritable conditions that are not associated with workplace exposures in employees or applicants. For example, employers used genetic screening in the early 1970s to identify African Americans who carried a gene mutation for sickle cell anemia. Those carrying the gene mutation were denied jobs—even though many of them were healthy and would never develop the disease. In these cases, genetic screening to identify the sickle cell trait often occurred without the consent of the individuals.

Genetic screening can also be used to detect the presence of genetically determined traits that render an employee susceptible, or "hypersusceptible," to a certain disease if exposed to specific environmental factors or substances that may be present in the workplace. In theory, genetic screening for occupationally relevant traits has the potential to be used to assign employees who are genetically susceptible to certain occupational diseases away from harmful exposure. However, no consensus currently exists regarding the validity of the scientific evidence or the usefulness of the genetic tests reported to predict an individual's susceptibility to exposure.

Genetic monitoring, a second type of testing, ascertains whether an individual's genetic material has changed over time due to workplace exposure to hazardous substances. Evidence of genetic changes in a population of workers could be used to target work areas for increased safety and health precautions and to indicate a need to lower exposure levels for a group exposed to a previously unknown hazard. The ultimate goal of genetic monitoring is to prevent or reduce the risk of disease caused by genetic damage.

Although genetic changes such as chromosomal damage have been associated with exposure to radiation and some chemical mutagens or carcinogens, little is known about which changes are predictive of subsequent disease risk. Much more research is required to establish the relationship, if any, between those changes and subsequent disease risk for affected populations and individuals. For this reason, use of genetic monitoring results to make employment decisions is rarely justifiable.

In addition, some employers may seek to use genetic tests to discriminate against workers—even those who have not yet or who may never show signs of disease—because the employers fear the cost consequences. Based on genetic information, employers may try to avoid hiring workers who they believe are likely to take sick leave, resign, or retire early for health reasons (creating extra costs in recruiting and training new staff), file for workers' compensation, or use health care benefits excessively. A 1989 survey of large businesses, private utilities, and labor unions found that 5 percent of the 330 organizations responding conducted genetic screening or monitoring of its workers. Another 1989 survey of 400 firms, conducted by Northwestern National Life Insurance, found that 15 percent of the companies planned, by the year 2000, to check the genetic status of prospective employees and their dependents before making employment offers. Thus, there is evidence that genetic information continues to be used to discriminate against qualified workers. The economic incentive to discriminate based on genetic information is likely to increase as genetic research advances and the costs of genetic testing decrease.

Real People—Real Discrimination

Genetic predisposition or conditions can lead to workplace discrimination, even in cases where workers are healthy and unlikely to develop disease or where the genetic condition has no effect on the ability to perform work. As a result, real people are denied employment opportunities.

One individual was screened and learned he was a carrier of a single mutation for Gaucher's disease. His carrier status indicates that he might pass this mutation to his children, but not that he would develop Gaucher's disease himself. He revealed this information when applying for a job and was denied the job because of his genetic mutation, even though it had no bearing on his present or future ability to perform a job.

A 53-year-old man at a job interview with an insurance company revealed that he had hemochromatosis but was asymptomatic. During the second interview, he was told that the company was interested in hiring him but would not be able to offer him health insurance because of his genetic condition. He agreed to this arrangement. During his third interview, the company representative told him that they would like to hire him, but were unable to do so because of his genetic condition.

An employee's parent developed Huntington's disease—indicating that the employee had a 50 percent chance of inheriting the mutated gene that would cause her to develop the disease. She decided to be tested. A genetic counselor advised her to secure life and health insurance before testing, because a positive test result would not only mean that she would get the disease but would probably prevent her from obtaining insurance as well. A co-worker who overheard her making arrangements to be tested reported the employee's conversations to their boss. Initially, the boss seemed empathetic and offered to help. When the employee eventually shared the news that her test results indicated that she did carry the mutated gene, she was fired from her job. In the 8-month period prior to her termination, she had received three promotions and outstanding performance reviews. Frightened by their sister's experience, none of her siblings are willing to undergo genetic testing for fear of losing health insurance or jobs. Consequently, they must live with the uncertainty of not knowing whether they have inherited the genetic trait that leads to Huntington's disease.

Efforts to Restrict Use of Genetic Information in the Workplace

There is no scientific evidence to substantiate a relationship between unexpressed genetic factors and an individual's ability to perform his or her job. Thus, most expert groups recommend prohibiting or severely restricting the use of genetic testing and access to genetic information in the workplace. The American Medical Association's (AMA) Council on Ethical and Judicial Affairs concludes that it is inappropriate to exclude workers with genetic risks for disease from the workplace because of that risk. In the future, however, the AMA

Council acknowledges there may be an appropriate but limited role for genetic testing in certain situations to protect workers who have a genetic susceptibility to occupational illness when health risks can be accurately predicted by the test.

The National Action Plan on Breast Cancer (NAPBC) and the National Institutes of Health-Department of Energy Working Group on Ethical, Legal, and Social Implications of Human Genome Research also has drafted recommendations for state and federal policy makers to protect against genetic discrimination in the workplace. Generally, the recommendations limit the collection, disclosure, and use of genetic information and support strong enforcement of these limitations through governmental agencies or private right of action. Exceptions are made for possible situations in the future that may arise if testing is shown to be scientifically valid to predict occupational risk and situations where an individual is unable to meet the performance requirements of a job.

Existing Protections Are Limited

There are no federal laws that directly and comprehensively protect against abuses in the gathering or use of genetic information in the workplace. A few protections exist incidentally under federal laws enacted to address other types of workplace discrimination. The incidental federal protections against workplace discrimination based on genetic information that do exist are narrow in scope and, in large measure, not well established. They are not sufficient to provide Americans with adequate protection against genetic discrimination in the workplace. States continue to enact legislation in response to growing concern over the specter of genetic discrimination in the workplace. Existing state laws, however, differ in coverage, protections afforded, and enforcement schemes. Federal leadership is necessary to ensure that all workers are protected against discrimination based on genetic information.

Federal Laws

The only federal law that directly addresses the issue of genetic discrimination is the 1996 Health Insurance Portability and Accountability Act (HIPAA). HIPAA prohibits group health plans from using any health status-related factor, including genetic information, as a basis for denying or limiting eligibility for coverage or for charging an individual more for coverage. In addition, the Administration has worked closely with Congress on legislation that would prevent an insurance company or HMO from disclosing genetic information or charging an entire plan or group more for health insurance on the basis of genetic information. These efforts, however, do not address the larger problems of the gathering or use of genetic information in the workplace outside of the health insurance context.

The most likely current source of protection against genetic discrimination in the workplace is provided by laws prohibiting discrimination based on disability. Title I of the Americans with Disabilities Act (ADA), enforced by the Equal Employment Opportunity Commission (EEOC), and similar disability-based anti-discrimination laws, such as the Rehabilitation Act of 1973, do not explicitly address genetic information, but they provide some protections against disability-related genetic discrimination in the workplace. Under the ADA, individuals with symptomatic genetic disabilities have the same protections against discrimination as individuals with other disabilities. However, as we make new advances in genetics, this protection will not be sufficient. More and more people will be vulnerable to genetic discrimination based on unexpressed genetic conditions that do not fall within the clear disability-based discrimination prohibitions of the ADA.

Protection against discrimination based on genetic information for those who do not currently have a symptomatic genetic disability is not well established. Individuals who do not currently have a symptomatic genetic disorder and, therefore, may not be protected against discrimination as a currently disabled person include unaffected carriers of a disease who may never get the disease themselves, individuals with late-onset genetic disorders who may be identified through genetic testing as being at high risk of developing the disease, and others who are identified through family history as being at high risk of developing the disease.

The EEOC has tried to provide ADA protection to individuals who do not have symptomatic genetic disabilities but who may be subject to discrimination based on genetic information. In 1995 the EEOC issued enforcement guidance advising that an employer who takes adverse action against an individual on the basis of genetic information relating to illness, disease, or other disorders regards that individual as having a disability within the meaning of the ADA. The ADA prohibits discrimination against a person who is regarded as having a disability. The guidance, however, is limited in scope and legal effect. It is policy guidance that does not have the same legally binding effect on a court as a statute or regulation and has not been tested in court. Moreover, many cases based on the argument that an employer has discriminated against workers by regarding them as disabled have not been well-received by the courts.

In addition, the ADA does not protect workers from requirements or requests to provide genetic information to their employers. Under the ADA, an employer generally may not make medical inquiries about a job applicant prior to extending a conditional offer of employment. However, once a conditional offer of employment has been extended, but before the individual begins work, the employer may obtain extensive medical information about the applicant, including genetic information. During this period an employer could, for example, obtain and store genetic samples of job applicants, require genetic screening as a condition of employment, or purchase genetic information about applicants from a genetic information data bank. In addition, once the applicant is hired the employer may request medical information that is job related and consistent with business necessity.

It is difficult to ensure that medical information is not used to discriminate. Detecting discrimination based on genetic information, which indicates a risk rather than a manifestation of disease, is particularly difficult. As a result, genetic information could be used to deny workers employment or opportunities regardless of their ability to do the job. This concern is especially significant because of the rapid advances in genetic research. For instance, genetic information obtained today may, in the future, be found to indicate a risk factor that could be the basis for discrimination. Moreover, this information also could be used to predict the health risks of an individual's family members—creating the potential that genetic information could be used to discriminate against future generations of workers.

Another federal law that may incidentally provide protection against some forms of genetic discrimination is Title VII of the Civil Rights Act of 1964. An argument could be made that genetic discrimination based on racially or ethnically linked genetic disorders constitutes unlawful race or ethnic discrimination. Protection under Title VII, however, is only available where an employer engages in discrimination against a particular racial or ethnic group based on a genetic trait that is substantially related to a race or ethnic group. Since a strong nexus between race or national origin has been established for only a few diseases, Title VII will not be an effective tool for combating most forms of genetic discrimination. Thus, it is clear that current anti-discrimination laws would not adequately address the issue of genetic-based discrimination in employment.

State Laws

A number of states have addressed the issue of genetic discrimination in employment through state legislation. As of October 1997, 14 states had enacted laws to provide protections against various forms of genetic discrimination in the workplace. There are wide variations among these state laws.

Some of the first state laws enacted to address this issue prohibited discrimination against individuals with specific genetic traits or disorders, such as the sickle cell trait (Florida and Louisiana) or the hemoglobin trait (North Carolina). Later laws cover broader categories of genetic traits and disorders. For example, a 1981 New Jersey statute (later broadened) prohibits discrimination in employment based on an "atypical hereditary cellular or blood traits" and a New York law prohibits employers from denying equal employment opportunities based on "unique genetic disorders."

Other state laws regulate both the use of genetic testing in employment decisions and the disclosure of genetic test results. These state laws generally prohibit employers from requiring workers and applicants to undergo genetic testing as a condition of employment. For example, Oregon state law prohibits employers from using genetic information to distinguish between or discriminate against applicants and employees and prohibits employers from subjecting applicants and employees to genetic testing. A recently enacted Texas law prohibits employers, labor organizations, licensing agencies, and employment agencies from discriminating against any individual on the basis of the results of a genetic test or because of the individual's refusal to submit to genetic testing.

Some states permit genetic testing when it is requested by the worker or applicant for the purpose of investigating a worker's compensation claim or determining the workers' susceptibility to potentially toxic chemicals in the workplace. These statutes often require the worker to provide informed written consent for such testing and contain specific restrictions governing disclosure and prevent the employer from taking adverse action against the employee.

Given the substantial gaps in state and federal protections against employment discrimination based on genetic information, comprehensive federal legislation is needed to ensure that advances in genetic technology and research are used to address the health needs of the nation—and not to deny individuals employment opportunities and benefits. Federal legislation would establish minimum protections that could be supplemented by state laws.

The need for federal protection has been recognized by Congress with the introduction of numerous bills with bipartisan support. Three stand-alone bills have been introduced that amend existing civil rights or labor laws to protect workers against employment discrimination based on genetic information (S. 1045, Sen. Daschle; H.R. 2275, Rep. Lowey; H.R. 2215, Rep. Kennedy). Two additional bills have been introduced that include worker protections against discrimination based on genetic information, as part of broader proposals addressing the use of genetic information (S. 422, Sen. Domenici; H.R. 2198, Rep. Stearns).

Guiding Principles for Federal Action

Federal legislation is needed to ensure that knowledge gained from genetic research is fully utilized to improve the health of Americans and not to discriminate against workers. This legislation should provide a floor or minimum level of protection and allow existing state laws to provide greater protection. Workers should not be forced to avoid tests that can help prevent disease because of fear of discrimination. At the same time, we must preserve the ability of scientists to continue the research, including studies of occupational health and safety that is so vital to expanding our knowledge of genetics and health.

The Administration proposes that Congress pass a law to ensure that discoveries made possible by the Human Genome Project are used to improve health and not to discriminate against workers or their families. Legislation generally should include the following basic protections against misuse of genetic information in the workplace.

- Employers should not require or request that employees or potential employees take a genetic test or provide genetic information as a condition of employment or benefits.
- Employers should not use genetic information to discriminate against, limit, segregate, or classify employees in a way that would deprive them of employment opportunities.
- Employers should not obtain or disclose genetic information about employees or potential employees under most circumstances.

Genetic testing and the use of genetic information by employers should be permitted in the following situations to ensure workplace safety and health and to preserve research opportunities. However, in all cases where genetic information about employees is obtained, the information should be maintained in medical files that are kept separate from personnel files, treated as confidential medical records, and protected by applicable state and federal laws.

- An employer should be permitted to monitor employees for the effects of a particular substance found in the workplace to which continued exposure could cause genetic damage under certain circumstances. Informed consent and assurance of confidentiality should be required.
- In addition, employers may only use the results to identify and control adverse conditions in the workplace and to take action necessary to prevent significant risk of substantial harm to the employee or others.
- The statutory authority of a federal agency or contractor to promulgate regulations, enforce workplace safety and health laws, or conduct occupational or other health research should not be limited.
- An employer should be able to disclose genetic information for research and other purposes with the written, informed consent of the individual.

These recommendations should apply to public and private-sector employers, unions, and labor management groups that conduct joint apprenticeship and other training programs. Employment agencies and licensing agencies that issue licenses, certificates, and other credentials required to engage in various professions and occupations also should be covered.

Individuals who believe they have been subjected to workplace discrimination based on genetic information should be able to file a charge with the Equal Employment Opportunity Commission, Department of Labor, or other appropriate federal agency for investigation and resolution. The designated agency should be authorized to bring lawsuits in the federal courts to resolve those issues that would not settle amicably. The courts should have the authority to halt the violations and order relief, such as hiring, promotion, back pay, and compensatory and punitive damages, to the individual. Alternatively, an individual should be able to elect to bring a private lawsuit in federal or state court to obtain the same type of relief plus reasonable costs and attorney's fees. In order to enforce these protections, the designated enforcement agency must be given sufficient additional resources to investigate and prosecute allegations of discrimination.

Chapter 22

Health Insurance in the Age of Genetics

As the Human Genome Project makes it ever easier to find genetic alterations associated with human disease, unprecedented opportunities are arising to treat or prevent those diseases. However, as knowledge grows about the genetic basis of disease, so too does the potential for discrimination and stigmatization based on genetic information. Too many Americans fear that their genetic information will be used to discriminate against them and too often they are right. Federal legislation is needed to guarantee access to health insurance coverage irrespective of an individual's genetic makeup.

The Promise of Genetic Testing

The Human Genome Project has brought with it the promise of a whole new way to understand, treat, and prevent many human diseases. For children born with a baffling inherited disorder, genetic technologies can put an end to the often long and agonizing search for a diagnosis. For healthy people from families prone to a later-onset disease, genetic technologies, such as simple DNA tests, can tell people and their health care providers who has an increased likelihood of developing the disorder and who does not. At one time, such medical clairvoyance seemed like science fiction, but not any more. Scientists have made tremendous strides in understanding genetics. In the next few years we will know the exact location and letter-by-letter sequence

Department of Health and Human Services, The National Human Genome Research Institute (NHGRI), July 1997.

of each of the 80,000 or so genes in the human genome and begin comprehensive studies to understand how they work.

Genetic tests for glaucoma, colon cancer, inherited kidney cancer, and other disorders are already helping to identify high-risk individuals before they become ill. In a Chicago hospital, for example, "Patty," who had tested positive for a cancer-related gene mutation called MEN2, has had her thyroid gland removed. She inherited the altered gene from her father who had thyroid cancer. Because his children have a 50-50 chance of inheriting the altered gene, doctors tested Patty and her only sibling. Patty turned out to carry the MEN alteration. Because this mutation placed Patty at very high likelihood of developing thyroid cancer, her doctors recommended that she have her thyroid removed. At the time of surgery, Patty's thyroid gland already contained small, potentially lethal, cancers. She now takes a pill every day to replace her thyroid hormones, but her chance of developing MEN-related cancer is very low.

During 1997 scientists discovered a mutated gene that leads to hereditary hemochromatosis (HH), a common disorder of iron metabolism, affecting about 1 in 400 individuals of Northern European descent. Because HH is so common and easily treatable, it potentially provides an excellent example for offering genetic testing on a large scale to identify people at risk for a disease and enabling them to avoid becoming ill. The major symptoms of HH—liver cirrhosis, heart deterioration, and other organ failures—don't occur until mid-life, and left untreated, the disease causes early death. But treatment by simple bloodletting to remove excess iron allows people with HH to live a normal life-span.

Today, genetic tests are available primarily in academic medical centers for some 450 disorders, most of which are rare. Genetic tests can identify DNA alterations in people who have already developed a disease, in healthy persons who may be at risk of developing a genetic disorder later in life, or in people who are at risk of having a child with an inherited disorder. Over the next decade, genetic testing will become ever more commonplace throughout the health care system. For example, a NIH Consensus Development Panel recently recommended that genetic testing for cystic fibrosis mutations be offered to all couples planning a pregnancy or seeking prenatal testing. This is the first time that offering genetic testing has been recommended for such a large population group. Genetic technologies will soon play a role in nearly every field of health care.

Genetic tests can save health care dollars by identifying those in high-risk families who might benefit from close medical surveillance, and who might not. "Beth," for instance, is a 47-year-old mother of two. Two of her brothers and her father were diagnosed with colon cancer, and her grandmother died of uterine cancer. Of course, Beth was concerned that she too might develop cancer. About 10 years ago, she asked her doctor about her colon cancer risk, but Beth's family history pattern did not fit a known syndrome at the time. With no genetic test available for her condition, her doctor could only say that her risk of colon cancer was higher than average. Worried about her risk, and wanting to detect any cancers early, Beth began an annual program of expensive and uncomfortable colonoscopies.

Six years after Beth first inquired about her cancer risk, an experimental genetic test became available that could tell Beth if she inherited the genetic alteration that caused the cancer in her family. Beth took this simple test and learned she had not inherited the cancer-causing alteration. Immediately, Beth stopped the annual colonoscopies, saved thousands of dollars for both her and her insurance company, and brought an end to the unnecessary medical procedure. Perhaps most importantly, because she now knew that her risk for colon cancer was no greater than that of the general population, Beth gained peace of mind for herself and for her two children.

Progress in Health Research

The Human Genome Project has given us the technology to decipher what were once an individual's most personal and intimate "family secrets," that is, the information contained in our DNA. The instructions encrypted in our genes affect nearly every function a human body carries out—in a moment, a day, or a lifetime. Research to understand those instructions offers the promise of better health because it gives researchers and clinicians critical information to work out therapies or other strategies to prevent or treat a disease.

What if we could prevent or reduce the effects of many common diseases by simple changes in lifestyle or avoidance of specific environmental substances? Many of the diseases we face—such as high blood pressure and other familiar diseases of the heart and circulatory system, diabetes, obesity, cancer, psychiatric illness, asthma, and arthritis—have been difficult to study and treat because almost all involve subtle actions of several genes and the environment. Scientists are rapidly developing advanced technologies to identify each of the genes that contribute to a complex disorder and study their interactions all at once. The goal is to tease apart which disease components are genetic and which are environmental.

The slowest part of a disease-gene hunt nowadays is sorting through all the genes in the target region on a chromosome and determining which one is responsible for the disease. But this is rapidly changing. New gene maps now pinpoint the locations of more than one-fourth of all human genes, and more are developed every day.

The complete set of genetic instructions will give researchers basic information about how a human cell works as a system, or how the cells of a brain or a heart work together, or how a single fertilized cell develops into a fully formed baby. Spelling out, letter by letter, the complete genetic instructions of a human being will bring with it new technologies that make identifying DNA differences effortless compared with what we can do today. Imagine analyzing your genetic composition on a computer chip, carrying your DNA "bar code" on a small plastic card, encrypted to protect privacy, that lets health care professionals instantly know your predisposition to disease, your reactions to drugs, or your susceptibility to certain environmental exposures. All of these will become realities as we continue to make advancements in genetics.

Genetic Discrimination: A New Twist on an Old Injustice

The ability to examine our DNA for the presence of disease-related alterations opens the door to a new twist on an old injustice: "genetic" discrimination—when people, either as groups or individuals, are treated unfairly because of the content of their DNA. The increased availability of genetic information raises concerns about who will have access to this potentially powerful information. Each of us has between 5 and 30 misspellings or alterations in our DNA; thus, we could all be targets for discrimination based on our genes. Like racism, sexism, and other forms of prejudice, genetic discrimination devalues diversity, squanders potential, and ignores achievement.

Genetic information has been used to discriminate against people in the past. In the early 1970's, some insurance companies denied coverage and some employers denied jobs to African Americans who were identified as carriers for sickle cell anemia, even though they were healthy and would never develop the disease.

Of particular concern is the fear of losing or being denied health insurance because of a possible genetic predisposition to a particular disease. For example, a woman who carries a genetic alteration associated with breast cancer, and who has close relatives with the disease, has an increased risk of developing breast and ovarian cancer. Knowledge of this genetic status can enable women in high-risk families, together with their health care providers, to better tailor surveillance and prevention strategies. However, because of a concern that she or her children may not be able to obtain or change health insurance coverage in the future, a woman currently in this situation may avoid or delay genetic testing.

These are real concerns for too many Americans. In a recent survey of people in families with genetic disorders, 22 percent indicated they, or a member of their family, had been refused health insurance on the basis of their genetic information. The overwhelming majority of those surveyed felt that health insurers should not have access to genetic information. A 1995 Harris poll of the general public found a similar level of concern.

Over 85 percent of those surveyed indicated they were very concerned or somewhat concerned that insurers or employers might have access to and use genetic information. Discrimination in health insurance, and the fear of potential discrimination, threaten both society's ability to use new genetic technologies to improve human health and the ability to conduct the very research we need to understand, treat, and prevent genetic disease.

To unravel the basis of complex disorders in the large numbers of individuals they affect, scientists must analyze the DNA of many hundreds of people for each disease they study. Valid research on complex disorders will require the participation of large numbers of volunteers. But a pall of mistrust hangs over research programs because study volunteers are concerned that their genetic information will not be kept confidential and will be used by insurers to discriminate against them. Information about research participant's genetic composition must be protected from misuse.

Participants in Dr. Barbara Weber's research program on breast cancer worry a great deal about genetic discrimination.[5] She and her coworkers in Pennsylvania are trying to understand how to keep women with breast cancer gene mutations healthy by studying them closely for several years. But nearly one-third of the high-risk people Dr. Weber invites into the study refuse because they fear discrimination and/or a loss of privacy. So strong is the fear of misuse of genetic information obtained in research programs that many physician-researchers leave genetic test results out of the study medical record or warn study participants not to give the information to their private physicians. In some instances, patients and/or their providers may be forced to tell outright lies about genetic test results.

In genetic testing studies at the National Institutes of Health (NIH), nearly 32 percent of eligible people offered a test for breast cancer risk decline to take it. The overwhelming majority of those who refuse cite concerns about health insurance discrimination and loss of privacy as the reason.

In an ongoing study, researchers are assessing individuals who have already had cancer and their families. Because individuals who have had cancer have already been categorized as a high risk by insurers, participants in this study are somewhat less concerned about the potential for health insurance discrimination. The vast majority of individuals invited to have genetic testing as a part of the research project have agreed to be tested. Those who have opted not to be tested state that knowledge of how this information might be used was a determining factor.

The Need for Legislation

In 1995, the National Action Plan on Breast Cancer (NAPBC, coordinated by the U.S. Public Health Service Office on Women's Health) and the NIH-DOE Working Group on Ethical, Legal and Social Implications of Human Genome Research (ELSI Working Group) tackled the issue of genetic discrimination and health insurance. This effort built on the ELSI Working Group's long standing interest in the privacy and fair use of genetic information and the NAPBC's mandate to address priority issues related to breast cancer. The following recommendations were published and made available to state and federal policy makers:

- Insurance providers should be prohibited from using genetic information, or an individual's request for genetic services, to deny or limit any coverage or establish eligibility, continuation, enrollment, or contribution requirements.
- Insurance providers should be prohibited from establishing differential rates or premium payments based on genetic information, or an individual's request for genetic services.
- Insurance providers should be prohibited from requesting or requiring collection or disclosure of genetic information.
- Insurance providers and other holders of genetic information should be prohibited from releasing genetic information without prior written authorization of the individual. Written authorization should be required for each disclosure and include to whom the disclosure would be made.

In developing these recommendations, the NAPBC and ELSI Working Group developed the following definitions:

- "Genetic information" refers to information about genes, gene products, or inherited characteristics that may derive from the individual or a family member.
- The term "insurance provider" refers to an insurance company, employer, or any other entity providing a plan of health insurance or health benefits including group and individual health plans whether fully insured or self-funded.

These recommendations would prevent insurers from having access to genetic information, from being able to misuse this information, and from disclosing it to others.

State Initiatives

At least 19 states have enacted laws to restrict the use of genetic information in health insurance. These range from very narrow prohibitions in earlier legislation (e.g., Alabama in 1982 prohibited insurers from denying coverage because an applicant had sickle cell anemia) to fairly comprehensive prohibitions with strong privacy protections in more recent legislation (e.g., Wisconsin in 1991, New Jersey in 1996, and California in 1994, 1995, and 1996). Since January 1997 at least 31 states have introduced legislation to prohibit genetic discrimination in insurance. The large volume of legislative activity at the state level is a positive indication of the level of concern about this important issue.

A law passed in Arizona prohibits health and disability insurers from rejecting an application or determining rates, terms, or conditions on the basis of a genetic condition and prohibits requiring the performance of a genetic test without written informed consent. Governor Symington signed the bill into law in spite of threats by the insurance industry to leave the state.

The Illinois Legislature passed the Genetic Information Privacy Act in May, 1997. The Act prohibits insurers from seeking genetic information derived from genetic testing and from using genetic testing information for non-therapeutic purposes. This bill was originally introduced by Representative Moffitt at the request of an ovarian cancer survivor whose mother and grandmother had died of ovarian cancer. This constituent wanted to be tested for BRCA1 in order to help her daughters and granddaughters. Her doctor warned, however, that if she tested positive, she and members of her family could lose health care coverage. Based on that threat, she chose not to be tested. (She has since been tested anonymously and tested negative.)

Why State Law Is Not Enough

The current patchwork of state legislative approaches does not provide a comprehensive solution to genetic discrimination in health insurance.

First, private sector employer-sponsored health plans that provide benefits for employees and their dependents through self-funded arrangements are generally exempt from state insurance laws pursuant to the Employee Retirement Income Security Act (ERISA) preemption. Thus, even if states enacted legislation modeled on the NAPBC-ELSI Working Group recommendations, approximately 125 million people, nearly one-half of all Americans, covered by such self-funded plans would not be protected.

Second, with the exception of a few states, these laws focus narrowly on genetic tests rather than more broadly on genetic information generated by family history, physical examination, or the medical record. Although insurers are prohibited from using the results of a chemical test of DNA, or the protein product of a gene, they may still use other physical/ physiological (phenotype) indicators, pattern of inheritance of genetic characteristics, or even a request for genetic testing as the basis for discrimination. Thus, meaningful protection against genetic discrimination requires that insurers be prohibited from using all information about genes, gene products, or inherited characteristics to deny or limit health insurance coverage.

HIPAA: Significant Steps But Serious Gaps

In 1996, Congress enacted a law, called The Health Insurance Portability and Accountability Act (HIPAA), which took a significant step toward expanding access to health insurance. But HIPAA doesn't go far enough. Americans are still largely unprotected by federal law against insurance rate hikes based on genetic information and against unauthorized people or institutions having access to the genetic information contained in their medical records. HIPAA includes genetic information among the factors that may not be used to deny or limit insurance coverage for members of a group plan. Further, HIPAA explicitly excludes genetic information from being considered a preexisting condition in the absence of a diagnosis of the condition related to such information. The law specifically uses the broad, inclusive definition of genetic information recommended by the NAPBC-ELSI Working Group. Finally, HIPAA prohibits insurers from charging one individual a higher premium than any other "similarly situated" individual in the group.

These steps towards preventing discrimination based on genetics are significant, but HIPAA left several serious gaps that can now be closed by Administration-supported legislation. First, the protections in HIPAA do not extend to the individual health insurance market. Thus, individuals seeking coverage outside of the group market may still be denied access to coverage and may be charged exorbitant premiums based on genetic information. While only approximately 5 percent of Americans obtain health insurance outside the group market today, many of us will, at some point in our lifetime, purchase individual health insurance coverage. Because genetic information persists for a lifetime and may be transmitted through generations, people who are now in group plans are concerned about whether information about their genes may, at some point later in their life, disallow them from being able to purchase health insurance outside of the group market.

Second, while HIPAA prohibits insurers from treating individuals within a group differently from one another, it leaves open the possibility that all individuals within a group could be charged a higher premium based on the genetic information of one or more members of the group.

Finally, HIPAA does nothing to limit an insurer's access to or release of genetic information. No federal law prohibits an insurer from demanding access to genetic information contained in medical records or family history or requiring that an individual submit to a genetic test. In fact, an insurer can demand that an individual undergo genetic testing as a condition of coverage. Further, there are no restrictions on an insurers' release of genetic information to others. For example, at present, an insurer may release genetic information, and other health-related information, to the Medical Information Bureau which makes information available to other insurers who can then use it to discriminate. Because genetic information is personal, powerful, and potentially predictive, it can be used to stigmatize and discriminate against people. Genetic information must be private.

Congressional Initiatives

Congressional interest in securing health insurance protection for genetic information is strong and bipartisan. Senator Hatfield and

Representative Stearns introduced the first bill on genetic discrimination in health insurance and employment in November 1995. Twelve bills addressing genetic information access and/or use were introduced in the 104th Congress. Many of these bills were reintroduced in the 1997 Congress.

Representative Solomon (R-NY) introduced H.R. 328, Genetic Information Health Insurance Nondiscrimination Act of 1996. This bill was rewritten to close the "loopholes" in HIPAA by addressing discrimination in the individual health insurance market, but it does not prohibit rate increases in the group health insurance market.

Genetic Confidentiality and Nondiscrimination Act of 1997 (S. 422) introduced by Senator Domenici (R-NM) is a broad bill that sought to address privacy and fair use of genetic information in many settings. The bill included a title that would prohibit health insurers from using genetic information that follows the NAPBC-ELSI Working Group recommendations. However, this bill refers only to "any molecular genetic information about a healthy individual or a healthy family member..." rather than the broader definition of genetic information that includes family history.

The Genetic Information Nondiscrimination in Health Insurance Act of 1997 (H.R. 306) introduced by Representative Slaughter (D-NY) most closely tracks the recommendations made by the NAPBC-ELSI Working Group. This bill successfully closes the "loopholes" in HIPAA by prohibiting rate increases in the group health insurance market based on genetic information, prohibiting the use of genetic information in the individual health insurance market, and placing restrictions on the collection and disclosure of genetic information by insurers. As of July 1, 1997, H.R. 306 had 132 co-sponsors and 67 supporting groups. The Senate companion bill, The Genetic Information Nondiscrimination in Health Insurance Act of 1997 (S. 89), was introduced by Senator Snowe (R-ME).

Recommendations for Federal Legislation

On May 18, 1997, President Clinton, in his commencement address at Morgan State University, urged "Congress to pass bipartisan legislation to prohibit insurance companies from using genetic information to determine the premium rate or eligibility of Americans for health insurance."

The Administration is proposing that Congress pass a law to ensure that the discoveries made possible by the Human Genome Project are used to improve the health of Americans and not used by health insurers to discriminate against individuals, families, or groups. The Administration recommends that the law build on the effort begun under HIPAA and encompass the NAPBC-ELSI Working Group's recommendations that seek to prevent health insurers from having access to genetic information, from being able to misuse this information, and from disclosing genetic information to others.

The bill should build on HIPAA and extend protection to insurance applicants and participants in four ways. It should—

- Explicitly prohibit health insurers from varying the rate charged to a group based on genetic information pertaining to one or more group members. This would expand the prohibition in HIPAA against using genetic information to vary the premium rates of an individual in a group plan.
- Prohibit insurers in the individual market from requesting or requiring genetic information from an individual, except where the information relates to a disease or condition for which the individual or dependent has been positively diagnosed, and prohibiting insurers from requiring individuals to undergo genetic testing.
- Prohibit insurers in the individual market from using genetic information in the absence of a diagnosis of disease to deny, limit or vary coverage, or to set rates.
- Protect the privacy and confidentiality of genetic information by prohibiting insurers from releasing this information for non-treatment purposes without the prior authorization of the individual. This would impose restrictions on the disclosure of genetic information to other insurers, to plan sponsors, and to other entities regulated by State insurance laws including life, disability, and long-term care insurers. It would also prohibit insurers from releasing genetic information to the Medical Information Bureau or any other entity that collects, compiles, or disseminates insurance information.

HIPAA does acknowledge that protections concerning access to and release of health information, including genetic information, were not provided in the law itself and directs the Department of Health and Human Services (DHHS) to develop recommendations to protect the privacy of health information. DHHS is preparing recommendations on privacy protections for all individually identifiable health information, including genetic information, as required by HIPAA. Congress may in the future enact legislation that would provide protections for personally identifiable health information in general. However, the public feels especially concerned about the unique properties of genetic information—its predictive nature, its fundamental linkage to personal identify and kinship ties, its history of abuse, and the speed of development of genetic technologies. Therefore, it is important to move forward with legislation prohibiting health insurance discrimination and restricting health insurers' use and dissemination of genetic information.

Conclusion

The technology of genetic testing offers great promise for better health. However, genetic tests and genetic information can also be used to deny insurance coverage or increase premiums. The Administration strongly supports efforts to protect individuals from misuse of genetic information by health insurers, while permitting providers and others who can positively use such information to continue to use genetic information in ways that will enhance the treatment and care of individuals.

We now have the opportunity to ensure that our social policy keeps pace with the scientific advances made possible through biomedical research. The American people and the Congress support protections against genetic discrimination in health insurance. Supporting the principles put forth by the NAPBC-ELSI Working Group could ensure that increasing knowledge about ourselves and our genetic heritage is used to benefit Americans, to improve their health and well-being, and not to stigmatize or discriminate against them. This is an issue that ultimately will concern all of us. The universal principles of fairness and justice compel an urgent solution to this growing problem.

References

1. Geller, Lisa N. et al, Individual, Family, and Societal Dimensions of Genetic Discrimination: A Case Study Analysis, *Science and Engineering Ethics*, Vol. 2, 71-88 (1996).

2. Lapham, E. Virginia et at, Genetic Discrimination: Perspectives of Consumers, *Science*, Vol. 274, 621-24 (October 25, 1996).

3. Harris Poll, 1995 #34.

4. Kolata, Gina, Advent of Testing for Breast Cancer Genes Leads to Fears of Disclosure and Discrimination, *New York Times*, C1 (Feb 4, 1997).

5. Cowley, Geoffrey, Flunk the Test and Lose Your Insurance, *Newsweek*, 48-50 (Dec 23, 1996).

6. Hudson, Kathy et al, Genetic Discrimination and Health Insurance: An Urgent Need for Reform, *Science*, Vol. 270, 391-93 (October 20, 1995).

7. Rothenberg, Karen H., Genetic Information and Health Insurance: State Legislative Approaches, *Journal of Law, Medicine and Ethics*, Vol. 23:4, 312-19 (Winter 1995).

8. Barbara Fuller, J.D., National Action Plan on Breast Cancer, unpublished data.

Part Four

The Impact of Chronic Diseases

Chapter 23

Asthma

Overview

Asthma is a growing concern in this country, particularly in inner-city African American and Latino populations. Asthma is a chronic lung disease characterized by episodes of airflow obstruction. Symptoms of an asthma attack include coughing, wheezing, shortness of breath, and chest tightness. Asthma occurs in people who are predisposed to develop asthma because of genetic and environmental factors that determine susceptibility. A variety of "triggers" may initiate or worsen an asthma attack, including viral respiratory infections, exercise, and exposure to allergens or to airway irritants such as tobacco smoke and certain environmental pollutants.

Once asthma sufferers learn what conditions prompt their attacks, they can take steps to control their environment and avoid these triggers. However, medical treatment with anti-inflammatory agents (especially inhaled steroids) and bronchodilators is usually necessary to prevent and control attacks. With optimal management, control of asthma is usually an attainable goal.

"Asthma: A Concern for Minority Populations," National Institute of Allergy and Infectious Diseases (NIAID), August 1996; and "Asthma Genes Linked to Regions Unique to Different Racial and Ethnic Groups, NHLBI Study Shows," National Heart, Lung, and Blood Institute (NHLBI), NIH Press Release, Monday, March 31, 1997.

The Impact of Asthma

Asthma affects nearly 15 million Americans, more than 5 percent of the U.S. population. In 1991, asthma claimed approximately 5,000 lives. After a decade of steady decline in the 1970s, the prevalence of asthma, hospitalizations for asthma, and mortality due to asthma each increased during the 1980s.

In 1993, among children and young adults, African Americans were three to four times more likely than whites to be hospitalized for asthma, and were four to six times more likely to die from asthma. Poverty, substandard housing that results in increased exposure to certain indoor allergens, lack of education, inadequate access to health care, and the failure to take appropriate medications may all contribute to the risk of having a severe asthma attack or, more tragically, of dying from asthma.

The scope of the health care problem caused by asthma lies not only in the large number of Americans with the disease, but also in the limitations that asthma can impose on daily life. Asthma is the leading cause of school absenteeism due to chronic illness and is the second most important respiratory condition as a cause of home confinement for adults. Each year, asthma causes more than 18 million days of restricted activity, and millions of visits to physicians' offices and emergency rooms. A recent study found that children with asthma lose an extra 10 million school days each year; this problem is compounded by an estimated $1 billion in lost productivity for their working parents. In 1990, asthma-related health care cost our nation approximately $6.2 billion.

National Cooperative Inner-City Asthma Studies

In 1991, to address the concerns about asthma in the Inner-City, the National Institute of Allergy and Infectious Diseases (NIAID), a component of the National Institutes of Health, launched the first National Cooperative Inner-City Asthma Study. The primary aim of the study was to identify factors responsible for the rise in asthma among inner-city children and to test new strategies for asthma intervention. The eight centers funded by NIAID included:

- Albert Einstein School of Medicine, New York, NY;
- Case Western Reserve University, Cleveland, OH;
- Children's Memorial Hospital, Chicago, IL;
- Henry Ford Hospital, Detroit, MI;

- Howard University, Washington, DC;
- The Johns Hopkins University, Baltimore, MD;
- Mt. Sinai Medical Center, New York, NY;
- Washington University, St. Louis, MO.

Phase I of the first National Cooperative Inner-City Asthma Study (1991-1994) was designed to identify factors associated with severity of asthma in children ages 4-11. The second phase, completed in February 1996, studied the effectiveness of a comprehensive program to develop improved knowledge about asthma, to promote better asthma self-management skills, and to eliminate or decrease exposure to environmental factors associated with increased morbidity from asthma.

Phase I enrolled 1,528 children and their families. The study population was 73 percent African American, 20 percent Latino, and 7 percent Caucasian. Asthma risk factors found to be present in these urban families included: high levels of indoor allergens, especially cockroach allergen; high levels of tobacco smoking among family members and caretakers; and high indoor levels of nitrogen dioxide, a respiratory irritant produced by inadequately vented stoves and heating appliances. Many patients also reported difficulties in obtaining follow-up care for their asthma. Low socioeconomic status and African American race were independent risk factors for allergic sensitization to cockroach allergens. Thus, new approaches to reduce exposure to cockroach allergens may be very useful in controlling asthma.

More than 1,000 children were enrolled in Phase II of the study. Several sites used a Spanish language program in addition to the standard English language program. These sites employed bilingual counselors and modified the intervention to account for cultural issues unique to a Latino population. A key component of the Phase II intervention was the use of an "asthma care counselor" whose primary role was to teach and monitor acquisition of asthma self-management skills. While the results are still preliminary, children in the intervention limb of the study had striking reductions in major symptoms, in school absenteeism, in hospitalizations, and in emergency room visits for asthma.

Based on the success of the first National Cooperative Inner-City Asthma Study, NIAID and the National Institute of Environmental Health Sciences (NIEHS) recently initiated a second cooperative multicenter study. A major objective is to extend and disseminate the findings of the first National Cooperative Inner-City Asthma Study. This continuation includes new educational programs for patients and physicians, and focuses on community-specific interventions and on the relationship between asthma morbidity and the environment. The seven Centers funded in FY1996 were:

- Albert Einstein School of Medicine, New York, NY;
- Boston University, Boston, MA;
- Children's Memorial Hospital, Chicago, IL;
- Mt. Sinai Medical Center, New York, NY;
- University of Arizona Health Sciences Center, Tucson, AZ;
- University of Texas Southwestern Medical Center, Dallas, TX;
- Odessa Brown Children's Clinic, Seattle, WA.

NIAID Asthma Demonstration and Education Research Projects

NIAID also supports 15 extramural Asthma, Allergic, and Immunologic Diseases Cooperative Research Centers to conduct basic and clinical research on mechanisms of disease and ways to prevent asthma, allergic, and immunologic diseases. Each Center supports a Demonstration and Education Research Project to study educational, behavioral, and environmental interventions in underserved populations, especially ethnic minorities. All but one of these projects focus on asthma. Additional Demonstration and Education Research Projects have been established at university and clinic sites in Atlanta, Boston, Miami, Dallas, and San Diego. At several of these sites, researchers are developing interactive video games about asthma as well as other educational and computer-based clinical management tools for inner-city health care providers. These projects focus on different inner-city populations and explore interventions other than those of the National Cooperative Inner-City Asthma Study.

Studies on the Genetic Basis of Asthma

In collaboration with the National Heart, Lung, and Blood Institute (NHLBI), NIAID is funding a cooperative study at four centers (Johns Hopkins University, Baltimore, MD; University of Chicago, Chicago, IL; University of Maryland, Baltimore, MD; and University of Minnesota, Minneapolis, MN) to explore the genetic basis of asthma. This study is enrolling asthmatic patients and their families (many of whom are from ethnic minorities) in order to identify genes for asthma and for responsiveness to allergens. This study has identified several candidate genes for asthma, some of which may be more common in African American populations. In other studies, investigators supported by NIAID have identified a genetic change in interleukin-4 (IL-4), an immune-signaling molecule involved in asthma and allergic responses, that correlates with asthma severity. This change appears to be several-fold more common among African Americans than among whites. Studies of such genes should facilitate development of new and more potent and selective therapies, and may help to identify patient populations who might respond best to a particular drug.

Through basic and clinical research, as well as intervention programs, NIAID seeks to improve the diagnosis, treatment, and management of asthma, particularly in the minority populations disproportionately affected by this disease.

Asthma Genes Linked to Regions Unique to Different Racial and Ethnic Groups

In the first search of the entire human genome in African Americans, Caucasians, and Hispanics with asthma, researchers supported by the National Heart, Lung, and Blood Institute (NHLBI) have found evidence for linkage of asthma susceptibility genes to six previously-unreported chromosomal regions. Evidence for linkage was also detected in 5 regions previously reported to be linked to asthma-associated traits, such as bronchial hyperresponsivity and allergic sensitivity. Of the 11 chromosomal regions identified, all but one were unique to only one racial or ethnic group, suggesting that the relative importance of specific asthma susceptibility genes and the effects of environmental exposures may vary by race or ethnicity.

According to NHLBI Director Dr. Claude Lenfant, "This is an intriguing study. It not only brings us one step closer to identifying all the important genes that contribute to the development of asthma, but it also provides a possible explanation for the substantial differences in disease prevalence and severity that we have observed among different racial and ethnic groups in the U.S." "Of course," he added, "these findings must be replicated in additional families with asthma."

The investigators currently are analyzing the 11 chromosomal regions in a new set of families to try to replicate the findings. The prevalence of asthma is greater for blacks (6.1 percent) than for whites (5.0 percent), while in Hispanics, it ranges from a low of 2.7 percent among Mexican-American children living in the Southwest to 11.2 percent for Puerto Rican children living in New York City. Both hospitalization and death rates for blacks are nearly triple those of whites. In the study, investigators at the 4 CSGA [Collaborative Study on the Genetics of Asthma] centers analyzed data on 380 children and adults with asthma (117 African Americans, 215 Caucasians, and 48 Hispanics). Each of the 140 families involved in the current analysis had at least 2 siblings with established asthma.

The CSGA centers are the University of Chicago, the Johns Hopkins University, the University of Maryland, and the University of Minnesota. The gene mapping was performed by the NHLBI Mammalian Genotyping Service in Marshfield, WI.

Chapter 24

Cardiovascular Disease

Cardiovascular disease, primarily coronary heart disease and stroke, kills nearly as many Americans as all other diseases combined and is among the leading causes of disability in the United States. Cardiovascular disease is the leading cause of death for all racial and ethnic groups. The impact of premature morbidity from cardiovascular disease on the ability of affected individuals to function independently or to participate fully in everyday life is devastating in terms of personal loss, pain, suffering, and effects on families and loved ones. The annual national economic impact of cardiovascular disease is estimated at $259 billion as measured in health care expenditures, medications, and lost productivity due to disability and death.

The major modifiable risk factors for cardiovascular disease are high blood pressure, high blood cholesterol, cigarette smoking, excessive body weight, and physical inactivity. The greatest potential for reducing coronary heart disease morbidity, disability, and mortality appears to be in prevention, by addressing these risk factors.

This chapter contains text from: "Cardiovascular Disease: How to Reach the Goals," Race and Health, September 13, 1999; "Asian American and Pacific Islander Workshops Summary Report on Cardiovascular Health," National Heart, Lung, and Blood Institute, NIH Publication No. 00-3793, March 2000; "Facts about Heart Disease and Stroke among American Indians and Alaska Natives," CDC Press Release, Friday, June 2, 2000; and "The Health of Minority Women," Office of Women's Health, U.S. Department of Health and Human Services, May 2000.

- Some people with high blood pressure have three to four times the risk of developing coronary heart disease and may have as much as seven times the risk of a stroke as do those with normal blood pressure. Clinical trials show that blood pressure reduction significantly reduces stroke mortality and can help to reduce deaths from coronary heart disease.
- Each 1 percent reduction in serum cholesterol level has been associated with a greater than 1 percent reduction in risk of coronary heart disease death.

Table 24.1. Stroke Death Rates Per 100,000

Ethnic/racial group	1990	1997
White	25.2	24.0
Black	48.4	42.5
Asian/Pacific Islander	25.0	24.4
American Indian/Alaska Native	19.3	19.9
Hispanic	21.6	19.4

Source: CDC, NCHG, National Vital Statistics System.

Table 24.2. Coronary Heart Disease Death Rates Per 100,000

Ethnic/racial group	1990	1997
White	111.4	97.7
Black	151.3	138.2
Asian/Pacific Islander	63.1	55.2
American Indian/Alaska Native	81.2	75.8
Hispanic	78.1	70.7

Source: CDC, NCHG, National Vital Statistics System.

- Prospective epidemiologic studies have documented a rapid and substantial reduction in coronary heart disease rates following smoking cessation. Reducing the proportion of youth who start to smoke and encouraging smoking cessation among current smokers are important preventive measures for reducing coronary heart disease incidence and mortality.
- A reduction in the proportion of Americans who are overweight and physically inactive can help lower coronary heart disease incidence and mortality. Risks of nonfatal myocardial infarction and coronary heart disease death increase with increasing levels of body mass index (BMI) (weight in kg divided by height in meter^2) and with weight gain. Risks are lowest in men and women with BMI's of 22 or less and increase with modest elevations of BMI. Persons who are physically active have one-half the risk of both coronary heart disease incidence and mortality compared to persons who are sedentary.

Major disparities exist among population groups, with a disproportionate burden of death and disability from cardiovascular disease in minority and low-income populations. The age-adjusted death rate for coronary heart disease for the total population declined by 20 percent from 1987 to 1995; for blacks, the overall decrease was only 13 percent. Compared with rates for whites, coronary heart disease mortality was 40 percent lower for Asian Americans but 40 percent higher for blacks in 1995. Stroke is the only leading cause of death for which mortality is higher for Asian American males than for white males.

Disparities also exist in the prevalence of risk factors for cardiovascular disease. Racial and ethnic minorities have higher rates of hypertension, tend to develop hypertension at an earlier age, and are less likely to undergo treatment to control their high blood pressure. For example, from 1988 to 1994, 35 percent of black males ages 20 to 74 had hypertension compared with 25 percent of all men. When age differences are taken into account, Mexican American men and women also have elevated blood pressure rates. Among adult women, the age-adjusted prevalence of overweight continues to be higher for black women (53 percent) and Mexican American women (52 percent) than for white women (34 percent). Furthermore, the rates for regular screening for cholesterol show disparities for certain racial and ethnic minorities—only 50 percent of American Indians/Alaska Natives, 44 percent of Asian Americans, and 38 percent of Mexican-Americans have had their cholesterol checked within the past 2 years. Although age-adjusted death rates for cardiovascular disease among other minority groups are lower than the national average, there are subgroups within these populations that have high mortality rates from heart disease and stroke.

Asian American and Pacific Islander Cardiovascular Health

Native Hawaiian Cardiovascular Health Profile

Among Pacific Islanders, Hawaiians comprise 57.8 percent of the population. In the State of Hawaii, Native Hawaiians comprise 19 percent of the total state population. Hawaiians represent about 211,000 persons of the overall Asian and Pacific Islander population, and Native Hawaiian inclusion in the groups masks and conceals the alarming health disparities that plague the Native Hawaiian community. Diseases of the circulatory system are the leading cause of death among Native Hawaiians. Among the conditions relating to circulatory diseases, heart disease accounts for 80 percent of deaths due to circulatory disease followed by cerebrovascular disease at 14 percent.

The burden of heart disease is disproportionate among Native Hawaiians. The death rate for Hawaiians for heart disease is 66 percent higher than for the total state population. Among Native Hawaiians, the mortality rates for heart disease for full-Hawaiians are the highest—271 percent higher than part-Hawaiians and 382 percent than non-Hawaiians. The prevalence of risk factors is also higher among Native Hawaiians than the state population.

Asian American and Pacific Islander Population Profile

AAPIs are the fastest growing ethnic/racial group nationwide. On July 1, 1998, AAPIs represented approximately 3.9 percent or 10.4 million of the U.S. population and its associated Pacific Island Jurisdictions as compared to only 0.4 percent of the Nation's population in 1960. From 1980 to 1990, the U.S. AAPI population increased over 95 percent as compared to the 51.5 percent increase in the Hispanic population, 27.7 percent in the Native American population, 13.2 percent increase in the African American population and 4.2 percent increase in the non-Hispanic white population in the same time period. Between July 1, 1990 and 1998, AAPIs again had a higher rate of population growth than any other race in the Nation—37 percent. The United States Census Bureau projects that the growth of the AAPI population will reach 34.4 million by the year 2050, representing almost 10 percent of all Americans. Immigration to the United States and resettlement of refugees from Southeast Asia in the mid-1970's account for much of the population growth (86 percent). However, several Asian groups (such as the Chinese and Japanese) have been in the United States for generations, relatively few Pacific Islanders are foreign born, and Native Hawaiians are the indigenous people of the State of Hawaii who settled there more than 2,000 years ago (U.S. Census Bureau, 1995).

The AAPI population is extremely heterogeneous with a high proportion of immigrants and refugees. The Asian and Pacific Islander single racial classification consists of approximately 30 Asian and 25 Pacific Island nations with distinct languages, culture, history of immigration, and community norms, relative to health and well-being. Some of the ethnic subgroups included in the category Pacific Islander include: Chamorro (Guam), Chuukese, Fijian, Hawaiian, Kosraean (Federated States of Micronesia), Mariana Islanders (Commonwealth of Northern Mariana Islands), Melanesian, Palauan (Republic of Palau), Papese, Pohnpeian, Samoan (American and Western Samoa), and Tongan. Some of the ethnic subgroups included in the category Asian include: Afghani, Asian Indian, Bangladeshi, Burmese, Cambodian, Chinese, Filipino, Hmong, Indonesian, Iwo-Jiman, Japanese, Korean, Laotian, Malaysian, Mien, Nepali, Okinawin, Pakistani, Sikkim, Sri Lankan, Thai, and Vietnamese.

Nearly 40 percent of the Nation's AAPI population lives in California, followed by New York (9.3 percent), Hawaii (8.3 percent), Texas (4.7 percent), New Jersey (3.9 percent), Illinois (3.8 percent), and Washington (3.0 percent). According to the March 1994 Current Population Survey, AAPIs were more likely than non-Hispanic whites to reside in metropolitan areas (95 percent vs. 75 percent). Although over 50 percent of all AAPIs live in the Western United States, the AAPI population has increased significantly in other regions: by 139 percent in the South and Northeast and by 97 percent in the Midwest (Takeuchi and Young, 1994).

These distinct ethnic subgroups not only reflect cultural and linguistic differences but also socioeconomic, educational, and generational differences that influence the decision-making skills and social support necessary for sustained reduction of cardiovascular-associated diseases. Historically AAPIs have been labeled as the "healthy minority" in part, as a result of grouping all AAPI subgroups into one homogenous category. Contrary to this stereotype, AAPIs show bipolar patterns in socioeconomic and health status (Lin-Fu, 1988).

Asian American and Pacific Islander Cardiovascular Health Status: What Does the Data Tell Us?

CVD is the leading cause of death and disability for Americans, accounting for approximately 960,000 deaths in 1995 alone. According to the U.S. DHHS, CVD kills nearly as many Americans as all other diseases combined. Estimated costs associated with CVD, both direct medical costs and indirect costs (lost productivity from morbidity and early mortality), are nearly $260 billion annually (NHLBI, 1997).

Disparities in cardiovascular health still persist among AAPIs as well as with other minority groups. For the majority of AAPI populations, CVD continues to be the leading cause of death. For example, in the State of Hawaii, Native Hawaiian mortality due to heart disease is 66 percent higher than the total state average (Johnson et al., 1996). Largely an immigrant population, AAPIs are particularly disadvantaged in benefiting from scientific and medical advancements in cardiovascular research. Despite increased awareness and a desire to seek CVD prevention and intervention services, the majority of AAPIs are precluded from doing so because of limitations to health services access including cultural, linguistic, and economic barriers.

Based on the 1998 American Heart Association's Statistical Update, CVD as a percent of total deaths for male AAPIs (35.4 percent) is second to that of white males (39.9 percent). For female AAPIs, the CVD mortality percentage ranked third (36.1 percent) following African American females (41.6 percent) and white females (44.9 percent).

Research reveals high rates of:

- Hypertension in Filipinos, Japanese, and Southeast Asians;
- Obesity and diabetes among Pacific Islanders;
- Stroke among South Asians; and
- Smoking among Korean and Southeast Asian men.

Cardiovascular Disease (CVD) Mortality

Heart disease and cancer are either the leading or second leading cause of death for each of the AAPI subgroups (Table 24.3). Stroke is the third leading cause of death for Chinese, Japanese, Hawaiians, and Filipinos. For the period of 1990-1995, stroke was the second leading cause of death for Filipino females in San Francisco, California (SF DHHS, 1998). For Asian Indians, Hawaiians, Guamanians, Filipinos, Samoans, Japanese, Chinese, and Koreans heart disease claimed over 22 percent of all deaths (National Center for Health Statistics, 1994). Alarming to note is that for both Hawaiians and Samoan groups, heart disease remains the leading cause of death beginning at the age of 25 and continues throughout their lifetime. In the State of Hawaii, Native Hawaiian mortality due to heart disease is significantly higher than the total state, 66 percent above the state average (Johnson et al., 1996). Similar to all racial groups, heart disease is the leading cause of death in the age group 65 years and older.

However, it is important to caution the validity of available mortality data. While all-cause death rates are reported to be lowest among AAPIs (350.5 per 100,000) from the National Center for Health Statistics (NCHS, 1991), ethnic-specific samples showed tremendous variation among AAPI subgroups (Hoyert and Kung, 1997). Moreover, the finding of only 82 percent concordance rate between race on death certificates and a population data source for the AAPI populations (Sorlie et a1.,1992) led some authors to conclude that the net effect of misclassification is an underestimation of deaths and death rates for AAPI populations (Yu and Liu, 1992; Uehara et al., 1994).

In American Samoa, CVD and diabetes-related mortality were determined from death records as part of the Pennsylvania University's Samoan Migration Project. Age-adjusted mortality rates of CVD and diabetes-related mortality in the period 1971-74 were reported higher than the period 1963-66. Although the presence of other CVD risk factors (e.g. tobacco, cholesterol) were not considered, CVD mortality was associated with baseline blood pressure and obesity. Higher mortality rates were also found in the modernized areas compared to traditional areas. The CVD death rate was also found to be associated with the physical activity level. Among sedentary men, the CVD death rate was reported to be 43 percent compared to 29 percent for those in more active occupation. In the San Francisco Samoan Study, higher incidences of premature (<50 years) CVD mortality were reported in comparison with Samoans in Hawaii and Samoa. Higher CVD mortality rates for immigrant Samoans were associated with excessive weight gain, elevated blood pressure, and high plasma blood glucose levels among the San Francisco Samoans (data collection period: 1966-78). Several papers from the Honolulu Heart Program reported CVD mortality among Japanese men. One paper compared coronary heart disease (CHD) incidence and mortality rates of the study population to the overall state rates. The state records showed a decline in CHD mortality between 1968 and 1978, while there was no evidence of a similar decline in the men in the Honolulu Heart Program. The relationship between glucose intolerance, diabetes, and sudden death was explored in another study. Almost 50 percent of these deaths were due to heart disease, stroke, or aneurysm. Men who were glucose intolerant or diabetic were found to be at significantly higher risk for sudden death.

Table 24.3. Heart Disease as Cause of Death, Percentage of All Deaths

Ethnic/racial group	Percentage
Asian Indian*	34.6
Hawaiian*	33.9
Guamanian*	33.7
Filipino*	31.7
Samoan*	30.4
Japanese*	29.4
Chinese	27.1
Korean	21.8
Vietnamese	19.5

*Heart disease is the leading cause of death.
Source: National Vital Statistics System, CDC, NCHS, 1994.

Cardiovascular Disease (CVD) Morbidity

There is a paucity of data on CVD morbidity patterns in AAPI and its subgroups. According to the 1993 California hospital discharge survey, psychoses, heart failure, and stroke were the three most common hospital discharge diagnoses unrelated to childbirth for AAPIs. Asian Indians have been reported to have one of the highest rates of coronary artery disease (CAD) of any ethnic group studied. This high risk has been reported for Asian Indians living in the United States and in other countries. In a longitudinal study among health plan members in California, the risk of hospitalization for CAD among Asian Indians was more than three times (relative risk of 3.7) that for whites in analyses that controlled for covariates including age, body mass index, total serum cholesterol, and blood glucose among others. The risk was more than six times greater for Asian Indians compared to Chinese in the same study (Klatsky, 1994).

Cardiovascular Disease (CVD) Risk Factors by AAPI Subgroup

Five risk factors are designated established because substantial amounts of data from many disciplines have demonstrated their significant role in the development of CVD. The following summary highlights these risk factors by AAPI ethnic subgroup from the articles reviewed, high blood cholesterol, high blood pressure or hypertension, diabetes, physical inactivity/nutrition, and tobacco use/exposure.

1. High Blood Cholesterol

According to the National Cholesterol Education Program (NCEP), average cholesterol levels have decreased from 220 mg/dL in 1961-1962 to 203 mg/dL (NHANES 111). For adults a normal blood cholesterol is 200 mg/dL; borderline is 200-239 mg/dL; and 240 mg/dL or above is considered high. Based on the 1998 Heart and Stroke Statistical Update, an estimated 96,800,000 American adults (51 percent) have blood cholesterol levels of 200 mg/dL or higher. According to the same 1998 update, a study of high blood cholesterol was examined for AAPIs in the aggregate which reported 27.4 percent of AAPI men and 25.8 percent of AAPI women age 18 and older have high blood cholesterol.

Chinese: Among 194 self-referred clinic patients at the New York City Chinatown Health Center self-reported rates for CVD were: 23 percent hypertension, 5 percent CHD, 4 percent stroke or peripheral vascular disease, and 4 percent diabetes (Pinnelas et al., 1992). Foreign-born Asians (presumed to be primarily Chinese based on place of birth) averaging 15 years in the United States had the same distribution of desirable (40 percent), borderline-high (37 percent), and high levels of blood cholesterol (23 percent) as the NHANESII study group. Although no difference in cholesterol levels for women and men were found before age 45, higher levels of cholesterol in women after age 45 were seen compared to the men in the study.

Southeast Asian: One hundred and fifty-four Southeast Asian refugees in a primary care clinic in Seattle, Washington were screened according to the NCEP's guidelines (Dodson et al., 1995). A high prevalence of smoking (27 percent) was reported. Hypertension was the most common CVD risk factor (26 percent). Fourteen percent of the Southeast Asian subjects required a therapeutic intervention for hypercholesterolemia. The authors conclude that CVD risk factors are common in Southeast Asian refugees among primary care clinic patients. In a 1991 study of a behavioral risk factor survey of Vietnamese in California, the estimated prevalence of hypercholesterolemia for men was 38 percent and for women 32 percent (Centers for Disease Control and Prevention, 1992).

Blood cholesterol screening is beneficial in personalizing the importance of keeping blood cholesterol levels normal. To date, overall AAPI blood cholesterol measurement is poor. Based on Centers for Disease Control and Prevention (CDC) reports, in 1992, a significant proportion of Vietnamese men (56 percent) and women (55 percent) had never checked their cholesterol level compared with 41 percent of men and 35 percent of women in the mainstream.

2. High Blood Pressure

High blood pressure (hypertension) is defined as a systolic blood pressure equal to or more than 140 mm Hg or the diastolic blood pressure equal to or more than 90 mm Hg or on antihypertensive medication. Hypertension is easily detected and usually controllable. As one of the pioneers of cardiovascular epidemiology, R. Stamler has stated, "Rise of blood pressure with age, which can move people from 'normal' to 'high' levels of blood pressure, is not an inevitable human condition, and prevention of that rise could eliminate epidemic hypertension, which is a major disease in industrialized countries as well as in many developing countries." It should be noted that high blood pressure is the leading cause of stroke, kidney disease, and cardiac disease. Based on decades of research, five major exposures have influenced the onset of high blood pressure in our society: high salt intake, low potassium intake, high ratio of dietary sodium to potassium, overweight, and high alcohol intake (Marmot et al., 1992). One in four adults has high blood pressure (NHLBI, 1996). Compared to white women and men, respectively, age-adjusted prevalence of hypertension for AAPI women is 8.35 percent versus 10.96 percent and for AAPI men 9.67 percent versus 10.32 percent. The majority of hypertension studies among AAPIs have been derived from studies conducted in Hawaii, California, and New York.

Chinese: In the California Hypertension Survey of 1979 (Stavig et al., 1984, 1988), Chinese had relatively low prevalence rates of hypertension. However, among those who were hypertensive, only 46 percent compared to 56 percent overall, were aware that they had high blood pressure. The data showed that Chinese had a lack of understanding about the consequences and nature of hypertension; only half responded correctly that high blood pressure leads to "serious" illnesses (79 percent overall), and only 15 percent knew that the symptoms of high blood pressure are "never felt" (31 percent overall). In another study of cardiovascular risk factors among Chinese, 346 elderly (age 60 and above) Chinese immigrants in Boston were reported to have a high prevalence rate of hypertension, 29.7 percent for men and 33.5 percent for women (Choi, 1990).

Filipino: Relatively high rates of hypertension prevalence have been reported for Filipino Americans. In the California Hypertension Survey of 1979 (Stavig et al., 1984, 1988), overall prevalence of hypertension was highest for blacks (33.8 percent), followed by Filipinos (26.6 percent). Higher rates of uncontrolled hypertension for Filipinos were consistent by gender and age. Among men ages 18-49, Filipinos had the highest rate (29.5 percent), followed by other AAPIs (28.5 percent), and blacks (25.4 percent); for men over age 50, the rate for Filipinos (50.8 percent) was comparable to that for blacks (52.9 percent), and the rates for Filipinos, Chinese (45.0 percent), and other AAPIs (45.2 percent) were all higher than the rate for whites (38.5 percent). Among women ages 18-49, rates for Chinese (6.4 percent) and Filipinos (6.5 percent) were slightly higher than that for whites (4.8 percent); for women over age 50, the rate for Filipinos (61.3 percent) was 1.7 times the rate for whites and 1.4 times the rate for blacks. Filipinos had significantly higher adjusted mean systolic and diastolic blood pressure compared to other Asian ethnic groups in a study among health plan members in Northern California. A higher rate for hypertension in Filipinos compared to Chinese remained in these analyses that controlled for age, relative body weight, marital status, education, and alcohol intake.

The California Hypertension Survey addressed awareness and rate of control of hypertension. The rate of uncontrolled hypertension for Filipinos was almost as high as the well-documented high rate for blacks. Although Filipinos who were hypertensive were more likely to be aware and to be treated compared to other AAPI groups, their control rate was poor (8 percent). All AAPI groups (Chinese, Japanese, Filipino, other AAPIs) had extremely low control rates (4 percent for other AAPIs, 13 percent for Chinese). Among Filipinos taking antihypertensive medicine, only 16 percent were controlled compared to 40 percent of the population overall.

Japanese: Data from the Honolulu Heart Program were combined with other data from Japan and the San Francisco Bay area for a study called "Ni-Hon-San" with sub-samples of Japanese men living in three regions. The article reviewed for this summary was a study of hypertension in the three sub-samples. The authors reported that the proportion of obese men was highest in California, lowest in Japan. The authors found that age, obesity, alcohol intake, and a parental history of hypertension were the most consistent correlates of blood pressure in Japanese men. The level of acculturation as measured by five items (reads in Japanese, educated in Japan, ethnicity of friends, frequency of Japanese celebration) was not associated with hypertension. According to NHLBI's Honolulu Heart Study (Phase 1: 1991-93), 73 percent of Japanese American men ages 71-93 had high blood pressure.

Another study reported on blood pressure among second- and third-generation Japanese Americans (men and women ages 34-75) living in King County, Washington. Overall, 41.5 percent of men and 33.8 percent of women were hypertensive. Among participants, 78 percent of men and 70 percent of women were aware of their hypertension. Among those who were hypertensive, 62 percent of men and 50 percent of women were taking antihypertensive medication, and of those treated, 44 percent of men and 39 percent of women had their hypertension controlled. In the California Hypertension Survey of 1979, prevalence of hypertension among Japanese was 14.1 percent (Stavig et al., 1984, 1988). Among the hypertensive, 57 percent were aware, 27 percent were being treated with antihypertensive medication, and 30 percent were treated and controlled. The composition of the Japanese by generation included in the survey is not known.

Pacific Islander: In the comparison study between San Francisco Samoans with populations in Western Samoa and American Samoa, weight in the San Francisco Samoan population was reported to be significantly greater in either the native population in Samoa or the migrant population in Hawaii (Pawson et al., 1982). Fifty-five percent of the men and 46 percent of the women exceeded the 95th percentile for weight. Mean blood pressure was higher among migrant men. Samoan men living in California exhibited higher overall rates of hypertension than those in Hawaii. Eighteen percent of the men and 9 percent of the women with a fasting blood sample were found to have abnormal plasma glucose levels. The exposure to modernization with exposure to a "Western" diet and lifestyle were suggested to be the cause for increased rates of hypertension and abnormal blood glucose among Samoans living in San Francisco. Similarly, a community-based study describing the dietary intake of American and Western Samoans reported substantial differences in nutrient intakes (Galanis et al., 1999). Intakes of cholesterol and sodium were higher among American Samoans regardless of age, gender, education, occupation, and material lifestyle. This study illustrates that the food choices of certain ethnic groups may be profoundly affected by the process of modernization within a country and by migration to a more economically developed locale.

Native Hawaiian: The data available from the population-based Moloka'i Heart Survey indicate that Native Hawaiians may be at higher risk of premature CHD and stroke because of obesity, hypertension and hypercholesterolemia, smoking, and diabetes mellitus (Curb et al., 1996). The prevalence of hypertension was reported to be 6 percent of men and 8 percent of women ages 20-24, 37 percent of men and 41 percent of women ages 45-54. At ages 55-59, the prevalence of hypertension for men was 31 percent and for women, 33 percent. Although they appear to be aware of hypertension (80 percent of men and 86 percent of women), control is poor (20 percent of men and 39.3 percent of women).

Southeast Asian: The ethnic groups represented in the Southeast Asian subgroup are primarily Cambodian, Hmong, Laotian, and Vietnamese. Based on the limited data concerning the levels of knowledge about CVD and its risk factors, it appears that newly arrived immigrants such as the Southeast Asian subgroups are unaware of lifestyle changes that can prevent or control many of the risk factors for CVD. For example, Southeast Asians were found to have lower treatment rates and knowledge levels concerning hypertension compared with hypertensive subjects of other race groups (Stavig et al. 1984, 1988). While 17 percent of Southeast Asian refugees in one sample were found to be hypertensive, only 2 percent were on hypertensive medication. In particular, Cambodians and Vietnamese were reported to have the lowest hypertension awareness rates, drug treatment levels, and control rates among all ethnic subgroups in California (Stavig et al., 1984). Based on a heart health study conducted in Ohio, the study revealed that Cambodian, Laotian, and Vietnamese immigrants had very poor knowledge of cardiovascular health: 94 percent had no knowledge of CVD and 85 percent had no knowledge of prevention (Chen et al., 1991).

In another study comparing CVD risk factors of newly arrived non-refugee Hmong in Fresno, California to Hmong who lived in Thailand, the consequences of migration and its impact on nutrition were examined. The researchers found that hypertension was one of the most commonly defined risk factors among the Hmong immigrants. The Hmong immigrants had a significant increase in both fat and salt compared to their comparison group in Thailand (Kurstadter et al., 1997).

3. Diabetes

High blood sugar level is the metabolic disorder named diabetes mellitus. In 1995, diabetes killed 59,254 Americans. The greatest burden of deaths was among females (55.9 percent of total deaths from diabetes). For males, a significant portion of deaths was due to diabetes, 44.1 percent. Based on the NCHS (1986-1990), AAPIs showed a prevalence of diabetes of 3.4 percent for AAPI men and 2.4 percent for AAPI women. In comparison to whites, the diabetes prevalence in AAPI men was higher than white men (2.5 percent) and equal to white women (2.4 percent).

Japanese: Two articles from the Seattle Japanese Diabetes Study (Filjimoto et al., 1996) were reviewed. In 1983, using a random sampling approach to achieve a representative sample of the Japanese male population, 229 second-generation Japanese American (Nisei) men living in King County Washington, were recruited for this study. Previous literature, not reviewed here, has consistently reported a higher prevalence of diabetes and glucose intolerance among Japanese Americans than among the white population in the United States and the native population of Japan. In the Seattle area study, the authors found that one-third had diabetes, and over 20 percent had impaired glucose tolerance. Prior to the study, only 13 percent reported a previous diagnosis of diabetes, suggesting a very high proportion of undiagnosed diabetes. A second study investigated the role of diet in this sample. The authors found that the Nisei men did not have the traditional low-protein, low-fat, high-complex-carbohydrate diet that their parents had in Japan, but rather diets more resembling other U.S. men, relatively high in fat and protein.

Among elderly Japanese men ages 71-93 in the NHLBI study (1991-93), 17 percent of the Japanese American men had diabetes. Of the population studied, 19 percent had unrecognized diabetes, and 32 percent had impaired glucose tolerance.

Native Hawaiian: Pacific Islanders and Hawaiians have high incidence of diabetes. One study on the Island of Moloka'i found that the prevalence of diabetes had significantly increased above 40 years of age. The increase in diabetes prevalence for the 40-49 age band and the 50-59 age band were 15 percent and 20 percent respectively (Aluli, 1991). Other Hawaii state data suggest that Native Hawaiians are twice as likely to be diagnosed with diabetes than whites (Hawaii Diabetes Control Program).

4. Physical Inactivity / Nutrition

Three risk behaviors in particular—lack of physical activity, poor nutrition, and tobacco use/exposure—are major contributors to both CVD and cancer. Based on the 1996 Surgeon General's Report on Physical Activity and Health, physical activity reduces the risk of premature death in general, CHD, hypertension, colon cancer, and diabetes in particular. The CDC 1994 Behavioral Risk Factor Surveillance Survey (BRFSS) reported that 60 percent or more of adults did not achieve the recommended amount of physical activity, and in half of the Nation 73 percent or more of adults had poor physical activity. In the United States, approximately 250,000 deaths (12 percent of total deaths) annually are attributed to a lack of regular physical activity (American Heart Association, 1998).

Japanese: The Honolulu Heart Program is the most comprehensive study of an AAPI group and CVD. The study began in 1965, when 8,006 men 45-68 years old of Japanese ancestry living in Oahu were recruited and given a baseline examination. For this review, articles that dealt with the CVD risk factors of interest or CVD morbidity or mortality were selected. Two articles investigated physical activity. Investigators reported that physical activity affected risk for CHD and that the effect is mediated through the effect of physical activity on hypertension, body mass index, cholesterol, and diabetes. In a subsequent report, the investigators found that physical activity was inversely and independently associated with cumulative incidence of diabetes. The association was graded and remained after taking into account age, obesity, body fat distribution, systolic blood pressure, triglycerides, glucose, hematocrit, and parental history of diabetes.

Pacific Islander: In a prospective study examining the associations between CVD risk factors (age, blood pressure, body weight, and fatness) and 6-year mortality, data on age, body weight, blood pressure, and skin folds were collected (Crews, 1988). High prevalence of obesity was reported in men (45.7 percent) and in women (66.1 percent). Although neither the body weight nor body mass index were found to be related to total or CVD mortality in men and women; elevated blood pressure was associated with increased total and CVD mortality in both sexes.

A community-based study describing the dietary intake of American Western Samoans reported that intakes of cholesterol and sodium were higher among American Samoans regardless of age, gender, education, occupation, and material lifestyle. This study illustrates that food choices of certain ethnic groups may be profoundly affected by the process of modernization within a country and by migration to a more economically developed locale (Galanis et al., 1999).

Korean: Korean Americans are less likely to exercise at least once in the past month than all Californians (69 percent vs. 79 percent). Acculturation is a significant factor which attributes to the likelihood of being physically active. Korean Americans born in the United States or those who immigrated before 1975 are more likely (80 percent) to have exercised in the past month than those who immigrated from 1975 to 1984 (66 percent) or those who immigrated from 1985 to 1994 (65 percent) (Wismer, 1994).

Chinese: In a study comparing dietary habits, physical activity, and body size among Chinese in North America (NA) and China (C), significant differences in the percentage of calories from protein (NA 18 percent, C 9 percent), fat (NA 35 percent, C 22 percent), and carbohydrates (NA 48 percent, C 65 percent) were reported (Lee et al., 1994). Although the majority of NA Chinese (90 percent) were born in Asia, the comparison group in China was found to have leaner body mass index and were more physically active than their counterparts in North America. The authors concluded that continuous assimilation into a Western lifestyle with changes in diet, physical activity, and body size explained observed differences in chronic disease rates between the two populations. As emphasized in the Healthy People 2000 work groups recommendations, it is important to understand the cultural context and health needs of different immigrant populations in order to effectively change behavior in health and diet.

Southeast Asian: A study assessed food preferences and food consumption patterns among 60 recently settled Southeast Asian refugee families in the United States with the use of a structured interview method. Although rice remains the staple food in their diet, high status foods, such as steak and soft drinks were highly preferred food items (Story and Harris, 1989). Within 4 years of arrival, 92 percent reported change in diet and 63 percent reported gaining weight on the average of 10 pounds. The study also found that 30 percent of teenagers in the families had major responsibility for meal preparation and 25 percent of the teenagers did most of the food shopping, pointing to the need for inclusion of this group in nutrition education programs.

South Asian: The published studies reviewed here were of Asian Indian Americans only. The South Asian American category includes immigrants and descendants of India, Pakistan, Sri Lanka, and Bangladesh.

Evidence suggests that South Asians have increased risk of heart disease within their country of origin and after migration (Enas et al., 1992). Much of the research on CVD in this ethnic group has been done in samples within the country of origin, primarily India, and in migrant groups to the United Kingdom.

The studies in the U.S. samples draw on the findings from other regions and begin with the premise that the conventional risk factors for heart disease in white and other populations are not the strongest correlates or predictors in Asian Indian populations. That is, high prevalence of heart disease has not been explained by elevated cholesterol levels, hypertension, smoking, or obesity. One study compared Asian Indian immigrants to whites and found that Asian Indians had higher prevalence of myocardial infarction in men only, higher prevalence of non-insulin-dependent diabetes, lower prevalence of cigarette smoking, lower prevalence of obesity, lower prevalence of hypertension in men only, lower HDL cholesterol, and lower hypertrigliceridemia. Two other studies of U.S. Asian Indians focused on the possibility of a greater role for other prominent risk variables, such as lipoprotein(a) levels, triglyceride levels, and insulin resistance.

5. Tobacco Use / Exposure

Cigarette smoking is the leading preventable cause of death and disability in the United States, where each year an estimated 420,000 smokers die from cigarette smoking and 50,000 nonsmokers die from exposure to environmental tobacco smoke. Patterns of tobacco use and exposure differ among and within AAPIs. Because of the heterogeneity of AAPIs including lifestyles, cultural beliefs and practices, genetic backgrounds, and environmental exposures, no single factor is the determinant of tobacco use or exposure. By comparison, AAPIs show a lower adult smoking prevalence rate than other race groups: AAPIs (15.3 percent); Hispanic/ Latinos (18.9 percent); whites (25.9 percent), African Americans (26.5 percent); and American Indians and Alaskan Natives (39.2 percent) (CDC, 1998). Based on the NHIS from 1978 to 1995, the AAPI overall prevalence of smoking decreased, however, patterns of decline differed between men and women. Throughout the period of the NHIS, the prevalence of smoking among men remained more than twice that among women; and during the years 1994-95, men were 4.3 times more likely than women to report current smoking. Research conducted by Hammond and Horn (1958) have shown that smokers had a 70 percent greater risk of mortality from CHD than nonsmokers. Because AAPIs are extremely heterogeneous, rigorous surveillance and prevention research is needed to unveil the specific factors that influence tobacco use. To date, only two community-based CVD intervention studies have been reported in AAPI communities even though high rates of C VD morbidity, mortality, and increased prevalence of CVD risk factors among AAPIs have been documented in the past three decades (Jenkins et al., 1995; Chen et al., 1991).

Chinese: In comparison, immigrant AAPIs who are limited English proficient have shown to be more likely smokers than their American-born counterparts. A study in Oakland Chinatown found that 40 percent of Chinese men did not know that smoking could cause heart disease (Chen et al., 1991).

Vietnamese: In a study conducted among Vietnamese in California, it was found that Vietnamese men had a smoking prevalence rate ranging from 35-56 percent, significantly higher than the national average for men (Jenkins et al., 1995).

Southeast Asian: Although rates for smoking in the United States are reported to be lowest among AAPIs (18.2 percent), ethnic-specific samples show that 92 percent of Laotians, 71 percent of Cambodians, and 65 percent of Vietnamese smoke (CDC, 1998).

Korean: There was only one study conducted among Korean Americans regarding heart disease risks and outcomes. However, data relevant to heart disease risks are available from the 1994 Korean American Community Health Survey (KACHS) (Wismer, 1994). A portion of the questions were adapted from the 1993 California Behavioral Risk Factor Survey (BRFS) and the 1992 NHIS Cancer Control Supplement. Some questions were modified to be culturally sensitive. The KACHS collected heart disease-related data including current tobacco use (39 percent of men, 6 percent of women), physical inactivity (31 percent), as well findings on whether the respondents had ever been told by a doctor or nurse that they had high blood pressure (12 percent), high cholesterol (12 percent), or diabetes (4 percent). A measurement of prevalence of smoking is the number of cigarettes smoked daily. In a study conducted in Alameda County in California, the percentage of Korean men who have ever smoked 100 cigarettes was significantly higher compared to the overall statewide prevalence rate for men only (70 percent vs. 50 percent). Regarding current smokers, Korean men have a significantly higher rate of smokers than the state rate (39 percent vs. 19 percent). Furthermore, Koreans show significantly higher prevalence of current smokers than the Healthy People 2000 Objective (21 percent vs. 15 percent). The level of spoken English has significant impact on the awareness of smoking being a risk factor to heart disease. Eighty-seven percent of Korean Americans who speak English fluently know that smoking is related to heart disease, compared to only 76 percent of those who speak little or no English (Wismer et al., 1994).

Facts about Heart disease and Stroke among American Indians and Alaska Natives

Heart disease and stroke, the principal causes of cardiovascular disease, are the first and fifth leading causes of death among American Indians and Alaska Natives (AI/AN). Risk factors often occur together and as the number of risk factors increases, so does the likelihood of heart disease and stroke.

Results from a national telephone survey by the Centers for Disease Control and Prevention (CDC) show that 63.7% of American Indian/Alaska Native (AI/AN) men and 61.4% of AI/AN women reported having one or more of the following risk factors for heart disease and stroke: high blood pressure, current cigarette smoking, high cholesterol, obesity, and diabetes.

- 22% of respondents (21.0% of men and 23.0% of women) said they had been told by a health professional that they had high blood pressure.
- 31% (32.8% of men and 28.8% of women) reported that they were current smokers.
- Almost 16% had been told by a health care professional that they had high cholesterol and more than 7% were told that they had diabetes.
- Nearly a fourth of men (23.6%) and nearly one-fifth of women (19.1%) were obese (21.5% of all AI/AN).

Having more than one risk factor was more common among older men and women, people with less education, the unemployed, and those reporting their health status as fair or poor.

- Having 2 or more risk factors was highest among people 65 and older.
- More than a fourth of AI/AN men with less than a high school education reported 2 or more risk factors, compared to almost 15% of AI/AN men who were college graduates.
- AI/AN women with less than a high school education were almost 3 times more likely to report 2 risk factors than AI/AN women who had graduated from college.
- The percentage of unemployed women having 2 or more risk factors was almost three times higher than the percentage of employed women.
- Half of those who reported their health status as fair or poor (men, 50%— women, 51%) reported having 2 or more risk factors compared with only about an eighth of those who reported health status as excellent or very good.

For men, having more 2 or more risk factors for heart disease and stroke was highest in the Midwest (26.1%) and lowest in the Northeast (13.8%). Less geographic variation was seen among women: having 2 or more risk factors was highest in the Northeast (28.0%) and lowest in the West (20.0%). Regional differences in heart disease and stroke risk factors and death rates may reflect differences in cultural backgrounds, historical circumstances, and socioeconomic conditions.

The high percentages of AI/AN men and women with multiple risk factors for heart disease and stroke highlights the importance of primary prevention activities among communities of AI/AN. Through the CDC's Racial and Ethnic Approaches to Community Health (REACH 2010) program, two AI/AN communities are mobilizing and organizing resources to support programs designed to eliminate racial and ethnic disparities in CVD and diabetes.

Tribal- and community-specific assessments of heart disease and stroke-related illness and deaths are needed to develop culturally relevant prevention programs and policies that support heart-healthy living and working conditions for AI/AN.

Minority Women's Heart Disease Health Concerns

Heart Disease

Heart disease is the leading cause of death for almost all American women, including those in minority populations. (Slightly more Asian American/Pacific Islander women die from all cancers combined than from heart disease.) Nearly twice as many women in the United States die of heart disease and stroke as from all forms of cancer. Several risk factors contribute to the likelihood of women getting heart disease: smoking, high blood pressure (hypertension), high blood cholesterol, obesity, physical inactivity, and a family history of the disease. Death rates from heart disease among minority populations vary greatly, from a low of 49.3 per 100,000 persons to a high of 147.6.

Although the term heart disease can refer to any heart ailment, it is usually associated with coronary heart disease. Blocked arteries in the heart severely restrict the amount of blood that can flow to the heart. In turn, this insufficient blood flow deprives the heart muscle of much-needed oxygen and nutrients. When the blood supply is interrupted, the muscle cells of the heart suffer irreversible injury and die. This condition is known as a heart attack.

African American women have the highest mortality rate from heart disease (147.6 per 100,000) of all American women. Of this minority population, 34% has elevated blood pressure, in contrast to 19% of Caucasian women. In addition, 21.3% of African American women 18 years of age and over reported smoking cigarettes in 1995, whereas

23.9% of Caucasian women in this age group smoke. More than one-third (38%) of these minority women are obese—defined as having a Body Mass Index (BMI) greater than or equal to 30—in contrast to slightly less than one-quarter (24%) of their Caucasian counterparts.

American Indian/Alaska Native women have significantly lower death rates from heart disease (73.9 per 100,000) than do Caucasian women (90.4 per 100,000), according to a U.S. Department of Health and Human Services document entitled Health, United States, 1999. However, when the data are adjusted to compensate for the miscoding of Indian race on death certificates, American Indian/Alaska Native women have a higher mortality rate (92.8) than Caucasian women (90.4), reports the Indian Health Service. (Persons identified as American Indian, Asian, or Hispanic are sometimes misreported as Caucasian or non-Hispanic on the death certificate, causing death rates to be underestimated by 22%-30% for American Indians, roughly 12% for Asians, and about 7 percent for persons of Hispanic origin. Almost one-third (32.9%) of American Indian/Alaska Native women smoke.

Hispanic women have lower death rates from heart disease (64.7) than do Caucasian women. Yet Hispanics, especially those in certain subgroups, have significantly high rates of obesity, physical inactivity, elevated blood pressure, and high blood cholesterol. In addition, 13.7% of Hispanic women smoke, which increases their risk of heart disease.

Asian American/Pacific Islander women have the lowest mortality rate from heart disease (49.3) of all population groups. Only 7.4% of Asian American/Pacific Islander smoke. However, heart disease ranks as the second leading cause of death among these minority women. One-fourth of these women's deaths can be attributed to this disease.

Stroke

Stroke and other cerebrovascular diseases (which refer to the blood supply to the brain) are another leading cause of death for minority women in the United States. An obstruction, rupture or other disorder in the blood vessels leading to the brain restricts the supply of oxygen to the brain. Insufficient oxygen to the brain usually results in a stroke. Cerebrovascular diseases can result in weakness, paralysis of some parts of the body, difficulties with speech, loss of consciousness, or death. Major risk factors for stroke are similar to those for heart disease, including smoking, high blood pressure, and high blood cholesterol.

African American women have the highest death rate from stroke of all women, at 37.9 deaths per 100,000 (in contrast to 22.5 for Caucasian women).

While 19.9 **American Indian/Alaska Native women** per 100,000 are reported to die from stroke, the proportion increases to 25.1 when adjusted to compensate for the miscoding of Indian race on death certificates.

Asian American/Pacific Islander women have a mortality rate from stroke of 21.4.

Hispanic women have the lowest death rate from stroke (17.0) of all women.

Chapter 25

Cancer Patterns of Ethnic and Racial Groups

Cancer is the second leading cause of death in the United States, accounting for more than 544,000 deaths each year. About 1.4 million new cases of cancer are expected to be diagnosed in 1997, and approximately 7.4 million Americans have or have had cancer. The chances of developing cancer in a lifetime are nearly 50 percent for men and nearly 40 percent for women. About half of those who develop the disease will die from it.

Many minority groups suffer disproportionately from cancer. Disparities exist in both mortality and incidence rates. For men and women combined, blacks have a cancer death rate about 35 percent higher than that for whites (171.6 vs. 127.0 per 100,000). The death rate for cancer for black men is about 50 percent higher than it is for white men (226.8 vs. 151.8 per 100,000). The death rate for lung cancer is about 27 percent higher for blacks than for whites (49.9 vs. 39.3 per 100,000). The prostate cancer mortality rate for black men is more than twice that of white men (55.5 vs. 23.8 per 100,000).

Paralleling the death rate, the incidence rate for lung cancer in black men is about 50 percent higher than in white men (110.7 vs. 72.6 per 100,000). Native Hawaiian men also have elevated rates of lung cancer compared with white men. Alaska Native men and women

---

"Cancer: How to Reach the Goals," Health and Human Services, 1999; "Questions and Answers: Annual Report to the Nation on the Status of Cancer, 1973-1996, With a Special Section on Lung Cancer and Tobacco Smoking," Office of Cancer Communications, National Cancer Institute (NCI), Tuesday, April 20, 1999.

suffer disproportionately higher rates of cancers of the colon and rectum than do whites. Vietnamese women in the United States have a cervical cancer incidence rate more than five times greater than white women (47.3 vs. 8.7 per 100,000). Hispanic women also suffer elevated rates of cervical cancer.

Much can be done to reduce the burden of cancer in the United States through prevention. Lifestyles can be modified to greatly reduce an individual's risk for cancer. Tobacco use is responsible for nearly one-third of all cancer deaths. Evidence suggests that diet and nutrition may be related to 30 to 40 percent of cancer deaths. Additionally, many of the estimated 900,000 skin cancer cases diagnosed each year could be prevented by reducing sun exposure. For some cancers that we do not yet know how to prevent, early detection can dramatically reduce the risk of death. Regular mammography screening and appropriate follow-up can reduce deaths from breast cancer by about 30 percent for women 50 years of age and older. Screening by Pap test for cervical cancer along with appropriate follow-up care can virtually eliminate the risk of developing this disease.

The goal is to improve screening and management of cancer. Although colorectal cancer screening is now recommended, few data on screening rates exist. Screening for prostate cancer remains controversial, and for this cancer as well, few data on screening rates exist. Indeed, there is a significant need for public education about what is known, what is not known, and what is believed about prostate cancer screening and treatment. Breast and cervical cancers, however, have proven screening modalities for which screening data, both baseline and continuing, are available.

Despite the considerable gains in screening in the black community, the mortality rate from breast cancer for black women is greater than for white women. Some of the reasons for this disparity include the fact that many women have not yet had a mammogram or a Pap smear, many more are not screened regularly, and still others are screened but have limited follow-up and treatment services available to them. Hispanic, American Indian and Alaska Native, and Asian and Pacific Islander women also have low rates of screening and treatment, limited access to health facilities and physicians, and barriers related to language, culture, and negative provider attitudes, which negatively affect their health status. Eliminating these differences is critical and is the focus of attention for the HHS initiative to help identify and understand approaches that have proven successful in some communities.

Five Most Common Cancers in Each Racial/Ethnic Group

The top five cancer age-adjusted incidence rates and mortality rates are displayed for men and women in each racial/ethnic group. Rankings for the total white population are identical to those for the non-Hispanic white population and are not shown in Tables 25.1 and 25.2. Among men, lung and bronchus, prostate and colorectal cancer appear among the top five cancer incidence rates in every racial/ethnic group. Prostate cancer is the highest reported cancer among American Indian, black, Filipino, Japanese, non-Hispanic white, and Hispanic men. Cancer of the lung and bronchus is highest among men in the remaining racial/ethnic groups. In women, breast cancer incidence rates are highest in all groups except Vietnamese, for whom cervical cancer ranks higher than breast cancer. Cancers of the breast, lung and bronchus, and colon and rectum appear among the top five cancer incidence rates for women in every racial/ethnic group except American Indians, for whom lung cancer does not appear. Unique to American Indian women in New Mexico is a high incidence rate for cancer of the gallbladder. Other studies have also documented elevated gallbladder cancer rates among American Indians. Stomach cancer appears among the top five cancers for men and women in each of the Asian populations with the exception of Filipinos and Chinese women.

Lung cancer is the leading cause of cancer death among men in all racial/ethnic groups except American Indians, who have higher mortality from cancers of the prostate, stomach, and liver. Cancer of the prostate or colon and rectum is the second leading cause of cancer death among men in most other racial/ethnic groups. The exception is Chinese men, for whom liver cancer ranks second in mortality. Stomach cancer appears in the top five causes of cancer deaths among men in all groups except blacks, Filipinos, and non-Hispanic whites. Cancer of the pancreas is among the top five causes of cancer deaths in men for all groups except Alaska Natives, American Indians, and Filipinos.

Among women, the leading cause of cancer death in most racial/ethnic groups is lung cancer. Breast cancer is the leading cause of cancer death in Filipino and Hispanic women and cancer of the gallbladder ranks highest in American Indian women in New Mexico (based on 19 deaths). Breast cancer is in second place among the groups where lung cancer mortality is highest, except for Alaska Native women, who experience higher mortality from cancers of the colon and rectum. Colorectal cancer appears among the top five cancer mortality rates for all groups except American Indians and cancer of the pancreas is in the top five cancers for all groups.

Table 25.1. Five Most Frequently Diagnosed Cancers; SEER Incidence Rates, 1988-1992 (Rates are "average annual" per 100,000 population, age-adjusted to 1970 standard)

Racial/ethnic group			
Men	**Rate**	**Women**	**Rate**
Alaska Native			
Lung and Bronchus	81.1	Breast	78.9
Colon and Rectum	79.7	Colon and Rectum	67.4
Prostate	46.1	Lung and Bronchus	50.6
Stomach	27.2	Kidney and Renal Pelvis	16.7*
Kidney and Renal Pelvis	19.0*	Cervix Uteri	15.8
American Indian (New Mexico)			
Prostate	52.5	Breast	31.6
Colon and Rectum	18.6	Ovary	17.5
Kidney and Renal Pelvis	15.6	Colon and Rectum	15.3
Lung and Bronchus	14.4	Gallbladder	13.2
Liver and Intrahep.	13.1*	Corpus Uteri	10.7
Black			
Prostate	180.6	Breast	95.4
Lung and Bronchus	117.0	Colon and Rectum	45.5
Colon and Rectum	60.7	Lung and Bronchus	44.2
Oral Cavity	20.4	Corpus Uteri	14.4
Stomach	17.9	Cervix Utari	13.2
Chinese			
Lung and Bronchus	52.1	Breast	55.0
Prostate	46.0	Colon and Rectum	33.6
Colon and Rectum	44.8	Lung and Bronchus	25.3
Liver and Intrahep.	20.8	Corpus Uteri	11.6
Stomach	15.7	Ovary	9.3
Filipino			
Prostate	69.8	Breast	73.1
Lung and Bronchus	52.0	Colon and Rectum	20.9
Colon and Rectum	35.4	Lung and Bronchus	17.5
Non-Hodgkin's Lymphoma	12.9	Thyroid	14.6
Liver and Intrahep.	10.5	Corpus Uteri	12.1
Hawaiian			
Lung and Bronchus	89.0	Breast	105.6
Prostate	57.2	Lung and Bronchus	43.1
Colon and Rectum	42.4	Colon and Rectum	30.5
Stomach	20.5	Corpus Uteri	23.9
Non-Hodgkin's Lymphoma	12.5	Stomach	13.0

Table 25.1. Continued.

NOTE to Table 25.1: *Rate is based on fewer than 25 cases and may be subject to greater variability than the other rates which are based on larger numbers.

Racial/ethnic group Men	Rate	Women	Rate
Japanese			
Prostate	88.0	Breast	82.3
Colon and Rectum	64.1	Colon and Rectum	39.5
Lung and Bronchus	43.0	Stomach	15.3
Stomach	30.5	Lung and Bronchus	15.2
Urinary Bladder	13.7	Corpus Uteri	14.5
Korean			
Lung and Bronchus	53.2	Breast	28.5
Stomach	48.9	Colon and Rectum	21.9
Colon and Rectum	31.7	Stomach	19.1
Liver and Intrahep	24.8	Lung and Bronchus	16.0
Prostate	24.2	Cervix Uteri	15.2
Vietnamese			
Lung and Bronchus	70.9	Cervix Uteri	43.0
Liver and Intrahep	41.8	Breast	37.5
Prostate	40.0	Lung and Bronchus	31.2
Colon and Rectum	30.5	Colon and Rectum	27.1
Stomach	25.8	Stomach	25.8
White Non-Hispanic			
Prostate	137.9	Breast	115.7
Lung and Bronchus	70.0	Lung and Bronchus	43.7
Colon and Rectum	57.6	Colon and Rectum	39.2
Urinary Bladder	33.1	Corpus Uteri	23.0
Non-Hodgkin's Lymphoma	19.1	Ovary	16.2
Hispanic (Total)			
Prostate	89.0	Breast	69.8
Lung and Bronchus	41.8	Colon and Rectum	24.7
Colon and Rectum	38.3	Lung and Bronchus	10.5
Urinary Bladder	15.8	Cervix Uteri	16.2
Stomach	15.3	Corpus Uteri	13.7
White Hispanic			
Prostate	92.8	Breast	73.5
Lung and Bronchus	44.0	Colon and Rectum	25.9
Colon and Rectum	40.2	Lung and Bronchus	20.4
Urinary Bladder	16.7	Cervix Uteri	17.1
Stomach	16.2	Corpus Uteri	11.5

Table 25.2. Five Most Common Types of Cancer Deaths United States Mortality Rates, 1988-1992 (Rates are "average annual" per 100,000 population, age-adjusted to 1970 U.S. standard)

Racial/ethnic group Men	Rate	Women	Rate
Alaska Native			
Lung and Bronchus	69.4	Lung and Bronchus	45.3
Colon and Rectum	27.2	Colon and Rectum	24.0
Stomach	18.9*	Breast	16.0*
Kidney and Renal Pelvis	13.4*	Pancreas	15.5*
Nasopharynx	11.6*	Kidney and Renal Pelvis	7.4*
American Indian (New Mexico)			
Prostate	16.2	Gallbladder	8.9*
Stomach	11.2*	Breast	8.7*
Liver and Intrahep	11.2*	Cervix Uteri	8.0*
Lung and Bronchus	10.4*	Pancreas	7.4*
Colon and Rectum	8.5*	Ovary	7.3*
Black			
Lung and Bronchus	105.6	Lung and Bronchus	31.5
Prostate	53.7	Breast	31.4
Colon and Rectum	28.2	Colon and Rectum	20.4
Esophagus	14.8	Pancreas	10.4
Pancreas	14.4	Cervix uteri	6.7
Chinese			
Lung and Bronchus	40.1	Lung and Bronchus	18.5
Liver and Intrahep	17.7	Breast	11.2
Colon and Rectum	15.7	Colon and Rectum	10.5
Stomach	10.5	Pancreas	5.1
Pancreas	6.7	Stomach	4.8
Filipino			
Lung and Bronchus	29.8	Breast	11.9
Prostate	13.5	Lung and Bronchus	10.0
Colon and Rectum	11.4	Colon and Rectum	5.8
Liver and Intrahep	7.8	Ovary	3.4
Leukemia	5.7	Ovary	3.4
Hawaiian			
Lung and Bronchus	88.9	Lung and Bronchus	44.1
Colon and Rectum	23.7	Breast	25.0
Prostate	19.9	Stomach	12.8
Stomach	14.4	Colon and Rectum	11.4
Pancreas	12.8	Pancreas	9.1

Table 25.2. Continued.

NOTE to Table 25.2: *Rate is based on fewer than 25 deaths and may be subject to greater variability than the other rates which are based on larger numbers.

Racial/ethnic group			
Men	**Rate**	**Women**	**Rate**
Japanese			
Lung and Bronchus	32.4	Lung and Bronchus	12.9
Colon and Rectum	20.5	Breast	12.5
Stomach	17.4	Colon and Rectum	12.3
Prostate	11.7	Stomach	9.3
Pancreas	8.5	Pancreas	6.7
White Non-Hispanic			
Lung and Bronchus	74.2	Lung and Bronchus	32.9
Prostate	24.2	Breast	27.7
Colon and Rectum	23.4	Colon and Rectum	15.6
Pancreas	9.8	Ovary	8.2
Leukemia	8.6	Pancreas	7.0
Hispanic (Total)			
Lung and Bronchus	32.4	Breast	15.0
Prostate	15.3	Lung and Bronchus	10.0
Colon and Rectum	12.8	Colon and Rectum	8.3
Stomach	8.4	Pancreas	5.2
Pancreas	7.1	Ovary	4.8
White Hispanic			
Lung and Bronchus	33.6	Breast	15.7
Prostate	15.9	Lung and Bronchus	11.2
Colon and Rectum	13.4	Colon and Rectum	8.6
Stomach	8.8	Pancreas	5.4
Pancreas	7.4	Ovary	5.1

Questions and Answers: Annual Report to the Nation on the Status of Cancer, 1973-1996, with a Special Section on Lung Cancer and Tobacco Smoking

1. What Is the Purpose of This Report and Who Created It?

This report provides an update on the trends in cancer death rates in the United States and presents information about trends in cancer incidence rates (new cases reported) that have not been published before. It also contains a special section on lung cancer and tobacco smoking. The American Cancer Society (ACS), the National Cancer Institute (NCI), and the Centers for Disease Control and Prevention (CDC), including the National Center for Health Statistics (NCHS), collaborated to create this annual report.

2. What Is the Source of the Data?

Data on cancer incidence come from the NCI's Surveillance, Epidemiology, and End Results Program (SEER). The SEER program collects cancer incidence data from 11 registries: five statewide registries (Connecticut, Hawaii, Iowa, New Mexico, and Utah) and six metropolitan area registries (Atlanta, Detroit, Los Angeles, San Francisco—Oakland, San Jose—Monterey, and Seattle—Puget Sound). These registries are population-based (collect information on every cancer in a geographic area) and include approximately 14 percent of the U.S. population. SEER sampling is designed to represent diverse populations. Cancer cases were diagnosed during 1973 to 1996.

Data on cancer mortality come from NCHS. Death certificates filed in every state are processed and consolidated into the NCHS database, so that 100 percent of the U.S. population is covered. Cancer deaths for this report occurred during 1950 to 1996.

Data on smoking behavior presented in the special section on lung cancer were collected by NCHS in nationwide household interviews for the National Health Interview Survey (1965 to 1996), and by CDC and state departments of health and education in two surveys, the Behavioral Risk Factor Surveillance system (1997), and the Youth Risk Behavior Surveillance system (1997).

3. What Is Happening with Cancer Rates Overall?

After increasing from 1973 to 1990, incidence rates for all cancer sites combined decreased 0.9 percent per year during 1990 to 1996.

The peak year was 1992; from 1992 to 1996 the rate decreased 2.2 percent per year. This confirms the continued downward trend that was reported to the nation in 1998 for the period 1990 to 1995.

Trends in incidence rates varied by gender and age at diagnosis. During 1990 to 1996, the largest annual decreases in incidence rates for all sites combined occurred in men ages 25 to 44 and men 75 years and older at diagnosis. The declines in cancer incidence rates among women were smaller. The largest trend among women was a decline in cancer incidence (all types combined) in women ages 35 to 44.

Cancer death rates also continued to decline during the 1990s. From 1990 to 1996, cancer deaths decreased on average 0.6 percent per year. The death rate decline is greater among males (on average 1.0 percent per year) than females (0.3 percent per year). Persons younger than age 65 had the greatest drops in cancer death rates. Rates among males declined in all age groups except for men ages 85 and older. Rates decreased for women younger than 65, but increased for women 75 years and older.

4. How Is the Cancer Burden Monitored among Ethnic and Racial Groups?

In this report, cancer incidence and death rates are analyzed for whites, blacks, Asian and Pacific Islanders, American Indians/Alaska Natives, and Hispanics. Hispanic is not mutually exclusive from whites, blacks, and Asian and Pacific Islanders. Cancer incidence rates for American Indians/Alaska Natives are based on data from Alaska plus all SEER registries.

5. What Is Happening with Cancer among Ethnic and Racial Groups?

Continued higher incidence and death rates among some racial and ethnic groups suggest that some populations may not have benefited equally from cancer prevention and control efforts. Such disparities may be due to multiple factors, such as late stage of disease at diagnosis, barriers to health care access, history of other diseases, biologic and genetic differences in tumors, health behaviors, and the presence of risk factors.

The four leading cancer incidence sites for the five racial and ethnic populations were: lung and bronchus, prostate, female breast, and colon/rectum. Together these four sites account for 54 percent of all new diagnoses.

When these four sites of new cancer cases were examined by race and ethnicity, it was found that except for breast cancer, blacks had higher incidence rates than the other racial and ethnic populations. Uterine cancer was common to all five groups as one of the top 10 sites. But some cancer sites tended to be unique to a specific population. For example, melanoma and leukemia were among the top 10 incidence sites only in whites; cancers of the pancreas and oral cavity and pharynx were among the top 10 only in blacks; liver cancer was among the top 10 only in Asian and Pacific Islanders and American Indians/Alaska Natives; cancer of the kidney and renal pelvis was among the top 10 only in American Indians/Alaska Natives; and bladder cancer was among the top 10 only in whites and Hispanics.

The top four causes of cancer death from 1990 to 1996 for the racial and ethnic groups, with one exception, were the same sites as incidence: lung and bronchus, prostate, female breast, and colon/rectum. Among Asian and Pacific Islanders, the excepted group, cancer of the liver, instead of female breast cancer, ranked among the four leading causes of cancer death. When these four mortality sites were examined by race and ethnicity, it was found that blacks had higher cancer death rates than whites, Asian and Pacific Islanders, American Indians/Alaska Natives, or Hispanics. Deaths due to leukemia and cancers of the stomach and ovary were among the top 10 sites in all five racial and ethnic groups.

Other top 10 leading cancer mortality sites varied by ethnic and racial group. For example, brain and nervous system cancers were among the top 10 cancer mortality sites only in whites; esophageal cancer and multiple myoloma were among the top 10 sites only in blacks; cervical cancer was among the top 10 sites only in blacks and American Indians/Alaska Natives; and kidney and renal pelvis cancer were among the top 10 sites only in American Indians/Alaska Natives.

6. Why Does the Report Emphasize Lung Cancer and Tobacco Smoking?

Lung cancer causes more deaths than any other cancer site, and is one of the top four incidence sites for each racial and ethnic group. Lung cancer accounts for 28 percent of all cancer deaths each year and about 14 percent of new cancer cases.

Historically, lung cancer has been a key factor driving overall cancer trends, and it continues to do so. As much as 90 percent of all lung cancer is caused by tobacco smoke, which includes cigarettes, pipes, cigars, and second-hand smoke. The prevalence of cigarette smoking among adults has declined over the past 25 years, but this trend has stalled during the past four to five years. At the same time, the number of high school students smoking cigarettes has increased during the 1990s, and unless this trend can be reversed, the lung cancer rates that are currently declining may increase again.

There has been much attention given in recent years at the state and local levels to the effects of tobacco use and efforts to effectively control it, especially among children and adolescents. This report reflects the need for more research in this area and illustrates how surveillance data can be illuminated further by comparing it with risk factor data.

7. What Does the Data Show about Lung Cancer Rates?

During 1990 to 1996, male lung cancer incidence and death rates decreased. By contrast, lung cancer incidence and death rates increased among females, although the rate of increase has slowed in recent years. Overall lung cancer incidence rates varied widely by race and ethnicity from a high of 73.9 per 100,000 among blacks to 27.6 per 100,000 among Hispanics. The overall rate for American Indians/ Alaska Natives was low at 29.7 per 100,000, but this group had wide-ranging rates across geographic areas.

Lung cancer incidence and death rates declined among males of all racial and ethnic groups except American Indians/Alaska Natives. Male lung cancer incidence rates during 1990 to 1996 decreased an average 2.6 percent per year. Male lung cancer death rates decreased on average 1.6 percent per year. These declines reflect the large decreases over the past several decades in active smoking and exposure to environmental tobacco smoke.

Among females during the 1990s, the average annual percent increase was 0.1 percent per year for incidence and 1.4 percent per year for mortality. Smoking patterns in women lag behind smoking patterns in men, although prevalence is higher in men. The impact of decreased smoking on female lung cancer rates over all ages and racial groups combined has not yet been observed. However, the age-specific patterns of declines seen for males are beginning to occur in females. Lung cancer incidence and death rates declined among women ages 40 to 49 and 50 to 59 years old; were approximately level among females 60 to 69 years old; and continued to increase among older women.

8. What Is Happening with Breast Cancer Rates in Women?

Female breast cancer incidence rates have been approximately level during the 1990s. Female breast cancer death rates declined on average 1.7 percent per year since 1989.

9. What Is Happening with Prostate Cancer Rates?

Prostate cancer incidence rates continued to decline after peaking in 1992, and prostate cancer death rates continued to decline.

10. What Is Happening with Colon and Rectum Cancer Rates?

Colorectal cancer incidence and death rates declined for males and females and for all racial and ethnic groups.

11. What Other Key Sites Had Significant Incidence and Mortality Findings?

During 1990 to 1996, incidence and death rates for non-Hodgkin's lymphoma continued to increase although the rates of increase are lower than in the 1980s. The slowing of the increase in death rates occurred among males.

Melanoma incidence rates also continued to increase on average 2.7 percent per year. Melanoma death rates have been unchanged during the 1990s.

12. Are the Rates of Childhood Cancer Increasing or Decreasing?

For children younger than 15 years of age, the incidence of cancer declined 0.4 percent per year between 1990 and 1996. The mortality rates declined 2.7 percent per year for the same time period.

How to Read the Report

13. How Is Progress Against Cancer Being Measured in This Report?

This report includes two different measures, the annual percent change in cancer rates and incidence and death rates. Annual percent change has been calculated for two time periods, 1990 to 1996, and the peak year to 1996, and by age. "Statistically significant" means that the annual percent change calculated is unlikely to have occurred by chance alone.

14. What Is an Annual Percent Change or APC?

The annual percent change is the averaged rate of change in a cancer rate per year in a given time frame, i.e. how fast or slow a cancer rate has increased or decreased each year over a period of years. Annual percent change, sometimes abbreviated as APC, was calculated for both incidence and death rates. The number is given as a percent—such as the 0.9 percent per year decrease in incidence of all cancers diagnosed from 1990 to 1996.

15. How Are Cancer Incidence and Death Rates Presented?

Cancer incidence rates and cancer death rates are measured as a number per 100,000 people and are age-adjusted to the 1970 U.S. standard million population. When a cancer affects only one gender, such as prostate cancer, the number is per 100,000 people of that gender.

16. Where Is This Report Being Published?

The report is published in the *Journal of the National Cancer Institute*, April 21, 1999, Volume 91, Number 8. It is titled, "The Annual Report to the Nation on the Status of Cancer, 1973-1996, With a Special Section on Lung Cancer and Tobacco Smoking." The authors are Phyllis A. Wingo, Ph.D., M.S. (ACS), Lynn A.G. Ries, M.S. (NCI), Gary A. Giovino, Ph.D. (CDC), Daniel S. Miller, M.D., M.P.H. (CDC), Harry M. Rosenberg, Ph.D. (NCHS), Donald R. Shopland (NCI), Michael J. Thun, M.D. (ACS), and Brenda K. Edwards, Ph.D. (NCI).

Cancer Information Internet Sites

National Cancer Institute's SEER Homepage
Website: http://www-seer.ims.nci.nih.gov

National Cancer Institute
Website: http://rex.nci.nih.gov

American Cancer Society
Website: http://www.cancer.org

CDC's Division of Cancer Prevention and Control
Website: http://www.cdc.gov/cancer

CDC's National Center for Health Statistics
Website: http://www.cdc.gov/nchswww

CDC's Youth Risk Behavior Surveillance System
Website: http://www.cdc.gov/nccdphp/youthris.htm

CDC's Behavioral Risk Factor Surveillance System
Website: http://www.cdc.gov/nccdphp/brfss

Chapter 26

Diabetes

Who Has Diabetes

Of the 16 million Americans suffering from diabetes, about 5.4 million of these people do not know they have the disease. Each year, an additional 798,000 people are diagnosed with diabetes, and the number of people with diagnosed diabetes has risen from 1.5 million in 1958 to 10.6 million in 1998—a six-fold increase.

The majority of people who suffer from diabetes have type 2 diabetes, which accounts for 90 to 95 percent of all diagnosed cases of the disease. Diabetes affects men and women at equal rates, with 7.5 million men (8.2 percent of all men), and 8.1 million women (8.2 percent of all women) having the disease. Diabetes strikes all age groups—it is most prevalent in older Americans, with 6.3 million age 65 and older having diabetes (18.4 percent of this age group), and 15.6 million Americans age 20 and older having diabetes (8.2 percent of this age group).

Minorities have particular reason to become aware and involved in the National Diabetes Education Program (NDEP) and other diabetes education and treatment programs. Among African Americans,

---

"Who Has Diabetes," by Jean Oxendine, *Closing the Gap,* February/March 1999; excerpts from "National Diabetes Fact Sheet," CDC, November 1998; "Diabetes in African Americans," National Institute of Diabetes and Digestive and Kidney Disease (NIDDK), NIH Pub No. 98-3266, August 1998; and "Prevalence of Diagnosed Diabetes among American Indians/Alaskan Natives—United States, 1996," *MMWR Weekly*, October 1998.

2.3 million people age 20 and older (10.8 percent) have diabetes. African Americans are 1.7 times as likely to have diabetes as Caucasians of similar age. Hispanic Americans are almost twice as likely to have diabetes as non-Hispanic whites of similar age. Both Mexican Americans and Puerto Ricans have higher rates of diabetes than non-Hispanic whites.

American Indians have the highest rates of diabetes in the world, ranging from 5 to 50 percent. Among the Pima Indians of Arizona, half of all the adults have type 2 diabetes. The data for diabetes among Asian Americans and Pacific Islanders are limited, but we do know that some groups within this population are at increased risk for diabetes. Data collected from 1988 to 1995 show Native Hawaiians are twice as likely to have diagnosed diabetes as Caucasian residents of Hawaii.

In 1995, diabetes contributed to 187,800 deaths, and was the seventh leading cause of death listed on U.S. death certificates (sixth leading cause of death by disease). Diabetes death rates vary considerably across racial and ethnic groups. Compared to non-Hispanic whites, diabetes death rates were 2.5 times higher among African Americans, 2.4 times higher among American Indian/Alaska Natives (AI/ AN), and 1.7 times higher among persons of Hispanic origin.

The complications from diabetes are numerous, affecting minorities at greater rates than non-minorities. According to NIDDK, African Americans experience higher rates of diabetes complications such as eye disease, kidney failure, and amputations, as compared to whites. The frequency of diabetic retinopathy is 40 percent to 50 percent higher in African Americans than in whites, according to the National Center for Health Statistics. African Americans with diabetes experience end-stage renal disease about four times more often than whites with diabetes. And they are more likely to undergo lower extremity amputations than whites with diabetes.

According to the American Diabetes Association, in 1995, the rate of diabetic end stage renal disease among AI/ANs was six times higher than the general population with diabetes. More than half of lower limb amputations in the U.S. occurred among people with diabetes, and amputation rates among AI/ANs were significantly higher than the general population.

Although studies don't universally agree, there is some evidence that suggests Mexican Americans have a higher incidence of microalbuminuria—an early indicator of diabetic nephropathy—than non-Hispanic whites. Other research shows Mexican Americans have higher rates of diabetic retinopathy than white Americans.

Diabetes costs the United States about $98.2 billion annually, for total health care and related costs for treatment. Of this total, direct medical costs (e.g. hospitalization, medial care, treatment supplies) account for about $44.1 billion. The other $54.1 billion covers indirect costs such as disability payments, time lost from work, and premature death.

As evidenced by these statistics, diabetes is a disease that affects everyone, regardless of age, race, or gender. The good news is that the NDEP campaign is making efforts to turn these numbers around.

Prevalence of Diabetes

- Total: 15.7 million people—5.9% of the population—have diabetes.
- Diagnosed: 10.3 million people
- Undiagnosed: 5.4 million people
- New cases diagnosed per year: 798,000

Deaths among Persons with Diabetes

- Studies have found death rates to be twice as high among middle-aged people with diabetes as among middle-aged people without diabetes.
- Based on death certificate data, diabetes contributed to 193,140 deaths in 1996.
- Diabetes was the seventh leading cause of death listed on U.S. death certificates in 1996, according to CDC's National Center for Health Statistics.
- Diabetes is believed to be underreported on death certificates, both as a condition and as a cause of death.

Prevalence of Diabetes by Age

- Age 65 years or older: 6.3 million. 18.4% of all people in this age group have diabetes.
- Age 20 years or older: 15.6 million. 8.2% of all people in this age group have diabetes.
- Under age 20: 123,000. 0.16% of all people in this age group have diabetes.

*Prevalence of Diabetes by Sex in People 20 Years or Older**

- Men: 7.5 million. 8.2% of all men have diabetes.
- Women: 8.1 million. 8.2% of all women have diabetes.

*These figures do not include the approximately 123,000 cases of diabetes in children and teenagers in the United States.

*Prevalence of Diabetes by Race/Ethnicity in People 20 Years or Older**

- Non-Hispanic whites: 11.3 million. 7.8% of all non-Hispanic whites have diabetes.
- Non-Hispanic blacks: 2.3 million. 10.8% of all non-Hispanic blacks have diabetes. On average, non-Hispanic blacks are 1.7 times as likely to have diabetes as non-Hispanic whites of similar age.
- Mexican Americans: 1.2 million. 10.6% of all Mexican Americans have diabetes. On average, Mexican Americans are 1.9 times as likely to have diabetes as non-Hispanic whites of similar age.
- Other Hispanic/Latino Americans: On average, Hispanic/Latino Americans are almost twice as likely to have diabetes as non-Hispanic whites of similar age. (Sufficient data are not currently available to derive more specific estimates.)
- American Indians and Alaska Natives: 9% of American Indians and Alaska Natives have diagnosed diabetes. On average, American Indians and Alaska Natives are 2.8 times as likely to have diagnosed diabetes as non-Hispanic whites of similar age.
- Asian Americans and Pacific Islanders: Prevalence data for diabetes among Asian Americans and Pacific Islanders are limited. Some groups within this population are at increased risk for diabetes. For example, data collected from 1988 to 1995 suggest that Native Hawaiians are twice as likely to have diagnosed diabetes as white residents of Hawaii.

*These figures do not include the approximately 123,000 cases of diabetes in children and teenagers in the United States.

Diabetes in African Americans

Today, diabetes mellitus is one of the most serious health challenges facing the United States. The following statistics illustrate the magnitude of this disease among African Americans.

- In 1998, of 35 million African Americans, about 1.5 million have been diagnosed with diabetes. This is almost 4 times the number known to have diabetes in 1968.
- About 730,000 African Americans have diabetes but do not know they have the disease. Identifying these undiagnosed cases and providing clinical care for their diabetes is a major challenge for the health care community.
- For every six white Americans who have diabetes, 10 African Americans have diabetes.
- Diabetes is particularly common among middle-aged and older adults and among African American women. Among African Americans age 50 years or older, 19 percent of men and 28 percent of women have diabetes.
- African Americans with diabetes are more likely to develop diabetes complications and experience greater disability from the complications than white Americans with diabetes.
- Death rates for people with diabetes are 27 percent higher for blacks compared with whites.

What Is Diabetes?

Diabetes mellitus is a group of diseases characterized by high levels of blood glucose. It results from defects in insulin secretion, insulin action, or both. Diabetes can be associated with serious complications and premature death, but people with diabetes can take measures to reduce the likelihood of such occurrences.

Most African Americans (about 90 percent to 95 percent) with diabetes have type 2 diabetes. This type of diabetes usually develops in adults and is caused by the body's resistance to the action of insulin and to impaired insulin secretion. It can be treated with diet, exercise, diabetes pills, and injected insulin. A small number of African Americans (about 5 percent to 10 percent) have type 1 diabetes, which usually develops before age 20 and is always treated with insulin.

Diabetes can be diagnosed by three methods:

- A fasting plasma glucose test and a value of 126 milligrams/deciliter (mg/dL) or greater.
- A non-fasting plasma glucose value of 200 mg/dL or greater in people with symptoms of diabetes.
- An abnormal oral glucose tolerance test, with a 2-hour glucose value of 200 mg/dL or greater.

Each test must be confirmed, on another day, by any one of the listed methods. The criteria used to diagnose diabetes were revised in 1997.

How Many African Americans Have Diabetes?

Table 26.1 shows the prevalence for African American men and women based on the most recent national study, the NHANES III survey conducted in 1988-94.[2] The proportion of the African American population that has diabetes rises from less than 1 percent for

Table 26.1. Prevalence of Diagnosed and Undiagnosed Diabetes in African Americans, U.S., 1988-1994.

Age	Percentage of Population
Men under 20	0.2
Women under 20	0.2
Men 20-39	3.0
Women 20-39	3.0
Men 40-49	10.0
Women 40-49	10.0
Men 50-59	16.0
Women 50-59	23.0
Men 60-74	23.0
Women 60-74	32.0
Men 75+	15.0
Women 75+	22.0

Note: Diabetes includes both previously diagnosed diabetes and undiagnosed diabetes (fasting plasma glucose greater than 126 mg/dL).

those aged younger than 20 years to as high as 32 percent for women age 65-74 years. In every age group, prevalence is higher for women than men: overall, among those age 20 years or older, the rate is 11.8 percent for women and 8.5 percent for men.

About one-third of total diabetes cases are undiagnosed among African Americans. This is similar to the proportion for other racial/ethnic groups in the United States.[2]

National health surveys during the past 35 years show that the percentage of the African American population that has been diagnosed with diabetes is increasing dramatically.[3] The surveys in 1976-80 and in 1988-94 measured fasting plasma glucose and thus allowed an assessment of the prevalence of undiagnosed diabetes as well as of previously diagnosed diabetes. In 1976-80, total diabetes prevalence in African Americans age 40-74 years was 8.9 percent; in 1988-94, total prevalence had increased to 18.2 percent—a doubling of the rate in just 12 years.[2]

Prevalence in African Americans is much higher than in white Americans. Among those age 40-74 years in the 1988-94 survey, the rate was 11.2 percent for whites, but was 18.2 percent for blacks—diabetes prevalence in blacks is 1.6 times the prevalence in whites.[2]

What Risk Factors Increase the Chance of Developing Type 2 Diabetes?

The frequency of diabetes in African American adults is influenced by the same risk factors that are associated with type 2 diabetes in other populations. Two categories of risk factors increase the chance of developing type 2 diabetes. The first is genetics. The second is medical and lifestyle risk factors, including impaired glucose tolerance, gestational diabetes, hyperinsulinemia and insulin resistance, obesity, and physical inactivity.

Genetic Risk Factors

The common finding that "diabetes runs in families" indicates that there is a strong genetic component to type 1 and type 2 diabetes. Many scientists are now conducting research to determine the genes that cause diabetes. For type 1 diabetes, certain genes related to immunology have been implicated. For type 2 diabetes, there seem to be diabetes genes that determine insulin secretion and insulin resistance. Some researchers believe that African Americans inherited a "thrifty gene" from their African ancestors. Years ago, this gene enabled

Africans, during "feast and famine" cycles, to use food energy more efficiently when food was scarce. Today, with fewer such cycles, the thrifty gene that developed for survival may instead make the person more susceptible to developing type 2 diabetes.

Table 26.2. Time Trends in the Percentage of Adolescents and Adults in the U.S. Who Are Overweight, U.S., 1988-1994.

	Adolescents		Men		Women	
	White	Black	White	Black	White	Black
1976-1980	17	17	24	26	24	45
1988-1991	17	28	32	32	34	49

Medical Risk Factors

Impaired Glucose Tolerance (IGT)

In some people, their blood glucose level after a meal or after an oral glucose test rises higher than is considered normal but not high enough for them to be diagnosed with diabetes. These individuals are described as having impaired glucose tolerance (IGT). IGT may be an early stage of diabetes, and people with IGT are at higher risk of developing type 2 diabetes than people with normal glucose tolerance. Rates of IGT among adults age 40-74 years in the NHANES III survey were similar for black (13 percent) and white (15 percent) Americans.[2]

Gestational Diabetes (GDM)

About 2 to 5 percent of pregnant women develop mild abnormalities in glucose levels and insulin secretion and are considered to have gestational diabetes. Although these women's glucose and insulin levels often return to normal after pregnancy, as many as 50 percent may develop type 2 diabetes within 20 years of the pregnancy.

Hyperinsulinemia and Insulin Resistance

Higher-than-normal levels of fasting insulin, called hyperinsulinemia, are associated with an increased risk of developing type 2 diabetes.

Hyperinsulinemia often predates diabetes by several years. Among people who did not have diabetes in the NHANES III survey, insulin levels were higher in African Americans than in whites, particularly African American women, indicating their greater predisposition for developing type 2 diabetes.[4] Another study showed a higher rate of hyperinsulinemia in African American adolescents compared with white American adolescents.[5]

Obesity

Overweight is a major risk factor for type 2 diabetes. The NHANES surveys found that overweight is increasing in the United States, both in adolescents and in adults. Table 26.2 illustrates these data and also shows that African American adults have substantially higher rates of obesity than white Americans.[6,7]

In addition to the overall level of obesity, the location of the excess weight is also a risk factor for type 2 diabetes. Excess weight carried above the waist is a stronger risk factor than excess weight carried below the waist. African Americans have a greater tendency to develop upper-body obesity, which increases their risk of diabetes.

Although African Americans have higher rates of obesity, researchers do not believe that obesity alone accounts for their higher prevalence of diabetes. Even when compared with white Americans with the same levels of obesity, age, and socioeconomic status, African Americans still have higher rates of diabetes. Other factors, yet to be understood, appear to be responsible.

Physical Activity

Regular physical activity is a protective factor against type 2 diabetes and, conversely, lack of physical activity is a risk factor for developing diabetes. Researchers suspect that a lack of exercise is one factor contributing to the high rates of diabetes in African Americans. In the NHANES III survey, 50 percent of black men and 67 percent of black women reported that they participated in little or no leisure time physical activity.[8]

How Does Diabetes Affect African American Young People?

African American children seem to have lower rates of type 1 diabetes than white American children. Researchers tend to agree that genetics probably makes type 1 diabetes less common among children with African ancestry compared with children of European ancestry.

How Does Diabetes Affect African American Women during Pregnancy?

Gestational diabetes, in which blood glucose values are elevated above normal during pregnancy, occurs in about 2 percent to 5 percent of all pregnant women. Perinatal problems such as macrosomia (large body size) and neonatal hypoglycemia (low blood sugar) are higher in these pregnancies. The women generally return to normal glucose values after childbirth. However, once a woman has had gestational diabetes, she has an increased risk of developing gestational diabetes in future pregnancies. In addition, experts estimate that about half of women with gestational diabetes develop type 2 diabetes within 20 years of the pregnancy. Several studies have shown that the occurrence of gestational diabetes in African American women may be 50 percent to 80 percent more frequent than in white women.

How Do Diabetes Complications Affect African Americans?

Compared with white Americans, African Americans experience higher rates of diabetes complications such as eye disease, kidney failure, and amputations. They also experience greater disability from these complications. Some factors that influence the frequency of these complications, such as high blood glucose levels, abnormal blood lipids, high blood pressure, and cigarette smoking, can be influenced by proper diabetes management.

Eye Disease

Diabetic retinopathy is a deterioration of the blood vessels in the eye that is caused by high blood glucose. It can lead to impaired vision and, ultimately, to blindness. The frequency of diabetic retinopathy is 40 percent to 50 percent higher in African Americans than in white Americans, according to NHANES III data.[9] Retinopathy may also occur more frequently in black Americans than in whites because of their higher rate of hypertension. Although blindness caused by diabetic retinopathy is believed to be more frequent in blacks than in whites, there are no valid studies that compare rates of blindness between the two groups.

Kidney Failure

African Americans with diabetes experience kidney failure, also called end-stage renal disease (ESRD), about four times more often than diabetic white Americans.[10] In 1995, there were 27,258 new cases of ESRD attributed to diabetes in black Americans.[11] Diabetes is the leading cause of kidney failure and accounted for 43 percent of the new cases of ESRD among black Americans during 1992-1996. Hypertension, the second leading cause of ESRD, accounted for 42 percent of cases. In spite of their high rates of ESRD, African Americans have better survival rates after they develop kidney failure than white Americans.[10]

Amputations

Based on the U.S. hospital discharge survey, there were about 13,000 amputations among black diabetic individuals in 1994, which involved 155,000 days in the hospital.[12] African Americans with diabetes are much more likely to undergo a lower-extremity amputation than white or Hispanic Americans with diabetes. The hospitalization rate of amputations for blacks was 9.3 per 1,000 patients in 1994, compared with 5.8 per 1,000 white diabetic patients. However, the average length of hospital stay was lower for African Americans (12.1 days) than for white Americans (16.5 days).

Does Diabetes Cause Excess Deaths in African Americans?

Diabetes was an uncommon cause of death among African Americans at the turn of the century. By 1994, however, death certificates listed diabetes as the seventh leading cause of death for African Americans. For those age 45 years or older, it was the fifth leading cause of death.[12]

Death rates (mortality) for people with diabetes are higher for blacks than for whites. In every age group and for both men and women, death rates for blacks with diabetes were higher than for whites with diabetes from 1971-1993. The overall mortality rate was 20 percent higher for black men and 40 percent higher for black women, compared with their white counterparts.

Points to Remember

- In 1993, 1.3 million African Americans were known to have diabetes. This is almost three times the number of African Americans who were diagnosed with diabetes in 1963. For every white American who gets diabetes, 1.6 African Americans get diabetes.

- The highest incidence of diabetes in blacks occurs between 65 and 74 years of age. Twenty-five percent of these individuals have diabetes.
- Obesity is a major medical risk factor for diabetes in African Americans, especially for women. Some diabetes may be prevented with weight control through healthy eating and regular exercise.
- African Americans have higher incidence of and greater disability from diabetes complications such as kidney failure, visual impairment, and amputations.
- If African Americans can prevent, reverse, or control diabetes, their risk of complications will decrease.
- Healthy lifestyles, such as eating healthy foods and getting regular exercise, are particularly important for people who are at increased risk of diabetes.

How Is NIDDK Addressing the Problem of Diabetes in African Americans?

Within many African American communities around the country, NIDDK supports centers that provide nutrition counseling, exercise, and screening for diabetes complications. These centers are called Diabetes Research and Training Centers.

Prevention

In 1996, NIDDK launched its Diabetes Prevention Program (DPP). The goal of this research effort is to learn how to prevent or delay type 2 diabetes in people with impaired glucose tolerance (IGT) and in women with IGT who have a history of gestational diabetes. Both conditions are strong risk factors for type 2 diabetes.

DPP will evaluate several interventions to prevent type 2 diabetes, including an intensive healthy eating and exercise program and the use of diabetes medication. Researchers are tailoring interventions to the cultural needs of individuals in the program. Recruitment into the study began in the summer of 1996, and participants will be followed for an average of 4.5 years, with findings to be released in 2002.

Education and Awareness Activities

NIDDK has joined the Centers for Disease Control and Prevention to sponsor the National Diabetes Education Program (NDEP). The goal of this program is to reduce the death and disability associated with diabetes and its complications. The NDEP conducts ongoing diabetes awareness and education activities for people with diabetes and their families. Special efforts are being made to address the needs of certain ethnic groups that are hardest hit by diabetes, including African Americans, Hispanic Americans, Asian Americans, Pacific Islanders, and Native Americans. Through these efforts, the NDEP hopes to improve the treatment and outcomes for people with diabetes, promote early diagnosis, and, ultimately, prevent the onset of diabetes.

References

1. American Diabetes Association. Report of the Expert Committee on the Diagnosis and Classification of Diabetes Mellitus. *Diabetes Care*, Vol. 20, p. 1183-1197, 1997.

2. Harris MI, Flegal KM, Cowie CC, et al. Prevalence of Diabetes, Impaired Fasting Glucose, and Impaired Glucose Tolerance in U.S. Adults: The Third National Health and Nutrition Examination Survey, 1988-94. *Diabetes Care* Vol. 21, p. 518-524, 1998.

3. Tull ES, Roseman JM. Diabetes in African Americans. Chapter 31 in Diabetes in America. 2nd Edition (NIH Publication No. 95-1468, pp. 613-630). Bethesda, MD: National Institute of Diabetes and Digestive and Kidney Diseases, National Institutes of Health, 1995. (http://diabetes-in-america.s-3.com)

4. Harris MI. Unpublished data from the Third National Health and Nutrition Examination Survey, 1988-94.

5. Jiang X, Srinivasan SR, Radhakrishnamurthy B, Dalferes ER, Berenson GS: Racial (black-white) differences in insulin secretion and clearance in adolescents: the Bogalusa heart study. *Pediatrics* 97:357-360, 1996.

6. Kuzmarski RJ, Flegal KM, Campbell SM, Johnson CL: Increasing prevalence of overweight among US adults. The National Health and Nutrition Examination Surveys, 1960 to 1991. *JAMA* 272:205-211, 1994.

7. Troiano RP, Flegal KM, Kuczmarski RJ, Campbell SM, Johnson CL: Overweight prevalence and trends for children and adolescents. *Arch Pediatr Adolesc Med* 149:1085-1091, 1995.

8. Crespo CJ, Keteyian SJ, Heath GW, Sempos CT: Leisure-time physical activity among US adults. *Arch Intern Med* 156:93-98, 1996.

9. Harris MI, Klein R, Cowie CC, Rowland M, Byrd-Holt DD: Is the risk of diabetic retinopathy greater in non-Hispanic blacks and Mexican Americans than in non-Hispanic whites with type 2 diabetes: a US population study. *Diabetes Care*, vol. 21, in press.

10. Cowie CC, Port FK, Wolfe RA, Savage PJ, Moll PP, Hawthorne VM: Disparities in incidence of diabetic end-stage renal disease by race and type of diabetes. *New Engl J Med* 321:1074-1079, 1989.

11. U.S. Renal Data System. USRDS 1997 Annual Data Report. Bethesda, MD: National Institute of Diabetes and Digestive and Kidney Disease, National Institutes of Health, 1997.

12. Geiss, LS (editor). Diabetes Surveillance, 1997. Centers for Disease Control and Prevention, Atlanta, Georgia, 1997.

13. Gu K, Cowie CC, Harris MI: Mortality in adults with and without diabetes in a national cohort of the US population, 1971-93. *Diabetes Care*, vol. 21, July 1998.

Prevalence of Diagnosed Diabetes among American Indians/Alaskan Natives—United States, 1996

Since the early 1960s, diabetes has disproportionately affected American Indians/Alaskan Natives (AIs/ANs) compared with other populations.[1,2] Diabetes is a major cause of morbidity (such as blindness, kidney failure, lower-extremity amputation, and cardiovascular disease) and premature mortality in this population.[3] To update information about the prevalence of diabetes among AIs/ANs, data were analyzed from the Indian Health Service (IHS) national outpatient database for 1996 and were compared with the prevalence of diabetes among non-Hispanic whites in the United States. This report presents the findings of this analysis, which indicate that the prevalence of diabetes among AIs/ANs remains high and is approximately three times the prevalence among non-Hispanic whites.

Outpatient data were reported from 141 of the 166 service units in four geographic groups of tribes;* 25 service units (representing 11% of the population served by IHS) were excluded because the reported data were incomplete. The International Classification of Diseases, Ninth Revision, Clinical Modification (ICD-9-CM) codes 250.0-250.9 were used to identify persons with diabetes. The outpatient database includes unduplicated case reports of persons who attended the service unit one or more times during 1996 and for whom there was a diagnostic code of diabetes. The number of persons residing within the IHS service units were estimated from the U.S. census and birth and death rates. Approximately 60% of the estimated 2.3 million AIs/ANs residing in the United States are eligible to receive IHS services and use IHS medical facilities.[4] The prevalence of diabetes in the United States was estimated from the 1995 National Health Interview Survey (NHIS).[5] Prevalence estimates were adjusted for age by the direct method using the 1980 U.S. population as the standard.

In 1996, an estimated 63,400 AIs/ANs who receive care from IHS had diabetes; 98.3% were aged greater than or equal to 20 years. Of those aged greater than or equal to 20 years, 49.7% were aged 45-64 years; 59.0% were women. The prevalence of diabetes increased with age—from 3.5% for persons aged 20-44 years to 21.5% for persons aged greater than or equal to 65 years. The overall crude prevalence for those aged greater than or equal to 20 years was 9.0% (Table 26.3). The prevalence was greater among women (10.1%) than men (7.7%). The age-specific prevalence among AI/AN women was higher than among men, but the age-specific prevalence among non-Hispanic white men was higher than among women.

Among AIs/ANs aged 20-44 years and 45-64 years, the prevalence of diabetes was more than three times that among non-Hispanic whites in the NHIS (3.5% versus 0.9% {95% confidence interval (CI)=0.6%-1.2%} for persons aged 20-44 years and 19.0% versus 5.2% {95% CI=4.2%-6.2%} for persons aged 45-64 years). Among persons aged greater than or equal to 65 years, the prevalence among AIs/ANs (21.5%) was approximately twice that among non-Hispanic whites (11.4% {95% CI=9.7%-13.1%}). The age-adjusted prevalence among persons aged greater than or equal to 20 years was 2.8 times that among non-Hispanic whites in the same age group (10.9% versus 3.9% {95% CI=3.5%-4.3%}).

The prevalence of diabetes varied by tribal group—12.7% among the Plains tribes, 10.5% among the Southwestern tribes, 9.3% among the Woodland tribes, and 4.5% among the Pacific Coastal tribes. The age-adjusted prevalence of diabetes ranged from 1.5 to 4.1 times the prevalence among non-Hispanic whites. Among the tribes of the Plains and the Southwest, the age-adjusted prevalence of diabetes (15.9% and 13.5%, respectively) was greater than that for the total IHS population and was more than three times that among non-Hispanic whites.

Reported by: Diabetes Program, Indian Health Service. Epidemiology and Statistics Br, Div of Diabetes Translation, National Center for Chronic Disease Prevention and Health Promotion, CDC.

Impact of Diabetes on American Indians and Alaska Natives

Diabetes is a serious disease associated with severe morbidity and premature death that affects approximately 9% of AI/AN adults. In persons with type 1 or type 2 diabetes, aggressive glycemic control may prevent or delay diabetes-related complications such as retinopathy, nephropathy, or neuropathy.[6,7] Interventions that promote healthy behaviors may prevent or delay the onset of diabetes in persons at risk for developing type 2 diabetes (also known as noninsulin-dependent or adult-onset diabetes).[8] As with other chronic disease prevention interventions, diabetes prevention efforts need to be ongoing and long-term before the impact on morbidity and mortality can be measured.

The findings in this analysis have at least four limitations. First, estimates of the AI/AN population are inaccurate because U.S. census estimates do not account for migration between service units and previously have underreported the number of AIs/ANs. Second, these data account only for those persons who are eligible to receive IHS services and use IHS medical facilities. The higher age-specific prevalence of diabetes among AI/AN women may be due to women seeking health care more frequently than men.[4] Moreover, the data represent diagnosed cases of diabetes being treated and underestimate the true prevalence. Data from the Navajo Health and Nutrition Survey showed that one third of Navajo adults with diabetes had not had diabetes diagnosed.[9] Third, under the Indian Self-Determination Act **, an increasing number of service units are becoming IHS sites operated by tribal governments that may choose not to report diabetes cases to the IHS outpatient database. Finally, 11% of the total IHS population was excluded from this analysis because of incomplete data.

Effective intervention strategies are needed to control diabetes and its complications among AIs/ANs. CDC provides technical assistance to the IHS Diabetes Program for surveillance of diabetes and its complications. CDC and the National Institute of Diabetes and Digestive and Kidney Disease of the National Institutes of Health are conducting the Diabetes Prevention Program, a clinical trial to evaluate three diabetes prevention interventions—including a program to increase exercise and reduce body weight—in four American Indian communities. CDC and IHS are collaborating to establish the National Diabetes Prevention Center in Gallup, New Mexico, that will 1) provide guidance and technical support in diabetes prevention and control strategies to AI/AN communities throughout the United States and 2) develop, evaluate, and disseminate culturally appropriate community-based interventions. IHS also has granted $30 million to tribal governments in 1998 to help develop and implement innovative interventions to prevent diabetes and its complications.

References

1. Bennett PH, Burch TA, Miller M. Diabetes mellitus in American (Pima) Indians. *Lancet* 1971; 2:125-8.

2. Valway S, Freeman W, Kaufman S, Welty T, Helgerson SD, Gohdes D. Prevalence of diagnosed diabetes among American Indians and Alaska Natives, 1987. *Diabetes Care* 1993;16(suppl 1):271-6.

3. Gohdes D. Diabetes in North American Indians and Alaska Natives. In: Harris MI, Cowie CC, Stern MP, Boyko EJ, Reiber GE, Bennett PH, eds. *Diabetes in America*. 2nd ed. Washington, DC: US Department of Health and Human Services, Public Health Service, National Institutes of Health, 1995; DHHS publication no. (NIH)95-1468.

4. Indian Health Service. *Trends in Indian Health*, 1996. Rockville, Maryland: US Department of Health and Human Services, Indian Health Service, Office of Planning, Evaluation, and Legislation, Division of Program Statistics, 1997.

5. Massey JT, Moore TF, Parsons VL, Tadros W. *Design and estimation for the National Health Interview Survey, 1985-1994*. Hyattsville, Maryland: US Department of Health and Human Services, Public Health Service, CDC, National Center for

Table 26.3. Prevalence[1] of Diagnosed Diabetes among American Indians/Alaskan Natives[2] and Non-Hispanic Whites[3] aged ≥ 20 Years, by Age and Sex—United States

Age group (years)	Men		Women		All	
	American Indians/ Alaskan Natives	Non-Hispanic Whites	American Indians/ Alaskan Natives	Non-Hispanic Whites	American Indians/ Alaskan Natives	Non-Hispanic Whites
20-44	3.1	0.6	3.8	1.3	3.5	0.9
45-64	16.7	5.4	21.1	5.1	19.0	5.2
≥65	19.1	11.8	23.3	11.2	21.5	11.4
≥20	7.7	3.9	10.1	4.5	9.0	4.2
Age-adjusted[4]	9.7	3.8	12.0	4.0	10.9	3.9

[1]Per 100 persons

[2]American Indians/Alaskan Natives in the 1996 Indian Health Service (HIS) Patient Comprehensive Care file; excludes data from 25 (representing 11% of the population served by HIS) of the 166 HIS service units because the data were incomplete.

[3]Non-Hispanic whites in the 1995 National Health Interview survey.

[4]To the 1980 population.

Health Statistics, 1989. (Vital and Health Statistics; vol 2, no. 110).

6. DCCT Research Group. The effect of intensive treatment of diabetes on the development and progression of long-term complications in insulin-dependent diabetes mellitus: The Diabetes Control and Complications Trial Research Group. *N Engl J Med* 1993;329:977-86.

7. U.K. Prospective Diabetes Study Group. Intensive blood-glucose control with sulphonylureas or insulin compared with conventional treatment and risk of complications in patients with type 2 diabetes (UKPDS 33). *Lancet* 1998;352:839-55.

8. Pan XR, Li GW, Hu YH, et al. Effects of diet and exercise in preventing NIDDM in people with impaired glucose tolerance: The Da Qing IGT and Diabetes Study. *Diabetes Care* 1997;20:537-44.

9. Will JC, Strauss KF, Mendlein JM, Ballew C, White LL, Peter DG. Diabetes mellitus among Navajo Indians: findings from the Navajo Health and Nutrition Survey. *J Nutrition* 1997;127 (suppl):2106-13.

Tribal Geographic Groups

- Woodland tribes—Alabama, Connecticut, Florida, Kansas, Louisiana, Maine, Michigan, Minnesota, Mississippi, New York, North Carolina, Oklahoma, Pennsylvania, Rhode Island, South Carolina, Tennessee, Texas, and Wisconsin;
- Plains tribes—Iowa, Montana, Nebraska, North Dakota, South Dakota, and Wyoming;
- Southwestern tribes—Arizona, Colorado, Nevada, New Mexico, and Utah; and
- Pacific Coastal tribes—Alaska, California, Idaho, Oregon, and Washington.

** Public Law 93-638.

Additional Resources

National Diabetes Information Clearinghouse

1 Information Way
Bethesda, MD 20892-3560
Tel: 301-654-3327
Fax: 301-907-8906
E-mail: ndic@info.niddk.nih.gov

The National Diabetes Information Clearinghouse (NDIC) offers additional information about diabetes including the following:

- The Diabetes Dictionary (booklet available in English and Spanish)
- Do Your Level Best: Start Controlling Your Blood Sugar Today (booklet, limited literacy).

Single copies are free. Bulk orders are available for health care professionals. For more information about diabetes and African Americans and to order publications, contact NDIC.

American Diabetes Association National Service Center

1701 North Beauregard Street
Alexandria, VA 22311
Tel: 800-342-2383
Fax: 703-549-6995
Website: http://www.diabetes.org

Centers for Disease Control and Prevention (CDC)

Toll Free: 877-232-3422
E-mail: ccdinfo@cdc.gov
Website: http://www.cdc.gov/diabetes

Division of Diabetes Translation

National Center for Chronic Disease Prevention and Health Promotion
4770 Buford Highway NE
Atlanta, GA 30341-3717

National Diabetes Education Program

Toll Free: 800-438-5383

Chapter 27

Hepatitis B and C

In October 1997, the Advisory Committee on Immunization Practices (ACIP) expanded its hepatitis B vaccination recommendations to include all unvaccinated children aged 0-18 years and made hepatitis B vaccine available through the Vaccines for Children program (VFC) for persons aged 0-18 years who are eligible for VFC. ACIP priorities for hepatitis B vaccination of children remain unchanged and include all infants; children in populations at high risk for hepatitis B virus (HBV) infection (e.g., Alaska Natives, Pacific Islanders, and children who reside in households of first-generation immigrants from countries where HBV infection is moderately or highly endemic); previously unvaccinated children aged 11-12 years; and older adolescents and adults in defined risk groups.

In 1991, the ACIP recommended a comprehensive hepatitis B vaccination strategy to eliminate HBV transmission in the United States.[1] Critical elements of this strategy include preventing perinatal HBV transmission by identifying and providing immunoprophylaxis to infants of hepatitis B surface antigen-positive mothers and universal hepatitis B vaccination of infants to interrupt transmission. In 1994, the ACIP expanded the recommendations to include previously

---

"Recommendations to Prevent Hepatitis B Virus Transmission—United States," *Morbidity and Mortality Weekly Report*, January 22, 1999; "NIDDK Workshop Examines Hepatitis C in African Americans," by Leslie Curtis, National Institutes of Health (NIH) Record, March 3, 2000; and "Draft Strategic Plan on Minority Health Disparities," National Institute of Diabetes and Digestive and Kidney Diseases (NIDDK), April 3, 2000.

unvaccinated children aged 11-12 years.[2] The percentage of children aged 19-35 months who have received three doses of hepatitis B vaccine has increased substantially from less than 10% in 1991 to 84% in 1997.[3] No nationwide vaccine coverage data are available to assess vaccine coverage among children aged 11-12 years; however, vaccine coverage in this group is expected to increase in states that have implemented middle school entry requirements for hepatitis B vaccination.[4]

To increase access to hepatitis B vaccine, the new recommendations encourage vaccination of previously unvaccinated children and adolescents aged 0-18 years whenever they are seen for routine medical visits. This expansion of the recommended age group for vaccination and for VFC eligibility simplifies previous recommendations and the eligibility criteria for VFC vaccine. Providers should ensure that vaccination records of children and adolescents presenting for vaccination are checked for receipt of previous doses.

Universal vaccination of infants and children aged 11-12 years will result in a highly immune population and is expected to eliminate HBV transmission in the United States. However, high rates of HBV infection continue to occur among Alaska Native and Pacific Islander children and among children residing in households of first-generation immigrants from countries where HBV infection is endemic.[5,6] As a result, targeted programs are needed to achieve high vaccination coverage among these children. In addition, because most HBV infections in the United States occur among adults, vaccinating infants and adolescents aged 11-12 years alone will not substantially lower disease incidence for several years. Most HBV infections in adults occur among persons who have defined risk factors for HBV infection, including persons with multiple sex partners (more than one partner during the preceding 6 months); men who have sex with men; and injecting-drug users.[7] The primary means to prevent these infections is to identify settings where adolescents and adults with high-risk drug and sexual practices can be routinely accessed and vaccinated (e.g., sexually transmitted disease clinics, family-planning clinics, drug-treatment clinics, community-based human immunodeficiency virus prevention sites, and correctional facilities).

References

1. CDC. Hepatitis B virus: a comprehensive strategy for eliminating transmission through universal childhood vaccination:

recommendations of the Immunization Practices Advisory Committee (ACIP). *MMWR* 1991;40(no. RR-13):1-20.

2. CDC. Update: recommendations to prevent hepatitis B virus transmission—United States. *MMWR* 1995;44:574-5.

3. CDC. National, state, and urban area vaccination coverage levels among children aged 19-35 months—United States, 1997. *MMWR* 1998;47:547-54.

4. CDC. Effectiveness of a seventh grade school entry vaccination requirement—statewide and Orange County, Florida, 1997-1998. *MMWR* 1998;47:711-5.

5. Hurie MB, Mast EE, Davis JP. Horizontal transmission of hepatitis B virus infection to United States-born children among refugees. *Pediatrics* 1992;89:269-73.

6. Mahoney FJ, Lawrence M, Scott K, Le Q, Farley T. Continuing risk for hepatitis B virus transmission among children born in the United States to southeast Asian children in Louisiana. *Pediatrics* 1995;95:1113-6.

7. CDC. Hepatitis surveillance report no. 56. Atlanta, Georgia: US Department of Health and Human Services, Public Health Service, CDC, 1995.

Hepatitis C in African Americans

Although there has been a four-fold decline in new cases of hepatitis C (HCV) in the U.S. population since 1989, identified cases of chronic HCV are rising, particularly in African Americans. The highest observed rate of HCV infection among all racial and ethnic groups is among Black males ages 40-49. They have a 9 percent rate of hepatitis C, according to researchers attending a recent NIH workshop on HCV in African Americans. Researchers also report that the onset of infection occurs at earlier ages in Blacks and, as a result, Blacks are infected longer.

"These general findings help crystallize some of our suspicions about racial differences of this disease," said meeting cosponsor Dr. Jay H. Hoofnagle, director, Division of Digestive Diseases and Nutrition, NIDDK. "But prospective studies that focus on complications, natural history, therapy and prevention involving African Americans and hepatitis C are still needed to confirm or disprove our suspicions."

According to the Centers for Disease Control and Prevention, 3.9 million Americans have been exposed to hepatitis C. Of these, 2.7 million are chronically infected with the virus. Hepatitis C is primarily spread by exposure to contaminated blood and blood products, with injection drug use now being the most common route of disease transmission.

CDC epidemiologist Dr. Miriam Alter said that even though sexual encounters account for 10 percent to 20 percent of HCV cases, they are an inefficient route of transmission that is difficult to assess because a health care provider does not know the number of infected sex partners a person has had.

Workshop participants also discussed how different races respond to interferon treatment. Although most studies reviewed included a limited number of African Americans, data from such diverse sites as the Miami Veterans Medical Center and the NIH Clinical Center indicate that African Americans respond to interferon at lower rates than Caucasians. The factors responsible for the different response rates between racial groups are unknown.

"The fact that African Americans are more likely to be infected with genotype 1b may also account for their poor response to treatment," said Dr. K. Rajender Reddy, professor, University of Miami. Future clinical trials using interferon and ribavirin may help determine whether combination therapy is more effective in African Americans.

Another topic of interest was increasing African American participation in clinical research, particularly hepatitis studies. The researchers acknowledged that the lack of African American participation in clinical research greatly limits researchers' understanding of the disease and how to treat it in this population. Numerous issues such as patient distrust of the medical community, rigid treatment schedules and lack of community outreach training for health professionals contribute to the low representation.

To begin to address these issues, researchers need to get to know the designated community and work with its local leaders such as ministers, said Dr. Claudia Baquet, associate dean, University of Maryland, Baltimore. "African Americans are interested in participating, but you need to build relationships with them before they are needed for a clinical trial."

Hepatitis C Virus Infection and Liver Disease

- Liver disease ranks as the tenth most common cause of death in the U.S., and disproportionately affects minority populations.

- The leading causes of end-stage liver disease in the U.S. are alcoholic liver disease and hepatitis C.
- Hepatitis C affects 1.5% of the U.S. population and is two-to-three fold more common among African Americans and Hispanics than Caucasians.
- Therapy for hepatitis C is evolving, and current recommended regimens are effective in only 40% of patients. The response rate in African Americans is lower than in Caucasians.
- The only therapy for end-stage liver disease is liver transplantation. At present approximately 4,000 liver transplants are done yearly, but waiting lists are lengthening and a shortage of organs has caused an increase in deaths among patients while awaiting transplantation.
- Although end-stage liver disease is more common in minority individuals, those individuals are less likely to undergo liver transplantation. Furthermore, the survival rate after liver transplantation appears to be lower for African Americans than for Caucasians.

Improving Our Understanding of Hepatitis C Virus and the Disease That It Causes.

Current Activities

Basic and clinical research into the transmission, host immune response, pathogenesis, and natural history of hepatitis C viral infection in collaboration with other Institutes/Centers has been encouraged by several initiatives: RFA DK 98-017, "Hepatitis C: Natural History, Pathogenesis, Therapy and Prevention;" RFA AI-99-007, Hepatitis C Cooperative Research Centers; the NIDDK supported clinical study of hepatitis C and long-term therapy with interferon aimed at preventing cirrhosis and hepatocellular cancer (HALT-C trial); and a surveillance study in cooperation with the CDC on incidence of chronic liver disease in the population.

Another initiative, PA-98-086, "Liver and Biliary Diseases among Women and Minorities," which was issued in collaboration with the NIH Offices of Research on Minority and Women's Health (ORMH and ORWH), NIDA, and NIAAA, solicits R03 and R01 grants for both clinical and basic research in these areas.

Potential Initiative

To determine how hepatitis C (HCV) is transmitted and what factors contribute to its pathogenesis.

Expected Outcome

Definition of the viral, host, and environmental factors contributing to the transmission and pathogenesis of HCV and the role of racial/ethnic and gender differences in the susceptibility to and outcomes of infection.

Improving the Therapy for Hepatitis C, Particularly for African Americans

Current Activities

The NIDDK convened a conference entitled "Hepatitis C in African Americans" held December 2, 1999, on the NIH campus. The workshop participants reviewed information on the prevalence, clinical course, complications, and therapy of hepatitis C among African Americans and focused on comparisons of epidemiology and spread, serological and virological markers, disease severity and outcome, and treatment responses and complications between African American and Caucasian populations. A central aim of that meeting was to plan future research directions. Also, the Hepatitis C Antiviral Long-Term Therapy to prevent Cirrhosis (HALT-C) Trial is designed to determine the ability of long term treatment with interferon to prevent the development of cirrhosis and hepatocellular cancer. The trial will also provide information on the natural history of HCV. As the largest and longest study of HCV, this trial should provide answers concerning disease management and provide clinical criteria for grading, staging, and assessing the prognosis of people infected with HCV. This trial will include emphasis on recruitment of minority individuals.

Potential Initiative

Initiate a large clinical trial of combination therapy for HCV that will enroll similar numbers of African American and Caucasian patients and provide intensive investigation of viral, cell biologic, and genomic resources for laboratory investigation of viral resistance and response in HCV infection.

Expected Outcome

Characterization of the poor response rates of African Americans to current anti-HCV therapies. This characterization of resistance to interferon is key to developing effective therapy for all patients with this disease.

Improving the Availability and Efficacy of Liver Transplantation for all Groups of Americans

Current Activities

The NIDDK continues to fund a long-term study on outcomes of liver transplantation. With the advent of technical advances for living donor liver transplantation, this modality of transplant has increased significantly.

Expected Outcome

Stimulation and development of clinical investigation and research on optimizing donor and patient selection, surgical techniques, safety, and improvement in survival of liver transplantation.

Preventing Infection with Hepatitis C through Vaccine Development

Current Activities

A group of intramural investigators at NIDDK has taken two complementary approaches to study the development of HCV vaccine. First, in collaboration with investigators in the Southwest Foundation for Biomedical Research, an NIH Regional Primate Center, the group is conducting studies on chimpanzees, the only non-human primate model for HCV infection. The investigators have developed methods of synthesizing and purifying large quantities of non-infectious hepatitis C virus-like particles (HCV-LP), and has demonstrated that HCV-LP are capable of eliciting a strong humoral immune response broadly directed against various regions of HCV structural proteins in mice and rabbits. In addition, the HCV-LP is capable of inducing a cytotoxic T cell response, which has been shown to be pivotal in controlling HCV infection. The other project involves detailed molecular, virologic and immunologic analyses of chimpanzees infected either acutely or chronically with HCV to dissect the viral factors and host immune responses (both cellular and humoral) in viral clearance and disease progression.

Potential New Initiative

In the next five years, the plan is to expand along the same line of the research program in progress. The investigators will begin testing the immunogenicity and efficacy of the HCV-like particles and other modalities in the chimpanzee model.

Expected Outcome

Given the higher prevalence of HCV infection (two-fold), increased incidence of liver cancer (three fold) and poorer response to treatment among African Americans (<50%), the impact of an effective HCV vaccine will be particularly relevant on the affected minority populations. These disparities could ultimately dissipate if the infection can be prevented.

Chapter 28

The Minority Acquired Immune Deficiency Syndrome (AIDS) Crisis

The face of AIDS in the United States is changing. Minorities, primarily African Americans and Hispanics, now constitute 54 percent of the more than 500,000 cases of AIDS reported since the epidemic began in 1981.

African Americans and Hispanics are disproportionately affected by AIDS, as illustrated by the following facts:

- African Americans and Hispanics represented 56 percent of AIDS cases reported among men in 1996 and 78 percent of those in women. For every 100,000 African Americans, there were 89.7 cases of AIDS reported in 1996. This is more than six times higher than among Caucasians (13.5) and more than twice as high as the rate among Hispanics (41.3).
- For the first time, in 1996, the proportion of adults/adolescents reported with AIDS who are African American (41 percent) exceeded the proportion who are Caucasian (38 percent). Yet African Americans make up only 13 percent of the U.S. population.

This chapter contains text from "Minorities and HIV Infection," Fact Sheet, National Institute of Allergy and Infectious Diseases (NIAID), May 1997; "Race and Health: HIV: How to Reach the Goals," Department of Health and Human Services, September 13, 1999; "HIV/AIDS Surveillance Report," Midyear edition Vol. 11, No. 1, National Center for HIV, STD, and TB Prevention, June 1999; and "The Minority AIDS Crisis," *Closing the Gap*, April 1999.

- Injection drug use (IDU) is a major factor in the spread of HIV in minority communities. During the period July 1994-June 1995, the rate of IDU-associated AIDS cases among African-American women was 31.8 cases per 100,000. The rate among Caucasian women was 1.9 per 100,000. The rate among African-American men was 78.7 vs. 5.8 for Caucasian men, 44.7 for Hispanic men and 15 for Hispanic women.
- AIDS is the number one killer of African American men and women ages 25 to 44.
- Hispanics make up less than 10 percent of the U.S. population, yet they accounted for 19 percent of the AIDS cases reported in 1996.
- In 1996, 85 percent of the children reported with AIDS were African American and Hispanic.
- The rates of reported AIDS cases in 1996 among American Indians/Alaska Natives and Asians and Pacific Islanders were 10.7 and 5.9 per 100,000 population respectively.

Eliminate Disparities in HIV Infection/AIDS

HIV infection/AIDS is a leading cause of death for all persons 25 to 44 years of age. Between 650,000 and 900,000 Americans are estimated to be living with HIV infection. Approximately 62 percent (375,000) of the 604,200 adults and adolescents reported with AIDS in the United States have died from the disease.

AIDS has disproportionately affected minority populations. Racial and ethnic minorities constitute approximately 25 percent of the total U.S. population, yet they account for nearly 54 percent of all AIDS cases. While the epidemic is decreasing in some populations, the number of new AIDS cases among blacks is now greater than the number of new AIDS cases among whites.

There are several different HIV epidemics occurring simultaneously in the United States, each of which must address the specific population affected and their associated risk factors. For example, although the number of AIDS diagnoses among gay and bisexual men has decreased dramatically among white men since 1989, the number of AIDS diagnoses among black men who have sex with men have increased. In addition, AIDS cases and new infections related to injecting drug use appear to be increasingly concentrated in minorities; of these cases, almost 75 percent were among minority populations (56 percent black and 20 percent Hispanic). Of cases reported among women and children, more than 75 percent are among racial and ethnic minorities.

During 1995 and 1996, AIDS death rates declined 23 percent for the total U.S. population while declining only 13 percent for blacks and 20 percent for Hispanics. Contributing factors for these mortality disparities include late identification of disease and lack of health insurance to pay for drug therapies. The cost of efficacious treatment, between $10,000 and $12,000 per patient per year, is a major hurdle in the effort to ensure equitable access to available drug therapies.

Inadequate recognition of risk, detection of infection, and referral to follow-up care are major issues for high-risk populations. About one-third of persons who are at risk of HIV/AIDS have never been tested.

Better prevention strategies are needed that are acceptable to the target community (i.e., they must be culturally and linguistically appropriate), and the capability of organizations serving at-risk populations to develop, implement, evaluate, and fund prevention and treatment programs must be improved. Efforts should include risk reduction counseling, street and community outreach, prevention case management services, and help for individuals at risk in gaining access to HIV testing, treatment, and related services.

At this moment, there are many causes for optimism in the fight against HIV/AIDS. HIV prevention efforts have contributed to slowing the spread of the disease. For the first 6 months of 1996, there was an overall decrease in deaths among persons with AIDS, attributed primarily to the effect of antiretroviral therapies on the survival of persons with HIV infection. The decrease in the growth of AIDS cases in minority populations, however, has not been so strong.

To enable HIV-infected persons to benefit from treatment advances, HIV counseling and testing programs in screening and health care settings must better facilitate early diagnosis of HIV infection and ensure that HIV-infected persons have access to care and treatment services. Continued emphasis on behavioral risk reduction and other prevention strategies targeted to these populations is still the most effective way to reduce HIV infections.

Although advances in prevention and treatment are improving the quality of life for individuals living with HIV/AIDS, not everyone is benefiting equally from this progress. Concerns regarding education about the benefits of knowing one's serostatus, access to counseling and testing, and referral and access to medical services, including efficacious therapies, will continue to guide the development and administration of Federal initiatives to prevent HIV transmission and improve access to care for individuals living with HIV/AIDS.

Table 28.1. HIV Infection Cases[1] by Sex, Age at Diagnosis, and Race/Ethnicity, Reporting Through June 1999, from the 33 Areas with Confidential HIV Infection Reporting

	White, not Hispanic		Black, not Hispanic		Hispanic		Asian/Pacific Islander		American Indian/ Alaska Native		Total[2]	
	No.	(%)	No.	(%)	No.	(%)	No.	(%)	No.	(%)	No.	(%)
Male												
Age at diagnosis (years)												
Under 5	159	(0)	490	(1)	83	(1)	3	(1)	1	(0)	738	(1)
5-12	90	(0)	105	(0)	31	(1)	3	(1)	1	(0)	236	(0)
13-19	680	(2)	1,178	(3)	95	(2)	6	(2)	12	(2)	1,993	(2)
20-24	4,626	(13)	4,715	(12)	704	(11)	39	(14)	93	(18)	10,292	(12)
25-29	8,264	(23)	7,026	(18)	1,360	(22)	68	(24)	134	(26)	17,088	(21)
30-34	8,590	(24)	8,196	(21)	1,473	(24)	78	(28)	117	(23)	18,719	(23)
35-39	6,225	(17)	7,115	(18)	1,153	(19)	33	(12)	71	(14)	14,809	(18)
40-44	3,595	(10)	4,908	(18)	668	(11)	24	(9)	43	(8)	9,380	(11)
45-49	1,851	(5)	2,541	(7)	325	(5)	13	(5)	16	(3)	4,818	(6)
50-54	976	(3)	1,188	(3)	145	(2)	7	(2)	11	(2)	2,365	(3)
55-59	401	(1)	605	(2)	73	(1)	3	(1)	5	(1)	1,098	(1)
60-64	223	(1)	297	(1)	46	(1)	2	(1)	2	(0)	580	(1)
65 or older	214	(1)	276	(1)	38	(1)	3	(1)			541	(1)
Male subtotal	**35,894**	**(100)**	**38,638**	**(100)**	**6,194**	**(100)**	**282**	**(100)**	**506**	**(100)**	**82,657**	**(100)**

Female Age at diagnosis (years)												
Under 5	163	(2)	528	(3)	83	(4)	4	(4)	7	(4)	793	(3)
5-12	44	(1)	112	(1)	29	(1)	2	(2)	1	(1)	189	(1)
13-19	521	(7)	1,794	(8)	120	(6)	4	(4)	18	(10)	2,477	(8)
20-24	1,284	(17)	3,460	(16)	300	(14)	25	(25)	33	(18)	5,140	(16)
25-29	1,607	(21)	4,082	(19)	434	(21)	21	(21)	31	(17)	6,236	(20)
30-34	1,511	(20)	4,073	(19)	456	(22)	17	(17)	33	(18)	6,155	(20)
35-39	1,098	(15)	3,145	(15)	291	(14)	9	(9)	27	(15)	4,615	(15)
40-44	578	(8)	2,003	(9)	171	(8)	7	(7)	20	(11)	2,806	(9)
45-49	351	(2)	964	(5)	113	(5)	5	(5)	9	(5)	1,457	(5)
50-54	138	(2)	431	(2)	51	(2)	2	(2)	2	(1)	630	(2)
55-59	86	(1)	241	(1)	36	(2)	2	(2)	1	(1)	372	(1)
60-64	39	(1)	133	(1)	13	(1)					185	(1)
65 or older	76	(1)	150	(1)	7	(0)	1	(1)		238	(1)	
Female subtotal	**7,496**	**(100)**	**21,116**	**(100)**	**2,104**	**(100)**	**99**	**(100)**	**182**	**(100)**	**31,293**	**(100)**
Total[3]	**43,390**		**59,756**		**8,298**		**381**		**688**		**113,959**	

[1]Includes only persons reported with HIV infection who have not developed AIDS.

[2]Includes 1,143 males, 296 females, and 7 persons of unknown sex whose race/ethnicity is unknown.

[3]Includes 9 persons whose sex is unknown.

Table 28.2. Deaths in Persons with AIDS, by Race/Ethnicity, Age at Death, and Sex, Reported Through June 1999, United States.

Race/ethnicity and age at death[1]	Males Cumulative total	Females Cumulative total	Both sexes Cumulative total
White, not Hispanic			
Under 18	553	409	962
15-24	2,491	461	2,952
25-34	53,347	4,457	57,804
35-44	77,536	4,731	82,267
45-54	35,003	1,826	36,829
55 or older	14,747	1,648	16,395
All ages	183,839	13,555	187,394
Black, not Hispanic			
Under 18	1,394	1,386	2,780
15-24	2,367	1,346	3,713
25-34	32,223	11,037	43,260
35-44	47,017	13,562	60,579
45-54	20,282	4,612	24,894
55 or older	8,598	2,048	10,646
All ages	111,985	34,025	146,010
Hispanic			
Under 18	617	561	1,178
15-24	1,304	464	1,768
25-34	19,555	4,304	23,859
35-44	24,833	4,542	29,375
45-54	9,936	1,586	11,522
55 or older	4,076	765	4,841
All ages	60,371	12,233	72,604

Table 28.2. Continued.

Race/ethnicity and age at death[1]	Males Cumulative total	Females Cumulative total	Both sexes Cumulative total
Asian/Pacific Islander			
Under 18	15	33	
15-24	36	5	41
25-34	687	73	760
35-44	1,070	96	1,166
45-54	519	59	578
55 or older	232	44	276
All ages	2,564	294	2,858
American Indian/Alaska Native			
Under 18	11	8	19
15-24	24	3	27
25-34	352	65	417
35-44	358	60	418
45-54	113	23	136
55 or older	39	8	47
All ages	900	167	1,067
All racial/ethnic groups			
Under 18	2,595	2,380	4,975
15-24	6,227	2,281	8,408
25-34	106,222	19,940	126,162
35-44	150,925	23,001	173,926
45-54	65,897	8,111	74,008
55 or older	27,713	4,516	32,229
All ages	359,902	60,299	420,201

[1]Data tabulated under "all ages" include 393 persons whose age at death is unknown. Data tabulated under "all racial/ethnic groups" include 268 persons whose race/ethnicity is unknown.

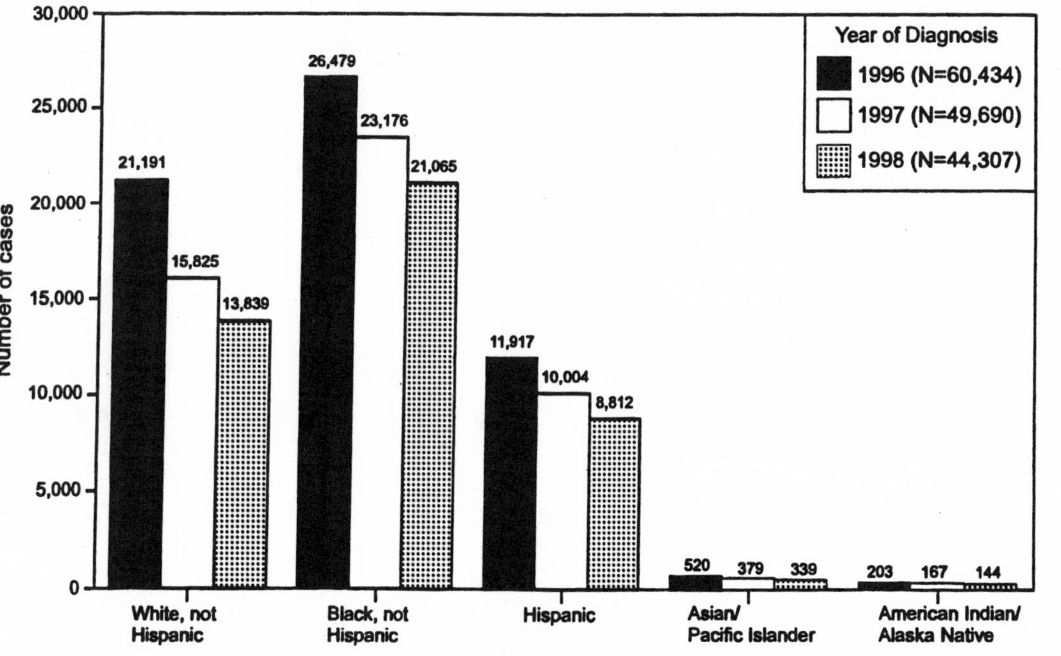

[1]These numbers do not represent actual cases of persons diagnosed with AIDS. Rather, these numbers are point estimates of persons diagnosed with AIDS adjusted for reporting delays, but not for incomplete reporting. Cases with missing or unknown gender or race/ethnicity data are included in the totals. Totals may vary between tables due to rounding. See Technical Notes.

Figure 28.1. *Estimated Adult/Adolescent AIDS Incidence, by Race/Ethnicity and Year of Diagnosis, 1996, 1997, and 1998, United States*[1]

Table 28.3. Estimated Persons Living with AIDS, by Race/Ethnicity and Year, 1993 Through 1998, United States[1]

Race/ethnicity	1993	1994	1995	1996	1997	1998
White, not Hispanic	80,582	86,999	92,172	99,202	108,031	116,445
Black, not Hispanic	60,752	72,029	81,489	92,540	105,719	118,525
Hispanic	31,241	36,579	41,169	46,371	52,455	58,185
Asian/Pacific Islander	1,284	1,447	1,606	1,849	2,088	2,230
American Indian/Alaska Native	559	657	710	796	890	971
Total[2]	**174,633**	**197,986**	**217,508**	**241,221**	**269,775**	**297,136**

[1]These numbers do not represent actual cases of persons living with AIDS. Rather these numbers are point estimates of persons living with AIDS derived by subtracting the estimated cumulative number of deaths in persons with AIDS from the estimated cumulative number of persons with AIDS. Estimated AUIDS cases and estimated deaths are adjusted for reporting delays, but not for incomplete reporting. Annual estimates are through the most recent year for which reliable estimates are available.

[2]Totals include estimates of persons whose race/ethnicity is unknown. Totals may vary between tables due to rounding.

Table 28.4. Estimated Deaths of Persons with AIDS, by Race/Ethnicity and Year of Death, 1993 Through 1998, United States[1]

Race/ethnicity	1993	1994	1995	1996	1997	1998
White, not Hispanic	21,501	22,297	21,549	14,230	7,033	5,454
Black, not Hispanic	15,352	17,785	18,803	15,753	10,199	8,401
Hispanic	7,665	8,787	8,958	6,816	3,985	3,133
Asian/Pacific Islander	307	144	186	120	74	64
Total[2]	**44,991**	**49,442**	**49,895**	**37,221**	**21,445**	**17,171**

[1]These numbers do not represent actual deaths of persons with AIDS. Rather, these numbers are point estimates adjusted for delays in the reporting of deaths, but not for incomplete reporting of deaths. Annual estimates are through the most recent year for which reliable estimates are available.

[2]Totals include estimates of persons whose race/ethnicity is unknown.

The Severity of the Minority HIV/AIDS Crisis

Every day, seven people contract HIV. Of those, three are African Americans, according to Dr. Beny J. Primm, executive director of Addiction Research and Treatment Corporation.

"African Americans are less likely to know their HIV status, get treatment, and be prescribed and take combination drug therapies for the disease." Dr. Primm said during the Congressional Black Caucus' (CBC) 1998 Spring Health Braintrust.

There has been a recent decline in HIV/AIDS death rates due to new treatment therapies. But current data from the Centers for Disease Control and Prevention (CDC) show HIV/AIDS rates among minorities—particularly African Americans—are on the rise. AIDS is the number one killer of African American men between the ages of 25 and 44, and is the second leading cause of death among African American women of the same age.

Several factors contribute to the severity of the AIDS epidemic among some minorities according to Eric P Goosby, M.D., director of HHS's Office of HIV/AIDS Policy. "First, within our population, we have individuals and groups that continue to practice high-risk behavior. Second, mixing of the virus into the population has occurred in African American and Hispanic groups whereas it hasn't occurred in Asian and American Indian populations." With Asians and American Indians, you have the same high-risk behavior taking place, but the virus has not been introduced into that population, according to Dr. Goosby.

The third factor is the stigma of HIV and AIDS. "In our community, the stigma associated with revealing yourself as an HIV positive individual, or as an individual who is in a group that is at higher risk—homosexuals or intravenous drug users—causes many individuals consciously to remain clandestine." According to Dr. Goosby. "It's about the patients. But it's also just as much if not more, about the impact it will have on their families."

Americans in general are living longer and healthier lives with HIV/AIDS due largely to medical advances and better drugs. But racial and ethnic health disparities also exist in quality of life for those living with the disease.

"No matter what health problem we have African Americans are hit harder." Said Congresswoman Christian Christensen. "It's not just an AIDS problem." She added. "It's a health infrastructure problem."

The Congresswoman said more basic problems need to be addressed like the ineffectiveness of many prevention programs, lack of access to quality and culturally appropriate services, and how managed care has failed the black community. "We need to look carefully at recent studies that show African Americans don't receive the same medical treatment by doctors as other Americans. Those are the systemic problems."

Of the 600,000 in the U.S. who are HIV positive, approximately half of them—300,000—are not getting care, according to Dr. Goosby. "Our goal is to identify high-risk populations; target them for testing; and move those that are positive, once tested, into a continuum of care and services. Those are our goals to increase the numbers of people getting treated."

AIDS in Blacks and Hispanics

Of the 641,086 AIDS cases reported to CDC through 1997, Blacks and Hispanics accounted for:

- 53 percent of total
- 76 percent of women
- 78 percent of heterosexuals*
- 81 percent of children

*Heterosexual injecting drug users and persons with heterosexually acquired HIV.

Blacks and Hispanics accounted for 65 percent of AIDS cases reported in 1997. (Source: Centers for Disease Control and Prevention.)

Part Five

Mental Health Services

Chapter 29

Overview of Cultural Diversity and Mental Health Services

The U.S. mental health system is not well equipped to meet the needs of racial and ethnic minority populations. Racial and ethnic minority groups are generally considered to be under-served by the mental health services system (Neighbors et al., 1992; Takeuchi and Uehara, 1996; Center for Mental Health Services [CMHS], 1998). A constellation of barriers deters ethnic and racial minority group members from seeking treatment, and if individual members of groups succeed in accessing services, their treatment may be inappropriate to meet their needs.

Awareness of the problem dates back to the 1960s and 1970s, with the rise of the civil rights and community mental health movements (Rogler et al., 1987) and with successive waves of immigration from Central America, the Caribbean, and Asia (Takeuchi and Uehara, 1996). These historical forces spurred greater recognition of the problems that minority groups confront in relation to mental health services.

Research documents that many members of minority groups fear, or feel ill at ease with, the mental health system (Lin et al., 1982; Sussman et al., 1987; Scheffler and Miller, 1991). These groups experience it as the product of white, European culture, shaped by research primarily on white, European populations. They may find only clinicians who represent a white middle-class orientation, with its

Excerpts from "Overview of Cultural diversity and Mental Health Services," Mental Health: A Report of the Surgeon General—Chapter 2, U.S. Public Health Service, 2000.

cultural values and beliefs, as well as its biases, misconceptions, and stereotypes of other cultures.

Research and clinical practice have propelled advocates and mental health professionals to press for "linguistically and culturally competent services" to improve utilization and effectiveness of treatment for different cultures. Culturally competent services incorporate respect for and understanding of, ethnic and racial groups, as well as their histories, traditions, beliefs, and value systems (CMHS, 1998). Without culturally competent services, the failure to serve racial and ethnic minority groups adequately is expected to worsen, given the huge demographic growth in these populations predicted over the next decades (Takeuchi and Uehara, 1996; CMHS, 1998; Snowden, 1999).

This section amplifies these major conclusions. It explains the confluence of clinical, cultural, organizational, and financial reasons for minority groups being under-served by the mental health system. The first task, however, is to explain which ethnic and racial groups constitute under-served populations, to describe their changing demographics, and to define the term "culture" and its consequences for the mental health system.

Introduction to Cultural Diversity and Demographics

The Federal government officially designates four major racial or ethnic minority groups in the United States: African American (black), Asian/Pacific Islander, Hispanic American (Latino),[1] and Native American/American Indian/Alaska Native/Native Hawaiian (referred to subsequently as "American Indians") (CMHS, 1998). There are many other racial or ethnic minorities and considerable diversity within each of the four groupings listed above. The representation of the four officially designated groups in the U.S. population in 1999 is as follows: African Americans constitute the largest group, at 12.8 percent of the U.S. population; followed by Hispanics (11.4 percent), Asian/Pacific Islanders (4.0 percent), and American Indians (0.9 percent) (U.S. Census Bureau, 1999). Hispanic Americans are among the fastest-growing groups. Because their population growth outpaces that of African Americans, they are projected to be the predominant minority group (24.5 percent of the U.S. population) by the year 2050 (CMHS, 1998).

Racial and ethnic populations differ from one another and from the larger society with respect to culture. The term "culture" is used loosely to denote a common heritage and set of beliefs, norms, and values. The cultures with which members of minority racial and ethnic groups identify often are markedly different from industrial societies of the West. The phrase "cultural identity" specifies a reference group "an identifiable social entity with whom a person identifies and to whom he or she looks for standards of behavior (Cooper and Denner, 1998). Of course, within any given group, an individual's cultural identity may also involve language, country of origin, acculturation,[2] gender, age, class, religious/spiritual beliefs, sexual orientation,[3] and physical disabilities (Lu et al., 1995). Many people have multiple ethnic or cultural identities.

The historical experiences of ethnic and minority groups in the United States are reflected in differences in economic, social, and political status. The most measurable difference relates to income. Many racial and ethnic minority groups have limited financial resources. In 1994, families from these groups were at least three times as likely as white families to have incomes placing them below the Federally established poverty line. The disparity is even greater when considering extreme poverty "family incomes at a level less than half of the poverty threshold" and is also large when considering children and older persons (O'Hare, 1996). Although some Asian Americans are somewhat better off financially than other minority groups, they still are more than one and a half times more likely than whites to live in poverty. Poverty disproportionately affects minority women and their children (Miranda & Green, 1999). The effects of poverty are compounded by differences in total value of accumulated assets, or total wealth (O'Hare et al., 1991).

Lower socioeconomic status—in terms of income, education, and occupation—has been strongly linked to mental illness. It has been known for decades that people in the lowest socioeconomic strata are about two and a half times more likely than those in the highest strata to have a mental disorder (Holzer et al., 1986; Regier et al., 1993b). The reasons for the association between lower socioeconomic status and mental illness are not well understood. It may be that a combination of greater stress in the lives of the poor and greater vulnerability to a variety of stressors leads to some mental disorders, such as depression. Poor women, for example, experience more frequent, threatening, and uncontrollable life events than do members of the population at large (Belle, 1990). It also may be that the impairments associated with mental disorders lead to lower socioeconomic status (McLeod and Kessler, 1990; Dohrenwend, 1992; Regier et al., 1993b).

Cultural identity imparts distinct patterns of beliefs and practices that have implications for the willingness to seek, and the ability to respond to, mental health services. These include coping styles and ties to family and community.

Coping Styles

Cultural differences can be reflected in differences in preferred styles of coping with day-to-day problems. Consistent with a cultural emphasis on restraint, certain Asian American groups, for example, encourage a tendency not to dwell on morbid or upsetting thoughts, believing that avoidance of troubling internal events is warranted more than recognition and outward expression (Leong and Lau, 1998). They have little willingness to behave in a fashion that might disrupt social harmony (Uba, 1994). Their emphasis on willpower is similar to the tendency documented among African Americans to minimize the significance of stress and to try to prevail in the face of adversity through increased striving (Broman, 1996).

Culturally rooted traditions of religious beliefs and practices carry important consequences for willingness to seek mental health services. In many traditional societies, mental health problems can be viewed as spiritual concerns and as occasions to renew one's commitment to a religious or spiritual system of belief and to engage in prescribed religious or spiritual forms of practice. African Americans (Broman, 1996) and a number of ethnic groups (Lu et al., 1995), when faced with personal difficulties, have been shown to seek guidance from religious figures.[4]

Many people of all racial and ethnic backgrounds believe that religion and spirituality favorably impact upon their lives and that well-being, good health, and religious commitment or faith are integrally intertwined (Taylor, 1986; Priest, 1991; Bacote, 1994; Pargament, 1997). Religion and spirituality are deemed important because they can provide comfort, joy, pleasure, and meaning to life as well as be means to deal with death, suffering, pain, injustice, tragedy, and stressful experiences in the life of an individual or family (Pargament, 1997). In the family/community-centered perception of mental illness held by Asians and Hispanics, religious organizations are viewed as an enhancement or substitute when the family is unable to cope or assist with the problem (Acosta et al., 1982; Comas-Diaz, 1989; Cook and Timberlake, 1989; Meadows, 1997).

Culture also imprints mental health by influencing whether and how individuals experience the discomfort associated with mental illness. When conveyed by tradition and sanctioned by cultural norms, characteristic modes of expressing suffering are sometimes called "idioms of distress" (Lu et al., 1995). Idioms of distress often reflect values and themes found in the societies in which they originate.

One of the most common idioms of distress is somatization, the expression of mental distress in terms of physical suffering. Somatization occurs widely and is believed to be especially prevalent among persons from a number of ethnic minority backgrounds (Lu et al., 1995). Epidemiological studies have confirmed that there are relatively high rates of somatization among African Americans (Zhang and Snowden, in press). Indeed, somatization resembles an African American folk disorder identified in ethnographic research and is linked to seeking treatment (Snowden, 1998).

A number of idioms of distress are well recognized as culture-bound syndromes. A culture-bound syndrome found among some Latino psychiatric patients is ataque de nervios, a syndrome of "uncontrollable shouting, crying, trembling, and aggression typically triggered by a stressful event involving family. . ." (Lu et al., 1995, p. 489). A Japanese culture-bound syndrome has appeared in that country's clinical modification of ICD-10 (WHO International Classification of Diseases, 10th edition, 1993). Taijin kyofusho is an intense fear that one's body or bodily functions give offense to others. Culture-bound syndromes sometimes reflect comprehensive systems of belief, typically emphasizing a need for a balance between opposing forces (e.g., yin/yang, "hot-cold" theory) or the power of supernatural forces (Cheung and Snowden, 1990). Belief in indigenous disorders and adherence to culturally rooted coping practices are more common among older adults and among persons who are less acculturated. It is not well known how applicable DSM-IV diagnostic criteria are to culturally specific symptom expression and culture-bound syndromes.

Family and Community as Resources

Ties to family and community, especially strong in African, Latino, Asian, and Native American communities, are forged by cultural tradition and by the current and historical need to assist arriving immigrants, to provide a sanctuary against discrimination practiced by the larger society, and to provide a sense of belonging and affirming a centrally held cultural or ethnic identity.

Among Mexican Americans (del Pinal and Singer, 1997) and Asian Americans (Lee, 1998) relatively high rates of marriage and low rates of divorce, along with a greater tendency to live in extended family households, indicate an orientation toward family. Family solidarity has been invoked to explain relatively low rates among minority groups of placing older people in nursing homes (Short et al., 1994).

The relative economic success of Chinese, Japanese, and Korean Americans has been attributed to family and communal bonds of association (Fukuyama, 1995). Community organizations and networks established in the United States include rotating credit associations based on lineage, surname, or region of origin. These organizations and networks facilitate the startup of small businesses.

There is evidence of an African American tradition of voluntary organizations and clubs often having political, economic, and social functions and affiliation with religious organizations (Milburn and Bowman, 1991). African Americans and other racial and ethnic minority groups have drawn upon an extended family tradition in which material and emotional resources are brought to bear from a number of linked households. According to this literature, there is "(a) a high degree of geographical propinquity; (b) a strong sense of family and familial obligation; (c) fluidity of household boundaries, with greater willingness to absorb relatives, both real and fictive, adult and minor, if need arises; (d) frequent interaction with relatives; (e) frequent extended family get-togethers for special occasions and holidays; and (f) a system of mutual aid" (Hatchett and Jackson, 1993, p. 92).

Families play an important role in providing support to individuals with mental health problems. A strong sense of family loyalty means that, despite feelings of stigma and shame, families are an early and important source of assistance in efforts to cope, and that minority families may expect to continue to be involved in the treatment of a mentally ill member (Uba, 1994). Among Mexican American families, researchers have found lower levels of expressed emotion and lower levels of relapse (Karno et al., 1987). Other investigators have demonstrated an association between family warmth and a reduced likelihood of relapse (Lopez et al., in press).

Epidemiology and Utilization of Services

One of the best ways to identify whether a minority group has problems accessing mental health services is to examine their utilization of services in relation to their need for services. As noted previously, a limitation of contemporary mental health knowledge is the lack of standard measures of "need for treatment" and culturally appropriate assessment tools. Minority group members' needs, as measured indirectly by their prevalence of mental illness in relation to the U.S. population, should be proportional to their utilization, as measured by their representation in the treatment population. These comparisons turn out to be exceedingly complicated by inadequate understanding of the prevalence of mental disorders among minority groups in the United States.[5] Nationwide studies conducted many years ago overlooked institutional populations, which are disproportionately represented by minority groups. Treatment utilization information on minority groups in relation to whites is more plentiful; yet, a clear understanding of health seeking behavior in various cultures is lacking.

The following paragraphs reveal that disparities abound in treatment utilization: some minority groups are underrepresented in the outpatient treatment population while, at the same time, over represented in the inpatient population.

African Americans

The prevalence of mental disorders is estimated to be higher among African Americans than among whites (Regier et al., 1993a). This difference does not appear to be due to intrinsic differences between the races; rather, it appears to be due to socioeconomic differences. When socioeconomic factors are taken into account, the prevalence difference disappears. That is, the socioeconomic status-adjusted rates of mental disorder among African Americans turn out to be the same as those of whites. In other words, it is the lower socioeconomic status of African Americans that places them at higher risk for mental disorders (Regier et al., 1993a).

African Americans are underrepresented in some outpatient treatment populations, but over represented in public inpatient psychiatric care in relation to whites (Snowden and Cheung, 1990; Snowden, in press). Their under-representation in outpatient treatment varies according to setting, type of provider, and source of payment. The racial gap between African Americans and whites in utilization is smallest, if not nonexistent, in community-based programs and in treatment financed by public sources, especially Medicaid (Snowden, 1998) and among older people (Padgett et al., 1995). The under-representation is largest in privately financed care, especially individual outpatient practice, paid for either by fee-for-service arrangements or managed care. As a result, under-representation in the outpatient setting occurs more among working and middle-class African Americans, who are privately insured, than among the poor. This suggests that socioeconomic standing alone cannot explain the problem of under-utilization (Snowden, 1998).

African Americans are, as noted, over-represented in inpatient psychiatric care (Snowden, in press-b). Their rate of utilization of psychiatric inpatient care is about double that of whites (Snowden and Cheung, 1990). This difference is even higher than would be expected on the basis of prevalence estimates. Over-representation is found in hospitals of all types except private psychiatric hospitals.[6] While difficult to explain definitively, the problem of over-representation in psychiatric hospitals appears more rooted in poverty, attitudes about seeking help, and a lack of community support than in clinician bias in diagnosis and overt racism, which also have been implicated (Snowden, in press-b). This line of reasoning posits that poverty, disinclination to seek help, and lack of health and mental health services deemed appropriate, and responsive, as well as community support, are major contributors to delays by African Americans in seeking treatment until symptoms become so severe that they warrant inpatient care.

Finally, African Americans are more likely than whites to use the emergency room for mental health problems (Snowden, in press-a). Their over-reliance on emergency care for mental health problems is an extension of their over-reliance on emergency care for other health problems. The practice of using the emergency room for routine care is generally attributed to a lack of health care providers in the community willing to offer routine treatment to people without insurance (Snowden, in press-a).

Asian Americans/Pacific Islanders

The prevalence of mental illness among Asian Americans is difficult to determine for methodological reasons (i.e., population sampling). Although some studies suggest higher rates of mental illness, there is wide variance across different groups of Asian Americans (Takeuchi and Uehara, 1996). It is not well known how applicable DSM-IV diagnostic criteria are to culturally specific symptom expression and culture-bound syndromes. With respect to treatment-seeking behavior, Asian Americans are distinguished by extremely low levels at which specialty treatment is sought for mental health problems (Leong and Lau, 1998). Asian Americans have proven less likely than whites, African Americans, and Hispanic Americans to seek care. One national sample revealed that Asian Americans were only a quarter as likely as whites, and half as likely as African Americans and Hispanic Americans, to have sought outpatient treatment (Snowden, in press-a). Asian Americans/Pacific Islanders are less likely than whites to be psychiatric inpatients (Snowden and Cheung, 1990). The reasons for the under-utilization of services include the stigma and loss of face over mental health problems, limited English proficiency among some Asian immigrants, different cultural explanations for the problems, and the inability to find culturally competent services.

These phenomena are more pronounced for recent immigrants (Sue et al., 1994).

Hispanic Americans

Several epidemiological studies revealed few differences between Hispanic Americans and whites in lifetime rates of mental illness (Robins and Regier, 1991; Vega and Kolody, 1998). A recent study of Mexican Americans in Fresno County, California, found that Mexican Americans born in the United States had rates of mental disorders similar to those of other U.S. citizens, whereas immigrants born in Mexico had lower rates (Vega et al., 1998a). A large study conducted in Puerto Rico reported similar rates of mental disorders among residents of that island, compared with those of citizens of the mainland United States (Canino et al., 1987).

Although rates of mental illness may be similar to whites in general, the prevalence of particular mental health problems, the manifestation of symptoms, and help-seeking behaviors within Hispanic subgroups need attention and further research. For instance, the prevalence of depressive symptomatology is higher in Hispanic women (46%) than men (almost 20%); yet, the known risk factors do not totally explain the gender difference (Vega et al., 1998a; Zunzunegui et al., 1998). Several studies indicate that Puerto Rican and Mexican American women with depressive symptomatology are under-represented in mental health services and over-represented in general medical services (Hough et al., 1987; Sue et al., 1991, 1994; Duran, 1995; Jimenez et al., 1997).

Native Americans

American Indians/Alaska Natives have, like Asian Americans and Pacific Islanders, been studied in few epidemiological surveys of mental health and mental disorders. The indications are that depression is a significant problem in many American Indian/Alaska Native communities (Nelson et al., 1992). One study of a Northwest Indian village found rates of DSM-III-R affective disorder that were notably higher than rates reported from national epidemiological studies (Kinzie et al., 1992). Alcohol abuse and dependence appear also to be especially problematic, occurring at perhaps twice the rate of occurrence found in any other population group. Suicide occurs at alarmingly high levels. (Indian Health Service, 1997). Among Native American veterans, post-traumatic stress disorder has been identified as especially prevalent in relation to whites (Manson, 1998). In terms of patterns of utilization, Native Americans are over-represented in psychiatric inpatient care in relation to whites, with the exception of private psychiatric hospitals (Snowden and Cheung, 1990; Snowden, in press-b).

References

1. The term “Latino(a)” refers to all persons of Mexican, Puerto Rican, Cuban, or other Central and South American or Spanish origin (CMHS, 1998).
2. Acculturation refers to the “social distance” separating members of an ethnic or racial group from the wider society in areas of beliefs and values and primary group relations (work, social clubs, family, friends) (Gordon, 1964). Greater acculturation thus reflects greater adoption of mainstream beliefs and practices and entry into primary group relations.
3. Research is emerging on the importance of tailoring services to the special needs of gay, lesbian, and bisexual mental health service users (Cabaj & Stein, 1996).
4. Of the 15 percent of the U.S. population that use mental health services in a given year, about 2.8 percent receive care only from members of the clergy (Larson et al., 1988).
5. In spring 2000, survey fieldwork began on an NIMH-funded study of the prevalence of mental disorders, mental health symptoms, and related functional impairments in African Americans, Caribbean blacks, and non-Hispanic whites. The study examines the effects of psychosocial factors and race-associated stress on mental health, and how coping resources and strategies influence that impact. The study will provide a database on mental health, mental disorders, and ethnicity and race. James Jackson, Ph.D., University of Michigan, is principal investigator.
6. African Americans are over-represented among persons undergoing involuntary civil commitment (Snowden, in press-b).

Chapter 30

Help-Seeking Behavior of Minorities

Barriers to the Receipt of Treatment

The under-representation in outpatient treatment of racial and ethnic minority groups appears to be the result of cultural differences as well as financial, organizational, and diagnostic factors. The service system has not been designed to respond to the cultural and linguistic needs presented by many racial and ethnic minorities. What is unresolved are the relative contribution and significance of each factor for distinct minority groups.

Help-Seeking Behavior

Among adults, the evidence is considerable that persons from minority backgrounds are less likely than are whites to seek outpatient treatment in the specialty mental health sector (Sussman et al., 1987; Gallo et al., 1995; Leong and Lau, 1998; Snowden, 1998; Vega et al., 1998a, 1998b; Zhang et al., 1998). This is not the case for emergency department care, from which African Americans are more likely than whites to seek care for mental health problems. Language, like economic and accessibility differences, can play an important role in why people from other cultures do not seek treatment (Hunt, 1984; Comas-Diaz, 1989; Cook and Timberlake, 1989; Taylor, 1989).

Excerpts from "Overview of Cultural Diversity and Mental Health Services," Mental Health: A Report of the Surgeon General—Chapter 2, U.S. Public Health Service, 2000.

Mistrust

The reasons why racial and ethnic minority groups are less apt to seek help appear to be best studied among African Americans. By comparison with whites, African Americans are more likely to give the following reasons for not seeking professional help in the face of depression: lack of time, fear of hospitalization, and fear of treatment (Sussman et al., 1987). Mistrust among African Americans may stem from their experiences of segregation, racism, and discrimination (Primm et al., 1996; Priest, 1991). African Americans have experienced racist slights in their contacts with the mental health system, called "microinsults" by Pierce (1992). Some of these concerns are justified on the basis of research, revealing clinician bias in over-diagnosis of schizophrenia and under-diagnosis of depression among African Americans.

Lack of trust is likely to operate among other minority groups, according to research about their attitudes toward government-operated institutions rather than toward mental health treatment per se. This is particularly pronounced for immigrant families with relatives who may be undocumented, and hence they are less likely to trust authorities for fear of being reported and having the family member deported. People from El Salvador and Argentina who have experienced imprisonment or watched the government murder family members and engage in other atrocities may have an especially strong mistrust of any governmental authority (Garcia and Rodriguez, 1989). Within the Asian community, previous refugee experiences of groups such as Vietnamese, Indochinese, and Cambodian immigrants parallel those experienced by Salvadoran and Argentine immigrants. They, too, experienced imprisonment, death of family members or friends, physical abuse, and assault, as well as new stresses upon arriving in the United States (Cook and Timberlake, 1989; Mollica, 1989).

American Indians' past experience in this country also imparted lack of trust of government. Those living on Indian reservations are particularly fearful of sharing any information with white clinicians employed by the government. As with African Americans, the historical relationship of forced control, segregation, racism, and discrimination has affected their ability to trust a white majority population (Herring, 1994; Thompson, 1997).

Stigma

The stigma of mental illness is another factor preventing African Americans from seeking treatment, but not at a rate significantly different from that of whites. Both African American and white groups report that embarrassment hinders them from seeking treatment (Sussman et al., 1987). In general, African Americans tend to deny the threat of mental illness and strive to overcome mental health problems through self-reliance and determination (Snowden, 1998). Stigma, denial, and self-reliance are likely explanations why other minority groups do not seek treatment, but their contribution has not been evaluated empirically, owing in part to the difficulty of conducting this type of research. One of the few studies of Asian Americans identified the barriers of stigma, suspiciousness, and a lack of awareness about the availability of services (Uba, 1994). Cultural factors tend to encourage the use of family, traditional healers, and informal sources of care rather than treatment-seeking behavior.

Cost

Cost is yet another factor discouraging utilization of mental health services. Minority persons are less likely than whites to have private health insurance, but this factor alone may have little bearing on access. Public sources of insurance and publicly supported treatment programs fill some of the gap. Even among working class and middle-class African Americans who have private health insurance, there is under-representation of African Americans in outpatient treatment (Snowden, 1998). Yet studies focusing only on poor women, most of whom were members of minority groups, have found cost and lack of insurance to be barriers to treatment (Miranda and Green, 1999). The discrepancies in findings suggest that much research remains to be performed on the relative importance of cost, cultural, and organizational barriers, and poverty and income limitations across the spectrum of racial and ethnic and minority groups.

Clinician Bias

Advocates and experts alike have asserted that bias in clinician judgment is one of the reasons for over-utilization of inpatient treatment by African Americans. Bias in clinician judgment is thought to be reflected in over-diagnosis or misdiagnosis of mental disorders. Since diagnosis is heavily reliant on behavioral signs and patients' reporting of the symptoms, rather than on laboratory tests, clinician judgment plays an enormous role in the diagnosis of mental disorders. The strongest evidence of clinician bias is apparent for African Americans with schizophrenia and depression. Several studies found that

African Americans were more likely than were whites to be diagnosed with schizophrenia, yet less likely to be diagnosed with depression (Snowden and Cheung, 1990; Hu et al., 1991; Lawson et al., 1994).

In addition to problems of over-diagnosis or misdiagnosis, there may well be a problem of under-diagnosis among minority groups, such as Asian Americans, who are seen as "problem-free" (Takeuchi and Uehara, 1996). The presence and extent of this type of clinician bias are not known and need to be investigated.

Improving Treatment for Minority Groups

The previous paragraphs have documented under-utilization of treatment, less help-seeking behavior, inappropriate diagnosis, and other problems that have beset racial and ethnic minority groups with respect to mental health treatment. This kind of evidence has fueled the widespread perception of mental health treatment as being uninviting, inappropriate, or not as effective for minority groups as for whites. The Schizophrenia Patient Outcome Research Team demonstrated that African Americans were less likely than others to have received treatment that conformed to recommended practices (Lehman and Steinwachs, 1998). Inferior treatment outcomes are widely assumed but are difficult to prove, especially because of sampling, questionnaire, and other design issues, as well as problems in studying patients who drop out of treatment after one session or who otherwise terminate prematurely. In a classic study, 50 percent of Asian Americans versus 30 percent of whites dropped out of treatment early (Sue and McKinney, 1975). However, the disparity in dropout rates may have abated more recently (O'Sullivan et al., 1989; Snowden et al., 1989). One of the few studies of clinical outcomes, a pre- versus post-treatment study, found that African Americans fared more poorly than did other minority groups treated as outpatients in the Los Angeles area (Sue et al., 1991). Earlier studies from the 1970s and 1980s had given inconsistent results (Sue et al., 1991).

Ethnopsychopharmacology

There is mounting awareness that ethnic and cultural influences can alter an individual's responses to medications (pharmacotherapies). The relatively new field of ethnopsychopharmacology investigates cultural variations and differences that influence the effectiveness of pharmacotherapies used in the mental health field. These differences are both genetic and psychosocial in nature. They range from genetic variations in drug metabolism to cultural practices that affect diet, medication adherence, placebo effect, and simultaneous use of traditional and alternative healing methods (Lin et al., 1997). Just a few examples are provided to illustrate ethnic and racial differences.

Pharmacotherapies given by mouth usually enter the circulation after absorption from the stomach. From the circulation they are distributed throughout the body (including the brain for psychoactive drugs) and then metabolized, usually in the liver, before they are cleared and eliminated from the body (Brody, 1994). The rate of metabolism affects the amount of the drug in the circulation. A slow rate of metabolism leaves more drug in the circulation. Too much drug in the circulation typically leads to heightened side effects. A fast rate of metabolism, on the other hand, leaves less drug in the circulation. Too little drug in the circulation reduces its effectiveness.

There is wide racial and ethnic variation in drug metabolism. This is due to genetic variations in drug-metabolizing enzymes (which are responsible for breaking down drugs in the liver). These genetic variations alter the activity of several drug-metabolizing enzymes. Each drug-metabolizing enzyme normally breaks down not just one type of pharmacotherapy, but usually several types. Since most of the ethnic variation comes in the form of inactivation or reduction in activity in the enzymes, the result is higher amounts of medication in the blood, triggering untoward side effects.

For example, 33 percent of African Americans and 37 percent of Asians are slow metabolizers of several antipsychotic medications and antidepressants (such as tricyclic antidepressants and selective serotonin reuptake inhibitors) (Lin et al., 1997). This awareness should lead to more cautious prescribing practices, which usually entail starting patients at lower doses in the beginning of treatment. Unfortunately, just the opposite typically had been the case with African American patients and antipsychotic drugs. Clinicians in psychiatric emergency services prescribed more oral doses and more injections of antipsychotic medications to African American patients (Segel et al., 1996). The combination of slow metabolism and overmedication of antipsychotic drugs in African Americans can yield very uncomfortable extrapyramidal[1] side effects (Lin et al., 1997). These are the kinds of experiences that likely contribute to the mistrust of mental health services reported among African Americans (Sussman et al., 1987).

Psychosocial factors also can play an important role in ethnic variation. Compliance with dosing may be hindered by communication difficulties; side effects can be misinterpreted or carry different connotations; some groups may be more responsive to placebo treatment; and reliance on psychoactive traditional and alternative healing methods (such as medicinal plants and herbs) may result in interactions with prescribed pharmacotherapies. The result could be greater side effects and enhanced or reduced effectiveness of the pharmacotherapy, depending on the agents involved and their concentrations (Lin et al., 1997). Greater awareness of ethnopsychopharmacology is expected to improve treatment effectiveness for racial and ethnic minorities. More research is needed on this topic across racial and ethnic groups.

Reference

1. Dystonia (brief or prolonged contraction of muscles), akathisia (an urge to move about constantly), or parkinsonism (tremor and rigidity) (Perry et al., 1997).

Mental Health Journals

Cultural Diversity and Mental Health
John Wiley and Sons
Subscription Dept.
605 Third Ave.
New York, NY 10158
Tel: 212-850-6000

Journal of Black Psychology and Hispanic Journal of Behavioral Sciences
Sage Publications
Customer Service Dept.
2455 Teller Rd.
Thousand Oaks, CA 91320
Tel: 805-499-9774

American Indian and Alaska Native Mental Health Research
University Press of Colorado
P.O. Box 849
Niwot, CO 80544
Tel: 720-406-8849

Chapter 31

Cultural Considerations in Treating Asians

Study after study has shown that Asians under-utilize mental health services much more than other populations, according to Stanley Sue, PhD, director of the National Research Center on Asian American Mental Health in Davis, California.

It's a trend that Dr. Sue discovered in the seventies when he was a graduate student intern at the University of California, Los Angeles Psychiatry Clinic. The clinic assessed information on the number of Asian student clients, as well as therapists' impressions of those clients. "Not only did we find that Asians under-utilized services," Dr. Sue said. "We also found that the Asian students exhibited more severe mental disturbances than the non-Asian students." The same patterns can be seen today. The National Research Center evaluated records of thousands of clients of the Los Angeles County mental health system for a six-year period. "What we found," said Dr. Sue, "was that Asians were underrepresented in the outpatient system, and they were more likely than African Americans, Whites, and Hispanics to have psychotic disorders." Contrary to popular belief, the fact that a certain population is not using mental health services does not indicate that the population is free of mental health problems, Dr. Sue added.

A key question then is why? Why aren't Asians seeking and receiving treatment from state services if their mental health needs are so significant? Several factors play into why people use or don't use

---

Closing the Gap, Office of Minority Health, September 1997.

mental health services, including the ease of accessing services and willingness to seek help. According to experts, culture is at the heart of such factors.

"For example, in traditional Chinese culture, many diseases are attributed to an imbalance of cosmic forces—yin and yang," Dr. Sue explained. "So the goal is to restore the balance, and that might be accomplished through exercise or diet," and not necessarily through a mainstream mental health system.

While there are cultural attitudes that can be seen across the Asian population, there are important differences between groups, according to Deborah S. Lee, CSW, director of Asian American Mental Health Services in New York City. "For all Asian groups, there is a stigma attached to going to an outsider to obtain treatment for mental health problems," Ms. Lee said. "But depending on the group, the stigma is expressed differently." This also can depend on educational background and how long a person has been in this country.

Ms. Lee's Chinese clients often interpret mental illness as punishment for some wrongdoing carried out by themselves, by their family members, or by their ancestors. For this reason, they may feel ashamed to seek or participate in treatment. People in the Chinese community often call Ms. Lee's clinic to say they have a friend who is experiencing some problems. After telling the caller to bring in the friend, she frequently discovers that the friend is really a relative of the person who called. "The caller was simply ashamed of having such problems in the family," she said.

For Asians, the individual is commonly viewed as a reflection of the entire family. "That's why the family should be included in treatment," Lee suggests.

In the case of a Cambodian woman who suffers from depression, her husband is against her receiving treatment from Lee's clinic. "He believes she has mental health problems because she is haunted by evil spirits," Ms. Lee said. "So we had to work on convincing him to keep letting us treat her here, while they also use cultural practices at home to ward off bad spirits. We had to let him know that we could include him in the process of developing a treatment plan for his wife. We also had to make sure that each practice would not interfere with the other."

Ms. Lee finds that because the Korean community is very religious, her Korean clients often confuse their hallucinations with spiritual voices. "Our Korean clients also rely very heavily on treating themselves with medication. We have to educate them and their families about the dangers of misusing drugs and the importance of understanding that treatment for mental health problems involves more than just medication." Lee also treats Japanese clients, who are very concerned about who knows that they are in treatment. Many people have failed to show up for appointments for fear of being seen. "Sometimes, we block in an extra 15 minutes between appointment so that there is less of a chance that people might run into someone they know," Lee noted.

Asian American Mental Health Services, a state-licensed program, is specifically designed for the New York Asian community. The program operates a Chinese unit, which has a continuing treatment program for patients who are chronically mentally ill. There is also a Japanese unit, a Korean unit, and a Southeast Asian unit, all with outpatient clinics.

Ms. Lee and her staff are Asian, and they possess specialized knowledge and skills about delivering mental health services to Asians. They know, for instance, that when a client comes in complaining of an inability to move a part of the body, it's important to conduct a culturally-sensitive psychological evaluation, rather that automatically sending the client away for a physical check-up. "It's very common among Asians," Ms. Lee said, "to report physical problems that are really a reflection of mental or emotional problems."

But what about those mainstream clinics that don't have insight into Asian culture? How can services be reorganized so that Asians can be treated there? According to Dr. Sue, mental health workers need to be trained on aspects of Asian culture, and mainstream facilities should make use of Asian consultants.

"Another valuable strategy," he added, "is targeting Asians through community education." It is possible to modify attitudes this way. Important points to make are that talking with others about problems can help, that early identification is crucial, and that providers are required to keep problems confidential.

—Michelle Meadows

Part Six

Ethnic Women's Health

Chapter 32

Asian American Women

Asian American and Pacific Islanders represent one of the fastest-growing and most diverse populations in the United States. There are 28 Asian and 19 Pacific Islander groups representing a vast array of languages and cultures. Some are 4th and 5th generation Asian Americans, while 75% are recent immigrants and refugees. Native Hawaiians and American Samoans are not immigrants, but indigenous peoples who are striving to preserve their culture and retain their relationship to the land.

Asian American women have the highest life expectancy (85.8 years) of any ethnic or racial group in the U.S. Yet there are wide disparities between Samoan (74.9 years), Native Hawaiian (77.2 years), Filipino (81.5 years), Japanese (84.5), and Chinese women (86.1 years).

Health Issues of Concern to Asian American Women

- Access to health care can be limited due to cultural and language differences, as well as economic and other barriers. Breast and cervical cancer screening rates are much lower than the national average.

- Tuberculosis is 13-times more common among Asian populations, especially those from Cambodia, China, Laos, Korea, India, Vietnam, and the Philippines.

"Women of Color Health Data Book," The National Women's Health Information Center, 1998.

- Hepatitis B is 25 to 75 times more common than the U.S. average among Samoans and immigrants from Cambodia, Laos, Vietnam, and China.
- Cervical cancer incidence rates among Vietnamese women are nearly 5-times those of white women.
- Breast cancer. Native Hawaiians have the highest mortality rate for any racial/ethnic group in the U.S. for breast cancer: 37.2 per 100,000. Chinese and Japanese American women have higher rates than in China and Japan.
- Suicide. Asian American women have the highest suicide rates among women ages 15 to 24 and those over age 65.
- Osteoporosis. Asian American women are at particular risk for osteoporosis due to their relatively lower bone mass and density, smaller frames, and lower intake of calcium compared to other population groups.

Factors Affecting the Health of Asian American Women

Although health issues for Asian Americans and Pacific Islander Americans often are analyzed jointly, in this chapter the groups are separated. Native Pacific Islanders are considered Native Americans and are discussed with American Indians/Alaska Natives. (See discussion of Pacific Islanders in section on Native Americans.) Asian populations are discussed together. This change is made because native Pacific Islanders are only 5 percent of the Asian and Pacific Islander total and often have health outcomes more akin to those of American Indians/Alaska Natives than to Asian populations. In addition, native Pacific Islanders are not immigrants to the United States as are Asian populations. Thus, an effort has been made throughout to disaggregate Asians from Pacific Islanders whenever possible, and to display data for the groups separately. Aggregate statistics for Asians and Pacific Islanders are used, however, when they are the best available.

Asian Americans are immigrants to the United States (and their descendants) from more than 20 countries who speak more than 100 different languages. They come from places such as China, India, Japan, the Philippines, Korea, Laos, Cambodia, Vietnam, and Thailand and represent more than 60 different ethnicities.[22] In 1990, the largest sub-populations (in descending order) were persons of Chinese,

Filipino, Japanese, Asian Indian, Korean, and Southeast Asian ancestry. By the year 2000, Filipinos are projected to be the largest Asian sub-population, followed by Chinese, Vietnamese, Korean, and Japanese Americans, in that order.[120]

The numbers of Asians and Pacific Islanders in the United States (both males and females) have grown from 1.5 million in 1970 to more than 7.2 million in 1990, and more than 9 million in 1996, making them the fastest growing minority group in the United States. The 1990 Census counted 6.9 million persons of Asian ancestry and more than 365,000 Pacific Islanders among the population of 7.2 million.[21] Asian and Pacific Islanders are currently more than 3 percent of the total U.S. population and nearly 13 percent of all people of color.[1] Asian and Pacific Islander women represent 13 percent of all women of color and 52 percent of all Asian and Pacific Islander Americans.[1]

The majority of Asian Americans—more than 90 percent—reside in metropolitan centers. The states with the largest shares of Asian and Pacific Islander Americans are California, Hawaii, and Washington. More than 55 percent of all Asians and Pacific Islanders live in these three states, with the remainder living in New York, New Jersey, Illinois, and Texas.[25] Among all the states, Asians and Pacific Islanders are the largest proportion of the population of Hawaii—62 percent.[2] When growth of the Asian and Pacific Islander population by state is examined between 1980 and 1990, however, the five states with the largest increases—Rhode Island (246 percent), New Hampshire (219 percent), Georgia (210 percent), Wisconsin (195 percent), and Minnesota (194 percent)—are neither West Coast states nor states traditionally considered as homes for large numbers of Asians and Pacific Islanders.[24]

Major Sub-Populations

The varied histories of the many Asian sub-populations who have immigrated to the United States contribute to the wide, bipolar distribution in their socioeconomic positions and health. Most Asian immigrants have come to the United States since 1965, when the Supreme Court struck down immigration quotas based on national origin and when only about 1 million Asians were in the United States. Chinese immigration to this country, however, dates back to the mid-1800s. With the decline of the African slave trade and the discovery of gold, waves of mostly male Chinese were brought to the United States as cheap, docile laborers to work in the mines and on the railroads in the Western states. This new servant class became the new "negro" for the white majority and was even referred to as "nagurs" by some.[121] Later labeled the "yellow peril," or disease-ridden and heathen, the Chinese were barred from entering the United States on the basis of race alone by the Chinese Exclusion Act of 1882. This ban remained in effect until 1943, and it was 1952 before immigrant Chinese were able to become U.S. citizens.[23,122]

In the 1960-1985 period, the **Chinese population of the United States** quadrupled, and immigrants from more diverse ethnic and social strata came to the United States.[23,122] Between 1980 and 1990, the Chinese American population doubled, mostly due to immigration; 63 percent of all Chinese Americans are foreign-born.[23] In 1990, more than 1.6 million persons of Chinese descent resided in the United States and constituted 23 percent of the Asian American population.[123] Although Chinese Americans live throughout the United States, the largest concentrations are found in California (more than 700,000) and in New York state (more than 284,000).[124] Because Chinese Americans are diverse in class, occupation, and regional and linguistic background, in many Chinese American communities, unity is an elusive goal.[25] Differences between foreign-born and American-born, urban residents and suburbanites, old timers and newcomers, northerners and southerners, Catholics and Protestants, Christians and Buddhists, professionals and laborers, and rich and poor frequently override a common ethnic identity.[125]

The second largest Asian American sub-population in the United States is **Filipino Americans**. Beginning with U.S. intervention in the Philippine Islands, Filipinos have migrated to both Hawaii and the mainland United States in three major waves.[23] Between 1903 and 1910, a first wave of Filipinos came to the United States to attend educational institutions; a second wave migrated after World War II to work in agriculture in Hawaii and on the mainland United States. The third wave, consisting of fewer single men, more family groups, and more highly educated people, began after 1965 and continues today.[25] Evidence of this third wave is the 81 percent increase in the Filipino population of the United States between 1980 and 1990. In 1990, Filipino Americans numbered 1.4 million and were 19 percent of the Asian American population.[123] More than 64 percent of Filipino Americans are foreign born.[23]

Immigration from Japan to both Hawaii and the mainland United States began in large numbers around 1885 and peaked between

1900 and 1910. The National Origins Act barred Japanese and other Asians from entering the United States after 1924 and contributed to the marked distinctions between the first-generation Japanese Americans (Issei) and second (Nisei) and subsequent generations.[23,25] Because first-generation Japanese Americans, many of whom were relocated and interned in prison camps in the United States during World War II, migrated to the United States when Japan had a single language without significant dialects, they have a stronger sense of nationalism than the immigrants constituting later generations.[23] This sense of national identity among the Issei has been posited as the explanation for the strong identity among this particular group of immigrants. Today's Japanese American population of 847,562 (11 percent of all Asian Americans) resides primarily in California and Hawaii. More than 70 percent of all Japanese Americans were born in the United States.

The more than 800,000 **Asian Indian Americans** (11 percent of all Asian Americans) live primarily in the Eastern United States, although nearly 160,000 Asian Indians live in California.[21,25,123] New York state is home to the second largest number (nearly 141,000) of Asian Indians. In 1992, the majority of births to Asian women in the states of Illinois (home to more than 64,000 Asian Indians) and New Jersey (home to more than 79,000 Asian Indians) were to Asian Indian women.[35] Asian Indians have migrated to the United States in largest numbers since 1965, though some had come to the Western United States in the early 1900s, after initially migrating to British Columbia. Although they are of differing ethnic groups and backgrounds, most share a common tradition of non-western medical practice (Ayurvedic), and many are highly educated professionals.[21,25]

Korean Americans, one of the most homogeneous Asian populations in terms of language, ethnicity, and culture, also are one of the fastest growing Asian sub-populations in the United States.[21] Their population increased more than tenfold between 1970 (70,000 population) and 1990 (800,000 population) to make Korean Americans 11 percent of the current total U.S. Asian population (123,126). Korean Americans first migrated to the United States in response to unstable conditions such as drought, famine, and epidemics in their homeland in the late 1800s and early 1900s, which sent them to Hawaii and the United States mainland primarily as contract laborers.[127] Others have migrated as a result of United States-Korean interaction during the Korean War (e.g., wives of servicemen; orphans adopted by Americans).[23]

The Korean population of the United States more than doubled between 1980 and 1990, with most of the growth due to immigration; in 1990, more than 80 percent of all Korean Americans were foreign born. Post-1965 Korean immigrants tend to come to the United States as families, and most tend to be well educated.

Southeast Asians began to migrate to the United States primarily after 1975, as the conflicts in that region in Cambodia, Laos, and Vietnam were winding down. The majority of refugees of these conflicts to come to the United States were Vietnamese (66 percent), with Cambodians and Laotians each constituting roughly 20 percent of Southeast Asian immigrants.[23] The earlier waves of refugees during the post-1975 period generally were better educated and wealthier than later arrivals, many of whom—especially Hmong (a Chinese-origin population that migrated to Laos and later to Thailand and the United States) and Laotians—were poor, illiterate, and not at all used to western culture at the time of their resettlement. The trauma of dislocation and resettlement is related to many of the health problems of these Asian sub-populations. About 615,000 Vietnamese, 149,000 Laotians, 147,000 Cambodians, and more than 90,000 Hmong resided in the United States in 1990.[23] Most Southeast Asians live in Western states, led by the 46 percent of Vietnamese and the 48 percent of Cambodians living in California.[128,129]

Factors Affecting Health

The "model minority" image replaced the negative stereotypes applied to Chinese and other Asian Americans in 1966. Coming shortly after the 1965 Watts riots in Los Angeles, the identification of a model minority is viewed by some as an attempt to provide proof that the U.S. social system does work for minorities.[24,121] However, Asians often are pitted against other minority groups and are made scapegoats by low-income whites and other minorities who indirectly blame Asians for their failure to succeed and claim that Asians take away their educational and job opportunities. The "model minority" epithet has direct implications for the health and economic status of Asian Americans. It tends to trivialize the health problems of Asians, suggesting that they can take care of these problems on their own and overlooks the diversity among Asians and the problems faced by some of the newest refugees.[130]

The health problems of Asian Americans are worsened by a complex set of cultural, linguistic, structural, and financial barriers to care. In 1980, a language other than English was spoken at home by nine out of 10 Asian Americans who were 5 years of age or older.[131] In 1992, 42 percent of the Vietnamese American population 5 years of age and older lived in a linguistically isolated household—that is, a household in which no person age 14 years and older speaks only English, and no person age 14 years and older, who speaks a language other than English, also speaks English "very well."[35] Nearly three-fifths of Asian Americans are foreign-born, and, in 1992, only 17 percent of all Asian mothers who gave birth in the United States had been born in the United States.[35] If residing illegally in the United States, Asian Americans may not seek out medical care for fear that this will expose their illegal status and result in deportation.

Since many Asians are unable to communicate in English, they are not readily employable. When employed, it is often in small businesses or sweatshop-type factories with unsafe and unhealthy working conditions and no fringe benefits such as health insurance. Three-fifths of all Asian and Pacific Islander women were in the labor force in 1990, with more than a fifth (22 percent) employed in administrative occupations. One-sixth (17 percent) of Asian and Pacific Islander females had professional specialty occupations, while an additional 16 percent had service occupations.[132]

Although only 15 percent of all Asians and Pacific Islanders and only 29 percent of all households headed by Asian and Pacific Islander females reported incomes below the federal poverty level in 1995, these averages mask considerable variation among sub-populations.[133] For example, the percentage of the population below the poverty level ranged from a low of 6 percent among Japanese Americans to a high of 66 percent among Laotians in 1990 (compared to about 13 percent for the entire U.S. population).[37] The proportion of Vietnamese families reporting incomes below the poverty level in 1990 (24 percent) was more than three times as great as that for Asian Indian families (7 percent).[35] Hmong and Cambodian Americans reported poverty levels above 45 percent.[23]

Both household and individual incomes for Asian Americans support the finding of disparate poverty rates among the sub-populations. In 1980, Asian Americans had average household income of $6,900, less than the United States average of $7,400. At that time, only Indonesian, Chinese, and Japanese Americans had average per capita incomes above the U.S. average.[23] In 1990, the median family income for Asian and Pacific Islanders was $35,900 (higher than the $35,000 median family income for non-Hispanic white Americans), and 37 percent of all Asian and Pacific Islander American households had annual incomes of at least $50,000. At the same time, more than 5 percent of Asian and Pacific Islander households had incomes of less than $5,000, and nearly 12 percent had incomes of less than $10,000.[134] The resettlement of more than 1 million Indochinese refugees in the 1970s and 1980s made the bimodal distribution even more pronounced because refugees arriving after 1979 have experienced higher rates of unemployment, underemployment, and poverty than other Asian Americans, and other minorities.[37] For example, in 1980, unemployment among the Hmong (20 percent), Laotians (15 percent), and Cambodians (11 percent) all exceeded the U.S. average.[23]

Health insurance coverage varies among Asian American women, as do employment and income levels. Eighty-one percent of all Asian and Pacific Islander women and 91 percent of Asian and Pacific Islander women ages 65 years and older reported having either private or public health insurance coverage in 1995.[133] Fourteen percent of Asian and Pacific Islander women reported Medicaid coverage and nearly 7 percent reported Medicare coverage. Nearly two-thirds (66 percent) of Asian and Pacific Islander women had private health insurance. Despite high rates of coverage in general, selected subpopulations of Asians lack health insurance, and this lack of health insurance causes some Asian American women to become frequent users of hospital emergency rooms. One study of Korean American residents in Los Angeles County found that 50 percent of those under 65 years of age and 45 percent of those 65 year of age and older had no health insurance.[135]

Healthful Behaviors and the Prevalence of Illness

Although Asian American women overall exhibit healthful lifestyle behaviors, such as a lower smoking prevalence (10 percent) than among other American women (25 percent), there is variation by subpopulation in both healthful behaviors and the prevalence of illness.[24] For example, this 10 percent overall smoking prevalence aggregates higher rates among Japanese American (19 percent of whom reported smoking in one California study) and Filipino American (11 percent of whom reported smoking in the same study) with the lower rates of Chinese women (7 percent of whom reported smoking in the California study).[136] The risk of hypertension also varies by sub-population. In another study of the California population, hypertension was found to be more of a problem for Filipino Americans (25 percent) than for either Chinese (16 percent) or Japanese (13 percent) Americans.[128] Only 9 percent of Vietnamese females in California reported hypertension compared to 16 percent of all females in the state population. The lowest hypertension rate was reported among Korean American females in California, only 3 percent of whom reported the condition.[128]

Other conditions, such as tuberculosis, are more common among Asian populations than among other racial/ethnic groups. The prevalence of tuberculosis among Asian Americans, the highest among all groups, is nearly 4 times that among the general population.[24,137] Hepatitis B and certain genetic abnormalities also are more common among Asian sub-populations.

Preventive Care Behaviors

The lack of knowledge of risk factors or preventive behaviors for various diseases also is a problem for Asian Americans. One study among Southeast Asian populations in central Ohio revealed that 94 percent of those surveyed did not know what blood pressure is, and 85 percent did not know what could be done to prevent heart disease.[128] The lack of knowledge about cancer risk factors, for example, results in the failure to conduct breast self-examinations or to get screening such as mammography or Pap smears to lessen the incidence of breast or cervical cancer.[24]

The failure of Asian women to get regular screenings relates not only to a lack of knowledge of risk factors but also to the belief that cancer is inevitably fatal. One survey of Vietnamese women in San Francisco found that more than half (52 percent) believed "there is little one can do to prevent cancer."[138] Although virtually all of the women surveyed (97 percent) had heard of cancer, many did not know common signs, symptoms, and risk factors for either breast or cervical cancer. Vietnamese women who have migrated to the United States more recently (post 1981) were more likely (76 percent) to have never had the Papanicolaou test for cervical cancer than women who had migrated before 1981 (33 percent).[138] In a survey of Vietnamese women in western Massachusetts, just over 50 percent of respondents reported having had the Pap test, less than the 57 percent of all U.S. women 18 years and older who reported having had this test in 1991.[139,140]

The failure to get mammograms is of particular concern because of the gradual increase in breast cancer rates among Asian women (especially Chinese, Japanese, and Filipino) over the generations after their migration to the United States, when compared to these same groups of women in Asia. Overall, Asian American women born in the United States have a breast cancer risk 60 percent higher than Asian American women born in Asia.[141]

Prenatal care is another form of preventive care that many Asian American women do not receive. Nearly half of Cambodian and Laotian American women do not begin prenatal care during their first trimester and have higher risk births because of this.[137,142] Of the five major Indochinese groups in Oregon (Khmer, Hmong, Mien, other Lao, and Vietnamese), Hmong American women had the least favorable birth risk profile.[142] Mean birth weight among Hmong infants born in California between 1985 and 1988 was significantly lower than mean birth weight among white infants.[143] The preterm and low-weight infants born to Hmong, Cambodian, and Laotian mothers in 1992 are reflected in the aggregate rates of 12 percent (preterm) and 7 percent (low birth weight) for births to all women in the category "Remaining Asian or Pacific Islander Total." These rates are higher than for Vietnamese mothers (10 percent preterm and 6 percent low birth weight), and also higher than for white non-Hispanic mothers (8 percent preterm and 5 percent low birth weight).[35]

Use of Traditional Health Practices and Medicines

Even with health insurance, culturally accepted medical models such as acupuncture and herbal medicines often are not covered services, a fact that further limits access to health care.[36] Asian American women are more likely to report using traditional health practices and medicines than Asian men—69 percent versus 39 percent. By ethnic group, nearly all Cambodian women (96 percent), nearly a fifth (18 percent) of Laotian women, and nearly two-thirds of Chinese women (64 percent) report using traditional health practices.[144] High non-compliance with western prescription medications among these populations clearly becomes a concern. Non-English-speaking Chinese hypertensives, for example, exhibit such non-compliance, perhaps in deference to traditional treatments.[24]

Communication with Health Care Providers

Fear of difficulties in communicating—compounded by shame, guilt, anger, depression, and other responses to certain stigmatized conditions such as mental retardation, substance abuse, and HIV/AIDS—also may deter Asian Americans from seeking care promptly.[37] Chinese Americans in particular have been documented to under-use mental health services.[145] The traumas due to war (e.g., torture, starvation, rape, forced labor, and witnessing murder), leaving one's homeland, and resettling in another land often result in unique medical conditions, such as the psychosomatic or non-organic blindness reported among Cambodian women 40 years of age and older. Even if Asian American patients seek care, language barriers make conditions such as this difficult to diagnose and treat.[129] To compound their stresses and trauma, many poor Southeast Asian immigrants resettle in violent, inner-city environments in the United States.[146] Depression is also found among Korean Americans, most of whom are recent immigrants but who migrated to the United States without war-related trauma; this mental health problem is more common among Korean Americans than it is among either Chinese, Japanese, or Filipino Americans.[126]

In addition, not all English medical/health terminology can be readily translated into the various Southeast Asian languages, nor can many Southeast Asian expressions describing physical and mental conditions be directly translated for U.S. health care providers. Cancer, for example, has a counterpart in Cantonese (the word nham, which loosely translates into English as "growth") but is not mentioned as a disease in texts on Chinese medicine. Thus, it may be difficult for Asian patients to accept their diagnoses as real or to accept western treatment regimens for them.[124]

If Asian Americans get to health care providers and translators are available, communication still is not guaranteed and appropriate care still may not be received.[147] For example, differences between the medical systems in the United States and China constitute a further deterrent to Chinese Americans born in China but in need of health care in the United States. In China, physicians generally prescribe and dispense medication, charging only a nominal fee for their services; the major cost for the visit is the medications.[124] Because the idea of a visit to a medical professional for a checkup without getting prescriptions for medications does not live up to the expectations of many Chinese Americans, they are reluctant to make visits for routine or preventive care. In addition, 90 percent of the obstetricians and gynecologists in China are female, a fact that makes it very difficult for foreign-born Chinese American women to be examined by or receive care from the predominantly male practitioners in these medical specialties in the United States.[124]

Some Korean American women, many of whom have extreme difficulty with English, report using han yak, a Korean medicine, and other over-the-counter Korean home remedies rather than going to physicians in the United States.[137] They avoid going to physicians because of "communication difficulties," "impatient" doctors and nurses, being "treated disrespectfully" because of their ethnicity, and other "bad experiences."[137]

Influence of Culture

Other cultural characteristics that influence the health of Asian Americans are familism, reverence for authority, and a sense of shame/pride. Asian cultures—like Hispanic cultures—often emphasize family decision-making. The practice of family decision-making may be heightened by necessity, or it may be rendered impotent within the socioeconomic context of U.S. society.[135] The reverence for authority common in Asian societies with hierarchical structures, such as in Korea, for example, may result in a Korean American patient not questioning a physician's diagnosis and treatment and indicating understanding, agreement, and compliance when there is none.[37] This reverence for authority also may combine with gender role differentiation to make Asian women reluctant to report domestic violence to either health providers or law enforcement authorities.[146,148]

The strong desire to "keep up appearances" within the community has resulted in low utilization of addiction treatment services for alcoholism and substance abuse by Asian Americans. Although little research has been done on either alcohol or substance abuse among Asian American women, available research suggests that Asians use and abuse alcohol and other substances less frequently than members of other racial/ethnic groups.[120] Low drinking rates among all Asian American groups seem to be due to high percentages of abstainers among the foreign-born populations.[120]

One study of Asian Americans in Los Angeles found that among women, Japanese Americans were the most likely to report being drinkers (73 percent), followed by Chinese (49 percent), and Koreans (25 percent).[149] High rates of alcohol consumption also have been noted among persons with one Asian and one Caucasian parent.[85] Filipino women are least likely to report the use of alcoholic beverages. Alcohol use among Asian American women tends to increase with acculturation. In addition, stressors such as divorce and widowhood are associated with both depression and substance abuse for these women.[85] Although risk factors for and patterns of substance use and abuse have been identified among selected Asian youth populations, prevalence is generally lower than among youth of other racial/ethnic groups.[120]

The vast differences between Asian societies and the United States mean that the most basic economic and socio-emotional needs of new immigrants may not be met by existing institutions. The painful process of acculturation produces high levels of stress and may produce a high prevalence of mental illness among Asian Americans.[94] Some of this mental illness results from frustration at not reaping benefits in the form of high-paying, high-status jobs, commensurate with their expectations based on the level of education attained and the benefits reaped by white Americans with comparable education.[150] Gender stereotyping of Asian women as docile and subservient also constitutes a stress that may contribute to depression and mental illness.[151] The major mental health problem for Asian Americans, though, is racism—which adversely affects their psycho-economic status, as well as the status of other peoples of color.[36]

References

1. Bureau of the Census. *US population estimates by age, sex, race, and Hispanic Origin*, 1990-1995, with associated tables for recent months. Population Division Release PPL-41, 1996.

2. Bureau of the Census. *We asked ... you told us: Race*. Census Questionnaire Content, 1990 CQC-4. Washington, DC: US Department of Commerce, 1992.

3. Alu Like, Inc. (Native Hawaiian Health Research Consortium). *E ola mau: The Native Hawaiian health needs study—Medical Task Force report*. Honolulu: Alu Like, Inc., 1985.

4. Kramer BJ. Health and aging of urban American Indians. *West J Med* 1992; 157(3):281-285.

5. Kingfisher PJ. The health status of indigenous women of the US: American Indian, Alaska Native, and Native Hawaiians. Background paper for the Canada-USA Forum on Women's Health, Ottawa, Canada, August 8-10, 1996.

6. Scott S, Suagee M. Enhancing health statistics for American Indian and Alaskan Native communities: An agenda for action—A report to the National Center for Health Statistics. St. Paul, MN: American Indian Health Care Association, 1992.

7. Bureau of the Census. CH-1-1 1990 Census of Housing, General housing characteristics. Washington, DC: US Government Printing Office, 1992.

8. Rousseau P. Native-American elders: Health care status. *Clin Geriatr Med* 1995; 11(1):83-95.

9. Indian Health Service. *Trends in Indian health*, 1996. Rockville, MD: US Public Health Service, 1997.

10. Cunningham PJ. *Access to care in the Indian Health Service*. AHRQ publication no. 94-0010. Rockville, MD: Agency for Healthcare Research and Quality, 1993.

11. Sugarman JR, Brenneman G, LaRoque W, Warren CW, Goldberg HI. The urban American Indian oversample in the 1988 National Maternal and Infant Health Survey. *Public Health Rep* 1994; 109(2):243-250.

12. Health Resources and Services Administration. HIV/AIDS workgroup on health care access issues for American Indians and Alaska Natives. Washington, DC: US Department of Health and Human Services, 1992.

13. Indian Health Service. *Indian women's health issues: Final report*. Tucson, AZ: US Public Health Service, 1991.

14. Campbell GR. The changing dimension of Native American health: A critical understanding of contemporary Native American health issues. *American Indian Culture and Research Journal* 1989; 13(3/4):1-20.

15. Bureau of the Census. CP-2-1 1990 Census of population, social and economic characteristics, United States. Washington, DC: US Government Printing Office, 1993, p. 95.

16. Indian Health Service. *Indian health focus: Women*. Rockville, MD: US Public Health Service, 1996.

17. Welty TK. Health implications of obesity in American Indians and Alaska Natives. *Am J Clin Nutr* 1991; 53: 1616S-1620S.

18. Alston D. Transforming a movement: People of color unite at summit against "Environmental Racism." Network News. New York: National Network of Grantmakers, 1992, p.1.

19. Indian Health Service. *The sanitation facilities construction program*—Public Law 86-121, Annual report for 1995. Rockville, MD: US Public Health Service, n.d.

20. Horton JA (ed). *The women's health data book: A profile of women's health in the United States*. Washington, DC: Jacobs Institute of Women's Health, 1992.

21. Selected Entries, in: *Grolier multimedia encyclopedia*. Version 8.01. San Jose, CA: Grolier Electronic Publishing Inc., 1996.

22. Ponce N. *Asian and Pacific Islander health data: Quality issues and policy recommendations*. In Policy Papers. San Francisco: Asian American Health Forum, Inc., 1990.

23. Takeuchi DT, Young KNJ, in: Zane NWS, Takeuchi DT, Young KNJ (eds). *Confronting critical health issues of Asian and Pacific Islander Americans*. Thousand Oaks, CA: Sage, 1994, pp. 3-21.

24. Chen MS, Hawks BL. A debunking of the myth of healthy Asian Americans and Pacific Islanders. *Am J Health Promot* 1995; 9(4):261-268.

25. Lum OM. Health status of Asians and Pacific Islanders. *Clin Geriatr Med* 1995; 11(1):53-67.

26. McCuddin CR, Miike LH, Pangelinan V, Franco RW. Pacific Americans and the National Health Care Act: Where we fit. *Asian American and Pacific Islander Journal of Health* 1994; 2(3):213-253.

27. Rubinstein DH. Epidemic suicide among Micronesian adolescents. *Soc Sci Med* 1983; 17(10):657-665.

28. Hirota S. Needs assessment of Pacific Islander Americans. In Summary of "Breaking the Barriers" conference by Asian American Health Forum, Inc. (AAHF). San Francisco: AAHF, 1988.

29. Office of Hawaiian Affairs. *Native Hawaiian data book*. Honolulu: Office of Hawaiian Affairs, 1994: http://planet-hawaii.com.

30. Chung CS, Tash E, Raymond J, Yasunobu C, Lew R. Health risk behaviors and ethnicity in Hawaii. *Int J Epidemiol* 1990; 19(4):1011-1018.

31. Curb JD, Aluli NE, Kautz JA, Petrovitch H, Knutsen SF, Knutsen R, O'Conner HK, O'Conner WE. Cardiovascular

risk factor levels in ethnic Hawaiians. *Am J Public Health* 1991; 81(2):164-167.

32. Wegner EL. *Hypertension and heart disease*. Social Progress in Hawaii 1989; 32:113-133.

33. Goodman MJ. Breast cancer in multi-ethnic populations: The Hawaii perspective. *Breast Cancer Res Treat* 1991; 18(suppl.1):S5-S9.

34. Bindon, JR, Crews DE. Measures of health and morbidity in Samoans. Abstract of a paper presented at the Third Asian American Health Biennial Forum, "Asian and Pacific Islanders: Dispelling the Myth of a Healthy Minority," Bethesda, MD, November 1990.

35. Martin JA. *Birth characteristics for Asian or Pacific Islander subgroups*, 1992. Monthly Vital Statistics Report 1995; 43(10):Supplement.

36. Asian American Health Forum, Inc. (AAHF). Fact sheets. San Francisco: AAHF, 1990.

37. Leung M, Lu MC. *Ethnocultural barriers to care*. In Policy Papers. San Francisco: Asian American Health Forum, Inc., 1990.

38. Health Resources and Services Administration. *HIV/AIDS workgroup on health care access issues for Hispanic Americans*. Washington, DC: US Department of Health and Human Services, 1991.

39. General Accounting Office. *Hispanic access to health care: Significant gaps exist*. GAO/PEMD-92-6. Washington, DC: US Government Printing Office, 1992.

40. Bureau of the Census. Statistical tables for the Hispanic Origin population from the March 1994 Current Population Survey. Washington, DC: 1995.

41. Leigh WA. *The health of US women: Minority/Diversity perspectives*. Background paper for the Canada-USA Forum on Women's Health, Ottawa, Canada, August 8-10, 1996.

42. Leigh WA. *Housing and neighborhood characteristics by race and ethnicity*. Washington, DC: Joint Center for Political and Economic Studies, 1994.

43. Bureau of the Census. Money income in the United States: 1995 (With separate data on valuation of noncash benefits). *Current Population Reports*, P60-193. Washington, DC: US Government Printing Office, 1996.

44. Lillie-Blanton M, Martinez RM, Taylor AK, Robinson BG. Latina and African American women: Continuing disparities in health. *Int J Health Serv* 1993; 23(3):555-584.

45. Bureau of the Census. *We asked ... you told us: Hispanic Origin*. Census Questionnaire Content, 1990 CQC-7. Washington, DC: US Department of Commerce, 1992.

46. Valdez RB, Delgado DJ, Cervantes RC, Bowler S. *Cancer in US Latino communities*. Santa Monica, CA: RAND, 1993.

47. Brown P. Race, class, and environmental health: A review and systematization of the literature. *Environ Res* 1995; 69:15-30.

48. Ginzberg E, in: Furino A. *Health policy and the Hispanic*. Boulder, CO: Westview Press, 1992, pp. 22-31.

49. Bastida E. *Macro structural factors impacting on Hispanic health*. Paper presented at the conference "Behavioral and Sociocultural Perspectives on Ethnicity and Health," Chapel Hill, NC, September 1992.

50. Zambrana RE, in: Grady ML, Schwartz H (eds). *Medical effectiveness research data methods*. Rockville, MD: US Department of Health and Human Services, 1992, pp. 221-227.

51. Higginbotham JC, Treviño FM, Ray LA. Utilization of curanderos by Mexican Americans: Prevalence and predictors—Findings from HHANES, 1982-1984. *Am J Public Health* 1990; 80(suppl.):32-35.

52. Wells KB, Hough RL, Golding JM, Burnam MA, Karno M. Which Mexican-Americans underutilize health services? *Am J Psychiatry* 1987; 144(7):918-922.

53. Wells KB, Golding JM, Hough RL, Burnam MA, Karno M. Factors affecting the probability of use of general and medical health and social/community services for Mexican American and Non-Hispanic whites. *Med Care* 1988; 26(5):441-452.

54. Sorel JE, Ragland DR, Syme SL. Blood pressure in Mexican Americans, whites, and blacks. *Am J Epidemiol* 1991; 134(4):370-378.

55. Pappas G, Gergen PJ, Carroll M. Hypertension prevalence and the status of awareness, treatment, and control in the Hispanic Health and Nutrition Examination Survey (HHANES), 1982-1984. *Am J Public Health* 1990; 80(12):1431-1436.

56. Baugher E, Lamison-white L. Poverty in the United States: 1995. Current Population Reports, Series P60-194. Washington, DC: US Government Printing Office, 1996.

57. Bureau of the Census. Unpublished tables from the March 1996 Current Population Survey. Washington, DC: 1997.

58. Sorenson SB. Violence against women: Examining ethnic differences and commonalities. *Eval Rev* 1996; 20(2):123-145.

59. Zambrana RE, Dunkel-Schetter C, Scrimshaw S. Factors which influence use of prenatal care in low-income racial-ethnic women in Los Angeles county. *J Community Health* 1991; 16(5):283-295.

60. Mobed K, Gold EB, Schenker MB. Occupational health problems among migrant and seasonal farm workers. *West J Med* 1992; 157:367-373.

61. Solis JM, Marks G, Garcia M, Shelton D. Acculturation, access to care, and use of preventive services by Hispanics: Findings from HHANES, 1982-1984. *Am J Public Health* 1990; 80(suppl.):11-19.

62. Rosenbach ML, Butrica B. *Issues in providing drug treatment services to racial and ethnic minorities*. Paper prepared for the Second Annual Advisory Committee Meeting for the National Institutes of Health, National Institute on Drug Abuse, Center for Drug Abuse Services Research, Tyngsboro, MA, May 1991.

63. Guendelman S, Gould JB, Hudes M, Eskenazi B. Generational differences in perinatal health among the Mexican American population: Findings from HHANES, 1982-1984. *Am J Public Health* 1990; 80(suppl.):61-65.

64. Burnam MA, Hough RL, Karno M, Escobar JI, Telles CA. Acculturation and lifetime prevalence of psychiatric disorders among Mexican Americans in Los Angeles. *J Health Soc Behav* 1987; 28:89-102.

65. Golding JM, Burnam MA. Immigration, stress, and depressive symptoms in a Mexican American community. *J Nerv Ment Dis* 1990; 178(3):161-171.

66. Wray LA. Health policy and ethnic diversity in older Americans—Dissonance or harmony? *West J Med* 1992; 157(3):357-361.

67. Zhang J, Markides KS, Lee DJ. Health status of diabetic Mexican Americans: Results from the Hispanic HHANES. *Ethn Dis* 1991; 1(3):273-279.

68. Lopez LM, Mâsse BR. Income, body fatness, and fat patterns in Hispanic women for the Hispanic Health and Nutrition Examination Survey. *Health Care Wom Int* 1993; 14:117-128.

69. Amaro H. *In the midst of plenty: Reflections on the economic and health status of Hispanic families*. Paper presented at the American Psychological Association convention, Washington, DC, August 14-18, 1992.

70. Markides K, Ray LA, Stroup-Benham CA, Trevño F. Acculturation and alcohol consumption in the Mexican American population of the Southwestern United States: Findings from HHANES, 1982-1984. *Am J Public Health* 1990; 80(suppl.):42-46.

71. Black SA, Markides KS. Acculturation and alcohol consumption in Puerto Rican, Cuban-American, and Mexican-American women in the United States. *Am J Public Health* 1993; 83(6):890-893.

72. Amaro H, Whitaker R, Coffman G, Heeren T. Acculturation and marijuana and cocaine use: Findings from the Hispanic Health and Nutrition Examination Survey (HHANES), 1982-1984. *Am J Public Health* 1990; 80(suppl.):54-60.

73. Nyamathi A, Bennett C, Leake B, Lewis C, Flaskerud J. AIDS-related knowledge, perceptions, and behaviors among

impoverished minority women. *Am J Public Health* 1993; 83(1):65-71.

74. Woodward AM, Dwinell AD, Arons BS. Barriers to mental health care for Hispanic Americans: A literature review and discussion. *J Ment Health Adm* 1992; 19(3): 224-236.

75. Scrimshaw SCM, Zambrana R, Dunkel-Schetter C, in: Ruzek S, Oleson V, Clarke A (eds). *Women's health: The dynamics of diversity*. Columbus, OH: Ohio State University Press, 1997, pp. 329-347.

76. Menendez BS. AIDS mortality among Puerto Ricans and other Hispanics in New York, 1981-1987. *J Acquir Immune Defic Syndr* 1990; 3:644-648.

77. Baker FM. Mental health issues in elderly African Americans. *Clin Geriatr Med* 1995; 11(1):1-13.

78. Savage PJ, Harlan WR. Racial and ethnic diversity in obesity and other risk factors for cardiovascular diseases: Implications for studies and treatment. *Ethn Dis* 1991; 1(2):200-211.

79. National Center for Health Statistics. Health United States, 1995. Hyattsville, MD: US Public Health Service, 1996.

80. National Institutes of Health. *A partnership for health: Minorities and biomedical research*. Bethesda, MD: National Institute of Allergy and Infectious Diseases, 1995-1996.

81. Norris SL, deGuzman M, Sobel E, Brooks S, Haywood LJ. Risk factors and mortality among black, Caucasian, and Latina women with acute myocardial infarction. *Am Heart J* 1993; 126(6):1312-1319.

82. Miller BA, Kolonel LN, Bernstein L, Young JL Jr., Swanson GM, West D, Key CR, Liff JM, Glover CS, Alexander GA, et al. (eds). *Racial/Ethnic patterns of cancer in the United States 1988-1992*. NIH publication no. 96-4104. Bethesda, MD: National Cancer Institute, 1996.

83. Darrow SL, Russell M, Cooper ML, Mudar P, Frone MR. Sociodemographic correlates of alcohol consumption among African-American and white women. *Women Health* 1992; 18(4):35-51.

84. Herd D. An analysis of alcohol-related problems in black and white women drinkers. *Addiction Research* 1993; 1(3):181-198.

85. Rebach H. Alcohol and drug use among American minorities. *Drugs and Society: A Journal of Contemporary Issues* 1992; 7:23-57.

86. Panel on Health and Demography, in: Jaynes GD, Williams RM. *A common destiny: blacks and American society*. Washington, DC: National Academy Press, 1989, pp. 391- 450.

87. David RJ, Collins JW. Bad outcomes in black babies: Race or racism? *Ethn Dis* 1991; 1:236-244.

88. Wilkinson DY, King G, in: Willis DP (ed). *Health policies and black Americans*. New Brunswick, NJ: Transaction Publishers, 1989, pp. 56-71.

89. Bureau of Labor Statistics. *Employment and Earnings*. Volume 42. Washington, DC: US Government Printing Office, 1996.

90. Himmelstein DU, Lewontin JP, Woolhandler S. Medical care employment in the United States, 1968 to 1993: The importance of health sector jobs for African Americans and women. *Am J Public Health* 1996; 86(4):525-528.

91. Gates-Williams J, Jackson MN, Jenkins-Monroe V, Williams LR. The business of preventing African-American infant mortality. *West J Med* 1992; 157(3):350-356.

92. Schoendorf KC, Hogue CJR, Kleinman JC, Rowley D. Mortality among infants of black as compared with white college-educated parents. *N Engl J Med* 1992; 326:1522-1526.

93. Lieberman E. Editorial: Low birth weight—Not a black-and-white issue. *N Engl J Med* 1995; 332(2):117-118.

94. Liu WT, Yu ESH, in: Maldonado L, Moore J (eds). *Urban ethnicity in the United States*. Beverly Hills, CA: Sage Publications, 1985, pp. 211-247.

95. Somervell PD, Leaf PJ, Weissman MM, Blazer DG, Bruce ML. The prevalence of major depression in black and white adults in five United States communities. *Am J Epidemiol* 1989; 130(4):725-735.

96. Repetti RL, Matthews KA, Waldron I. Employment and women's health: Effects of paid employment on women's mental and physical health. *Am Psychol* 1989; 44(11):1394-1401.

97. Snapp MB. Occupational stress, social support, and depression among black and white professional-managerial women. *Women Health* 1992; 18(1):41-79.

98. Miller SM, in: Willis DP (ed). *Health policies and black Americans*. New Brunswick, NJ: Transaction Publishers, 1989, pp. 500-531.

99. Sexton K, Gong H, Bailar JC, Ford JG, Gold DR, Lambert WE, Utell MJ. Air pollution health risks: Do class and race matter? *Toxicol Ind Health* 1993; 9(5):843-878.

100. Headen AE Jr., Headen SW. General health conditions and medical insurance issues concerning black women. *Review of Black Political Economy* 1985-86; 14:183-197.

101. Calle EE, Flanders D, Thun MJ, Martin LM. Demographic predictors of mammography and pap smear screening in US women. *Am J Public Health* 1993; 83(1):53-60.

102. Wilcox LS, Mosher WD. Factors associated with obtaining health screening among women of reproductive age. *Public Health Rep* 1993; 108(1):76-86.

103. Makuc DM, Freid VM, Kleinman JC. National trends in the use of preventive health care by women. *Am J Public Health* 1989; 79(1):21-26.

104. Dooley SL, Metzger BE, Cho NH. Influence of race on disease prevalence and perinatal outcome in the US population. *Diabetes* 1991; 40(suppl. 2):25-29.

105. Hogue CJR, Hargraves MA. Class, race, and infant mortality in the United States. *Am J Public Health* 1993; 83(1):9-12.

106. Folsom AR, Burke GL, Byers CL, Hutchinson RG, Heiss G, Flack JM, Jacobs DR Jr., Caan B. Implications of obesity for cardiovascular disease in blacks: the CARDIA and ARIC studies. *Am J Clin Nutr* 1991; 53:1604S-1611S.

107. Smith GD, Egger M. Socioeconomic differences in mortality in Britain and the United States. *Am J Public Health* 1992; 82:1079-1081.

108. Krieger N, Sidney S. Racial discrimination and blood pressure: The CARDIA study of young black and white adults. *Am J Public Health* 1996; 86(10):1370-1378.

109. Bachman R. *Violence against women: A national crime victimization survey report*. Publication no. NCJ-145325. Washington, DC: US Department of Justice, 1994.

110. Bachman R, Saltzman LE. *Violence against women: Estimates from the redesigned survey*. Publication no. NCJ-154348. Washington, DC: US Department of Justice, 1995.

111. Sorenson SB, Telles CA. Self-reports of spousal violence in a Mexican American and Non-Hispanic white population. *Violence Vict* 1991; 6(1):3-15.

112. Ewbank DC, in: Willis DP (ed). *Health policies and black Americans*. New Brunswick, NJ: Transaction Publishers, 1989, pp. 100-128.

113. Rawlings JS, Rawlings VB, Read JA. Prevalence of low-birth-weight and preterm delivery in relation to the interval between pregnancies among white and black women. *N Engl J Med* 1995; 332(2):69-74.

114. Elledge RM, Clark GM, Chamness GC, Osborne CK. Tumor biologic factors and breast cancer prognosis among white, Hispanic, and black women in the United States. *J Natl Cancer Inst* 1994; 86(9):705-712.

115. Baquet CR, Horm JW, Gibbs T, Greenwald P. Socio-economic factors and cancer incidence among blacks and whites. *J Natl Cancer Inst* 1991; 83(8):551-556.

116. Manton KG, Patrick CH, Johnson KW, in: Willis DP (ed). *Health policies and black Americans*. New Brunswick, NJ: Transaction Publishers, 1989, pp. 129-199.

117. Friedman SJ, Sotheran JL, Abdul-Quader A, Primm BJ, Des Jarlais DC, Kleinman P, Mauge C, Goldsmith DS, El-Sadr W, Maslansky R, in: Willis DP (ed). *Health policies and*

black Americans. New Brunswick, NJ: Transaction Publishers, 1989, pp. 455-499.

118. Centers for Disease Control and Prevention. *HIV/AIDS Surveillance Report* 1996; 8(2).

119. Harrison DF, Byers JB, Levine P, Quadagno DM, Jones MA. AIDS knowledge and risk behavior among culturally diverse women. *AIDS Educ Prev* 1991; 3(2):79-89.

120. Zane NWS, Kim JH, in: Zane NWS, Takeuchi DT, Young KNJ (eds). *Confronting critical health issues of Asian and Pacific Islander Americans*. Thousand Oaks, CA: Sage, 1994, pp. 316-343.

121. Hu-DeHart E. From yellow peril to model minority: The Columbus legacy and Asians in America. *In The New World*. Washington, DC: Smithsonian Institution, 1992.

122. Yu ESH. *Health of the Chinese elderly*. Research on Aging 1986; 8:84-109.

123. Leong F. Guest editor's introduction. *Asian American and Pacific Islander Journal of Health* 1994; 2(2):89-91.

124. Mo B. Modesty, sexuality, and breast health in Chinese-American women. *West J Med* 1992; 157(3):260-264.

125. Yu ESH, in: Liu WT (ed). *Methodological problems in minority research*. Chicago: Pacific/Asian American Mental Health Research Center, 1982, pp. 93-118.

126. Hurh WM, Kim KC. Correlates of Korean immigrants' mental health. *J Nerv Ment Dis* 1990; 178(11):703-711.

127. Han E. Korean health survey in southern California: A preliminary report on health status and health care needs of Korean immigrants. Abstract of a paper presented at the Third Asian American Health Biennial Forum, "Asian and Pacific Islanders: Dispelling the Myth of a Healthy Minority," Bethesda, MD, November 1990.

128. Tamir A, Cachola S, in: Zane NWS, Takeuchi DT, Young KNJ (eds). *Confronting critical health issues of Asian and Pacific Islander Americans*. Thousand Oaks, CA: Sage, 1994, pp. 209-247.

129. Rozee PD, Van Boemel G. The psychological effects of war trauma and abuse on older Cambodian refugee women. *Women and Therapy* 1989; 8(4):23-50.

130. Liu WT, Yu ESH, Chang C, Fernandez M, in: Stiffman AR, Davis LE (eds). *Ethnic issues in adolescent mental health*. New York: Sage Publications, 1990, pp. 92-112.

131. Yu ESH, Liu WT, in: Liu WT (ed). *The Pacific/Asian American Mental Health Research Center: A decade review*. Chicago: University of Illinois, 1987, pp. 19-28.

132. Bureau of the Census. CP-2-1 1990 Census of population, social and economic characteristics, United States. Washington, DC: US Government Printing Office, 1993, p. 115.

133. Bureau of the Census. Unpublished tables from the March 1996 Current Population Survey. Washington, DC: 1997.

134. Bureau of the Census. The Asian and Pacific Islander population in the United States: March 1991 and 1990. *Current Population Reports*, Series P-20, No. 459. Washington, DC: US Government Printing Office, 1992.

135. Crews DE, in: Zane NWS, Takeuchi DT, Young KNJ (eds). *Confronting critical health issues of Asian and Pacific Islander Americans*. Thousand Oaks, CA: Sage, 1994, pp. 174-207.

136. Klatsky AL, Armstrong MA. Cardiovascular risk factors among Asian Americans living in northern California. *Am J Public Health* 1991; 81(11):1423-1428.

137. Luluquisen EM, Groessl KM, Puttkammer NH. The health and well-being of Asian and Pacific Islander American women. Oakland, CA: *Asian and Pacific Islanders for Reproductive Health,* 1995.

138. Pham CT, McPhee SJ. Knowledge, attitudes, and practices of breast cancer and cervical cancer screening among Vietnamese women. *J Cancer Educ* 1992; 7(4):305-310.

139. Brown ER, Wyn R, Cumberland WG, Yu H, Abel E, Gelberg L, Ng L. Women's health-related behaviors and use of clinical preventive services: A report of The Commonwealth Fund. Los Angeles: UCLA Center for Health Policy Research, 1996.

140. Yi JK. Factors associated with cervical cancer screening behavior among Vietnamese women. *J Community Health* 1994; 19(3):189-200.

141. Ziegler RG, Hoover RN, Pike MC, Hildsheim A, Nomura AMY, West DW, Wu-Williams AH, Kolonel LN, Horn-Ross PL, Rosenthal JF, Hyer MB. Migration patterns and breast cancer risk in Asian American women. *J Natl Cancer Inst* 1993; 85(22):1819-1827.

142. Kulig JC. A review of the health status of Southeast Asian refugee women. *Health Care Wom Int* 1990; 11:49-63.

143. Helsel D, Petitti DB, Kunstadter P. Pregnancy among the Hmong: Birthweight, age and parity. *Am J Public Health* 1992; 82(10):1361-1364.

144. Buchwald D, Panwala S, Hooton TM. Use of traditional health practices by Southeast Asian refugees in a primary care clinic. *West J Med* 1992; 156:507-511.

145. Ying Y. Explanatory models of major depression and implications for help-seeking among immigrant Chinese-American women. *Cult Med Psychiatry* 1990; 14:393-408.

146. Frye BA, D'Avanzo CD. Cultural themes in family stress and violence among Cambodian refugee women in the inner city. *Adv Nurs Sci* 1994; 16(3):64-77.

147. US Commission on Civil Rights. *Civil rights issues facing Asian Americans in the 1990s*. Washington, DC: US Commission on Civil Rights, 1992.

148. Cheung FK. Asian American and Pacific Islanders' mental health issues: A historical perspective. *Asian American and Pacific Islander Journal of Health* 1994; 2(2):94-107.

149. Chi I, Lubben JE, Kitano H. Differences in drinking behavior among three Asian-American groups. *J Stud Alcohol* 1989; 50(1):15-23.

150. Takeuchi DT, Mokuau N, Chun C. Mental health services for Asian Americans and Pacific Islanders. *J Ment Health Adm* 1992; 19(3):237-245.

151. Woods NF, Lentz M, Mitchell E, Oakley LD. Depressed mood and self esteem in young Asian, black and white women in America. *Health Care Wom Int* 1994; 15:243-262.

152. Bureau of the Census. CPH-5 1990 Census of Population and Housing, Summary social, economic, and housing characteristics. Washington, DC: US Government Printing Office, 1993.

153. Hoberman HM. Ethnic minority status and adolescent mental health services utilization. *J Ment Health Adm* 1992; 19(3):246-267.

154. Coiro MJ, Zill N, Bloom B. Health of our nation's children. *Vital Health Stat* 1994; 10(191).

155. Blum RW, Harmon B, Harris L, Bergeisen L, Resnick MD. American Indian-Alaska Native youth health. *JAMA* 1992; 267(12):1637-1644.

156. Kann L, Warren CW, Harris WA, Collins JL, Williams BI, Ross JG, Kolbe LJ, State and Local YRBSS Coordinators. Youth risk behavior surveillance—United States, 1995. *MMWR CDC Surveill Summ* September 27, 1996; 45(No.55-4).

157. Grossman DC, Milligan BC, Deyo RA. Risk factors for suicide attempts among Navajo adolescents. *Am J Public Health* 1991; 81(7):870-874.

158. Chavez EL, Swaim RC. Hispanic substance use: Problems in epidemiology. *Drugs and Society: A Journal of Contemporary Issues* 1992; 7:211-230.

159. Liu LL, Slap GB, Kinsman SB, Khalid N. Pregnancy among American Indian adolescents: Relations and prenatal care. *J Adolesc Health* 1994; 15(4):336-341.

160. Ventura SJ, Clarke SC, Matthews TJ. Recent declines in teenage birth rates in the United States: Variations by state, 1990-1994. Monthly Vital Statistics Report 1996; 45(5): Supplement.

161. Bachman JG, Wallace JM, O'Malley PM, Johnston LD, Kurth CL, Neighbors HW. Racial/Ethnic differences in smoking, drinking, and illicit drug use among American

high school seniors, 1976-89. *Am J Public Health* 1991; 81(3):372-377.

162. Bruerd B. Smokeless tobacco use among Native American school children. *Public Health Rep* 1990; 105(2):196-201.

163. Welte JW, Barnes GM. Alcohol use among adolescent minority groups. *J Stud Alcohol* 1987; 48(4):329-336.

164. Bureau of the Census. *We the American...elderly*. Series WE-9. Washington, DC: US Government Printing Office, 1993.

165. Bureau of the Census, National Institutes of Health. *Profiles of America's elderly: Racial and ethnic diversity of America's elderly population*. Current Population Reports, Series POP/93-1. Washington, DC: US Government Printing Office, 1993.

166. Wallace SP, Lew-Ting C. Getting by at home—Community-based long-term care of Latino elders. *West J Med* 1992; 157(3):337-344.

167. Brangman SA. African American elders: Implications for health care providers. *Clin Geriatr Med* 1995; 11(1):15-23.

168. Proctor EK. *Posthospital care for African American elderly*. Research Activities, Agency for Health Care Policy and Research 1996; 196:19-20.

169. Douglas KC, Fujimoto D. Asian Pacific elders: Implications for health care providers. *Clin Geriatr Med* 1995; 11(1):69-81.

170. National Coalition of Hispanic Health and Human Services Organizations. *Hispanic women's health: A nuestros numeros fact sheet*. Washington, DC: COSSMHO, 1996.

171. Lefkowitz D, Underwood C. *Personal health practices: Findings from the Survey of American Indians and Alaska Natives*. Publication No. 91-0034. National Medical Expenditure Survey, Research Findings 10, Agency for Health Care Policy and Research. Rockville, MD: US Public Health Service, 1991.

172. Eng E, Smith J. Natural helping functions of lay health advisors in breast cancer education. *Breast Cancer Res Treat* 1995; 35:23-29.

173. Earp JAL, Altpeter M, Mayne L, Viadro CI, O'Malley MS. The North Carolina breast cancer screening program: Foundations and design of a model for reaching older, minority, rural women. *Breast Cancer Res Treat* 1995; 35:7-22.

174. Callahan LF, Rao J, Boutaugh M. Arthritis and women's health: Prevalence, impact, and prevention. *Am J Prev Med* 1996; 12(5):401-409.

175. Grisso JA, Kelsey JL, Storm BL, O'Brien LA, Maislin G, LaPann K, Samuelson L, Hoffman S, Northeast Hip Fracture Study Group. Risk factors for hip fracture in black women. *N Engl J Med* 1994; 330(22):1555-1559.

176. Johnson A, Taylor A. *Prevalence of chronic diseases: A summary of data from the Survey of American Indians and Alaska Natives*. National Medical Expenditure Survey Data Summary 3, Agency for Health Care Policy and Research. Rockville, MD: US Public Health Service, 1991.

177. National Institutes of Health. *Diabetes in Black America*. NIH publication no. NIH 93-3266. Bethesda, MD: National Institute of Diabetes and Digestive and Kidney Diseases, 1992.

178. Mui AC. Self-reported depressive symptoms among black and Hispanic frail elders: A sociocultural perspective. *J Appl Geront* 1993; 12(2):170-187.

179. Diego AT, Yamamoto J, Nguyen LH, Hifumi SS. Suicide in the elderly: Profiles of Asians and whites. *Asian American and Pacific Islander Journal of Health* 1994; 2(1):49-57.

Chapter 33

African American Women

Editor's Note: Please refer to Chapter 32, pp. 329–58 to investigate the numbered references listed in this chapter.

Major Health Concerns of African American Women

- Diabetes—a condition that increases the risk of kidney disease, hearth disease, eye and foot problems and other health complications—is 60% more common in African American women compared to white women.
- High blood pressure is also more frequent among African American women, increasing the risks of stroke and heart disease.
- Obesity affects more than half of all adult African American women. It carries with it an increased risk of heart disease, diabetes, high blood pressure, respiratory disorders, arthritis, and some cancers.
- Kidney disease disproportionately affects African American women, often as a complication of high blood pressure or diabetes.
- Arthritis is more prevalent and leads to more activity limitations in African American women compared with white women.

"Women of Color Health Data Book," The National Women's Health Information Center, 1998.

- HIV/AIDS disproportionately affects African American women, and is a leading cause of death for African American women between the ages of 25 and 44.
- Lupus, an autoimmune disease in which the body attacks its own health tissues and organs, is more than twice as common in African American women compared with white women.
- Breast cancer, although more prevalent in white women, is more likely to lead to death when it affects African American women.
- Maternal mortality and infant mortality among African Americans are five and 2.5 times greater, respectively, than the national average.

Factors Affecting the Health of African American Women

The black population of the United States consists primarily of African Americans, although sizable numbers of African and African Caribbean immigrants have become part of this group in the last 15 years.[77] The African ancestors of the group known today as African Americans were brought to the shores of what is now the United States as slaves by Europeans, beginning in 1619. Today, there are more than 32 million black Americans in this country, more than 12 percent of the total population, and they are currently the largest minority group.[1] More than half of all black Americans (nearly 17 million) are females, and many are of mixed ancestry, including individuals with Caribbean, Indian, and European lineage.[44] Approximately 5 percent of black Americans are foreign born, mainly French-speaking Haitians and other non-Spanish-speaking Caribbean people, some of whom are farm workers in the United States.[35] Though seldom studied, marked differences in acculturation exist among black women and contribute to the diversity of their health.[73]

Black Americans are a largely urban population (87 percent of all black households in 1995) and can be found in all 50 states.[43,77] In spite of their urbanity and their wider distribution among the United States than other racial/ethnic groups, more than half of all black Americans live in these 13 Southern states—Alabama, Arkansas, Florida, Georgia, Kentucky, Louisiana, Maryland, Mississippi, North Carolina, South Carolina, Tennessee, Texas, and Virginia.[77]

Differences in the health of blacks and whites are many and varied. Blacks have more undetected diseases, higher disease and illness rates (from infectious conditions such as tuberculosis and sexually transmitted diseases), more chronic conditions (such as hypertension and diabetes), and shorter life expectancies than whites.[78,79,80,81] Morbidity and mortality rates for blacks from many conditions (cancer, HIV/AIDS, pneumonia, and homicide) exceed those for whites.[80,82] These findings exist even though black females are generally less likely than white females to report risk behaviors such as smoking cigarettes, consuming alcohol, or using other substances.[79,83,84,85]

Explanations for racial differences in health outcomes have been sought by experts, and many contributing factors have been identified. Although the interactive mechanisms have not been specified, three factors—genetics, poverty, and racism—generally are believed to have the greatest influence on the health of black Americans.[78]

The murkiness of race as a concept to define black Americans, who range from fair-skinned and blue-eyed with straight hair to dark-skinned with dark eyes and coarse hair, makes purely genetic explanations of the health differences between blacks and whites questionable. Biology appears to explain very little of the differences in health between blacks and whites if the proportion of excess deaths among blacks—that is, deaths that would not have occurred if blacks had the same age- and sex-related death rates as whites—due to hereditary conditions is examined. Less than 0.5 percent of black deaths have been attributed to hereditary conditions such as sickle cell anemia, for which genetic patterns have been established.[86,87] On the other hand, researchers studying the prevalence of hypertension among blacks have found that it varies with skin color. That is, lighter-pigmented blacks often have a lower prevalence of hypertension than darker-skinned blacks, and pigment is related to the degree of admixture with whites, whose overall prevalence of hypertension is lower than that of blacks.[88] One study found that darker-skinned individuals who identified with higher social class status were the most likely to have elevated blood pressures. Individuals with both light skin and high social status and with both dark skin and low social status reported lower blood pressure.[87]

Environmental Health Stresses

Instead of looking at population-related genetic differences, others link the racial differences in health to black sub-populations that are exposed to multiple risks—such as intravenous drug users, those living and working in hazardous environments, and the like. Environmental stresses that may increase obesity, for example, have been noted as contributors to the high prevalence of hypertension among black Americans.[78] Those health conditions common among blacks that are considered to be genetic in origin are likely to receive more public attention and resources, however, than conditions that arise from behavior or life style choices. For example, conditions such as sickle cell anemia receive more research attention and public support than health conditions attributable to accidents, substance abuse, and environmentally caused illness.[88]

Poverty affected 29 percent of all black Americans and nearly a third (32 percent) of all black women in 1995.[56] In addition, around two-fifths of black females both under 18 years of age (42 percent) and 75 years of age and older (38 percent) reported incomes below the poverty level. Single-parent, female-headed households, 47 percent of all black-family households in 1995, were mired in poverty to a greater degree than the entire black population.[56] Forty-eight percent of all people in black female-headed families, but only 10 percent of all people in black married-couple families, had incomes below the poverty level in 1995. In addition, 80 percent of the more than 2 million black families in poverty were maintained by women with no husbands present.[56] Median income for all black households in 1995 was nearly $22,400, with median household income for married-couple black families at nearly $41,400.[43] For female-headed family households, 1995 median income was nearly $15,600.

More than half of the black work force (52 percent) is female, with many of these workers earning poverty level wages. Although nearly 8 million black women (out of the total of 17 million black women) worked in 1995, one-sixth (nearly 17 percent) of them earned incomes at or below the federal poverty level.[56] More than a fourth of all young black female workers ages 18-24 earned incomes at or below the poverty level.

The largest shares of employed black women—28 percent and 21 percent—have administrative support occupations (including clerical) and service occupations, respectively.[89] Many of the black women in the work force—19 percent in 1993—held lower level, low-wage jobs in the health care sector. Black women held 20 percent of all jobs in nursing homes and 26 percent of all positions as nursing home aides.[90] Black women also held about a fifth of all food service jobs (21 percent) and cleaning, building service, and laundry jobs (18 percent) in the health care sector.

Inadequate income carries over into other aspects of daily life that impinge upon health. These include inadequate housing (which may quicken the spread of communicable diseases), malnutrition, the stress of constantly struggling to make ends meet, dangerous jobs, and little or no preventive medical care.[87] Malnutrition in little black girls may later result in low-birth-weight babies and high infant mortality rates when these girls become mothers. The high black infant mortality rate also has been related to the intergenerational effects of socioeconomic conditions on the growth and development of a mother from her pre-birth to childhood, which may in turn influence the intrauterine growth of her child.[91,92] Since many middle-class blacks are the first generation in their families to achieve that status, a black middle-class mother may be giving birth to an infant whose health is markedly determined by maternal childhood poverty.[86] An ongoing cohort study of middle-class black women that suggests an improvement in the incidence of low birth weights among infants born to subsequent generations of these women supports this explanation.[93]

The stresses of constantly struggling to make ends meet also may translate directly into the finding that blacks living below the poverty level, many of whom work, have the highest rate of depression for any racial/ethnic group.[94] Symptoms of depression have been found with greater frequency among black women ages 18-24 years than among white women.[95] In addition, studies of the effect of employment on women have found that working outside the home can have harmful effects on both mental and physical health if associated with occupational hazards, heavy job demands, or poor social relations at work.[96] Snapp (1992) has found that black professional/managerial workers report significantly lower levels of co-worker support than white professional/managerial workers, a finding that could place this group of women at risk of health problems.[97]

Dangerous jobs may expose blacks to certain cancers to a much greater extent than whites.[82,98] Black women are more likely than white women to work in hazardous jobs. Nearly 75 percent of the poultry plants in this nation—similar to the one that caught fire and killed 25 people in Hamlet, N.C., in 1991—are located in the South, in predominantly poor and black neighborhoods. The fire was fatal because locked safety doors prevented people from escaping. Two-thirds of the workforce at this plant (both males and females) was black.[44]

Hazards in their living environments also detract from the health of black Americans. One of the first major studies to link race with environmental hazards was a 1983 study by the U.S. General Accounting Office that found that three of the four hazardous waste landfills in the Southeast were located in predominantly poor or black areas.[47] A 1992 report by the Environmental Equity Workgroup at the Environmental Protection Agency (EPA) found both that blacks suffer higher rates of lung cancer and chronic obstructive pulmonary disease and that blacks have greater exposure to poor air quality in the environments in which they live and work. This report, however, did not make a causal connection between these findings. The share of black Americans living in EPA-designated air quality nonattainment areas exceeds that of whites for the following air pollutants—particulate matter, carbon monoxide, ozone, sulfur dioxide, and lead.[99] More than three-fifths of blacks (62 percent) lived in non-attainment areas for ozone, while nearly half (46 percent) lived in non-attainment areas for carbon monoxide. Exposure to environmental lead (via air, water, soil/dust, and food) and the prevalence of high lead levels in the blood (greater than 15 $\mu g/dl$) also are most common among black Americans (relative to other racial/ethnic groups), but especially so among black children.[99]

Preventive Care

Exposure to hazards in the work and living environments suggests that black Americans might have a greater need than other groups for preventive health care. In reality, many blacks get little or no preventive care for a variety of reasons, including:

- parental ignorance of disease symptoms and when to seek medical care;
- lack of health insurance to enable access to health care; lack of neighborhood facilities in which to seek health care;
- persistent use of emergency rooms to treat chronic conditions, which are better managed in other settings; and
- racial discrimination encountered when seeking care.[86,100]

Older black women are especially likely to report under-using both the Pap smear and mammography, the main screening technologies for cervical cancer and breast cancer, respectively.[101] Lifetime risk for cervical cancer among black women is 2 per 100, more than double that for white women, and age-adjusted death rates for black women are more than 2.5 times that for whites.[82,102,103] Estimated lifetime risk of developing breast cancer was 10 per 100 white women born in 1980 and 7 per 100 black women born that same year.[102] However, significantly fewer black than white women survive five years after diagnosis with breast cancer.[82]

Racial Discrimination and Racism

Racial discrimination and racism have remained significant operative factors in the health and health care of blacks over time. From as early as 1867, black spokespersons concluded that racism was a major contributor to the poor health of black Americans in two significant ways. First, "structural racism" creates barriers to getting access to adequate care, and second, dealing with both structural barriers and racial insults may contribute to stress-related health problems such as pregnancy-induced hypertension among black women.[104,105] Stress related to racism also may underlie the overeating and resultant obesity common in black women and may be associated with the more than a twofold prevalence of hypertension and the more than fourfold prevalence of diabetes among black women relative to white women 18 to 30 years of age, one study found.[106]

"John Henryism," defined as the behavioral predisposition to work hard and strive determinedly against the constraints of one's environment, has been advanced as one explanation for the black-white differences in hypertension rates. High blood pressure in blacks is a response to the incongruity between the social position one's work would typically merit and the position one actually occupies.[107] Other research suggests that blood pressure becomes elevated among blacks in connection with racial discrimination at work, in reaction to movie scenes depicting angry and racist confrontations, and as an internalized response to racial discrimination and unfair treatment.[108] A recent analysis of the relationship between self-reported experiences of racial discrimination and blood pressure among working class black men and women indicates that blood pressure is lower among those who reported they challenged unfair treatment than among those who accepted racial discrimination as an unalterable part of the fabric of United States society.[108]

Another response to racism that affects the health of black women is the internalized rage of black men against their mistreatment, that too often is manifest in anger and violent behavior against black women.[109,110] This violence has resulted in the highest reported spousal homicide rates among black women—more than 4 per 100,000.[111] Racism even influences the response of black women to domestic violence. They often are unwilling to call police, for fear that the police will brutalize the men who have battered them.[58]

Racial discrimination has limited the access of blacks to higher incomes, improved health care, adequate housing, and better education—all of which are necessary to achieve modern levels of health and mortality.[112] Racial discrimination probably "...exacerbates the mental health-damaging effects of poverty status among blacks."[98] Being black impinges upon health, even at higher income levels. A study of stress found its severity highest in lower-class blacks and lowest in middle-class whites. Even more notable is the fact that middle-class blacks and lower-class whites were found to have similar levels of stress.[98]

Another example of what may be a psychophysiological response to racism is pregnancy outcome. Although there is a significant gap in mortality rates between the infants of all white and black mothers, there is an even greater gap between the infant mortality rates of white and black mothers of higher socioeconomic status.[87] Mortality rates for infants born to college-educated black parents (from 1983 to 1985) were 90 percent higher than the rates among infants born to college-educated white parents. This excess mortality was due primarily to higher rates of death associated with premature delivery and low birth weights of black babies.[92] Although the relationship with the father of a baby has been found to be critical to the early timing of prenatal care, and black women often do not live with the fathers of their unborn children while they are pregnant, differences in the use of prenatal care do not fully account for disparities between black and white women in the incidence of births of infants with low and very-low weights.[59,91] Other factors such as the frequency of intervals of less than nine months between pregnancies (which is greater among black than white women) also have been associated with the greater incidence of low-weight infants born to black women. A complete explanation for this disparity is yet to be provided, however.[113]

Immigrant black couples, when compared to native black couples, have a lower incidence of low-birth-weight babies. The incidence of low-birth-weight babies among immigrant blacks is similar to that among white couples. Black babies born in more segregated cities have higher rates of infant mortality than their counterparts born in less segregated cities, another suggestive finding that does not fully explain the differential incidence.[105]

Mortality Rates from Disease

The impact on health of responses to racism can be seen by the high mortality rates for blacks from diseases such as cancer, HIV infection, and AIDS. Black breast cancer patients have a worse prognosis overall, a worse prognosis at each stage, and are diagnosed at a more advanced stage than either Hispanic or white breast cancer patients.[114] A greater incidence of more aggressive tumors could result in a later stage at diagnosis and the poorer survival rates that make breast cancer a disease with lower incidence but higher mortality among black than white women. Baquet et al. (1991) found a significant inverse relationship between socioeconomic status and the incidence of both cervical cancer and lung cancer, and attribute part of the elevated incidence of these cancers to the disproportionately low socioeconomic status of blacks.[115] Blacks generally are less educated about the danger signs and more pessimistic about treatment for cancer than are whites. Both of these facts also contribute to making cancer the terminal disease many blacks conceive it to be.[116]

It has been suggested that the experience of fighting HIV/AIDS is different for most whites than for minorities and the poor. For whites with HIV/AIDS, the fact that they have education and employment contributes to their sense of outrage about the disease and motivates them to fight for what is being lost. Blacks and members of other minority groups, who may never have had these advantages, do not have this sense of loss or the associated drive and the educational tools with which to fight against the loss. Delays in seeking medical care, differences in preexisting health, and differences in drugs administered as treatment generate a mean survival time of six months for blacks after diagnosis with HIV/AIDS, while whites have a mean survival time of 18 to 24 months.[117]

Women represent a small but growing share of the cases of acquired immunodeficiency syndrome (AIDS) reported in the United States. In 1996, 20 percent of all AIDS cases reported were among women, a somewhat larger share than the nearly 15 percent of all AIDS cases (i.e., reported between 1981 and 1996) for which women accounted. Both cumulatively since 1981 (47,367 cases) and during 1996 (8,147 cases), black women reported the greatest number of cases of AIDS among women. Over these same periods, 20,026 cases and 2,888 cases, respectively, were reported among white women.[118] Fifty-nine percent of all cases of AIDS reported among women in 1996 and 55 percent of all cases of AIDS reported among women between 1981 and 1996 were among black women.

Among black women during 1996, heterosexual contact (37 percent of cases) was the major source of infection by the human immunodeficiency virus (HIV) that causes AIDS. Injecting drug use was the cause of AIDS for half (47 percent) of all cases ever reported among black women. This dual pattern among causes of transmission is the same for white women, although among both Hispanic and Asian and Pacific Islander women, heterosexual contact is reported as the major cause of AIDS both in 1996 and since 1981.[118] Among American Indian/Alaska Native women, injecting drug use has consistently been the major reported cause of AIDS.

Research in both Los Angeles and in south Florida suggests that black women continue to engage in behaviors that place themselves at high risk of infection.[73,119] Ten percent of the black women in the Los Angeles survey reported intravenous drug use in the past month, while 10 percent of the Florida sample indicated that their sexual partners were injecting drug users. More than half (53 percent) of the black women in the Florida survey reported that they had unprotected sex with their main partner, and one-fifth (20 percent) indicated they would not use a condom if their sexual partner were HIV-positive.[119] Nearly a third of the black women in the Los Angeles survey reported having sex with multiple partners.[73] Haitian women in Florida also reported unprotected sex with their main partner (71 percent) and that they would not use a condom with an HIV-positive partner (44 percent).[119] These high percentages of both black American and Haitian women who report that they would not use a condom with an HIV-positive partner may reflect the cultural realities these women face; they know that they are unable to override economic and gender role norms to engage in "safer" sexual intercourse.

Resentment by others at the unfair advantages presumably accorded blacks under affirmative action programs contributes to the sense of exclusion from and inequality in mainstream America felt by blacks, a sense that bears on them economically, socially, and physically. Even if poverty in America is reduced, as long as economic, social, and political inequalities persist, the health of black Americans is likely to remain impaired.[98]

Chapter 34

Hispanic American Women

Editor's Note: Please refer to Chapter 32, pp. 329–58 to investigate the numbered references listed in this chapter.

Major Health Issues Facing Hispanic American Women

- Health care access. There are more uninsured Latina women than any other race/ethnic group (30%) even though many of them are employed or live with someone who is employed. Only 26% have private health insurance, 27% receive Medicaid coverage, and 7% are covered by Medicare. Difficulties with language, transportation, childcare, immigration status, or cultural differences act as further barriers to health care services.
- Diabetes, including gestational diabetes that occurs during pregnancy, is two to three times more common in Mexican American, Cuban American, and Puerto Rican adults that in non-Hispanic whites.
- Obesity is 1.5 times more common in Mexican American women than in the general female population—reaching 52%.
- HIV/AIDS. The rate of HIV infection is seven times higher in Latina women than in white women, highlighting the need for greater prevention and treatment in this community.

"Women of Color Health Data Book," The National Women's Health Information Center, 1998.

- Prenatal care. Many Latina women do not get timely prenatal care (in the first three months of pregnancy). The rates are 89% (Cuban American), 74% (Puerto Rican), 73% (Central and South American), and 69% (Mexican American). Yet Latina women have infant mortality rates comparable to those of white women (7%) and far lower than those of African American women (17%) and Native American women (13%).

Factors Affecting the Health of Hispanic American Women

The earliest forebearers of the group known today as Hispanic Americans or Latinos were Spanish colonists in the late 1500s who came from Mexico to live in what is now the Southwestern United States. The descendants of these forebearers are included among "other Hispanics" and made up 7 percent of the more than 28 million Hispanics in the United States in 1996.[38,39,40] The other major Hispanic subgroups are Mexican Americans (64 percent), Central and South Americans (14 percent), Puerto Ricans (10 percent), and Cuban Americans (4 percent).[40] More than a third (36 percent) of all Hispanic Americans were foreign born, and 51 percent of the infants born to Hispanic women in 1992 were born to women who themselves were born outside the 50 states and Washington, DC.[35,41] The nearly 14 million Hispanic women were about half of the total Hispanic population in 1996.[1]

More than 90 percent of the nation's Hispanic population is urban, with 58 percent living in the central cities of metropolitan areas.[42,43] Seventy percent of the Hispanic population resides in six of the most populous states (California, Texas, New York, Florida, New Jersey, and Illinois), with the largest concentrations in four cities —New York City, Los Angeles, Chicago, and San Antonio.[44,45] The South (34 percent) and the West (42 percent) combined are home to three-fourths of all Hispanics.[43]

The Hispanic population in the United States is diverse by many measures. The population ranges from dark-skinned to light-skinned and includes all the shades in between; Hispanics include people who are admixtures with Indians, blacks, whites, and Asians.[44,46] The Hispanic population includes 75 percent of all United States farmworkers, the laborers in this nation with a life expectancy of 49 years, infant mortality rates 25 percent higher than the United States average, and higher rates of cancers and reproductive disorders than the general population.[47] Ten million people on both sides of the U.S.-Mexico border between California and Brownsville, Texas, are Hispanic, with many living in colonias, unincorporated areas often lacking septic tanks, sewers, and running water.[48] Hispanics also include people from Spanish-speaking countries (such as certain parts of El Salvador and various regions of Mexico) whose primary language is not Spanish.[49,50] Although median age for the Hispanic population is 26 years (compared to a median age of 34 years for the non-Hispanic United States population), this median includes Mexicans with a median age of 24, as well as Cubans whose median age is 43 years.[40]

Among Hispanic sub-populations, Mexican Americans appear to enjoy better health than would be predicted, given their socioeconomic status and the fact that they have low utilization rates for health care services for both physical and mental conditions.[51,52,53] Specifically, Mexican American women are less likely than Cuban, white, or black American women to have hypertension, despite their greater likelihood of being poor than either Cuban or white American women.[54,55] Puerto Ricans and Cuban Americans, however, use health care facilities at rates comparable to whites. Puerto Rican women are less likely to be hypertensive and more likely to be poor than Mexican American women. In short, there is such variation in the health of the Hispanic American subgroups that looking at aggregated measures can obscure meaningful intragroup differences.

Economics and Employment

The socioeconomics and employment of Hispanics, as of all populations in the United States, influence their access to health insurance, and thereby to health care. In 1995, 30 percent of the U.S. Hispanic population had incomes below the poverty line.[56] A third of Hispanic women had incomes below the poverty line that year as well. This third reflects the 43 percent of Puerto Rican females with poverty level incomes in 1995, along with the 34 percent of Mexican American females with similarly low incomes at that time.[57] Twenty-seven percent of all Hispanic families had poverty level incomes, as did 19 percent of all Hispanic married-couple families.

Rates of unemployment and labor force participation account for the poverty levels of Hispanics in part. In 1993, the unemployment rate for the Hispanic origin population (both males and females) of 11 percent exceeded the unemployment rate for the non-Hispanic population of 6.6 percent overall, 7 percent for males and 6 percent for females.[40] The 65 percent share of the Hispanic population in the labor force reflects both the 78 percent share for Hispanic males (which exceeds the 73 percent labor force participation rate for non-Hispanic males) and the 52 percent share for Hispanic females (which falls short of the 59 percent labor force participation rate for non-Hispanic females).[40] As with other measures, for Hispanics, there is variation by subgroup in unemployment and labor force participation rates. Unemployment rates for Mexican Americans and populations from Central and South America are near the Hispanic population average, while rates for Puerto Ricans are above and rates for Cubans and other Hispanics are below this level.

Hispanic households also are more likely than non-Hispanic white households to be headed by females; these female-headed households also are more likely to have incomes below the federal poverty line than other types of households. Forty-four percent of Puerto Rican households are headed by women, as are 24 percent of Cuban households, and 19 percent of both Mexican American and Central and South American households.[40] Although 34 percent of all non-Hispanic female-headed households had incomes below the poverty level in 1993, the corresponding share of Hispanic female-headed households was 52 percent. This 52 percent share includes the 61 percent of all female-headed Puerto Rican households with poverty level incomes, along with the 39 percent of female-headed Cuban households with comparably low incomes.[40] Overall, nearly half (47 percent) of poor Hispanic families are female-headed and are likely to face the combined stresses of poverty, lack of health insurance, lack of health care for themselves and their children, and lack of social support.[56] This arsenal of stressors places these women at risk for mental health problems as well as for substance and alcohol abuse. The lack of citizenship may be an added stressor for poor Hispanic women and may make them unwilling to use public clinics and other health facilities for fear of detection and deportation.[58,59]

When Hispanic women are employed, they tend to hold jobs of low status and with low pay. Hispanics are more likely than other Americans to be among the working poor, with 17 percent of all Hispanics and 16 percent of Hispanic women reporting that they work but earn poverty level wages.[56] Only 6 percent of all non-Hispanic people and 7 percent of non-Hispanic women reported working for poverty-level wages in 1995.

Partly as a reflection of this, 30 percent of the Hispanic population was not covered by health insurance in 1995.[57] Medicaid coverage of Hispanics with comparably low incomes varies by state of residence, as do eligibility requirements and administrative practices under this health insurance program for the poor. Hispanic residents of New York and California are more likely to be enrolled in Medicaid than are equally poor Hispanics in either Florida or Texas.[48] Beyond the likely lack of employer-sponsored health insurance, the working poor face double jeopardy with respect to health care because they cannot afford to pay costly medical bills out-of-pocket and because they do not qualify for federal programs such as Medicaid. Some of the Hispanic working poor have the added disadvantage of lacking United States citizenship and thus are ineligible for federal health assistance programs, even if their incomes are low enough.

Although 54 percent of Hispanic women worked in 1995, half of them worked only part-time.[43] The major occupation of Hispanic women was technical, sales, and administrative support (39 percent), with the next largest share (28 percent) in service occupations.[40] This pattern is replicated among Mexican American women and among women who are "Other Hispanic." However, managerial and professional occupations are the second leading category for both Cuban and Puerto Rican women. Hispanic women from Central and South America are most likely to have service occupations, followed by technical, sales, and administrative support occupations. The median earnings for Hispanic women (1993) of $10,631 falls short of the median earnings for non-Hispanic women ($14,346) by nearly $4,000.[40] In addition, large proportions of Hispanic women work in the semiconductor and agriculture industries, both of which have occupational hazards.[44] Workers in the semiconductor industry experience occupational illnesses at three times the rate of workers in other manufacturing industries. Agricultural workers are exposed to pesticides, the use of faulty equipment, and to a range of health problems such as dermatitis, musculoskeletal and soft-tissue problems, communicable diseases, and reproductive disorders, as well as health problems related to climate.[44,60]

Cultural Factors and Health Care

Along with socioeconomic status, cultural context or acculturation—the process of change that occurs as a result of continuous contact between cultural groups—plays a major role in the access of Hispanic populations to health care.[61] More acculturated Hispanics (as reflected by greater use and skill with the English language, lessened contact with their homeland, and greater involvement with the Anglo American culture) would be expected to adopt behaviors and have health outcomes similar to the dominant Anglo culture.[62] In cancer studies in Los Angeles, for example, Hispanics born in the United

States, regardless of their socioeconomic status, appear to lose the low cancer risk associated with being born abroad and replace it with the higher cancer risk of their non-Hispanic Angeleno neighbors.[46]

Less acculturated Hispanic immigrants, however, have a significantly lower likelihood of outpatient visits for health problems (both physical and mental). One example is the incidence of low-birth-weight infants (which is highly correlated with the infant mortality rate) among less acculturated, first-generation Mexican American women. Less acculturated, first-generation Mexican American women have a lower incidence of low-birth-weight infants (4 percent of live births) than white non-Hispanic women (6 percent of live births) and than second-generation Mexican American women (6 percent of live births).[63]

Similarly, immigrants from Mexico to the United States have been found to have lower lifetime prevalence of phobias, alcohol abuse or dependence, drug abuse or dependence, and major depression than native-born Mexican Americans.[64] One possible explanation for this is that, even if equally poor, immigrants from Mexico may have less of a sense of deprivation than native-born Mexican Americans, and it is this sense of deprivation that contributes to the prevalence of psychiatric disorders. If immigrants have lower social status than their native-born counterparts, they may be less distressed (than the native-born) by their socioeconomic position because it far surpasses their standard of living in Mexico.[64,65]

Hispanics, in general, are more obese, less physically active, and less likely to participate in lifestyles that promote cardiovascular health. As a consequence, they are more likely to have diabetes than the general U.S. population. The prevalence of diabetes among Mexican Americans is two to five times that among other racial/ethnic groups.[66,67] In addition, the San Antonio Heart Study has shown that Mexican American diabetics are about six times as likely to have end-stage renal disease and three times as likely to have retinopathy as are non-Hispanic white diabetics.[67] Hispanics who are more acculturated tend to have less centralized body fatness than their less acculturated peers, however, and are, therefore, at lower risk for chronic diseases such as diabetes and heart disease. More acculturated Hispanics are likely to have intermarried with groups other than Indian populations, who have a high prevalence of obesity and associated health problems, and, thereby, to have altered their genetic material enough to reduce their risk factors for these diseases.[68] The admixture of Indian genes has been found to be more prevalent in Mexican

Americans of low socioeconomic status than in Mexican Americans of higher socioeconomic status. Coupled with the fact that Mexican Americans of low socioeconomic status are more likely to be obese and to have a less favorable distribution of body fat than other Hispanics, these findings partially explain the differentially greater prevalence of diabetes among Mexican Americans.[67]

Another aspect of acculturation for the Hispanic American is encountering discrimination, prejudice, and exclusion (based either on language or skin color), perhaps for the first time, and incorporating into her or his identity a newly acquired "minority status." Experiences with discrimination and exclusion can frustrate expectations of improved socioeconomic status when the dominant culture's values are adopted.[69] This may explain the fact that among more acculturated, younger Hispanic women, alcohol consumption has been found to be greater than among less acculturated, younger Hispanic women.[70] When measured by language use and a series of sociodemographic variables (such as education, marital status, income, and employment), greater acculturation is found to be associated with the likelihood of being a drinker and with the frequency of consuming alcohol among Puerto Rican, Cuban, and Mexican American women.[71] For example, better educated Mexican American women were more likely to be drinkers and to drink frequently than those with less education. However, Mexican American women living in poverty were less likely to be drinkers than those not living in poverty. This is true even though Mexican American women drinkers living in poverty consumed more drinks per occasion and were more likely to be heavy drinkers than women with higher incomes.[71]

Highly acculturated Mexican Americans and Puerto Ricans, who are frustrated because they have not enjoyed access to the educational resources of the United States, are the most likely to report marijuana and cocaine use.[72] Intravenous drug use, along with other high-risk health behaviors, is most prevalent among high-acculturated Hispanic women.[73] In one study, 23 percent of high-acculturated Hispanic women reported intravenous drug use, while 4 percent of low-acculturated Hispanic women reported the same. Also varying with acculturation is the frequency with which Hispanic women have multiple sex partners, a high-risk behavior for sexually transmitted diseases and HIV infection/AIDS that affects disproportionately high percentages of Hispanic women. Only 13 percent of low-acculturated, but 31 percent of high-acculturated, Hispanic women reported having had more than one sexual partner within the past 6 months.[73]

Health Beliefs

Other aspects of culture that can influence health are religion, folk healing, and “familism,” or family mores. The health beliefs of many Hispanics relate to their views about God as the omnipotent creator of the universe, with personal behavior subject to God’s judgment.[62] Beliefs such as these make it difficult to establish the importance of preventive health behaviors and also can make it difficult for Hispanic women to leave abusive relationships. Sometimes religion gives Hispanic women the strength to leave, and, in other cases, it provides the guilt that keeps women in abusive relationships.[58]

The reluctance of users of indigenous healers and folk medicines to disclose their use, and the associated delays in seeking biomedical care while using these treatments, also can jeopardize the health of Hispanics.[38] Family mores that dictate that Hispanics must seek the advice of family members before getting professional health care also can build delays into the care-seeking process that may be costly in terms of either morbidity or mortality.[62,74] Thus, low utilization of health care services, including preventive tests such as the Pap smear and mammography, can result from cultural beliefs as well as from socioeconomic barriers.[75]

HIV/AIDS

Finally, HIV/AIDS, as it affects the Hispanic community, illustrates the many barriers to effective care that are socioeconomic, cultural, and political. Puerto Ricans, on the mainland United States and on the island of Puerto Rico, have the highest incidence of HIV/AIDS among Hispanics. They also have several characteristics that distinguish them from other Hispanic subgroups and may contribute to their high rates of infection.[76] All Puerto Ricans have U.S. citizenship and therefore have no need to marry non-Puerto Ricans to maintain residency in the United States. Thus, Puerto Ricans marry each other in greater proportions than do other Hispanic sub-populations in the United States, and are, therefore, more likely to have sex with other Puerto Ricans than they are with non-Puerto Rican Hispanics or non-Hispanic people.[76] This has contributed to the heterosexual spread of HIV/AIDS among Puerto Ricans, as has the existence of racially and ethnically homogeneous needle-sharing networks. The frequent and relatively cheap flights between New York City and Puerto Rico, and continuous work-related migration between the two, have added to the difficulty in counting and providing continuous care to Puerto Ricans diagnosed with HIV/AIDS.

Cultural factors influence the spread of HIV infection and AIDS among Hispanics because they often are unwilling to discuss intimate and emotional matters such as illness and sex unless they are able to speak to someone in Spanish. Low-acculturated Hispanic women, although less likely to engage in the high-risk behaviors through which they may contract HIV infection, may be at greater risk than their behavior would suggest because they may have little knowledge of their bodies and have little clout when it comes to negotiating condom use with their husbands or sexual partners.[73] Educational programs to prevent HIV/AIDS, which instruct Hispanic women to encourage their sex partners who are intravenous drug users to use condoms, ignore the riskiness of speaking out for Latinas. Suggesting the use of a condom may cause her partner to believe that the Latina either knows too much about sex or is being unfaithful and may place her at risk of either physical or emotional abuse. Successful educational programs for poor Hispanic (and black) women have been difficult to establish, partly because these women need help in surviving in their daily environments before they can become receptive to skill-building and informational strategies.[73]

Chapter 35

Native American Women

Editor's Note: Please refer to Chapter 32, pp. 329–58 to investigate the numbered references listed in this chapter.

Health Concerns for Native American Women

Native American women come from more than 550 tribes, ranging in size from 20 to 250,000 people. Descending from the original inhabitants of this nation, they face new health risks associated with cultural dislocation, poverty, and the historical neglect of Indian rights and treaties.

- Accidental deaths among Native American women are nearly three times the national average. Many are associated with a lack of seatbelt use and drunk driving.
- Diabetes rates range from 5% to as much as 50% in different Indian tribes. Diabetes is the fourth-ranked cause of death in Native American Women.
- Native American women die from alcoholism at five to six times the national rate. Drinking during pregnancy is three times the national average. Deaths from tuberculosis are five times the national rate.

"Women of Color Health Data Book," The National Women's Health Information Center, 1998.

- Native American women have some of the highest smoking rates in the country (44%), compared to white (29%), African American (23%), Hispanic (16%) and Asian (6%).
- Suicide death rates for young Native American women are nearly twice the national average, but are lower than average in older women.
- The average infant mortality rate among Native American women is 30% higher than the national average, and sudden infant death syndrome (SIDS), is nearly two times higher.
- Gallstones. Native Americans have the highest prevalence of gallstones in the United States. Among the Pima Indians of Arizona, 70% of women have gallstones by age 30.

Factors Affecting the Health of Native Americans

Under Title VIII of the 1975 Native American Programs Act, the following groups are defined as Native Americans—American Indians, Alaska Natives (Eskimos and Aleutians), Native Hawaiians, Samoans, and other native Pacific Islanders.[3,4,5] Health data for Native Hawaiians, Samoans, and other Pacific Islanders, however, often are aggregated with data for Asian Americans under the rubric Asian and Pacific Islanders, a practice that obscures both the differences between the Asian and the native Pacific Islander sub-populations and the similarities in outcomes for native Pacific Islanders and American Indians/Alaska Natives. To the extent that data allow, this chapter discusses Native Hawaiian and other native Pacific Islander women as Native Americans and covers Asian American women separately.

American Indians/Alaska Natives

The ancestors of the people known today as American Indians/ Alaska Natives lived in North America many centuries before Europeans came. Although 12 to 15 million Indians were here when Columbus arrived in 1492, today their progeny number around 2 million.

American Indians/Alaska Natives are the smallest of the four major racial/ethnic sub-populations discussed in this report. They are constituted as 535 federally recognized (plus 100 not recognized) tribes in seven nations (such as the Navajo or Iroquois) on nearly 300 reservations in the lower 48 states and in approximately 500 government units in Alaska.[4,5,6] The many American Indian/Alaska Native subpopulations are culturally distinctive, diverse, and complex—and are growing three times more rapidly than the white population. American Indians/Alaska Natives speak more than 300 distinct languages, which makes their dialects more diverse than the entire Indo-European language family.[5]

This diversity, coupled with their many small population groups scattered throughout the United States, has made it difficult to provide a uniform, readily accessible health care system for American Indians/Alaska Natives. The 1990 Census reported that nearly three-fifths (59 percent) of the 2.2 million American Indians lived in urban areas, in contrast to a somewhat smaller share of Eskimos (50 percent) and a larger share of Aleuts (69 percent).[7] Others estimate that a third live in urban areas, another third live on reservations, and a third move back and forth between the two.[5]

Although American Indians/Alaska Natives are culturally diverse to the point that it often becomes meaningless to classify them together for any but the most gross comparisons, their shared experiences include:

- the rapid and forced change from a cooperative, clan-based society to a capitalistic and nuclear family-based system;
- the outlawing of language and spiritual practices;
- the death of generations of elders to infectious diseases or war; and
- the loss of the ability to use the land walked by their ancestors for thousands of years.[6]

These experiences have fostered the development of several characteristics among American Indians/Alaska Natives that influence their behavior when seeking and responding to health care services. Native people are generally strongly autonomous, are non-linear thinkers (especially about time), use indirect communication and styles, and have a historical suspicion of authority.[5]

Access to Health Services

Receiving health services via the Federal Government, as American Indians/Alaska Natives do because of treaty obligations, influences their ability to access and use these services. The U.S. Government has signed over 800 treaties with tribes, obligating them to maintain a reasonable level of education and health among American Indians/ Alaska Natives.[5] The Indian Health Service (IHS)—since 1955 a part of the United States Public Health Service—provides health care through its clinics and hospitals to all American Indians/Alaska Natives who belong to federally recognized tribes and live on or near the reservations in its 12 service areas. These service areas contain 144 service units (analogous to county or city health departments) that operate hospitals, and health centers and stations.[8] Of the 144 units, the 68 operated by the IHS administer 38 hospitals and 112 health centers and stations in fiscal year 1996. The remaining 76 service units operated by American Indian and Alaska Native tribal governments administer 11 hospitals and 372 health centers and stations. As of October 1, 1995, 34 Indian-operated urban projects, either health clinics or community services and referrals, provided care for the American Indians/Alaska Natives who live in urban areas and, therefore, have lost eligibility for IHS care near their reservations as the result of living away from them for 180 days.[4,9]

Although the IHS reports that it serves approximately 60 percent of all American Indians/Alaska Natives, services in urban areas and in non-reservation rural areas often are very limited and uncoordinated.[6,9] In 1987, only 41 percent of all American Indians/Alaska Natives included in the 1987 Survey of American Indians and Alaska Natives (SAIAN) reported having IHS facilities as a source of health care all year.[10] An additional 25 percent reported having private coverage and 18 percent reported public coverage throughout the year. The remaining 16 percent indicated that they had some other type of health insurance coverage for part of the year. The SAIAN also found that, among residents of metropolitan statistical areas (MSAs), only 24 percent reported the IHS as their form of health insurance throughout the year, with 35 percent of the residents of MSAs stating that they had private coverage.[10]

Geographic disparities in the location of facilities and the small number of facilities in urban areas account in part for urban American Indian women having both greater difficulties in obtaining access to prenatal care and less likelihood of getting such care than either black or white women.[11] For example, there are only two IHS health units east of the Mississippi River (a clinic in Nashville, Tenn., and a hospital in Cherokee, N.C.) to serve all the American Indians from Maine to Florida.[12] In addition, the Phoenix service area (with a population of 139,993 in fiscal year 1997) has eight hospitals, while there are none in the Portland, Ore., service area, or in the state of California (with populations of 147,887 and 123,208, respectively).[8,9]

Effects of Forced Relocation

How has the legacy of American Indians/Alaska Natives in this country influenced the health of Indian women? The major legacy of the forced relocation of American Indians throughout the United States has been to place them in communities in which they confront racism and hostility from their non-Native neighbors.[13] Forced relocation took place both in the 1830-1850 period, when tribes were relocated from lands east of the Mississippi River to Oklahoma, and in the 1950s, when, in an attempt to mainstream them, American Indians were given one-way transportation by the Bureau of Indian Affairs to relocate to urban areas.[4,8,14] Instead of mainstreaming, urban living brought continued unemployment and poverty to many American Indians/Alaska Natives. When compared to forced migrants from Indian reservations to urban areas, such as Los Angeles, voluntary migrants tend to be more successful.[4]

Racism, coupled with a mistrust of the U.S. Government, has engendered low self-esteem among many American Indians/Alaska Natives. Racism and discrimination also have contributed to the poverty in which 27 percent of American Indians/Alaska Natives live. Specifically, 27 percent of American Indians, 26 percent of Eskimos, and 13 percent of Aleutians reported incomes below the federal poverty level in 1990.[15] Poverty rates among female-headed American Indian/Alaska Native households are even greater than poverty rates for individuals. Although 26 percent of all American Indian/Alaska Native households were female-headed, 50 percent of these households had incomes below the poverty level. Fifty-one percent of all female-headed American Indian households had incomes below the poverty level, as did 39 percent and 31 percent of comparable Eskimo and Aleutian households.[15] Half of all American Indian/Alaska Native children under the age of six are estimated to live in poverty.*

This poverty stems from the high unemployment rates among both American Indian/Alaska Native men and women. In 1990, although unemployment for men of all races was 6 percent, among American Indian men the rate was 16 percent (16). Although slightly better off than American Indian men, 13 percent of American Indian women were unemployed when the rate for women of all races was 6 percent.

Poverty and unemployment have in turn fostered welfare dependency and diets replete with government commodity foods, high both in fat and calories. The malnutrition that was a problem among American Indians/Alaska Natives two generations ago has been replaced by obesity.[17] Sixty percent of both male and female urban

American Indians/Alaska Natives are reported to be overweight and, therefore, at risk for diabetes and other illnesses. Approximately 20 percent of American Indians have diabetes, a rate twice that of the general United States population. Non-insulin dependent diabetes mellitus has reached epidemic proportions among some tribes.[4,5] Although it remains less of a problem for Alaska Natives than for American Indians, the prevalence of diabetes mellitus among Alaska Natives has increased tenfold in the past 30 years.[8] End-stage renal (kidney) disease is 2.8 times more common among American Indians than among whites, and the diabetes-attributable prevalence of end-stage renal disease is 5.8 times that of whites.[17] Neuropathy and amputations also are common among American Indian diabetics. Age-adjusted death rates from diabetes mellitus among American Indians are 4.3 times that for whites and twice that for black Americans.[8] A sedentary lifestyle and sharp decreases in hunting and gathering are implicated in the high prevalence of obesity and related health problems and mortality among American Indians/Alaska Natives.

Poverty has combined with the historical suppression of indigenous religions and medical practices to place American Indians/Alaska Natives at health risks due to environmental degradation. These health risks result from living in poor quality housing (often with lead-based paint that poisons the children) and exposure to local toxins. Half of all American Indians/Alaska Natives live in areas with uncontrolled toxic waste sites.[18] Lacking a safe water supply or sewage disposal system or both, which characterized 28,700 American Indian/Alaska Native homes in fiscal year 1995, also places American Indians/Alaska Natives at risk of illness and disease.[19] On some reservations one of every five homes lacks indoor plumbing.

The loss of access to traditional environments or ecosystems and the suppression of religious and medical practices threaten the body of knowledge developed from plants and herbs. As the environments supporting plant-derived compounds such as digitoxin and ephedrine are vanishing, the knowledge base among American Indians/Alaska Natives about the use of plants and herbs is vanishing even more rapidly.[5] The fact that the IHS, in several of its facilities both on the mainland United States and in Alaska, allows medicine men and other traditional healers to hold clinic hours and treat patients in its facilities is a cooperative activity that may help counteract this. Sharing facilities in this manner not only may help foster and preserve American Indian/Alaska Native heritage, but also may expose IHS health professionals to non-western healing practices from which they may be able to learn.[5]

Family Violence

The loss of access to the lands their ancestors roamed freely has extinguished the traditional gender roles for American Indian/Alaska Native males (as hunters, horsemen, and protectors). American Indian/Alaska Native men often have channeled their rage about this against American Indian/Alaska Native women, who must still fulfill the caretaker role for their families. Family violence among American Indians/Alaska Natives takes many forms—child abuse and neglect, elder abuse, spouse battering, spouse abandonment, and sexual abuse of young children.[13] Violence is reported in 16 percent of all marital relationships among American Indians/Alaska Natives, with severe violence reported in 7 percent of these relationships.[5]

Both the lack of tribal ordinances to deal with family violence and the refusal of local non-Indian law enforcement officials to take rapes reported by American Indian/Alaska Native women seriously (especially if they are alcoholics or substance abusers) limit the recourse of American Indian/Alaska Native women who seek help. In addition, many American Indian/Alaska Native women are reluctant to report mistreatment by the men in their lives to non-Indian authorities because of the history of harsh treatment of American Indian/Alaska Native men by the U.S. justice system.

Alcoholism

Alcoholism and its multigenerational effects is at the root of many of the health problems experienced by American Indian/Alaska Native women, as evidenced by the magnitudes of their death rates from alcoholism, cirrhosis, and other liver diseases. Native American women often cope with prior victimization (from incest, rape, and other forms of sexual assault) by escaping into alcohol and drugs; doing so, though, contributes to higher mortality rates.[20] Among American Indian and Alaska Native women, death rates associated with alcoholism are much higher than among women of all races. For the 1990-1992 period, mortality due to alcoholism among American Indian/Alaska Native women ages 25-34 years was nearly 21 per 100,000 population, in contrast to the nearly 2 per 100,000 rate for women of all races.[16] American Indian/Alaska Native women ages 35-44 had a mortality rate due to alcoholism of 47 per 100,000 in 1990-1992, nearly 10 times the rate of U.S. women of all races.

American Indian/Alaska Native women who are alcoholics or substance abusers, however, seldom receive hospitalization, detoxification, or counseling for their addictions. Instead they are often jailed and lose their parental rights.[5] In addition, alcoholism and substance abuse among their daughters often adds to the stresses of elderly American Indian/Alaska Native women who wind up parenting their grandchildren and/or great-grandchildren, as well as managing the chronic diseases typical in older women.[13] The failure of addiction treatment programs, in particular, to incorporate healing elements from Native cultures, such as the medicine wheel, into their service offerings creates another barrier to seeking care. Many Natives view the use of Euro-American treatment models that focus on a single disease rather than the whole person as another form of oppression. This view thus renders the programs ineffective for American Indians/Alaska Natives.[5]

Preventive Health Care

The prevailing life circumstances for many American Indian/ Alaska Native women jeopardize their health in yet another way, because poverty, low self-esteem, alcoholism, and substance abuse may interfere with their ability to seek preventive health care. The necessity of patronizing culturally insensitive providers located at great distances limits preventive health practices and places the day when measures such as breast self-examination have been adequately taught and accepted in American Indian/Alaska Native communities far into the future.[13] Preventive health care for cancers may be even longer in becoming a reality because there are no words for cancer in some of the languages of indigenous people. Many feel that talking about the disease will bring it on and hold fatalistic views of it. In other Native traditions, cancer survivors are stigmatized.[5]

The response to the human immunodeficiency virus/acquired immune deficiency syndrome (HIV/AIDS) by American Indians/Alaska Natives reflects their long history of mistreatment by the U.S. Government and, consequently, the complexities related to providing treatment to them. HIV infection and AIDS also have not been given a meaning in indigenous languages. Thus, these conditions cannot be discussed in local tongues, nor can indigenous healing processes be applied to them. Consequently, HIV/AIDS is discussed solely as a "white man's disease," like the many other infectious diseases to which whites have exposed American Indians/Alaska Natives.[12] This perception, coupled with the fact that the Federal Government does not pay American Indians/Alaska Natives to be tested for HIV infection—as it has paid them to participate in other federal health programs—

leaves many American Indians/Alaska Natives both skeptical of the need for testing and unwilling to get it. The lack of confidentiality in IHS clinics also keeps many American Indians/Alaska Natives from getting tested and treated.[5]

Many American Indians/Alaska Natives also view the Federal Government's emphasis on multicultural outreach in funding for HIV/AIDS prevention as favoring black Americans and as resulting in ethnic minority groups competing among themselves for very limited resources. American Indians/Alaska Natives find it difficult to identify HIV/AIDS as something that can affect them, without a spokesperson who is an American Indian/Alaska Native to bring the message home in the way former basketball star Magic Johnson has for many young people and for black Americans.[12]

Native Hawaiians and Other Pacific Islanders

The more than 365,000 Pacific Islander Americans come from more than 22 islands—either Polynesian, Micronesian, or Melanesian—and speak as many as 1,000 different languages.[21,22] The vast majority are from the Polynesian islands, the islands in the central and south Pacific that are farthest from Asia. In 1990, 85 percent of Pacific Islanders—to be exact, more than 211,000 Native Hawaiians, nearly 47,000 American Samoans, and nearly 18,000 Tongans—were Polynesians.[21,23] Native Hawaiians are the largest sub-population, constituting 66 percent of all Pacific Islanders, with Samoans the next largest group at 15 percent.[24,25] Ninety-three percent of the residents of American Samoa are Polynesian, including both Samoans and Tongans (who are 4 percent of the population), along with the 2 percent who are white, and the 5 percent who are of other racial/ethnic groups.

Micronesians are the second largest Pacific Islander group—about one in every seven Pacific Islanders—and Guamanians (more than 49,000 in 1990) are the largest Micronesian population.[21,23] Making up 12 percent of all Pacific Islanders, most Guamanians are of mixed ancestry, descended from the native Chamorros of Guam, who have intermarried with settlers primarily from Spain, Japan, the Philippines, and the 50 U.S. states. The Chamorro are nearly half of the residents of Guam, with Filipinos a fourth, Chinese and Japanese together close to a fifth, and whites 10 percent.[26] The second largest group of Micronesians are Belauans (formerly Palauans), who numbered just over 1,400 in 1990.[21] Other Micronesian Islands include the Carolines, the Marianas, the Marshalls, and the Gilberts (now the Republic of Kiribati).[27] Melanesians are only 2 percent of Pacific

Islander Americans, with the more than 7,000 Fijians (including both natives and descendants of the Asian Indians who came to work the coconut plantations in the late 1800s and early 1900s) the dominant group.

Close to half (45 percent) of all Pacific Islander Americans lived in Hawaii in 1990; an additional 30 percent lived in California, 4 percent in Washington, and 2 percent each in Texas and Utah.[21] Half of the Samoans counted in the 1990 Census lived in California, while a fourth of all Tongan Americans lived in Utah, many of them Mormon converts brought to the United States by missionaries.[21]

Citizens of the autonomous governments of the islands in the Pacific Ocean to the west of Hawaii have a variety of political relationships with the United States and, partly as a result of this, have several different tiers of health care. Guam, the most developed of the islands in the western Pacific, has a relatively advanced system of health care. The Commonwealth of the Northern Marianas, however, provides a lesser tier of health facilities and care to its residents. The Republic of Belau and the Federated States of Micronesia have old hospitals and provide a generally poorer level of care than the other islands already noted.[28]

Native Hawaiians

Native Hawaiians are individuals whose ancestors were natives of the Hawaiian Islands prior to initial contact with Europeans in 1778.[3,5] Although the 1778 Native population of the seven inhabited Hawaiian islands is estimated as 300,000, one century after European contact (i.e., in 1878), the Native Hawaiian population had declined by more than 80 percent, to 57,985.[29] During the past 200 years, Native Hawaiians have faced traumatic social changes, resulting in the loss of their traditions and threatening their survival as a distinct group. Most of this decline was due to venereal diseases (resulting in sterility), miscarriages, and epidemics such as small pox, measles, whooping cough, and influenza. Poor housing, inferior sanitation, hunger, malnutrition, alcohol, and tobacco use also contributed to the decline.[29]

The **political and economic transformation** of Hawaii associated with statehood and with the development of a modern commercial/service economy has resulted in the loss of land and political power for Native Hawaiians.[3] In the early 1900s, demands for labor to work in the expanding plantation economy, which could not be met locally, were satisfied by the immigration of more than 250,000 foreign laborers, most of them Japanese and Filipino. In later waves and smaller numbers, laborers also came to Hawaii from Portugal, Puerto Rico, Spain, and Korea.

As a result, the population of Hawaii today is multi-racial/ethnic with only an estimated 8,000 full-blooded Native Hawaiian descendants remaining.[29] Native Hawaiians—today defined to include both "pure" Hawaiians and part-Hawaiians—own less than 1 percent of the Hawaiian islands, although they are attempting to regain their sovereignty over more of the state.[5] Part Hawaiians, however, number more than 200,000, comprising a fifth of the islands' population, and are the fastest growing racial/ethnic group on Hawaii. Native Hawaiians are 13 percent of the population and one of every three newborns on the Hawaiian islands.[29]

Although 70 percent of Native Hawaiians reside in the West (i.e., the Mountain or Pacific states), more than a third of Native Hawaiians reside outside of the state of Hawaii.[29] Nearly three-fifths (59 percent or 42,285) of the Native Hawaiian population on the mainland United States lives in the states of California, Oregon, and Washington. In addition, 12 states report 1,000 or more Native Hawaiians. Most statistics for Native Hawaiians, however, represent the two-thirds of the population resident in the state of Hawaii.

The health problems of Native Hawaiians today in large measure reflect their socioeconomic status. In 1990, more than 12 percent of Native Hawaiians lived in households with incomes less than $15,000, and these Native Hawaiians constituted 22 percent of all the individuals in the state of Hawaii in households with incomes at this level.[29] In addition, although 6 percent of all families in Hawaii had incomes below the poverty level in 1989, 14 percent of all Native Hawaiian families had poverty level incomes.[29] Median household income of $36,135 for Native Hawaiians, however, was close to the state median of $38,829 in 1989. Households headed by Native Hawaiian females and with no husband present had 1989 median income of $17,493, though, considerably below the state median.[29] Thirty-five percent of these female household heads had incomes below the poverty level. Of the 77,900 recipients of government aid in Hawaii in 1990, 26 percent were Native Hawaiian, double their share of the state population.[29] Of the Native Hawaiian recipients of government assistance, 73 percent received Aid to Families with Dependent Children (AFDC), the former version of the federal welfare program.

Poverty among Native Hawaiian women is associated with their labor market outcomes. Although Native Hawaiian women were 11 percent of the females in the civilian labor force, they were 15 percent of the unemployed females in the civilian labor force in 1991.[29] The 1991 unemployment rate for Native Hawaiian females of nearly 4 percent exceeds the statewide female unemployment rate of about 3 percent. In addition to often being unemployed, Native Hawaiians frequently are employed part-time or are marginally self-employed in agriculture or fishing.[3]

Many Native Hawaiians engage in **high-risk behaviors**, and the group as a whole has poorer health outcomes (such as a lower life expectancy) than other groups in Hawaii. In one study comparing whites, Japanese, Native Hawaiians, Filipinos, and Chinese in Hawaii, Native Hawaiians ranked highest in all the behavioral risk factors (not using seat belt, being overweight, smoking cigarettes, using alcohol, and driving while intoxicated) except physical inactivity.[30] Although the National Health and Nutrition Examination Survey (NHANES) II reported that 27 percent of all U.S. adults 20 to 59 years of age were overweight in 1985, a study of residents of Hawaiian Homestead lands (allocated for long-term lease in individual parcels to persons with at least 50 percent Native Hawaiian ancestry) on the largely rural island of Molokai found that 65 percent of these Native Hawaiians ages 20 to 59 were overweight. Being overweight is defined as having a body mass index [weight/height] 20 percent or more above the average body mass index for whites. By this measure, Native Hawaiian females had a 50 percent greater prevalence of overweight than all U.S. females.[31] Smoking rates among the Molokai Native Hawaiian females—34 percent reported being current smokers—also were slightly higher than the 31 percent share of United States females who reported that they were current smokers at that time. An additional 15 percent of the Molokai Native Hawaiian females indicated that they were past smokers.

Obesity is implicated in the high rates of diabetes among Native Hawaiians, especially those 35 years and older, who account for 44 percent of all cases reported in the state of Hawaii.[29] Among Native Hawaiians in the Molokai Homestead study, evidence was found not only of diabetes but also of inadequate control for it, even among persons who knew that they had the condition.[31] The levels of sugar measured in the blood and detected in the urine of Native Hawaiians known to have diabetes indicate poor control of this chronic disease.

As suggested by the evidence with diabetes, Native Hawaiians often enter medical treatment at late stages of diseases. They sometimes seek medical treatment only when self-care and traditional practices have not brought sufficient relief.[3] This pattern shows up in the entry into prenatal care by Native Hawaiian women, who are 24 percent of the pregnant women on Hawaii.[29] Although 60 percent of Native Hawaiian women began prenatal care in the first trimester in 1989 and 1990, this falls short of the 70 percent of all women in Hawaii who got care early in their pregnancies. More than one-third of the women who waited until the third trimester to seek prenatal care were Native Hawaiian women. In addition, 36 percent of those who received no prenatal care were Native Hawaiian mothers.[29] Late or no prenatal care often is implicated in low birth weights among infants. In 1990, Native Hawaiian newborns with low birth-weight (less than 2,500 grams) were 25 percent of all infants born in Hawaii with low birth weight.

Heart disease and cancer are the **major causes of death among Native Hawaiians**, as among other populations in the United States. Hypertension, a major risk factor for both coronary heart disease and stroke, is a problem for Native Hawaiians of all ages.[29] Even among Native Hawaiians between the ages of 6 and 18 years, the rate per 1,000 of 1.2 is double that for other ethnic groups in the state (0.6 per 1,000). Among Native Hawaiians ages 36 to 65, the rate per 1,000 of 197 exceeds the rate of 130 per 1,000 reported by the other racial/ethnic groups on Hawaii. The fact that the incidence of hypertension and heart disease among Native Hawaiians throughout the life span exceeds those among Hawaiians who are not natives suggests that the process underlying these diseases begins early in the lives of Native Hawaiians. To address this health problem, screening and prevention programs for circulatory diseases should be aimed at young Native Hawaiians.[32]

Breast cancer is the most common cancer among Native Hawaiian females, with the peak incidence of all cancers occurring among 65-74 year olds. Cases of cancer among Native Hawaiian females younger than 45 years of age, however, comprise nearly a quarter of all cases among women on the islands.[29] Because the perception of cancer in Hawaiian culture is bound up with beliefs about guilt and retribution, Native Hawaiian breast cancer patients often are fatalistic and do not vigorously fight their disease.[33]

AIDS also affects Native Hawaiian females more than other females in Hawaii. Between 1980 and 1993, 12 cases of AIDS were reported among Native Hawaiian females, 40 percent of all AIDS cases reported among females in the state of Hawaii during that period. A third of all AIDS deaths among women during this period also occurred to Native Hawaiian women.[29]

Efforts to modify behavior among Native Hawaiians and other Pacific Islanders and to improve their health are fraught with obstacles. For example, obesity is acceptable within Polynesian cultures where large body size is equated with power and respect.[3] In addition, efforts from outsiders to bring about behavior changes are viewed by Native Hawaiians as infringements on their traditions, which value integration, balance, and continuity among person, nature, and the spiritual world. Changes may be resisted for this reason alone.[5] For example, Native Hawaiian culture emphasizes the preservation of harmony, which sometimes results in the tendency for individuals to minimize the importance of events such as illnesses that may set them apart or reflect disharmony. This tendency results in delays in seeking services.[3] Previous experiences with white and other non-Native people also have made Native Hawaiians suspicious of medical researchers and their advice.[31] It may not be realistic to expect Native Hawaiians to give up high-risk behaviors without first solving the socioeconomic problems and cultural conflicts that contribute to these behaviors.[3]

One way to address the cultural barriers related to delivering health care services to Native Hawaiian women would be to incorporate traditional cultural systems such as Ho'oponopono (a family conference that ensures understanding, harmony, and agreement). Because Native Hawaiian culture is focused on affiliation and close personal bonds to solve or cope with problems, Native Hawaiians are uncomfortable with impersonal bureaucracies and the reliance on expert authority within these systems.[3] Respect for the importance of 'Ohana (family, or interdependence and mutual help and connectedness from the same root of origin) also is critical to developing effective health care delivery systems for Native Hawaiians.[5] The Papa Ola Lokahi clinics of the Native Hawaiian Health Service are an example of community-based health care centers culturally sensitive to the needs of Native Hawaiians.

Other Pacific Islander

Samoa, a group of volcanic islands in the southern Pacific Ocean about halfway between Honolulu and Sydney (Australia), is divided into two parts—the United States Territory of American Samoa and Western Samoa, which has been an independent country since 1962.[21] Most Samoans on U.S. soil, the second most populous native Pacific Islander group after Native Hawaiians, reside primarily in American Samoa, Hawaii, and California.[26] More Samoans live on the U.S.

mainland (nearly 48,000) than on American Samoa, although mainland residents maintain close ties to families in Samoa by visiting on ritual occasions and sending monthly remittances. Many return to the U.S. Territory of American Samoa to live permanently at some point.[26]

Regardless of residence, though, Samoans show high rates of non-insulin dependent diabetes mellitus, with associated morbidity due to hypertension, renal failure, cardiovascular disease, blindness, and amputation.[26] Samoans are among the most obese populations in the world, with Samoans in Hawaii and California even more obese than those in American Samoa.[34] Hypertension also is a problem for adult Samoans, with 13 percent of Samoan women in Hawaii and 18 percent of Samoan women in California reporting this condition.[34] Samoans born in the United States have an increased prevalence of hypertension relative to Samoans born in American Samoa. Average life expectancy at birth for Samoans is around 72 years, with Samoans sharing the major causes of death with other American sub-populations.[26] In decreasing order of frequency, the major causes of death among adult Samoans are: heart disease, cancer, accidents, cerebrovascular disease, chronic obstructive pulmonary disease (and allied conditions), influenza, and pneumonia. Breast cancer accounted for 22 percent of cancer deaths, while cancers of the lung and bronchus were the causes of 19 percent of cancer deaths among Samoan women. Cervical cancer accounted for 8 percent of all female cancer deaths.[26]

Access to health care among Samoans living on American Samoa is unique, in part because of the political relationship between the United States and its territory. Although this set of islands, located 240 miles southwest of Hawaii (the nearest site for tertiary care for residents of American Samoa), is medically under-served, American Samoa has operated a locally appropriate form of Medicaid since 1983.[26] All inpatient and most outpatient services are provided at the Lyndon Baines Johnson Tropical Medical Center (LBJ) in the village of Faga'alu on the island of Tutuila. For persons living in the urban areas of Tutuila, this aging facility built in 1968 is convenient; however, for persons in rural areas of Tutuila or on other islands within the United States Territory of American Samoa, it is difficult to access care. Financial access to services at LBJ is not a problem for the Samoan population because of the Medicaid program. However, other things, such as an insufficient number and scope of needed health professionals, the unavailability of sophisticated diagnostic tools, and the lack of financing to replace the aging and increasingly outdated medical center hinder the access to quality care in American Samoa.[26]

Samoans living on the United States mainland are more likely to be poor than other Americans and also are less likely to hold higher paying jobs that provide insurance coverage for families.[26] Twenty-five percent of all urban American Samoan families have incomes below the poverty level, compared to 10 percent of all white families. Poverty and low-wage jobs among Samoans are related to their lower levels of education. Samoan women complete high school at lower rates than other U.S. female populations.[26]

Other barriers in access to health care for American Samoans result from their **linguistic isolation, their culture and traditions, and their beliefs about the etiology of disease**. Among groups on the U.S. mainland, urban American Samoans are one of the most linguistically isolated, as defined by the percentage of households that contain no persons who speak only English or that contain no persons who speak English "very well." Nearly two-thirds of Samoans on the U.S. mainland report that no one in their households age 14 years or older speaks only English, and nearly a third report that no one in their households age 14 or older speaks English "very well."[26,35] Linguistic isolation makes it difficult for Samoans to seek and receive appropriate health care. Samoan traditions as practiced in the U.S. Territory of American Samoa include a simple, close-knit way of life centered around the family (aiga), the chief (matai), the church, and the village. Although Samoans living in California, Hawaii, and Washington tend to live in similarly close-knit, well-defined communities and to establish close ties to their churches, only in Hawaii, where the Samoan community is visible and concentrated in three distinct areas (Laie, Kalihi, and Waianae), have community-centered clinics been developed to provide culturally appropriate health care and education.[26]

Part of the difference in hypertension prevalence between Samoans in American Samoa and on the mainland United States has been attributed to the loss of the protective effect of the strong traditional social structure among older Samoans.[36] The high rates of suicide among Samoans have been explained in a similar way. Some see the high Samoan suicide rates as a continuation of a "culturally sanctioned response to inescapable stressful situations."[37] Others see the suicides as the result of the conflict between traditional Samoan values and newly introduced values.

Finally, Samoan beliefs about the etiology of disease often constitute a barrier for them when seeking care. Samoans attribute disease states to such factors as too much work, too little sleep, the weather, certain foods, interpersonal frictions, or moral/religious issues. They thus often delay seeking care for conditions that are treatable or preventable.

Other Pacific Islanders, especially if living in urbanized/westernized areas, also report glucose intolerance or diabetes and have been identified as at risk for mental health problems (which may underlie suicide attempts). For example, 11 percent of urban Polynesian women (other than Native Hawaiians and Samoans) report diabetes, while in rural areas between 1 percent and 4 percent report the condition.[31] Micronesians from Nauru, an affluent and relatively westernized place, have a 30 percent prevalence rate for diabetes, while Melanesians on Fiji report low rates—1 percent in the rural areas and 4 percent in the urban areas.[31]

*The poverty level differs for individuals and families by household composition and by size. For example, in 1995, although the poverty income level, or threshold, for four-person families averaged $15,569, this average includes a threshold of $15,455 for a four-person family with two children and two adults along with a threshold of $15,976 for a four-person family with one child and three adults. Thus, it is difficult to report the income levels that represent poverty for the populations discussed.

Chapter 36

Drug Use during Pregnancy

More than 5 percent of the 4 million women who gave birth in the United States in 1992 used illegal drugs while they were pregnant, according to the first nationally representative survey of drug use among pregnant women. The National Institute on Drug Abuse (NIDA) sponsored survey, which was in the fall of 1994, provides the best estimates to date of the number of women who use drugs during pregnancy, their demographic characteristics, and their patterns of drug use.

"Information from NIDA's National Pregnancy and Health Survey can help to guide public health policymakers who have to make decisions about prevention and treatment programs aimed at reducing the problem of drug abuse during pregnancy," said NIDA Director Dr. Alan I. Leshner. Dr. Leshner reported the survey's findings at a press briefing held during NIDA's conference on Drug Addiction Research and the Health of Women.

The survey gathered self-report data from a national sample of 2,613 women who delivered babies in 52 urban and rural hospitals during 1992. Based on these data, an estimated 221,000 women who gave birth in 1992 used illicit drugs while they were pregnant. Marijuana and cocaine were the most frequently used illicit drugs—2.9 percent, or 119,000 women, used marijuana and another 1.1 percent, or 45,000 women, used cocaine at some time during their pregnancy.

"NIDA Survey Provides First National Data on Drug Use during Pregnancy," *NIDA Notes*, Volume 10, Number 1, January/February 1995.

The survey found a high incidence of cigarette and alcohol use among pregnant women. At some point during their pregnancy, 20.4 percent, or 820,000, pregnant women smoked cigarettes and 18.8 percent, or 757,000, drank alcohol.

"We know for certain that these [legal] substances affect the health of the fetus and a woman during and after pregnancy," said Dr. Loretta D. Finnegan, NIDA's former senior advisor on women's issues. Health care practitioners should ask women about their use of cigarettes and alcohol during prenatal checkups and educate them about the health risks of licit drugs, said Dr. Finnegan, who now directs the Women's Health Initiative at the National Institutes of Health.

Table 36.1. Drug Use during Pregnancy* among Racial and Ethnic Groups

Blacks	
Any Illicit Drug	11.3 %
Marijuana	4.6%
Cocaine	4.5%
Alcohol	15.8%
Cigarettes	19.8%
Whites	
Any Illicit Drug	4.4%
Marijuana	3.0%
Cocaine	0.4%
Alcohol	22.7%
Cigarettes	24.4%
Hispanics	
Any Illicit Drug	4.5%
Marijuana	1.5%
Cocaine	0.7%
Alcohol	8.7%
Cigarettes	5.8%

*Percent of American women who gave birth in 1992 and used drugs during pregnancy.

The survey also uncovered a strong link between cigarette smoking and alcohol use and the use of illicit drugs in this population. Among those women who used both cigarettes and alcohol, 20.4 percent also used marijuana and 9.5 percent took cocaine. Conversely, of those women who said they had not used cigarettes or alcohol, only 0.2 percent smoked marijuana and 0.1 percent used cocaine. "This finding reinforces the need for health practitioners to monitor the status of both licit and illicit drug use during pregnancy," said Dr. Leshner.

Besides providing the first national estimates of drug use during pregnancy, the survey also examined differences in the amount and types of drugs used by several racial and ethnic groups of women. Overall, 11.3 percent of African American women, 4.4 percent of white women, and 4.5 percent of Hispanic women used illicit drugs while pregnant. While African Americans had higher rates of drug use, in terms of actual numbers of users, most women who took drugs while they were pregnant were white. The survey found that an estimated 113,000 white women, 75,000 African American women, and 28,000 Hispanic women used illicit drugs during pregnancy.

The survey also described different patterns of licit and illicit drug use among white women and ethnic minorities. African American women had the highest rates of cocaine use, mainly "crack," during pregnancy. About 4.5 percent of African American women used cocaine compared with 0.4 percent of white women and 0.7 percent of Hispanic women who did so.

White women had the highest rates of alcohol and cigarette use. Nearly 23 percent of white women drank alcohol and 24.4 percent smoked cigarettes. By comparison, 15.8 percent of African American women and 8.7 percent of Hispanic women drank alcohol; and 19.8 percent of African American women and 5.8 percent of Hispanic women smoked cigarettes. "These findings point to the importance of attending to cultural issues in drug abuse prevention and treatment efforts," said Dr. Finnegan.

Although women who used drugs during pregnancy generally decreased their rates of drug use throughout their pregnancy, they did not discontinue drug use, Dr. Leshner noted. "This finding indicates how gripping an illness drug addiction can be, even in the face of what may seem to be the ultimate incentive to stay drug free," Dr. Leshner said. Nevertheless, "it is a disease that can be treated and managed with appropriate interventions," he stressed.

"With the information the survey provides about the patterns of drug use by women during pregnancy, we will be better able to identify priorities we must address," said Dr. Finnegan. This will enable researchers to develop and test more effective approaches to the differential drug abuse treatment and prevention needs of women of childbearing age, she concluded.

—Robert Mathias

Robert Mathias is a *NIDA Notes* staff writer.

Chapter 37

Life Expectancy and Leading Causes of Death among Women by Ethnic and Racial Group

Life Expectancy

- Among both whites and people of color, life expectancy (or expected remaining years of life) from birth is greater for women than for men, with the greatest gaps (of 9 years) reported between black women and men, and between Puerto Rican women and men.[1,2,3] The life expectancy for white men exceeds that of all men of color, while the life expectancy of white women exceeds that of most women of color. However, life expectancies for many Asian women living in Hawaii and for Puerto Rican women (living in Puerto Rico) exceed that of white women.[1,2,3]
- Based on current mortality data, the life expectancy for all Hispanics in the United States (both males and females) is 79 years.[4] For the population living in Puerto Rico, female life expectancy from birth is close to 80 years, while for men it is nearly 71 years.
- Hispanic women have a longer life expectancy (more than 77 years) than either black American or American Indian/Alaska Native women (both more than 74 years).[1,2,3]

"Life Expectancy," and "Major Causes of Death," and "Other Causes of Death," *Women of Color Health Data Book*, 1998, National Women's Health Information Center (NWHIC); and "Facts about Maternal Mortality among Black and White Women by State: United States, 1987-1996," Centers for Disease Control and Prevention (CDC), June 18, 1999.

- The predominantly black population of the U.S. Virgin Islands reports life expectancies at birth (for both men and women) that exceed these expectancies for other black Americans. Life expectancy for females in the Virgin Islands is 79 years, compared to slightly more than 74 years for black American females elsewhere in the United States. The gap in life expectancy is even greater between males in the Virgin Islands (more than 70 years) and black American males elsewhere in the United States (close to 65 years).[1,5]
- Life expectancy from birth for Native Hawaiian females living in Hawaii was slightly more than 77 years in 1990. Life expectancy for Samoan women living in the U.S. Territory of American Samoa is close to 75 years; for Guamanian women, life expectancy is slightly more than 76 years.[5,6]
- American Indian/Alaska Native women in the majority of Indian Health Service (IHS) service areas have a life expectancy of 74 years. This average life expectancy for American Indian/Alaska Native women reflects service areas such as Albuquerque and Nashville in which life expectancy is 78 years, along with the Aberdeen service area where life expectancy is 69 years.[3]

Table 37.1. Total Life Expectancy in Years by Race and Sex, 1989, 1991-1993, 1994.

Ethnic Group	Males	Females
American Indian/Alaska Native	66.1	74.4
Native Hawaiian	71.5	77.2
Samoan	71.0	74.9
Guamanian	72.4	76.1
Hispanic Origin	69.6	77.1
Puerto Rican	70.8	79.7
Black	64.9	74.1
U.S. Virgin Islander	70.1	79.0
Chinese	79.8	86.1
Japanese	79.5	84.5
Filipino	77.6	81.5
White	73.2	79.6
All Races	64.9	74.1

- Life expectancy at birth for all U.S. Asian populations (both males and females) is estimated at nearly 83 years.[4] Life expectancies based on the female sub-populations in Hawaii in 1990 are as follows: white—nearly 79 years; Chinese—over 86 years; Filipino—nearly 82 years; and Japanese—nearly 85 years.[6]

Major Causes of Death

- Diseases of the heart are the major cause of death for all females, except Asian and Pacific Islander females, for whom they are the second major cause of death.[1] In 1993, diseases of the heart accounted for as much as 34 percent of all deaths to white females and as little as 22 percent of all deaths to American Indian/Alaska Native females.[1]

- Age-adjusted death rates from diseases of the heart ranged from a high of 164 per 100,000 black women to 56 per 100,000 Asian and Pacific Islander women between 1991 and 1993. Death rates for Hispanic women and American Indian/Alaska Native women—70 per 100,000 and 74 per 100,000, respectively—are less than the rates reported by both black women and white women (99 per 100,000).[1]

- Cancers (malignant neoplasms) are the second most common cause of death for all females except Asian and Pacific Islander females, for whom it is the main cause of death. Twenty-eight percent of all deaths to Asian and Pacific Islander females in 1993 were due to cancer.[1]

- Black and white women reported the highest death rates from all forms of cancer in the 1991-1993 period. The death rate for black women of 136 per 100,000 exceeded the rate of white women (111 per 100,000), as well as the rates of American Indian/Alaska Native (71 per 100,000), Hispanic (67 per 100,000), and Asian and Pacific Islander women (66 per 100,000).[1]

- The third-ranked killer of most females is cerebrovascular diseases (primarily strokes). American Indian/Alaska Native women provide the only exception to this because unintentional injuries is their third-ranked killer. Cerebrovascular diseases rank fifth among the causes of death for American Indian/Alaska Native women.[1]

Table 37.2. Leading Causes of Death for Women, 1993 Numbers of Deaths According to Sex, Detailed Race, and Hispanic Origin

American Indian/Alaskan Native	
All causes	4,145
Diseases of heart	932
Malignant neoplasms	720
Unintentional Injuries	377
Diabetes mellitus	275
Cerebrovascular diseases	256
Chronic liver disease and cirrhosis	181
Pneumonia and influenza	152
Chronic obstructive pulmonary disease	142
Nephritis, nephrotic syndrome, and nephrosis	64
Suicide	58
Hispanic*	
All causes	34,758
Diseases of heart	9,567
Malignant neoplasms	7,253
Unintentional Injuries	2,222
Diabetes mellitus	1,872
Cerebrovascular diseases	1,680
Chronic liver disease and cirrhosis	1,253
Pneumonia and influenza	906
Chronic obstructive pulmonary disease	795
Nephritis, nephrotic syndrome, and nephrosis	784
Suicide	712
Black	
All causes	128,649
Diseases of heart	40,654
Malignant neoplasms	26,802
Unintentional Injuries	9,958
Diabetes mellitus	5,732
Cerebrovascular diseases	3,807
Chronic liver disease and cirrhosis	3,673
Pneumonia and influenza	2,995
Chronic obstructive pulmonary disease	2,582

Table 37.2. Continued.

***Black*, continued**	
Nephritis, nephrotic syndrome, and nephrosis	2,522
Suicide	2,297
Asian/Pacific Islander	
All causes	10,854
Diseases of heart	3,011
Malignant neoplasms	2,832
Unintentional Injuries	1,074
Diabetes mellitus	519
Cerebrovascular diseases	430
Chronic liver disease and cirrhosis	307
Pneumonia and influenza	239
Chronic obstructive pulmonary disease	172
Nephritis, nephrotic syndrome, and nephrosis	139
Suicide	133
White	
All causes	963,108
Diseases of heart	331,563
Malignant neoplasms	219,996
Unintentional Injuries	79,772
Diabetes mellitus	43,803
Cerebrovascular diseases	40,569
Chronic liver disease and cirrhosis	25,703
Pneumonia and influenza	24,105
Chronic obstructive pulmonary disease	10,052
Nephritis, nephrotic syndrome, and nephrosis	9,685
Suicide	9,609

*Excludes data from States lacking an Hispanic-origin item on their death certificates.

Source: National Center for Health Statistics, Health United States, 1995, Hyattsville, MD: US Public Health Service, 1996.

- Death rates from cerebrovascular diseases also were highest among black women (40 per 100,000). The second highest death rates from cerebrovascular diseases during the 1991-1993 period were reported for white women (23 per 100,000) and for Asian and Pacific Islander women (22 per 100,000). Mortality rates for American Indian/Alaska Native (19 per 100,000) and Hispanic (17 per 100,000) women were the lowest during that period.[1]

- Unintentional injuries kill many females, although their ranking among the top 10 causes of death varies by racial/ethnic group. They are the third-ranked killer of American Indian/ Alaska Native women. They are the fourth-ranked killer of Asian and Pacific Islander females, the fifth-ranked killer of black and Hispanic females, and the sixth-ranked killer of white females.[1]

- Although its ranking varies, diabetes mellitus is among the top 10 causes of death for all women. It is the fourth-ranked cause of death for black, American Indian/Alaska Native, and Hispanic females, and the sixth-ranked cause of death for Asian and Pacific Islander females. Diabetes mellitus is the seventh-ranked killer of white females.[1]

- Chronic obstructive pulmonary diseases (COPD), the fourth-ranked cause of death for white females, is a major killer of other women, but to a lesser extent. It is the seventh-ranked killer of Asian and Pacific Islander females, the eighth-ranked killer of American Indian/Alaska Native females, and the ninth-ranked killer of black females.[1]

- Several conditions are notable because they cause large numbers of deaths only among women of color. HIV infection is among the top 10 causes of death only for black (seventh-ranked) and Hispanic (ninth-ranked) women. Suicide is a major cause of death for Asian and Pacific Islander women (eighth-ranked) and American Indian/Alaska Native women (tenth-ranked). Homicide and legal intervention is the tenth-ranked cause of death for black and Asian and Pacific Islander females. Chronic liver disease and cirrhosis are major killers (sixth-ranked) only for American Indian/Alaska Native women.[1]

Other Causes of Death

- In 1993, among women, blacks had the highest mortality rates from homicides and firearms-related events (more than 13 per 100,000 and nearly 9 per 100,000, respectively). Approximately half as many American Indian/Alaska Native women died from each of these causes (5 per 100,000) as did black women. The homicide rate was nearly 5 per 100,000 Hispanic women and 3 per 100,000 for both Asian American and white women. Firearm-related mortality rates ranged from nearly 3 per 100,000 to nearly 5 per 100,000 among American Indian/Alaska Native, Asian and Pacific Islander, Hispanic, and white women.[1]
- The motor-vehicle death rate for most women of color was between 8 per 100,000 and 10 per 100,000, except for American Indian/Alaska Native women. More than twice as many American Indian/Alaska Native women (22 per 100,000) died in motor-vehicle-related accidents in 1993 as did black, Hispanic, Asian and Pacific Islander, and white women.[1]
- Unintentional injuries took the lives of more white, black, and American Indian/Alaska Native women than did firearm-related and motor-vehicle-related deaths and homicides in 1993. The mortality rate for unintentional injuries among American Indian/Alaska Native women was nearly 42 per 100,000, compared to 20 per 100,000 black women and 17 per 100,000 white women.[1]

Maternal Mortality among Black and White Women by State: United States, 1987-1996

- Total maternal mortality has not declined in the United States since 1982. Between 1982 and 1996 the national maternal mortality ratio (MMR), using vital statistics as the source of data, has remained approximately 7.5 maternal deaths per 100,000 live births.
- The United States has not reached an irreducible minimum in maternal mortality. The Healthy People 2000 goal of 3.3 maternal deaths per 100,000 live births has been achieved in three states for white women (Massachusetts, Nebraska, and Washington) and eight other states are close to achieving the goal for white women with maternal morbidity rates (MMRs) of less than 4 per 100,000 live births.

Table 37.3. Leading Causes of Death for American Women by Racial/Ethnic Group (1996)

Rank	All American Women	African American	Asian/Pacific Islanders	Caucasian	Hispanic/Latina	Native Americans/ Alaskans
1st	Heart Disease	Heart Disease	Cancer	Heart Disease	Heart Disease	Heart Disease
2nd	Cancer	Cancer	Heart Disease	Cancer	Cancer (HIV ages 22-44)	Cancer
3rd	Cerebrovascular Diseases (includes stroke)	Cerebrovascular Diseases (includes stroke)	Cerebrovascular Diseases (includes stroke)	Cerebrovascular Diseases (includes stroke)	Cerebrovascular Diseases (includes stroke)	Unintentional Injuries
4th	Chronic Obstructive Pulmonary Diseases	Diabetes Mellitus	Unintentional Injuries	Chronic Obstructive Pulmonary Diseases	Diabetes Mellitus	Diabetes Mellitus
5th	Pneumonia and Influenza	Unintentional Injuries	Pneumonia and Influenza	Pneumonia and Influenza	Unintentional Injuries	Cerebrovascular Diseases (includes stroke)
6th	Diabetes Mellitus	Pneumonia and Influenza	Diabetes Mellitus	Unintentional Injuries	Pneumonia and Influenza	Chronic Liver Disease and Cirrhosis
7th	Unintentional Injuries	HIV/AIDS	Chronic Obstructive Pulmonary Diseases	Diabetes Mellitus	Chronic Obstructive Pulmonary Diseases	Pneumonia and Influenza
8th	Alzheimer's Disease	Chronic Obstructive Pulmonary Diseases	Suicide	Alzheimer's Disease	HIV/AIDS	Chronic Obstructive Pulmonary Diseases
9th	Kidney Disease	Kidney Disease	Kidney Disease	Kidney Disease	Chronic Liver Disease and Cirrhosis	Kidney Disease
10th	Septicemia	Septicemia	Congenital Anomalies	Septicemia	Conditions Originating in the Perinatal Period	Suicide

- MMRs could be reliably calculated for black women in 26 states and ranged from 8.7 per 100,000 live births in Massachusetts to 28.7 in New York. MMRs could be calculated for white women in 41 states and ranged from 2.7 in Massachusetts to 9.2 in Vermont. There is little overlap between the MMRs for black women and those for white women. The lowest black MMR reported for black women equals approximately the highest MMR reported for white women.

- The four-fold increase in risk of maternal death among black women compared to white women is one of the largest racial disparities among the public health indicators. A black woman's risk of dying is higher for every specific cause of death reported including all the most frequent causes: hemorrhage, embolism, and pregnancy-induced hypertension. The risk is higher for black women of every age group but increases from a two-fold increase among black women in younger age groups to a six-fold increase among black women older than 40.

- The risk of maternal death is higher for black women no matter what level of prenatal care they receive.

- Early diagnosis and effective treatment of pregnancy complications are critical to reduce maternal mortality. The finding that a black woman's risk of dying from pregnancy or its complications is four times greater than for white women contrasts with the fact that her risk of developing maternal complications is less than twice that of white women.

- Although U.S. vital statistics data indicate that between 1987 and 1996, 3,086 women died as a consequence of pregnancy or its complications in the United States, misclassification on death certificates causes these data to underestimate maternal mortality. The true number of maternal deaths is estimated to be 1.3 to 3 times higher than that reported in vital statistics records, indicating the need for improved surveillance (public health monitoring) of this outcome.

- To assess the problem and develop appropriate interventions to reduce the number of maternal deaths, all states should implement active surveillance of maternal mortality by reactivating maternal mortality review committees and identifying and investigating all deaths, discussing each case in a multi-disciplinary process, and disseminating findings and recommendations for preventing future deaths.

- Both public health surveillance and prevention research are needed to understand the continued marked disparity between black and white maternal mortality. In return, this understanding will guide the development of appropriate interventions and improvements in maternal health care. By investing in public health surveillance and prevention research to monitor and identify causes of maternal mortality, and maternal health programs to promote maternal health, the risk of maternal mortality and morbidity can be reduced for all women in the United States.

References

1. National Center for Health Statistics. Health United States, 1995. Hyattsville, MD: US Public Health Service, 1996.
2. National Institutes of Health. *Report of the National Institutes of Health: Opportunities for research on women's health.* Bethesda, MD: Office of Research on Women's Health, 1991.
3. Indian Health Service. *Regional differences in Indian health* 1996. Rockville, MD: US Public Health Service, 1997.
4. Bureau of the Census, National Institutes of Health. *Profiles of America's elderly: Racial and ethnic diversity of America's elderly population.* Current Population Reports, Series POP/93-1. Washington, DC: US Government Printing Office, 1993 Honorable D Christian-Green, Member of Congress, personal communication, February 1997.
5. Yee BWK. Health status of Asian and Pacific Islander women: Many unanswered questions. Paper presented at conference "Bridging the Gap: Enhancing Partnerships To Improve Minority Women's Health," Washington, DC, January 27-28, 1997.
6. Hartmann HI, Kuriansky JA, Owens CL, in: Falik MM, Collins KS (eds). *Women's health: The Commonwealth Fund survey*. Baltimore: Johns Hopkins University Press, 1996, pp. 296-323.

Chapter 38

Health Status of Older Minority Women

Editor's Note: Please refer to Chapter 32, pp. 329–58 to investigate the numbered references listed in this chapter.

Introduction

The United States has the third largest population of 65-year olds and the largest and oldest population in the world (Aging America, 1987). Racial/ethnic older women have rich heritages in America. They transported with them traditions of survival that have served to provide them with unprecedented stamina to endure a lifetime struggle often in a hostile society.

These women have been the key components of family stability, abiding by family traditions and culture. Yet, they have encountered a lowly status in society. However, their contributions laid the foundation for future generations to have a better chance at elevating their personal status to the highest levels.

Racial/ethnic women have traditionally experienced prolonged poverty, in part due to discriminatory practices in the workforce, housing, and social living. The result of being old and a minority woman poses a "Double Jeopardy" in American society. An important concern about racial/ethnic older women is that they bring with them unique

---

"Health Status of Racial/Ethnic Older Women," Health Resources and Services Administration (HRSA), December 18, 1996, and excerpts from "Elderly Women of Color," *Women of Color Health Data Book,* 1998, National Women's Health Information Center.

historical legacies and rich cultural backgrounds including physical identification, such as black, red, brown, and yellow skin. Many authors refer to women of different skin tones as "Women of Color." These women constitute a growing concern in this nation because they are now living longer than in earlier years and are estimated to increase dramatically in numbers by the year 2030.

Poverty has been and continues to be a major concern for racial/ethnic elderly women. Coupled with poverty is social isolation and the inability to change their lifestyles at this latter stage of their lives. Limited education is another major factor adding to poverty among these elderly groups.

Since 1900, major statistical reports have investigated the health status primarily of African Americans (which was the largest minority group at that time) in comparison to whites. The comprehensive data reports indicate that over a 95-year period of time African Americans have consistently had higher mortality rates than their white counterparts across the older ages. Life expectancy has and continues to be lower for African American women during this extended period of time. A vast amount of research literature now exists, in greater detail than earlier reports. The literature reveals the health disparities in more recent disease categories, such as heart disease, malignant neoplasms, cerebrovascular diseases, etc., than those at the turn of the century which were primarily infectious and communicable diseases. Again, racial/ethnic women when compared to white women of comparable ages, did not fair well. Yet, a major contrast exists, racial/ethnic women are growing in number despite the health-disparity paradigms.

This chapter will examine the health status and cultural traditions of older women of the four major racial/ethnic groups in this country today. They include: (1) African American, (2) American Indians/Alaska Natives, (3) Asian/Pacific Islanders, and (4) Hispanics/Latinos.

African American Older Women

- African Americans, age 65 and over represent approximately 9 percent of this black population, compared to 12 percent for whites in this age group. Interestingly, this segment of the African American population is accelerating more rapidly than whites. During the 1970 to 1980 decade, African Americans age 65 and over increased 40 percent and whites increased by 25 percent. This finding raises questions about the reasons for this discrepancy among the races. The rationale for the discrepancy has been described as the "crossover effect," which notes that if African American women reach age 65, the life expectancy rate is higher for African Americans than whites. About one-fifth of the African American older population lives in rural America compared to one-fourth of the white elders.

- More than 59 percent are dispersed in Southeastern states. Others are concentrated in the North Central or Northeast regions (AARP, 1988).
- Harper and Alexander (1990) reported that the African American elderly encounter increased susceptibility to economic loss. They live on private pensions, and government pensions. Many retired elderly undertake second careers after retirement.
- Many elderly African Americans have never learned to participate in leisure time activities such as outdoor sports, etc. Households consisting of families headed by African American elderly age 65 and over had an annual income of $18,489 (AARP, 1994). The median income for African American elderly women is $2,825.
- One out of three rural African American elderly live in poverty. About 68 percent of rural African American elderly women are in or near poverty.
- Between 1990 and the year 2030, African American elderly will increase 160 percent.
- Six percent of the African American elderly had no formal education compared to 2 percent white elderly.
- Only 17 percent of the African American elderly completed high school compared to 41 percent whites. African Americans have not always had equal access to a public school education.
- In 1983, African American elderly women had a median of 8.7 years of education. A disproportionate number of African American women suffer from coronary heart disease primarily due to hypertension, elevate blood cholesterol levels, diabetes mellitus, obesity, and smoking (Gillum and Liu, 1984).
- An estimated 1.5 million Americans suffer from severe dementia. Vascular dementia is prevalent among African Americans, primarily related to obesity and hypertension (Folstein, Anthony, and Parhad, 1985).

- The need for a change in the lifestyles of the African American elderly women is a major concern. Reduction in smoking, alcohol intake, drug abuse, and an increase in exercise could diminish the mortality rates in this population.
- There are a number of health problems related to heart disease, cancer, cerebrovascular disease, unintentional injuries, homicide, and elder abuse that affect the health and well-being of these elderly women. The African American older woman adheres to many cultural beliefs in determining how sick she is and what form of medicine should be undertaken.
- African American elders tend to rely on emergency rooms for health care services and seek this service as a last resort.
- Outreach is one of the most important aspects of delivering appropriate and quality health care to African American older women. Because these women rely heavily on cultural traditions, health care is not always a first choice. Home remedies are often used to provide cures for illnesses.
- Health care services are expensive and often inaccessible to African American elderly women who are poor and have multiple health problems.
- Health care services in the future must be culturally sensitive to the folk medicines used by this target population and work with the patients to improve their use of traditional health care systems.
- Medicare and Medicaid have assisted the African American elderly woman in receiving quality health care. Some exceptions are due to physicians who do not accept Medicaid. In these instances, the patient is left with few choices, therefore leading them to emergency services.

Asian American Older Women

- This is the fastest growing population in the U.S. It is anticipated that this population will have the largest expansion among the Filipinos, Chinese, Vietnamese, Korean, Japanese, and other Asian groups.
- There is a great diversity among Asian/Pacific Islanders.

- While the health research literature is sporadic, the Asian traditions have been that elders were highly respected and to a large extent taken care of in their old age by younger members of the family.
- The elderly refugee Asian populations tend to be poor and face a number of health problems in this country.
- In 1980, six percent of Asian Americans were over 65 years of age and over 60 percent were living in Western states in the U.S.
- The second major dilemma is poverty which leads them to seek out social services for survival and for health care.
- In this country, the Asian elderly often feel powerless, isolated and depressed along with the growing physical problems of old age. They learn about health and social services available to them through their tightly knitted community structure.
- Health care services must provide services that are tailored to the multiple languages of these cultures as well as embrace the cultural diversity surrounding their traditions in order to give them optimal health care. Further, the elderly patient is often accompanied by younger family members to assist in the translation of physicians' instructions.

Hispanic American Older Women

- There is a growing body of research on this population. The literature consists of the problems facing the elderly in terms of health care, education, and poverty.
- This population is quite diverse and has a number of cultural similarities and differences.
- It is estimated that only five percent are over age 65. Hispanics tended to be a young population group. However, there is a rapid growth patterns among the elderly and by the year 2030, Hispanics are expected to show a 555 percent increase in the overall population.
- Fifty-seven percent of older Hispanics are females and among Puerto Ricans the percentage is 64.

- Language barriers are deterrents to health care among older Hispanic women. In 1985, about one-third of older Hispanics had 5 years of schooling. Older Cubans tended to have higher education levels.
- Hispanic older women tend to be poor and cannot afford health care services despite the language barriers.
- One study showed that older Hispanic women who lived alone reported the greatest number of illnesses and had increased levels of arthritis, high blood pressure, and circulation problems.
- Diabetes was the third most prevalent problem in this group. Dental services were those needed the most by this population. They tended to be hospitalized much less than their white counterparts.
- About 85 percent reported having chronic diseases and 45 percent reported having difficulty in daily living activities.
- Breast cancer was a concern for older Hispanic women. Cardiovascular disease was increased due to older women with high levels of obesity, diabetes mellitus, and hypertension.
- Hispanic elders follow their cultural traditions when they are sick and health care providers must factor these concerns into their caregiving protocols.
- Spiritual and folk healing are strong traditions among older Hispanic women.
- It is strongly suggested that future health care services include time-oriented health plans for older Hispanic women and include family members in the regimens.
- Hispanic elderly women live in "Triple Jeopardy." They are old, poor, and they are members of a minority group.
- Heart disease, cancer, and stroke are the three main causes of death among Hispanic elders. With the expected increase in population in the year 2030, the health system should prepare to handle the diversity of problems faced by this population in their older years of life.
- Health costs are also a major barrier to the elder Hispanic woman in receiving health care.

- Health care models need to factor in health care systems that can effectively meet the special needs of older Hispanic women.

American Indians and Alaska Natives

- There are inherent differences among elder American Indians and Alaska Natives in the 460 nations, tribes, organizations, villages, and rancheros.
- There are 250 distinct languages among these nations.
- More than 50 percent of these populations are women.
- The leading causes of death among these populations are heart disease, accidents (motor vehicle and others), and malignant neoplasms, cerebrovascular disease, chronic liver disease, and diabetes mellitus. The Indian Health Service (IHS) operates 50 hospitals and several hundred health clinics and health stations throughout the U.S.
- Approximately 1.4 million American Indian and Alaska Natives are eligible for health services under the IHS.
- Traditional Indian healing is important in the health service delivery for older American Indian and Alaska Native women.
- Geographically, the Midwest and the West contain the largest number of older Indian women who live predominantly in rural areas.
- More than half of the American Indians and Alaska older women tend to be living below the U.S. poverty level.
- About three-fourths of the elderly ages 65 to 74 live with their families.
- Significant numbers of elderly Indians suffer Organic Brain Syndrome in the mental disorders portfolio.
- Health care systems need to develop language specific protocols to work effectively with the Indian nations because the elderly require a large number of health care services.
- Effective health care and counseling to the American Indian and Alaska Native older women populations should consist of

nonthreatening approaches that are in harmony with the Indian traditions and cultures.

- An understanding of the basic teachings of Indian Medicine will provide several methodologies utilizing traditions that emphasize values that can be applied to their lifestyles today for bringing people back to health.

Health Assessment

Elderly people of color, especially Hispanics and African Americans, are known to have a greater number of functional disabilities, as measured by restricted activity and bed-disability days, than are elderly whites of the same ages.[65] Activity limitations due to arthritis increase with age for all women, but are especially severe for African American and American Indian/Alaska Native women among the 2.5 million women 65 years of age and older reporting this condition.[174] In addition, although the age-specific incidence of hip fractures in black women is about half that of white women, the rates in black women are considerable and are associated with higher subsequent rates of disability and even mortality.[175] Osteoporosis, often the cause of hip fractures among elderly women, is widely known to be more common in Asian women than in other racial/ethnic groups of elderly women.[169] Although the decrease in calcium absorption with age is implicated in the incidence of osteoporosis among Asian women, the lack of exercise among this sub-population also is a causal factor.

American Indian/Alaska Native women ages 65 and older included in the SAIAN reported greater incidence than all United States women of gallbladder disease and of diabetes mellitus, two chronic conditions that may contribute to functional disability and impairment.[176] Diabetes continues to be a problem among black and Hispanic women 65 years of age and older as it was in earlier adult years. Among black women, diabetes can be termed epidemic, with one in four black women older than 55 years of age with the disease, double the rate among white women.[177] Mexican American (15 percent) and Puerto Rican (16 percent) women ages 45 to 74 years have a higher prevalence of diabetes mellitus than both non-Hispanic white (6 percent) and black women (11 percent).[170] Hypertension, especially among Filipino women, and high levels of cholesterol are two major causes of morbidity among Asian women.[25]

Racial/ethnic minority elders have been found to be somewhat more likely than other elderly persons to experience psychosocial distress.[178]

This is especially true for those elderly people of color who have experienced lives with low incomes, minimal education, substandard housing, and a general lack of opportunity, and thus have fewer social and psychological coping resources available to them. At the same time, the accuracy of reports of psychiatric illnesses among African Americans has been questioned.[77] Diagnostic biases have been found to result in greater likelihood of a diagnosis of schizophrenia among blacks than is warranted upon re-examination of patients. Erroneous diagnoses are attributed to the social distance between the treating psychiatrists and the patients, the presence of racism, and unconscious fears related to working with patients different from themselves. These erroneous diagnoses often result in the increased use of restraints and higher doses of drugs being prescribed for black elderly patients (than for white elderly patients) with mental health problems.[77]

Effective responses to mental problems vary by racial/ethnic group. For example in one study family help has been found to buffer psychological distress among elderly blacks, while higher levels of family interaction were associated with greater depression among elderly Mexican Americans.[178]

The major causes of death for racial/ethnic minority elderly populations include diabetes and hypertension, which are prominent as causes of deaths among African American, Hispanic, and Native American elders.[66] The six leading causes of death for elderly American Indians/Alaska Natives are heart disease, cancer, cerebrovascular disorders, pneumonia and influenza, diabetes mellitus, and accidents.[8] Cancer survival rates among elderly American Indians/Alaska Natives are the lowest among all United States sub-populations.

In one state survey, elderly Hispanics (both male and female) were found to have lower death rates than elderly non-Hispanic whites (both male and female) for almost all causes, especially diseases of the heart, chronic obstructive pulmonary disease and allied conditions, and cancers.[166] Older Hispanics had higher death rates due to diabetes mellitus, motor vehicle accidents, kidney ailments (such as nephritiis, nephrotic syndrome, and nephrosis), and chronic liver disease and cirrhosis than did non-Hispanic whites.

Although age-adjusted mortality rates generally are lower for Asian Americans than for whites, there is great variety in the rates reported by subgroups of Asians.[25] Asian and Pacific Islander women 65 years of age and older have a death rate from suicide (more than 8 per 100,000), that is four times that of elderly black women (2 per 100,000) and 1.3 times that of elderly white women (more than 6 per

100,000). Suicide rates among elderly Chinese American and Japanese American women, in particular, are known to exceed suicide rates among non-Asian women the same ages.[25] Social isolation is posited as an explanation for this, although health problems are mentioned most often as the reason for suicide when suicide notes are left.[179]

Death rates among some racial/ethnic elderly populations differ from those among whites due in part to the "mortality crossover effect" observed among African Americans and American Indians/Alaska Natives. The mortality crossover effect is a pattern of selective survival in which the least robust African Americans and American Indians/Alaska Natives die at earlier ages and hardier ones survive to much older ages.[66] This explains why life expectancy for whites exceeds that for African Americans at age 65, but the reverse becomes true around age 75—that is, life expectancy for African Americans exceeds that for whites.[66]

Summary

In summary, racial/ethnic older Americans are at great risk in accessing health care systems to receive quality health care. The major barriers are: poverty, language difficulty, isolation, poor health, lack of transportation, and a deep sense of being left out of the mainstream of health service systems.

Future policies must address the growing population increases in racial/ethnic groups in the 21st century and the ability of the U.S. health care systems to effectively meet their special and unique needs. Both Medicare and Medicaid programs are essential in the provision of some support to older Americans who would not survive the onset of major diseases without these types of compensations. More importantly, our health systems must be more flexible in meeting the language needs of these diverse populations to facilitate the treatment modalities that will extend their lives. Health care access is a real challenge in the 21st century and careful planning is needed to contribute effectively to the well-being of racial/ethnic older women. The White House Conference on Older Americans emphasized the necessity of maintaining programs focused on older Americans.

Part Seven

Improving the Health of Ethnic and Racial Groups

Chapter 39

Health Insurance and Access to Health Care

Health Insurance

Health insurance plays a critical role in ensuring that Americans obtain timely medical care and have protection against expensive health care costs. This section describes the health insurance coverage of various racial and ethnic groups. The Medical Expenditure Panel Survey (MEPS) groups health insurance into three categories. Those people grouped as "any private" had private health insurance at any time during the study. For example, people who had health care coverage from their workplace for 1 month would be considered privately insured. People who had no private coverage at any time during the study but who had public insurance such as Medicaid or Medicare are described as "public only." People who did not have private or public insurance at any time during the study are described as "uninsured."

Who Has Coverage and Who Doesn't?

Black and Hispanic Americans were more likely than whites to be uninsured. Blacks were the most likely to be publicly insured, while whites were the most likely to have private insurance.

"Racial and Ethnic Differences in Health," Medical Expenditure Panel Survey (MEPS), AHCPR Publication No. 99-0001, February 1999; and "Barriers Limiting Access to Health Care," The Health of Minority Women, Office of Women's Health, U.S. Department of Health and Human Services, 2000.

- Less than half of all Hispanics and blacks had private health insurance, compared to three-fourths of whites.
- Over one-fifth of all Hispanics and over one-fourth of blacks had only public insurance, compared to one-tenth of whites.
- Hispanics and blacks were much more likely than whites to be uninsured.

Are Some Racial and Ethnic Groups More Likely to Have Job-Related Insurance?

Employers are the most common source of private health insurance coverage in the United States. Overall Hispanic and black workers ages 16-64 were less likely than white workers to have job-related health insurance.

- Slightly more than half of Hispanic workers and two-thirds of black workers had job-related insurance, compared to over three-quarters of white workers.

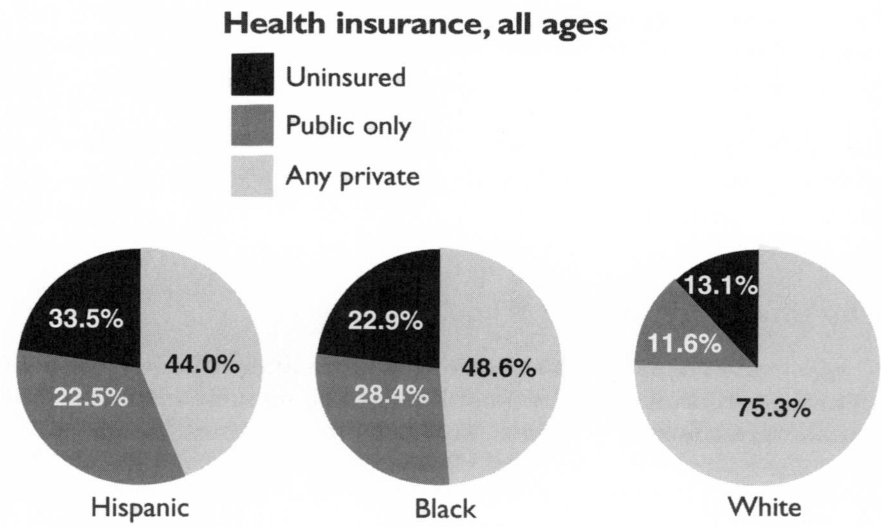

Figure 39.1. *Health Insurance, All Ages*

Are Certain Racial/Ethnic Groups More Likely to Be Uninsured?

Although people in the white/other group represented more than half of the uninsured population, Hispanics and blacks were disproportionately represented among the uninsured.

- Hispanics represented only 11.6 percent of the U.S. population under age 65 but accounted for 21.2 percent of the uninsured population.
- Similarly, blacks represented 13.1 percent of the non-elderly U.S. population but 16.9 percent of the uninsured population.
- In contrast, the white/other group represented 75.3 percent of the non-elderly U.S. population but only 61.9 percent of the uninsured population.

What Is the Role of Gender in Insurance Coverage?

Gender is an important factor in the relationship between race/ethnicity and health insurance coverage.

- Private insurance coverage was similar for males and females in each racial/ethnic group.

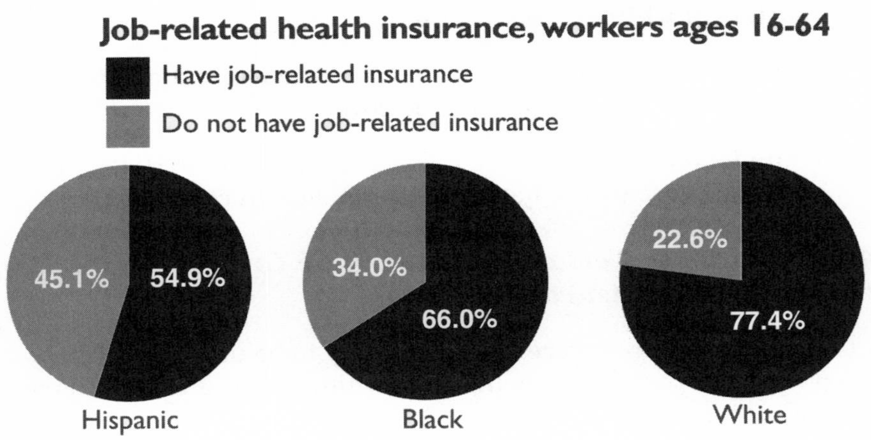

Figure 39.2. *Job-Related Health Insurance, Workers Ages 16-64*

- Among all racial/ethnic groups, females were more likely than males to have public insurance.
- Hispanic males were substantially more likely to be uninsured than any other group.

Is Health Insurance Different for Young Adults?

Young adults ages 19-24 were the age group most likely to lack health care coverage.

- About one-third of Hispanic and black young men and women had private insurance coverage. In contrast, more than 60 percent of white young adults had such coverage.
- Among young adults, Hispanic and black women were far more likely to be publicly insured than their male counterparts. They were also more likely than young white women to have public coverage.

Are There Gender Differences in Job-Related Health Insurance among Racial/Ethnic Groups?

- Hispanic male workers were far less likely than all other workers to have health coverage from an employer. Only half of Hispanic male workers obtained job-related health coverage, compared with two-thirds of black male workers and three-quarters of white male workers.
- Hispanic female workers were much more likely than Hispanic male workers to have job-related coverage.
- White female workers were more likely than their Hispanic or black counterparts to have job-related health coverage.

Are Children in Certain Racial/Ethnic Groups More Likely to Lack Health Insurance?

- Hispanic children were the most likely to be uninsured. They were more than twice as likely as white children to have no insurance coverage.
- White children were far more likely than either black or Hispanic children to have private health insurance.

- Black children were the most likely to have public health care coverage (40.8 percent), followed by Hispanic (32.5 percent) and white (13.1 percent) children.

Access to Health Care

Adequate access to health care services can significantly influence health care use and health outcomes. One way to measure access to care is to ask whether people have a usual source of care—a person or place they usually go to if they are sick or need advice about their health. Lacking a usual source of care may also have important implications for the quality and continuity of care received. In addition, even people who have a usual source of care may experience barriers to receiving services because of financial or insurance restrictions, lack of availability of providers at night or on weekends, or other difficulties.

This section describes racial and ethnic differences in usual sources of care and barriers to obtaining needed health care.

Are Different Racial/Ethnic Groups Less Likely to Have A Usual Source of Care?

Hispanic and black Americans were substantially less likely than other Americans to have a usual source of health care.

- Hispanics were the least likely to have a usual source of care.

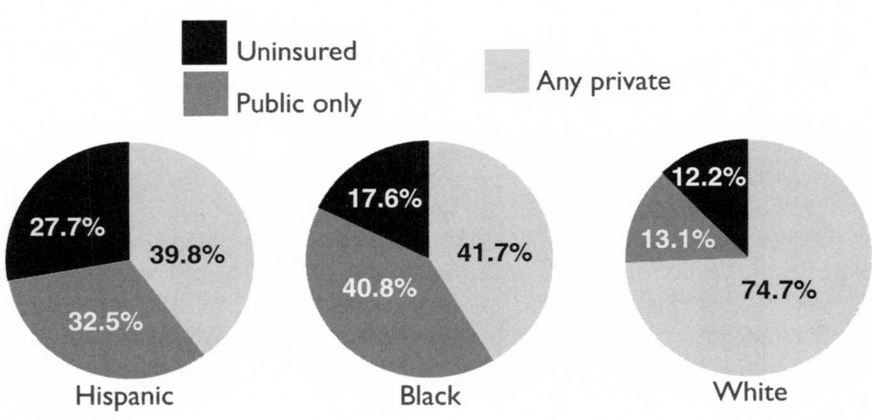

Figure 39.3. *Health Insurance, Children under Age 18*

- Over three-fourths of the white/other group (76.3 percent) had an office-based usual source of care, compared with 57.9 percent of Hispanics and 63.6 percent of blacks.
- Blacks and Hispanics were more likely than the white/other group to have a hospital-based usual source of care.

Are Children in Some Racial/Ethnic Groups More Likely to Be without a Usual Source of Care?

Hispanic and black children were less likely than white children both to have a usual source of care and to have an office-based source of care.

- Hispanic children were less likely than children in any other racial/ethnic group to have a usual source of health care.
- Black children were twice as likely as white children to have no usual source of health care.
- Hispanic and black children were less likely than white children to have an office-based usual source of care and were more likely to have a hospital-based source of care.

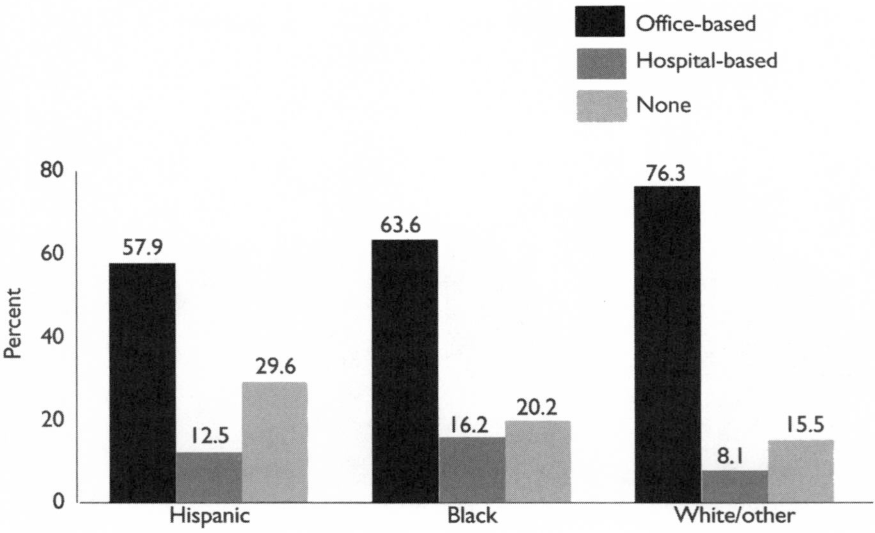

Figure 39.4. *Usual Source of Care, All Ages*

Health Care Barriers Experienced by Different Racial/ Ethnic Groups

Families headed by Hispanics were the most likely to report having difficulty, delaying, or not receiving health care they needed.

Among families that encountered problems in receiving care, those headed by Hispanics (69.1 percent) were more likely than those headed by persons in the white/other group (58.5 percent) to be unable to afford health care.

Barriers Limiting Access to Health Care

The Health Care System Itself

The current state of medical practice, medical education, medical research, and medical leadership in the United States creates its own obstacles for minority women. These four areas of medicine have traditionally ignored the health of both women and minorities.

1. **Medical practice**. Obstacles for minority women include inadequate numbers of primary care physicians, the tendency of physicians not to practice in either rural or urban low-income

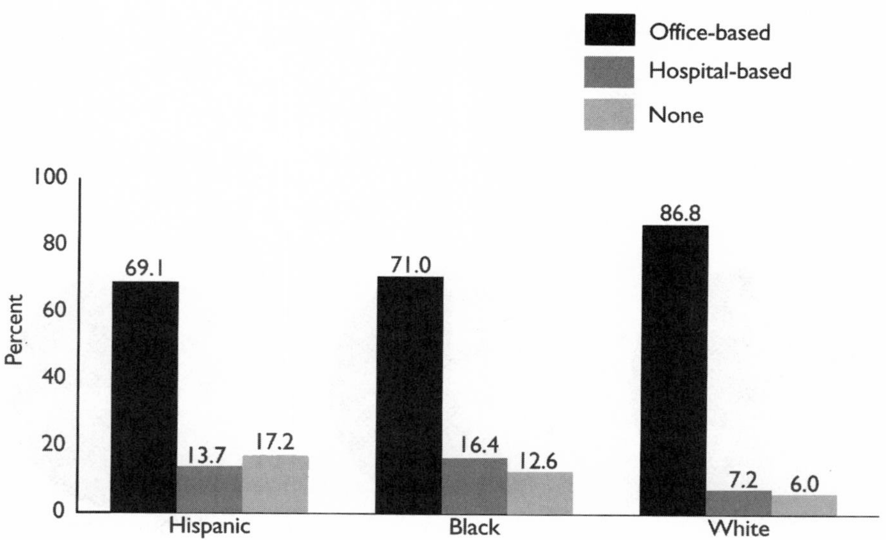

Figure 39.5. *Usual Source of Care, Children under Age 18*

areas in which many minority women live, the absence of nearby health care facilities, and the communication barriers presented by physicians who do not speak or understand the native language of their patients. Minority women who live in poverty face yet another problem. Most receive care in community health centers, hospital outpatient clinics, or other facilities that have high-volume practices. Consequently, physicians in these settings spend less time with patients and provide less preventive care counseling than is common in other medical practices.

2. **Medical education**. Medical education offers little training in cultural competence. Ultimately, cultural competence—more than gender, race, or ethnicity—fosters an environment in which patients of diverse backgrounds will be understood, appropriately diagnosed, and appropriately treated. Only recently has medical education promoted community-based training and increased its focus on primary care, which is desperately needed by minority women in under-served communities.

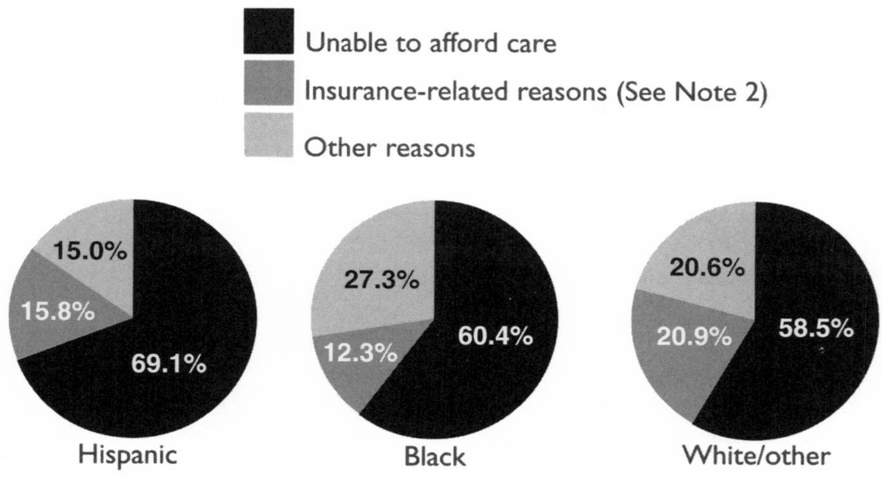

***Figure 39.6.** Main Problem Encountered by Families with Barriers to Care*

3. **Medical research**. Few minority women participate in research studies, which results in inadequate or inaccurate data on these populations. Many research studies and data collection efforts misreport the race and ethnicity of minority women. Moreover, data are typically gathered from a limited number of subgroups, and then the conclusions are erroneously applied to the entire minority group.

4. **Medical leadership**. In addition, too few women and minorities serve as physicians, administrators, researchers, medical faculty, nurses, dentists, or other health care providers. Many health care professionals and facilities are, consequently, insensitive to the needs and preferences of minority women. Inadequate communication between patients and health care providers commonly occurs, often as a result of stereotyping, language barriers, and health care materials written at inappropriate literacy levels. Health care services that are relevant to the social concerns, cultural attitudes, health needs, and health practices of minority women do not typically exist.

Economic Barriers

2. **Income levels**. While minority women are found in all socioeconomic levels, they are more likely to have lower incomes and to live in poverty than Caucasian women. Despite more than 30 years of progress in this society, minority women continue to have less formal education than Caucasian women. Even minority women who have similar levels of education as their Caucasian counterparts earn less money and have fewer assets. Minority women also hold a disproportionate share of low-wage jobs, and they experience higher unemployment rates. Low income, in particular, is strongly associated with the decreased use of health services and poor health outcomes. The tendency of economically disadvantaged women to delay seeking treatment—often until the advanced stages of disease—points to the need for early prevention efforts.

2. **Health insurance**. More minority women than Caucasian women are uninsured or rely on public, rather than private, health insurance. Since 1965, the federal government's Medicare and Medicaid programs have helped increase minority women's access to health care. Program benefits are limited, however, and frequently do not meet all of these women's

health care needs. Unfortunately, the gaps between Caucasian and minority women in socioeconomic status and health insurance coverage appear to be growing.

3. **Social and cultural barriers**. Several other factors limit the access of minority women to the U.S. health care system. They include social disadvantages, cultural values, discrimination, the lack of culturally appropriate services, inadequate childcare, and transportation, among many others.

   Substantial numbers of minority women

   - may distrust the health care system, which is perceived by many to be hostile and insensitive;
   - may be single parents;
   - can have cultural values about health that lead to seeking traditional, ancestral, or spiritual healing first and seeking Western medicine only when other interventions fail;
   - can experience racial, ethnic, gender, and other forms of discrimination which could interfere with appropriate diagnosis and treatment;
   - may be dissatisfied with their health care plans and service providers; and
   - may experience language barriers and religious differences when being treated by providers.

Chapter 40

Cultural Competency in Health Care

Defining Cultural Competency

The culturally and linguistically appropriate services (CLAS) in health care project uses a working definition of cultural competency that's an adaptation of a definition cited by the Office of Women and Minority Health in the Bureau of Primary Health Care, Health Resources and Services Administration.

"Cultural and linguistic competence is a set of congruent behaviors, attitudes, and policies that come together in a system, agency, or among professionals that enables effective work in cross cultural situations. 'Culture' refers to integrated patterns of human behavior that include the language, thoughts, communications, actions, customs, beliefs, values, and institutions of racial, ethnic, religious, or social groups. 'Competence' implies having the capacity to function effectively as an individual and an organization within the context of the cultural beliefs, behaviors, and needs presented by consumers and their communities."

As an example, the CLAS project report describes an elderly Bosnian woman being admitted to a health facility with terminal cancer. She doesn't read, speak, or understand English, her Muslim faith requires modesty during physical exams, and cultural beliefs make her family member shy away from discussing end-of-life matters.

"Many providers are looking for guidance on how to respond to these situations appropriately," said Julia Puebla Fortier, principal

Excerpts from *Closing the Gap*, January 2000, Office of Minority Health.

investigator with Resources for Cross Cultural Health Care. The draft standards will give providers a context for understanding and responding to the role of culture and language in health, she said.

Valerie Welsh, evaluation officer and public health analyst in OMH's Division of Policy and Data, said cultural competence is not just a matter of diversity. "It's one of many factors that affect health care quality," she says, and can even be considered a route to better quality care.

Making Cultural Competency Work

All it takes to see the need for cultural competency in health care is looking around, whether it's looking at the people you work with or the people driving by you in rush-hour traffic. The great variety of race and ethnicity in both urban and rural areas is here to stay. Think of how many people don't look like you, think like you, or talk like you. Now consider how these differences impact basic communication.

The implications for communications in health care can be a matter of life or death. For example, culture and language can affect whether a patient takes a proper dose of medication or even agrees to take medication at all. Not offering appropriate translation services could lead a hospital to misdiagnose the condition of a person with limited English-speaking skills. Distributing a brochure with culturally insensitive health messages can backfire and discourage a person from getting a check-up.

A first step for health care organizations interested in developing a cultural competency program is understanding what cultural competency means in health care. Some mistakenly equate it to cultural diversity or affirmative action. Some think cultural competency is only an issue for mainstream America. But at the crux of the concept is how well health workers of all races can reach, serve, and treat those people that don't look like them, think like them, and speak like them.

The need for culturally competent approaches is important in all health care settings, from managed care organizations to clinics. Here are more tips for integrating cultural competency into your organization.

- Tap into good cultural competency resources. Some organizations rule out cultural competency because they consider it too expensive. Too expensive to buy those training videos or too expensive to bring in a consultant. But many good resources that are free or low-cost can support your efforts. For example, the

National Center for Cultural Competence offers a useful checklist called "Getting Started." The free publication is on the Web: http://www.dml.georgetown.edu/depts/pediatrics/gucdc/cultural.html. Also look for experts who may volunteer time to help you. The Office of Minority Health Resource Center (800-444-6472) is a good starting place with its Resource Persons Network of experts who may be able to provide technical assistance as you develop a program.

- Assess your staff's understanding of cultural competency. Use a pre- and post-test as part of staff training. This will help you assess your people and your organization, a requirement for setting goals and identifying staff development needs.
- Make training reflective of real life. Use guest speakers who can talk about how cultural competency has improved patient outcomes for their organization. Both best practice approaches and input on what kind of challenges to expect will help shape your program. Case Studies and role play scenarios can also be used to get health care workers truly involved.
- Include minorities in leadership roles. It's a simple enough concept, but many times decisions are made for minorities without their involvement. Empower minorities to take on leadership roles with your program's advisory committee or task force on cultural competency.
- Put your organization's plans in writing. Not only are you showing staff that cultural competency requires a real commitment, but a written plan will make everyone in your organization aware of your goals, your approach, and the rationale for your efforts. Look for models that work for organizations similar to yours. The National Black Nurses Association recently developed guidelines for its institute to train nurses on cultural competency.
- Put ideas into action. The National Mental Health Association states it well in its position paper on cultural competency (http://www.nmha.org). "Many health systems simply pay lip service to the concept. Some organizations claim to be culturally competent, but don't have appropriate procedures in place to address diversity." Evaluate your current communication vehicles such as printed materials and your telephone system. Assess your target populations and make sure there's a clear communication path for each group.

Promoting Cultural Diversity and Cultural Competency

Self-Assessment Checklist for Personnel Providing Services to Children with Special Health Needs and their Families

This checklist was developed by HRSA's Maternal and Child Health Bureau/Children with Special Health Needs component of the National Center for Cultural Competence. It is for personnel providing health services and supports to children with special health needs and their families and is intended to heighten the awareness and sensitivity of personnel to the importance of cultural diversity and cultural competence in human service settings. The checklist provides concrete examples of the kinds of values and practices that foster such an environment.

Directions: Select A, B, or C for each item listed.

A = Things I do frequently, B = Things I do occasionally, C = Things I do rarely or never.

Physical Environment, Materials, and Resources

1. I display pictures, posters and other materials that reflect the cultures and ethnic backgrounds of children and families served by my program or agency.
2. I insure that magazines, brochures, and other printed materials in reception areas are of interest to and reflect the different cultures of children and families served by my program or agency.
3. When using videos, films or other media resources for health education, treatment, or other interventions, I insure that they reflect the cultures of children and families served by my program or agency.
4. When using food during an assessment, I insure that meals provided include foods that are unique to the cultural and ethnic backgrounds of children and families served by my program or agency.
5. I insure that toys and other play accessories in reception areas and those which are used during assessment are representative of the various cultural and ethnic groups within the local community and the society in general.

Communication Styles

6. For children who speak languages or dialects other than English, I attempt to learn and use key words in their language so that I am better able to communicate with them during assessment, treatment, or other interventions.

7. I attempt to determine any familial colloquialisms used by children and families that may impact on assessment, treatment, or other interventions.

8. I use visual aids, gestures, and physical prompts in my interactions with children who have limited English proficiency.

9. I use bilingual staff or trained volunteers to serve as interpreters during assessment, meetings, or other events for parents who would require this level of assistance.

10. When interacting with parents who have limited English proficiency I always keep in mind that:
    - limitations in English proficiency are in no way a reflection of their level of intellectual functioning.
    - their limited ability to speak the language of the dominant culture has no bearing on their ability to communicate effectively in their language of origin.
    - they may or may not be literate in their language of origin or English.

11. When possible, I insure that all notices and communiqués to parents are written in their language of origin.

12. I understand that it may be necessary to use alternatives to written communications for some families, as word of mouth may be a preferred method of receiving information.

Values and Attitudes

13. I avoid imposing values that may conflict or be inconsistent with those of cultures or ethnic groups other than my own.

14. In group therapy or treatment situations, I discourage children from using racial and ethnic slurs by helping them understand that certain words can hurt others.

15. I screen books, movies, and other media resources for negative cultural, ethnic, or racial stereotypes before sharing them with children and their parents served by my program or agency.

16. I intervene in an appropriate manner when I observe other staff or parents within my program or agency engaging in behaviors that show cultural insensitivity or prejudice.

17. I understand and accept that family is defined differently by different cultures (e.g. extended family members, fictive kin, godparents).

18. I recognize and accept that individuals from culturally diverse backgrounds may desire varying degrees of acculturation into the dominant culture.

19. I accept and respect that male and female roles in families may vary significantly among different cultures (e.g. who makes major decisions for the family, play, and social interactions expected of male and female children).

20. I understand that age and life cycle factors must be considered in interactions with individuals and families (e.g. high value placed on the decisions of elders or the role of the eldest male in families).

21. Even though my professional or moral viewpoints may differ, I accept the family/parents as the ultimate decision-makers for services and supports for their children.

22. I recognize that the meaning or value of medical treatment and health education may vary greatly among cultures.

23. I accept that religion and other beliefs may influence how families respond to illnesses, disease, and death.

24. I recognize and accept that folk and religious beliefs may influence a family's reaction and approach to a child born with a disability or later diagnosed with a disability or special health care needs.

25. I understand that traditional approaches to disciplining children are influenced by culture.

26. I understand that families from different cultures will have different expectations of their children for acquiring toileting, dressing, feeding, and other self-help skills.

27. I accept and respect that customs and beliefs about food, its value, preparation, and use are different from culture to culture.

28. Before visiting or providing services in the home setting, I seek information on acceptable behaviors, courtesies, customs, and expectations which are unique to families of specific cultures and ethnic groups served by my program or agency.

29. I seek information from family members or other key community informants, which will assist in service adaptation to respond to the needs and preferences of culturally and ethnically diverse children and families served by my program or agency.

30. I advocate for the review of my program's or agency's mission statement, goals, policies, and procedures to insure that they incorporate principles and practices that promote cultural diversity and cultural competence.

There is no answer key. However, if you frequently responded "C," you may not necessarily demonstrate values and engage in practices that promote a culturally diverse and culturally competent service delivery system for children and families.

Source: Adapted from "Promoting Cultural Competence and Cultural Diversity in Early Intervention and Early Childhood Settings" (Revised 1999).

American Association of Medical Colleges and Medical Schools Want Help in Providing Cultural Competence Curriculum

Learning how to interview patients and take a medical history is a requirement of all medical schools. Some schools go even further and train students on culture and how it impacts the care they give. For example, Dartmouth/Brown Medical School's "Clinical Experience" class covers cultural beliefs and values, race, ethnicity, and sexual orientation. Dave Osborne, a White student in his third year at the school, said he learned how to work with an interpreter for the many patients from Hispanic and Portuguese backgrounds he encounters.

"It was helpful to learn that it is important to maintain eye contact with your patient and to keep the interpreter in the background. You need to speak directly to your patient," he said. Osborne said the class content on culture was good, but there could have been more.

AAMC Studies Culture in Medical Schools

In late 1997, staff in the Division of Medical Education at the American Association of Medical Colleges (AAMC) began gathering information on the activities in place at medical schools regarding cultural competence curriculum. AAMC's ongoing study aims to find out if medical schools considered it their responsibility to teach cultural competency and to find out what schools needed to do it better, said Deborah Danoff, MD, assistant vice president of AAMCs Division of Medical Education.

So far, AAMC has surveyed 141 medical education programs in the United States and Canada, of which 96 percent responded. Of those who responded, 67 percent indicated that they had some form of teaching on cultural competence already in place. Fourteen percent have plans to introduce the topic. The study also found that:

- At least 86 percent of medical schools provided at least one opportunity in multicultural medicine.
- Seventy-one percent said that multicultural medicine was part of a required course.
- Only one school teaches multicultural medicine as a separately required course.

Survey results also showed that most of the medical schools thought they needed assistance in developing or implementing a cultural competency program, said Dr. Danoff. Approximately 60 percent of schools that already had some form of cultural competency training in place indicated they would like additional help. That figure jumped to 80 percent for the schools who did not have a program in place.

The most commonly requested forms of assistance were information on model programs, faculty development materials, formal teaching materials, and evaluation instruments. Of the schools that don't have a program in place, over 40 percent asked for help in the form of justifying the need for cultural competency training. "This is an indication that some medical schools need to learn how to fit cultural competency into the rest of the medical school curriculum," said Dr. Danoff.

But medical schools soon may not have a choice about including cultural competency in their curriculum. The Liaison Committee on Medical Education (LCME) proposed a standard on cultural diversity that would hold faculty and students accountable for recognizing and dealing with cultures and belief systems and how this impacts perceived health, illness, and responses to various symptoms, diseases, and treatments. LCME is the nationally recognized accrediting authority for medical education programs leading to the medical degree in U.S. and Canadian medical schools. LCME voted on the adoption of the standard in February 2000.

Although AAMC's survey indicates most medical schools are providing some cultural competence training for students and are asking for assistance, some are questioning whether this is enough. "Most U.S. medical schools are not providing adequate instruction in cultural competency," said Glen Flores, MD, assistant professor of pediatrics and public health at Boston University Schools of Medicine and Public Health. For example, little is known about how to teach cultural issues in medical school.

AAMC continues to gather information on cultural competence efforts at medical schools. The association will collect information from course directors on cultural competency programs or courses in place at medical schools, identify model programs, and share techniques for implementation with other schools.

American Indian Traditional Healers, IHS Policy Ensures American Indian Beliefs are Respected

Many American Indians use traditional healers in addition to using Western medicine and Indian Health Service (IHS) facilities. Approximately 62 percent of Navajo patients have used a native healer in their lifetime and 39 percent have used native healers in the last year, according to research published in the *Archives of Internal Medicine* (Volume 158, November 9, 1998). "If they know the healer is there, they'll try it," said Wilbur Woodis, management analyst at IHS and information specialist at the Behavioral Health Alcoholism and Substance Abuse Program in the Albuquerque area IHS.

Health in Relation to the Earth

For many American Indians/Alaska Natives (AI/ANs), and other aboriginal groups all over the world, health is seen in relation to the Earth, said Ervin W Lewis, MD, director of the Behavioral Health Program in Albuquerque. Many native people see themselves as part of the Earth, not separate from it, Dr. Lewis said. This has a profound effect on the way native healers view and treat medical problems.

"If you are dehydrated, a Western doctor would tell you that drinking water will alleviate your sickness," said Woodis. "A traditional healer might bless you with a feather and water and tell you that you are not respecting the water. These are two very different ways of looking at health, but you get to the same place," Woodis said.

Helping American Indians Locate Healers

To ensure the cultural values, beliefs, and traditional healing practices of AI/ANs are respected and affirmed by IHS employees in all services and programs, in 1994 the agency developed a set of policies and procedures called the Traditional Cultural Advocacy Program (TCAP).

TCAP states IHS staff must inform its patients of their right to practice native religions and healing practices. When a patient or family member requests help in obtaining the service of a native practitioner or healer, every effort will be made to comply. These efforts might include contracting a native healer, providing space or privacy within a hospital room for a ceremony, or authorizing contract health care funds to pay for native health consultation. The policy also states the following:

- IHS area offices have the responsibility to consult and obtain the consent of AI/ANs in their area concerning each tribe's desire concerning the following: autopsy or other postmortem operations, disposition of body, disposal of a limb, and disposal/burial of fetus.

- The patient's right to privacy must be respected. No IHS employee can interfere with a patient's private belief.

- IHS support, in whatever form, should not become a wedge that creates dependency or wrests control from chosen native health practitioners. IHS must work to maintain a system of healing which has a long history.

"Each tribe uses TCAP as it sees fit," Woodis said. The local communities decide where services will be provided, what those will be, who to go to for traditional healing, and what relationship they have with IHS. The agency can provide support to tribes through funding and resources, but it does not oversee the individual tribal use of the policy. This is in accordance with tribal self-governance regulations, Woodis said.

Woodis said health facilities in his area often point persons back to the community if they want to use traditional healing practices. A facility in Gallup, NM, has a hogan style building-used for traditional healing purposes on-site. A hogan is a round building made of wood where life is propagated. Another IHS facility in Winslow, AZ, provides after-hours services for traditional healing ceremonies and a reimbursement program for traditional medicine costs.

Chapter 41

Eating Healthy with Ethnic Food

The new National Heart, Lung, and Blood Institute Obesity Guidelines recommend trying different ethnic cuisine to give yourself a taste treat while counting calories and fat. Many ethnic cuisines offer lots of low fat, low calorie choices. So if you want to eat healthy and still have lots of different choices, take a taste adventure with ethnic foods. Here's a sample of healthy food choices (lower in calories and fat) and terms to look for when making your selection:

Chinese

- Steamed
- Jum (poached)
- Kow (roasted)
- Shu (barbecued)
- Steamed rice
- Dishes without MSG added

Italian

- Red sauces
- Primavera (no cream)
- Piccata (lemon)
- Sun-dried tomatoes
- Crushed tomatoes
- Lightly sauteed
- Grilled

"Tip Sheet: Eating Healthy with Ethnic Food," Obesity Education Initiative, National Heart, Lung, and Blood Institute (NHLBI); "Traditional Foods Can Be Healthy," National Cancer Institute (NCI), NIH Publication No. 96-3548, September 1996; and "Down Home Healthy Cookin'," National Cancer Institute (NCI), NIH Publication No. 96-3408SV, September 1996.

Mexican

- Spicy chicken
- Rice & black beans
- Salsa or Picante
- Soft corn tortillas

Traditional Foods Can Be Healthy

During traditional times, American Indians rarely had:

- Cancer
- Heart Disease
- Diabetes
- Obesity

Why Was This Healthy?

- Traditionally, American Indians were very active and ate smaller amounts of food than American Indian people do today.
- The foods eaten in the past by many American Indians were low in fat like fish and game (such as deer).
- The elders have told us that the amount of food eaten in a meal was as much as a person could put into the palm of the hand. That was much smaller than what we eat today!

What Can You and Your Family Do Today?

- Record what types of traditional foods you and your family use in your meals today.
- Decide what types of foods you and your family could add to your meals.
- Discuss how you and your family could reduce the amounts of food eaten.

Traditional Foods in Today's World That Make a Healthy Diet

Fruits: Chokecherries, currants, buffalo berries, cactus fruit, plums, strawberries, and blackberries.

Vegetables: Wild turnips, onions, corn, carrots, cucumber, squash, and leafy green vegetables.

Meats, dry beans, and nuts: Buffalo, deer, elk, moose, antelope, raccoon, rabbit, squirrel, beans, nuts (acorns), and seeds.

Fish: Salmon, bass, king fish, catfish, trout, walleye, and bullhead.

Fowl: Pheasant, grouse, prairie chicken, and dove.

Grains and bread: Wild rice, barley, and wheat.

Down Home Healthy Cookin' Recipes

20-Minute Chicken Creole

4 medium chicken breast halves (1½ lbs total), skinned, boned, and cut into 1-inch strips*

1 14-oz can tomatoes, cut up **

1 cup low-sodium chili sauce

1 ½ cups chopped green pepper (1 large)

1/2 cup chopped celery

1/4 cup chopped onion

2 cloves garlic, minced

1 Tbsp chopped fresh basil or 1 tsp dried basil, crushed

1 Tbsp chopped fresh parsley or 1 tsp dried parsley

1/4 tsp crushed red pepper

1/4 tsp salt

Nonstick spray coating

1. Spray deep skillet with nonstick spray coating. Preheat pan over high heat. Cook chicken in hot skillet, stirring for 3 to 5 minutes or until no longer pink.
2. Reduce heat. Add tomatoes and their juice, low-sodium chili sauce, green pepper, celery, onion, garlic, basil, parsley, crushed red pepper, and salt. Bring to boiling; reduce heat and simmer covered for 10 minutes, Serve over hot, cooked rice or whole-wheat pasta.

Makes 4 servings

*You can substitute 1 lb boneless, skinless, chicken breasts, cut into 1-inch strips.

**To cut back on sodium, try low-sodium canned tomatoes.

Nutrition Content Per Serving:

- Calories: 255
- Total fat: 3 g
- Saturated fat: 0.8 g
- Carbohydrates: 16 g
- Protein: 31 g
- Cholesterol: 100 mg
- Sodium: 465 mg
- Dietary fiber: 1.5 g

Garlic Mashed Potatoes

1 lb potatoes (2 large)
1/2 cup skim milk
2 large cloves garlic, chopped
1/2 tsp white pepper

1. Peel potatoes; cut in quarters. Cook, covered, in a small amount of boiling water for 20 to 25 minutes or until tender. Remove from heat. Drain. Recover the pot.
2. Meanwhile, in a saucepan over low heat, cook garlic in milk until garlic is soft, about 30 minutes.
3. Add milk-garlic mixture and white pepper to potatoes. Beat with an electric mixer on low speed or mash with a potato masher until smooth.

Microwave Directions

1. Scrub potatoes, pat dry, and prick with a fork. On a plate, cook potatoes, uncovered, on 100% (high) until tender, about 12 minutes, turning potatoes over once. Let stand 5 minutes. Peel and quarter potatoes.
2. Meanwhile, in a 4-cup glass measure, combine milk and garlic. Cook, uncovered, on 50%power (medium) until garlic is soft, about 4 minutes, Continue as directed above.

Makes 4 servings.

Nutrition Content Per Serving:

- Calories: 141
  Total fat: 0.3 g
- Saturated fat: 0.2 g
- Carbohydrates 29 g
- Protein: 6 g
- Cholesterol: 2.0 mg
- Sodium: 70 mg
- Dietary fiber: 2 g

Catfish Stew and Rice

2 medium potatoes

1 14 ½-oz can tomatoes,* cut up

1 cup chopped onion

1 8-oz bottle (1 cup) clam juice or water

1 cup water

2 cloves garlic, minced

1/2 head cabbage, coarsely chopped

1 lb catfish fillets

1 ½ Tbsp Hot 'n Spicy Seasoning (recipe follows)

sliced green onion for garnish (optional)

2 cups hot, cooked rice (white or brown)

1. Peel potatoes and cut into quarters. In a large pot, combine potatoes, tomatoes and their juice, onion, clam juice, water, and garlic. Bring to boiling; reduce heat. Cook, covered, over medium-low heat for 10 minutes.
2. Add cabbage. Return to boiling. Reduce heat; cook, covered, over medium h-low heat for 5 minutes, stirring occasionally.
3. Meanwhile, cut fillets into 2-inch lengths. Coat with Hot 'n Spicy Seasoning. Add fish to vegetables. Reduce heat; simmer, covered, for 5 minutes or until fish flakes easily with a fork.
4. Serve in soup plates, garnished with sliced green onion. Top with an ice cream scoop of hot, cooked rice. Or, ladle stew over hot, cooked rice in soup plates and garnish with green onion.

Makes 4 servings.

*To reduce sodium, try low-sodium canned tomatoes.

Nutrition Content Per Serving:

- Calories: 355
- Total fat: 5 g
- Saturated fat: 1.3 g
- Carbohydrates: 49 g
- Protein: 28 g
- Protein: 28 g
- Cholesterol: 65 mg
- Sodium: 454 mg
- Dietary fiber: 7 g

Hot 'n Spicy Seasoning

1/4 cup paprika
2 Tbsp dried oregano, crushed
2 tsp chili powder
1 tsp garlic powder
1 tsp black pepper
1/2 tsp red (cayenne) pepper
1/2 tsp dry mustard

Mix together all ingredients. Store in an airtight container.

Makes about 1/3 cup.

Old-Fashioned Bread Pudding with Apple Raisin Sauce

10 slices whole wheat bread
1 egg
3 egg whites
1½ cups skim milk
1/4 cup sugar
1/4 cup brown sugar
1 tsp vanilla extract
1/2 tsp cinnamon
1/4 tsp nutmeg
1/4 tsp cloves
2 tsp sugar

1. Preheat the oven to 350 degrees F. Spray an 8-inch x 8-inch baking dish with vegetable oil spray. Lay the slices of bread in the baking dish in two rows. Overlapping them like shingles.
2. In a medium mixing bowl, beat together the egg, egg whites, milk, ¼ cup sugar brown sugar, and vanilla. Pour the egg mixture over the bread.
3. In a small bowl, stir together the cinnamon, nutmeg, cloves, and 2 tsp sugar. Sprinkle the spiced sugar over the bread pudding. Bake the pudding for 30 to 35 minutes, until it has browned on top and is firm to the touch.
4. Serve warm or at room temperature, with warm apple-raisin sauce.

Makes 9 servings

Nutrition Content Per Serving:

- Calories: 233
- Total fat: 3 g
- Saturated fat: 1 g
- Carbohydrates: 46 g
- Protein: 7 g
- Cholesterol: 24 mg
- Sodium: 252 mg
- Dietary Fat: 3 g

Apple-Raisin Sauce

1¼ cups apple juice
1/2 cup apple butter
2 Tbsp molasses
1/2 cup raisins
1/4 tsp ground cinnamon
1/4 tsp ground nutmeg
1/2 tsp orange zest (optional)

Stir all the ingredients together in a medium saucepan. Bring to a simmer over low heat. Let the sauce simmer 5 minutes. Serve warm.

Makes 2 cups.

New Orleans Red Beans

1 lb dry red beans

2 quarts water

1½ cups chopped onion

1 cup chopped celery

4 bay leaves

1 cup chopped sweet green pepper

3 Tbsp chopped garlic

3 Tbsp chopped parsley

2 tsp dried thyme, crushed

1 tsp salt

1 tsp black pepper

1. Pick through beans to remove bad beans; rinse thoroughly. In a 5-quart pot, combine beans, water, onion, celery, and bay leaves, Bring to boiling; reduce heat. Cover and cook over low heat for about 1½ hours or until beans are tender. Stir and mash beans against side of pan.
2. Add green pepper, garlic, parsley, thyme, salt, and black pepper. Cook, uncovered, over low heat until creamy, about 30 minutes. Remove bay leaves.
3. Serve over hot, cooked brown rice, if desired.

Makes 8 servings.

Nutrition Content Per Serving:

- Calories: 171
- Total fat: 0.5 g
- Saturated fat: 0.1 g
- Carbohydrates: 32 g
- Protein: 10 g
- Cholesterol: 0 mg
- Sodium: 285 mg
- Dietary fiber: 7.2 g

Mixed Greens

2 bunches mustard greens or kale

2 bunches turnip greens

pepper to taste (optional)

1 tsp salt, or to taste (optional)

1. Rinse greens well, removing stems. In a large pot of boiling water, cook greens rapidly, covered, over medium heat for about 25 minutes or until tender.
2. Serve with some of the pot liquor. If desired, cut greens in pan with a sharp knife and kitchen fork before serving.

Note: If desired, add 2 Tbsp of lean cooked ham, Canadian bacon, or split turkey thighs to greens before serving. However, this will increase calorie, sodium, and fat content.

Makes 8 servings.

Nutrition Content Per Serving:

- Calories 18
- Total fat: 0.1 g
- Saturated fat: 0 g
- Carbohydrates: 3 g
- Protein: 1 g
- Cholesterol: 0 mg
- Sodium: 153 mg
- Dietary fiber: 2 g

Baked Pork Chops

Note: If desired, substitute skinless, boneless chicken, turkey pieces, or fish for pork chops and bake for 20 minutes.

6 lean center-cut pork chops, ½-inch thick

1 egg white

1 cup evaporated skim milk

1 cup cornflake crumbs

1/4 cup fine dry bread crumbs

2 Tbsp Hot 'n Spicy Seasoning

1/2 tsp salt

Nonstick spray coating

1. Trim all fat from chops.
2. Beat egg white with evaporated skim milk. Place chops in milk mixture; let stand for 5 minutes, turning chops once.
3. Meanwhile, mix together cornflake crumbs, breadcrumbs, Hot 'n Spicy Seasoning and salt. Remove chops from milk mixture. Coat thoroughly with crumb mixture.
4. Spray a 13-inch x 9-inch baking pan with nonstick spray coating. Place chops in pan; bake in 375 degree F oven for 20 minutes. Turn chops; bake 15 minutes longer or until no pink remains.

Nutrition Content Per Serving:

- Calories: 186
- Total fat: 4.9 g
- Saturated fat: 1.8 g
- Carbohydrates: 16 g
- Protein: 17 g
- Cholesterol: 31 mg
- Sodium: 393 mg
- Dietary fiber: 0.2 g

Sweet Potato Custard

1 cup mashed, cooked sweet potato
½ cup mashed banana (about 2 small)
1 cup evaporated skim milk
2 Tbsp packed brown sugar
2 beaten egg yolks (or 1/3-cup egg substitute)
1/2 tsp salt
1/4 cup raisins
1 Tbsp sugar
1 tsp ground cinnamon
Nonstick spray coating

1. In a medium bowl, stir together sweet potato and banana. Add milk, blending well. Add brown sugar, egg yolks, and salt, mixing thoroughly.
2. Spray a 1-quart casserole with nonstick spray coating. Transfer sweet potato mixture to casserole.
3. Combine raisins, sugar, and cinnamon; sprinkle over top of sweet potato mixture. Bake in preheated 300 degree F oven for 45 to 50 minutes or until a knife inserted near center comes out clean.

Makes 6 servings.

Nutrition Content Per Serving:

- Calories: 144
- Total fat: 2 g
- Saturated fat: 0.7 g
- Carbohydrates: 20 g
- Protein: 6 g
- Cholesterol: 92 mg
- Sodium: 235 mg
- Dietary fiber: 1.4 g

Note: If made with egg substitute, the amount of cholesterol will be lower.

Winter Crisp

Filling
1/2 cup sugar
3 Tbsp all-purpose flour
1 tsp grated lemon peel
5 cups unpeeled, sliced apples
1 cup cranberries

Topping
2/3 cup rolled oats
1/3 cup packed brown sugar
1/4 cup whole wheat flour
2 tsp ground cinnamon
3 Tbsp soft margarine, melted

1. **Filling:** In a medium bowl, combine sugar, flour, and lemon peel; mix well. Add apples and cranberries; stir to mix. Spoon into a 6-cup baking dish.
2. **Topping:** In a small bowl, combine oats, brown sugar, flour, and cinnamon. Add melted margarine; stir to mix. Sprinkle topping over filling.
3. Bake in a 375 degree F oven for 40 to 50 minutes or until filling is bubbly and top is brown. Serve warm or at room temperature.

Summer Crisp

Prepare as directed, substituting 4 cups fresh, or unsweetened frozen, peaches and 2 cups fresh, or unsweetened frozen, blueberries for apples and cranberries. If frozen, thaw fruit completely (do not drain).

Nutrition Content Per Serving:

- Calories: 284
- Total fat: 6 g
- Saturated fat: 1 g
- Carbohydrates: 54 g
- Protein 3 g
- Cholesterol: 0 mg
- Sodium: 56 mg
- Dietary fiber: 5 g

Chillin' Out Pasta Salad

8 oz (2½ cups) medium shell pasta

1 8 oz carton (1 cup) plain nonfat yogurt

2 Tbsp spicy brown mustard

2 Tbsp salt-free herb seasoning

1½ cups chopped celery

1 cup sliced green onion

1 lb cooked small shrimp

3 cups coarsely chopped tomatoes (about 3 large)

1. Cook pasta according to package directions. Drain; cool.
2. In a large bowl stir together yogurt, mustard, and herb seasoning. Add pasta, celery, and green onion; mix well. Chill at least 2 hours.
3. Just before serving, carefully stir in shrimp and tomatoes.

Makes 12 servings.

Nutrition Content Per Serving:

- Calories: 140
- Total fat: 1 g
- Saturated fat: 0.1 g
- Carbohydrates: 19 g
- Protein: 14 g
- Cholesterol: 60 mg
- Sodium: 135 mg
- Dietary fiber: 1.3 g

Spaghetti with Turkey Meat Sauce

1 lb ground turkey

1 28-oz can tomatoes, cut up

1 cup finely chopped sweet green pepper

1 cup finely chopped onion

2 cloves garlic, minced

1 tsp dried oregano, crushed

1 tsp black pepper

1 lb spaghetti

Nonstick spray coating

1. Spray a large skillet with nonstick spray coating. Preheat over high heat. Add turkey; cook, stirring occasionally, for 5 minutes. Drain fat.
2. Stir in tomatoes with their juice, green pepper, onion, garlic, oregano, and black pepper. Bring to boiling; reduce heat. Simmer, covered, for 15 minutes, stirring occasionally.
3. Remove cover; simmer for 15 minutes more. (For a creamier sauce, give sauce a whirl in a blender or food processor.)
4. Meanwhile, cook spaghetti according to package directions; drain well. Serve sauce over spaghetti with crusty, whole-grain bread.

Makes 6 servings

Nutrition Content Per Serving:

- Calories: 330
- Total fat: 5 g
- Saturated fat: 1.3 g
- Carbohydrates: 42 g
- Protein: 29 g
- Cholesterol: 60 mg
- Sodium: 280 mg
- Dietary fiber: 2.7 g

Black Skillet Beef with Greens and Red Potatoes

1 lb beef top round

1½ Tbsp Hot 'n Spicy Seasoning

8 red-skinned potatoes, halved

3 cups finely chopped onion

2 cups beef broth

2 large cloves garlic, minced

2 large carrots, peeled, cut into very thin 2 ½-inch strips

2 bunches (1/2 lb each) mustard greens, kale, or turnip greens, stems removed, coarsely torn

Nonstick spray coating

1. Partially freeze beef. Thinly slice across the grain into long strips, 1/8-inch thick. Thoroughly coat strips with Hot 'n Spicy Seasoning.
2. Spray a large, heavy skillet (cast iron is good) with nonstick spray coating. Preheat pan over high heat. Add meat; cook, stirring for 5 minutes.
3. Add potatoes, onion, broth, and garlic. Cook, covered, over medium heat for 20 minutes. Stir in carrots; lay greens over top and cook, covered, until carrots are tender (about 15 minutes). Serve in large serving bowl, with crusty bread for dunking.

Makes 6 servings.

Nutrition Content Per Serving:

- Calories: 342
- Total fat: 4 g
- Saturated fat: 1.4 g
- Carbohydrates: 52 g
- Protein: 24 g
- Cholesterol: 45 mg
- Sodium: 101 mg
- Dietary fiber: 10 g

Garden Potato Salad

3 lbs potatoes (6 large)

1 cup chopped celery

1/2 cup sliced green onion

2 Tbsp chopped parsley

1 cup low-fat cottage cheese

3/4 cup skim milk

3 Tbsp lemon juice

2 Tbsp cider vinegar

1/2 tsp celery seed

1/2 tsp dillweed

1/2 tsp dry mustard

1/2 tsp white pepper

1. Scrub potatoes; boil in jackets until tender. Cool; peel. Cut into ½-inch cubes. Add celery, green onion, and parsley.

2. Meanwhile, in a blender, blend cottage cheese, milk, lemon juice, vinegar, celery seed, dillweed, dry mustard, and white pepper until smooth. Chill for 1 hour.

3. Pour chilled cottage cheese mixture over vegetables; mix well. Chill at least 30 minutes before serving.

Makes 10 servings.

Nutrition Content Per Serving:

- Calories: 151
- Total fat: 0.5 g
- Saturated fat: 0.2 g
- Carbohydrates: 30 g
- Protein: 6 g
- Cholesterol: 2.3 mg
- Sodium: 118 mg
- Dietary fiber: 3.1 g

Healthy Cooking Tips

1. Use low-fat (1% or 2%) nonfat/skim milk instead of whole milk.

2. Broil, steam, roast/bake, microwave, grill, braise/stew, boil, simmer, or stir-fry with a small amount of oil *instead of* frying, basting with fat, or cooking in fatty sauces and gravies.

3. When baking or cooking, use 3 egg whites and 1 yolk instead of 2 whole eggs, and 2 egg whites instead of 1 whole egg.

4. Substitute bean and grain dishes for high-fat meats.

5. Cook vegetables without added fat.

6. Use evaporated skim milk *instead of* cream.

7. When a recipe calls for butter, lard, or shortening, choose margarine with vegetable oil listed as the first ingredient on the label.

8. Use nonfat or low-fat dressing yogurt, or mayonnaise *instead of* regular mayonnaise in salads and sandwiches.

9. Use ground (boneless) turkey breast *instead of* ground beef and pork.

10. Use lean meat cuts, such as round, sirloin, chuck arm, pot roast, and loin *instead of* high-fat meats.

Part Eight

Additional Help and Information

Chapter 42

Glossary of Important Terms

A

Acquired mutations: Gene changes that arise within individual cells and accumulate throughout a person's lifetime; also called somatic mutations. (See Hereditary mutation.)

Acculturation: The "social distance" separating members of an ethnic or racial group from the wider society in areas of beliefs and values and primary group relations (work, social clubs, family, friends) (Gordon, 1964). Greater acculturation thus reflects greater adoption of mainstream beliefs and practices and entry into primary group relations.

Alleles: Variant forms of the same gene. Different alleles produce variations in inherited characteristics such as eye color or blood type.

Alzheimer's disease: A disease that causes memory loss, personality changes, dementia and, ultimately, death. Not all cases are inherited, but genes have been found for familial forms of Alzheimer's disease.

Amino acid: Any of a class of 20 molecules that combine to form proteins in living things. Compounds that link together to make proteins.

This chapter includes text from "Understanding Gene Testing-Glossary," National Cancer Institute, and "Dr. Roscoe Brady and Gaucher Disease—Glossary," National Institutes of Health (NIH).

Essential amino acids are released in the intestines when food containing protein is digested—the body cannot make them. Non-essential amino acids can be made by the body. Amino acids contain carbon, hydrogen, oxygen, nitrogen, and sometimes sulfur.

Amyotrophic lateral sclerosis: An inherited, fatal degenerative nerve disorder; also known as Lou Gehrig's disease.

Anemia: Results when the blood doesn't have enough red blood cells, hemoglobin, or total volume. Causes of anemia include loss of blood, an iron deficiency (so that not enough blood is formed), or a bone marrow dysfunction where the blood is made. Symptoms include being tired and bone pain.

Autosome: Any of the non-sex-determining chromosomes. Human cells have 22 pairs of autosomes.

B

Base pairs: The two complementary, nitrogen-rich molecules held together by weak chemical bonds. Two strands of DNA are held together in the shape of a double helix by the bonds between their base pairs. (See Chemical base.)

BRCA1: A gene that normally helps to restrain cell growth.

BRCA1 breast cancer susceptibility gene: A mutated version of BRCA1, which predisposes a person toward developing breast cancer.

C

Carbohydrate: A compound produced mainly by plants, made up of carbon, hydrogen, and oxygen. Carbohydrates are found as sugars, starches, and cellulose in food.

Carrier: A person who has a recessive mutated gene, together with its normal allele. Carriers do not usually develop disease but can pass the mutated gene on to their children.

Carrier testing: Testing to identify individuals who carry disease-causing recessive genes that could be inherited by their children.

Carrier testing is designed for healthy people who have no symptoms of disease, but who are known to be at high risk because of family history.

Cell: Small, watery, membrane-bound compartment filled with chemicals; the basic subunit of any living thing. The smallest structural unit of life capable of functioning by itself, a cell has a membrane which allows some things to pass through. Inside the cell is nucleus and other cellular parts. Cells contain DNA and make up our bodies.

Central nervous system: The brain and spinal cord together. They coordinate the rest of the nervous system, receiving sensory information from nerves and sending out messages to respond to stimulation.

Chemical base: An essential building block. DNA contains four complementary bases: adenine, which pairs with thymine, and cytosine, which pairs with guanine. In RNA, thymine is replaced by uracil.

Chromosomes: Structures found in the nucleus of a cell, which contain the genes. Chromosomes come in pairs, and a normal human cell contains 46 chromosomes, 22 pairs of autosomes and two sex chromosomes.

Chronic disease(s): Diseases which last a long time or frequently reoccur, and that progress slowly, such as arthritis, heart disease, and many genetic diseases.

Clone: A group of identical genes, cells, or organisms derived from a single ancestor.

Cloning: The process of making genetically identical copies.

Contig maps: Types of physical DNA maps that consist of overlapping segments of DNA (contigs) that, taken together, completely represent that section of the genome. (See Physical maps.)

Colonoscopy: Examination of the colon through a flexible, lighted instrument called a colonoscope.

Crossing over: A phenomenon, also known as recombination, that sometimes occurs during the formation of sperm and egg cells (meiosis);

a pair of chromosomes (one from the mother and the other from the father) break and trade segments with one another.

Cystic fibrosis: An inherited disease in which a thick mucus clogs the lungs and blocks the ducts of the pancreas.

Cytoplasm: The cellular substance outside the nucleus in which the cell's organelles are suspended.

D

Dementia: Severe impairment of mental functioning.

DNA: The substance of heredity; a large molecule that carries the genetic information that cells need to replicate and to produce proteins.

DNA repair genes: Certain genes that are part of a DNA repair pathway; when altered, they permit mutations to pile up throughout the DNA.

DNA sequencing: Determining the exact order of the base pairs in a segment of DNA.

Dominant allele: A gene that is expressed, regardless of whether its counterpart allele on the other chromosome is dominant or recessive. Autosomal dominant disorders are produced by a single mutated dominant allele, even though its corresponding allele is normal. (See Recessive allele.)

Dystonia: Distortion of posture caused by muscle contractions.

E

Enzyme: A protein that facilitates a specific chemical reaction. Enzymes control digestion, muscle contraction, and many other functions of metabolism.

Esterification: The transport of cholesterol in the cells is studied by measuring conversion of the cholesterol from one form to another.

Ethnopsychopharmacology: A new field that investigates cultural variations and differences that influence the effectiveness of pharmacotherapies used in the mental health field. These differences are both genetic and psychosocial in nature.

Familial adenomatous polyposis: An inherited condition in which hundreds of potentially cancerous polyps develop in the colon and rectum.

Familial cancer: Cancer, or a predisposition toward cancer, that runs in families.

Fibroblasts: Cells grown in a laboratory from a small piece of skin obtained through a skin biopsy.

Filipin: A compound that glows under ultraviolet light used to stain cells and then assess their ability to store cholesterol.

Functional gene tests: Biochemical assays for a specific protein, which indicates that a specific gene is not merely present but active.

G

Gene: A working subunit of DNA. Each of the body's 50,000 to 100,000 genes contains the code for a specific product, typically, a protein such as an enzyme. Usually a gene is found on a specific place on a chromosome, genes reproduce exactly during cell division, and usually occur in pairs, except for those genes on the sex chromosomes X and Y.

Gene deletion: The total loss or absence of a gene.

Gene expression: The process by which a gene's coded information is translated into the structures present and operating in the cell (either proteins or RNAs).

Genetic inheritance patterns: A classification of **dominant** or **recessive**. If a parent passes on the gene for a dominant disorder (such as Marfan's syndrome, a connective-tissue disease), her child has a 50 percent chance of inheriting it. If both parents carry a gene for a recessive disorder (such as cystic fibrosis), their child has a 25 percent chance of inheriting it. If only one parent has the gene for a recessive trait, it will be overridden by the other parent's normal gene and will not cause the child to be affected.

Gene markers: Landmarks for a target gene, either detectable traits that are inherited along with the gene, or distinctive segments of DNA.

Gene mapping: Determining the relative positions of genes on a chromosome and the distance between them.

Gene testing: Examining a sample of blood or other body fluid or tissue for biochemical, chromosomal, or genetic markers that indicate the presence or absence of genetic disease.

Gene therapy: Treating disease by replacing, manipulating, or supplementing nonfunctional genes.

Genetic linkage maps: DNA maps that assign relative chromosomal locations to genetic landmarks—either genes for known traits or distinctive sequences of DNA—on the basis of how frequently they are inherited together. (See Physical maps.)

Genetics: The scientific study of heredity: how particular qualities or traits are transmitted from parents to offspring.

Genome: All the genetic material in the chromosomes of a particular organism.

Genome maps: Charts that indicate the ordered arrangement of the genes or other DNA markers within the chromosomes.

Genotype: The actual genes carried by an individual (as distinct from phenotype—that is, the physical characteristics into which genes are translated).

Germ cells: The reproductive cells of the body, either egg or sperm cells.

Germline mutation: (See Hereditary mutation.)

Glucocerebroside: A fatty substance (lipid), used by the body as a building block to make cell membrane materials.

H

Hemoglobin: A protein in red blood cells that contains iron and transports oxygen from the lungs to the rest of the body.

Hereditary mutation: A gene change in the body's reproductive cells (egg or sperm) that becomes incorporated in the DNA of every cell in the body; also called germline mutation. (See Acquired mutations.)

Human genome: The full collection of genes needed to produce a human being.

Human Genome Project: An international research effort (led in the United States by the National Institutes of Health and the Department of Energy) aimed at identifying and ordering every base in the human genome.

Huntington's disease: An adult-onset disease characterized by progressive mental and physical deterioration; it is caused by an inherited dominant gene mutation.

I

Imprinting: A biochemical phenomenon that determines, for certain genes, which one of the pair of alleles, the mother's or the father's, will be active in that individual.

Inborn errors of metabolism: Inherited diseases resulting from alterations in genes that code for enzymes.

Inherit(s): To receive a gene from a parent during reproduction; in humans, we inherit half of our genes from our fathers and half from our mothers.

L

Leukemia: Cancer that begins in developing blood cells in the bone marrow.

Li-Fraumeni syndrome: A family predisposition to multiple cancers, caused by a mutation in the p53 tumor-suppressor gene.

Linkage analysis: A gene-hunting technique that traces patterns of heredity in large, high-risk families, in an attempt to locate a disease-causing gene mutation by identifying traits that are co-inherited with it.

Liver: A large organ that conditions many of the substances in the blood. The liver secretes bile, converts and stores sugars in useable forms, and produces urea (the main component of urine).

M

Macrophage(s): A large cell that stores materials and helps to protect the body against infections and foreign substances.

Melanoma: A cancer that begins in skin cells called melanocytes and spreads to internal organs.

Metabolism: The entire process by which living cells get energy for their activities and new material is added. Metabolism involves the buildup and breakdown of many substances by the use of amino acids and enzymes.

Molecule: A group of atoms arranged to interact in a particular way; one molecule of any substance is the smallest physical unit of that particular substance.

Mutation: To change the hereditary substances (DNA, chromosomes, or genes) by affecting the physical location of genes on a chromosome or changing or altering the gene itself. A change in the number, arrangement, or molecular sequence of a gene.

N

Newborn screening: Examining blood samples from a newborn infant to detect disease-related abnormalities or deficiencies in gene products.

Nucleotide: A subunit of DNA or RNA, consisting of one chemical base plus a phosphate molecule and a sugar molecule.

Nucleus: The cell structure that houses the chromosomes.

O

Oncogenes: Genes that normally play a role in the growth of cells but, when overexpressed or mutated, can foster the growth of cancer.

P

p53: (See Tumor-suppressor genes.)

Pharmacotherapies: Ethnic and cultural influences that can alter an individual's responses to medications.

Penetrance: A term indicating the likelihood that a given gene will actually result in disease.

Phenylketonuria (PKU): An inborn error of metabolism caused by the lack of an enzyme, resulting in abnormally high levels of the amino acid phenylalanine; untreated, PKU can lead to severe, progressive mental retardation.

Physical maps: DNA maps showing the location of identifiable landmarks, either genes or distinctive short sequences of DNA. The lowest resolution physical map shows the banding pattern on the 24 different chromosomes; the highest resolution map depicts the complete nucleotide sequence of the chromosomes. (See Contig maps.)

Placenta: The organ that connects a fetus to the mother's uterus and that processes the exchange of nourishment and other functions.

Platelet: A small disk-shaped part of the blood that helps in blood clotting.

Precancerous polyps: Growths in the colon that often become cancerous.

Predictive gene tests: Tests to identify gene abnormalities that may make a person susceptible to certain diseases or disorders.

Prenatal: Occurring, existing, or performed before birth.

Prenatal diagnosis: Examining fetal cells taken from the amniotic fluid, the primitive placenta (chorion), or the umbilical cord for biochemical, chromosomal, or gene alterations.

Probe: A specific sequence of single-stranded DNA, typically labeled with a radioactive atom, which is designed to bind to, and thereby single out, a particular segment of DNA.

Proofreader genes: (See DNA repair genes.)

Prophylactic surgery: Surgery to remove tissue that is in danger of becoming cancerous, before cancer has the chance to develop. Surgery to remove the breasts of women at high risk of developing breast cancer is known as prophylactic mastectomy.

Protein: A large, complex molecule composed of amino acids. The sequence of the amino acids—and thus the function of the protein—is determined by the sequence of the base pairs in the gene that encodes it. Proteins are essential to the structure, function, and regulation of the body. Examples are hormones, enzymes, and antibodies.

Protein product: The protein molecule assembled under the direction of a gene.

R

Recessive allele: A gene that is expressed only when its counterpart allele on the matching chromosome is also recessive (not dominant). Autosomal recessive disorders develop in persons who receive two copies of the mutant gene, one from each parent who is a carrier. (See Dominant allele.)

Recombination: (See Crossing over.)

Renal cell cancer: A type of kidney cancer.

Reproductive cells: Egg and sperm cells. Each mature reproductive cell carries a single set of 23 chromosomes.

Restriction enzymes: Enzymes that can cut strands of DNA at specific base sequences.

Retinoblastoma: An eye cancer caused by the loss of a pair of tumor-suppressor genes; the inherited form typically appears in childhood, since one gene is missing from the time of birth.

RNA: A chemical similar to DNA. The several classes of RNA molecules play important roles in protein synthesis and other cell activities.

S

Sarcoma: A type of cancer that starts in bone or muscle.

Screening: Looking for evidence of a particular disease such as cancer in persons with no symptoms of disease.

Sex chromosomes: The chromosomes that determine the sex of an organism. Human females have two X chromosomes; males have one X and one Y.

Sickle-cell anemia: An inherited, potentially lethal disease in which a defect in hemoglobin, the oxygen-carrying pigment in the blood, causes distortion (sickling) and loss of red blood cells, producing damage to organs throughout the body.

Somatic cells: All body cells except the reproductive cells.

Somatic mutations: (See Acquired mutations.)

Somatization: the expression of mental distress in terms of physical suffering.

Spleen: An organ near the stomach that filters and stores blood, destroys old red blood cells, and helps produce lymphocytes (specialized cells that help fight infections).

T

Tay-Sachs disease: An inherited disease of infancy characterized by profound mental retardation and early death; it is caused by a recessive gene mutation.

Transcription: The process of copying information from DNA into new strands of messenger RNA (mRNA). The mRNA then carries this information to the cytoplasm, where it serves as the blueprint for the manufacture of a specific protein.

Translation: The process of turning instructions from mRNA, base by base, into chains of amino acids that then fold into proteins. This process takes place in the cytoplasm, on structures called ribosomes.

Tumor-suppressor genes: Genes that normally restrain cell growth but, when missing or inactivated by mutation, allow cells to grow uncontrolled.

W

White blood cells: Different kinds of colorless blood cells that fight invaders to the body.

Wilms' tumor: A kidney cancer (tumor) that occurs in children, usually before age 5.

X

X chromosome: A sex chromosome; normal females carry two X chromosomes.

Y

Y chromosome: A sex chromosome; normal males carry one Y and one X chromosome.

Chapter 43

Minority Health Resources

Minority Health Information

Office of Minority Health
Division of Information and Education
Rockwall II Building, Suite 1000
5600 Fishers Lane
Rockville, MD 20857
Tel: 301-443-5224
Fax: 301-443-8280
Website: http://www.omhrc.gov

The Office of Minority Health (OMH) advises the Secretary and Office of Public Health and Science on public health program activities affecting Blacks/African Americans, American Indians/Alaska Natives, Asian Americans, Native Hawaiians, and other Pacific Islanders, and Hispanics/Latinos. The goal of OMH is to improve and protect the health of racial and ethnic minority populations through the development of health policies and programs that will address health disparities.

"Pocket Guide to Minority Health Resources," Office of Minority Health (OMH), U.S. Department of Health and Human Services, Fall 1999.

Office of Minority Health Resource Center (OMH-RC)
P.O. Box 37337
Washington, DC 20013-7337
Toll Free: 800-444-6472
Tel: 301-230-7198
Fax: 301-230-7199
TDD: 301-230-7199
E-mail: info@omhrc.gov
Website: http://www.omhrc.gov

Office of Minority Health Resource Center (OMH-RC) information resources on minority health include databases (funding, media, research, data, and listings of volunteer resource persons) as well as scientific reports, journals, and documents. OMH-RC services are free, and can be obtained by calling the Toll Free number. Information specialists are available from 9:00 a.m. to 5:00 p.m., Eastern Time, Monday through Friday, to assist callers in English and Spanish.

African Americans

Association of Black Cardiologists
6849-B2 Peachtree Dunwoody Rd., NE
Atlanta, GA 30328
Tel: 678-302-4ABC
Fax: 678-302-4223
E-mail: Jacquelyn butts@abcardio.org
Website: http://www.abcardio.org

Association of Black Nursing Faculty, Inc.
7219 Saddle Creek
San Antonio, TX 78238
Tel: 210-680-2064
Fax: 210-680-1678
Website: http://www.abnf.org

Association of Black Psychologists
P.O. Box 55999
Washington, DC 20040-5999
Tel: 202-722-0808
Fax: 202-722-5941
E-mail: admin@abpsi.org
Website: http://www.abpsi.org

Black Congress on Health Law and Economics
1025 Vermont Avenue, NW, Suite 910
Washington, DC 20005
Tel: 202-347-2800
Fax: 202-347-2424

Black Women's Agenda, Inc. (BWA)
1 Dupont Circle, NW, Suite 430
Washington, DC 20036
Tel: 202-223-9401
Fax: 202-296-9194

The Congress of National Black Churches, Inc. (CNBC)
1225 "I" Street, NW, Suite 750
Washington, DC 20005
Tel: 202-371-1092
Fax: 202-371-0908
Website: http://www.cnbc.org

International Society on Hypertension in Blacks
2045 Manchester Street, NE
Atlanta, GA 30324-4110
Tel: 404-875-6263
Fax: 404-875-6334
E-mail: ishib@mindspring.com
Website: http://www.ishib.org

Joint Center for Political and Economic Studies
1090 Vermont Ave., NW
Suite 1100
Washington, DC 20005-4928
Tel: 202-789-3500
Fax: 202-789-6390
E-mail:
dduckett@jointcenter.org
Website: http://
www.jointcenter.org

Minority Health Professions Foundation
3 Executive Park Drive, NE,
Suite 100
Atlanta, GA 30329
Tel: 404-634-1993
Fax: 404-634-1903
E-mail:
mail@minorityhealth.org
Website: http://
www.minorityhealth.org

National Association for the Advancement of Colored People (NAACP)
4805 Mt. Hope Drive
Baltimore, MD 21215
Tel: 410-521-4939
Fax: 410-486-9255
Website: http://www.naacp.org

National Association for Equal Opportunity in Higher Education (NAFEO)
8701 Georgia Avenue, Suite 200
Silver Spring, MD 20910
Tel: 301-650-2440
Fax: 301-495-3306
Website: http://www.nafeo.org

National Association of Black Social Workers, Inc. (NABSW)
8436 West McNichols
Detroit, MI 48221
Tel: 313-862-6700
Fax: 313-862-6998
E-mail: questions@nabsw.org
Website: http://www.nabsw.org

National Association of Health Services Executives (NAHSE)
8630 Fenton Street, Suite 126
Silver Spring, MD 20910
Tel: 202-628-3953
Fax: 301-588-0011
E-mail:
nahse_hq@compuserve.com
Website: http://www.nahse.org

National Black Alcoholism and Addictions Council (NBAC)
1101 14th Street, N.W.
Washington, DC 20005
Tel: 202-296-2696
E-mail: nbac@borg.com
Website: http://www.borg.com/tb~nbac

National Black Child Development Institute, Inc. (NBCDI)
1023 15th Street, NW, Suite 600
Washington, DC 20005
Tel: 202-387-1281
Fax: 202-234-1738
E-mail: moreinfo@mbcdi.org
Website: http://www.nbcdi.org

National Black Nurses' Association, Inc. (NBNA)
8630 Fenton Street, Suite 330
Silver Spring, MD 20910-3803
Tel: 301-589-3200
Fax: 301-589-3223
E-mail: nbna@erols.com
Website: http://www.nbna.org

National Black Women's Health Project (NBHP)
600 Pennsylvania Ave, SE
Suite 310
Washington, DC 20003
Tel: 202-543-9311
Fax: 202-543-9743
E-mail: nbwhp@nbwhp.org
Website: http://www.nbwhp.org

National Caucus and Center on Black Aged, Inc. (NCBA)
1424 K Street, NW, Suite 500
Washington, DC 20005
Tel: 202-637-8400
Fax: 202-347-0895
E-mail: ncba@aol.com
Website: http://www.ncba-blackaged.org

National Center for the Advancement of Blacks in the Health Professions
PO Box 21121
Detroit, MI 48235
Tel: 313-342-1522
Fax: 313-345-4480

National Coalition of 100 Black Women
38 West 32nd Street, Suite 1610
New York, NY 10001-3816
Tel: 212-947-2196
Fax: 212-947-2477
E-mail: nc100bw@aol.com
Website: http://www.ncbw.org

National Council of Negro Women (NCNW)
633 Pennsylvania Avenue, NW
Washington, DC 20004
Tel: 877-912-7366 or 202-383-9134
Fax: 202-383-9135
E-mail: webadmin@ncnw.com
Website: http://www.ncnw.com

National Dental Association
3517 16th Street, NW
Washington, DC 20010
Tel: 202-588-1697
Fax: 202-588-1244
E-mail: kmcdavid@natdent.org
Website: http://www.natdent.org

National Hypertension Association (NHA)
324 East 30th Street
New York, NY 10016
Tel: 212-889-3557
Toll Free: 800-575-9355
Fax: 212-447-7032

National Medical Association (NMA)
1012 Tenth Street, NW
Washington, DC 20001
Tel: 202-347-1895
Fax: 202-842-3293
E-mail: feedback@nmaonline.com
Website: http://www.nmanet.org

National Optometric Association (NOA)
3723 Main Street
P.O. Box F
East Chicago, IN 46312
Tel: 877-397-2020 or 212-398-1832
Fax: 219-398-1077
E-mail: info@natoptassoc.org
Website: http://www.natoptassoc.org

National Organization of Blacks in Dietetics and Nutrition (NOBIDAN)
P.O. Box 221-884
Beachwood, OH 44118
Tel: 817-292-1824
Website: http://www.nobidan.org

National Pharmaceutical Association
The Courtyards Office Complex
107 Kilmayne Drive, Suite C
Cary, NC 27511
Toll Free: 800-944-6742
Fax: 919-469-5870

National Urban League, Inc. (NUL)
120 Wall Street, 8th Floor
New York, NY 10005
Tel: 212-558-5300
Fax: 212-344-5332
E-mail: info@nul.org
Website: http://www.nul.org

Sickle Cell Disease Association of America, Inc.
200 Corporate Pointe, Suite 495
Culver City, CA 90230-8727
Toll Free: 800-421-8453
Tel: 310-216-6363
Fax: 310-245-3722
E-mail:
scdaa@sicklecelldisease.org
Website: http://
www.sicklecelldisease.org

American Indiana/Alaska Native

All Indian Pueblo Council (AIPC)
P.O. Box 3256
3939 San Pedro NE, Suite E
Albuquerque, NM 87190-3256
Tel: 505-883-7360
Fax: 505-884-1474
E-mail: fvigil@aipcinc.com
Website: http://www.aipcinc.com

American Indian Health Care Association, Inc. (AIHCA)
7050 West 120th Ave, Suite 206A
Brommfield, CO 80020
Tel: 303-460-7420
Fax: 303-460-7426

American Indian Rehabilitation Research and Training Center
Northern Arizona University
P.O. Box 5630
Flagstaff, AZ 86011-5630
Toll Free: 800-553-0714
Tel: 520-523-4791
TTY: 520-523-1695
Fax: 520-523-9127
E-mail: ihd.uap@nau.edu
Website: http://www.nau.edu/
~ihd

Association of American Indian Physicians, Inc. (AAIP)
1225 Sovereign Row, Suite 103
Oklahoma City, OK 73108
Tel: 405-946-7072
Fax: 405-946-7651
E-mail: aaip@aaip.com
Website: http://www.aaip.com

Indian Health Board of Minneapolis
1315 East 24th Street
Minneapolis, MN 55404-3959
Tel: 612-721-9800
Fax: 612-721-7870
E-mail: cwindal@aol.com

Indian Health Service (IHS)
Parklawn Building, Room 6-35
56500 Fishers Lane
Rockville, MD 20857
Tel: 301-443-1083
Fax: 301-443-0507
E-mail: feedback@ihs.gov
Website: http://www.ihs.gov

Indians Into Medicine (INMED) Program
University of North Dakota
School of Medicine
501 North Columbia Road
Grand Forks, ND 58203
Tel: 707-777-3037
Fax: 701-777-3277
E-mail:
inmed@mail.med.und.nodak.edu
Website: http://
www.med.und.nodak.edu/depts/
inmed/home.htm

National Association for Native American Children of Alcoholics (NANACOA)
P.O. Box 2708
Seattle, WA 98111-2708
Tel: 206-903-6574
Fax: 206-624-4452
E-mail: nanacoa@nanacoa.org
Website: http://www.nanacoa.org

National Center for American Indian and Alaska Native Mental Health Research
4455 East 12th Avenue
Campus Box A011-13
Denver, CO 80220
Tel: 303-315-9232
Fax: 303-315-9579
Website: http://
www.hsc.colorado.edu/sm/
ncaianmhr

National Congress of American Indians
1301 Connecticut Ave. NW,
Suite 200
Washington, DC 20036
Tel: 202-466-7767
Fax: 202-466-7797
Website: http://www.ncai.org

National Indian Child Welfare Association
3611 SW Hood Street, Suite 201
Portland, OR 97201
Tel: 503-222-4044
Fax: 503-222-4007
E-mail: info@nicwa.org
Website: http://www.nicwa.org

National Indian Council on Aging (NICOA)
10501 Montgomery Blvd, NE,
Suite 210
Albuquerque, NM 87111
Tel: 505-292-2001
Fax: 505-292-1922
E-mail: dave@nicoa.org
Website: http://www.nicoa.org

National Indian Health Board
1385 South Colorado Blvd.
Suite A-707
Denver, CO 80222
Tel: 303-759-3075
Fax: 303-759-3674
E-mail: yjoseph@nihb.org
Website: http://www.nihb.org

National Native American AIDS Prevention Center
436 14th Street, Suite 1020
Oakland, CA 94126
Tel: 510-444-2051
Fax: 510-444-1593
E-mail: information@nnaapc.org
Website: http://www.nnaapc.org

Nez Perce Tribal Council
P.O. Box 305
Lapwai, ID 83540
Tel: 208-843-2253
Fax: 208-843-7354
E-mail: NPTEC@nezperce.org
Website: http://www.nezperce.org

Northwest Portland Area Indian Health Board
527 SW Hall, Suite 300
Portland, OR 97201
Tel: 503-843-2391 or 208-935-4117
Website: http://www.npaihb.org

Pawhuska Indian Health Center
715 Grand View
Pawhuska, OK 74056
Tel: 918-287-4491
Fax: 918-287-2347

Seattle Indian Health Board
P.O. Box 3364
Seattle, WA 98114-3364
Tel: 206-324-9360
Fax: 206-324-8910
E-mail: info@sihb.org
Website: http://www.sihb.org

United National Indian Tribal Youth, Inc. (UNITY)
P.O. Box 25042
Oklahoma City, OK 73125
Tel: 405-236-2800
Fax: 405-971-1071
E-mail: unity@unityinc.org
Website: http://www.unityinc.org

Asian Americans and Pacific Islanders

Asian and Pacific Islander American Health Forum, Inc.
942 Market Street, Suite 200
San Francisco, CA 94102
Tel: 415-954-9988
Fax: 415-954-9999
E-mail: hforum@apiahf.org
Website: http://www.apiahf.org

Asian and Pacific Islanders for Reproductive Health
310 8th Street, Suite #305A
Oakland, CA 94607
Tel: 510-268-8988
Fax: 510-268-8181
Website: http://www.apirh.org

Association of Asian/Pacific Community Health Organizations (AAPCHO)
1440 Broadway, Suite 510
Oakland, CA 94612
Tel: 510-272-9536
Fax: 510-272-0817
Website: http://www.aapcho.org

Chinese American Medical Society, Inc.
281 Edgewood Avenue
Teaneck, NJ 07666
Tel: 201-833-1506
Fax: 201-833-8252
E-mail: hw5@columbia.edu
Website: http://www.camsociety.org

Japanese American Citizens' League
1765 Sutter Street
San Francisco, CA 94115
Tel: 415-921-5225
Fax: 415-931-4671
E-mail: jacl@jacl.org
Website: http://www.jacl.org

National Asian Pacific American Families Against substance Abuse (NAPAFASA)
340 East Second Street
Suite 409
Los Angeles, CA 90012
Tel: 213-625-5795
Fax: 213-625-5796
E-mail: napafasa@napafasa.org
Website: http://www.napafasa.org

National Asian Women's Health Organization
250 Montgomery Street
Suite 1500
San Francisco, CA 94104
Tel: 415-989-9747
Fax: 415-989-9758
E-mail: nawho@nawho.org
Website: http://www.nawho.org

National Asian Pacific Center on Aging
P.O. Box 21668
Melbourne Tower
1511 3rd Ave., Suite 914
Seattle, WA 98101
Tel: 206-624-1221
Fax: 206-624-1023
E-mail: web@napca.org
Website: http://www.napca.org

National Research Center of Asian American Mental Health (NRCAAMH)
Department of Psychology
University of California
One Shields Avenue
Davis, CA 95616-8686
Tel: 530-752-1400
Fax: 530-752-3747
Website: http://psychology.ucdavis.edu/asianamerican/nrcaamh.htm

Organization of Chinese American Women
4641 Montgomery Ave.
Suite 208
Bethesda, MD 20814
Tel: 301-907-3898
Fax: 301-907-3899

Papa Ola Lokahi
222 Merchant Street, 2nd Floor
Honolulu, HI 96813
Tel: 808-536-9453
Fax: 808-545-1783
Website: http://papaolalokahi.8m.com

Refugee Health Issues Center
American Refugee Committee
2344 Nicollet Ave. South
Suite 350
Minneapolis, MN 55404
Tel: 612-872-7060
Fax: 612-607-6499
E-mail: info@archq.org
Website: http://www.archq.org

Hispanics/Latinos

Asociacion Nacional Pro Personas Mayores
National Association for Hispanic Elderly
1452 West Temple St., Room 100
Los Angeles, CA 90026
Tel: 213-487-1922
Fax: 213-385-3014

ASPIRA Association, Inc.
1444 I Street, NW, Suite 800
Washington, DC 20005
Tel: 202-835-3600
Fax: 202-835-3613
E-mail: info@aspira.org
Website: http://www.aspira.org

Cuban American National Council, Inc.
1223 SW 4th Street
Miami, FL 33135
Tel: 305-642-3484
Fax: 305-642-9122
E-mail: info@cnc.org
Website: http://www.cnc.org

The Hispanic Serving Health Professions Schools
1700 17th Street, NW, Suite 405
Washington, DC 20009
Tel: 202-667-9788
Fax: 202-234-5468

Interamerian College of Physicians and Surgeons
1712 I Street NW, Suite 200
Washington, DC 20006
Tel: 212-777-3642
Fax: 212-505-7984
E-mail: icps@icps.org
Website: http://www.icps.org

Inter-University Program for Latino Research (IUPLR)
University of Notre Dame
P.O. Box 764
230 McKena Hall
Notre Dame, IN 46556-0764
Tel: 219-631-4440
Fax: 219-631-3522
E-mail: latino@nd.edu
Website: http://www.nd.edu/~iupir

League of United Latin American Citizens (LULAC)
2000 L Street, NW, Suite 610
Washington, DC 20036
Tel: 202-833-6130
Website: http://www.lulac.org

Mana National Latina Organization
1725 K Street, NW, Suite 501
Washington DC 20006
Tel: 202-833-0060
Fax: 202-496-0588
E-mail: hermana2@aol.com
Website: http://www.hermana.org

National Association of Hispanic Nurses, Inc. (NAHN)
c/o COSSMHO
1501 16th Street, NW
Washington, DC 20036-1401
Tel: 202-387-5000
Fax: 202-797-4353
E-mail:
alliance@hispanichealth.org
Website: http://www.cossmho.org

National Association of Latino Elected and Appointed Officials (NALEO)
5800 South Eastern Ave, Ste. 365
Los Angeles, CA 90040
Tel: 323-720-1932
Fax: 323-720-9519
E-mail: olopez@naleo.org
Website: http://www.naleo.org

National Coalition of Hispanic Health & Human Services Organization (COSSMHO)
1501 16th Street, NW
Washington, DC 20036
Tel: 202-387-5000
Fax: 202-797-4353
E-mail:
alliance@hispanichealth.org
Website: http://www.cossmho.org

National Conference of Puerto Rican Women (NACOPRW)
5 Thomas Circle
Washington, DC 20005
Tel: 202-387-4716
E-mail: imilan@prfaa-govpr.org
Website: http://www.nacoprw.org

National Council of La Raza (NCLR)
1111 19th Street, NW, Suite 1000
Washington, DC 20036
Toll Free: 800-311-6257
Tel: 202-785-1670
Fax: 202-776-1792
Website: http://www.nclr.org

National Hispanic Council on Aging (NHCoA)
2713 Ontario Road, NW
Washington, DC 20009
Tel: 202-265-1288
Fax: 202-745-2522
E-mail: nhcoa@worldnet.att.net
Website: http://www.nhcoa.org

National Hispanic Medical Association (NHMA)
141 K Street, N.W., Suite 200
Washington, DC 20009
Tel: 202-628-5895
Fax: 202-628-5898
Website: http://
home.earthlink.net/~nhma

National Hispanic Religious Partnership for Community Health
5 Thomas Circle, NW, 4th Floor
Washington, DC 20005
Tel: 202-265-3338
Fax: 202-265-3339

National Latino Children's Institute
1412 West Sixth Street
Austin, TX 78703
Tel: 512-472-9971
Fax: 512-472-5845
E-mail: nlci@nlci.org
Website: http://www.nlci.org

National Latino/z Lesbian and Gay Organization (LLEGO)
1612 K Street, NW, Suite 500
Washington, DC 20006
Tel: 202-466-8240
Fax: 202-466-8530
E-mail: pjserrano@llego.org
Website: http://www.llego.org

National League of Cuban American Community Based Centers
2513 S. Calhoun Street
Fort Wayne, IN 46807
Tel: 219-745-5421
Fax: 219-744-1363

National Latina Institute for Reproductive Health (NLIRH)
1200 New York Ave., NW
Suite 206
Washington, DC 20005
Tel: 202-326-8970
Fax: 202-371-8112
E-mail: mail@nlirh.org
Website: http://www.nlirh.org

National Puerto Rican Coalition
1700 K Street, NW, Suite 500
Washington, DC 20006
Tel: 202-223-3915
Fax: 202-429-2223

National Puerto Rican Forum
31 East 32nd Street, 4th Floor
New York, NY 10016-5536
Tel: 212-685-2311
Fax: 212-685-2349
Website: http://www.nprf.org

Organizacion Nacional de la Salud de la Mujer Latina
National Latina Health Organization
P.O. Box 7567
Oakland, CA 94601
Tel: 510-534-1362
Fax: 510-435-1364

Pan American Development Foundation
2600 16th Street, NW, 4th Floor
Washington, DC 20009-4202
Tel: 202-458-3969
Fax: 202-458-6316

Pan American Health Organization (PAHO)
525 23rd Street NW
Washington, DC 20037
Tel: 202-974-3000
Fax: 202-974-3663
Website: http://www.paho.org

Multicultural

Association for Multicultural Counseling and Development
5999 Stevenson Avenue
Alexandria, VA 22304
Toll Free: 800-347-6647
Tel: 703-823-9800
Fax: 703-823-0252
E-mail: lpeele@counseling.org
Website: http://
www.counseling.org

Intercultural Cancer Council
1720 Dryden, Suite C
Houston, TX 77030
Tel: 713-798-4617
Fax: 713-798-3990
E-mail: icc@bcm.tmc.edu
Website: http://icc.bcm.tmc.edu

International Minority Affairs Cooperative (IMAC)
P.O. Box 276
Beltsville, MD 20704
Tel: 301-595-4747
Fax: 301-595-4748

Multicultural and Gender Equity Resource Center
College of Education, Room 119
University of New Mexico
Albuquerque, NM 87131-1231
Tel: 505-277-7260
Fax: 505-277-8427

National Center for Primary Care at Morehouse School of Medicine
720 Westview Drive SW
Atlanta, GA 30310-1495
Tel: 404-756-5740
Fax: 404-756-1492
E-mail: murrayv@msm.edu
Website: http://www.msm.edu/
ncpc/ncpcpage.html

National Minority AIDS Council
1931 13th Street, NW
Washington, DC 20009-4432
Tel: 202-483-6622
Fax: 202-483-1135
E-mail: info@nmac.org
Website: http://www.nmac.org

National Minority Organ and Tissue Transplant Education Program (MOTTEP)
Howard University Hospital
Ambulatory Care Center
2041 Georgia Avenue, NW
Suite 3100
Washington, DC 20060
Toll Free: 800-393-2839
Tel: 202-865-4888
Fax: 202-865-4880
E-mail:
ccallender@fac.howard.edu

Public Health Foundation
1220 L Street, NW, Suite 350
Washington, DC 20005
Tel: 202-898-5600
Fax: 202-898-5609

The Quality Education for Minorities (QEM) Network
1818 N Street, NW, Suite 350
Washington, DC 20036
Tel: 202-659-1818
Fax: 202-659-5408

Chapter 44

Sources of Health Education Materials

Contents

Section 44.1

African American

"1999 Sources of Health Education Materials," Office of Minority Health Resource Center (OMH-RC).

African Americans account for almost 13 percent of the U.S. population according to the current U.S. Bureau of Census Resident Population estimates. By the year 2010, there will be approximately 40 million African Americans, accounting for the 2nd largest minority group in the United States behind Hispanics.

The search for publications concentrated on the minority health priority identified by the DHHS Secretary's Task Force on Black and Minority Health—cancer, chemical dependency, diabetes, heart disease and stroke, infant mortality, homicide, suicide, and unintentional injuries, and the associated risk factors. Although this resource list indicates some of what is available, it is important to note that some materials were not identified in some subject areas. There is a need to develop additional materials to address these "gaps."

The following list includes culturally sensitive health materials for African Americans, including resources on nutrition, exercise, and AIDS educational materials. Although as many publications as possible are included, this guide is not a comprehensive listing of all such materials.

Organizations included in this section should be contacted directly to determine the cost and availability of bulk quantities for permission to copy.

The Office of Minority Health Resource Center has not evaluated the materials included in the resource list. It is the responsibility of the reader to review the materials to determine their appropriateness for the intended audience. Inclusion does not imply endorsement by the OMH-RC, the Office of Minority Health, the U.S. Public Health Service, or the U.S. Department of Health and Human Services.

OMH-RC is continually seeking health information resources for the U.S. minority populations. If you are aware of sources of health materials that have not been included, please share the information with OMH-RC by calling 1-800-444-6472 or TDD: 301-230-7199.

Subject Topics

Adolescent Pregnancy Prevention

ABCD Boston Family Planning
March of Dimes Birth Defects Foundation
Office of Population Affairs
Planned Parenthood of Summit, Portage, and Medina Counties

Aging

American Association of Retired Persons

AIDS

AIDS Foundation Houston
CDC National Prevention Information Network
Center for AIDS Prevention Studies
Channing L. Bete Company, Inc.
Health Education Resource Organization
Minority AIDS Project
National Maternal and Child Health Clearinghouse
New York State Department of Health

Asthma

American Lung Association

Bibliographies

National Information Center on Health Services Research
National Library of Medicine

Breast Cancer

American Cancer Society

Cancer

American Cancer Society
American Lung Association
Cancer Information Service
National Women's Health Information Center
New York State Department of Health

Child-Health

March of Dimes Birth Defects Foundation
National Clearinghouse on Families and Youth
National Maternal and Child Health Clearinghouse

Consumer Information

Consumer Information Center

Cultural Competence

American Association of Retired Persons
Scarecrow Press, Inc

Diabetes

American Diabetes Association
National Diabetes Information Clearinghouse

Digestive Diseases

National Digestive Diseases Information Clearinghouse

Disability

National Institute on Deafness and Other Communication Disorders
Parent Advocacy Coalition for Education Rights

Exercise

Cancer Information Service

Eye Care

National Eye Institute

Family Planning

ABCD Boston Family Planning
Office of Population Affairs Clearinghouse

Heart Disease

American Heart Association
National Heart, Lung, and Blood Institute

National Women's Health Information Center
New York State Department of Health

High Blood Pressure

American Heart Association
National Heart, Lung, and Blood Institute

Kidney Disease

National Kidney and Urologic Disease Information Clearinghouse

Lung Disease

American Lung Association

Lupus

Lupus Foundation of Northern California
National Institute of Arthritis and Musculoskeletal and Skin Diseases Information Clearinghouse

Mental Health

National Mental Health Association

Nutrition

American Diabetes Association
American Dietetic Association
Cancer Information Service
National Heart, Lung, and Blood Institute

Organ Transplant

National Minority Organ and Tissue Transplant Education Program

Osteoporosis

National Institutes of Health Osteoporosis and Related Bone Disease National Resource Center

Parenting

National Clearinghouse on Families and Youth
National Maternal and Child Health Clearinghouse

Pregnancy

ABCD Boston Family Planning
March of Dimes Birth Defects Foundation
National Maternal and Child Health Clearinghouse

Prenatal Care

ABCD Boston Family Planning
March of Dimes Birth Defects Foundation
National Maternal and Child Health Clearinghouse

Reports

Commonwealth Fund
Grantmakers in Health
Office of Research on Women's Health

Sickle Cell Disease

Agency for Healthcare Research and Quality
American Sickle Cell Anemia Association
National Maternal and Child Health Clearinghouse

Smoking/Tobacco

American Lung Association
Office on Smoking and Health

Stroke

American Heart Association

Substance Abuse

Alcoholics Anonymous
Hazelden Educational Materials
National Clearinghouse on Alcohol and Drug Information
National Council on Alcoholism and Drug Dependence
Wisconsin Clearinghouse for Prevention Resources

Women's Health

National Women's Health Information Center

New York State Department of Health
Office of Research on Women's Health

Organizations Offering Health Education Materials

ABCD Boston Family Planning
Action for Boston Community Development Inc.
178 Tremont St.
Boston, MA 02111-1093
Tel: 617-357-6000 x 263
TTY: 617-423-9215
Fax: 617-357-6810
Website: http://www.bostonabcd.org

Distributes low-literacy contraceptive pamphlets providing step-by-step instructions for each method: birth control pills, IUDs, diaphragms, vaginal contraceptive films, cervical caps, condoms, Norplant, Depo-Provera, and contraceptive foam. "AIDS Alert" section promotes condom use for disease prevention. Pamphlets are available in English and Haitian Creole.

Agency for Healthcare Research and Quality (AHCPR)
AHCPR Publications Clearinghouse
P.O. Box 8547
Silver Spring, MD 20907-8547
Tel: 800-358-9295
TDD: 888-586-6340
Outside the U.S.: 410-381-3150
Fax: 301-594-2800
E-mail: info@ahrq.gov
Website: http://www.ahcpr.gov

Distributes three publications on sickle cell disease. "Sickle Cell Disease: Screening, Diagnosis, Management, and Counseling in Newborns and Infants." "Clinical Practice Guideline No. 6" is intended for the practitioner. It presents the findings and recommendations of AHCPR's panel on sickle cell disease and provides supporting evidence and references. #AHCPR 93-0562. "Sickle Cell Disease: Comprehensive Screening & Management in Newborns and Infants. Quick Reference Guide for Clinicians," a brief summary of the clinical practice guideline, serves as a companion volume to the guideline. #AHCPR 93-0563. "Sickle Cell Disease in Newborns and Infants. A Guide for Parents" is a brochure for consumers on sickle cell trait and disease, screening, and medical management published in English and Spanish, #AHCPR 930564 and 93-0564.

AIDS Foundation Houston
3202 Weslayan Annex
Houston, TX 77027
Toll Free: 888-524-AIDS
Tel: 713-623-6796
In Houston Hotline: 713-524-AIDS
Fax: 713-623-4029
E-mail: afh@aidshelp.org
Website: http://www.aidshelp.org

Offers publications on the risks of AIDS. A brochure, "AIDS/ HIV & The African American Community" presents facts about AIDS/HIV and discusses risky behaviors to avoid. "An African American Woman's Story" tells a story of an African American Women who is infected with AIDS. "Protect the Blood" tells African Americans how they can protect themselves from the HIV virus. "Listen Up" tells how the virus is transmitted and how to protect yourself.

Alcoholics Anonymous
Grand Central Station
Box 459
New York, NY 10163
Tel: 212-870-3400
Fax: 212-870-3003
Website: http://www.alcoholics-anonymous.org

Publishes books and pamphlets. A free catalog of materials and price listings are available.

American Association of Retired Persons
601 E Street, NW
Washington, DC 20049
Tel: 800-424-3410
E-mail: member@aarp.org
Website: http://www.aarp.org

"A Profile of Older Americans" is a brochure that provides demographic and health related information regarding older Americans, including African Americans, Hispanics, Asians! Pacific Islanders, and American Indians.

American Cancer Society
National Headquarters
1599 Clifton Road NE
Atlanta, GA 30329
Toll Free: 800-ACS-2345
Website: http://www.cancer.org

Offers a booklet called "Facts on Prostate Cancer" code #26209 "Being There!" a pamphlet on breast cancer, code #3035, and a booklet, "Cancer Statistics for African Americans" code #8617. Also distributes a booklet called "Cancer Facts and Figures for African Americans 1998-1999."

American Diabetes Association
1701 North Beauregard Street
Alexandria, VA 22311
Toll Free: 800-DIABETES (1-800-342-2383)
E-mail: customerservice@diabetes.org
Website: http://www.diabetes.org

Offers "New Soul Food Cookbook for People with Diabetes." Dig into sensational low-fat recipes from the first African American cookbook for people with diabetes. More than 150 recipes in all; including appetizers, snacks, soups, salads, main dishes, vegetables, side dishes, and desserts. To order, contact the Order Fulfillment Department at 1-800-232-673. Contact the American Diabetes Association for information on the African American Program, which provides information, materials, and programming on their initiative to stop diabetes in the African American community.

American Dietetic Association
216 West Jackson Boulevard
Chicago, IL 60606-6995
Toll Free: 800-877-1600 ext. 5000
Tel: 312-899-0040
Fax: 312-899-4899
E-mail: sales@eatright.org
Website: http://www.eatright.org

Distributes materials for professionals and clients, including the guides, "Ethnic and Regional Food Practices: Soul and Traditional Southern Food Practices, Customs, and Holidays," and "Cajun & Creole Food Practices, Customs, and Holidays." Cost is $8.50 per guide for ADA members and $10.00 per guide for non-members. Call for a free catalog.

American Heart Association
National Center
7272 Greenville Avenue
Dallas, Texas 75231
Toll Free: 800-AHA-USAI (800-242-8721)
Fax: 800-499-6464
E-mail: patientinfo@heart.org
Website: http://www.americanheart.org

"Heart and Stroke, 1999" is a report that provides annual statistics for heart disease, stroke, and other related diseases. It provides charts on mortality and morbidity in the general population and minority populations. It also offers statistics on behavioral risk factors, related surgeries, and hospital stays. Includes a biostatistical factsheet, "African Americans and Cardiovascular Diseases." Distributes "High Blood Pressure in African Americans," a pamphlet, written jointly with the International Society on Hypertension in Blacks. The pamphlet helps African Americans understand high blood pressure, what it is, the risks of developing it, and what can be done about it. It has also been approved by the Association of Black Cardiologists. Contact the American Heart Association for a complete list of publications.

American Lung Association
1740 Broadway
New York, NY 10019
Toll Free: 800-LUNG-USA (800-586-4872)
Tel: 212-315-8700
E-mail: info@lungusa.org
Website: http://www.lungusa.org

Produces materials for African Americans on asthma, emphysema, and the dangers of smoking. A booklet entitled "Asthma ...At My Age? Facts about Asthma for Older Americans" discusses several issues dealing with asthma. Order # 1553. "Facts about ...Emphysema" provides basic information about emphysema in pamphlet form. Order # 0301.

A pamphlet entitled "Don't Let Your Dreams Go Up In Smoke..." targets African Americans and discusses the dangers of smoking.

Order # 1032. The posters are available from State and local affiliates of the American Lung Association. Offers the following fact sheets "African Americans and Tobacco," and "African Americans and Lung Disease."

Also offers "Lung Disease in Minorities, 98." Please contact the American Lung Association for a complete list of publications.

American Sickle Cell Anemia Association
10300 Carnegie Avenue
Cleveland Clinic/East Office Building (EEb18)
Cleveland, OH 44106
Tel: 216-229-8600
Fax: 216-229-4300
Website: http://www.ascas.org

Produces a brochure entitled "Sickle cell anemia and sickle cell trait" which describes the condition, how people get, and who has it. It also discusses the symptoms and risks.

Cancer Information Service
National Cancer Institute
31 Center Drive MSC-2580
Building 31, Room 10A16
Bethesda, MD 20892-2580
Toll Free: 800-4-CANCER (800-422-6237)
TTY: 800-332-8615
Fax: 301-330-1968
Website: http://cis.nci.nih.gov

"Down Home Healthy Cookin'" is a booklet listing 12 recipes that are low-fat, high-fiber versions of traditional favorites of black Americans (#P886) and "Make Low Fat Cooking Taste Great! The Down Home Healthy Way" bookmark (#Z965). "Your Best Body: A Story about Losing Weight" targets African American women, providing information on making lifestyle changes to lose weight. Offers bookmarks with breast cancer facts for African American women, (#Z274). Two fact sheets offered include, "Lung Cancer and Cigarette Smoking Facts among Men and Women of Different Races and Ethnic Groups" and "Racial Differences in Breast Cancer Survival."

CDC National Prevention Information Network

P.O. Box 6003
Rockville, MD 20849-6003
Toll Free: 800-458-5231
TTY: 800-243-7012
Fax: 888-282-7681
E-mail: info@cdcnpin.org
Website: http://www.cdcnpin.org

Provides posters and fact sheets warning about the dangers of AIDS. "What Have You Got Against a Condom?" is available in versions posed to young Black men and young Black women, and urges readers to use condoms every time they have sexual intercourse. "If He Doesn't Have a Condom, You Just Have to Take a Deep Breath and Tell Him To Go Get One" urges females to tell their male sex partners to obtain and use condoms. "If Your Man Is Dabbling in Drugs ... He Could Be Dabbling with Your Life" pictures a Black female and urges the reader to talk to her partner, to urge him to seek counseling, and to insist that he wear a condom during sexual intercourse to prevent spreading HIV. A poster "If You're Dabbling in Drugs ... You Could Be Dabbling With Your Life" pictures a young Black male in a basketball uniform and emphasizes that sharing needles involves the risk of contracting HIV and that just one exposure can result in infection.

"Since I Got HIV, All I Want to Do Is Tell Women That Love Alone Won't Protect Them, Will You Protect Yourself?" features a message from Frankie Alston, a woman with HIV infection. Also provides "African Americans and HIV/AIDS Pathfinder: A Guide to Selected Resources."

Center for AIDS Prevention Studies at the AIDS Research Institute

University of California, San Francisco
74 New Montgomery, Suite 600
San Francisco, CA 94105
Tel: 415-597-9100
Fax: 415-597-9213
E-mail: capsweb@psg.uscf.edu
Website: http://www.caps.ucsf.edu/

Offers many fact sheets on HIV/AIDS in both English and Spanish including "What Are African Americans' HIV Prevention Needs?" (15E). Contact CAPS for a complete publications list.

Channing L. Bete Company, Inc.
200 State Road
South Deerfield, MA 01373
Toll Free: 800-477-4776
Tel: 413-665-7611
Fax: 800-499-6464
E-mail: custsvcs@channing-bete.com
Website: http://www.channing-bete.com

Provides African American specific booklets on AIDS/HIV: "My Brother Got AIDS" (#41228), "AIDS and My Brother" (#74048), "AIDS: An African American Woman's Story" (#41632), and "AIDS and My Sister: The Story of Two African American Women" (#74-007).

Commonwealth Fund
One East 75th Street
New York, NY 10021-2692
Tel: 212-606-3800
Fax: 212-606-3500
E-mail: nb@cmwf.org
Website: http:///www.cmwf.org

"U.S. Minority Health: A Chartbook" a report comparing findings from several surveys and national data sources to provide a clear and graphics based presentation of racial and ethnic disparities in health. Contact the Commonwealth Fund for pricing.

Consumer Information Center
GSA, Room 6142
18th & F Streets NW
Washington, DC 20405
Tel: 202-501-1794
Fax: 202-501-4281
E-mail: catalog.pueblo@gsa.gov
Website: www.pueblo.gsa.gov

Provides consumer information for African Americans. Contact for Consumer Information Center for a complete list:

Grantmakers in Health (GIH)
1100 Connecticut Avenue, Suite 1200
Washington, DC 20036
Tel: 202-452-8331
Fax: 202-452-8340
E-mail: mbackley@gih.org
Website: http://www.gih.org

"Eliminating Racial and Ethnic Disparities in Health: A Chartbook" presents data on the disparities in health among American racial and ethnic populations in the six health areas identified by President Clinton in the February 1998 radio address: infant mortality, cancer, heart disease, diabetes, HIV/AIDS; and immunizations. Data are also presented on risk factors, access to care, and minority participation in the health professions. Contact GIH for pricing information.

Hazelden Educational Materials
P.O. Box 11
Center City, MN 55012-0011
Toll Free: 800-257-7810
Tel: 612-257-4010
E-mail: info@hazelden.org
Website: http://www.hazelden.org

Distributes many materials targeted toward African Americans. Some of the titles offered are pamphlets, "Chemical Dependency and the African American Counseling Strategies and Community Issues" and "African Americans in Treatment—Dealing with Cultural Differences." Also offered is a three video series; "Brother Earl's..." which explains addiction and its effects. Offers "Growing Up Black and Proud" curriculum that focuses on preventing alcohol and other drug problems through building a positive racial identity in adolescents. Contact Hazelden for a complete list of African American publications.

Health Education Resource Organization (HERO)
1734 Maryland Avenue
Baltimore; MD 21201
Tel: 410-685-1180
Fax: 410-752-3353

Disseminates an AIDS poster and an AIDS pamphlet for the African American community. The poster, "AIDS in the Black Community" notes that females can acquire AIDS from having sex with drug users or bisexual men, that babies are being born with AIDS, that African American men are three times as likely to acquire AIDS as white men; and asks if you know what to do to avoid AIDS. The pamphlet, "You Don't Have To Be White Or Gay To Get AIDS" details the cause and transmission of AIDS, how IV drug users are at risk for AIDS, AIDS statistics in the African American community, and how African Americans can reduce the risks of AIDS through safer sex, and eliminating IV drug use and needle sharing. Also distributes "Yo! Get to Know about AIDS," "Don't let AIDS block your shot at life" and "Reach for the bleach." A poster, "Sisters stay alive!" is also available. Contact HERO for a complete list of publications.

Lupus Foundation of Northern California
2635 North First Street, Suite 206
San Jose, CA 95134
Tel: 408-954-8600
Fax: 408-954-8129
E-mail: admin@thebalf.com
Website: http://www.balf.org

Offers articles relating to high incidence of occurrence of lupus in the African American community and two books on lupus.

March of Dimes Birth Defects Foundation
1275 Mamroneck Avenue
White Plains; NY 10605
Toll Free: 888-MODIMES (663-4637)
Tel: 914-428-7100
Fax: 914-997-4763
Website: http://www.modimes.org

Offers over forty health information sheets on issues related to pregnancy, birth defects, and perinatal loss. Also has various brochures and palm cards dealing with pregnancy, preterm labor, folic acid, and other topics.

Minority AIDS Project (MAP)
5149 West Jefferson Boulevard
Los Angeles, CA 90016
Tel: 323-935-4949
Fax: 323-936-4973

Disseminates AIDS educational materials for African Americans via pamphlets, posters, and brochures. Contact MAP for a complete publications list.

National Clearinghouse on Alcohol and Drug Information
Center for Substance Abuse Prevention
5600 Fishers Lane
Rockwall II Room 9D-10
Rockville, MD 20857
Toll Free: 800-729-6686
Tel: 301-443-0365
E-mail: nnadal@samhsa.gov
Website: http://www.samhsa.gov/csap/index.htm

Provides a prevention resource guide on substance abuse for African Americans.

National Clearinghouse on Families & Youth
P.O. Box 13505
Silver Spring, MD 20911-3505
Tel: 301-608-8098
Fax: 301-608-8721
Website: www.ncfy.com

Provides "A Guide to Enhancing the Cultural Competence of Runaway and Homeless Youth Programs."

National Council on Alcoholism and Drug Dependence
12 West 21st Street, 7th Floor
New York, NY 10410
Tel: 212-206-6770
Hope Line: 800-NCA-CALL (24 hour affiliate referral)
Fax: 212-645-1690
E-mail: national@ncadd.org
Website: http://www.ncadd.org

Distributes a pamphlet "Who's Got the Power? You ...Or Drugs?" Single copies are free. Call NCADD for bulk orders.

National Diabetes Information Clearinghouse
1 Information Way
Bethesda, MD 20892-3560
Tel: 301-654-3327
Fax: 301-907-8906
E-mail: dkocpl@extra.niddk.nih.gov
Website: http://www.niddk.nih.gov/ndic

Provides a fact sheet, "Diabetes in African Americans" (DM-113). Maintains a database of patient and professional education materials that contains materials for African Americans from which literature searches are generated.

National Digestive Diseases Information Clearinghouse
2 Information Way
Bethesda, MD 20892-3570
Tel: 301-654-3810
Fax: 301-907-8906
E-mail: niddc@info.niddk.nih.gov
Website: http://www.niddk.nih.gov

Provides a bibliographic database search on "Digestive Diseases in Minority Populations." Maintains a database of patient and professional education materials that are geared toward African Americans.

National Eye Institute
2020 Vision Place
Bethesda, MD 20892-3655
Tel: 301-496-5248
Fax: 301-402-1065
Website: http://www.nei.nih.gov

Offers two pamphlets on African Americans and eye care: "Don't Lose Sight of Glaucoma" and "Don't Lose Sight of Diabetic Eye Disease." Contact for a complete publications list.

National Heart, Lung, and Blood Institute—NHLBI Information Center
P.O. Box 39105
Bethesda, MD 20824-0105
Tel: 301-592-8573
Fax: 301-592-8563
E-mail: NHLBIinfo@rover.nhlbi.nih.gov
Website: http://www.nhlbi.nih.gov/health/infoctr/index.htm

Offers several publications for African Americans including "Embrace Your Health! Lose Weight if You are Overweight," "Heart-Healthy Home Cooking African American Style," "Refresh Yourself! Stop Smoking," and "Spice Up Your Life! Eat Less Salt and Sodium." Contact the Information Center for a complete list of publications.

National Information Center on Health Services Research
Building 38A, RM 4S-410, Mail Stop 20
8600 Rockville Pike
Bethesda, MD 20894
Tel: 301-496-0176
Fax: 301-402-3193
E-mail: nichsr@nlm.nih.gov
Website: http://www.nlm.nih.gov/nichsr/nichsr.html

HealthSTAR database can be accessed for literature citations.

National Institute of Arthritis and Musculoskeletal and Skin Diseases Information Clearinghouse
National Institutes of Health
1 AMS Circle
Bethesda, MD 20892-3675
Tel: 301-495-4484
Fax: 301-718-6366
TTY: 301-565-2966
E-mail: niamsINFO@mail.nih.gov
Website: http://www.nih.gov/niams/

Offers "What Black Women Should Know about Lupus: Ideas for Community Programs" as well as "LUPUS: A Patient Care Guide for Nurses and Other Health Professionals."

National Institute on Deafness and Other Communication Disorders
Information Clearinghouse
1 Communication Avenue
Bethesda, MD 20892-3456
Toll Free: 800-241-1044
TTY: 800-241-1055
Fax: 301-907-8830
E-mail: nidcdinfo@nidcd.nih.gov
Website: http://www.nih.gov/nidcd

Provides information for African Americans. Contact agency for additional information and listings.

National Institutes of Health Osteoporosis and Related Bone Diseases National Resource Center
1232 22nd Street, NW
Washington, DC 20037-1292
Toll Free: 800-624-BONE
Tel: 202-223-0344
Fax: 202-293-2356
TTY: 202-466-4315
E-mail: orbdnrc@nof.org
Website: http://www.osteo.org

Offers a fact sheet "African American Women and Osteoporosis" as well as a bibliography on "Osteoporosis Research in African Americans."

National Kidney and Urologic Diseases
Information Clearinghouse
3 Information Way
Bethesda, MD 20892-3580
Tel: 301-654-4415
Fax: 301-097-8906
E-mail: nkudic@aerie.com
Website: http://www.niddk.nih.gov

Maintains a database of patient and professional education materials that are geared towards African Americans.

National Library of Medicine
8600 Rockville Pike
Bethesda, MD 20894
Toll Free: 888-346-3656
Tel: 301-594-5983
Fax: 301-496-2809
E-mail: custserv@nlm.nih.gov
Website: http://www.nlm.nih.gov/

National Library of Medicine collects worldwide medical literature in all languages as well as health information on various minority and ethnic groups. Call for specific topics.

National Maternal and Child Health Clearinghouse
2070 Chain Bridge Road, Suite 450
Vienna, VA 22182-2536
Toll Free: 888-434-4MCH
Tel: 703-356-1964
Fax: 703-821-2098
E-mail: nmchc@circsol.com
Website: http://www.nmchc.org

Offers "A Parents' Handbook for Sickle Cell Disease, Part II: Six to Eighteen Years of Age" (H033); and "Parents' Handbook for Sickle Cell Disease, Part I: Birth to Six Years of Age" (F060). Also offers publications in Haitian Creole, "Groses ak HIV Eske AZT se Meye Chwa pou Ou ak pou Pitit Ou? (Pregnancy and HIV: Is AZT the Right Choice for You and Your Baby?)" (I078); and "Koneksyon Familial: Tras Selil Falsifom (Family Connection: Sickle Cell Trait)" (G055).

National Mental Health Association
Order Department
1021 Prince Street
Alexandria, VA 22314-2971
Toll Free: 800-969-NMHA
Tel: 703-684-7722
TTY: 800-433-5959
Fax: 703-684-5968
Website: http://www.nmha.org

Offers a pamphlet on "Depression in African Americans" which discusses depression and how the African American culture views depression, the treatments, and sources of help. #262. Call for a complete publications and pricing list.

National Minority Organ and Tissue Transplant Education Program (MOTTEP)
Howard University Hospital
Ambulatory Care Center
2041 Georgia Avenue, NW, Suite 3100
Washington, DC 20060
Toll Free: 800-393-2839
Tel: 202-865-4888
Fax: 202-865-4880
E-mail: ccallender@fac.howard.edu

Provides information on the need for organ transplantation and donation in minority communities.

National Women's Health Information Center
8550 Arlington Boulevard, Suite 300
Fairfax, VA 22031
Toll Free: 800-994-WOMAN (994-9662)
TDD: 888-220-5446
Fax: 703-560-6598
E-mail: 4woman@soza.com
Website: http://www.4woman.org

Fact sheets offered include "Heart Disease and Stroke," "Women and AIDS/HIV," and "Women's Health Issues: An Overview." "The Health of Minority Women" fact sheet addresses socioeconomic and cultural issues as well as health system barriers which limit minority women's access to preventive health care and diagnostic and treatment services. Contact the Center for a complete list of publications, reports, and documents.

New York State Department of Health
Publications
Box 2000
Albany, NY 12220
Tel: 518-474-5370
E-mail: telecom.directory@ogs.state.ny.us
Website: http://www.health.state.ny.us/home.html

Offers many publications on health issues ranging from AIDS to cancer to heart disease to women's health. Provides materials in Albanian, Amheric, Arabic, Chinese, English, French, Greek, Haitian, Hebrew, Hindi, Hmong, Italian, Japanese, Laotian, Polish, Romanian, Russian, Spanish, Urdu, Vietnamese, and Yiddish. Call for a free publications catalog.

Office of Research on Women's Health
Office of the Director
National Institutes of Health
1 Center Drive, Room 201, MSC 0161
Bethesda, MD 20892-0161
Tel: 301-402-1770
Fax: 301-402-1798
Website: http://www4.od.nih.gov/orwh/orwhpubs.html

"Women of Color Health Data Book: Adolescents to Seniors" examines the role of culture, ethnicity, race, socioeconomic background, geographic location, and other social and economic factors as important contributors to health status.

Office of Population Affairs Clearinghouse (OPA)

P.O. Box 30696
4350 East West Highway
Suite 200 West
Bethesda, MD 20814
Tel: 301-654-6190
Fax: 301-215-7731
E-mail: opa@osophs.dhhs.gov
Website: http://www.hhs.gov/progorg/opa

Offers facts sheets on topics ranging from sterilization to pap smears to alcohol and drugs and pregnancy. Also offers a video on HIV and African Americans. Contact OPA for a complete publications list.

Office on Smoking and Health

CDC/NCCDPHP
Mail Stop K-50
4770 Buford Highway, NE
Atlanta, GA 30341-3724
Toll Free: 800-CDC-1311 (800-232-1311)
General information/publication requests: 770-488-5705
Tel: 770-488-5707
Fax: 770-488-2552
E-mail: tobacco@cdc.gov
Website: http://www.cdc.gov/tobacco

Provides a fact sheet on "African Americans and Tobacco." Also has the Surgeon General's Report, "Tobacco Use among U.S. Racial/Ethnic-Minority Groups." A citation database is also available for the latest tobacco related information and research.

Parent Advocacy Coalition for Educational Rights
4826 Chicago Avenue South
Minneapolis, MN 55417-1098
Toll Free: 800-53-PACER (in MN) or 888-248-0822 (nationally)
Tel: 612-827-2966
TDD: 612-827-7770
E-mail: pacer@pacer.org
Website: http://www.pacer.org

Provides books for African American parents of children with disabilities.

Planned Parenthood of Summit, Portage, and Medina Counties
444 West Exchange Street
Akron, OH 44302
Tel: 330-535-2671
Fax: 330-536-7145

Disseminates a pamphlet "Nobody's Fool Again" which presents the true stories of three African American teenage mothers who experienced unintended pregnancies and the problems they faced raising their children alone.

Scarecrow Press, Inc.
4720 Boston Way
Lanham, MD 20706
Toll Free: 800-462-6420
Tel: 301-459-3366
Fax: 301-459-1705
Website: http://www.scarecrowpress.com

Offers "Ethnic Minority Health: A Selected Annotated Bibliography" a guide that encompasses in one volume various minority health issues for the four major U.S. ethnic minority groups (Native Americans/Alaska Natives; African Americans, Hispanic Americans, and Asian/Pacific Islander Americans). Features nine quick access sections that are divided first by material format or broad subject area and then by ethnic group. (ISBN: 0-8108-3225-9).

Wisconsin Clearinghouse for Prevention Resources
University of Wisconsin-Madison
1552 University Avenue
Madison, WI 53705-4085
Toll Free: 800-322-1468
Tel: 608-262-9157
Fax: 608-262-6346
Website: http://www.uhs.wisc.edu/wch/

"Brain Drain" is a multicultural poster for middle schoolers that uses creative, high-tech graphics to show the effects of alcohol on the brain. "Mouth Off" another new FACE poster which, through the use of attention-getting; high-tech graphics, grabs kids and teaches them the importance of saying. "no" to alcohol use: "Growing Up Black and Proud—Preventing Alcohol and Other Drug Problems Through Building a Positive Racial Identity" is a curriculum for African American youth that helps teens learn the information and skills they need to grow into healthy, drug-free adults. The curriculum addresses identity, overcoming racism, communicating feelings, making decisions, solving problems, resolving conflicts, dealing with peer pressure, and more. Includes a facilitator's guidebook, the video, and a guide for teenagers. Contact the Clearinghouse for a complete publications list.

Section 44.2

American Indian/Alaska Native

"1999 Sources of Health Education Materials," Office of Minority Health Resource Center (OMH-RC).

American Indians and Alaska Natives combine to make up one of the smallest minority groups in the United States with a population of 2.4 million, according to the current U.S. Bureau of Census Population Estimates. By the year 2010, they are expected to reach 2.7 million, 0.9 percent of the total U.S. population.

The search for publications concentrated on the minority health priority identified by the DHHS Secretary's Task Force on Black and Minority Health—cancer, chemical dependency, diabetes, heart disease and stroke, infant mortality, homicide, suicide, and unintentional injuries, and the associated risk factors. Although this resource list indicates some of what is available, it is important to note that some materials were not identified in some subject areas. There is a need to develop additional materials to address these "gaps."

The following list includes culturally sensitive health materials for American Indians and Alaska Natives. Resources on nutrition, exercise, and AIDS educational materials are included. Although as many publications as possible are included, this guide is not a comprehensive listing of materials.

Organizations included in this section should be contacted directly to determine the cost and availability of bulk quantities for permission to copy.

The Office of Minority Health Resource Center has not evaluated the materials included in the resource list. It is the responsibility of the reader to review the materials to determine their appropriateness for the intended audience. Inclusion does not imply endorsement by the OMH-RC, the Office of Minority Health, the U.S. Public Health Service, or the U.S. Department of Health and Human Services.

OMH-RC is continually seeking health information resources for the U.S. minority populations. If you are aware of sources of health materials that have not been included, please share the information with OMH-RC by calling 1-800-444-6472.

Subject Topics

Aging

American Association of Retired Persons
National Indian Policy Center

AIDS

CDC National Prevention Information Network
National Native American AIDS Prevention Center
San Diego American Indian Health Center
Seneca Nation of Indians Health Department

Bibliographies

National Information Center on Health Services Research
National Library of Medicine
Scarecrow Press, Inc.

Breast Cancer

American Cancer Society
Center for American Indian Research and Education
Native American Women's Health Education Resource Center

Cancer

American Lung Association
Cancer Information Service
National Women's Health Information Center

Child Health

National Clearinghouse on Families and Youth

Cultural Competence

American Association of Retired Persons
Indians Into Medicine Program (INMED)
Sage Publications
Scarecrow Press, Inc

Diabetes

National Diabetes Information Clearinghouse
USPHS Indian Health Service Diabetes Program

Digestive Diseases

National Digestive Diseases Information Clearinghouse

Disability

Native American Research and Training Center
Parent Advocacy Coalition for Education Rights

Education

Indians Into Medicine Program (INMED)

Fetal Alcohol Syndrome

Alaska Department of Health and Social Services
American Indian Institute
National Organization on Fetal Alcohol Syndrome

Heart Disease

American Heart Association
National Women's Health Information Center

Kidney Disease

National Kidney and Urologic Disease Information Clearinghouse

Lung Disease

American Lung Association

Nutrition

American Dietetic Association
Cancer Information Service

Organ Transplant

National Minority Organ and Tissue Transplant Education Program

Osteoporosis

National Institutes of Health Osteoporosis and Related Bone Disease
National Resource Center

Parenting

National Clearinghouse on Families and Youth

Post-Traumatic Stress Disorder

National Center for Post-Traumatic Stress Disorder

Pregnancy/Prenatal Care

Native American Women's Health Education Resource Center
WWAMI Rural Health Research Center

Reports

Commonwealth Fund
Grantmakers in Health
Office of Research on Women's Health

Smoking/Tobacco

American Lung Association
Office on Smoking and Health

Substance Abuse

Alcoholics Anonymous
Hazelden Educational Materials
National Clearinghouse on Alcohol and Drug Information

Women's Health

Indian Health Service
National Women's Health Information Center
Native American Women's Health Education Resource Center
Office of Research on Women's Health

Organizations Offering Health Education Resources

Alaska Department of Health and Social Services (DHSS)
Statewide FAS Coordinator
DHSS, Office of the Commissioner
P.O. Box 110607
Juneau, AK 99811
Toll Free: 800-478-2072 Statewide
Tel: 907-465-3033
Fax: 907-465-2185
E-mail: Diane Worley@health.state.ak.us
Website: http://hss.state.ak.us/fas/

DHSS publications related to Fetal Alcohol Syndrome available for distribution include: "Fetal Alcohol Syndrome Alaska's Guide to Prevention, Intervention, and Services," "Fetal Alcohol Syndrome—Alaska's Medical Provider's Guide," and "Fetal Alcohol Syndrome: Alaska's #1 Preventable Birth Defect: An Update on the Status of Alaska's Response to FAS." To request copies of these publications and get a complete list, contact the Alaska Department of Health and Social Services.

Alcoholics Anonymous
Grand Central Station
Box 459
New York, NY 10163
Tel: 212-870-3400
Fax: 212-870-3003
Website: http://www.alcoholics-anonymous.org

"AA for the Native North American" describes how 13 Native American men and women successfully gave up drinking and are now living fruitful lives as sober people. Single copies are free.

American Association of Retired Persons
601 E Street, NW
Washington, DC 20049
Toll Free: 800-424-3410
Tel: 202-434-2277
E-mail: member@aarp.org
Website: http://www.amp.org

"A Profile of Older Americans" is a brochure that provides demographic and health-related information regarding older Americans including African Americans, Hispanics, Asians/Pacific Islanders, and American Indians.

American Dietetic Association (ADA)
216 West Jackson Boulevard
Chicago, IL 60606-6995
Toll Free: 800-877-1600; ext. 5000
Tel: 312-899-0040
Fax: 312-899-4899
E-mail: sales@eatright.org
Website: http://www.eatright.org

Distributes "Ethnic and Regional Food Practices: Alaska Native Food Practices, Customs, and Holidays" and "Ethnic and Regional Food Practices: Navajo Food Practices, Customs, and Holidays," professional guides, $8.50 each for ADA members, $10 each for non-members: Call for a free catalog.

American Heart Association
National Center
7272 Greenville Avenue
Dallas, Texas 75231
Toll Free: 800-AHA-USAI (800-242-8721)
Fax: 800-499-6464
E-mail: patientinfo@heart.org
Website: http://www.americanheart.org

"Heart and Stroke, 1999" is a report that provides annual statistics for heart disease, stroke, and other related diseases. It provides charts on mortality and morbidity in the general population and minority populations. It also offers statistics on behavioral risk factors, related surgeries, and hospital stays. Includes a biostatistical fact sheet, "American Indian/Alaska Natives and Cardiovascular Diseases."

American Indian Institute
College of Continuing Education
Engineering Annex Building
P.O. Box 879909
Tempe, Arizona 85287-9909
Tel: 480-965-8044
Fax: 480-965-7201
E-mail: amerind@mainex1.asu.edu
Website: http://aii.asu.edu

"Remembering What We Know" is 12-minute movie/presentation kit that informs adolescents about the dangers of fetal alcohol syndrome and the dangers of drinking while pregnant. "Faces Yet To Come" is a 10-minute video and 19 lesson curriculum on fetal alcohol syndrome. If shows how the American Indian views spirituality, the Earth, and the significance of the Seventh Generation promoting the well-being of future generations.

American Lung Association
1740 Broadway
New York, NY 10019
Toll Free: 800-LUNG-USA (800-586-4872)
Tel: 212-315-8700
E-mail: info@lungusa.org
Website: http://www.lungusa.org

Offers the following fact sheets "American Indians/Native Alaskans and Tobacco" and "American Indians/Alaskan Natives and Lung Disease." Also offers "Lung Disease in Minorities, 1998." Please contact for a complete list of publications.

Cancer Information Service
National Cancer Institute
31 Center Drive MSC-2580
Building 31, Room 10A16
Bethesda, MD 20892 2580
Toll Free: 800-4-CANCER (800-422-6237)
TTY: 800-332-8615
Fax: 301-330-1968
Website: http://cis.nci.nih.gov

Two fact sheets offered include, "Lung Cancer and Cigarette Smoking Facts among Men and Women of Different Races and Ethnic Groups" and "Racial Differences in Breast Cancer Survival." Offers bookmarks with breast cancer facts for American Indian women, #Z375. One brochure, "Traditional Foods Can Be Healthy" targets Native Americans and suggests that they practice the nutritional balance that was common in traditional diets from their past. It shows that the ancestors stayed active, ate low-fat foods, and broiled, boiled, smoked, or dried vegetables, meat, and fish.

CDC National Prevention Information Network

P.O. Box 6003
Rockville, MD 20849-6003
Toll Free: 800-458-5231
TTY: 800-243-7012
Fax: 888-282-7681
E-mail: info@cdcnpin.org
Website: http://www.cdcnpin.org

"Native Americans and HIV/AIDS: A Guide to Selected Resources" includes the most up-to-date information from the Clearinghouse's Resources and Services, Educational Materials, and Periodical databases on a variety of HIV/AIDS related topics. The Guide includes lists of: HIV/AIDS related organizations in the U.S. and Canada that serve Native Americans, clinic/health centers operating under Indian Health Service Contract 638, Indian Health Service offices, urban Indian health program branch coordinators, a bibliography of "AIDS 101" materials targeting Native Americans, newsletters, journals and other periodicals about HIV/AIDS, and Internet sites that provide information targeting Native Americans and/or provide general health and AIDS-related information. Provides "MMWR: HIV/AIDS among American Indians and Alaska Natives—United States, 1981-1997," March 6;1998,47(6).

Center for American Indian Research and Education

1918 University Avenue, Suite 2A
Berkeley, CA 94704-1051
Tel: 510-843-8661
Fax: 510-843-8611
E-mail: CAIREberk@aol.com
Website: http://www.caire.org

The "American Indian Women's Breast Cancer Guide" is designed to reach all women so they can actively participate in their medical care and become knowledgeable about all risk factors related to breast cancer. Included is information about breast cancer risk and treatment, the patient-physician relationship, patient rights, Indian Health Service, and breast cancer information resources. There is a nominal charge for postage and handling. The companion "American Indian Women's Breast Cancer Resource Directory" provides information on resources for American Indian women affected by breast cancer. It lists California Indian Health Clinics, Northern, Central and

Southern California resources, a glossary of terms, product manufacturers, national and state organizations, and support group and programs. Each entry includes the resource name, address, contact, and a description of the activities and services. Contact for pricing information.

Commonwealth Fund
One East 75th Street
New York, NY 10021-2692
Tel: 212-606-3800
Fax: 212-606-3500
E-mail: nb@cmwf.org
Website: http://www.cmwf.org

"U.S. Minority Health: A Chartbook" is a report that compares the findings from several surveys and national data sources to provide a clear and graphics-based presentation of racial and ethnic disparities in health: Contact the Commonwealth Fund for pricing.

Grantmakers in Health (GIH)
1100 Connecticut Avenue, Suite 1200
Washington, DC 20036
Tel: 202-452-8331
Fax: 202-452-8340
E-mail: mbackley@gih.org
Website: http://www.gih.orgvv

"Eliminating Racial and Ethnic Disparities in Health: A Chartbook" presents data on the disparities in health among American racial and ethnic populations in the six health areas identified by President Clinton in the February 1998 radio address: infant mortality, cancer, heart disease; diabetes, HIV/AIDS, and immunizations. Data are also presented on risk factors, access to care, and minority participation in the health professions. Contact GIH for pricing information.

Hazelden Educational Materials
P.O. Box 11
Center City, MN 55012-0011
Toll Free: 800-257-7810
Tel: 612-257-4010
E-mail: bookstore@hazelden.org
Website: http://www.hazelden.org

Distributes many materials targeted toward American Indians. The following are just 2 of many offered. "The Red Road Audio—Native American Paths to Recovery" follows in the oral tradition of American Indians, using native spirituality in recovery. Audio tape is 10 minutes, $11. (#5634). "Recovery from the Heart" is an interactive program designed to assist American Indians set goals and create strategies for results. Uses a system of principles, values, and laws common to many American Indian tribes. Contact Hazelden for a complete list of American Indian materials.

Indian Health Service
Program Statistics Team
Twinbrook Metro Plaza
12300 Twinbrook Parkway, Suite 450
Rockville, MD 20852
Tel: 301-443-1180
Fax: 301-443-1522
Website: http://www.ihs.gov

"Highlights of Indian Health Focus: Women" presents the highlights of a report that examines the health status of Indian women. It is based on data published in the "Trends in Indian Health and Regional Differences in Indian Health."

Indians Into Medicine (INMED) Program
University of North Dakota School of Medicine & Health Sciences
501 North Columbia Road
Grand Forks, ND 58203
Tel: 701-777-3037
Fax: 701-777-3277
E-mail: inmed@mail.med.und.nodak.edu
Website: http//www.med.und.nodak.edu/depts/inmed/home.htm

"Good Medicine for Our People" is a coloring book with pictures of doctors, nurses, and patients. The book also describes the current need for American Indians in health careers. Suitable for elementary students. Single copies are free. "Serpent, Staff, and Drum" (newsletter). INMED's quarterly newsletter describes program activities and includes information pertinent to college counselors and American Indian health careers students. Suitable for junior high students through adult. Single copies are free. "Indians into Medicine" (program information book), describes summer enrichment sessions and academic year support services for American Indians preparing for health careers at the University of North Dakota. Suitable for junior high students through adult. Single copies are free. "Healthy Games and Teasers" (activity book) includes puzzles, mazes, word searches, and other games to test knowledge of the human body and awareness of Native Indian tribes. Suitable for upper elementary students through adult. Single copies are free. "INMED...Our Way of Giving—Remembering the Indian Way" (poster) gives a brief description of the INMED program. Single copies are free.

National Center for Post-Traumatic Stress Disorder
VA Medical Center (116D)
White River Junction, VT 05009
Tel: 802-296-5132
Fax: 802-296-5135
E-mail: ptsd@dartmouth.edu
Website: http://www.ncptsd.org

Provides two publications for American Indians: "Challenging the Hidden Enemy: the legacy of psychological trauma of the Vietnam War for American Indian military personnel" and "Evaluation and Treatment of Post-Traumatic Stress Disorder with American Indian Vietnam veterans."

National Clearinghouse on Alcohol and Drug Information
Center for Substance Abuse Prevention
5600 Fishers Lane
Rockwall II Room 9D-10
Rockville, MD 20857
Toll Free: 800-729-6686
Tel: 301-443-0365
E-mail: nnadal@samhsa.gov
Website: http://www.samhsa.gov/csap/index.htm

Provides a prevention resource guide on substance abuse for American Indians and Alaska Natives.

National Clearinghouse on Families and Youth
P.O. Box 13505
Silver Spring, MD 20911-3505
Tel: 301-608-9098
Fax: 301-608-8721
Website: www.ncfy.com

Provides "A Guide to Enhancing the Cultural Competence of Runaway and Homeless Youth Programs."

National Diabetes Information Clearinghouse
1 Information Way
Bethesda, MD 20892-3560
Tel: 301-654-3327
Fax: 301-907-8906
E-mail: dkocpl@extra.niddk.nih.gov
Website: http://www.niddk.nih.gov/ndic

Provides a publication on diabetes and American Indians called "The Pima Indians: Pathfinders for Health" (DM-170). Maintains a database of patient and professional education materials that address American Indians.

National Digestive Diseases Information Clearinghouse
2 Information Way
Bethesda, MD 20892-3570
Tel: 301-654-3810
Fax: 301-907-8906
E-mail: niddc@info.niddk.nih.gov
Website: http://www.niddk.nih.gov

Provides a bibliographic database search on "Digestive Diseases in Minority Populations." Maintains a database of patient and professional education materials that are American Indian/Alaskan Native specific.

National Information Center on Health Services Research
Building 38A, RM 4S-410, Mail Stop 20
8600 Rockville Pike
Bethesda, MD 20894
Tel: 301-496-0176
Fax: 301-402-3193
E-mail: nichsr@nlm.nih.gov
Website: http://www.nlm.nih.gov/nichsr/nichsr.html

HealthSTAR database can be accessed for literature citations.

National Kidney and Urologic Diseases
Information Clearinghouse
3 Information Way
Bethesda, MD 20892-3580
Tel: 301-654-4415
Fax: 301-097-8906
E-mail: nkudic@aerie.com
Website: http://www.niddk.nih.gov

Maintains a database of patient and professional education materials that are American Indian/Alaskan Native specific.

National Library of Medicine
8600 Rockville Pike
Bethesda, MD 20894
Toll Free: 888-346-3656
Tel: 301-594-5983
Fax: 301-496-2809
E-mail: custserv@nlm.nih.gov
Website: http://www.nlm.nih.gov/

National Library of Medicine collects worldwide medical literature in all languages, as well as health information on various minority and ethnic groups. Call for specific topics.

National Minority Organ and Tissue Transplant Education Program (MOTTEP)
Howard University Hospital
Ambulatory Care Center
2041 Georgia Avenue, NW, Suite 3100
Washington, DC 20060
Toll Free: 800-393-2839
Tel: 202-865-4888
Fax: 202-865-4880
E-mail: ccallender@fac.howard.edu

Provides information on the need for organ transplantation and donation in minority communities.

National Native American AIDS Prevention Center (NNAAPC)

436 14th Street, Suite 1020
Oakland, CA 94612
Tel: 510-444-2051
Fax: 510-444-1593
E-mail: information@nnaapc.org
Website: http://www.nnaapc.org

NNAAPC offers materials, resources, and information on American Indians and HIV/AIDS. NNAAPC Prevention Services publishes the journal "Seasons." NNAAPC Media Services publishes a current awareness newsletter, "In The Wind," and distributes press packets with statistics, press releases, articles on HIV/AIDS and Native Americans, and occasional ad slicks or public service announcements.

National Organization on Fetal Alcohol Syndrome (NOFAS)

216 G Street, NE
Washington, DC 20002
Tel: 202-785-4585
Fax: 202-466-6456
E-mail: information@nofas.org
Website: http://www.nofas.org

NOFAS offers publications, resources, and other information on fetal alcohol syndrome. Contact NOFAS for a complete listing of fetal alcohol syndrome information.

National Women's Health Information Center

8550 Arlington Boulevard, Suite 300
Fairfax, VA 22031
Toll Free: 800-994-WOMAN (994-9662)
TDD: 888-220-5446
Fax: 703-560-6598
E-mail: 4woman@soza.com
Website: http://www.4woman.org

Fact sheets offered include "Heart Disease and Stroke," "Women and AIDS/HIV," and "Women's Health Issues: An Overview." "The Health of Minority Women" fact sheet addresses socioeconomic and cultural issues as well as health system barriers which limit minority women's access to preventive health care and diagnostic and treatment services. Contact the Center for a complete list of publications, reports, and documents.

Native American Research and Training Center (NARTC)
University of Arizona, Tucson
1642 E. Helen
Tucson, AZ 85719
Tel: 520-621-5075 (voice/TTY)
Fax: 520-621-9802
E-mail: lclore@u.Arizona.edu
Website: http://www.ahsc.arizona.edu/nartc/nartc.html

NARTC publishes a monograph series on topics ranging from government policies to specific health and rehabilitation problems affecting American Indians. NARTC also produces instructional videos that cover topics ranging from the training of nursing care personnel to discussion of cultural sensitivity issues in working with Indian peoples.

The Native American Women's Health Education Resource Center
P.O. Box 572
Lake Andes, SD 57356-0572
Tel: 605-487-7072
Fax: 605-487-7964
E-mail: nativewoman@igc.apc.org
Website: http://www.nativeshop.org

Provides various materials, brochures, posters, and products on fetal alcohol syndrome, diabetes, domestic violence and other topics as they relate to American Indian women's health. Contact the Center for a complete publications list.

Office of Research on Women's Health
Office of the Director
National Institutes of Health
1 Center Drive, Room 201, MSC 0161
Bethesda, MD 20892-0161
Tel: 301-402-1770
Fax: 301-402-1798
Website: http://www4.od.nih.gov/orwh/orwhpubs.html

"Women of Color Health Data Book: Adolescents to Seniors" examines the role of culture, ethnicity, race, socioeconomic background, geographic location, and other social and economic factors as important contributors to health status.

Office on Smoking and Health
CDC/NCCDPHP
Mail Stop K-50
4770 Buford Highway, NE
Atlanta, GA 30341-3724
Toll Free: 800-CDC-1311 (800-232-1311)
General information/publication requests: 770-488-5705
Tel: 770-488-5707
Fax: 770-488-2552
E-mail: tobacco@cdc.gov
Website: http://www.cdc.gov/tobacco

Provides a fact sheet on "American Indians and Alaska Natives and Tobacco." Also has the Surgeon General's Report, "Tobacco Use among U.S. Racial/Ethnic Minority Groups." A citation database is also available for the latest tobacco related information and research.

Parent Advocacy Coalition for Educational Rights
4826 Chicago Avenue South
Minneapolis, MN 55417-1098
Toll Free: 800-53-PACER (in MN) or 888-248-0822 (nationally)
Tel: 612-827-2966
TDD: 612-827-7770
E-mail: pacer@pacer.org
Website: http://www.pacer.org

Provides books for American Indian parents of children with disabilities.

Sage Publications, Inc.
2455 Teller Road
Thousand Oaks, CA 91320
Tel: 805-499-0721
Fax: 805-499-0871
E-mail: info@sagepub.com
Website: http://www.sagepub.com

Offers "Counseling with Native American Indians and Alaska Natives—Strategies for Helping Professionals." A supplementary text for counseling, clinical psychology, and social work courses emphasizing strategies for meeting the needs of diverse populations, this book provides a thorough background to helping professionals on the developmental, cultural, and special mental health needs and concerns of Native American Indian clients. Contact Sage for pricing information.

San Diego American Indian Health Center
2630 1st Avenue
San Diego, CA 92103
Tel: 619-234-2158
Fax: 619-234-0206
E-mail: editor@sdaihc.com
Website: http://www.sdaihc.com

The Center publishes "The Speaking Tree Newsletter: About Native Women's Health Issues," which is a publication of the women's HIV prevention project. "The Lone Tree" is the Center's general newsletter.

Scarecrow Press, Inc.
4720 Boston Way
Lanham, MD 20706
Toll Free: 800-462-6420
Tel: 301-459-3366
Fax: 301-459-1705
Website: http://www.scarecrowpress.com

Offers "Ethnic Minority Health: A Selected Annotated Bibliography," a guide that encompasses in one volume various minority health issues for the four major U.S. ethnic minority groups (Native Americans/Alaska Natives, African Americans, Hispanic Americans, and Asian/Pacific Islander Americans). Features nine quick access sections that are divided first by material format or broad subject area and then by ethnic group. (ISBN: 0-8108-3225-9)

Seneca Nation of Indians Health Department
Lionel R. John Health Center
P.O. Box 480
Salamanca, NY 14779
Tel: 716-945-5894
Fax: 716-945-5889

Provides "AIDS Can Find Many Roads to the Reservation" (pamphlet). Lists the telephone numbers of the local health centers, the

State AIDS Hotline, and the National Indian AIDS Hotline. Single copies are free.

USPHS Indian Health Service Diabetes Program
5300 Homestead Road, NE
Albuquerque, NM 87110
Tel: 505-248-4539
Fax: 505-248-4656
E-mail: rgollub@SMTP.his.gov
Website: http://www.ihs.gov

Provides description of the Indian Health Service "Comprehensive Healthcare Program for American Indians and Alaska Natives." "Family Food Choices: A Guide to Weight and Diabetes Control" is an illustrated booklet designed to help Native Americans with diabetes make appropriate choices for weight control. It includes tips on weight loss, fats, fiber, sugar, and alcohol. Fat and fiber charts give calorie and exchange listings. Food choices use dishes from the Native American diet.

Wisconsin Clearinghouse for Prevention Resources
University of Wisconsin-Madison
1552 University Avenue
Madison, WI 53705-4085
Toll Free: 800-322-1468
Tel: 608-262-9157
Fax: 608-262-6346
Website: http://www.uhs.wisc.edu/wch/

Offers videos, curricula, posters, and other prevention materials for American Indians. Contact for a complete list.

WWAMI Rural Health Research Center
Department of Family Medicine, School of Medicine, University of Washington
Box 354696
Seattle, WA 98195-4696
Tel: 206-685-0401
Fax: 206-616-4768
E-mail: wamirhrc@fammed.washington.edu
Website: http://www.fammed.washington.edu/wamirhrc

"Perinatal and Infant Health among Rural and Urban American Indians/Alaska Natives" is a report that looks at the maternal risk factors, prenatal care use, and birth outcomes for American Indian and Alaska Native women living in rural and urban areas that not necessarily covered by the Indian Health Service.

Section 44.3

Asian Americans

"1999 Sources of Health Education Materials," Office of Minority Health Resource Center (OMH-RC).

Asian Americans, combined with Pacific Islanders, account for 4 percent of the U.S. population according to the current U.S. Bureau of Census Population Estimates. By the year 2010 there will be close to 15 million Asian and Pacific Islanders, 5 percent of the total U.S. population. Although there are over 20 different countries represented by Asians in the U.S., the three most common countries of origin are China, Japan, and Korea with significant portions from Cambodia; Vietnam, and Laos.

The search for publications concentrated on the minority health priority identified by the DHHS Secretary's Task Force on Black and Minority Health—cancer, chemical dependency, diabetes, heart disease and stroke, infant mortality, homicide, suicide, and unintentional injuries, and the associated risk factors. Although this resource list indicates some of what is available, it is important to note that some materials were not identified in some subject areas. There is a need to develop additional materials to address these "gaps."

The following list includes culturally sensitive health materials for Asians as well as materials in various Asian languages. It includes resources on nutrition, exercise, and AIDS educational materials. Although as many publications as possible are included, this section is not a comprehensive listing of all such materials.

Organizations included in the this section should be contacted directly to determine the cost and availability of bulk quantities for permission to copy.

The Office of Minority Health Resource Center has not evaluated the materials included in the resource list. It is the responsibility of the reader to review the materials to determine their appropriateness for the intended audience. Inclusion does not imply endorsement by the OMH-RC, the Office of Minority Health, the U.S. Public Health Service, or the U.S. Department of Health and Human Services.

OMH-RC is continually seeking health information resources for the U.S. minority populations. If you are aware of sources of health materials that have not been included; please share the information with OMH-RC by calling 1-800-444-6472.

Subject Topics

Aging

American Association of Retired Persons
National Asian Pacific Center on Aging

AIDS

Association of Asian Pacific Community Health Organizations
CDC National Prevention Information Network
Center for AIDS Prevention Studies
Chinatown Health Clinic
Chinatown Service Center
Korean Health Education, Information and Research Center
New York State Department of Health

Bibliographies

Asian and Pacific Islander American Health Forum, Inc.
National Information Center on Health Services Research
National Library of Medicine
Scarecrow Press, Inc

Breast Cancer

Agency for Healthcare Research and Quality
Asian and Pacific Islander American Health Forum, Inc.
Family Health and Social Service Center

Cancer

American Cancer Society

American Lung Association
Cancer Information Service
National Women's Health Information Center
New York State Department of Health

Child Health

Asian Community Mental Health Services
Association of Asian Pacific Community Health Organizations
National Clearinghouse on Families and Youth
National Maternal and Child Health Clearinghouse

Consumer Safety

U.S. Consumer Product Safety Commission

Cultural Competence

American Association of Retired Persons
Scarecrow Press, Inc

Diabetes

Chinatown Health Clinic
National Diabetes Information Clearinghouse
North East Medical Services

Digestive Diseases

National Digestive Diseases Information Clearinghouse

Disability

Parent Advocacy Coalition for Education Rights

Environmental Health

Indoor Air Quality Information Clearinghouse

Family Planning

Education Programs Associates
San Francisco Department of Public Health

Health Education

Kalihi Palama Health Center
Korean Health Education, Information, and Research Center
National Clearinghouse for Primary Care Information
South Cove Community Health Center

Heart Disease

American Heart Association
National Women's Health Information Center
New York State Department of Health

Hepatitis

Asian Pacific Health Care Venture, Inc.
National Maternal and Child Health Clearinghouse

Immunization

Channing L. Bete Company

Kidney Disease

National Kidney and Urologic Disease Information Clearinghouse

Lung Disease

American Lung Association

Lupus

Lupus Foundation of Northern California

Managed Care

National Asian Pacific Center on Aging

Mental Health

Asian Community Mental Health Services
National Asian Pacific American Families Against Substance Abuse

Nutrition

American Dietetic Association

University of California

Oral Health

Dental Health Foundation

Organ Transplant

National Minority Organ and Tissue Transplant Education Program

Osteoporosis

National Institutes of Health Osteoporosis and Related Bone Disease National Resource Center

Parenting

Chinatown Youth Center
National Clearinghouse on Families and Youth
National Maternal and Child Health Clearinghouse
Washington Department of Social and Health Services

Pregnancy

La Leche League International

Prenatal Care

ABCD Boston Family Planning
March of Dimes Birth Defects Foundation
National Maternal and Child Health Clearinghouse

Reports

Asian and Pacific Islander American Health Forum, Inc.
Commonwealth Fund Grantmakers in Health
Office of Research on Women's Health

Sickle Cell Disease

American Sickle Cell Anemia Association
National Maternal and Child Health Clearinghouse

Smoking/Tobacco

Agency for Healthcare Research and Quality

American Lung Association
Office on Smoking and Health

Substance Abuse

Al-Anon and Alateen
Alcoholics Anonymous
Asian Community Mental Health Services
Hazelden Educational Materials
National Asian Pacific American Families Against Substance Abuse
National Clearinghouse on Alcohol and Drug Information
National Council on Alcoholism and Drug Dependence
Pacific Asian Alcohol and Drug Program

Thalessemia

Association of Asian Pacific Community Health Organizations

Women's Health

Asian and Pacific Islander American Health Forum, Inc.
National Asian Women's Health Organization
National Women's Health Information Center
New York State Department of Health
Office of Research on Women's Health

Organizations Offering Health Education Resources

Agency for Healthcare Research and Quality (AHRQ)

AHRQ Publications Clearinghouse
P.O. Box 8547
Silver Spring, MD 20907-8547
Tel: 800-358-9295
TDD: 888-586-6340
Outside the U.S.: 410-381-3150
Fax: 301-594-2800
E-mail: info@ahrq.gov
Website: http://www.ahcpr.gov

Provides mammogram information and smoking cessation information in Chinese, Korean, Laotian, Tagalog, Vietnamese, and Cambodian.

Al-Anon and Alateen
1600 Corporate Landing Parkway
Virginia Beach, VA 23454-5617
Toll Free: 888-245-2666
Tel: 757-563-1600
Fax: 757-563-1655
E-mail: WSO@al-anon.org
Website: http://www.al-anon.alateen.org

Offers limited quantities of alcohol-related materials approved by the Al-Anon/Alateen Conference in Chinese, Japanese, and Korean.

Alcoholics Anonymous
Grand Central Station
Box 459
New York, NY 10163
Tel: 212-870-3400
Fax: 212-870-3003
Website: http://www.alcoholics-anonymous.org

Publishes books and pamphlets. A free catalog of materials and price listings are available.

American Association of Retired Persons
601 E Street, NW
Washington, DC 20049
Toll Free: 800-424-3410
E-mail: member@aarp.org
Website: http://www.aarp.org

"A Profile of Older Americans" is a brochure that provides demographic and health-related information regarding older Americans, including African Americans, Hispanics, Asian/ Pacific Islanders, and American Indians.

American Cancer Society (ACS)
National Headquarters
1599 Clifton Road NE
Atlanta, GA 30329
Toll Free: 800-ACS-2345-(800-227-2345)
Website: http://www.cancer.org

Offers posters with Asian Americans featured depicting dangers of smoking, Code #5752, and #5742. Contact your local ACS for Asian specific information.

American Dietetic Association
216 West Jackson Boulevard
Chicago, IL 60606-6995
Toll Free: 800-877-1600 ext. 5000
Tel: 312-899-0040
Fax: 312-899-4899
E-mail: sales@eatright.org
Website: http://www.eatright.org

Distributes materials for professionals and clients, including "Ethnic and Regional Food Practices: Chinese Food Practices, Customs, and Holidays," "Ethnic and Regional Food Practices: Filipino American Food Practices, Customs, and Holidays," and "Ethnic and Regional Food Practices: Hmong Food Practices, Customs, and Holidays," professional guides, $8.50 each for ADA members, $10 each for nonmembers. Call for a catalog.

American Heart Association
National Center
7272 Greenville Avenue
Dallas, Texas 75231
Toll Free: 800-AHA-USAI (800-242-8721)
Fax: 800-499-6464
E-mail: patientinfo@heart.org
Website: http://www.americanheart.org

"Heart and Stroke, 1999" is a report that provides annual statistics for heart disease, stroke, and other related diseases. It provides charts on mortality and morbidity in the general population and minority populations. It also offers statistics on behavioral risk factors, related surgeries, and hospital stays. It also includes a biostatistical fact sheet, "Asian/Pacific Islanders and Cardiovascular Diseases."

American Lung Association
1740 Broadway
New York, NY 10019
Toll Free: 800-LUNG-USA (800-586-4872)
Tel: 212-315-8700
E-mail: info@lungusa.org
Website: http://www.lungusa.org

Offers the following fact sheets "Asian and Pacific Islanders and Tobacco" and "Asian and Pacific Islanders and Lung Disease." Also offers "Lung Disease in Minorities, 98." Contact for a complete list of publications.

American Sickle Cell Anemia Association
10300 Carnegie Avenue
Cleveland Clinic/East Office Building (EEb18)
Cleveland, OH 44106
Tel: 216-229-8600
Fax: 216-229-4300
Website: http://www.ascas.org

Call for a list of Asian language materials.

Asian and Pacific Islander American Health Forum, Inc.
942 Market Street, Suite 200
San Francisco, CA 94-102
Tel: 415-954-9988
Fax: 415-954-9999
E-mail: hforum@apiahf.org
Website: http://www.apiahf.org

Offers reports, bibliographies, and newsletters on Asian and Pacific Islander health issues. Provides a fact sheet on cancer, as well as fact sheets on women's health and chronic disease, access and utilization of health services, and maternal and child health.

Asian Community Mental Health Services
310 8th Street, Suite 201
Oakland, CA 94607
Tel: 510-451-6729
Fax: 510-268-0202
E-mail: email@acmhs.org
Website: http://www.acmhs.org

Publishes pamphlets and booklets on child mental health in English, Chinese, Vietnamese, Cambodian, Korean, and Japanese. Substance abuse prevention—child and parent versions in Cambodian, Chinese, Laotian, Tagalog, and Vietnamese.

Asian Pacific Health Care Venture, Inc.
1530 Hillhurst Avenue, Suite 200
Los Angeles, CA 90027
Tel: 213-346-0370
Fax: 213-346-0373

Materials for distribution available from APHCV include "Understanding Hepatitis B" and "Join Our Forces Against Hepatitis B" in English, Chinese, Korean, Thai, and Cambodian.

Association of Asian Pacific Community Health Organizations
1440 Broadway, Suite 510
Oakland, CA 94612
Tel: 510-272-9536
Fax: 510-272-0817
E-mail: aapcho@egroups.com
Website: http://aapcho.org

Distributes a videotape about AIDS in different languages: English, Cantonese, Cambodian, Korean, Laotian, Mandarin, Mien, Samoan, Tagalog, and Vietnamese. Brochures on hepatitis come in Chinese, English, Korean, Laotian, Samoan, Tagalog, and Vietnamese. Also information on thalassemia and a parental guide on childhood illness comes in Chinese, English, Korean, Laotian, Samoan, Tagalog, and Vietnamese.

Cancer Information Service
National Cancer Institute
31 Center Drive MSC-2580
Building 31, Room 10A16
Bethesda, MD 20892 2580
Toll Free: 800-4-CANCER (800-422-6237)
TTY: 800-332-8615
Fax: 301-330-1968
Website: http://cis.nci.nih.gov

Two fact sheets offered include, "Lung Cancer and Cigarette Smoking Facts among Men and Women of Different Races and Ethnic Groups" and "Racial Differences in Breast Cancer Survival." Offers bookmarks with breast cancer facts for Asian American women, #Z301

CDC National Prevention Information Network
P.O. Box 6003
Rockville, MD 20849-6003
Toll Free: 800-458-5231
TTY: 800-243-7012
Fax: 888-282-7681
E-mail: info@cdcnpin.org
Website: http://www.cdcnpin.org

Provides fact sheets on AIDS in Cambodian, Chinese, and Vietnamese. Provides fact sheets on HIV/AIDS and Asian and Pacific Islanders.

Center for AIMS Prevention Studies at the AIDS Research Institute
University of California, San Francisco
74 New Montgomery, Suite 600
San Francisco, CA 94105
Tel: 415-597-9100
Fax: 415-597-9213
E-mail: CAPSWeb@psq.ucsf.edu
Website: http://www.caps.ucsf.edu/

Offers many fact sheets on HIV/AIDS including "What Are Asian and Pacific Islander HIV Prevention Needs?" (33E) In Tagalog, "Ano ang mga pangangailangan ng mga Asyano at Pacific Islander tungkol sa HIV prevention?" (33T).

Channing L. Bete Company, Inc.
200 State Read
South Deerfield, MA 01373
Toll Free: 800-477-4776
Tel: 413-665-7611
Fax: 800-499-6464
E-mail: custsvcx@channing-bete.com
Website: http://www.channing-bete.com

"Give Your Child a Shot at Good Health" pamphlet and the "My Book about Shots" coloring book are available in Chinese, Vietnamese, and Cambodian.

Chinatown Health Clinic
Health Education Department
125 Walker Street, 2nd Floor
New York, NY 10013
Tel: 212-226-1872
Fax: 212-226-2289
E-mail: easy@aweb.com
Website: http://www.asianweb.net/news/text/chc.htm

Distributes pamphlets in Chinese on AIDS, baby's health, cancer, cardiovascular/heart health, children/adolescent health, dental care, diabetes, heart disease, high blood pressure, mental health, nutrition, prenatal care, respiratory disease, smoking, tuberculosis, and women's health.

Chinatown Service Center
Family Health Clinic
767 North Hill Street, Suite 200
Los Angeles, CA 90012
Toll Free: 800-733-2882
Tel: 213-808-1718
Fax: 213-680-9427
E-mail: cscinfo@csc.apanet.org
Website: http://csc.apanet.org/index.html

Offers pamphlets on the following topics: AIDS, birth control methods, family planning, breast self-examination, prenatal care, menopause, pap smear, prematura syndrome, sexually transmitted diseases, teen pregnancy, and tobacco control in Chinese.

Chinatown Youth Center
1693 Polk Street
San Francisco, CA 94109
Tel: 415-775-2636
Fax: 415-775-1345
E-mail: cyc@cycsf.org
Website: http://www.cycsf.org

Provides a workbook on parenting, "Ten Principles on Raising Chinese-American Teens" available in Chinese and English.

Commonwealth Fund
One East 75th Street
New York, NY 10021-2692
Tel: 212-606-3800
Fax: 212-606-3500
E-mail: nb@cmwf.org
Website: http:///www.cmwf.org

"U.S. Minority Health: A Chartbook" is a report that compares the findings from several surveys and national data sources to provide a clear and graphics-based presentation of racial and ethnic disparities in health. Contact the Commonwealth Fund for pricing.

Dental Health Foundation
520 Third Street, Suite 205
Oakland, CA 94607
Tel: 510-663-3727
Fax: 510-663-3733
E-mail: tdhf@pacbell.net
Website: http://www.dentalhealthfoundation.org

Offers brochures on baby bottle tooth decay in Cambodian, Chinese, Laotian, Thai, and Vietnamese.

Education Program Associates
1 West Campbell Avenue, #45
Campbell, CA 95008-1004
Tel: 408-374-3720
Fax: 408-374-7385

Offers IUD, pill, and shot wallet cards detailing danger signs and other instructions for each type of birth control in Chinese and Korean languages.

Family Health and Social Service Center
Southeast Asian Health Program
26 Queen Street
Worcester, MA 01610
Tel: 508-860-7700
Fax: 508-860-7990

Develops and distributes educational fact sheets in Vietnamese and Cambodian on breast and cervical cancer, pap smear and breast self-examination, tuberculosis, diabetes, hepatitis B, and mammograms. Also produces a video on breast self-examination and mammography in Vietnamese and Cambodian.

Grantmakers in Health (GIH)
1100 Connecticut Avenue, Suite 1200
Washington, DC 20036
Tel: 202-452-8331
Fax: 202-452-8340
E-mail: mbackley@gih.org
Website: http://www.gih.org

"Eliminating Racial and Ethnic Disparities in Health: A Chartbook" presents data on the disparities in health among American racial and ethnic populations in the six health areas identified by President Clinton in the February 1998 radio address: infant mortality, cancer, heart disease, diabetes, HIV/ AIDS, and immunizations. Data are also presented on risk factors, access to care, and minority participation in the health professions. Contact GIH for pricing information.

Indoor Air Quality Information Clearinghouse
P.O. Box 37133
Washington, DC 20013-7133
Toll Free: 800-438-4318
Tel: 703-356-4020
Fax: 703-356-5386
Website: http//www.epa.gov/iaq/

Provides the following. "What You Can Do about Secondhand Smokers as Parents, Decision Makers, and Building Occupants" available in Chinese; "Protecting Your Family and Yourself from Carbon Monoxide Poisoning" available in Korean, Chinese, Vietnamese (developed by Association of Asian Pacific Community Health Organizations). They offer pamphlets in Chinese on "Secondhand Smoke," and a CO fact sheet for Chinese, Korean, and Vietnamese.

Kalihi Palama Health Center
915 North King Street
Honolulu, HI 96817
Tel: 808-848-1438

Provides Filipino, Chinese, Vietnamese, and Korean language materials on various health topics. Contact for additional information.

Korean Health Education, Information and Research Center
545 South Gramercy Place
Los Angeles, CA 90020-4914
Tel: 213-427-4000
Fax: 213-427-4008

Offers brochures and pamphlets on various health topics including cancer, diabetes, heart disease, and HIV/AIDS in Korean language.

La Leche League International
P.O. Box 4079
1400 North Meacham Road
Schaumburg, IL 60168-4079
Tel: 847-519-7730
Fax: 847-519-0035
E-mail: prdept@llli.org
Website: http://www.lalecheleague.org

Distributes pamphlets on breastfeeding in Japanese language.

Lupus Foundation of Northern California
2635 North First Street, Suite 206
San Jose, CA 95134
Tel: 408-954-8600
Fax: 408-954-8129
E-mail: admin@thebalf.com
Website: http://www.balf.org

"Lupus and Women of Color" briefly explains the symptoms and characteristics of systemic lupus erythematosus (SLE) in Vietnamese. Some articles in Vietnamese and Chinese are available.

National Asian Pacific American Families against Substance Abuse
340 East Second Street, Suite 409
Los Angeles, CA 90012
Tel: 213-625-5795
Fax: 213-625-5796
Website: http://www.napafasa.org

Provides information and referral regarding substance abuse, mental health, and related services to API populations. Also offers mental health and substance abuse information and materials, as well as a newsletter and publications list.

National Asian Pacific Center on Aging

Melbourne Tower
P.O. Box 21668
1511 3rd Avenue, Suite 914
Seattle, WA 98101
Tel: 206-624-1221
Fax: 206-624-1023
E-mail: web@napca.org
Website: http://www.napca.org

Offers publication on Medicare, Medicaid, and other managed care issues in Chinese, Khmer, Korean, and Vietnamese.

National Asian Women's Health Organization

250 Montgomery Street, Suite 1500
San Francisco, CA 94104
Tel: 415-989-9747
Fax: 415-989-9758
E-mail: nawho@nawho.org
Website: http://'www.nawho.org

Offers several publications on Asian American women's health. One title, "Perceptions of Risk: The Factors Influencing Use of Reproductive and Sexual Health Services by Asian American Women" is a breakthrough report on Asian women's attitudes and views on health and health care services. A useful resource for practitioners and educators serving this diverse population. Contact for pricing information and a complete publications catalog.

National Clearinghouse for Primary Care Information

2070 Chain Bridge Road, Suite 450
Vienna, VA 22182
Tel: 703-821-8955
TTY: 703-556-4831
Fax: 703-821-2098
E-mail: info@circsol.com
Website: http://www.circsol.com

Provides materials in various Asian languages. Contact the Clearinghouse for a publication listing.

National Clearinghouse on Alcohol and Drug Information
Center for Substance Abuse Prevention
5600 Fishers Lane
Rockwall II Room 9D-10
Rockville, MD 20857
Toll Free: 800-729-6686
Tel: 301-443-0365
E-mail: nnadal@samhsa.gov
Website: http://www.samhsa.gov/csap/index.htm

Provides a prevention resource guide for Asians and Pacific Islanders (English). Contact for a complete publications list.

National Clearinghouse on Families and Youth
P.O. Box 13505
Silver Spring, MD 20911-3505
Tel: 301-608-8098
Fax: 301-608-8721
Website: http://www.ncfy.com

Provides "A Guide to Enhancing the Cultural Competence of Runaway and Homeless Youth Programs."

National Council on Alcoholism and Drug Dependence
12 West 21st Street, 7th Floor
New York, NY 10410
Tel: 212-206-6770
Hope Line: 800-NCA-CALL (24 hour affiliate referral)
Fax: 212-645-1690
E-mail: national@ncadd.org
Website: http://www.ncadd.org

"What Are the Signs of Alcoholism: The NCADD Self Test" is available in Chinese; Vietnamese, Laotian, and Thai. Single copies are free; reproduction is permitted.

National Diabetes Information Clearinghouse
1 Information Way
Bethesda, MD 20892-3560
Tel: 301-654-3327
Fax: 301-907-8906
E-mail: dkocpl@extra.niddk.nih.gov
Website: http://www.niddk.nih.gov/ndic

Maintains a database of patient and professional education materials that contain Asian language materials, from which literature searches are generated.

National Digestive Diseases Information Clearinghouse

2 Information Way
Bethesda, MD 20892-3570
Tel: 301-654-3810
Fax: 301-907-8906
E-mail: niddc@info.niddk.nih.gov
Website: http://www.niddk.nih.gov

Provides a bibliographic database search on "Digestive Diseases in Minority Populations." Maintains a database of patient and professional education materials that contain Asian language materials.

National Information Center on Health Services Research

Building 38A, RM 4S-410, Mail Stop 20
8600 Rockville Pike
Bethesda, MD 20894
Tel: 301-496-0176
Fax: 301-402-3193
E-mail: nichsr@nlm.nih.gov
Website: http://www.nlm.nih.gov/nichsr/nichsr.html

HealthSTAR database can be accessed for literature citations.

National Institutes of-Health Osteoporosis and Related Bone Diseases National Resource Center

1232 22nd Street, NW
Washington, DC 20037-1292
Toll Free: 800-624-BONE
Tel: 202-223-0344
Fax: 202-293-2356
E-mail: orbdnrc@nof.org
Website: http://www.osteo.org

Offers a fact sheet "Asian American Women and Osteoporosis" as well as a bibliography on "Osteoporosis Research in Asian Populations." Both documents are in English.

National Kidney and Urologic Diseases Information Clearinghouse
3 Information Way
Bethesda, MD 20892-3580
Tel: 301-654-4415
Fax: 301-097-8906
Website: http://www.niddk.nih.gov

Maintains a database of Asian language educational materials. Also provides a bibliographic search on "Foreign Language Materials on Kidney and Urologic Diseases."

National Library of Medicine
8600 Rockville Pike
Bethesda, MD 20894
Toll Free: 888-346-3656
Tel: 301-594-5983
Fax: 301-496-2809
E-mail: custserv@nlm.nih.gov
Website: http://www.nlm.nih.gov/

National Library of Medicine collects worldwide medical literature in all languages as well as health information on various minority and ethnic groups. Call for specific topics.

National Maternal and Child Health Clearinghouse
2070 Chain Bridge Road, Suite 450
Vienna, VA 22182-2536
Toll Free: 888-434-4MCH
Tel: 703-356-1964
Fax: 703-821-2098
E-mail: nmchc@circsol.com
Website: http://www.nmchc.org

Offers information on hepatitis B in Korean–F042, Samoan–F044; Tagalog–F045, and Vietnamese–F046. "Parent's Guide to Common Childhood Illnesses" is offered in Laotian–F050, Samoan–F051, Tagalog–F052, and Vietnamese–F053. "Protect Your Child's Teeth! Put Your Baby to Bed with Love, Not a Bottle" comes in Cambodian–D041, Chinese–D043, Laotian–D039, and Thai–D040. "Thalassemia among Asians" is provided in Korean–F056, Tagalog–F058, and Vietnamese–F059.

National Minority Organ and Tissue Transplant Education Program (MOTTEP)
Howard University Hospital
Ambulatory Care Center
2041 Georgia Avenue, NW, Suite 3100
Washington, DC 20060
Toll Free: 800-393-2839
Tel: 202-865-4888
Fax: 202-865-4880
E-mail: ccallender@fac.howard.edu

Provides information on the need for organ transplantation and donation in minority communities.

National Women's Health Information Center
8550 Arlington Boulevard, Suite 300
Fairfax, VA 22031
Toll Free: 800-994-WOMAN (994-9662)
TDD: 888-220-5446
Fax: 703-560-6598
E-mail: 4woman@soza.com
Website: http://www.4woman.org

Fact sheets offered include "Heart Disease and Stroke," "Women and AIDS/HIV," and "Women's Health Issues: An Overview." "The Health of Minority Women" fact sheet addresses socioeconomic and cultural issues as well as health system barriers which limit minority women's access to preventive health care and diagnostic and treatment services. Contact the Center for a complete list of publications, reports, and documents.

New York State Department of Health
Publications
Box 2000
Albany, NY 12220
Tel: 518-474-5370
E-mail: telecom.directory@ogs.state.ny.us
Website: http://www.health.state.ny.us/home.html

Offers many publications on health issues ranging from AIDS to cancer, and heart disease to women's health. Provides materials in Albanian, Amheric, Arabic, Chinese, English, French, Greek, Haitian, Hebrew, Hindi, Hmong, Italian, Japanese, Laotian, Polish, Romanian,

Russian, Spanish, Urdu, Vietnamese, and Yiddish. Call for a free publications catalog.

North East Medical Services
1520 Stockton Street
San Francisco, CA 94133
Tel: 415-391-9686
Fax: 415-433-4726

Offers brochures on diabetes-related topics including insulin injections, diabetic foot care, and dietary restrictions. Materials are also available on high blood pressure and weight control in Chinese.

Office of Research on Women's Health
Office of the Director
National Institutes of Health
1 Center Drive, Room 201, MSC 0161
Bethesda, MD 20892-0161
Tel: 301-402-1770
Fax: 301-402-1798
Website: http://www4.od.nih.gov/orwh/orwhpubs.html

"Women of Color Health Data Book: Adolescents to Seniors" examines the role of culture, ethnicity, race, socioeconomic background, geographic location, and other social and economic factors as important contributors to health status.

Office on Smoking and Health
CDC/NCCDPHP
Mail Stop K-50
4770 Buford Highway, NE
Atlanta, GA 30341-3724
Toll Free: 800-CDC-1311 (800-232-1311)
General information/publication requests: 770-488-5705
Tel: 770-488-5707
Fax: 770-488-2552
E-mail: tobacco@cdc.gov
Website: http://www.cdc.gov/tobacco

Provides a fact sheet "Asian Americans and Pacific Islanders and Tobacco." Also has the Surgeon General's Report, "Tobacco Use among U.S. Racial/Ethnic Minority Groups." A citation database is also available for the latest tobacco related information and research.

Pacific Asian Alcohol and Drug Program
532 S. Vermont Ave., Suite 102
Los Angeles, CA 90020
Tel: 213-738-3362
Fax: 213-389-4512

Distributes educational materials on alcoholism in Chinese, Japanese, Korean, Filipino, Tagalog, Tongan, and Vietnamese. Distributes pamphlets on drunk driving in Cambodian, Chinese, Hmong, Japanese, Korean, Laotian, Thai, and Vietnamese. Makes available a directory on alcohol-related services.

Parent Advocacy Coalition for Educational Rights
4826 Chicago Avenue South
Minneapolis, MN 55417-1098
Toll Free: 800-53-PACER (in MN) or 888-248-0822 (nationally)
Tel: 612-827-2966
TDD: 612-827-7770
E-mail: pacer@pacer.org
Website: http://www.pacer.org

Produces booklets for parents of children with disabilities in Hmong.

San Francisco Department of Public Health
Chinatown Public Health Center
1490 Mason Street
San Francisco, CA 94133
Tel: 415-705-8500
Fax: 415-705-8578
Website: http://www.dph.sf.ca.us

Various health education materials in Chinese. Same materials in Southeast Asian languages. Topics include: TB, nutrition, AIDS, family planning, perinatal care, hypertension, arthritis, and low-fat eating.

Scarecrow Press, Inc.
4720 Boston Way
Lanham, MD 20706
Toll Free: 800-462-6420
Tel: 301-459-3366
Fax: 301-459-1705
Website: http://www.scarecrowpress.com

Offers "Ethnic Minority Health: A Selected Annotated Bibliography," a guide that encompasses in one volume various minority health issues for the four major U.S. ethnic minority groups (Native Americans/Alaska Natives, African Americans, Hispanic Americans, and Asian/Pacific Islander Americans). Features nine quick access sections that are divided first by material format or broad subject area and then by ethnic group. (ISBN: 0-8108-32259)

South Cove Community Health Center
885 Washington St.
Boston, MA 02111-1415
Tel: 617-482-7555
Fax: 617-482-2930
Website: http://www.scchc.org

Distributes brochures in Chinese, English, and Vietnamese on various health topics including AIDS/STD, alcohol, child care, cholesterol, diabetes, domestic violence, hepatitis, hypertension, smoking, women's health, menopause, thalassemis, tuberculosis, breast cancer, glaucoma, depression, lead poisoning, carbon monoxide poisoning, and managed care.

University of California
Cooperative Extension in Alameda County
1131 Harbor Bay Parkway, Suite 131
Alameda, CA 94502
Tel: 510-567-6812
Fax: 510-567-6813
E-mail: cealameda@ucdavis.edu

Provides materials on nutrition and diet in Chinese and Vietnamese languages.

U.S. Consumer Product Safety Commission
Western Regional Office
600 Harrison St.
San Francisco, CA 94107-1397
Tel: 510-637-4050
Website: http://www.cpsc.gov

Provides materials on flammable materials and toxic substances in Chinese.

Washington State Department of Health
1112 SE Quince Street
P.O. Box 47890
Olympia, WA 98504-7890
Tel: 360-236-4010

Offers "A Family's Guide to Early Intervention Services in Washington State," "Developmental Prescreen Chart," and "Parents Rights Brochure," in Cambodian, Chinese, Laotian, and Vietnamese.

Section 44.4

Hispanics

"1999 Sources of Health Education Materials," Office of Minority Health Resource Center (OMH-RC).

Currently, Hispanics are the second largest minority group in the United States, with a population of approximately 31 million, 11 percent of the total population. Persons of Hispanic origin are considered an ethnic group and may be of any race. According to the U.S. Bureau of Census Population Estimates, Hispanics will be the largest minority group in the year 2010, with 41 million people, almost 14 percent of the total population.

The search for publications concentrated on the minority health priority identified by the DHHS Secretary's Task Force on Black and Minority Health—cancer, chemical dependency, diabetes, heart disease and stroke, infant mortality, homicide, suicide, and unintentional injuries, and the associated risk factors. Although this resource list indicates some of what is available, it is important to note that some materials were not identified in some subject areas. There is a need to develop additional materials to address these "gaps."

The following list includes culturally sensitive health materials for Hispanics as well as Spanish language materials. Also included are resources on nutrition, exercise, and AIDS educational materials. Although as many publications as possible are included, this guide is not a comprehensive listing of all such materials.

Organizations included in the this section should be contacted directly to determine the cost and availability of bulk quantities for permission to copy.

The Office of Minority Health Resource Center has not evaluated the materials included in the resource list. It is the responsibility of the reader to review the materials to determine their appropriateness for the intended audience. Inclusion does not imply endorsement by the OMIT-RC, the Office of Minority Health, the U.S. Public Health Service, or the U.S. Department of Health and Human Services.

OMH-RC is continually seeking health information resources for the U.S. minority populations. If you are aware of sources of health materials that have not been included, please share the information with OMH-RC by calling 1 800-444-6472.

Subject Topics

Adolescent Pregnancy Prevention

ABCD Boston Family Planning
March of Dimes Birth Defects Foundation
Office of Population Affairs Clearinghouse
Planned Parenthood of Summit, Portage, and Medina Counties

Aging

Alzheimer's Disease Education and Referral Center
American Association of Retired Persons

AIDS

AIDS Clinical Trials Information Service
AIDS Foundation Houston
AIDS Project Rhode Island
Aims Media
CDC National Prevention Information Network
Center for AIDS Prevention Studies
Channing L. Bete Company, Inc.
Education Programs Associates
Health Education Resource Organization
HIV/AIDS Treatment Information Service

National Clearinghouse for Primary Care Information
National Coalition of Hispanic Health and Human Services Organizations
National Consumers League
National Council of La Raza
National Institutes of Allergy and Infectious Diseases
National Maternal and Child Health Clearinghouse
National Women's Health Information Center
New York State Department of Health

Bibliographies

National Information Center on Health Services Research
National Library of Medicine
Scarecrow Press, Inc.

Breast Cancer

American Cancer Society
Cancer Information Service
Hartford Gay and Lesbian Health Center
National Women's Health Information Center
Y-ME National Breast Cancer Organization

Cancer

American Cancer Society
American Lung Association
Cancer Information Service
National Women's Health Information Center
New York State Department of Health

Child Health

March of Dimes Birth Defects Foundation
National Clearinghouse on Families and Youth
National Institute of Child Health and Human Development Clearinghouse
National Maternal and Child Health Clearinghouse

Consumer Information

Consumer Information Center
National Highway Traffic Safety Administration

U.S. Consumer Product Safety Commission

Cultural Competence

American Association of Retired Persons
Scarecrow Press, Inc

Diabetes

American Diabetes Association
National Diabetes Information Clearinghouse
National Council of La Raza

Digestive Diseases

National Digestive Diseases Information Clearinghouse

Disability

National Institute on Deafness and Other Communication Disorders
National Library Service for the Blind and Physically Handicapped
Parent Advocacy Coalition for Education Rights

Environmental Health

Environmental Protection Agency
Indoor Air Quality Information Clearinghouse

Eye Care

National Eye Institute

Family Planning

ABED Boston Family Planning
Education Programs Associates
Office of Population Affairs Clearinghouse
Planned Parenthood Federation of America, Inc
Planned Parenthood Golden Gate

Health Education

Fenway Community Health Center

National Coalition of Hispanic Health and Human Services Organizations
National Council of La Raza

Heart Disease

American Heart Association
National Council of La Raza
National Heart, Lung, and Blood Institute
National Women's Health Information Center
New York State Department of Health

Kidney Disease

National Kidney and Urologic Disease Information Clearinghouse

Lung Disease

American Lung Association
National Heart, Lung, and Blood Information Center

Lupus

Lupus Foundation of Northern California
National Institute of Arthritis and Musculoskeletal and Skin Diseases Information Clearinghouse

Mental Health

National Institute of Mental Health
National Mental Health Association

Migrant Health

Migrant Clinicians Network
National Center for Farmworker Health, Inc.

Nutrition

American Diabetes Association
American Dietetic Association
Cancer Information Service
National Dairy Council
National Heart, Lung, and Blood Institute
University of California

Oral Health

Dental Health Foundation
National Oral Health Information Center

Organ Transplant

National Minority Organ and Tissue Transplant Education Program

Osteoporosis

National Institutes of Health Osteoporosis and Related Bone Disease National Resource Center

Parenting

National Clearinghouse on Families and Youth
National Maternal and Child Health Clearinghouse

Pregnancy/Prenatal Care

ABCD Boston Family Planning
La Leche League International
March of Dimes Birth Defects Foundation
National Institute of Child Health and Human Development Clearinghouse
National Maternal and Child Health Clearinghouse

Reports

Commonwealth Fund
Grantmakers in Health
National Coalition of Hispanic Health and Human Services Organizations
National Council of La Raza
Office of Research on Women's Health

Sickle Cell Disease

Agency for Healthcare Research and Quality
American Sickle Cell Anemia Association
National Heart, Lung, and Blood Institute
National Maternal and Child Health Clearinghouse

Smoking/Tobacco

American Lung Association
Office on Smoking and Health

Substance Abuse

Al-Anon and Alateen
Alcoholics Anonymous
Hazelden Educational Materials
National Clearinghouse on Alcohol and Drug Information
National Council on Alcoholism and Drug Dependence
Wisconsin Clearinghouse for Prevention Resources

Women's Health

National Coalition of Hispanic Health and Human Services Organizations
National Council of La Raza
National Women's Health Information Center
New York State Department of Health
Office of Research on Women's Health

Organizations Offering Health Education Materials

ABCD Boston Family Planning

Action for Boston Community Development Inc.
178 Tremont St
Boston, MA 02111-1093
Tel: 617-357-6000 x 263
Fax: 617-357-6810

Distributes low-literacy contraceptive pamphlets providing step-by-step instructions for each method; birth control pills, IUD, diaphragms, vaginal contraceptive film, cervical caps, condoms, Norplant, Depo-Provera, and contraceptive foam. "AIDS Alert" section promotes condom use for disease prevention. Pamphlets are available in Spanish. Translations to Portuguese are in progress.

Agency for Healthcare Research and Quality (AHRQ)
AHRQ Publications Clearinghouse
P.O. Box 8547
Silver Spring, MD 20907-8547
Toll Free: 800-358-9295
TDD: 888-586-6340
Outside the U.S.: 410-381-3150
Fax: 301-594-2800
E-mail: info@ahrq.gov
Website: http://www.ahcpr.gov

"Sickle Cell Disease in Newborns and Infants: A Guide for Parents" is a brochure for consumers on sickle cell trait and disease, screening, and medical management published in English and Spanish. #AHCPR 93-0564. Also offers materials on pain management, depression, heart disease, smoking cessation, Alzheimer's disease, prostate cancer, and HIV.

AIDS Clinical Trials Information Service
P.O. Box 6421
Rockville, MD 20849-6421
Toll Free: 800-TRIALS-A
International Line: 301-519-0459
TTY/TDD: 888-480-3739
Fax: 301-519-6616
E-mail: actis@actis.org
Website: http://www.actis.org

Provides information on HIV treatment and clinical trials via bilingual service.

AIDS Foundation Houston
3202 Weslayan Annex
Houston, TX 77027
Toll Free: 888-524-AIDS
Tel: 713-623-6796
In Houston Hotline: 713-524-AIDS
Fax: 713-623-4029
E-mail: afh@aidshelp.org
Website: http://www.aidshelp.org

Offers two brochures for the Hispanic Community on HIV. "Think about It," is in Spanish and discusses what the virus is and how to protect yourself. "Be Smart about HIV," is also in Spanish and talks about HIV and how the virus is treated.

AIDS Project Rhode Island
232 West Exchange Street, 2nd Floor
Providence, RI 02903-1024
Tel: 401-831-5522
Hotline: 800-726-3010
Fax: 401-454-0299
Website: http://www.aidsprojectri.org

Distributes a newsletter in Spanish about AIDS to the Hispanic/Latino community of Rhode Island. Contact the agency for information on distribution.

Aims Media
9710 De Soto Avenue
Chatsworth, CA 91311
Toll Free: 818-773-4300

Distributes videos in Spanish for Hispanics/Latinos about AIDS, alcohol abuse, family violence, peer intervention, and other titles. Contact for a complete list of Spanish language materials.

Al-Anon and Alateen
1600 Corporate Landing Parkway
Virginia Beach, VA 23454-5617
Toll Free: 888-245-2666
Tel: 757-563-1600
Fax: 757-563-1655
E-mail: WSO@al-anon.org
Website: http://www.al-anon.alateen.org

Distributes a wide variety of publications on alcoholism in Spanish and Portuguese. Free Spanish language publications catalog and price list are available.

Alcoholics Anonymous
Grand Central Station, Box 459
New York, NY 10163
Tel: 212-870-3400
Fax: 212-870-3003
Website: http://www.alcoholics-anonymous.org

Publishes books and pamphlets. A free catalog of Spanish language materials and price listings are available.

Alzheimer's Disease Education and Referral Center
P.O. Box 8250
Silver Spring, MD 20907-8250
Toll Free: 800-438-4380
Tel: 301-495-3311
Fax: 301-495-3334
Website: http://www.alzheimers.org

Distributes fact sheets produced by the Suncoast Gerontology Center: "Boletin de la edad avanzada: Cuando alguien que usted conoce sufre de la enfermedad de Alzheimer" (Agelines: When someone you know suffers from Alzheimer's disease); "Boletin de la edad avanzada: Las siete senales de alarma de laenfermedad de Alzheimer" (Agelines: The seven warning signs of Alzheimer's disease), and "Edad y Novedad: La mala memoria no siempre es to que usted cree" (Age Page Forgetfulness: It's not always what you think). Also provides a brochure, "Seguridad en el hogar para el paciente con laenferniedad de Alzheimer" (Home safety for the Alzheimer's patient), on a cost recovery basis.

American Association of Retired Persons
601 E Street, NW
Washington, DC 20049
Toll Free: 800-424-3410
E-mail: member@aarp.org
Website: http://www.aarp.org

"A Profile of Older Americans" is a brochure provides demographic and health related information regarding older Americans including African Americans, Hispanics, Asian/Pacific Islanders, and American Indians.

American Cancer Society
National Headquarters
1599 Clifton Road NE
Atlanta, GA 30329
Toll Free: 800-ACS-2345 (800-227-2345)
Website: http://www.cancer.org

Offers a variety of documents in Spanish on cancer, cancer prevention, and treatment. Single copies are free. Contact for a complete of publications.

American Diabetes Association
1701 North Beauregard Street
Alexandria, VA 22311
Toll Free: 800-DIABETES (1-800-342-2383)
E-mail: customerservice@diabetes.org
Website: http://www.diabetes.org

Provides several titles in Spanish including topics on weight loss, eating right, and diabetes related foot health. Contact the American Diabetes Association for a complete list of publications.

American Dietetic Association
216 West Jackson Boulevard
Chicago, IL 60606-6995
Toll Free: 800-877-1600 ext. 5000
Tel: 312-899-0040
Fax: 312-899-4899
E-mail: sales@eatright.org
Website: http://www.eatright.org

Available in Spanish are 11 copy-ready fact sheets on topics including breastfeeding, feeding young children, food safety, physical activity, health, weight, lactose intolerance, calcium intake, and healthy eating with the pyramid. Cost is $14.95. Distributes materials in Spanish for professionals and clients, including "Como Escoger Alimentos Saludables" (Healthy Food Choices)—a handout/poster, and "Comp Vivir Mejor con VIH y con el SIDA: Una Gala para Alimentarse Sanamente" (Living Well with HIV and AIDS: A Guide to Healthy Eating), softbound. Produces Spanish language materials on breastfeeding, cholesterol, diabetes, pregnancy, and weight reduction. Also publishes "Mexican-American Food Practices, Customs, and Holidays," $8.50 each for ADA members, $10 each for non-members. Call for a free catalog.

American Heart Association
National Center
7272 Greenville Avenue
Dallas, Texas 75231
Tel: 800-AHA-USAI (800-242-8721)
Fax: 800-499-6464
E-mail: patientinfo@heart.org
Website: http://www.americanheart.org

"Heart and Stroke, 1991" is a report that provides annual statistics for heart disease, stroke, and other related diseases. It provides charts on mortality and morbidity in the general population and minority populations. It also offers statistics on behavioral risk factors, related surgeries, and hospital stays. Includes a biostatistical fact sheet, "Hispanics and Cardiovascular Diseases." Also offers many Spanish language publications such as: "Ataque al corazon y derrame cerebral: Senales y accion" (Heart Attack and Stroke: Signals and Action), "¿Por quo hater ejercicio?" (Why Exercise?), "Diez mandamientos para el paciente con alto presion arterial" (Ten Commandments for the Patient with High Blood Pressure); and "Como hater comida mexicana saludable para el corazon," (Making Mexican Food Heart Healthy). Contact for a complete publications list.

American Lung Association
1740 Broadway
New York, NY 10019
Toll Free: 800-LUNG-USA (800-586-4872)
Tel: 212-315-8700
E-mail: info@lungusa.org
Website: http://www.lungusa.org

Offers the following fact sheets "Hispanics and Tobacco" and "Hispanics and Lung Disease." Also offers "Lung Disease in Minorities, 98." "TB—lo quo usted debe saber" is designed to inform the Spanish speaking population about tuberculosis—Order #0200. Please contact the American Lung Association for a complete list of publications

American Sickle Cell Anemia Association

10300 Carnegie Avenue
Cleveland Clinic/East Office Building (EEb18)
Cleveland, OH 44106
Tel: 216-229-8600
Fax: 216-229-4300
Website: http://www.ascas.org

Call for a list of Spanish language materials.

Cancer Information Service

National Cancer Institute
31 Center Drive MSC-2580
Building 31, Room 10A16
Bethesda, MD 20892 2580
Toll Free: 800-4-CANCER (800-422-6237)
TTY: 800-332-8615
Fax: 301-330-1968
Website: http://cis.nci.nih.gov

Offers Spanish language materials on various treatments for cancer, clinical trials, healthy eating, mammograms, Pap smears, and other cancer related topics. Some of the titles are "Celebre la cocina Hispanic" (Healthy Hispanic Recipes), a bilingual booklet with healthy and nutritional recipes, #P929; "Rompa con el vico: Una guia para dejar de fumar," a self-help smoking cessation booklet, #P157; and "Hagase un mamograma...Por su salud y sy famila," a poster encouraging getting a mammogram, #G415. Also offers bookmarks with breast cancer facts for Hispanic women, #Z463. Two fact sheets offered include "Lung Cancer and Cigarette Smoking Facts among Men and Women of Different Races and Ethnic Groups" and "Racial Differences in Breast Cancer Survival."

CDC National Prevention Information Network

P.O. Box 6003
Rockville, MD 20849-6003
Toll Free: 800-458-5231
TTY: 800-243-7012
Fax: 888-282-7681
E-mail: info@cdcnpin.org
Website: http://www.cdcnpin.org

Provides information and materials on AIDS and AIDS-related organizations and their services. Spanish language publications distributed by CDC-NPIN include: “The Surgeon General’s Report on AIDS” and “Facts about AIDS,” available free and online. Other resources for AIDS-related Spanish language materials are available from NPIN. Distributes brochures, flyers, and fact sheets produced by the National Institute on Allergy and Infectious Diseases (NIAID). Also provides “Hispanics and HIV/AIDS Pathfinder: A Guide to Selected Resources.”

Center for AIDS Prevention Studies at the AIDS Research Institute
University of California, San Francisco
74 New Montgomery, Suite 600
San Francisco, CA 94105
Tel: 415-597-9100
Fax: 415-597-9213
E-mail: capsweb@psg.uscf.edu
Website: http://www.caps.ucsf.edu/

Offers many fact sheets on HIV/AIDS in both English and Spanish, including “What Are Latinos’ HIV Prevention Needs?” (17E) (Que Necesitan los Latinos en la Provencion del VIH?, 17S).

Channing L. Bete Company, Inc.
200 State Road
South Deerfield, MA 01373
Toll Free: 800-477-4776
Tel: 413-665-7611
Fax: 800-499-6464
E-mail: custsvcs@channing-bete.com
Website: http://www.channing-bete.com

Distributes scriptographic booklets and coloring books on more than 300 topics. Spanish language resources are available on the following subjects: alcohol and drug abuse, aging, contraception, pregnancy and childbirth, infant and child health, child abuse and neglect, cardiovascular diseases, domestic violence, mental health, nutrition, occupational safety, personal hygiene, physical fitness and exercise, prescription drugs, sexually transmitted diseases, smoking and smoking cessation, and women’s health. For price information and catalog of publications, contact the company.

Commonwealth Fund
One East 75th Street
New York, NY 10021-2692
Tel: 212-606-3800
Fax: 212-606-3500
E-mail: nb@cmwf.org
Website: http:///www.cmwf.org

"U.S. Minority Health: A Chartbook" is a report that compares the findings from several surveys and national data sources to provide a clear and graphics-based presentation of racial and ethnic disparities in health. Contact the Commonwealth Fund for pricing.

Consumer Information Center
GSA, Room 6142
18th & F Streets NW
Washington, DC 20405
Tel: 202-501-1794
Fax: 202-501-4281
E-mail: catalog.pueblo@gsa.gov
Website: www.pueblo.gsa.gov

Provides "La Lista," the Consumer Information Catalog in Spanish. Contact for complete list.

Dental Health Foundation
520 Third Street, Suite 205
Oakland, CA 94607
Tel: 510-663-3727
Fax: 510-663-3733
E-mail: tdhf@pacbell.net
Website: http://www.dentalhealthfoundation.org

Offers brochures on baby bottle tooth decay and fluoridation in both Spanish and English.

Education Program Associates
1 West Campbell Avenue, #45
Campbell, CA 95008-1004
Tel: 408-374-3720
Fax: 408-374-7385

"What is Right for You? Choosing a Birth Control Method" covers the basic information needed for informed consent. Publications on STDs/HIV include: "STDs: What You Need to Know" written in Spanish and English and a series of pamphlets, the "Infection Series" for those who have been diagnosed with an STD infection. Offers Spanish language IUD, pill, shot wallet cards, birth control consent forms, birth control information sheets, and pamphlets on sexually transmitted diseases, women's health, and prenatal care. Also offers a booklet, "Two Heads Are Better Than One," on male sexuality and responsibility. Contact EPA for complete list and pricing.

Environmental Protection Agency Information Resources Center
401 M Street, SW, Suite 3404
Washington, DC 20460
Tel: 202-260-5922
Fax: 202-260-5153
E-mail: library-hq@epamail.epa.gov
Website: http://www.epa.gov

Provides Spanish language materials. Contact for complete listing of publications.

Fenway Community Health Center
7 Haviland Street
Boston, MA 02115
Toll Free: 888-242-0900
Tel: 617-2267-0900
TTY: 617-859-1256
Fax: 617-247-3460
Website: http://www.fenwayhealth.org

Offers a patient guide and brochure in Spanish. Contact for a complete list.

Grantmakers in Health (GIH)
1100 Connecticut Avenue, Suite 1200
Washington, DC 20036
Tel: 202-452-8331
Fax: 202-452-8340
E-mail: mbackley@gih.org
Website: http://www.gih.org

"Eliminating Racial and Ethnic Disparities in Health: A Chartbook" presents data on the disparities in health among American racial and ethnic populations in the six health areas identified by President Clinton in the February 1998 radio address: infant mortality, cancer, heart disease, diabetes, HIV/AIDS, and immunizations. Data are also presented on risk factors, access to care, and minority participation in the health professions. Contact GIH for pricing information.

Hartford Gay and Lesbian Health Collective
P.O. Box 2094
1841 Broad Street
Hartford, CT 06415-2094
Tel: 860-278-4163
Fax: 860-278-5995
E-mail: info@hglhc.org
Website: http://www.hglhc.org

Provides information and materials on breast and cervical cancer in Spanish.

Hazelden Educational Materials
P.O. Box 11
Center City, MN 55012-0011
Toll Free: 800-257-7810
Tel: 612-257-4010
E-mail: info@hazelden.org
Website: http://www.hazelden.org

There are many Spanish language materials offered at Hazelden. Contact for a complete list. Some of the titles offered are "Libre de Adicciones (Free from Addictions) #6294, and "Alcoholics Anonymous—Big Book" #2130.

Health Education Resource Organization (HERO)
1734 Maryland Avenue
Baltimore, MD 21201
Tel: 410-685-1180
Fax: 410-752-3353

Offers "Como usar un condon" (How to use a condom) and "Enterate" (Get to Know about AIDS).

HIV/AIDS Treatment Information Service
P.O. Box 6303
Rockville, MD 20849-6303
Toll Free: 800-448-0440
TTY: 800-480-3739
Fax: 301-519-6616
International fax: 301-519-0459
E-mail: atis@hivatis.org
Website: http://www.hivatis.org

Provide materials on HIV/AIDS in Spanish and in English.

Indoor Air Quality Information Clearinghouse
P.O. Box 37133
Washington, DC 20013-7133
Toll Free: 800-438-4318
Tel: 703-356-4020
Fax: 703-356-5386
E-mail: iaqinfo@aol.com
Website: http://www.epa.gov/iaq

Provides the following "Proteja A Su Familia: Ese Humo Es Un Amenaza" (What You Can Do about Secondhand Smokers as Parents, Decision Makers, and Building Occupants) and "El Radon: Guia para su proteccion y la de su familia" (Protecting Your Family and Yourself from Carbon Monoxide Poisoning).

La Leche League International
P.O. Box 4079
1400 North Meacham Road
Schaumburg, IL 60168-4079
Tel: 847-519-7730
Fax: 847-519-0035
E-mail: prdept@llli.org
Website: http://www.lalecheleague.org

Distributes a range of materials in Spanish on maternal and child health topics that focus on breastfeeding. These include: the diabetic mother, working mother, increasing milk, inverted nipples, weaning, weight loss while nursing, lactation and women's sexuality, nursing twins, nursing an adopted baby, and sore breasts. Also provides breastfeeding information in Portuguese. A publications list is available free from the agency.

Lupus Foundation of Northern California
2635 North First Street, Suite 206
San Jose, CA 95134
Tel: 408-954-8600
Fax: 408-954-8129
E-mail: admin@thebalf.com
Website: http://www.balf.org

Provides a 30-minute educational video and a 50-page manual for instructors to teach. education classes in Spanish. Has a listing of over 20 articles in Spanish language.

March of Dimes Birth Defects Foundation
1275 Mamroneck Avenue
White Plains, NY 10605
Toll Free: 888-MODIMES (663-4637)
Tel: 914-428-7100
Fax: 914-997-4763
Website: http://www.modimes.org

Offers over 40 health information sheets in Spanish on issues related to pregnancy, birth defects, and perinatal loss. Also has various brochures and palm cards dealing with pregnancy, pre-term labor, folic acid, and other topics.

Migrant Clinicians Network
P.O. Box 164285
Austin, TX 78716
Tel: 512-327-2017
Fax: 512-327-0719
E-mail: webmaster@migrantclinicians.org
Website: http://www.migrantclinician.org

Offers the following manuals in Spanish, "Tuberculosis Tracking and Referral for Mobile Populations," "Eye Care," "Binational Tuberculosis," and Domestic Violence video and curriculum.

National Center for Farmworker Health, Inc.
P.O. Box 150009
Austin, TX 78715
Tel: 512-312-2700
Fax: 512-312-2600
E-mail: mckay@ncfh.org
Website: http://www.ncfh.org

The organization distributes a newsletter, "Farmworker News," a bilingual diabetic meal planning booklet, a bilingual patient education portfolio, materials on back pain, prenatal care, heatstroke, and several bilingual and Spanish EPA pesticide safety materials. Some titles include breast and cervical cancer, "Recuerdos para la vida/Reminders for Life" (#5695), and back pain "Me Duele la Espalda!/My Back Hurts" (#5696).

National Clearinghouse for Primary Care Information
2070 Chain Bridge Road, Suite 450
Vienna, VA 22182
Tel: 703-821-8955
TTY: 703-556-4831
Fax: 703-821-2098
E-mail: info@circsol.com
Website: http://www.circsol.com

Provides booklets in Spanish that describe HIV and AIDS and the basic facts that people with HIV should understand, providing care for AIDS patients at home and information on HIV and your child. Other Spanish titles include an English/Spanish Guide for Medical Personnel who work with Spanish clientele and a poster promoting vaccinations for children. Contact the clearinghouse directly for publication listing.

National Clearinghouse on Alcohol and Drug Information
Center for Substance Abuse Prevention
5600 Fishers Lane
Rockwall II Room 9D-10
Rockville, MD 20857
Toll Free: 800-729-6686
Tel: 301-443-0365
E-mail: nnadal@samhsa.gov
Website: http://www.samhsa.gov/csap/index.htm

Provides a prevention resource guide on substance abuse for Hispanics. Contact for additional information on Spanish language materials.

National Clearinghouse on Families and Youth
P.O. Box 13505
Silver Spring, MD 20911-3505
Tel: 301-608-8098
Fax: 301-608-8721
Website: http://www.ncfy.com

"Como Apoyar a un Hijo Adolescente: Sugerencias para los Padres" (Supporting Your Adolescent: Tips for Parents). Provides "A Guide to Enhancing the Cultural Competence of Runaway and Homeless Youth Programs."

National Coalition of Hispanic Health and Human Services Organizations (COBS-MHOS)
1501 16th Street, NW
Washington, DC 20036-1401
Tel: 202-387-5000
Fax: 202-797-4353
E-mail: alliance@hispanichealth.org
Website: http://www.hispanichealth.org

COSSHMO offers publications and reports on the health status of Hispanics in the United States. Also provides the book, "¡Salud! A Latina's Guide to Total Health—Body, Mind, and Spirit." Contact for a complete publications list.

National Consumers League
1701 K Street, NW, Suite 1201
Washington, DC 20006
Tel: 202-835-3323
Fax: 202-835-0747
E-mail: info@nclnet.org
Website: http://www.ntlconsumersleague.org

Distributes these new brochures "La interaccion de Drogas y Alimentos," "Take care with..." (series of 6 brochures, easy to read, on over-the-counter medications), "AIDS: Women at risk," "No todas las medicinal se deben mezclar: Previniendo la interaccion de las drogas," and "Dolores de cabeza" (headaches). The brochures cost $1, and bulk discounts are available.

National Council of La Raza
1111 19th Street, NW, Suite 1000
Washington, DC 20036
Toll Free: 800-311-6257
Tel: 202-785-1670
Fax: 202-785-0851
Website: http://www.nclr.org

Offers publications and reports on HIV/AIDS, farmworker health issues, heart disease, diabetes, and other topics. Contact for a complete list of publications.

National Council on Alcoholism and Drug Dependence
12 West 21st Street, 7th Floor
New York, NY 10410
Tel: 212-206-6770
Hope Line: 800-NCA-CALL (24 hour affiliate referral)
Fax: 212-645-1690
E-mail: national@ncadd.org
Website: http://www.ncadd.org

Distributes a pamphlet, "¿Quien Tiene: EI Poder El Alcohol o Tu?" and a poster, "Don't Let Drinking Take Your Power Away," in Spanish and English. Single copies are free.

National Dairy Council
Order Department
3030 Airport Road
La Crosse, WI 54603
Toll Free: 800-426-8271
Fax: 800-974-6455
E-mail: ndc@bsmg.com
Website: http://www.nationaldairycouncil.org

Offers "Guia-para la buena alimentacion" (Guide to good eating). A publications catalog and price list are available from the agency.

National Diabetes Information Clearinghouse
1 Information Way
Bethesda, MD 20892-3560
Tel: 301-654-3327
Fax: 301-907-8906
E-mail: dk_ocpl@extra.niddk.nih.gov
Website: http://www.niddk.nih.gov/ndic

Provides a fact sheet, “Diabetes in Hispanic Americans” (DM-114, English). Also provides booklets in Spanish on diet and diabetes; DM-190, DM-191, DM-192. Develops and distributes publications about diabetes written in Spanish language. Maintains a database of patient and professional education materials that contain Spanish. Contact for complete list.

National Digestive Diseases Information Clearinghouse
2 Information Way
Bethesda, MD 20892-3570
Tel: 301-654-3910
Fax: 301-907-8906
Website: http://www.niddk.nih.gov

Offers the following in Spanish—“H. pyloriy Ulcera Peptica” (DD–182, H. pylor iand Peptic Ulcer) and “Lo que necesito saber sobre la Hepatitis A, B, y C” (What I need to know about Hepatitis A, B and C). Also provides bibliographic database searches on Spanish language materials and “Digestive Diseases in Minority Populations.”

National Eye Institute
2020 Vision Place
Bethesda, MD 20892-3655
Tel: 301-496-5248
Fax: 301-402-1065
Website: http://www.nei.nih.gov

“¡Ojo con su vision!” is a “fotonovela” explaining the risk of diabetic eye disease. Includes a place for the patients to track the results of eye exams. “¿Cuanto sabe sobra la enfermedad diabetica del ojo? Tome esta pueba” (Diabetic Eye Disease Eye-Q Test) is a 10-question true-false quiz that can help Hispanics with diabetes learn more about diabetic eye disease. Contact for a complete publications list.

National Heart, Lung, and Blood Institute
NHLBI Information Center
P.O. Box 30-105
Bethesda, MD 20824-0105
Tel: 301-592-8573
Fax: 301-592-8563
Website: http://www.nhlbi.nih.gov/health/infoctr/index.htm

Offers several Spanish language titles including "El asma: como controlar esta enfermedad," the Spanish equivalent of "Facts about Controlling Your Asthma," and "Datos Sobre La Anemia Falciforme" (Facts about Sickle Cell Anemia). Also provides "Delicious Heart-Healthy Latino Recipes," as well as materials on smoking cessation, high blood pressure, and obesity. "An Ounce of Prevention: A Guide to Heart Health," a bilingual guide, is a simple, entertaining, and colorful photonovela with five brief stories on how to prevent heart disease. It features tips on ways the Ramirez family has made lifestyle changes to protect their hearts with proper heart health. Each story includes a workbook segment to help the readers write down their personal pledges to improve their heart health and chart their own progress. Contact the Information Center for a complete publications list.

National Highway Traffic Safety Administration Department of Transportation
400 Seventh Street SW, NTS-13
Washington, DC 20590
Toll Free: 800-424-9393
Tel: 202-366-0123
TTY: 800-424-9153
Fax: 202-493-2062
E-mail: kklass@nhtsa.dot.gov
Website: http://www.nhtsa.dot.gov/

Provides single copies of two posters in Spanish: "Bienvenidos a Safetyville" (Welcome to Safetyville) and "¿Quienes de Estos Ninos Deben Viajar En Asientos Infantiles para Automoviles? Todos!" (Which of these Children Should Be in a Car Seat? All of Them!). Also distributes single copies of bilingual and Spanish-language brochures and flyers on transportation safety.

National Information Center on Health Services Research
Building 38A, RM 4S-410, Mail Stop 20
8600 Rockville Pike
Bethesda, MD 20894
Tel: 301-496-0176
Fax: 301-402-3193
E-mail: nichsr@nlm.nih.gov
Website: http://www.nlm.nih.gov/nichsr/nichsr.html

HealthSTAR database can be accessed for literature citations.

National Institute of Allergy and Infectious Diseases
Building 31, Room 7A–50
31 Center Drive, MSC 2520
Bethesda, MD 20892-2520
Tel: 301-496-5717
Fax: 301-402-0120
E-mail: lf7j@nih.gov
Website: http://www.niaid.nih.gov

Provides Spanish language materials on HIV, toxoplasmosis, and AIDS related diseases. Call for a complete list.

National Institute of Arthritis and Musculoskeletal and Skin Diseases Information Clearinghouse
National Institutes of Health
1 AMS Circle
Bethesda, MD 20892-3675
Tel: 301-495-4484
Fax: 301-718-6366
TTY: 301-565-2966
E-mail: niamsINFO@mail.nih.gov
Website: http://www.nih.gov/niams/

Offers "El Puiso dela Salud: Lupus" (Spanish magazine reprint, regular print), as well as "LUPUS: A Patient Care Guide for Nurses and Other Health Professionals."

National Institute of Child Health and Human Development Clearinghouse
P.O. Box 3006
Rockville, MD 20847
Toll Free: 800-370-2743
Fax: 301-954-1473
Website: http://www.nichd.nih.gov

Distributes a brochure "Proteja a su bebe del sindrome de muerte infantil subita (smis)" (Reduce the risk of Sudden Infant Death Syndrome), and "El Sindrome de Downs" (Facts about Down's Syndrome). Also offers a brochure "Milk Matters for Your Child's Health" in Spanish.

National Institutes of Health Osteoporosis and Related Bone Diseases National Resource Center
1232 22nd Street, NW
Washington, DC 20037-1292
Toll Free: 800-624-BONE
Tel: 202-223-0344
Fax: 202-293-2356
TTY: 202-466-4315
E-mail: orbdnrc@nof.org
Website: http://www.osteo.org

Offers a fact sheet "Tiene sus huesos sanos? Lo que la mujer latina debe saber sobre la osteoporosis." Available in both large and regular print versions. Other fact sheets include "Are your bones healthy: What Latino Women Should Know about Osteoporosis" and "Latino Women and Osteoporosis." A bibliography "Osteoporosis Research in Hispanic Populations" is also available.

National Institute of Mental Health
6001 Executive Boulevard
Room 8184, MSC 9663
Bethesda, MD 20892-9663 U.S.A.
Tel: 301-443-4513
Fax: 301-443-4279
Website: http://www.nimh.nih.gov

Offers facts sleets on mental health in Spanish. Some titles includes "Pro Depresion" (Depression), "Trastornos de Ansiedad" (Anxiety Disorders), "Trastorno Obsesivo Compulsivo" (Obsessive-Compulsive Disorders), and "Trastorno Hiperactivo de Deficit cit de Atencif" (Attention Deficit Hyperactivity Disorder). Contact for a complete publications list.

National Institute on Deafness and Other Communication Disorders
Information Clearinghouse
1 Communication Avenue
Bethesda, MD 20892-3456
Toll Free: 800-241-1044
TTY: 800-241-1055
Fax: 301-907-8830
E-mail: nidcdinfo@nidcd.nih.gov
Website: http://www.nih.gov/nidcd

Provides some information on deafness and disability in Spanish. Contact agency for additional information and listings

National Kidney and Urologic Diseases
Information Clearinghouse
3 Information Way
Bethesda, MD 20892-3580
Tel: 301-654-4415
Fax: 301-097-8906
E-mail: nkudic@aerie.com
Website: http://www.niddk.nih.gov

Offers the booklet "Insuficiencia Renal Cronica Terminal: Eleccion del Tratamiento que le Conviene a Usted" (KU-54 End-Stage Renal Disease: Choosing a Treatment That's Right for You). "Impotencia" (KU-129—Impotence) is also offered in fact sheet format. Also provides a bibliographic search on "Foreign Language Materials on Kidney and Urologic Diseases."

National Library of Medicine
8600 Rockville Pike
Bethesda, MD 20894
Toll Free: 888-346-3656
Tel: 301-594-5983
Fax: 301-496-2809
E-mail: custserv@nlm.nih.gov
Website: http://www.nlm.nih.gov/

National Library of Medicine collects worldwide medical literature in all languages as well as health information on various minority and ethnic groups. Call for specific topics.

National Library Service for the Blind and Physically Handicapped
Library of Congress
1291 Taylor Street, NW
Washington, DC 20542
Tel: 202-707-5100
TDD: 202-707-0744
Fax: 202-707-0712
E-mail: nls@loc.gov
Website: http://lcweb.loc.gov/nls

Provides some brochures on reading, talking books, and other topics in Spanish. Call for additional information.

National Maternal and Child Health Clearinghouse
2070 Chain Bridge Road, Suite 450
Vienna, VA 22182-2536
Toll Free: 888-434-4MCH
Tel: 703-356-1964
Fax: 703-821-2098
E-mail: nmchc@circsol.com
Website: http://www.nmchc.org

Offers "¡Los ninos pequenos se pueden estrangular accidentalmente en los bucles de los cordones de las ventanas!" (Young Children Can Strangle on Looped Window Cords!) #J111, "Explorando una Alimentacion Saludable: Actividades para los Padres a Hijos en Conjunto" (Exploring Healthy Eating: Activities for Parents and Children Together) #K086, and many other topics in Spanish language. Contact for a complete publications list.

National Mental Health Association
Order Department
1021 Prince Street
Alexandria, VA 22314-2971
Toll Free: 800-969-NMHA
Tel: 703-684-7722
TTY: 800-433-5959
Fax: 703-684-5968
Website: http://www.nmha.org

"La Salud Mental Es 1-2-3" describes the characteristics of a mentally healthy person, #264. "La Familia Jiminez Responde a Sus Preguntas Sobre la Depresion Clinica," discusses clinical depression, its treatments, and sources of help. Call for a complete publications and pricing list.

National Minority Organ and Tissue Transplant Education Program (MOTTEP)
Howard University Hospital
Ambulatory Care Center
2041 Georgia Avenue, NW, Suite 3100
Washington, DC 20060
Toll Free: 800-393-2839
Tel: 202-865-4888
Fax: 202-865-4880
E-mail: ccallender@fac.howard.edu

Provides information on the need for organ transplantation and donation in minority communities.

National Oral Health Information Clearinghouse
One NOHIC Way
Bethesda, MD 20892-3500
Tel: 301-462-7364
Fax: 301-907-8830
TDD: 301-656-7581
E-mail: nidr@aerie.com
Website: http://www.aerie.com/nohicweb

Distributes materials produced by the National Institute of Dental and Craniofacial Research (NIDCR). Titles include "Meriendas Sanas para Dientes Sanos" (Snack Smart for Healthy Teeth) #NR-39, "Una Boca Saludable Para Su Bebe" (A Healthy Mouth for Your Baby) #NR-26, "Diabetes: Consejos Dentales" (Diabetes: Dental Tips) #OP-10, and "Prevenga el Dano Que Causa el Biberon (Prevent Baby Bottle Tooth Decay). Call for a complete list.

National Women's Health Information Center
8550 Arlington Boulevard, Suite 300
Fairfax, VA 22031
Toll Free: 800-994-WOMAN (994-9662)
TDD: 888-220-5446
Fax: 703-560-6598
E-mail: 4woman@soza.com
Website: http://www.4woman.org

Offers the following fact sheets on Hispanic women's health issues: "Autoimmune Disease," "Breast Cancer: Increasing 5-Year Survival Rates in Hispanic Women," "Cardiovascular Disease in Hispanic

Women," "Diabetes Mellitus in Hispanic Women," "Hispanic Women and HIV/AIDS," "Hypertension/High Blood Pressure: A Silent Killer of Hispanic Women," and "Problems with Health Care Access: Hispanic Women." Also provides Spanish language information. "The Health of Minority Women" fact sheet addresses socioeconomic and cultural issues as well as health system barriers which limit minority women's access to preventive health care and diagnostic and treatment services. Contact the Center for a complete list of publications, reports, and documents, both in English and Spanish.

New York State Department of Health
Publications
Box 2000
Albany, NY 12220
Tel: 518-474-5370
E-mail: telecom.directory@ogs.state.ny.us
Website: http://www.health.state.ny.us/home.html

Offers many publications on health issues ranging from AIDS to cancer, and heart disease to women's health. Provides materials in Albanian, Amheric, Arabic, Chinese, English, French, Greek, Haitian, Hebrew, Hindi, Hmong, Italian, Japanese, Laotian, Polish, Romanian, Russian, Spanish, Urdu, Vietnamese, and Yiddish. Call for a free publications catalog.

Office of Population Affairs Clearinghouse (OPA)
P.O. Box 30696
4350 East West Highway
Suite 200 West
Bethesda, MD 20814
Tel: 301-654-6190
Fax: 301-215-7731
E-mail: opa@osophs.dhhs.gov
Website: http://www.hhs.gov/progorg/opa

Provides facts sheets on topics ranging from sterilization to Pap smears, alcohol, drugs, and pregnancy in Spanish. Some titles offered include "Informacion para el Hombre sobre la Esterilizacion" (Male Sterilization Brochure), "Informacion para la Mujer sobre la Esterilizacion" (Female Sterilization Brochure), "¿Que Es La Prueba Pap?" (What Is a Pap Smear?), and "¿Embarazada? Tomar Drogas o Alcohol Puede Danar..." (Pregnant? Drugs & Alcohol Can Hurt Your

Unborn Baby). Also offers a video on HIV and Hispanics. Contact OPA for a complete publications list.

Office of Research on Women's Health

Office of the Director
National Institutes of Health
1 Center Drive, Room 201, MSC 0161
Bethesda, MD 20892-0161
Tel: 301-402-1770
Fax: 301-402-1798
Website: http://www4.od.nih.gov/orwh/orwhpubs.html

"Women of Color Health Data Book: Adolescents to Seniors" examines the role of culture, ethnicity, race, socioeconomic background, geographic location, and other social and economic factors as important contributors to health status.

Office on Smoking and Health

CDC/NCCDPHP
Mail Stop K-50
4770 Buford Highway, NE
Atlanta, GA 30341-3724
Toll Free: 800-CDC-1311 (800-232-1311)
General information/publication requests: 770-488-5705
Tel: 770-488-5707
Fax: 770-488-2552
E-mail: tobacco@cdc.gov
Website: http://www.cdc.gov/tobacco

Provides a fact sheet "Hispanics and Tobacco,"(English). Also has the Surgeon General's Report, "Tobacco Use Among U.S. Racial/Ethnic Minority Groups." A citation database is also available for the latest tobacco related information and research.

Parent Advocacy Coalition for Educational Rights

4826 Chicago Avenue South
Minneapolis, MN 55417-1098
Toll Free: 800-53-PACER (in MN) or 888-248-0822 (nationally)
Tel: 612-827-2966
TDD: 612-827-7770
E-mail: pacer@pacer.org
Website: http://www.pacer.org

Provides books in Spanish for parents of children with disabilities.

Planned Parenthood Federation of America, Inc.
Marketing Department
810 Seventh Avenue
New York, NY 10010
Tel: 212-541-7800
Fax: 212-245-1845
E-mail: communications@ppfa.org
Website: http://www.plannedparenthood.org

Offers publications on family planning: "Anticoncepcion de Emergencia" (Emergency Contraception) and "Tus Alternativas Anticonceptivas" (Methods of Contraception). For additional information, contact the agency.

Planned Parenthood Golden Gate
815 Eddy Street, 3rd Floor
San Francisco, CA 94109
Tel: 415-441-7858
E-mail: info@ppgg.org
Toll Free: 800-967-7526

Brochures in Spanish are available on numerous topics including birth control methods, sexually transmitted diseases, and vaginal discharges and infections. For price and shipping information, contact the organization at the number listed above.

Scarecrow Press, Inc.
4720 Boston Way
Lanham, MD 20706
Toll Free: 800-462-6420
Tel: 301-459-3366
Fax: 301-459-1705
Website: http://www.scarecrowpress.com

Offers "Ethnic Minority Health: A Selected Annotated Bibliography," a guide that encompasses in one volume various minority health issues for the four major U.S. ethnic minority groups (Native Americans/Alaska Natives, African Americans, Hispanic Americans, and Asian/Pacific Islander Americans). Features nine quick access sections that are divided first by material format or broad subject area and then by ethnic group. (ISBN: 0-8108-3225-9)

University of California
Cooperative Extension in Alameda County
1131 Harbor Bay Parkway, Suite 131
Alameda, CA 94502
Tel: 510-567-6812
Fax: 510-567-6813
E-mail: cealameda@ucdavis.edu

Provides materials on nutrition and diet in Spanish.

U.S. Consumer Product Safety Commission
Publication Request
Office of Information and Public Affairs
U.S. Consumer Product Safety Commission
Washington, DC 20207
Toll Free: 800-638-2772
Fax on demand: 301-504-0051
Website: http://www.cpsc.gov

Provides the following: "Locked-up Poisons"—#382S, "Home Safety Checklist for Older Consumers"—#702S, "Protect Your Family from Lead in Your Home"—#426S. Additional publications include Childcare Safety (242S), Poison Lookout (383S), Toy Safety (281S), and Childproofing Your Home (252S). Call for complete list.

Wisconsin Clearinghouse for Prevention Resources
University of Wisconsin-Madison
1552 University Avenue
Madison, WI 53705-4085
Toll Free: 800-322-1468
Tel: 608-262-9157
Fax: 608-262-6346
Website: http://www.uhs.wisc.edu/wch/

"Los Ninos y Las Drogas" (Young Children and Drugs: What Parents Can Do) offers guidelines on raising healthy children, parent role modeling, building self-esteem, effective communication, and how to avoid alcohol and other drugs. "Autoexamen Para El/Los Padre(s) Una Guia para Ayudar a Padres Evaluar el propio use de Substancias Quimicas" is a brief questionnaire (22 questions) to help focus on alcohol and other drug-related attitudes and behaviors, which children are likely to copy from their parents. "Como Pueden Los Padres Ayudar A Sus, Hijos Con Problemas De Alcohol Y Otras Drogas" is a pamphlet that gives warning signs of AODA problems, tips for communication, and information on where to find help. Contact for a complete list of publications in Spanish.

Y-ME, National Breast Cancer Organization
212 West Van Buren, 4th Floor
Chicago, IL 606-3908
Toll Free: 800-221-2141
Latina Breast Cancer Hotline: 800-986-9505
E-mail: nabcoinfo@aol.com
Website: http://www.nabco.org

Offers a bilingual newsletter, "Noticias Latinas," which looks at the latest developments in breast cancer diagnosis and treatment. Y-Me also offers almost all of its publications and information in Spanish. Call for a complete list of Spanish language materials.

Section 44.5

Pacific Islanders

"1999 Sources of Health Education Materials," Office of Minority Health Resource Center (OMH-RC).

Pacific Islanders, combined with Asians, account for 4 percent of the U.S. population according to the current U.S. Bureau of Census Population estimates. By the year 2010, there will be close to 15 million Asian and Pacific Islanders, 5 percent of the total U.S. population.

The search for publications concentrated on the minority health priority identified by the DHHS Secretary's Task Force on Black and Minority Health—cancer, chemical dependency, diabetes, heart disease and stroke, infant mortality, homicide, suicide, and unintentional injuries, and the associated risk factors. Although this resource list indicates some of what is available, it is important to note that some materials were not identified in some subject areas. There is a need to develop additional materials to address these "gaps."

The following list includes culturally sensitive health materials for Pacific Islanders as well as materials in various Pacific Islander languages. Includes resources on nutrition, exercise, and AIDS educational materials. Although as many publications as possible are included, this guide is not a comprehensive listing of all such materials.

Organizations included in the this listing should be contacted. directly to determine the cost and availability of bulk quantities for permission to copy.

The Office of Minority Health Resource Center has not evaluated the materials included in the resource list. It is the responsibility of the reader to review the materials to determine their appropriateness for the intended audience. Inclusion does not imply endorsement by the OMH-RC, the Office of Minority Health, the U.S. Public Health Service, or the U.S. Department of Health and Human Services.

OMH-RC is continually seeking health information resources for the U.S. minority populations. If you are aware of sources of health materials that have not been included, please share the information with OMB-RC by calling 1-800-444-6472.

Subject Topics

Aging

American Association of Retired Persons
National Asian Pacific Center on Aging

AIDS

AIDS Community Care Team
AIDS Education Project
Association of Asian Pacific Community Health Organizations
Big Island AIDS Project
CDC National Prevention Information Network
Center for AIDS Prevention Studies
Hawaii AIDS Research Department
Hawaii State Health Department
National Women's Health Information Center

Bibliographies

Asian and Pacific Islander American Health Forum, Inc.
National Information Center on Health Services Research

National Library of Medicine
Scarecrow Press, Inc

Breast Cancer

Agency for Healthcare Research and Quality
American Cancer Society
Asian and Pacific Islander American Health Forum, Inc.

Cancer

American Cancer Society
American Lung Association
Cancer Information Service
Hawaii State Health Department
National Women's Health Information Center

Child Health

Asian Community Mental Health Services
Association of Asian Pacific Community Health Organizations
National Clearinghouse on Families and Youth
National Maternal and Child Health Clearinghouse

Cultural Competence

American Association of Retired Persons
Scarecrow Press, Inc

Diabetes

Hawaii State Health Department
National Diabetes Information Clearinghouse

Digestive Diseases

National Digestive Diseases Information Clearinghouse

Health Education

Kalihi Palama Health Center
Papa Ola Lokahi
Waianae Coast Comprehensive Health Center

Heart Disease

American Heart Association
Hawaii State Health Department
National Women's Health Information Center

Hepatitis

Asian Pacific Health Care Venture, Inc.
Association of Asian Pacific Community Health Organization
National Maternal and Child Health Clearinghouse

Kidney Disease

National Kidney and Urologic Disease Information Clearinghouse

Lung Disease

American Lung Association

Mental Health

Asian Community Mental Health Services
National Asian Pacific American Families Against Substance Abuse

Nutrition

American Dietetic Association

Oral Health

Dental Health Foundation

Organ Transplant

National Minority Organ and Tissue Transplant Education Program

Parenting

National Clearinghouse on Families and Youth
National Maternal and Child Health Clearinghouse

Post-Traumatic Stress Disorder

National Center for Post-Traumatic Stress Disorder

Reports

Asian and Pacific Islander American Health Forum, Inc.
Commonwealth Fund
Grantmakers in Health
Office of Research on Women's Health

Smoking/Tobacco

Agency for Healthcare Research and Quality
American Lung Association
Office on Smoking and Health

Substance Abuse

Alcoholics Anonymous
Asian Community Mental Health Services
Coalition for a Drug-Free Hawaii
National Asian Pacific American Families Against Substance Abuse
National Clearinghouse on Alcohol and Drug Information
National Council on Alcoholism and Drug Dependence
Native Hawaiian Safe and Drug-Free Schools/Communities Program
Pacific Asian Alcohol and Drug Program

Thalessemia

Association of Asian Pacific Community Health Organizations

Women's Health

Asian and Pacific Islander American Health Forum, Inc.
National Women's Health Information Center
Office of Research on Women's Health

Organizations Offering Health Education Resources

Agency for Healthcare Research and Quality (AHRQ)
AHRQ Publications Clearinghouse
P.O. Box 8547
Silver Spring, MD 20907-8547
Toll Free: 800-358-9295
TDD: 888-586-6340
Outside the U.S.: 410-381-3150
Fax: 301-594-2800
E-mail: info@ahrq.gov
Website: http://www.ahcpr.gov

Provides mammogram information and smoking cessation information in Tagalog.

AIDS Community Care Team
1314 South King Street, Suite 964
Honolulu, HI 96813
Tel: 808-521-0077

A consortium of 10 direct service providers in social services. Call for publications.

AIDS Education Project University of Hawaii
Department of Psychiatry
1319 Punahou Street, Suite 625
Honolulu, HI 96826
Tel: 808-941-6322
Fax: 808-942-5725

Offers a training tape on AIDS in Hawaii, available only within the state of Hawaii. Call for details.

Alcoholics Anonymous
Grand Central Station
Box 459
New York, NY 10163
Tel: 212-870-3400
Fax: 212-870-3003
Website: http://www.alcoholics-anonymous.org

Publishes books and pamphlets. A free catalog of materials and price listings are available:

American Association of Retired Persons
601 E Street, NW
Washington, DC 20049
Toll Free: 800-424-3410
E-mail: member@aarp.org
Website: http://www.aarp.org

"A Profile of Older Americans" is a brochure that provides demographic and health-related information regarding older Americans including African Americans, Hispanics, Asian/ Pacific Islanders, and American Indians.

American Cancer Society
Hawaiian Division
2370 Nuuanu Avenue
Honolulu, HI 96817
Toll Free: 800-ACS-2345 (800-227-2345)
Tel: 808-595-7544
E-mail: mbustama@cancer.org
Website: http://www.hi-cancer.org

Contact for Pacific Islander specific materials.

American Cancer Society
National Headquarters
1599 Clifton Road NE
Atlanta, GA 30329
Toll Free: 800-ACS-2345 (800-227-2345)
Website: http://www.cancer.org

Contact your local American Cancer Society for Pacific Islander specific materials.

American Dietetic Association
216 West Jackson Boulevard
Chicago, IL 60606-6995
Toll Free: 800-877-1600 ext. 5000
Tel: 312-899-0040
Fax: 312-899-4899
E-mail: sales@eatright.org
Website: http://www.eatright.org

Distributes materials for professionals and clients, including "Ethnic and Regional Food Practices: Filipino American Food Practices, Customs, and Holidays," a professional guide, $8.50 for ADA members, $10 for non-members. Call for a free catalog.

American Heart Association
National Center
7272 Greenville Avenue
Dallas, Texas 75231
Toll Free: 800-AHA-USAI (800-242-8721)
Fax: 800-499-6464
E-mail: patientinfo@heart.org
Website: http://www.americanheart.org

"Heart and Stroke, 1999" is a report that provides annual statistics for heart disease, stroke, and other related diseases. It provides charts on mortality and morbidity in the general population and minority populations. It also offers statistics on behavioral risk factors, related surgeries, and hospital stays. Includes a biostatistical fact sheet, "Asian/Pacific Islanders and Cardiovascular Diseases."

American Lung Association
1740 Broadway
New York, NY 10019
Toll Free: 800-LUNG-USA (800-586-4872)
Tel: 212-315-8700
E-mail: info@lungusa.org
Website: http://www.lungusa.org

Offers a fact sheet, "Asian and Pacific Islanders and Tobacco" as well as "Lung Disease in Minorities, 98." Please contact for a complete list of publications.

Asian and Pacific Islander American Health Forum, Inc.
942 Market Street, Suite 200
San Francisco, CA 94102
Tel: 415-954-9988
Fax: 415-954-9999
E-mail: hforum@apiahf.org
Website: http://www.apiahf.org

Offers reports, bibliographies, and newsletters on Asian and Pacific Islander health issues. Provides a fact sheet on cancer, as well as fact sheets on women's health and chronic disease, access and utilization of health services, and maternal and child health.

Asian Community Mental Health Services
310 8th Street, Suite 201
Oakland, CA 94607
Tel: 510-451-6729
Fax: 510-268-0202
E-mail: email@acmhs.org
Website: http://www.acmhs.org

Publishes pamphlets and booklets on substance abuse prevention—child and parent versions in Cambodian, Chinese, Laotian, Tagalog, and Vietnamese.

Asian Pacific Health Care Venture, Inc.
1530 Hillhurst Avenue, Suite 200
Los Angeles, CA 90027
Tel: 213-346-0370
Fax: 213-346-0373

Materials for distribution available from APHCV include "Understanding Hepatitis B" and "Join Our Forces Against Hepatitis B" in English, Chinese, Korean, Thai, and Cambodian.

Association of Asian Pacific Community Health Organizations
1440 Broadway, Suite 510
Oakland, CA 94612
Tel: 510-272-9536
Fax: 510-272-0817
E-mail: aapcho@egroups.com
Website: http://aapcho.org

Distributes a videotape about AIDS in different languages (English, Cantonese, Cambodian, Korean, Laotian, Mandarin, Mien, Samoan, Tagalog, and Vietnamese), brochures on hepatitis (Chinese, English, Korean, Laotian, Samoan, Tagaiog, and Vietnamese), thalassemia (Chinese, English, Korean, Laotian, Samoan, Tagalog, and Vietnamese), and parental guide on childhood illness (Chinese, English, Korean, Laotian, Samoan, Tagalog, and Vietnamese).

Big Island AIDS Project
P.O. Box 11510
Hilo, Hawaii 96721
Tel: 808-935-6711
Fax: 808-969-9329

Provides culturally appropriate materials on HIV/AIDS for Pacific Islanders. Please contact for additional information.

CDC National Prevention Information Network
P.O. Box 6003
Rockville, MD 20849-6003
Toll Free: 800-458-5231
TTY: 800-243-7012
Fax: 888-282-7681
E-mail: info@cdcnpin.org
Website: http://www.cdcnpin.org

Provides fact sheets on HIV/AIDS and Asian and Pacific Islanders.

Cancer Information Service
National Cancer Institute
31 Center Drive MSC-2580
Building 31, Room 10A16
Bethesda, MD 20892-2580
Toll Free: 800-4-CANCER (800-422-6237)
TTY: 800-332-8615
Fax: 301-330-1968
Website: http://cis.nci.nih.gov

Two fact sheets offered, "Lung Cancer and Cigarette Smoking Facts among Men and Women of Different Races and Ethnic Groups" and "Racial Differences in Breast Cancer Survival."

Center for AIDS Prevention Studies at the AIDS Research Institute
University of California, San Francisco
74 New Montgomery, Suite 600
San Francisco, CA 94105
Tel: 415-597-9100
Fax: 415-597-9213
E-mail: capsweb@psg.uscf.edu
Website: http://www.caps.ucsf.edu/

Offers many fact sheets on HIV/AIDS including "What Are Asian and Pacific Islander HIV Prevention Needs?" (33E). In Tagalog, "Ano ang mga pangangailangan ng mga Asyano at Pacific Islander tungkol sa HIV prevention?" (33T).

Drug Addiction Services of Hawaii, Inc. (DASH)
1130 North Nimitz Highway, Suite #C-302
Honolulu, HI 96817
Tel: 808-538-0704

Conducts an ongoing statewide educational campaign to reduce, and ultimately prevent, drug use, and to increase capacities to create drug-free environments in schools, homes, and workplaces. Contact for curriculum materials.

Commonwealth Fund
One East 75th Street
New York, NY 10021-2692
Tel: 212-606-3800
Fax: 212-606-3500
E-mail: nb@cmwf.org
Website: http://www.cmwf.org

"U.S. Minority Health: A Chartbook" is a report that compares the findings from several surveys and national data sources to provide a clear and graphics-based presentation of racial and ethnic disparities in health. Contact the Commonwealth Fund for pricing.

Dental Health Foundation
520 Third Street, Suite 205
Oakland, CA 94607
Tel: 510-663-3727
Fax: 510-663-3733
E-mail: tdhf@pacbell.net
Website: http://www.dentalhealthfoundation.org

Offers brochures on baby bottle tooth decay.

Grantmakers in Health (GIH)
1100 Connecticut Avenue, Suite 1200
Washington, DC 20036
Tel: 202-452-8331
Fax: 202-452-8340
E-mail: mbackley@gih.org
Website: http://www.gih.org

"Eliminating Racial and Ethnic Disparities in Health: A Chartbook" presents data on the disparities in health among American racial and ethnic populations in the six health areas identified by President Clinton in the February 1998 radio address: infant mortality, cancer, heart disease, diabetes, HIV/ AIDS, and immunizations. Data are also presented on risk factors, access to care, and minority participation in the health professions. Contact GIH for pricing information.

Hawaii AIDS Clinical Research Program (HACRP)
Leahi Hospital
Young Building, 6th Floor
3675 Kilauea Avenue
Honolulu, HI 96816
Toll Free: 800-806-8208
Tel: 808-737-2751
Fax: 808 735-8529
E-mail: hiactu2@pixi.com
Website: http://www.pixi.com/~hiactu2

A group of 95 physicians have joined to improve the qualify of life and health care of infants, children, and adults with HIV infection within Hawaii's established health care system. Contact for publication information.

Hawaii State Health Department
1250 Punchbowl Street
Honolulu, HI 96813
Tel: 808-586-4442
E-mail: webmail@mail.health.state.hi.us
Website: http://www.state.hi.us/doh/

Offers many publications in Asian and Pacific Islander languages. Various health topics from AIDS to cancer to diabetes to heart disease are covered. Contact to get a complete list of publications.

Kalihi Palama Health Center
915 North King Street
Honolulu, HI 96817
Tel: 808-848-1438

Distributes health materials in Samoan and Hawaiian. Contact for additional information.

National Asian Pacific American Families Against Substance Abuse
340 East Second Street, Suite 409
Los Angeles, CA 90012
Tel: 213-625-5795
Fax: 213-625-5796
Website: http://www.napafasa.org

Provides information and referral regarding substance abuse, mental health, and related services to API populations. Also offers mental health and substance abuse information and materials, as well as a newsletter and publications list.

National Asian Pacific Center on Aging
Melbourne Tower
P.O. Box 21668
1511 3rd Avenue, Suite 914
Seattle, WA 98101
Tel: 206-624-1221
Fax: 206-624-1023
E-mail: web@napca.org
Website: http://www.napca.org

Offers publications on Medicare, Medicaid, and other managed care issues in Tagalog, Tongan, and Samoan.

National Center for Post-Traumatic Stress Disorder
VA Medical Center (116D)
White River Junction, VT 05009
Tel: 802-296-5132
Fax: 802-296-5135
E-mail: ptsd@dartmouth.edu
Website: http://www.ncptsd.org

Provides two publications for Pacific Islanders: "In Search of Peace and Harmony: the legacy of psychological trauma of the Vietnam War for Native Hawaiian and American of Japanese Ancestry military personnel," and "Evaluation and Treatment of Post-Traumatic Stress Disorder with Native Hawaiian and American of Japanese Ancestry Vietnam Veterans."

National Clearinghouse on Alcohol and Drug Information
Center for Substance Abuse Prevention
5600 Fishers Lane
Rockwall II Room 9D-10
Rockville, MD 20857
Toll Free: 800-729-6686
Tel: 301-443-0365
E-mail: nnadal@samhsa.gov
Website: http://www.samhsa.gov/csap/index.htm

Provides a prevention resource guide for Asians and Pacific Islanders (English).

National Clearinghouse on Families and Youth
P.O. Box 13505
Silver Spring, MD 20911-3505
Tel: 301-608-8099
Fax: 301-608-8721
Website: http://www.ncfy.com

Provides "A Guide to Enhancing the Cultural Competence of Runaway and Homeless Youth Programs."

National Council on Alcoholism and Drug Dependence
12 West 21st Street, 7th Floor
New York, NY 10410
Tel: 212-206-6770
Hope Line: 800-NCA-CALL (24 hour affiliate referral)
Fax: 212-645-1690
E-mail: national@ncadd.org
Website: http://www.ncadd.org

"What Are the Signs of Alcoholism: The NCADD Self Test" is available in Thai and Tongan. Single copies are free and reproduction is permitted.

National Digestive Diseases Information Clearinghouse
2 Information Way
Bethesda, MD 20892-3570
Tel: 301-654-3810
Fax: 301-907-8906
E-mail: niddc@info.niddk.nih.gov
Website: http://www.niddk.nih.gov

Provides a bibliographic database search on "Digestive Diseases in Minority Populations." Maintains a database of patient and professional education materials that are Pacific Islander specific.

National Information Center on Health Services Research
Building 38A, RM 4S-410, Mail Stop 20
8600 Rockville Pike
Bethesda, MD 20894
Tel: 301-496-0176
Fax: 301-402-3193
E-mail: nichsr@nlm.nih.gov
Website: http://www.nlm.nih.gov/nichsr/nichsr.html

HealthSTAR database can be accessed for literature citations:

National Kidney and Urologic Diseases
Information Clearinghouse
3 Information Way
Bethesda, MD 20892-3580
Tel: 301-654-4415
Fax: 301-097-8906
E-mail: nkudic@aerie.com
Website: http://www.niddk.nih.gov

Maintains a database of patient and professional education materials that are Pacific Islander specific.

National Library of Medicine
8600 Rockville Pike
Bethesda, MD 20894
Toll Free: 888-346-3656
Tel: 301-594-5983
Fax: 301-496-2809
E-mail: custserv@nlm.nih.gov
Website: http://www.nlm.nih.gov/

National Library of Medicine collects worldwide medical literature in all languages, as well as health information on various minority and ethnic groups. Call for specific topics.

National Maternal and Child Health Clearinghouse
2070 Chain Bridge Road, Suite 450
Vienna, VA 22182-2536
Toll Free: 888-434-4MCH
Tel: 703-356-1964
Fax: 703-821-2098
E-mail: nmchc@circsol.com
Website: http://www.nmchc.org

Offers the following in Samoan—a fact sheet on "Hepatitis B," F044, and the "Parent's Guide to Common Childhood Illnesses in Samoan," F051.

National Minority Organ and Tissue Transplant Education Program (MOTTEP)
Howard University Hospital
Ambulatory Care Center
2041 Georgia Avenue, NW, Suite 3100
Washington, DC 20060
Toll Free: 800-393-2839
Tel: 202-865-4888
Fax: 202-865-4880
E-mail: ccallender@fac.howard.edu

Provides information on the need for organ transplantation and donation in minority communities.

National Women's Health Information Center
8550 Arlington Boulevard, Suite 300
Fairfax, VA 22031
Toll Free: 800-994-WOMAN (994-9662)
TDD: 888-220-5446
Fax: 703-560-6598
E-mail: 4woman@soza.com
Website: http://www.4woman.org

Fact sheets offered include "Heart Disease and Stroke," "Women and AIDS/HIV," and "Women's Health Issues: An Overview." "The Health of Minority Women" fact sheet addresses socioeconomic and cultural issues as well as health system barriers which limit minority women's access to preventive health care and diagnostic and treatment services. Contact the Center for a complete list of publications, reports, and documents.

Native Hawaiian Safe and Drug Free Schools/ Communities Program
1850 Makuakane Street, Building B
Honolulu, HI 96817
Tel: 808-842-8508
Fax: 808-842-8515

Develops, disseminates, and implements culturally appropriate violence and substance abuse prevention curricula, activities, and services to support Native Hawaiians in developing and strengthening effective and productive skills to be healthy participants in their schools and communities.

Office of Research on Women's Health
Office of the Director
National Institutes of Health
1 Center Drive, Room 201, MSC 0161
Bethesda, MD 20892-0161
Tel: 301-402-1770
Fax: 301-402-1798
Website: http://www4.od.nih.gov/orwh/orwhpubs.html

"Women of Color Health Data Book: Adolescents to Seniors" examines the role of culture, ethnicity, race, socioeconomic background, geographic location, and other social and economic factors as important contributors to health status.

Office on Smoking and Health
CDC/NCCDPHP
Mail Stop K-50
4770 Buford Highway, NE
Atlanta, GA 30341-3724
Toll Free: 800-CDC-1311 (800-232-1311)
General information/publication requests: 770-488-5705
Tel: 770-488-5707
Fax: 770-488-2552
E-mail: tobacco@cdc.gov
Website: http://www.cdc.gov/tobacco

Provides a fact sheet on "Asian Americans and Pacific Islanders and Tobacco." Also has the Surgeon General's Report, "Tobacco Use among U.S. Racial/Ethnic Minority Groups." A citation database is also available for the latest tobacco related information and research. related information and research.

Pacific Asian Alcohol and Drug Program
1720 W. Beverly Boulevard, Suite 200
Los Angeles, CA 90026
Tel: 213-738-3361

Distributes educational materials on alcoholism in Japanese, Filipino, Tagalog, and Tongan. Distributes pamphlets on drunk driving in Japanese and Thai. Makes available a directory on alcohol-related services.

Papa Ola Lokahi (POL)222
Kawaiah'o Plaza, Suite 102
Honolulu, HI 96813
Tel: 808-536-9453

Provides planning, administrative, and technical assistance for the Native Hawaiian Health Care Systems. POL offers a research information clearinghouse for Native Hawaiians: data collection, research, project funds, health research collaboration, and health information dissemination.

Scarecrow Press, Inc.
4720 Boston Way
Lanham, MD 20706
Toll Free: 800-462-6420
Tel: 301-459-3366
Fax: 301-459-1705
Website: http://www.scarecrowpress.com

Offers "Ethnic Minority Health: A Selected Annotated Bibliography," a guide that encompasses in one volume various minority health issues for the four major U.S. ethnic minority groups (Native Americans/Alaska Natives, African Americans, Hispanic Americans, and Asian/Pacific Islander Americans). Features nine quick access sections that are divided first by material format or broad subject area and then by ethnic group. (ISBN: 0-8108-3225-9)

Waianae Coast Comprehensive Health Center
86-260 Farrington Highway
Waianae, HI 96792-3199
Tel: 808-696-7081
Fax: 808-696-7093
E-mail: wcchc@wcchc.com
Website: http://www.wcchc.com

Offers low literacy materials for the Pacific Islanders on various health topics. Contact for a complete list of materials.

Chapter 45

Genetic Testing Laboratories in the United States

Table 45.1. Legend for Laboratory Information in This Chapter

Code	Description
S Serum Test	Blood test used to screen population for carriers of the Tay-Sachs gene.
L Leukocyte Test	Blood test to detect carriers of the Tay-Sachs gene which is used for pregnant women; to confirm inconclusive results and for those individuals taking insulin.
G Genetic Counseling	Professional counseling dealing with all aspects of inherited disorders as they affect the family and future generations.

Please Note: An asterisk (*) indicates that the laboratory has successfully participated in the Quality Control Program established by the International Tay-Sachs Screening, Reference Standard and Quality Control Center for the type of carrier test indicated (Serum and/or Leukocyte).

*Quality Control—Serum
**Quality Control—Serum & Leukocytes

California

Los Angeles

Cedars-Sinai Medical Center
Medical Genetics
Steven Spielberg Bldg., Suite 378
8700 Beverly Blvd.
Los Angeles, CA 90048
Tel: 310-967-1644
Fax: 310-659-0491
David Rimoin, M.D., Director
E-mail:
drimoin@xchg.peds.csmc.edu
Website: http://www.csmc.edu/genetics
CG

U.C.L.A.
760 Westwood Plaza
68-225 NPI
Los Angeles, CA 90024-1759
Tel: 310-825-4529
CG

Children's Hospital of Los Angeles
4650 Sunset Blvd.
Los Angeles, CA 90027
Tel: 323-669-2271
Fax: 323-660-7072
CG
Website: http://www.childrenshospitals.org

UC-Irvine Medical Center
101 The City Dr. S.
Bldg. 27—Z0T 4482
Orange, CA 92868-3298
Tel: 714-456-5791
Toll Free: 877-UCI-DOCS
CG

Kaiser-Panorama City
13652 Cantara Street
Panorama City, CA 91402
Tel: 818-375-2073
CG

Encino-Tarzana Regional Health Center
18321 Clark Street
Tarzana, CA 91356
Tel: 818-881-1061
CG

Fresno

Kaiser—Fresno
7300 North Fresno Street
Fresno, CA 93720
Tel: 209-448-4393
CG

Valley Children's Hospital
3151 North Millbrook
Fresno, CA 93703
Tel: 209-243-6626
CG

Northern California—Bay Area

Children's Hospital Medical Center
Dept. of Medical Genetics
747 52nd Street
Oakland, CA 94609
Tel: 510-428-3550
Fax: 510-450-5874
E-mail:
genetics@chogenetics.org
CG

Kaiser—Oakland
280 West MacArthur Blvd.
Oakland, CA 94611
Tel: 510-596-6298
CG

UC—San Francisco Medical Center
533 Parnassus, U-262
San Francisco, CA 94143
Tel: 415-476-4080
CG

Kaiser—San Francisco
Genetics Dept.
2350 Geary Boulevard, 3rd floor
San Francisco, CA 94115
Tel: 415-202-2998
CG

Kaiser—San Jose Reg. Gen. Lab
260 International Circle
San Jose, CA 95119
Tel: 408-972-3300
CG

Stanford Medical Center
Dept. of Gyn/Ob, #HH333
300 Pasteur Drive
Stanford, CA 94305
Tel: 650-723-5680
CG

Sacramento

Kaiser Permanente—Sacramento
2345 Fair Oaks Blvd.
Sacramento, CA 95825
Tel: 916-978-1402
CG

UC Davis Medical Center
Prenatal Diagnosis
1621 Alhambra Blvd.
Rm 2719
Sacramento, CA 95816
Tel: 916-734-6124
CG

San Diego

California Tay-Sachs Prevention Program
8110 Birmingham Way
San Diego, CA 92123
Tel: 619-495-7737
Fax: 619-279-8379
E-mail: ccoffey@ucsd.edu
SLG**

Santa Barbara

Tri-Counties Regional Center
520 E. Montecito Street
Santa Barbara, CA 93103
Tel: 805-884-7204
CG

Colorado

Univ. of Colorado Health Sciences Center
4200 East Ninth Ave.
Box C-233
Denver, CO 80262
Tel: 303-315-0409
Fax: 303-315-0407
SG*

Connecticut

State of Connecticut
Dept. of Public Health Labs
P.O. Box 1689, 10 Clinton Street
Hartford, CT 06144
Tel: 860-509-8509
S*

District of Columbia

Children's Hospital
Dept of Laboratory Medicine
111 Michigan Avenue, NW
Molecular Genetics
Washington, DC 20010
Tel: 202-884-3991
SL**

Florida

Miami Children's Hospital Research Institute
3100 SW 62nd Avenue
Miami, FL 33155
Tel: 305-666-6511
Fax: 305-669-6429
SL**

Georgia

Emory University
Dept. of Pediatrics/Div. of Medical Genetics,
2040 Ridgewood Drive
Atlanta, GA 30322
Tel: 404-727-5782
Toll Free: 800-366-1502
Fax: 404-727-9398
SLG**

Illinois

Children's Memorial Hospital
2300 Children's Plaza, #59
Chicago, IL 60614
Tel: 773-880-4462
SL**

Lutheran General Hospital
Genetics Laboratory
1775 Dempster Street
Park Ridge, IL 60068-1174
Tel: 847-723-6385
SG*

University of Illinois
Pediatrics—Biochem Genetics Lab
Rm. 1311 N CSB M/C 856
840 S. Wood Street
Chicago, IL 60612
Tel: 312-996-5326
Fax: 312-996-8205
SL**

Louisiana

Tulane University School of Medicine
1430 Tulane Ave, Room 5550
New Orleans, LA 70112
Tel: 504-584-2993
or 504-588-5229
Fax: 504-584-1763
E-mail:
handers@tmcpop.tmc.tulane.edu
SL**

Maryland

Kennedy Krieger Institute
707 North Broadway, Room 506
Baltimore, MD 21205
Tel: 410-502-9405
SL**

Univ. of Maryland Baltimore
Division of Human Genetics
655 W. Baltimore St.
Rm. 11-047
Baltimore, MD 21201
Tel: 410-706-2810
SLG**

Michigan

Wayne State University
Pediatrics
46.1 Landis Building
550 East Canfield Ave.
Detroit, MI 48201
Tel: 313-577-8504
SLG**

Minnesota

Mayo Clinic—Metabolism Lab
Mayo Clinic, Hilton 330
200 First Street, SW
Rochester, MN 55905
Tel: 800-533-1710
SLG**

Missouri

Cardinal Glennon Children's Hospital
Biochemical Genetics Lab
Room BN 14
1465 S. Grand Blvd.
St. Louis, MO 63104
Tel: 314-577-5600
SL**

New Jersey

New Jersey Medical School
Department of Pediatrics
185 S. Orange Avenue, MSB
Room F 545
Newark, NJ 07103-2714
Tel: 973-972-3326 or 973-972-5420
SLG**

New Mexico

Genzyme Genetics
2000 Vivigen Way
Santa Fe, NM 87505
Tel: 505-438-2156 or 505-438-2144
SL**

New York

Montefiore Medical Center
Division of Reproductive Genetics
1695 Eastchester Rd., Suite 301
Bronx, NY 10461
Tel: 718-405-8150
Fax: 718-405-8154
S*

Robert Guthrie Biochem. Lab
936 Delaware, Room 405
Buffalo, NY 14209
Tel: 716-878-7513
LG*

NYU Medical Center
Neuro-Genetics Lab
Rusk Bldg—RR2101
400 E. 34th St.
New York, NY 10016
Tel: 212-263-0577 (Lab) or 212-263-6347
SLG**

Center of Jewish Genetic Diseases
Mt Sinai School of Medicine
Department of Human Genetics
Fifth Avenue & 100th Street
New York, NY 10029
Tel: 212-241-6947
SLG**

Specialty Clinic Laboratories at the NYS
Institute for Basic Research
1050 Forest Hill Road
Staten Island, NY 10314
Tel: 718-494-5345
Fax: 718-494-0694
SLG**

North Carolina

Lab Corp
Director of Biochem Genetics
1912 Alexander Drive
Research Triangle Park, NC 27709
Toll Free: 800-533-0567
Fax: 919-361-7755
SG*

Ohio

Metrohealth Medical Center
Department of Pediatrics
2500 Metrohealth Drive
Cleveland, OH 44109-1998
Tel: 216-459-4271
SL**

Oregon

Biochemical Genetics Laboratory/L473
3181 SW Sam Jackson Park Rd, BH 2029
Portland, OR 97201-3098
Tel: 503-494-8392
Fax: 503-494-7645
E-mail: bcgenlab@ohsu.edu
SLG**

Pennsylvania

Thomas Jefferson University
Tay-Sachs Prevention Program
1100 Walnut Street, 411-MOB
Philadelphia, PA 19107
Tel: 215-955-8320 or 215-955-8321
SL**

Satellite Programs
University of Pittsburgh MC
5845 Main Tower—UPMC
200 Lothrop Street
Pittsburgh, PA 15213-2582
Tel: 412-647-6526
SL**

Texas

TDH/Genetic Testing Center
3600 E. McKinney
Denton, TX 76201
Tel: 940-383-3561 x276
SLG**

Baylor College of Medicine
Biochemical Genetics Lab
Department of Molecular & Human Genetics
One Baylor Plaza, Room T-530
Houston, TX 77030
Tel: 713-798-4982
Fax: 713-798-8937
S*

Virginia

University of Virginia Health Sciences Center
Old Medical School Building
Room 1806—Box 386
Charlottesville, VA 22908
Tel: 804-924-2665 or 804-982-3850
SLG**

Washington

Children's Hospital
LAB CH-37
4800 San Point Way, NE
Seattle, WA 98105-0371
Tel: 206-526-2216
SL**

Wisconsin

Univ. of Wisconsin
Waisman Center
1500 Highland Avenue, Room 361
Madison, WI 53705-2280
Tel: 608-263-5993 or 608-263-4619
Fax: 608-263-0530
E-mail: rasmussm@vms2.macc.wisc.edu
SG*

Index

Index

Page numbers followed by 'n' indicate a footnote. Page numbers in *italics* indicate a table or illustration.

A

B

D

E

F

G

H

I

J

K

L

M

N

O

P

Q

R

S

T

U

V

W

X

Y

Z

Health Reference Series

COMPLETE CATALOG

AIDS Sourcebook, 1st Edition

Basic Information about AIDS and HIV Infection, Featuring Historical and Statistical Data, Current Research, Prevention, and Other Special Topics of Interest for Persons Living with AIDS

Along with Source Listings for Further Assistance

Edited by Karen Bellenir and Peter D. Dresser. 831 pages. 1995. 0-7808-0031-1. $78.

"One strength of this book is its practical emphasis. The intended audience is the lay reader . . . useful as an educational tool for health care providers who work with AIDS patients. Recommended for public libraries as well as hospital or academic libraries that collect consumer materials."
—*Bulletin of the Medical Library Association, Jan '96*

"This is the most comprehensive volume of its kind on an important medical topic. Highly recommended for all libraries." —*Reference Book Review, '96*

"Very useful reference for all libraries."
—*Choice, Association of College and Research Libraries, Oct '95*

"There is a wealth of information here that can provide much educational assistance. It is a must book for all libraries and should be on the desk of each and every congressional leader. Highly recommended."
—*AIDS Book Review Journal, Aug '95*

"Recommended for most collections."
—*Library Journal, Jul '95*

■

AIDS Sourcebook, 2nd Edition

Basic Consumer Health Information about Acquired Immune Deficiency Syndrome (AIDS) and Human Immunodeficiency Virus (HIV) Infection, Featuring Updated Statistical Data, Reports on Recent Research and Prevention Initiatives, and Other Special Topics of Interest for Persons Living with AIDS, Including New Antiretroviral Treatment Options, Strategies for Combating Opportunistic Infections, Information about Clinical Trials, and More

Along with a Glossary of Important Terms and Resource Listings for Further Help and Information

Edited by Karen Bellenir. 751 pages. 1999. 0-7808-0225-X. $78.

"Highly recommended."
—*American Reference Books Annual, 2000*

"Excellent sourcebook. This continues to be a highly recommended book. There is no other book that provides as much information as this book provides."
—*AIDS Book Review Journal, Dec-Jan 2000*

"Recommended reference source."
—*Booklist, American Library Association, Dec '99*

"A solid text for college-level health libraries."
—*The Bookwatch, Aug '99*

Cited in *Reference Sources for Small and Medium-Sized Libraries, American Library Association, 1999*

■

Alcoholism Sourcebook

Basic Consumer Health Information about the Physical and Mental Consequences of Alcohol Abuse, Including Liver Disease, Pancreatitis, Wernicke-Korsakoff Syndrome (Alcoholic Dementia), Fetal Alcohol Syndrome, Heart Disease, Kidney Disorders, Gastrointestinal Problems, and Immune System Compromise and Featuring Facts about Addiction, Detoxification, Alcohol Withdrawal, Recovery, and the Maintenance of Sobriety

Along with a Glossary and Directories of Resources for Further Help and Information

Edited by Karen Bellenir. 613 pages. 2000. 0-7808-0325-6. $78.

"Recommended reference source."
—*Booklist, American Library Association, Dec '00*

"Presents a wealth of information on alcohol use and abuse and its effects on the body and mind, treatment, and prevention." —*SciTech Book News, Dec '00*

"Important new health guide which packs in the latest consumer information about the problems of alcoholism." —*Reviewer's Bookwatch, Nov '00*

SEE ALSO *Drug Abuse Sourcebook, Substance Abuse Sourcebook*

■

Allergies Sourcebook

Basic Information about Major Forms and Mechanisms of Common Allergic Reactions, Sensitivities, and Intolerances, Including Anaphylaxis, Asthma, Hives and Other Dermatologic Symptoms, Rhinitis, and Sinusitis

Along with Their Usual Triggers Like Animal Fur, Chemicals, Drugs, Dust, Foods, Insects, Latex, Pollen, and Poison Ivy, Oak, and Sumac; Plus Information on Prevention, Identification, and Treatment

Edited by Allan R. Cook. 611 pages. 1997. 0-7808-0036-2. $78.

■

Alternative Medicine Sourcebook

Basic Consumer Health Information about Alternatives to Conventional Medicine, Including Acupressure, Acupuncture, Aromatherapy, Ayurveda, Bioelectromagnetics, Environmental Medicine, Essence

Therapy, Food and Nutrition Therapy, Herbal Therapy, Homeopathy, Imaging, Massage, Naturopathy, Reflexology, Relaxation and Meditation, Sound Therapy, Vitamin and Mineral Therapy, and Yoga, and More

Edited by Allan R. Cook. 737 pages. 1999. 0-7808-0200-4. $78.

"Recommended reference source."
—*Booklist, American Library Association, Feb '00*

"A great addition to the reference collection of every type of library." —*American Reference Books Annual, 2000*

■

Alzheimer's, Stroke & 29 Other Neurological Disorders Sourcebook, 1st Edition

Basic Information for the Layperson on 31 Diseases or Disorders Affecting the Brain and Nervous System, First Describing the Illness, Then Listing Symptoms, Diagnostic Methods, and Treatment Options, and Including Statistics on Incidences and Causes

Edited by Frank E. Bair. 579 pages. 1993. 1-55888-748-2. $78.

"Nontechnical reference book that provides reader-friendly information."
—*Family Caregiver Alliance Update, Winter '96*

"Should be included in any library's patient education section." —*American Reference Books Annual, 1994*

"Written in an approachable and accessible style. Recommended for patient education and consumer health collections in health science center and public libraries." —*Academic Library Book Review, Dec '93*

"It is very handy to have information on more than thirty neurological disorders under one cover, and there is no recent source like it." —*Reference Quarterly, American Library Association, Fall '93*

***SEE ALSO** Brain Disorders Sourcebook*

■

Alzheimer's Disease Sourcebook, 2nd Edition

Basic Consumer Health Information about Alzheimer's Disease, Related Disorders, and Other Dementias, Including Multi-Infarct Dementia, AIDS-Related Dementia, Alcoholic Dementia, Huntington's Disease, Delirium, and Confusional States

Along with Reports Detailing Current Research Efforts in Prevention and Treatment, Long-Term Care Issues, and Listings of Sources for Additional Help and Information

Edited by Karen Bellenir. 524 pages. 1999. 0-7808-0223-3. $78.

"Provides a wealth of useful information not otherwise available in one place. This resource is recommended for all types of libraries."
—*American Reference Books Annual, 2000*

"Recommended reference source."
—*Booklist, American Library Association, Oct '99*

Arthritis Sourcebook

Basic Consumer Health Information about Specific Forms of Arthritis and Related Disorders, Including Rheumatoid Arthritis, Osteoarthritis, Gout, Polymyalgia Rheumatica, Psoriatic Arthritis, Spondyloarthropathies, Juvenile Rheumatoid Arthritis, and Juvenile Ankylosing Spondylitis

Along with Information about Medical, Surgical, and Alternative Treatment Options, and Including Strategies for Coping with Pain, Fatigue, and Stress

Edited by Allan R. Cook. 550 pages. 1998. 0-7808-0201-2. $78.

". . . accessible to the layperson."
—*Reference and Research Book News, Feb '99*

■

Asthma Sourcebook

Basic Consumer Health Information about Asthma, Including Symptoms, Traditional and Nontraditional Remedies, Treatment Advances, Quality-of-Life Aids, Medical Research Updates, and the Role of Allergies, Exercise, Age, the Environment, and Genetics in the Development of Asthma

Along with Statistical Data, a Glossary, and Directories of Support Groups, and Other Resources for Further Information

Edited by Annemarie S. Muth. 628 pages. 2000. 0-7808-0381-7. $78.

"Highly recommended." —*The Bookwatch, Jan '01*

■

Back & Neck Disorders Sourcebook

Basic Information about Disorders and Injuries of the Spinal Cord and Vertebrae, Including Facts on Chiropractic Treatment, Surgical Interventions, Paralysis, and Rehabilitation

Along with Advice for Preventing Back Trouble

Edited by Karen Bellenir. 548 pages. 1997. 0-7808-0202-0. $78.

"The strength of this work is its basic, easy-to-read format. Recommended."
—*Reference and User Services Quarterly, American Library Association, Winter '97*

■

Blood & Circulatory Disorders Sourcebook

Basic Information about Blood and Its Components, Anemias, Leukemias, Bleeding Disorders, and Circulatory Disorders, Including Aplastic Anemia, Thalassemia, Sickle-Cell Disease, Hemochromatosis, Hemophilia, Von Willebrand Disease, and Vascular Diseases

Along with a Special Section on Blood Transfusions and Blood Supply Safety, a Glossary, and Source Listings for Further Help and Information

Edited by Karen Bellenir and Linda M. Shin. 554 pages. 1998. 0-7808-0203-9. $78.

"Recommended reference source."
—*Booklist, American Library Association, Feb '99*

"An important reference sourcebook written in simple language for everyday, non-technical users."
—*Reviewer's Bookwatch, Jan '99*

■

Brain Disorders Sourcebook

Basic Consumer Health Information about Strokes, Epilepsy, Amyotrophic Lateral Sclerosis (ALS/Lou Gehrig's Disease), Parkinson's Disease, Brain Tumors, Cerebral Palsy, Headache, Tourette Syndrome, and More

Along with Statistical Data, Treatment and Rehabilitation Options, Coping Strategies, Reports on Current Research Initiatives, a Glossary, and Resource Listings for Additional Help and Information

Edited by Karen Bellenir. 481 pages. 1999. 0-7808-0229-2. $78.

"Belongs on the shelves of any library with a consumer health collection." —*E-Streams, Mar '00*

"Recommended reference source."
—*Booklist, American Library Association, Oct '99*

SEE ALSO *Alzheimer's, Stroke & 29 Other Neurological Disorders Sourcebook, 1st Edition*

■

Breast Cancer Sourcebook

Basic Consumer Health Information about Breast Cancer, Including Diagnostic Methods, Treatment Options, Alternative Therapies, Self-Help Information, Related Health Concerns, Statistical and Demographic Data, and Facts for Men with Breast Cancer

Along with Reports on Current Research Initiatives, a Glossary of Related Medical Terms, and a Directory of Sources for Further Help and Information

Edited by Edward J. Prucha and Karen Bellenir. 600 pages. 2001. 0-7808-0244-6. $78.

SEE ALSO *Cancer Sourcebook for Women, 1st and 2nd Editions, Women's Health Concerns Sourcebook*

■

Burns Sourcebook

Basic Consumer Health Information about Various Types of Burns and Scalds, Including Flame, Heat, Cold, Electrical, Chemical, and Sun Burns

Along with Information on Short-Term and Long-Term Treatments, Tissue Reconstruction, Plastic Surgery, Prevention Suggestions, and First Aid

Edited by Allan R. Cook. 604 pages. 1999. 0-7808-0204-7. $78.

"This key reference guide is an invaluable addition to all health care and public libraries in confronting this ongoing health issue."
—*American Reference Books Annual, 2000*

"This is an exceptional addition to the series and is highly recommended for all consumer health collections, hospital libraries, and academic medical centers." —*E-Streams, Mar '00*

"Recommended reference source."
—*Booklist, American Library Association, Dec '99*

SEE ALSO *Skin Disorders Sourcebook*

■

Cancer Sourcebook, 1st Edition

Basic Information on Cancer Types, Symptoms, Diagnostic Methods, and Treatments, Including Statistics on Cancer Occurrences Worldwide and the Risks Associated with Known Carcinogens and Activities

Edited by Frank E. Bair. 932 pages. 1990. 1-55888-888-8. $78.

Cited in *Reference Sources for Small and Medium-Sized Libraries, American Library Association, 1999*

"Written in nontechnical language. Useful for patients, their families, medical professionals, and librarians."
—*Guide to Reference Books, 1996*

"Designed with the non-medical professional in mind. Libraries and medical facilities interested in patient education should certainly consider adding the *Cancer Sourcebook* to their holdings. This compact collection of reliable information . . . is an invaluable tool for helping patients and patients' families and friends to take the first steps in coping with the many difficulties of cancer."
—*Medical Reference Services Quarterly, Winter '91*

"Specifically created for the nontechnical reader . . . an important resource for the general reader trying to understand the complexities of cancer."
—*American Reference Books Annual, 1991*

"This publication's nontechnical nature and very comprehensive format make it useful for both the general public and undergraduate students."
—*Choice, Association of College and Research Libraries, Oct '90*

■

New Cancer Sourcebook, 2nd Edition

Basic Information about Major Forms and Stages of Cancer, Featuring Facts about Primary and Secondary Tumors of the Respiratory, Nervous, Lymphatic, Circulatory, Skeletal, and Gastrointestinal Systems, and Specific Organs; Statistical and Demographic Data; Treatment Options; and Strategies for Coping

Edited by Allan R. Cook. 1,313 pages. 1996. 0-7808-0041-9. $78.

"An excellent resource for patients with newly diagnosed cancer and their families. The dialogue is simple, direct, and comprehensive. Highly recommended for patients and families to aid in their understanding of cancer and its treatment."
—*Booklist Health Sciences Supplement, American Library Association, Oct '97*

"The amount of factual and useful information is extensive. The writing is very clear, geared to general readers. Recommended for all levels."

—*Choice, Association of College and Research Libraries, Jan '97*

Cancer Sourcebook, 3rd Edition

Basic Consumer Health Information about Major Forms and Stages of Cancer, Featuring Facts about Primary and Secondary Tumors of the Respiratory, Nervous, Lymphatic, Circulatory, Skeletal, and Gastrointestinal Systems, and Specific Organs

Along with Statistical and Demographic Data, Treatment Options, Strategies for Coping, a Glossary, and a Directory of Sources for Additional Help and Information

Edited by Edward J. Prucha. 1,069 pages. 2000. 0-7808-0227-6. $78.

"Recommended reference source."

—*Booklist, American Library Association, Dec '00*

Cancer Sourcebook for Women, 1st Edition

Basic Information about Specific Forms of Cancer That Affect Women, Featuring Facts about Breast Cancer, Cervical Cancer, Ovarian Cancer, Cancer of the Uterus and Uterine Sarcoma, Cancer of the Vagina, and Cancer of the Vulva; Statistical and Demographic Data; Treatments, Self-Help Management Suggestions, and Current Research Initiatives

Edited by Allan R. Cook and Peter D. Dresser. 524 pages. 1996. 0-7808-0076-1. $78.

". . . written in easily understandable, non-technical language. Recommended for public libraries or hospital and academic libraries that collect patient education or consumer health materials."

—*Medical Reference Services Quarterly, Spring '97*

"Would be of value in a consumer health library. . . . written with the health care consumer in mind. Medical jargon is at a minimum, and medical terms are explained in clear, understandable sentences."

—*Bulletin of the Medical Library Association, Oct '96*

"The availability under one cover of all these pertinent publications, grouped under cohesive headings, makes this certainly a most useful sourcebook."

—*Choice, Association of College and Research Libraries, Jun '96*

"Presents a comprehensive knowledge base for general readers. Men and women both benefit from the gold mine of information nestled between the two covers of this book. Recommended."

—*Academic Library Book Review, Summer '96*

"This timely book is highly recommended for consumer health and patient education collections in all libraries."

—*Library Journal, Apr '96*

SEE ALSO *Breast Cancer Sourcebook, Women's Health Concerns Sourcebook*

Cancer Sourcebook for Women, 2nd Edition

Basic Consumer Health Information about Specific Forms of Cancer That Affect Women, Including Cervical Cancer, Ovarian Cancer, Endometrial Cancer, Uterine Sarcoma, Vaginal Cancer, Vulvar Cancer, and Gestational Trophoblastic Tumor; and Featuring Statistical Information, Facts about Tests and Treatments, a Glossary of Cancer Terms, and an Extensive List of Additional Resources

Edited by Karen Bellenir. 600 pages. 2001. 0-7808-0226-8. $78.

SEE ALSO *Breast Cancer Sourcebook, Women's Health Concerns Sourcebook*

Cardiovascular Diseases & Disorders Sourcebook, 1st Edition

Basic Information about Cardiovascular Diseases and Disorders, Featuring Facts about the Cardiovascular System, Demographic and Statistical Data, Descriptions of Pharmacological and Surgical Interventions, Lifestyle Modifications, and a Special Section Focusing on Heart Disorders in Children

Edited by Karen Bellenir and Peter D. Dresser. 683 pages. 1995. 0-7808-0032-X. $78.

". . . comprehensive format provides an extensive overview on this subject."

—*Choice, Association of College and Research Libraries, Jun '96*

". . . an easily understood, complete, up-to-date resource. This well executed public health tool will make valuable information available to those that need it most, patients and their families. The typeface, sturdy non-reflective paper, and library binding add a feel of quality found wanting in other publications. Highly recommended for academic and general libraries."

—*Academic Library Book Review, Summer '96*

SEE ALSO *Healthy Heart Sourcebook for Women, Heart Diseases & Disorders Sourcebook, 2nd Edition*

Caregiving Sourcebook

Basic Consumer Health Information for Caregivers, Including a Profile of Caregivers, Caregiving Responsibilities, Tips for Specific Conditions, Care Environments, and the Effects of Caregiving

Along with Legal Issues, Financial Concerns, Future Planning, a Glossary, and a Listing of Additional Resources

Edited by Joyce Brennfleck Shannon. 550 pages. 2001. 0-7808-0331-0. $78.

Colds, Flu & Other Common Ailments Sourcebook

Basic Consumer Health Information about Common Ailments and Injuries, Including Colds, Coughs, the Flu, Sinus Problems, Headaches, Fever, Nausea and Vomiting, Menstrual Cramps, Diarrhea, Constipation, Hemorrhoids, Back Pain, Dandruff, Dry and Itchy Skin, Cuts, Scrapes, Sprains, Bruises, and More

Along with Information about Prevention, Self-Care, Choosing a Doctor, Over-the-Counter Medications, Folk Remedies, and Alternative Therapies, and Including a Glossary of Important Terms and a Directory of Resources for Further Help and Information

Edited by Chad T. Kimball. 600 pages. 2001. 0-7808-0435-X. $78.

"Both public and academic libraries will want to have a copy in their collection for readers who are interested in self-education on health issues."

—*American Reference Books Annual, 2000*

"The editor has researched the literature from government agencies and others, saving readers the time and effort of having to do the research themselves. Recommended for public libraries."

—*Reference and User Services Quarterly, American Library Association, Spring '99*

"Recommended reference source."

—*Booklist, American Library Association, Dec '98*

■

Communication Disorders Sourcebook

Basic Information about Deafness and Hearing Loss, Speech and Language Disorders, Voice Disorders, Balance and Vestibular Disorders, and Disorders of Smell, Taste, and Touch

Edited by Linda M. Ross. 533 pages. 1996. 0-7808-0077-X. $78.

"This is skillfully edited and is a welcome resource for the layperson. It should be found in every public and medical library." —*Booklist Health Sciences Supplement, American Library Association, Oct '97*

■

Congenital Disorders Sourcebook

Basic Information about Disorders Acquired during Gestation, Including Spina Bifida, Hydrocephalus, Cerebral Palsy, Heart Defects, Craniofacial Abnormalities, Fetal Alcohol Syndrome, and More

Along with Current Treatment Options and Statistical Data

Edited by Karen Bellenir. 607 pages. 1997. 0-7808-0205-5. $78.

"Recommended reference source."

—*Booklist, American Library Association, Oct '97*

SEE ALSO *Pregnancy & Birth Sourcebook*

■

Consumer Issues in Health Care Sourcebook

Basic Information about Health Care Fundamentals and Related Consumer Issues, Including Exams and Screening Tests, Physician Specialties, Choosing a Doctor, Using Prescription and Over-the-Counter Medications Safely, Avoiding Health Scams, Managing Common Health Risks in the Home, Care Options for Chronically or Terminally Ill Patients, and a List of Resources for Obtaining Help and Further Information

Edited by Karen Bellenir. 618 pages. 1998. 0-7808-0221-7. $78.

■

Contagious & Non-Contagious Infectious Diseases Sourcebook

Basic Information about Contagious Diseases like Measles, Polio, Hepatitis B, and Infectious Mononucleosis, and Non-Contagious Infectious Diseases like Tetanus and Toxic Shock Syndrome, and Diseases Occurring as Secondary Infections Such as Shingles and Reye Syndrome

Along with Vaccination, Prevention, and Treatment Information, and a Section Describing Emerging Infectious Disease Threats

Edited by Karen Bellenir and Peter D. Dresser. 566 pages. 1996. 0-7808-0075-3. $78.

■

Death & Dying Sourcebook

Basic Consumer Health Information for the Layperson about End-of-Life Care and Related Ethical and Legal Issues, Including Chief Causes of Death, Autopsies, Pain Management for the Terminally Ill, Life Support Systems, Insurance, Euthanasia, Assisted Suicide, Hospice Programs, Living Wills, Funeral Planning, Counseling, Mourning, Organ Donation, and Physician Training

Along with Statistical Data, a Glossary, and Listings of Sources for Further Help and Information

Edited by Annemarie S. Muth. 641 pages. 1999. 0-7808-0230-6. $78.

"Recommended reference source."

—*Booklist, American Library Association, Aug '00*

"This book is a definite must for all those involved in end-of-life care." —*Doody's Review Service, 2000*

■

Diabetes Sourcebook, 1st Edition

Basic Information about Insulin-Dependent and Non-insulin-Dependent Diabetes Mellitus, Gestational Diabetes, and Diabetic Complications, Symptoms, Treatment, and Research Results, Including Statistics on Prevalence, Morbidity, and Mortality

Along with Source Listings for Further Help and Information

Edited by Karen Bellenir and Peter D. Dresser. 827 pages. 1994. 1-55888-751-2. $78.

". . . very informative and understandable for the layperson without being simplistic. It provides a comprehensive overview for laypersons who want a general understanding of the disease or who want to focus on various aspects of the disease."
—*Bulletin of the Medical Library Association, Jan '96*

■

Diabetes Sourcebook, 2nd Edition

Basic Consumer Health Information about Type 1 Diabetes (Insulin-Dependent or Juvenile-Onset Diabetes), Type 2 (Noninsulin-Dependent or Adult-Onset Diabetes), Gestational Diabetes, and Related Disorders, Including Diabetes Prevalence Data, Management Issues, the Role of Diet and Exercise in Controlling Diabetes, Insulin and Other Diabetes Medicines, and Complications of Diabetes Such as Eye Diseases, Periodontal Disease, Amputation, and End-Stage Renal Disease

Along with Reports on Current Research Initiatives, a Glossary, and Resource Listings for Further Help and Information

Edited by Karen Bellenir. 688 pages. 1998. 0-7808-0224-1. $78.

"This comprehensive book is an excellent addition for high school, academic, medical, and public libraries. This volume is highly recommended."
—*American Reference Books Annual, 2000*

"An invaluable reference." —*Library Journal, May '00*

Selected as one of the 250 "Best Health Sciences Books of 1999." —*Doody's Rating Service, Mar-Apr 2000*

"Recommended reference source."
—*Booklist, American Library Association, Feb '99*

". . . provides reliable mainstream medical information . . . belongs on the shelves of any library with a consumer health collection." —*E-Streams, Sep '99*

"Provides useful information for the general public."
—*Healthlines, University of Michigan Health Management Research Center, Sep/Oct '99*

■

Diet & Nutrition Sourcebook, 1st Edition

Basic Information about Nutrition, Including the Dietary Guidelines for Americans, the Food Guide Pyramid, and Their Applications in Daily Diet, Nutritional Advice for Specific Age Groups, Current Nutritional Issues and Controversies, the New Food Label and How to Use It to Promote Healthy Eating, and Recent Developments in Nutritional Research

Edited by Dan R. Harris. 662 pages. 1996. 0-7808-0084-2. $78.

"Useful reference as a food and nutrition sourcebook for the general consumer." —*Booklist Health Sciences Supplement, American Library Association, Oct '97*

"Recommended for public libraries and medical libraries that receive general information requests on nutrition. It is readable and will appeal to those interested in learning more about healthy dietary practices."
—*Medical Reference Services Quarterly, Fall '97*

"An abundance of medical and social statistics is translated into readable information geared toward the general reader." —*Bookwatch, Mar '97*

"With dozens of questionable diet books on the market, it is so refreshing to find a reliable and factual reference book. Recommended to aspiring professionals, librarians, and others seeking and giving reliable dietary advice. An excellent compilation." —*Choice, Association of College and Research Libraries, Feb '97*

SEE ALSO *Digestive Diseases & Disorders Sourcebook, Gastrointestinal Diseases & Disorders Sourcebook*

■

Diet & Nutrition Sourcebook, 2nd Edition

Basic Consumer Health Information about Dietary Guidelines, Recommended Daily Intake Values, Vitamins, Minerals, Fiber, Fat, Weight Control, Dietary Supplements, and Food Additives

Along with Special Sections on Nutrition Needs throughout Life and Nutrition for People with Such Specific Medical Concerns as Allergies, High Blood Cholesterol, Hypertension, Diabetes, Celiac Disease, Seizure Disorders, Phenylketonuria (PKU), Cancer, and Eating Disorders, and Including Reports on Current Nutrition Research and Source Listings for Additional Help and Information

Edited by Karen Bellenir. 650 pages. 1999. 0-7808-0228-4. $78.

"This book is an excellent source of basic diet and nutrition information." —*Booklist Health Sciences Supplement, American Library Association, Dec '00*

"This reference document should be in any public library, but it would be a very good guide for beginning students in the health sciences. If the other books in this publisher's series are as good as this, they should all be in the health sciences collections."
—*American Reference Books Annual, 2000*

"This book is an excellent general nutrition reference for consumers who desire to take an active role in their health care for prevention. Consumers of all ages who select this book can feel confident they are receiving current and accurate information."
—*Journal of Nutrition for the Elderly, Vol. 19, No. 4, '00*

"Recommended reference source."
—*Booklist, American Library Association, Dec '99*

SEE ALSO *Digestive Diseases & Disorders Sourcebook, Gastrointestinal Diseases & Disorders Sourcebook*

■

Digestive Diseases & Disorders Sourcebook

Basic Consumer Health Information about Diseases and Disorders that Impact the Upper and Lower Digestive System, Including Celiac Disease, Constipation, Crohn's Disease, Cyclic Vomiting Syndrome, Diarrhea, Diverticulosis and Diverticulitis, Gallstones, Heart-

burn, Hemorrhoids, Hernias, Indigestion (Dyspepsia), Irritable Bowel Syndrome, Lactose Intolerance, Ulcers, and More

Along with Information about Medications and Other Treatments, Tips for Maintaining a Healthy Digestive Tract, a Glossary, and Directory of Digestive Diseases Organizations

Edited by Karen Bellenir. 335 pages. 1999. 0-7808-0327-2. $48.

"This title is recommended for public, hospital, and health sciences libraries with consumer health collections." —*E-Streams, Jul-Aug '00*

"Recommended reference source."
—*Booklist, American Library Association, May '00*

SEE ALSO *Diet & Nutrition Sourcebook, 1st and 2nd Editions, Gastrointestinal Diseases & Disorders Sourcebook*

■

Disabilities Sourcebook

Basic Consumer Health Information about Physical and Psychiatric Disabilities, Including Descriptions of Major Causes of Disability, Assistive and Adaptive Aids, Workplace Issues, and Accessibility Concerns

Along with Information about the Americans with Disabilities Act, a Glossary, and Resources for Additional Help and Information

Edited by Dawn D. Matthews. 616 pages. 2000. 0-7808-0389-2. $78.

"An excellent source book in easy-to-read format covering many current topics; highly recommended for all libraries."
—*Choice, Association of College and Research Libraries, Jan '01*

"Recommended reference source."
—*Booklist, American Library Association, Jul '00*

"An involving, invaluable handbook."
—*The Bookwatch, May '00*

■

Domestic Violence & Child Abuse Sourcebook

Basic Consumer Health Information about Spousal/Partner, Child, Sibling, Parent, and Elder Abuse, Covering Physical, Emotional, and Sexual Abuse, Teen Dating Violence, and Stalking; Includes Information about Hotlines, Safe Houses, Safety Plans, and Other Resources for Support and Assistance, Community Initiatives, and Reports on Current Directions in Research and Treatment

Along with a Glossary, Sources for Further Reading, and Governmental and Non-Governmental Organizations Contact Information

Edited by Helene Henderson. 1,064 pages. 2001. 0-7808-0235-7. $78.

Drug Abuse Sourcebook

Basic Consumer Health Information about Illicit Substances of Abuse and the Diversion of Prescription Medications, Including Depressants, Hallucinogens, Inhalants, Marijuana, Narcotics, Stimulants, and Anabolic Steroids

Along with Facts about Related Health Risks, Treatment Issues, and Substance Abuse Prevention Programs, a Glossary of Terms, Statistical Data, and Directories of Hotline Services, Self-Help Groups, and Organizations Able to Provide Further Information

Edited by Karen Bellenir. 629 pages. 2000. 0-7808-0242-X. $78.

"Highly recommended." —*The Bookwatch, Jan '01*

SEE ALSO *Alcoholism Sourcebook, Substance Abuse Sourcebook*

■

Ear, Nose & Throat Disorders Sourcebook

Basic Information about Disorders of the Ears, Nose, Sinus Cavities, Pharynx, and Larynx, Including Ear Infections, Tinnitus, Vestibular Disorders, Allergic and Non-Allergic Rhinitis, Sore Throats, Tonsillitis, and Cancers That Affect the Ears, Nose, Sinuses, and Throat

Along with Reports on Current Research Initiatives, a Glossary of Related Medical Terms, and a Directory of Sources for Further Help and Information

Edited by Karen Bellenir and Linda M. Shin. 576 pages. 1998. 0-7808-0206-3. $78.

"Overall, this sourcebook is helpful for the consumer seeking information on ENT issues. It is recommended for public libraries."
—*American Reference Books Annual, 1999*

"Recommended reference source."
—*Booklist, American Library Association, Dec '98*

■

Endocrine & Metabolic Disorders Sourcebook

Basic Information for the Layperson about Pancreatic and Insulin-Related Disorders Such as Pancreatitis, Diabetes, and Hypoglycemia; Adrenal Gland Disorders Such as Cushing's Syndrome, Addison's Disease, and Congenital Adrenal Hyperplasia; Pituitary Gland Disorders Such as Growth Hormone Deficiency, Acromegaly, and Pituitary Tumors; Thyroid Disorders Such as Hypothyroidism, Graves' Disease, Hashimoto's Disease, and Goiter; Hyperparathyroidism; and Other Diseases and Syndromes of Hormone Imbalance or Metabolic Dysfunction

Along with Reports on Current Research Initiatives

Edited by Linda M. Shin. 574 pages. 1998. 0-7808-0207-1. $78.

"Omnigraphics has produced another needed resource for health information consumers."
—*American Reference Books Annual, 2000*

"Recommended reference source."
—*Booklist, American Library Association, Dec '98*

Environmentally Induced Disorders Sourcebook

Basic Information about Diseases and Syndromes Linked to Exposure to Pollutants and Other Substances in Outdoor and Indoor Environments Such as Lead, Asbestos, Formaldehyde, Mercury, Emissions, Noise, and More

Edited by Allan R. Cook. 620 pages. 1997. 0-7808-0083-4. $78.

"Recommended reference source."
—*Booklist, American Library Association, Sep '98*

"This book will be a useful addition to anyone's library." —*Choice Health Sciences Supplement, Association of College and Research Libraries, May '98*

". . . a good survey of numerous environmentally induced physical disorders . . . a useful addition to anyone's library."
—*Doody's Health Sciences Book Reviews, Jan '98*

". . . provide[s] introductory information from the best authorities around. Since this volume covers topics that potentially affect everyone, it will surely be one of the most frequently consulted volumes in the *Health Reference Series.*" —*Rettig on Reference, Nov '97*

■

Ethnic Diseases Sourcebook

Basic Consumer Health Information for Ethnic and Racial Minority Groups in the United States, Including General Health Indicators and Behaviors, Ethnic Diseases, Genetic Testing, the Impact of Chronic Diseases, Women's Health, Mental Health Issues, and Preventive Health Care Services

Along with a Glossary and a Listing of Additional Resources

Edited by Joyce Brennfleck Shannon. 664 pages. 2001. 0-7808-0336-1. $78.

■

Family Planning Sourcebook

Basic Consumer Health Information about Planning for Pregnancy and Contraception, Including Traditional Methods, Barrier Methods, Hormonal Methods, Permanent Methods, Future Methods, Emergency Contraception, and Birth Control Choices for Women at Each Stage of Life

Along with Statistics, a Glossary, and Sources of Additional Information

Edited by Amy Marcaccio Keyzer. 600 pages. 2001. 0-7808-0379-5. $78.

SEE ALSO *Pregnancy & Birth Sourcebook*

Fitness & Exercise Sourcebook, 1st Edition

Basic Information on Fitness and Exercise, Including Fitness Activities for Specific Age Groups, Exercise for People with Specific Medical Conditions, How to Begin a Fitness Program in Running, Walking, Swimming, Cycling, and Other Athletic Activities, and Recent Research in Fitness and Exercise

Edited by Dan R. Harris. 663 pages. 1996. 0-7808-0186-5. $78.

"A good resource for general readers."
—*Choice, Association of College and Research Libraries, Nov '97*

"The perennial popularity of the topic . . . make this an appealing selection for public libraries."
—*Rettig on Reference, Jun/Jul '97*

■

Fitness & Exercise Sourcebook, 2nd Edition

Basic Consumer Health Information about the Fundamentals of Fitness and Exercise, Including How to Begin and Maintain a Fitness Program, Fitness as a Lifestyle, the Link between Fitness and Diet, Advice for Specific Groups of People, Exercise as It Relates to Specific Medical Conditions, and Recent Research in Fitness and Exercise

Along with a Glossary of Important Terms and Resources for Additional Help and Information

Edited by Kristen M. Gledhill. 600 pages. 2001. 0-7808-0334-5. $78.

■

Food & Animal Borne Diseases Sourcebook

Basic Information about Diseases That Can Be Spread to Humans through the Ingestion of Contaminated Food or Water or by Contact with Infected Animals and Insects, Such as Botulism, E. Coli, Hepatitis A, Trichinosis, Lyme Disease, and Rabies

Along with Information Regarding Prevention and Treatment Methods, and Including a Special Section for International Travelers Describing Diseases Such as Cholera, Malaria, Travelers' Diarrhea, and Yellow Fever, and Offering Recommendations for Avoiding Illness

Edited by Karen Bellenir and Peter D. Dresser. 535 pages. 1995. 0-7808-0033-8. $78.

"Targeting general readers and providing them with a single, comprehensive source of information on selected topics, this book continues, with the excellent caliber of its predecessors, to catalog topical information on health matters of general interest. Readable and thorough, this valuable resource is highly recommended for all libraries."
—*Academic Library Book Review, Summer '96*

"A comprehensive collection of authoritative information." —*Emergency Medical Services, Oct '95*

Food Safety Sourcebook

Basic Consumer Health Information about the Safe Handling of Meat, Poultry, Seafood, Eggs, Fruit Juices, and Other Food Items, and Facts about Pesticides, Drinking Water, Food Safety Overseas, and the Onset, Duration, and Symptoms of Foodborne Illnesses, Including Types of Pathogenic Bacteria, Parasitic Protozoa, Worms, Viruses, and Natural Toxins

Along with the Role of the Consumer, the Food Handler, and the Government in Food Safety; a Glossary, and Resources for Additional Help and Information

Edited by Dawn D. Matthews. 339 pages. 1999. 0-7808-0326-4. $48.

"This book is recommended for public libraries and universities with home economics and food science programs." —*E-Streams, Nov '00*

"This book takes the complex issues of food safety and foodborne pathogens and presents them in an easily understood manner. [It does] an excellent job of covering a large and often confusing topic."
—*American Reference Books Annual, 2000*

"Recommended reference source."
—*Booklist, American Library Association, May '00*

■

Forensic Medicine Sourcebook

Basic Consumer Information for the Layperson about Forensic Medicine, Including Crime Scene Investigation, Evidence Collection and Analysis, Expert Testimony, Computer-Aided Criminal Identification, Digital Imaging in the Courtroom, DNA Profiling, Accident Reconstruction, Autopsies, Ballistics, Drugs and Explosives Detection, Latent Fingerprints, Product Tampering, and Questioned Document Examination

Along with Statistical Data, a Glossary of Forensics Terminology, and Listings of Sources for Further Help and Information

Edited by Annemarie S. Muth. 574 pages. 1999. 0-7808-0232-2. $78.

"There are several items that make this book attractive to consumers who are seeking certain forensic data. . . . This is a useful current source for those seeking general forensic medical answers."
—*American Reference Books Annual, 2000*

"Recommended for public libraries."
—*Reference & User Services Quarterly, American Library Association, Spring 2000*

"Recommended reference source."
—*Booklist, American Library Association, Feb '00*

"A wealth of information, useful statistics, references are up-to-date and extremely complete. This wonderful collection of data will help students who are interested in a career in any type of forensic field. It is a great resource for attorneys who need information about types of expert witnesses needed in a particular case. It also offers useful information for fiction and nonfiction writers whose work involves a crime. A fascinating compilation. All levels." —*Choice, Association of College and Research Libraries, Jan '00*

Gastrointestinal Diseases & Disorders Sourcebook

Basic Information about Gastroesophageal Reflux Disease (Heartburn), Ulcers, Diverticulosis, Irritable Bowel Syndrome, Crohn's Disease, Ulcerative Colitis, Diarrhea, Constipation, Lactose Intolerance, Hemorrhoids, Hepatitis, Cirrhosis, and Other Digestive Problems, Featuring Statistics, Descriptions of Symptoms, and Current Treatment Methods of Interest for Persons Living with Upper and Lower Gastrointestinal Maladies

Edited by Linda M. Ross. 413 pages. 1996. 0-7808-0078-8. $78.

". . . very readable form. The successful editorial work that brought this material together into a useful and understandable reference makes accessible to all readers information that can help them more effectively understand and obtain help for digestive tract problems."
—*Choice, Association of College and Research Libraries, Feb '97*

SEE ALSO *Diet & Nutrition Sourcebook, 1st and 2nd Editions, Digestive Diseases & Disorders Sourcebook*

■

Genetic Disorders Sourcebook, 1st Edition

Basic Information about Heritable Diseases and Disorders Such as Down Syndrome, PKU, Hemophilia, Von Willebrand Disease, Gaucher Disease, Tay-Sachs Disease, and Sickle-Cell Disease, Along with Information about Genetic Screening, Gene Therapy, Home Care, and Including Source Listings for Further Help and Information on More Than 300 Disorders

Edited by Karen Bellenir. 642 pages. 1996. 0-7808-0034-6. $78.

"Recommended for undergraduate libraries or libraries that serve the public."
—*Science & Technology Libraries, Vol. 18, No. 1, '99*

"Provides essential medical information to both the general public and those diagnosed with a serious or fatal genetic disease or disorder."
—*Choice, Association of College and Research Libraries, Jan '97*

"Geared toward the lay public. It would be well placed in all public libraries and in those hospital and medical libraries in which access to genetic references is limited." —*Doody's Health Sciences Book Review, Oct '96*

■

Genetic Disorders Sourcebook, 2nd Edition

Basic Consumer Health Information about Hereditary Diseases and Disorders, Including Cystic Fibrosis, Down Syndrome, Hemophilia, Huntington's Disease, Sickle Cell Anemia, and More; Facts about Genes, Gene Research and Therapy, Genetic Screening, Ethics of Gene Testing, Genetic Counseling, and Advice on Coping and Caring

Along with a Glossary of Genetic Terminology and a Resource List for Help, Support, and Further Information

Edited by Kathy Massimini. 768 pages. 2001. 0-7808-0241-1. $78.

■

Head Trauma Sourcebook

Basic Information for the Layperson about Open-Head and Closed-Head Injuries, Treatment Advances, Recovery, and Rehabilitation

Along with Reports on Current Research Initiatives

Edited by Karen Bellenir. 414 pages. 1997. 0-7808-0208-X. $78.

■

Health Insurance Sourcebook

Basic Information about Managed Care Organizations, Traditional Fee-for-Service Insurance, Insurance Portability and Pre-Existing Conditions Clauses, Medicare, Medicaid, Social Security, and Military Health Care

Along with Information about Insurance Fraud

Edited by Wendy Wilcox. 530 pages. 1997. 0-7808-0222-5. $78.

"Particularly useful because it brings much of this information together in one volume. This book will be a handy reference source in the health sciences library, hospital library, college and university library, and medium to large public library."
—*Medical Reference Services Quarterly, Fall '98*

Awarded "Books of the Year Award"
—*American Journal of Nursing, 1997*

"The layout of the book is particularly helpful as it provides easy access to reference material. A most useful addition to the vast amount of information about health insurance. The use of data from U.S. government agencies is most commendable. Useful in a library or learning center for healthcare professional students."
—*Doody's Health Sciences Book Reviews, Nov '97*

■

Healthy Aging Sourcebook

Basic Consumer Health Information about Maintaining Health through the Aging Process, Including Advice on Nutrition, Exercise, and Sleep, Help in Making Decisions about Midlife Issues and Retirement, and Guidance Concerning Practical and Informed Choices in Health Consumerism

Along with Data Concerning the Theories of Aging, Different Experiences in Aging by Minority Groups, and Facts about Aging Now and Aging in the Future; and Featuring a Glossary, a Guide to Consumer Help, Additional Suggested Reading, and Practical Resource Directory

Edited by Jenifer Swanson. 536 pages. 1999. 0-7808-0390-6. $78.

"Recommended reference source."
—*Booklist, American Library Association, Feb '00*

SEE ALSO *Physical & Mental Issues in Aging Sourcebook*

Healthy Heart Sourcebook for Women

Basic Consumer Health Information about Cardiac Issues Specific to Women, Including Facts about Major Risk Factors and Prevention, Treatment and Control Strategies, and Important Dietary Issues

Along with a Special Section Regarding the Pros and Cons of Hormone Replacement Therapy and Its Impact on Heart Health, and Additional Help, Including Recipes, a Glossary, and a Directory of Resources

Edited by Dawn D. Matthews. 336 pages. 2000. 0-7808-0329-9. $48.

"Contains very important information about coronary artery disease that all women should know. The information is current and presented in an easy-to-read format. The book will make a good addition to any library."
—*American Medical Writers Association Journal, Summer '00*

"Important, basic reference."
—*Reviewer's Bookwatch, Jul '00*

SEE ALSO *Cardiovascular Diseases & Disorders Sourcebook, 1st Edition, Heart Diseases & Disorders Sourcebook, 2nd Edition, Women's Health Concerns Sourcebook*

■

Heart Diseases & Disorders Sourcebook, 2nd Edition

Basic Consumer Health Information about Heart Attacks, Angina, Rhythm Disorders, Heart Failure, Valve Disease, Congenital Heart Disorders, and More, Including Descriptions of Surgical Procedures and Other Interventions, Medications, Cardiac Rehabilitation, Risk Identification, and Prevention Tips

Along with Statistical Data, Reports on Current Research Initiatives, a Glossary of Cardiovascular Terms, and Resource Directory

Edited by Karen Bellenir. 612 pages. 2000. 0-7808-0238-1. $78.

"Recommended reference source."
—*Booklist, American Library Association, Dec '00*

"Provides comprehensive coverage of matters related to the heart. This title is recommended for health sciences and public libraries with consumer health collections."
—*E-Streams, Oct '00*

SEE ALSO *Cardiovascular Diseases & Disorders Sourcebook, 1st Edition, Healthy Heart Sourcebook for Women*

■

Immune System Disorders Sourcebook

Basic Information about Lupus, Multiple Sclerosis, Guillain-Barré Syndrome, Chronic Granulomatous Disease, and More

Along with Statistical and Demographic Data and Reports on Current Research Initiatives

Edited by Allan R. Cook. 608 pages. 1997. 0-7808-0209-8. $78.

Infant & Toddler Health Sourcebook

Basic Consumer Health Information about the Physical and Mental Development of Newborns, Infants, and Toddlers, Including Neonatal Concerns, Nutrition Recommendations, Immunization Schedules, Common Pediatric Disorders, Assessments and Milestones, Safety Tips, and Advice for Parents and Other Caregivers

Along with a Glossary of Terms and Resource Listings for Additional Help

Edited by Jenifer Swanson. 585 pages. 2000. 0-7808-0246-2. $78.

■

Kidney & Urinary Tract Diseases & Disorders Sourcebook

Basic Information about Kidney Stones, Urinary Incontinence, Bladder Disease, End Stage Renal Disease, Dialysis, and More

Along with Statistical and Demographic Data and Reports on Current Research Initiatives

Edited by Linda M. Ross. 602 pages. 1997. 0-7808-0079-6. $78.

■

Learning Disabilities Sourcebook

Basic Information about Disorders Such as Dyslexia, Visual and Auditory Processing Deficits, Attention Deficit/Hyperactivity Disorder, and Autism

Along with Statistical and Demographic Data, Reports on Current Research Initiatives, an Explanation of the Assessment Process, and a Special Section for Adults with Learning Disabilities

Edited by Linda M. Shin. 579 pages. 1998. 0-7808-0210-1. $78.

Named "Outstanding Reference Book of 1999."
—*New York Public Library, Feb 2000*

"An excellent candidate for inclusion in a public library reference section. It's a great source of information. Teachers will also find the book useful. Definitely worth reading."
—*Journal of Adolescent & Adult Literacy, Feb 2000*

"Readable . . . provides a solid base of information regarding successful techniques used with individuals who have learning disabilities, as well as practical suggestions for educators and family members. Clear language, concise descriptions, and pertinent information for contacting multiple resources add to the strength of this book as a useful tool."
—*Choice, Association of College and Research Libraries, Feb '99*

"Recommended reference source."
—*Booklist, American Library Association, Sep '98*

"This is a useful resource for libraries and for those who don't have the time to identify and locate the individual publications."
—*Disability Resources Monthly, Sep '98*

Liver Disorders Sourcebook

Basic Consumer Health Information about the Liver and How It Works; Liver Diseases, Including Cancer, Cirrhosis, Hepatitis, and Toxic and Drug Related Diseases; Tips for Maintaining a Healthy Liver; Laboratory Tests, Radiology Tests, and Facts about Liver Transplantation

Along with a Section on Support Groups, a Glossary, and Resource Listings

Edited by Joyce Brennfleck Shannon. 591 pages. 2000. 0-7808-0383-3. $78.

"This title is recommended for health sciences and public libraries with consumer health collections."
—*E-Streams, Oct '00*

"Recommended reference source."
—*Booklist, American Library Association, Jun '00*

■

Medical Tests Sourcebook

Basic Consumer Health Information about Medical Tests, Including Periodic Health Exams, General Screening Tests, Tests You Can Do at Home, Findings of the U.S. Preventive Services Task Force, X-ray and Radiology Tests, Electrical Tests, Tests of Blood and Other Body Fluids and Tissues, Scope Tests, Lung Tests, Genetic Tests, Pregnancy Tests, Newborn Screening Tests, Sexually Transmitted Disease Tests, and Computer Aided Diagnoses

Along with a Section on Paying for Medical Tests, a Glossary, and Resource Listings

Edited by Joyce Brennfleck Shannon. 691 pages. 1999. 0-7808-0243-8. $78.

"A valuable reference guide."
—*American Reference Books Annual, 2000*

"Recommended for hospital and health sciences libraries with consumer health collections."
—*E-Streams, Mar '00*

"This is an overall excellent reference with a wealth of general knowledge that may aid those who are reluctant to get vital tests performed."
—*Today's Librarian, Jan 2000*

■

Men's Health Concerns Sourcebook

Basic Information about Health Issues That Affect Men, Featuring Facts about the Top Causes of Death in Men, Including Heart Disease, Stroke, Cancers, Prostate Disorders, Chronic Obstructive Pulmonary Disease, Pneumonia and Influenza, Human Immunodeficiency Virus and Acquired Immune Deficiency Syndrome, Diabetes Mellitus, Stress, Suicide, Accidents and Homicides; and Facts about Common Concerns for Men, Including Impotence, Contraception, Circumcision, Sleep Disorders, Snoring, Hair Loss, Diet, Nutrition, Exercise, Kidney and Urological Disorders, and Backaches

Edited by Allan R. Cook. 738 pages. 1998. 0-7808-0212-8. $78.

"This comprehensive resource and the series are highly recommended."

—*American Reference Books Annual, 2000*

"Recommended reference source."

—*Booklist, American Library Association, Dec '98*

■

Mental Health Disorders Sourcebook, 1st Edition

Basic Information about Schizophrenia, Depression, Bipolar Disorder, Panic Disorder, Obsessive-Compulsive Disorder, Phobias and Other Anxiety Disorders, Paranoia and Other Personality Disorders, Eating Disorders, and Sleep Disorders

Along with Information about Treatment and Therapies

Edited by Karen Bellenir. 548 pages. 1995. 0-7808-0040-0. $78.

"This is an excellent new book . . . written in easy-to-understand language." —*Booklist Health Sciences Supplement, American Library Association, Oct '97*

". . . useful for public and academic libraries and consumer health collections."

—*Medical Reference Services Quarterly, Spring '97*

"The great strengths of the book are its readability and its inclusion of places to find more information. Especially recommended." —*Reference Quarterly, American Library Association, Winter '96*

". . . a good resource for a consumer health library."

—*Bulletin of the Medical Library Association, Oct '96*

"The information is data-based and couched in brief, concise language that avoids jargon. . . . a useful reference source." —*Readings, Sep '96*

"The text is well organized and adequately written for its target audience." —*Choice, Association of College and Research Libraries, Jun '96*

". . . provides information on a wide range of mental disorders, presented in nontechnical language."

—*Exceptional Child Education Resources, Spring '96*

"Recommended for public and academic libraries."

—*Reference Book Review, 1996*

■

Mental Health Disorders Sourcebook, 2nd Edition

Basic Consumer Health Information about Anxiety Disorders, Depression and Other Mood Disorders, Eating Disorders, Personality Disorders, Schizophrenia, and More, Including Disease Descriptions, Treatment Options, and Reports on Current Research Initiatives

Along with Statistical Data, Tips for Maintaining Mental Health, a Glossary, and Directory of Sources for Additional Help and Information

Edited by Karen Bellenir. 605 pages. 2000. 0-7808-0240-3. $78.

"Recommended reference source."

—*Booklist, American Library Association, Jun '00*

Mental Retardation Sourcebook

Basic Consumer Health Information about Mental Retardation and Its Causes, Including Down Syndrome, Fetal Alcohol Syndrome, Fragile X Syndrome, Genetic Conditions, Injury, and Environmental Sources

Along with Preventive Strategies, Parenting Issues, Educational Implications, Health Care Needs, Employment and Economic Matters, Legal Issues, a Glossary, and a Resource Listing for Additional Help and Information

Edited by Joyce Brennfleck Shannon. 642 pages. 2000. 0-7808-0377-9. $78.

"The strength of this work is that it compiles many basic fact sheets and addresses for further information in one volume. It is intended and suitable for the general public. The sourcebook is relevant to any collection providing health information to the general public."

—*E-Streams, Nov '00*

"From preventing retardation to parenting and family challenges, this covers health, social and legal issues and will prove an invaluable overview."

—*Reviewer's Bookwatch, Jul '00*

■

Obesity Sourcebook

Basic Consumer Health Information about Diseases and Other Problems Associated with Obesity, and Including Facts about Risk Factors, Prevention Issues, and Management Approaches

Along with Statistical and Demographic Data, Information about Special Populations, Research Updates, a Glossary, and Source Listings for Further Help and Information

Edited by Wilma Caldwell and Chad T. Kimball. 376 pages. 2001. 0-7808-0333-7. $48.

■

Ophthalmic Disorders Sourcebook

Basic Information about Glaucoma, Cataracts, Macular Degeneration, Strabismus, Refractive Disorders, and More

Along with Statistical and Demographic Data and Reports on Current Research Initiatives

Edited by Linda M. Ross. 631 pages. 1996. 0-7808-0081-8. $78.

■

Oral Health Sourcebook

Basic Information about Diseases and Conditions Affecting Oral Health, Including Cavities, Gum Disease, Dry Mouth, Oral Cancers, Fever Blisters, Canker Sores, Oral Thrush, Bad Breath, Temporomandibular Disorders, and other Craniofacial Syndromes

Along with Statistical Data on the Oral Health of Americans, Oral Hygiene, Emergency First Aid, Information on Treatment Procedures and Methods of Replacing Lost Teeth

Edited by Allan R. Cook. 558 pages. 1997. 0-7808-0082-6. $78.

"Unique source which will fill a gap in dental sources for patients and the lay public. A valuable reference tool even in a library with thousands of books on dentistry. Comprehensive, clear, inexpensive, and easy to read and use. It fills an enormous gap in the health care literature." —*Reference and User Services Quarterly, American Library Association, Summer '98*

"Recommended reference source."
—*Booklist, American Library Association, Dec '97*

Osteoporosis Sourcebook

Basic Consumer Health Information about Primary and Secondary Osteoporosis and Juvenile Osteoporosis and Related Conditions, Including Fibrous Dysplasia, Gaucher Disease, Hyperthyroidism, Hypophosphatasia, Myeloma, Osteopetrosis, Osteogenesis Imperfecta, and Paget's Disease

Along with Information about Risk Factors, Treatments, Traditional and Non-traditional Pain Management, a Glossary of Related Terms, and a Directory of Resources

Edited by Allan R. Cook. 600 pages. 2001. 0-7808-0239-X. $78.

SEE ALSO *Women's Health Concerns Sourcebook*

Pain Sourcebook

Basic Information about Specific Forms of Acute and Chronic Pain, Including Headaches, Back Pain, Muscular Pain, Neuralgia, Surgical Pain, and Cancer Pain

Along with Pain Relief Options Such as Analgesics, Narcotics, Nerve Blocks, Transcutaneous Nerve Stimulation, and Alternative Forms of Pain Control, Including Biofeedback, Imaging, Behavior Modification, and Relaxation Techniques

Edited by Allan R. Cook. 667 pages. 1997. 0-7808-0213-6. $78.

"The text is readable, easily understood, and well indexed. This excellent volume belongs in all patient education libraries, consumer health sections of public libraries, and many personal collections."
—*American Reference Books Annual, 1999*

"A beneficial reference." —*Booklist Health Sciences Supplement, American Library Association, Oct '98*

"The information is basic in terms of scholarship and is appropriate for general readers. Written in journalistic style . . . intended for non-professionals. Quite thorough in its coverage of different pain conditions and summarizes the latest clinical information regarding pain treatment." —*Choice, Association of College and Research Libraries, Jun '98*

"Recommended reference source."
—*Booklist, American Library Association, Mar '98*

Pediatric Cancer Sourcebook

Basic Consumer Health Information about Leukemias, Brain Tumors, Sarcomas, Lymphomas, and Other Cancers in Infants, Children, and Adolescents, Including Descriptions of Cancers, Treatments, and Coping Strategies

Along with Suggestions for Parents, Caregivers, and Concerned Relatives, a Glossary of Cancer Terms, and Resource Listings

Edited by Edward J. Prucha. 587 pages. 1999. 0-7808-0245-4. $78.

"A valuable addition to all libraries specializing in health services and many public libraries."
—*American Reference Books Annual, 2000*

"Recommended reference source."
—*Booklist, American Library Association, Feb '00*

"An excellent source of information. Recommended for public, hospital, and health science libraries with consumer health collections." —*E-Streams, Jun '00*

Physical & Mental Issues in Aging Sourcebook

Basic Consumer Health Information on Physical and Mental Disorders Associated with the Aging Process, Including Concerns about Cardiovascular Disease, Pulmonary Disease, Oral Health, Digestive Disorders, Musculoskeletal and Skin Disorders, Metabolic Changes, Sexual and Reproductive Issues, and Changes in Vision, Hearing, and Other Senses

Along with Data about Longevity and Causes of Death, Information on Acute and Chronic Pain, Descriptions of Mental Concerns, a Glossary of Terms, and Resource Listings for Additional Help

Edited by Jenifer Swanson. 660 pages. 1999. 0-7808-0233-0. $78.

"Recommended for public libraries."
—*American Reference Books Annual, 2000*

"This is a treasure of health information for the layperson." —*Choice Health Sciences Supplement, Association of College & Research Libraries, May 2000*

"Recommended reference source."
—*Booklist, American Library Association, Oct '99*

SEE ALSO *Healthy Aging Sourcebook*

Podiatry Sourcebook

Basic Consumer Health Information about Foot Conditions, Diseases, and Injuries, Including Bunions, Corns, Calluses, Athlete's Foot, Plantar Warts, Hammertoes and Clawtoes, Club Foot, Heel Pain, Gout, and More

Along with Facts about Foot Care, Disease Prevention, Foot Safety, Choosing a Foot Care Specialist, a Glossary of Terms, and Resource Listings for Additional Information

Edited by M. Lisa Weatherford. 600 pages. 2001. 0-7808-0215-2. $78.

Pregnancy & Birth Sourcebook

Basic Information about Planning for Pregnancy, Maternal Health, Fetal Growth and Development, Labor and Delivery, Postpartum and Perinatal Care, Pregnancy in Mothers with Special Concerns, and Disorders of Pregnancy, Including Genetic Counseling, Nutrition and Exercise, Obstetrical Tests, Pregnancy Discomfort, Multiple Births, Cesarean Sections, Medical Testing of Newborns, Breastfeeding, Gestational Diabetes, and Ectopic Pregnancy

Edited by Heather E. Aldred. 737 pages. 1997. 0-7808-0216-0. $78.

"A well-organized handbook. Recommended."
—*Choice, Association of College and Research Libraries, Apr '98*

"Recommended reference source."
—*Booklist, American Library Association, Mar '98*

"Recommended for public libraries."
—*American Reference Books Annual, 1998*

SEE ALSO *Congenital Disorders Sourcebook, Family Planning Sourcebook*

Public Health Sourcebook

Basic Information about Government Health Agencies, Including National Health Statistics and Trends, Healthy People 2000 Program Goals and Objectives, the Centers for Disease Control and Prevention, the Food and Drug Administration, and the National Institutes of Health

Along with Full Contact Information for Each Agency

Edited by Wendy Wilcox. 698 pages. 1998. 0-7808-0220-9. $78.

"Recommended reference source."
—*Booklist, American Library Association, Sep '98*

"This consumer guide provides welcome assistance in navigating the maze of federal health agencies and their data on public health concerns."
—*SciTech Book News, Sep '98*

Reconstructive & Cosmetic Surgery Sourcebook

Basic Consumer Health Information on Cosmetic and Reconstructive Plastic Surgery, Including Statistical Information about Different Surgical Procedures, Things to Consider Prior to Surgery, Plastic Surgery Techniques and Tools, Emotional and Psychological Considerations, and Procedure-Specific Information

Along with a Glossary of Terms and a Listing of Resources for Additional Help and Information

Edited by M. Lisa Weatherford. 400 pages. 2001. 0-7808-0214-4. $48.

Rehabilitation Sourcebook

Basic Consumer Health Information about Rehabilitation for People Recovering from Heart Surgery, Spinal Cord Injury, Stroke, Orthopedic Impairments, Amputation, Pulmonary Impairments, Traumatic Injury, and More, Including Physical Therapy, Occupational Therapy, Speech/ Language Therapy, Massage Therapy, Dance Therapy, Art Therapy, and Recreational Therapy

Along with Information on Assistive and Adaptive Devices, a Glossary, and Resources for Additional Help and Information

Edited by Dawn D. Matthews. 531 pages. 1999. 0-7808-0236-5. $78.

"Recommended reference source."
—*Booklist, American Library Association, May '00*

Respiratory Diseases & Disorders Sourcebook

Basic Information about Respiratory Diseases and Disorders, Including Asthma, Cystic Fibrosis, Pneumonia, the Common Cold, Influenza, and Others, Featuring Facts about the Respiratory System, Statistical and Demographic Data, Treatments, Self-Help Management Suggestions, and Current Research Initiatives

Edited by Allan R. Cook and Peter D. Dresser. 771 pages. 1995. 0-7808-0037-0. $78.

"Designed for the layperson and for patients and their families coping with respiratory illness. . . . an extensive array of information on diagnosis, treatment, management, and prevention of respiratory illnesses for the general reader." —*Choice, Association of College and Research Libraries, Jun '96*

"A highly recommended text for all collections. It is a comforting reminder of the power of knowledge that good books carry between their covers."
—*Academic Library Book Review, Spring '96*

"A comprehensive collection of authoritative information presented in a nontechnical, humanitarian style for patients, families, and caregivers."
—*Association of Operating Room Nurses, Sep/Oct '95*

Sexually Transmitted Diseases Sourcebook, 1st Edition

Basic Information about Herpes, Chlamydia, Gonorrhea, Hepatitis, Nongonoccocal Urethritis, Pelvic Inflammatory Disease, Syphilis, AIDS, and More

Along with Current Data on Treatments and Preventions

Edited by Linda M. Ross. 550 pages. 1997. 0-7808-0217-9. $78.

Sexually Transmitted Diseases Sourcebook, 2nd Edition

Basic Consumer Health Information about Sexually Transmitted Diseases, Including Information on the Diagnosis and Treatment of Chlamydia, Gonorrhea, Hepatitis, Herpes, HIV, Mononucleosis, Syphilis, and Others

Along with Information on Prevention, Such as Condom Use, Vaccines, and STD Education; And Featuring a Section on Issues Related to Youth and Adolescents, a Glossary, and Resources for Additional Help and Information

Edited by Dawn D. Matthews. 538 pages. 2001. 0-7808-0249-7. $78.

■

Skin Disorders Sourcebook

Basic Information about Common Skin and Scalp Conditions Caused by Aging, Allergies, Immune Reactions, Sun Exposure, Infectious Organisms, Parasites, Cosmetics, and Skin Traumas, Including Abrasions, Cuts, and Pressure Sores

Along with Information on Prevention and Treatment

Edited by Allan R. Cook. 647 pages. 1997. 0-7808-0080-X. $78.

". . . comprehensive, easily read reference book."
—Doody's Health Sciences Book Reviews, Oct '97

SEE ALSO *Burns Sourcebook*

■

Sleep Disorders Sourcebook

Basic Consumer Health Information about Sleep and Its Disorders, Including Insomnia, Sleepwalking, Sleep Apnea, Restless Leg Syndrome, and Narcolepsy

Along with Data about Shiftwork and Its Effects, Information on the Societal Costs of Sleep Deprivation, Descriptions of Treatment Options, a Glossary of Terms, and Resource Listings for Additional Help

Edited by Jenifer Swanson. 439 pages. 1998. 0-7808-0234-9. $78.

"This text will complement any home or medical library. It is user-friendly and ideal for the adult reader."
—American Reference Books Annual, 2000

"Recommended reference source."
—Booklist, American Library Association, Feb '99

"A useful resource that provides accurate, relevant, and accessible information on sleep to the general public. Health care providers who deal with sleep disorders patients may also find it helpful in being prepared to answer some of the questions patients ask."
—Respiratory Care, Jul '99

Sports Injuries Sourcebook

Basic Consumer Health Information about Common Sports Injuries, Prevention of Injury in Specific Sports, Tips for Training, and Rehabilitation from Injury

Along with Information about Special Concerns for Children, Young Girls in Athletic Training Programs, Senior Athletes, and Women Athletes, and a Directory of Resources for Further Help and Information

Edited by Heather E. Aldred. 624 pages. 1999. 0-7808-0218-7. $78.

"Public libraries and undergraduate academic libraries will find this book useful for its nontechnical language." *—American Reference Books Annual, 2000*

"While this easy-to-read book is recommended for all libraries, it should prove to be especially useful for public, high school, and academic libraries; certainly it should be on the bookshelf of every school gymnasium." *—E-Streams, Mar '00*

■

Substance Abuse Sourcebook

Basic Health-Related Information about the Abuse of Legal and Illegal Substances Such as Alcohol, Tobacco, Prescription Drugs, Marijuana, Cocaine, and Heroin; and Including Facts about Substance Abuse Prevention Strategies, Intervention Methods, Treatment and Recovery Programs, and a Section Addressing the Special Problems Related to Substance Abuse during Pregnancy

Edited by Karen Bellenir. 573 pages. 1996. 0-7808-0038-9. $78.

"A valuable addition to any health reference section. Highly recommended."
—The Book Report, Mar/Apr '97

". . . a comprehensive collection of substance abuse information that's both highly readable and compact. Families and caregivers of substance abusers will find the information enlightening and helpful, while teachers, social workers and journalists should benefit from the concise format. Recommended."
—Drug Abuse Update, Winter '96/'97

SEE ALSO *Alcoholism Sourcebook, Drug Abuse Sourcebook*

■

Traveler's Health Sourcebook

Basic Consumer Health Information for Travelers, Including Physical and Medical Preparations, Transportation Health and Safety, Essential Information about Food and Water, Sun Exposure, Insect and Snake Bites, Camping and Wilderness Medicine, and Travel with Physical or Medical Disabilities

Along with International Travel Tips, Vaccination Recommendations, Geographical Health Issues, Disease Risks, a Glossary, and a Listing of Additional Resources

Edited by Joyce Brennfleck Shannon. 635 pages. 2000. 0-7808-0384-1. $78.

Women's Health Concerns Sourcebook

Basic Information about Health Issues That Affect Women, Featuring Facts about Menstruation and Other Gynecological Concerns, Including Endometriosis, Fibroids, Menopause, and Vaginitis; Reproductive Concerns, Including Birth Control, Infertility, and Abortion; and Facts about Additional Physical, Emotional, and Mental Health Concerns Prevalent among Women Such as Osteoporosis, Urinary Tract Disorders, Eating Disorders, and Depression

Along with Tips for Maintaining a Healthy Lifestyle

Edited by Heather E. Aldred. 567 pages. 1997. 0-7808-0219-5. $78.

"Handy compilation. There is an impressive range of diseases, devices, disorders, procedures, and other physical and emotional issues covered . . . well organized, illustrated, and indexed." —*Choice, Association of College and Research Libraries, Jan '98*

SEE ALSO *Breast Cancer Sourcebook, Cancer Sourcebook for Women, 1st and 2nd Editions, Healthy Heart Sourcebook for Women, Osteoporosis Sourcebook*

■

Workplace Health & Safety Sourcebook

Basic Consumer Health Information about Workplace Health and Safety, Including the Effect of Workplace Hazards on the Lungs, Skin, Heart, Ears, Eyes, Brain, Reproductive Organs, Musculoskeletal System, and Other Organs and Body Parts

Along with Information about Occupational Cancer, Personal Protective Equipment, Toxic and Hazardous Chemicals, Child Labor, Stress, and Workplace Violence

Edited by Chad T. Kimball. 626 pages. 2000. 0-7808-0231-4. $78.

"Highly recommended." —*The Bookwatch, Jan '01*

■

Worldwide Health Sourcebook

Basic Information about Global Health Issues, Including Malnutrition, Reproductive Health, Disease Dispersion and Prevention, Emerging Diseases, Risky Health Behaviors, and the Leading Causes of Death

Along with Global Health Concerns for Children, Women, and the Elderly, Mental Health Issues, Research and Technology Advancements, and Economic, Environmental, and Political Health Implications, a Glossary, and a Resource Listing for Additional Help and Information

Edited by Joyce Brennfleck Shannon. 614 pages. 2001. 0-7808-0330-2. $78.

Health Reference Series Cumulative Index 1999

A Comprehensive Index to the Individual Volumes of the Health Reference Series, Including a Subject Index, Name Index, Organization Index, and Publication Index

Along with a Master List of Acronyms and Abbreviations

Edited by Edward J. Prucha, Anne Holmes, and Robert Rudnick. 990 pages. 2000. 0-7808-0382-5. $78.

"Essential for collections that hold any of the numerous *Health Reference Series* titles." —*Choice, Association of College and Research Libraries, Nov '00*